THE MA S
IN
MY MANY ROADS

Reflections on a Full and Active Life

KEITH D. BUSHEY

High School Dropout • Burglar • Marine Mustang Colonel • Parent
Police Commander • Sheriff's Deputy Chief • Marshal • Game Warden
Foster & Adoptive Father • College Professor • FBI LEEDA Instructor
Undercover Agent • Pilot • Writer & Author • Motivational Speaker

Library of Congress Control Number: 2012951268

ISBN 978-1508669463 (*Softcover*)

Printed and bound in the United States of America

Cover design by John Hollenbeck

Graphic Publishers
Santa Ana, California 92705-8753 USA
1 800 4-YOUR-BOOK

—DEDICATION—

THIS BOOK IS DEDICATED to my late father and mother, David D. and Mary J. Bushey, and my late brother, Laurence D. Bushey.

Special love and thanks go to my wonderful mom, who was always there for her family in every way—including during some truly challenging times.

AND TO my great wife, Cathy Bushey, and all of the wonderful kids, young and old.

Cathy—against all odds—is somtimes able to keep me organized and appropriately focused (*kinda*).

AND TO my two favorite non-profit organizations, which will be the beneficiaries of the royalties from the sale of this book:

Devil Pups, Inc.

A wonderful, USMC-oriented youth program that has been strengthening the fiber of America's young men—and for the last decade, its young women, as well—since 1954.

The Desert Refuge for Peace Officers

A non-demoninational spiritual retreat for peace officers and their families, both in daily living and when confronted by the special challenges that often face cops and their loved ones. Father Michael McCullough, a dear friend, is the founder and executive director.

—OTHER TITLES BY KEITH BUSHEY—

The Centurions' Shield
(co-authored with Ray Sherrard and Jake Bushey)

My USMC Journey—From Private to Colonel

My LAPD Journey—From Street Cop to Commander

—INTRODUCTION—

ALL OF US CAN REFLECT on situations in our lives that some of us refer to as "forks in the road," where a slight change could have completely altered our life. The chance encounter that yielded the lifetime spouse—the cop who decided not to arrest you for DUI because there was someone to drive you home—the boss who fired you for something foolish when he could just as easily have allowed you to resign—the soldier who overstayed his leave but returned to a lenient sergeant—the party you did not go to, and the people you never met—the list goes on. In such instances, the alternative—that which did not occur—might easily have completely changed your life forever. The title I have chosen for this book, *The Many Forks in My Many Roads*, is a reflection of some truly interesting "forks" I have encountered in the many roads that I have traveled.

I can only hope that each person who reads these pages is someone who recognizes the unfairness and pitfalls of judging yesterday's actions by today's standards. I am not aware of anyone, and I have known a lot of folks, who is the same person today that he or she was three or four decades ago; certainly I am not. I am not suggesting that the core of our souls changes, but many of our viewpoints and behaviors become radically different; again, I fall into this category. The reader will find plenty of things for which I could be criticized, but hopefully these are all things that occurred decades ago when society as well was a different place. In addition to a number of things that are good, wholesome, and funny, these pages also reflect some pretty tough stuff: violent deaths, brutality, inappropriate behavior, profanity, pain, misery, sordid actions, sexual deviancy, and other unpleasantries. These pages reflect several years of wracking my brain in an attempt to recall as many events as possible. I am sure there must be a thing or two that I missed, but not much. These have all been part of my life, as a result of the roads that I have traveled in the careers that I have chosen.

For better or worse, I am the person I am today because of the cumulative impact of the situations found on these pages. It could be argued—and I probably wouldn't disagree too vigorously—that some of these experiences have hardened and warped me just a bit too much. I have occasionally used language and expressions that some of my friends and acquaintances may find troubling. Oh well, now you know the real me! I have spent a good chunk of my life being politically correct, where it is necessary, and I will continue to be politically correct where and when necessary. But these pages are a reflection of the real world as I have seen it, and the way I see that world when I am bluntly honest. I must also be brutally honest in acknowledging that I have occasionally found humor in situations that I absolutely would never engage in. Anyone who may be troubled by what I have to say is encouraged to abandon these memoirs and get the latest copy of a more socially acceptable publication.

I hope these pages will also be of interest to the future generations of my relatives. I wish I could know you personally, but realize that the aging process will keep that from occurring; but at least you will have the opportunity to know quite a bit about this one earlier family member. I would really liked to have had this type of information about my many loved ones who long ago made that transition into eternal life.

These pages also reflect what I call my "defining experiences," in which several incidents affected me in very immediate and profound ways, and from that moment on changed the way I thought or behaved in certain instances. In addition to the defining experiences, these pages also reflect scores of situations that affected me in more subtle ways. Some of these incidents may not seem interesting or significant to you, the reader, but they did make an impact on me. For better or for worse, the reader will be able to immediately recognize the cumulative impact that much of what is said would have on a person; it sure made an impact on me.

I have been completely honest in every situation that is described, and often in ways that are a poor reflection on me personally. However, there are a few things that I have wisely chosen to leave out. No, I have not committed any murders or other serious crimes, nor have I engaged in inappropriate behavior with kids or small animals. But I have stayed clear of my social activity during the PB & PC Era (post-Barbara and pre-Cathy). Such silence is essential to maintaining martial bliss. I have some pretty good stories about my activities during that era, but will reserve those stories for nights out with the boys after a few drinks. Some of those stories will require more than just a few drinks!

These memoirs are very much of a catharsis in some instances. While it took me a while to realize it, much of what I have written, including many of my other writings that have been published, have served as a catharsis for pain that I have experienced. The passage of time is the best, and arguably the only real method, for me to expunge some of my sadness and anger toward certain people and situations; it has resulted in me "toning down" some of the things I wrote several years ago in the first draft of these memoirs. Without a doubt, my most severe and longest enduring pain was from what I observed and personally experienced in my last several months on the LAPD, in watching first-hand the self-serving and unethical actions of some folks I had previously liked and respected. Their behavior in failing to seriously challenge the actions of a struggling chief, in taking advantage of the leadership void in pursuit of their own selfish interests, and in taking care of their pals to the exclusion of more qualified and deserving persons, validated my long-term belief (and writings) that poor leadership brings out the worst in some people.

A few comments about the organization of these memoirs are in order. My life has not been lived in simple chronological order; rather, I have traveled down a series of parallel paths. For most of my adult life I held at least three jobs simultaneously: whatever law enforcement agency I was with, the Marine Corps, and Citrus College. Additionally, many of the actions and events that I discuss are interwoven with other activities. For simplicity and convenience of the reader, I have tried to organize the material in some semblance of order, and somewhat chronological, with the main activities (such as Marine Corps service) in one section from start to finish, LAPD service in one section start to finish, etc. To the extent that the reader occasionally comes across mention of something that has not yet been fully discussed, I apologize and ask your patience.

I hope the reader finds these pages to be interesting and informative, and that they even yield a few laughs. I also hope that my critics will not condemn me too harshly—a little harshly is okay, but not too much! We are all products of multiple influences, including our experiences, and I am clearly a product of what lies inside the following pages.

—Contents—

CHAPTER ONE

MY PARENTS & BROTHER

DAVID DELIAH BUSHEY—MY FATHER

My father, whose legal given name was David Deliah Bushey, was born October 14, 1902 in York, Pennsylvania. He did not care for his middle name and always just used the initial "D." He died in Duarte, California, on January 19, 1963. Dad's father, my grandfather Jacob Wesley Bushey, was born August 26, 1858, in Adams County, Pennsylvania, and died in Alhambra, California on April 19, 1941. Dad's mother, my grandmother Cora Myers Bushey, was born May 10, 1872 in Pennsylvania (unknown city) and died in Pennsylvania (unknown city) on October 6, 1906. My dad's siblings were Russell, Harold, Earl, and Clay.

My father was a Pennsylvania Dutchman who was born and spent his early years in York, Pennsylvania. On his father's side the clan first came to the United States in 1753, when Nicholas Buschi arrived. I have visited his gravesite at the Lower Burmudian Cemetery just outside of East Berlin, Pennsylvania. My dad and all his brothers entered the military (dad and Uncle Earl the Army, Uncle Clay the Ambulance Corps (Army), Uncle Russ the Navy, and Uncle Harold the Army (I think) during World War One. Afterward, they gravitated to California. All of the brothers have since passed on. Because of his young age, dad actually entered the Army at the very end of the war and did not see overseas service. I really do not know much about my dad's mother, except that she died when he was young and that he had a stepmother. My cousin, Steve Garrett, is the family historian and has a great grasp of all details of the family.

MARY JEAN BUSHEY—MY MOTHER

My mother, whose legal given name was Mary Amelia Hood, was born on October 26, 1906 in Sheridan Borough, Allegheny County,

Pennsylvania. She did not care for the name Amelia and used "Jean" as her middle name. She died at the Beverly Manor in Monrovia, California on March 2, 1998. Her father, my grandfather Archibald Stewart Hood, was born on December 23, 1876 in Liberton Parish, Edinburgh, Scotland, and died in Monrovia, California on June 19, 1965. Mom's mother, my grandmother Bessie Sherrill Armstrong, was born on September 20, 1879, in Schoolcraft, Michigan and died in Alhambra, California in approximately 1950. Mom's siblings were Stuart, Reid, Keith, and Dorothy; all have passed on.

LAURENCE DAVID BUSHEY—MY BROTHER

Larry was born at the Vorbeck Maternity Hospital, 2712 New Avenue in Wilmar, California on December 28, 1932. The attending physician was Dr. Dewey Aday. The city of Wilmar was absorbed into other cities many years ago, and the above location is now in Monterey Park. Neither the address nor the facility that was the hospital exists today.

At the time of my brother's birth the family lived in Alhambra at 1414 S. Campbell Avenue, in a 1920s era stucco motor lodge where access to the dozen or so small units is through an archway next to the sidewalk. The motor court is still there, and most likely today looks much as it did when my parents and brother lived there. The family's little bungalow was pretty close to the things happening in their lives. At the time my dad worked for his brother, Earl, at a barbecue stand located around Valley Boulevard and Atlantic Avenue. My mom's dad, Arch Hood, was a long-term employee at the "supermarket" located at 910 W. Valley Boulevard; the structure, now a Chinese "supermarket," is still there.

I think it was a bit of a difficult time for my parents. On several occasions, mom told me that Earl accused her of pocketing money from the cash register. The resulting rift, with my dad being outraged at the accusation, caused the brothers to be estranged for some period of time. After a while the rift blew over, but my mom was always somewhat sensitive to what she believed was Earl's "mean side." Thankfully, she also recognized and put the greatest emphasis on his good qualities. I loved my Uncle Earl and his wonderful wife Florence (who baked lemon pies just for me), but I did observe that occasional "mean streak." My mom and dad were as honest and ethical as the day is long, and any suggestion that my mom would have taken money from their business is not plausible. Funny, even when dad was a "bookie," he was very ethical and pro-police. Dad just felt that bookmaking should not have been illegal.

Chapter Two

MY RESIDENCES

221 West Adams Street
Alhambra

At least two noteworthy things happened on November 12, 1944: the WWII Battle of Leyte Gulf in the Philippine Islands, and the birth of another son, Keith Douglas Bushey, to David D. and Mary J. Bushey in Alhambra, California. My only sibling, brother Laurence David, was called "Dave" by just about everyone other than me and our parents. We have a photo of my brother holding me in his arms in front of our home at 221 West Adams Street when I was brought home from the hospital. Having found a dated American Kennel Club registration for a cocker spaniel there many years later, I know that we lived at that address at least through November of 1945; in fact, I am of the belief that we lived there until we moved to the Wells residence.

163 W. Wells Street
San Gabriel

This was a nice house built for my mom and dad by dad's brother Earl, who was also a contractor. At the time the house was built, probably in late 1946 or early 1947, my family was doing pretty well financially. Unfortunately, dad soon made a decision that did not work out too well. He sold "Dave's Drive-In," which was located on the northeast corner of 2nd Street and Valley Boulevard in Alhambra (the building is still there, but now a Chinese restaurant), and became a bookmaker (an illegal activity involving betting on horses). He apparently then became the victim of a more organized criminal operation, which put him out of business by orchestrating a situation where one of the horses he took a great deal of bets on did not perform anywhere near what the "odds" anticipated. Overnight, dad went deeply into debt because of his inability to pay off many of the people who had placed bets with him. We had to get out of town, *fast*—and that is how we ended up developing a chicken ranch in a remote part of the Antelope Valley.

My wonderful aunt and uncle, Dorothy "Dot" and Matt Twomey (she was mom's younger sister), lived just down the street from us at 229 W. Wells in San Gabriel. The only thing I recall about their house was a decorative, octagonal window by the front door (it is still there). Matt was a Navy "Seabee" (Construction Battalion-Metalsmith) who had spent most of World War II overseas in the Pacific Theatre with the Marines, where he'd been active in many of the most difficult campaigns. Sadly, he came home with a terrible case of malaria. While growing up I spent many good times at the homes of Dot and Matt, and remember vividly his misery, nightmares and profuse sweating at night. I remained close to them throughout their lives, including frequent visits to the nursing home in their later years, and coordinated the final services for both of them. They were cremated and laid to rest at the Riverside National Cemetery. Matt passed away last, on December 31st of 1999. I still think of them often for their love and the wonderful role they played in my life and that of my family.

90TH STREET WEST & AVENUE I
LANCASTER

We moved to this location with a great deal of haste in about 1948. The bottom had just fallen out of dad's "bookie" business in L.A. after he took in quite a number of bets on a horse that was doomed to fail. By the time dad realized he'd been "set up" by a competitor (or competitors), it was pretty much too late. The horse that supposedly was good only for the glue factory came in at the front of the pack, and dad did not have anywhere near the amount of money needed to pay off all the winners. We literally went to Lancaster in exile, to avoid all the people that were after him for money. There dad created a chicken ranch, where we lived for a year or so before returning to the Alhambra-San Gabriel area. I was just a little fellow and do not recall very much about it. But the things I do recall were the constant wind, stink bugs, watching my dad build the chicken coops, a mail biplane that flew over each day, watching our Kaiser automobile being repossessed in the middle of the night, and eating red-colored popcorn when my parents went to the small community of Pearblossom for a few drinks.

4

1011 SOUTH 4TH STREET
ALHAMBRA

We moved to Alhambra around 1949, just in time for me to start kindergarten at Ramona School, where I remained through the fourth grade. We moved in with my maternal grandparents, Arch and Bess Hood. Mom's brother, my Uncle Reid, also lived there. My brother Larry went into the Marines about the time we moved there, but returned home for visits when he was on leave or liberty. These were formative years for me, and a number of my activities occurred there that are discussed elsewhere in these memoirs. The house still stands, and occasionally I drive by and reminisce. A couple of times over the years I've walked around it and peered in the windows when the house was vacant and on the real estate market. There are still many memories in that house for me.

14023 DONALDALE STREET
PUENTE

My parents, brother, and I moved to this brand-new tract home around 1955. As I recall, the purchase price was $12,500 and was obtained via my brother's G.I. Bill. At the time Puente was a rural area that was rapidly being transformed into tract homes to feed the housing appetites of servicemen returning from World War II and Korea. Our house was in the first phase of "Sunkist Gardens," located in a tract to the immediate southwest of the intersection of Puente Avenue and Francisquito Road. At the time, just about the entire east side of Puente Avenue between Garvey Avenue (soon-to-be adjacent to the San Bernardino/Interstate 10 Freeway that was built through the area during the time we lived there) and Valley Boulevard were alfalfa fields. There was a cattle stockyard immediately north of the railroad tracks on the northeast side of Valley and Puente. In the northeast quadrant of Francisquito and Puente were dichondra fields, which were really great because of all the fun we had slipping and sliding between the berms just after watering (very much like the shallow rice paddies I later encountered in Southeast Asia).

It was a wonderful and developmental time in my life because of all the kids, the diversity, and the open areas in which to play. In the short time we were there I attended three elementary schools: Keenan, Bassett, and Van Wig. Of special glee to me, because every family had a military veteran, was the fact that just about every house had closets and garages full of military uniforms, equipment, and war trophies. As someone who has always had a fascination with the military (some might call it a *fetish*), I was in heaven and was always horse-trading with my pals for the stuff in their dads' duffle bags and locker boxes. I still recall one situation in particular, where every time one of my buddies needed another quarter or fifty cents it meant another trip into his Marine brother's locker box in the garage.

236 South California Street
San Gabriel

After a couple of years in Puente, my parents and I left the Donaldale house and moved into the home owned by Matt and Dot Twomey in San Gabriel. My brother had married his first wife, Marie Dingalo, who was a dispatcher on the Baldwin Park Police Department during my brother's brief tenure there. Larry soon got a job with the Buena Park Police Department and he and Marie moved to that city, which I guess is the reason we left Puente. Larry needed to devote his pay to his new life, yet my parents could not swing the monthly payments on Donaldale without my brother's added income. Life back in San Gabriel wasn't a very good time for me. I just didn't seem to fit in with the very few other kids in the neighborhood, and didn't make any long-term buddies while we lived there. Nothing big or catastrophic happened; it just wasn't a good fit, for whatever reason. I went to Washington School where I really didn't much care for the teacher, and at times actually had trouble understanding her (she was from the Philippines). As I recall, she did not care much for me, either.

Because I did not like Washington School I was hoping my parents would enroll me in the Christian school just up the street, but as it turned out they could not afford to do so. I was a lousy student, and have occasionally wondered whether I might have done better in a private school.

There was something really neat about our house, however—it was the room at the back of the garage that was all mine. It was my little corner of the world and full of all the stuff I liked, especially military junk. I spent many fun hours wearing various military uniforms, including the Navy Seabees tunic with Metalsmith 2nd Class insignia that I'd found in the garage. It had been my Uncle Matt's during World War II.

1964 CINCO ROBLES DRIVE
DUARTE

My mom worked at the City of Hope in Duarte. Around 1956 she found a house for rent immediately adjacent to the hospital grounds; literally just a couple of hundred yards from the personnel office where she worked. George Barnes, a wonderful old fellow who had served in the British armed forces before and during World War I, had just built two small stucco homes on the front part of his one-acre parcel to the immediate west of the hospital, and we rented one of them. George's wife was named Merle, a nice lady who was a nurse at the City of Hope. George was a real Western buff and called his acre the "Lazy Y Ranch," a term that I quickly embraced. I was moving to a ranch! George and my pop helped me build a small shack at the back of the property; naturally, it was soon full of my military stuff. The old Lazy Y ranch, consisting of George's "ranch house" (it really was just that—very rustic), several out-buildings, and the two stucco houses, are long gone. The property is now a parking lot for the hospital. My first school in Duarte was Beardslee Elementary; later I attended Northview Junior High School.

1956 CINCO ROBLES DRIVE
DUARTE

After a couple of years we moved again, but only next door to the house at 1956 Cinco Robles Drive. About that time I began my two years at Duarte High School. This move was pretty much just an economic decision, because it meant paying less rent. I recall the owner was a fellow named Chris Biller. The house supposedly had been some type of ranch outbuilding in the past, then it was converted into a residence. It was quaint but very homey, being the structure where most of my teen recollections are based. It had a fairly large shed in the rear that became my Shangri-La. From this home my pop and I traveled into downtown Los Angeles on November 13, 1961—the day I was shipping off to Marine Corps boot camp.

By the mid-1990s the house had been abandoned and was obviously about to be torn down. I took my son, Jake, to the old home (and my shed in the back!) and spent a few minutes reflecting on all that had occurred there when I was a teenager. The structures were torn down, and the entire area is fenced (as of January 2012) and obviously owned by the hospital, most likely part of an anticipated facility expansion.

1636 COTTER AVENUE
DUARTE

During my service in Cuba pursuant to the 1962 Missile Crisis, my mom and dad purchased a house of their very own! It had also been a farm outbuilding, a chicken house that had been turned into a residential dwelling. It was a bit of a strange place, with some walls that were really just partitions, and some features that were more a result of whatever construction materials were available as opposed to conscious design. But all in all it was a warm and cozy home. This was home for my last three years on active USMC enlisted duty and first four years on the LAPD. My mom sold it and moved into an apartment complex in the early 1970s.

459 WEST LAUREL AVENUE
GLENDORA

Barbara Beck and I were married on April 11, 1970. We were already in the process of purchasing this home, which was only a couple of hundred feet from her parents' home. It was a very nice house—three bedrooms and two baths with a detached double-car garage—and I could not believe that I really owned a home (well, along with the bank). The purchase price was the princely sum of $25,000 and the monthly payments were $220.00! We purchased it from the former wife of an Azusa physician whose last name was Goodman. In the late 1990s this house sold again, for something like $450,000.

Interestingly, before moving into our next home, we looked at a house on an acre parcel in the nearby foothills (where we now live), which at that time was listed at $44,000. We liked the location but realized we would have to add a room in order to suit our needs, and we felt we could not swing the monthly payments for both the house and an addition.

717 W. COUNTRY CLUB
BIG BEAR CITY
(VACATION HOME)

Barbara and I had spent a couple of weekends in Big Bear with my friend and his wife, Chuck and Evelyn Alexander, and decided to see if we could buy a place up there. In 1970 we bought this house for $10,000, and made the roughly $100 a month payments with my Marine Corps Reserve drill pay check. It was very small, I think about 500 square feet, but on a 50-by-100-foot lot. This was the first of four homes in Big Bear City—two with Barbara and two with Cathy—that were largely paid for with my Marine Corps drill checks. My neighbor across the street was a San Bernardino County sheriff's deputy assigned to Big Bear Station, Jim Stauffer, and my neighbor over the back fence was a fellow who had been arrested (but not charged due to inadequate evidence) by LAPD for the murder of his wife. I got along well with both of them. Some 35 years later, when I was appointed as San Bernardino County Sheriff's deputy chief, I tried unsuccessfully to locate Jim. But no record of his service was still maintained, nor could I find him in any other way, either.

215 Circledell Drive
Azusa

After about three years on Laurel Avenue we now had three kids, Jim (Barbara's son from a previous marriage), Jake and Stacy. That situation translated into a need for three bedrooms, which meant that I would have to give up my beloved den (the third bedroom on Laurel). We were exploring the option of putting on an addition when Chris Beck's (Barbara's dad) close pal, Bill Pickering, offered to let us assume the $37,000 note on a beautiful four bedroom home in the hills above Azusa. We sold the Laurel Avenue home and took over the Circledell home. It was a nice house in a nice neighborhood, overlooking a lovely view of part of the San Gabriel Valley. Jim was our only school-age kid at the time, and for the most part he attended Christian private schools in neighboring Glendora.

Hillside Community
San Gabriel Valley

We spent about four years on Circledell. During that time I was promoted to lieutenant with LAPD, continued to be promoted in the Marine Corps Reserve, and by then was also working part-time as an instructor at Citrus College. We were thinking that we would like to have horses and a bigger place. By then we were also in the position financially where we could afford to put an addition on that neat piece of property that we had looked at previously. A very nice couple had owned the house, but the man had unexpectedly died of a heart attack. The most recent owners added a pool in the front yard and had been growing all kinds of stuff, including some of the biggest pumpkins I've ever seen.

In the summer of 1977 we purchased the property for $99,500. While there, Zak was conceived and born, and we added a pretty nice addition to the house consisting of an office and a massive family room. But a couple of years later Barbara and I decided to go our separate ways. By the time I made captain (LAPD) in July of 1980, Jake and I were the sole residents; Barbara and the two younger children had moved to an apartment in Glendora. We decided to sell the house, but the timing could not have been worse: the 17% interest rates in the early 1980s precluded our ability to sell the house at any price even remotely close to reasonable. So, as another entry discusses, I bought Barbara out with a quitclaim process in 1984, and have remained in the house to this day.

The quality of the property really went into high gear with my marriage to Cathy in 1988. She diplomatically got rid of some old cars and equipment and started turning our crash pad (Barbara had been gone for eight years, and the occasional female visitors had not made any lasting impact) into a home. The improvements under Cathy's leadership have included a massive remodeling, addition of several rooms, a second story museum, a massive garage with an attic, and a video and alarm system second to none. I can only imagine what it would look like had I remained a bachelor!

HILLENDALE & FAIRWAY
BIG BEAR CITY
(VACATION HOME)

With our growing prosperity in the late '70s, Barbara and I decided to get a bigger weekend home in Big Bear City. In 1977 we sold the Country Club cabin and bought a corner lot immediately adjacent to the Big Bear City Airport, on the northeast corner of Hillendale and Fairway. We then had a nice two-story home built on the lot, which as I recall cost us another $37,000. Within a year or so, however, our marriage started to deteriorate, and we sold the place when we split up. Interestingly, halfway through escrow the purchasers also decided to divorce, but as an investment went through with purchase anyway—*whew*!

913 BEAR MOUNTAIN
BIG BEAR CITY
(VACATION HOME)

In 1988, while engaged, Cathy and I found a very nice two-story home on the North Shore in Big Bear City. The area is known as "Whispering Forest." Escrow on this property closed within a couple of days of our marriage in September of 1988. Things went pretty well until it was all but destroyed during the Big Bear earthquake around 1991. It was "red tagged" for close to a year and then our contractor, who had been a childhood friend of Cathy's, disappointed us with lousy and unfinished repair work. After the repairs were finally made, we enjoyed it for another couple of years before setting our sights on something even bigger, better, and with a commanding view of the Big Bear Valley.

Whispering Forest Community
Big Bear City
(Vacation Home)

By 1994 I had been promoted to commander on the LAPD and full colonel in the USMCR, and we were in the position to step up to a bigger house with a commanding view of the Big Bear Valley. We found and fell in love with the hilltop property and, after an unpleasant experience with a problematic realtor, bought the house directly from the sellers. We paid $185,000 at somewhat of a depressed time; it is now easily worth twice that. Our improvements have included turning the former dirt basement into a really great game and rumpus room for the kids. As of this writing (July 2012) we still own and enjoy this home. Unfortunately, all of the kids' activities prevent us from going up there as often as we like. But our several close friends sure enjoy it!

CHAPTER THREE
THE EARLY YEARS

SAM & THELMA ENGLAND—MY GODPARENTS

Sam and Thelma England were two of my parents' best friends. They lost their son, Navy Ensign John Charles England, who as a member of the crew of the U.S.S. *Oklahoma* was killed on December 7, 1941 at Pearl Harbor, Hawaii during the attack that triggered World War II for America. As dear family friends, it was the loss of their son that caused my parents to ask Sam and Thelma to be my godparents. While remaining good friends, as I got older my parents saw less and less of the Englands; I met and visited with them on a couple of occasions, but wish I had gotten to know them better. They passed away many years ago.

In September 1943 my godmother had the honor of christening the USS *England*, DE635, a destroyer escort named for their late son. The ship was placed into commission in December of 1943, and went on to become one of the most distinguished fighting ships of World War II, with an unsurpassed record of sinking six Japanese submarines as well as other achievements before the war was over. Toward the end of the war, during the battle for Okinawa, the *England* was struck by a Japanese kamikaze pilot and sustained severe damage, with 37 of her men dead or missing and another 25 wounded. This ship was decommissioned and scrapped after the war.

Because of its combat record and sinking of the Japanese submarines, in late 1944 the Chief of Naval Operations, Admiral Ernest King, stated: "There'll always be an England in the United States Navy!" King's pledge was partially kept when in November 1963 the USS *England*, DLG-22, was launched in Long Beach, California. At the time I was a lance corporal on Okinawa and was invited to attend the ceremony. But the Marine Corps did not feel that I needed to be there. Also, this christening occurred during the thirty-day mourning period following the assassination of President John F. Kennedy, and was not the gala event that it otherwise would have been. Like the original *England*, this ship is no longer in service and I suspect has been scrapped as well.

Wells & Manley—My First Recollection

My very first recollection of anything was as a toddler, when we lived at 163 West Wells Street in San Gabriel Village. I vaguely recall climbing up a dirt hill with my brother, a bug in a bottle in a basement (probably a crawl space), and visiting my Aunt Dot and Uncle Matt at their home several houses away at 229 West Wells Street. It was during this time that my dad was making the transition from owning and operating his own restaurant to being a bookmaker. Although he had no problem with being a bookie, he was very pro-police.

A Foster Kid Who Did Not Work Out

While living on Wells Street when I was just a toddler we had a young boy living with us. As I recall my mom telling me, the boy was a friend of my brother's from school who was taken into our home as a foster child at Larry's urging. For whatever reason, he did not work out, and after some period of time (several months?), he was removed. When I first joined the LAPD, at my mom's urging I went to the Records & Identification Division and pulled his file and his photograph (you could do those types of things in that era). Then in his mid-30s, by that time he had quite a troubling and extensive criminal record. Mom immediately recognized him and was saddened, but not surprised, that he had pretty much turned into an opportunist criminal.

Ate A Lotta Chicken In Lancaster

While a bookmaker, things went sideways for dad around 1947 or 1948. He was the "back office" for several bookies, and one day took in a lot of suspicious action on a horse that should not have done well. By the time he realized that he was being set up, he was unable to "lay off" some of the bets to others, and the horse—which really had high odds against it—came in well. With the benefit of hindsight and as a student of local history, I think it very likely that my dad was put out of business by the notorious mobster Mickey Cohen, who ran the wire services that notified the various bookies of how horses came in at the various tracks throughout the country, and was able to get last-minute bets placed when he already knew how the horse had placed (a process known as "past-posting"). Not only did we become destitute overnight, but my dad also was unable to pay off some of his customers. So we literally went into hiding, ending up on a ten-acre chicken ranch about ten miles east of Lancaster. We Busheys ate a great deal of chicken during that era. After a year or so we moved back to Alhambra, moving in with my mom's parents at 1011 South 4th Street. My maternal grandmother, Bess Hood, died of a stroke around 1950. My recollections of her are very positive, but not very clear—I wish I had known her better. Funny, the things people remember: our phone number was ATlantic 29047. This was a fairly new telephone number, because it was about that time that telephone numbers went from six to seven digits.

Among my great regrets is not having had the sophistication when my dad was still alive to discuss and truly understand his demise as a bookie. A book was written and released in 2009, called *L.A. Noir*, which describes well the activities of Mickey Cohen. The shenanigans and dates of many events in the book coincide with the downfall of my dad's bookmaking operation.

Fire Truck Chases Our Car

I still recall what could have been a tragic incident. It occurred as my mother was driving a car, pulling a trailer, bringing our worldly goods from Lancaster to the house on South 4th Street in Alhambra. We were somewhere in the Los Angeles basin when we noticed that a fire truck, with red lights on and siren blaring, was following us. Obviously, my mom immediately pulled over.

But it was chasing us! Our trailer was on fire, and a number of our possessions were burning. Apparently my mother, who was a smoker at the time, had thrown her cigarette out of the window and it had landed in the furniture and ignited some of the contents in the trailer. Fortunately, we didn't lose too much. But one of the casualties was one of the two wooden toy boxes that my dad had custom-made for my brother and me—my toy box and some of the toys went up in flames. The firemen quickly put out the trailer fire. Lucky for me, Larry, who was a teenager by this time, no longer cared about his toy box and it became mine.

CHAPTER FOUR
GRADE SCHOOL ERA (K-8)

JOE THE ICE MAN

After returning from exile in Lancaster we lived with my maternal grandparents in Alhambra. Among my many recollections there is that we did not own a refrigerator, but an icebox. It stood on the rear porch, and ice for it was delivered to our home every day or so. I still remember "Joe the ice man," carrying a big block held in large pincers up the back steps and into the enclosed back porch.

TELEVISION WITH MAGNIFIER ON SCREEN

The first television I can recall was in the home of our next-door neighbor in Alhambra, a very nice and kind elderly woman whose first name was Dovey. The TV had a small screen with a magnifying device covering the screen to make the images appear larger. Obviously, it was black-and-white. Dovey really loved wrestling, and was addicted to the TV and her beloved wrestling matches. I still recall that wonderful lady with great fondness.

MY FIRST LAW ENFORCEMENT BADGE

To the best of my recollection, I was in either first or second grade (actually a three-year period, because I flunked the second grade and got to do it twice!) when during a trip to the PTA Thrift Shop in Alhambra (I loved that place!) I saw a metal badge in the display case. The price was five cents. I bought it, and it turned out to be a federal agent's badge, circa WWI, with the letters "MTD" on the top ribbon. In the 1990s I gave this badge to one of my closest friends, retired IRS treasury investigator and badge collector Ray Sherrard. He specializes in Treasury badges and believes the letters stand for the "Miscellaneous Tax Division," which was an entity that existed during the early part of the 20th century.

My Favorite Toys

As a little kid my taste in toys remained pretty consistent. I liked toy guns and toy soldiers (not cowboys or Indians or gladiators, but toy soldiers). Christmas pretty much yielded the same things every year, all exactly what I wanted. I always got toys soldiers, military trucks and airplanes, toy guns, and often either a red wagon or a new sleeping bag, or both. I was one of those kids who spent a lot of time in sleeping bags, and just loved the warmth and comfort that went with a flannel sleeping bag. My mom and dad really knew what I liked.

My Closest Boy Cousin While Growing Up

Steve Garrett is the son of a wonderful older cousin who was about twenty-some years older than me, Dorothy Brady. He's also the grandson of my dad's brother, Earl Bushey. Because the Bushey brothers were close over the years, and just about always lived near to one another, Steve and I grew up together in the Alhambra-San Gabriel-Temple City area. Steve went into the Air Force for one term of enlistment, where he served as a medical technician. Like the rest of us he has a previous spouse, but for many years he's been married to a real sweetheart (hot, too!) named Marge. He has two great kids, Stacy and Brian, and is justifiably proud of them both. After a successful career in financial investments, Steve has achieved a prosperous and comfortable life style. He presently lives in northern Arcadia, has become the Bushey family historian, and really knows his stuff. Like Cousin Diana, after many years of sporadic visits we now see each other on a more frequent basis. I like that very much.

My Closest Girl Cousin While Growing Up

Diana Hood is the daughter of my mom's brother, Keith Hood, and his wife Ilene. Both of those wonderful people are gone now. Diana and I were about the same age, our parents were very close, and reciprocal childcare destined us to spend a great deal of time together. Like everyone else, Diana has had more than one spouse, and at present is single. She has a son, Lance, and a daughter, Jennifer, both now adults. After years of sporadic visits we have once again become close, for which I am very grateful. Diana recently confided that, when younger, she long thought that she and I would end up getting married. I confided that there was a time when my thoughts about her were definitely non-platonic and non-cousinly, and that it was only the evil eye and subtle comments of her dad that kept those amorous covert thoughts from becoming overt intentions! As long as I am confessing to the sins of my mind, I must also acknowledge that a few other female cousins also looked pretty hot and were also the object of a non-platonic thought or two during my young and reckless years.

KICKED OUT OF THE CUB SCOUTS!

Around 1953 I was a student at Ramona Elementary School in Alhambra, and also a member of the Cub Scouts. The den mother was a Mrs. Tedford, who was the mother of a kid I did not get along with, Jimmy Tedford. One day, he and I got into some type of a verbal disagreement, not unlike the kind of squabbles that kids often get into. Prior to a Cub Scout meeting, Mrs. Tedford called my mom and explained that I was a disruptive force in the den and that perhaps I should consider leaving the scouts! Then she reminded my mom it was my week to bring the donuts, but that if I was to leave it was still our responsibility to supply the donuts for the meeting! My mom was indignant, and did not think much of Mrs. Tedford's meddling in the squabbles of little kids. So we drove to a donut shop, got a box of donuts, then drove to the Tedford home (on the east side of 4th Street, just a few houses north of Valley Boulevard) where my mom told me to deliver the donuts. She also instructed me to tell them that I was too good for the den and I would no longer be a member. That is what I did—and that was the end of my Cub Scout career!

As soon as I got home I removed all the Cub Scout patches from my blue uniform shirt and sewed on Marine Corps chevrons! I vividly recall then going outside in my new "Marine Corps shirt," with a Marine Corps hat given to me by my brother, and strutting up the street! I still remember leaning against the fire hydrant on the southwest corner of Linda Vista and 4th Streets, and having a few other kids make fun of me in my new outfit. I also recall not being the least bit fazed by their scorn. That fire hydrant is still there, and I occasionally drive by the old home at 1011 South 4th Street. Among other things and recollections, I always look with affection and amusement at the hydrant!

This incident forever formed for me skepticism of the role of mothers in the organizations of young boys. Moms are super, but I think they sometimes become troublesome meddlers when their own kids are involved, with the result that they sometimes do foolish things and become tools in kids' cruelty toward one another. Scouting is great, but I must confess that the incident have left a negative impression for me that exists to this day.

My Dog, "Apache"

At some point in the mid-1950s while living on Fourth Street in Alhambra, I acquired a mangy dog that I named "Apache." I think he came from the pound. Like most kids, I really loved my dog. One day another child came to the door and Apache went crazy, barking and snarling and throwing himself against the screen that stood between him and the kid at the door. My parents became concerned that Apache might hurt a child, and got rid of him (probably returned him to the pound). I recall being upset. But even at that young age, I reluctantly understood the wise decision of my mom and dad.

Collecting and Selling Magazines in My Red Wagon

I honestly cannot remember a time when I didn't have some type of job. When I was just a little fellow I had a pretty good enterprise going with my little red wagon: I would go around our Alhambra neighborhood collecting various types of magazines. Once I had a good stock of magazines, I would arrange them neatly in the wagon and go door-to-door selling them! I actually did reasonably well and made a few bucks here and there, as it was very common for the woman of the house to pick through the magazines and select several, typically at the price of five or ten cents. As someone who was always a voracious reader, especially of detective magazines, this was a good deal for me, too. Not only did I get to read the magazines, which I'd got for nothing, but then I'd make a little bit of money selling them.

Shoeshine Stand at Tops Market

Another of my enterprises was a temporary shoeshine stand, which I established at the main entrance to Tops Market on the north side of Valley Boulevard between Fourth and Fifth Streets. I actually spent quite a bit of time there with my fairly extensive array of shoeshine equipment, offering to shine shoes to anyone who was willing to pay me the grand sum, as I recall, of about ten cents.

Cutting Lawns

When I was a kid it was fairly common for young boys to cut lawns in order to earn some money. I cut a great many lawns, for which the fee was usually about fifty cents. We did not have gas-powered mowers in that era; or, if they did exist they surely were not down at my level. I always used a push-mower, whose only propulsion came from me! Today, the mere thought of a push-mower is unthinkable, but I don't recall the use of one as being all that bad. I recall there was a knack to using it on heavier sections of the grass, by getting a run at the thicker portion and revving up the blade so that it was turning pretty fast when it hit the grass. I cut lawns from the age of about eight to the age of about twelve. Worked fine for me.

The Railroad Culvert at Sixth Street and Mission Road

This was one of those activities that would've caused my parents heart attacks had they known what I was doing. From time to time, one or two of my young buddies and I would crawl into a small culvert-type opening underneath the railroad tracks located on Sixth Street immediately south of Mission Road, and lay there as the trains rushed overhead. The roar of the train engine, the whoosh of the passing cars, and the vibration was nearly overwhelming. But, more importantly, it was great fun! This location no longer exists, as the tracks were lowered into a trench for sound abatement and to avoid interfering with vehicular traffic, a number of years ago.

Bicycle Tire Explodes

My hearing is lousy, and this event may have been the beginning of my hearing loss. One day when I was around eight or nine years old I rode my bike to the gas station then located on the northwest corner of Fifth Street and Valley Boulevard in Alhambra. I ended up pumping far too much air into my tire, and it exploded. Part of the shredded tire slapped me upside the face, which really stung, and the loud explosion caused a ringing in my ears that lasted for quite a while. The owner was nice enough to put my bike in his truck and drive me home. It was a pretty tough way to learn, but it was the last time I put too much air in a tire.

I don't think there was anything I enjoyed more than having a little bit of money in my pocket and going to a military surplus store. When I was a little kid, World War II had not been over that long and there was an absolutely wonderful abundance of surplus stores with all kinds of neat goodies. I was always using my allowance to buy items such as gas masks, helmets, hats, insignia, and just about anything else you can imagine. I recall purchasing a number of electronic gadgets, never knowing what they were for. I remember one of my favorite items was the control stick out of a fighter plane. I had hours of fun with it between my legs, pretending I was flying around and participating in aerial dogfights. Wonder whatever happened to that joystick? Don't know what I would do with it, but sort of wish I still had it.

MARY BUSHEY AND HER CATS

There was never a time when my mom did not have at least one cat. She was clearly one of the world's greatest lovers of cats, an affection she passed on to me and my kids. She often spoke of cats that she'd had as a child, and dearly loved every one of them. We had a lot of cats. All of them eventually made the transition into cat heaven, some tragically (like one in the clothes dryer!). Each death of one of her beloved cats took a toll on her. She always initially rejected getting another, saying the one that had just died could never be replaced. But within days another kitten always popped up. God, how my mom loved her cats.

My mom's love of cats, and the companionship and love they return to their owners, has convinced me that God put cats on earth to keep us laughing. I also see cats for what they are: short-term animals of affection that usually do not last all that long, and which must be immediately replaced with another loving kitten!

CHASING THE DOGS—FINALLY (DEFINING EXPERIENCE IN MY LIFE)

Up until the time I was about ten or eleven years old, I ran from dogs when they chased me, and was bitten quite a few times. I guess the absence of leash laws resulted in a great many more dogs running loose in neighborhoods than is the case today. I still recall an incident that occurred on the north side of Adams Street just east of Fourth Street, when a dog running loose bit me several times on the legs. Mom was indignant and took me to the owner's house and showed the woman all my bites, which were still fresh and bleeding. She then took me to Alhambra Receiving Hospital (on the west side of Sixth Street just north of Valley Boulevard, it was a large brick structure co-located with a fire station), where I was treated and given a tetanus shot. I was taken there several times for different reasons.

Then something in my brain snapped. I started chasing any dog that started to chase me! I yelled at them and threatened them just as they threatened me, and chased them home or wherever. No dog never again bit me—except accidently, while playing!

End of My Musical Career

At some point in the early to mid-1950s, as a student at Ramona Elementary School, I signed up for a music class. I wanted to play the trumpet, but had to rent one from the local store in town, Pedrini's. I was given a note to take to the music store in order to rent the instrument, which as I recall was something like fifty cents a week (maybe a month). When I went to Pedrini's, the man saw my name and asked if I was related to Dave Bushey, to which I proudly responded that he was my dad. The man said something to the effect that nothing was too good for Dave Bushey's kid, and to bring my dad back with me and I would get the best trumpet they had! I was thrilled and ran home to get my dad, who told me we would not be going back to the store and, basically, that my musical career was over! It turned out that old man Pedrini was among the folks my dad owed money to from his days as a bookie, not someone he was anxious to see again. If not for that situation, I might have become a famous musician (then again, probably not).

German Machine Gun Nest in Neighbor's Garage

As a child growing up it was very common for my young friends to have dads and uncles who had served during World War II, and who had brought home all sorts of war souvenirs. Probably the most significant and interesting of all the war souvenirs I encountered was a complete German machine gun nest that was located in the rafters of the Bensted home, just a couple of doors south of our home on South 4th Street in Alhambra. In addition to the machine gun nest, there were several German rifles. I really fell in love with those guns and felt fortunate that the Bensteds would occasionally let me fondle them. Today, because of all the laws, it would be unheard of for a machine gun of any sort to be found at a private home.

Telephone "Party Lines"

As a small child and up to my teen years, just about every household had a telephone that was part of a "party line" network. During that era technology had not advanced to anywhere near what we have today, and there were more phones than lines to accommodate those phones. As a consequence, it was commonplace to have several households on one common circuit. Although only the number being called would ring, if any of the other households on the circuit picked up their phone they could hear the entire conversation, regardless of it being directed to some other phone on the circuit. Today if somebody comes on the line, it is another person in the same household. But many years ago it might have been a complete stranger (usually) from some other household. In small towns where everyone knew everyone else's business, party lines were among the reasons why.

The Racists Whom I Loved

So much has changed in the last five or so decades, and much of that change has been for the better. As a child I had a couple of uncles who, by today's standards, would have to have been called horrible racists. To them, Blacks were "niggers," Mexicans were "spics," Jews were "kikes," etc. They were loving and caring men, and relatives whom I loved. But they came from an environment that was pretty troublesome, and a long-past generation. I was just a little kid and quite frankly did not think much about what they said, good or bad. In later life they both settled down a bit, with fewer racial comments coming from either. In the final years of their lives, I do not recall hearing any such troubling comments. I always think of these two wonderful men and the positive changes that occurred during their lives, and of the phenomenal societal changes that have taken place during my own lifetime.

Teacher Drags Little Keith Out of the Classroom

My first day in the sixth grade was pretty memorable. Van Wig was a new school constructed for all the kids living in the hundreds of new homes being built in the area. Our teacher was an Army Korean War veteran, Mr. Wilson. During the first hour of so of the class, Mr. Wilson was doing what teachers do—telling us what was expected, etc. I don't recall the issue, but I made some wisecrack that apparently irritated Mr. Wilson, at which point he grabbed me by the collar, pulled me out of my seat, dragged me outside and jacked me up against the wall! I don't recall his exact words, but there was some profanity. In essence, he said I was a little shithead and that I had better knock off my nonsense! He got my attention. I ended up loving (well, kinda) and respecting this man, and this became my only year of getting good grades in either grammar or high school! I was also in the school safety patrol and attained the coveted gold certificate (most of them were green) for my performance. My safety badge from Mr. Wilson is displayed in my office to this day. I would like to meet this man again, but such is not to be the case. Several years ago I met with the then-superintendent of Bassett School District, but Mr. Wison was long gone. The name "Robert Wilson" is common, and my further attempts to locate him were futile.

I drive through the old neighborhood from time to time, looking at my old home and my childhood haunts. I never fail to look at that wall where one teacher was able to truly get my year-long attention.

That Guy Was a Colonel?

I still remember my shock—and certainly my awe and resulting respect—on learning the background of one of my pals from Van Wig School. His dad was a soft-spoken and humble Mexican man who struck me as a hard-working laborer. Then one day my friend showed me his dad's military uniform: he had been a full colonel and pilot in the China-Burma Theatre during WWII! This incident helped me to realize that "you cannot always tell a book by its cover."

Negroes Move into the Neighborhood

There was quite a fuss one day on Donaldale Street. The kid across the street said that a big meeting was planned to determine how to deal with the fact that a black family had moved into the neighborhood. The neighbor kid asked me to have my mom and dad to come to the meeting that night. He was breathless and excited, and I guess I was too when I told my parents about his request. But they were clearly unimpressed with the concerns of the man across the street, and explained that the color of a person's skin has no bearing on what type of person they are. My dad took me outside, pointed to the house where the black family lived, and asked me if I saw any problems with the house or yard, which I did not. He made some comment about *that* was all the counted, and that was the end of the conversation. This was not a big topic of conversation in our house, and there was no heated discussion. But it was an experience that stuck with me, and made an impression.

In 1956 I was fourteen, and clearly in love with and obsessed with the Marine Corps. In addition to a room and garage full of Marine surplus uniforms, insignias, etc., I was a member of the San Gabriel Valley Junior Marine Drill & Rifle Team. In the Junior Marines I participated in virtually every parade and meeting, and loved every minute of it. The leader of the Junior Marines was a former Marine named Jim Smith, who lived on a street off Del Mar Avenue in South San Gabriel. I still recall that he hauled all the kids around in a 1938 LaSalle hearse, and the horror in my mom's eyes the first time he picked me up for a function.

Jim Smith was somehow affiliated with Devil Pups, Inc., and had the ability to send kids to the organization's ten-day summer encampment at Camp Pendleton. I wanted more than anything in the world to go. Smith apparently decided to use the Devil Pups as a recruiting incentive for either the American Legion or the Veterans of Foreign Wars (I do not recall which). I was told I could go, if I could get either my dad or my brother, both of whom were veterans, to join the concerned veterans' organization. My dad was ill and not really able, and my brother scoffed at the idea and apparently did not think much of the organization. Neither of them joined, with the result that I was unable to attend Devil Pups. I was upset beyond description and remember crying all night over my inability to attend.

Not long after this incident there was a big battle among the adults in the San Gabriel Valley Junior Marines, and in a coup the organization was taken over by the parents of another cadet/member named George Little. Jim Smith was pretty much thrown out. I was devastated, as were my parents. We were among some of the families who left the organization because of the rift and our unhappiness with the way Smith had been treated (even through he did not send me to Devil Pups!). I recall seeing a news article several years later, showing a picture of Private First Class George Little as a Marine Corps boot camp graduate.

Forty-some years later, as a Marine colonel (USMCR) performing my active duty training out in the middle of the Mojave Desert at the Marine Corps Air-Ground Training Center in Twenty-Nine Palms, Sergeant Major George Little (also USMCR) was temporarily assigned to my command. The name was familiar, but it took each of us a while to connect the dots. Then we had a number of good conversations about the old times. The animosity from many years before did not surface in the least. In civilian life George was a sergeant with the Alameda County Sheriff's Department. A few years later I was saddened to learn that George had died as a result of injuries sustained during a fall.

Also a number of years later, probably in the early 1970s, my brother joined the VFW in Monrovia and encouraged me to become a member. I did join, but then he lost interest and I never attended a meeting. As I write this, I am a life member of the VFW and still have not attended a meeting. I have also been a member of American Legion Post #381 (LAPD) since 1967, and have attended a couple of meetings, but not on a regular basis.

Now, fifty-some years later, I am a vice president of Devil Pups, Inc., and have been affiliated with this great organization since right after the Vietnam War. I still recall my youthful pain at not being able to go to camp, and as a recruiter, in addition to my vice president status, I have always found a way to send a kid who is as motivated as I was. In addition to being a member of the board, I have also retained the position as liaison officer for the San Gabriel Valley, the same position that Jim Smith held over fifty years ago! I remember a situation twenty or thirty years ago where a dear friend and fellow Marine, Tom Vetter, and I exceeded our quota at that time. Although our quota was for 35 kids, we jammed 105 young boys on the bus. Like I said, a kid who really wants to go will have the opportunity as long as I am in a position of leadership.

Military Medals and the Half-Hour Wait

I was about eleven or twelve and living at 236 South California Street in San Gabriel (the house we rented from Uncle Matt and Aunt Dot Twomey), when a strange and painful situation occurred. My brother Larry said he had something to show me. But before showing me what it was, Larry made me promise to wait one-half-hour before calling the telephone number that was given. I agreed. He then showed me an ad in the newspaper where a private party was selling a collection of military medals and insignias for $5.00. Wow, right up my alley! I wanted to immediately pick up the phone, but he made me stick to my half-hour promise before calling! It was a horrible half hour. There was nothing I cared for more than military insignias, and I was afraid they would already be sold if I didn't call right away. As soon as the half-hour passed (I sat fidgeting at the kitchen table with my eyes glued to the clock the whole time—mom was also present), I immediately called the number. But the collection had just been sold. I was hurt and pissed, and I know that mom felt bad and was not pleased with the situation. She tried to make amends a day or so later by taking me to a surplus store and giving me a few bucks—which I really appreciated.

I loved my brother dearly, but he occasionally did some foolish and painful things. He apparently found some amusement in this incident that was very painful for me. I would never do this to someone, nor would I permit someone else to behave this way. My guess is that my mom would have never permitted something like this to happen again, either.

THE "LAZY Y RANCH," GEORGE BARNES, GRETEL, AND MY BB GUN

About 1957 or 1958 mom, dad and I moved from San Gabriel to 1964 Cinco Robles Drive in Duarte. I really loved the place we moved into. It was on an acre next to the City of Hope Medical Center, and adjacent to hundreds of acres of open area (undeveloped hospital property and the Santa Fe Dam). Our landlord was an old World War I Veteran named George Barnes and his wife, Merle, who was a nurse at City of Hope. George really liked the Western motif, and their house was essentially a big cabin in which cowboy accoutrements were everywhere. He baked his own bread, which was delicious, and entertained me for hours with his military stories. He still had the uniform with kilts that he'd worn in his Highlander Regiment. He was a crusty old fart, but very kind to me. He made an impact on my life.

Every day after school, and all day during the long days of summer, I went out into those open areas with my beloved dog, Gretel, and my trusty BB gun. It was something that I just loved doing. Today, seldom a time passes when I am on the 605 Freeway, literally driving over my old stomping grounds, that I fail to glance at the open spaces and reflect back on those pleasant youthful pastimes.

MY FAVORITE DAY—HALLOWEEN

Nothing—absolutely nothing—provided me more happiness than wearing a military uniform. From as far back as I can remember, I was fascinated with military uniforms from all branches, and frequently bought surplus shirts and hats and whatever else I could find at thrift stores. I'm sure I was responsible for a great many chuckles when, as a little kid, I would parade around dirt lots wearing uniforms that were too big, a helmet that my head pretty much disappeared into, a gas mask, and leggings covering my feet and ankles, while carrying a genuine replica military training rifle! Halloween was the best day of the year, however, because I could parade around in uniform with some scintilla of dignity and legitimacy, and where my obsessive-compulsive uniform fetish was not out of place because of all the other people were wearing costumes, as well.

My Go-Kart

I still don't know how I talked them into it, but when in the eighth grade my mom and dad bought me a go-kart. I still recall that it cost $99, and that we got it from Angel's Hardware, which was located around Huntington Drive and Los Lomas. I drove that thing all over town for months, and was never once stopped by the sheriff. I had a few crashes, including a speed run into the garage that resulted in me obliterating a big mirror when I couldn't stop in time (thankfully, I did not suffer seven years of bad luck as a result!). I recall my kart had a belt drive, and that as the belt became worn and loose I had to drive with one hand on the engine to increase the belt tension for speed. My mom did not like to cook, so I made dozens of trips from our house to the "Hi Ho" hamburger stand on the northeast corner of Huntington Drive and Buena Vista Street. Can you imagine a kid driving a go-kart on those streets today?

I still shudder with horror when recalling one incident. A pretty little gal named Jackie lived down the street. One day Jackie asked if she could take a spin in my go-kart. Since the belt was badly worn and very loose and the thing would hardly pull me, I mistakenly assumed it would barely pull her as well. I did not factor into consideration that she weighed much less than I. When she sat down and hit the gas the thing took off like a rocket, heading toward Duarte Road! I was unable to catch up on foot and stop her. Jackie didn't know how to engage the brake and was screaming at the top of her lungs. She went westbound on Duarte Road and somehow flipped over just short of Buena Vista Avenue, resulting in a great deal of road rash and looking like hell. Thank goodness she was not badly injured, or worse, as the incident could have had a much sadder ending. Funny, but we didn't have much of a relationship after that day.

My Pal Rick Crippen and Our Mo-Peds

Rick Crippen was one of my best pals in high school. His parents were very nice, as was his sister Barbara. Rick and I both had Mo-Ped motorbikes, made by the Puche Corporation in Germany. We rode all over the San Gabriel Valley on our motorbikes, and had great fun. I will always recall one time when I was invited to join his family for a Sunday afternoon dinner at a nice restaurant in Pasadena. After high school Rick entered the Navy and served on the USS *Boxer* during Vietnam. He later married a nice gal named Claire and had a couple of fine sons; unfortunately, their marriage did not last. For quite a while Rick served as an aide to Congressman John Russolott, a Republican. Later Rick went into investments and seemed to get by okay, but unfortunately he started drinking.

In later life Rick met and resided with a great gal, Mary Lou Marshall, in San Clemente. They and Cathy and I were good friends and we especially liked to visit at Big Bear, where Mary Lou also had a nice home on Georgia Street. But Rick's health started going downhill around 2005, and he almost did not survive due to a severe heart problem. Then in May 2011 while driving in San Clemente he had a fatal heart attack, ran off the road, and crashed his car. It was my honor to coordinate the appearance of a Navy honor guard for his services in San Clemente. Rick's sons and his mother were both present, and it was especially nice for me to be able to visit with her as she still had most of her faculties even into her 90s. Unfortunately, Rick's sister Barbara is pretty much permanently housed in a facility for those who have suffered the consequences of permanent damage due to substance abuse.

Rest in peace, Rick.

Academic Performance and Homework

I hesitate to be absolutely candid on the issue of my school homework. However, my desire to be accurate is going to win out. Although I do not expect the reader to believe what I'm about to say, it is absolutely true. In all of my years of grammar school, junior high school, and my two undistinguished years of high school, I almost never did any homework. In fact, I don't think it is too much of a stretch to suggest that what my kids do in one week today is probably pretty close to what I did during all my years in public schools, prior to entering the Marine Corps! As I write this I am a pretty well-educated person, with degrees up to and including master of science. But I think the two factors that served me well, despite my mediocre academic performance, were the fact that I have always been a voracious reader, and while on active duty in the military I typically wrote two or three letters a day (not only to my mom and other relatives, but to any number of young women who were my pen-pals—and sometimes a little bit more).

Mediocre Plans for the Future Stopped at My 17th Birthday!

The only thing I knew for certain before turning seventeen, was that I would enter the Marine Corps the very day I turned seventeen. In those days the lack of a high school diploma was not a disqualifying factor, and in fact I think that a very high percentage of enlistees were high school dropouts during the era. I had fleeting thoughts about maybe being a cop, but feared that my burglary arrest (discussed in the subsequent chapter) might exclude me from that occupation. Realistically, I had no serious thoughts—absolutely none—that extended beyond becoming a Marine the day I turned seventeen. In my earlier teens I had given some consideration to the Navy; but it was always secondary to the Marine Corps.

Unique Men Played a Positive Role in My Development

As a kid growing up, I was fortunate to have a number of adult men who played fairly significant roles in my development. Interestingly, most of these men were not pillars of society, and in fact were pretty much at the opposite end of the spectrum. The most significant for me was Sam Nusenoff, a wonderful man who was among the hardest workers I have ever met, but who as I recall liked his beer to a considerable extent. Then there were two fellows who operated the Duarte Shoe Repair shop, George and Russ, both of whom were a little bit on the sleazy side with respect to their attraction to women. And I don't want to forget old Mr. Rogers, who lived just north of our home on Cinco Robles Drive in Duarte. I don't believe I ever saw him sober. All these men, and several others of similar backgrounds whose names I have forgotten, were very good to me. Despite their own questionable existences, they had a very positive influence on my life. I know they all liked me and wanted the very best for me. I think the situation is a pretty good example of the good that exists in all people.

Tropicana Liquor

In about the seventh and eighth grades, I worked as a stock boy at the Tropicana Liquor Store located on the corner of the Duarte Road and Buena Vista Street. The owners were very nice people, a husband-and-wife from some Eastern European nation, possibly Romania, as I recall. It was a good job, part-time of course, and it paid minimum wage, with the only real downside being quite a bit of time in a cold locker restocking the various types of beverages.

My mom and dad apparently got quite a kick out of this situation, as they both repeated it a number of times to a number of people. As an 8th grader I had a brief romance with another eighth grader, who was very well (and prematurely) endowed. Naturally, I wanted to introduce and show her off to my parents, so we walked from her house to mine. My pop saw us coming down the street and was apparently stunned and incredulous at my young girlfriend's enormous attributes, and yelled to my mom, "My god, Keith is coming down the street and is arm-in-arm with Tits Mallory!" I don't know who that Mallory gal was, but assume she also must have been very well endowed.

FIGHTING BACK IN DUARTE (DEFINING INCIDENT IN MY LIFE)

In moving to Duarte from San Gabriel midway through the sixth grade, as I recall, I encountered something new. That was being continually challenged to fight. I was the new kid at Beardslee School, and an apparent juicy target for bullies and those who wanted to be bullies. I still recall some of the kids who continually "chose me off." They were Richard Arias, Henry Rodriguez, Laverne Wetzel, Rick McCloud, and a few others. For several months I continually declined to fight them. But the situation just got worse. It seemed that every declination to fight caused those who challenged me to challenge me even more, and resulted in other little shitheads starting to challenge me, as well.

On day I'd apparently had enough and agreed to fight Laverne Wetzel after school. We met in a dirt lot between Beardslee School and Buena Vista Avenue (now occupied by apartments), where we were were joined by a few spectators. We exchanged blows, Laverne ended up with a bloody lip, and the fight really did not last that long.

My whole world changed after that fight! It was now known that I would not back down, and people stopped challenging me to fight. Laverne Wetzel and Rick McCloud became two of my best friends. My days of worrying about being challenged, and feeling fearful as I walked home, were over. My way of looking at the world was changed by five minutes in that dirt lot: the best defense is a strong and vociferous offense! I have shared this lesson with my sons, and it is pretty much a behavior that I have demonstrated (but not foolishly; after all, I'm a cop and don't want to jeopardize my careers) throughout my life. In the great majority of instances, a confident demeanor that sends out the message that you are willing to go to blows will in the end prevent those blows.

Chapter Five
HIGH SCHOOL ERA (2 Years!)

Pop Reading the Dictionary

My dad was a very wise and intelligent man. But academically he never went beyond the seventh grade! One of my lasting impressions of him is sitting by the door in our house at 1956 Cinco Robles Drive, waiting up for me to return home after going out with my pals, or whatever, and reading the dictionary. We moved to Duarte when I was in the sixth grade, living first at 1964 Cinco Robles Drive, later next-door at 1956 Cinco Robles Drive and, still later when I was in Cuba during the 1962 Missile Crisis, moved to 1636 Cotter Avenue. None of these houses survives. The two on Cinco Robles were leveled for the City of Hope, and the one on Cotter was leveled to make room for a new home.

DeMolay

While I was a freshman in high school a fine young man and a friend, Bill Trusdell, invited me to join DeMolay. It was a youth extension of the Masons, and a fine organization that places a high premium on all things positive, from honesty to Christianity to fidelity to truthfulness and beyond. Only "good" kids were in DeMolay, and my parents were very supportive. I jumped through all the hoops, memorized all the required oaths, went through the ceremony, and became a full-fledged DeMolay. This was a very good thing for me, because it kept me in the company of good kids and good people during my limited high school years, when I could have easily drifted in bad directions. Toward the end of my USMC enlistment I became briefly re-associated as an advisor, and successfully made application to be designated a "Representative DeMolay."

Sam Nussenoff was a hard-working, blue-collar guy who did not leave much of an impact on the world. But he played a big role in my life and in my development. I first met Sam when I was about ten or eleven years old. He was one of two people who ran a little market and sundries store at the City of Hope, across the parking lot and due west from mom's personnel office. When the store was shut down, he got some other type of relatively low-level job at the hospital. Sam had the additional job of running the projector and showing movies one night a week in an old auditorium, where he permitted me to be his assistant. I still remember the old, arc-light projectors, which had "Dual Peerless Super Simplex" in gold leaf lettered on their sides. These were real, first-run movies that the studios permitted the hospital to show for the benefits of its patients; some employees also attended. I remember making a big mistake one night that resulted in burning some of the film and damaging one of the projectors (the two worked in tandem, seamlessly switching from one to the other in a manner that did not interrupt the movie). I know it created a big problem for Sam that necessitated a trip into Los Angeles to get parts, but he was gentle and understanding. He was a wonderful man with a strong work ethic and a fine character, always available to me as a friend. I believe he helped shape the person that eventually I became. At some point Sam left the City of Hope and went to work for Columbia Ribbon & Carbon, a long-time plant that then existed alongside the north side of the railroad track a block or so west of Buena Vista. He was a long-time resident of the Filly Motel on Huntington Drive, drove an old beat-up car, and lived somewhat of a "hand-to-mouth" existence. I regret that I slipped away from him as I entered the military and adulthood, and believe he passed on due to cancer long ago. God bless that wonderful man.

Duarte Shoe Repair

Duarte Shoe Repair was located on the north side of Huntington Drive, roughly across from Pops Road, in a small building that is long gone. The owner was a crippled old man named George, and his only employee was named Russ. I worked there on Saturdays for quite a while when in high school. They were nice men and it was a fun little job. In fact, I always had a part-time job of some type, and this was one of the longer-lasting ones.

We never took a family vacation, *per se*. But every couple of years, mom, dad, and I would go to San Diego and spend a couple of days in a motel on Pacific Coast Highway. From there was always a trip to Tijuana, where I bought some fireworks.

But my greatest joy was walking up and down Broadway in the presence of all the Marines and sailors, and going into the locker clubs soliciting the used stripes and patches that had been removed from the sleeves of uniforms as servicemen were promoted (or demoted). The patches usually littered the floor around the sewing machines, and I was always told to help myself. I also really enjoyed hanging out at the pier at the bottom of Broadway, watching all the Navy personnel come and go on the water taxis. Further north stood the Port Building (still there), from where I could watch the PBY aircraft take off and land in the bay.

At night, it was fascinating to watch the flashing signal lights going from one ship to another, probably by bored signalmen who had the duty.

This was the era where families often went camping on their vacations, which was pretty neat. I always thought it would have been nice to go camping, but my dad was older and not well, and my mom was not really the camping type. My brother took me up to Chantry Flats one night, where we slept out, but that was about it. I occasionally camped out in our back yards, and really enjoyed those times. In hindsight, given my obsession with the military, the limited San Diego mini-vacations gave me more joy than probably any other type of family vacation.

The pier at the foot of Broadway has a lot of significance for me. Both my brother during the Korean War, and me in the early Vietnam stages, shipped out and returned aboard troop ships. Each of those four times we embarked from and returned to that same pier. I still remember, as a child with my mom, waving goodbye to my brother (we were able to make him out among the hundreds of Marines on deck). We stood on that pier watching his troop ship, the USS *Mann*, fade from view as it set out to sea enroute to Korea.

That was 1953, I was about nine, and I cried at the departure of my brother. He got to Korea shortly before the end of hostilities, serving in the 1st Marine Division Embarkation Section. A lot of construction and changes have taken place in San Diego, but whenever I'm there I go to the foot of Broadway to reflect on my experiences there, and think about my brother.

As an 8th grader, I spent some time hanging out with a kid who was really not much of a good influence (maybe I was the bad influence on him!). His name was Bruce Robertson (pseudonym). Bruce lived with his mom and a sister in a home that had a back house, on the south side of Duarte Road about three houses east of Cinco Robles Drive (the house is gone and the property is now part of the City of Hope Medical Center). He also had a brother in prison and a sister in a mental hospital.

We were a couple of little turds who skipped school and did stupid stuff. It was kinda neat because he had the back house to himself, and that is where he and I and a few others (who I do not recall) hung out. One night during a nocturnal outing, three or four of us found an open door on the west side of the boy's gym at Duarte High School. A chain through the push levers secured the building, but we were all thin and managed to open the doors enough to slip in. As I recall, we each took a football jersey (I think that was all?). We then returned to Bruce's back house and fell asleep in the chairs (it must have been a weekend and I would have had my parents' permission to sleep over, but not if they knew I was running wild around town). Bruce apparently told his sister about what we had done and she apparently snitched us off to the sheriff's department. As I recall, she didn't care for any of us.

I was awakened by a big deputy whose name was Billy Malone, who told me to step outside for a little chat. I recall playing the tough guy when he asked what had occurred, replying that I had no idea of what he was talking about. He then picked me up, shook me a few times, repeated his question, and my mouth started going like a duck's butt. I spilled the beans and confessed what we had done.

We were all taken to the Temple City sheriff's station and booked for burglary. I was in a cell for five or six hours before my dad came and got me. My parents did not make a real big deal out of it, but they were clearly disappointed in me. I think they thought I was basically a pretty good kid (despite cutting school all the time) and that my conduct had been an aberration. Also, my dad was old beyond his years, and sick, and my mom didn't really have the energy to deal with it. I did not go to court, but was put on probation. My probation officer was a very nice man named Ignacio Hernandez. He visited me about once a month for a few months, followed by unsupervised probation for some unremembered additional period of time.

About ten years later, as a relatively new policeman I ran across Ignacio Hernandez in a downtown courtroom. I believe he was genuinely glad to see me and to learn that I was doing well. Then around 1981, as a police captain in uniform attending the funeral of a sheriff's retiree, I ran across retired Sergeant Billy Malone! I reminded him of the arrest incident that night long ago, and he said he recalled the event. He was probably just being polite, but we shared a nice conversation. It is a small world, indeed.

Dave Bushey, Sick but Always There for His Son

My dad was in his forties when I was born. He was a heavy smoker and at one time a heavy drinker, and not in good health any time during my life that I recall. He had his tonsils taken out while in the Army, circa 1918, and the years of cigarette smoke and tar on that spot in his throat resulted in throat cancer. After a long period of radiation that killed his taste buds and did a lot of damage to his system, and following the failure of the radiation treatment, he had radical surgery to remove the cancer, which in so doing removed about a third of his neck and throat. Because of not eating well (everything had a metallic taste), his system became weakened and he contracted tuberculosis. He also ended up with emphysema. Toward the end of his life he was in bed just about all the time, getting up only briefly to tend to personal matters and take some nutrition.

Anyway, during my life dad was always sick to some degree. Nevertheless, he always found the time and energy to assist me, usually by taking me places—to the movies and back, to friends' houses, whatever. He was a very kind and considerate person, and clearly loved me. He did what he could and I will always be grateful for him.

I never drive by 1031 South Broadway in downtown Los Angeles without looking at the exact spot where he dropped me off early on the morning of November 13, 1961, at the military induction station. He did not hesitate to kiss me goodbye. I also never drive past the weed-strewn area that used to be a parking lot adjacent to what had been the "Mike" Company area of the Infantry Training Regiment at Camp Pendleton, without remembering him picking me up for my first Marine Corps ten-day leave.

How I wish he could have lived longer so that I could have known him as an adult! Beyond his love, he was very kind to me. I hope that I have been equally kind to my kids. Upon his death the coroner returned his belongings including his wallet, which contained three pictures of me. That wallet sits in my center desk drawer to this day. I love you, Pop.

THE CROSS-COUNTY STAR—NOT!

I have always been an outdoor type of fellow, but never much of an athlete. As a high school freshman I went out for football, but quit after several weeks because I did not like staying so long after school. So I went out for track and cross-country because, except for the competitive meets at other schools, it didn't require staying after school. I was so mediocre at it that the coaches lumped my points together from track and cross-county so I had enough to earn a school letter (a chenille letter that went on my "letterman's sweater"). Only the varsity players got jackets in those days. I'll never forget one cross country meet, where I was so far behind everyone else that as I ran past the bleachers the people stood up and cheered, thinking I was out front in a new race! That was my level of fitness when I entered the Marine Corps. But when I came home on my first leave from boot camp I ran with the team one day and beat just about everyone! Funny, what the Marine Corps can do for a person.

BIG DADDY AND THE KNIFE

There was a punk at Duarte High School named Henry "Big Daddy" Rodriguez (pseudonym). One day he pulled a knife and said he was going to cut me up. I chose to bullshit him out of the knife. As he was threatening me, I was verbally admiring the knife and asking him how much he wanted for it. He finally stopped the threatening, and we agreed on a price for the knife. He was part of a bad Mexican crowd with some other shithead pals, and I did not want trouble from any of the others, either. I bought the knife, and afterward always said hi to "Big Daddy" when I saw him. It is my understanding that after high school he went to work for CALTRANS, and was struck and killed by a car on the San Bernardino Freeway. I assume that he had grown and matured and become a decent person as an adult.

I have always been a pretty decent bullshitter, and this was a reflection of my early skills. As those skills were further developed they became pretty helpful as I moved through life, hopefully in either fun or legitimate ways. These same abilities were further developed and used with great value when I infiltrated subversive, terrorist, and un-American organizations as an undercover policeman.

My First Driver's License—A Learner's Permit

In those days a kid had to be 15½ years old to obtain a learner's permit, subsequent to a written test. I was green with envy when accompanying my pal, Jim Dowdle (and his dad) when Jim reached that magic age, and went to the DMV to get his permit. I hovered over every bit of the process, and to my amazement saw that the examiner did not require Jim to provide his birth certificate indicating his birth date. Having his dad present was apparently sufficient; probably the examiner was just plain lazy. Anyway, I called my dad then and there and asked him to come to the DMV and attest to my age, which meant saying that I was six months older than I really was. Dad hustled right over to the DMV office on Garvey alongside the San Bernardino Freeway—and Jim and I both got our permits that day.

Two Phony Squids and the Chief Petty Officer

Don Middleton was another of my good pals. He was as jazzed about joining the Navy as I was about joining the Marines. We both had an interest in electronics, but he knew what he was doing and I did not. By the time I began high school I had a virtual costume shop of military uniforms, mostly Marine and Navy, and everything that went along with them. One night, Don and I put on a couple of Navy uniforms that were 100 percent accurate in every detail. Even though we were only fourteen or fifteen years old at the time, we could easily pass for a couple of sailors on liberty as it was a pretty common sight in those days. Our goal—never achieved that night—was to "score on a couple of chicks," so we hitchhiked around the San Gabriel Valley. But on the way home, on Arrow Highway we were picked up by two real sailors, one of whom was a chief petty officer. We pretty much knew what to say (although I don't recall what we said), and engaged in some small talk. But mostly we sat in silence until reaching the point for us to get out of his car. That was the last time we put on uniforms we were not entitled to wear. Later Don did join the Navy, and we even met once in Yokosuka where his destroyer was tied up. He was in the electronics field and made rank very quickly, but got out after just the one enlistment. We never visited without reflecting on that crazy hitchhiking experience. The last time we visited was about twenty years ago when he was moving his land mobile radio business to Illinois. He is a great guy and I hope we have another visit in our future.

Every day after school, I went home and got my BB gun and my dog and went out shooting in the area that is now the Santa Fe Dam. One such day as we returned to our house I saw this really bad kid, one grade behind me. Gene Harris (pseudonym) was walking away from the area of my house with what appeared to be my BB gun. I entered the house, saw that my gun was gone, and chased the kid down. I caught him under the flood control drainage area on the south side of Duarte Road about 100 yards west of Cinco Robles Drive. I took my back gun and threatened to kick his ass. But he begged me to let him go, which I did.

Later, when in the Marine Corps, I was interviewed by sheriff's homicide investigators about Harris. He was apparently the person who had committed a hot prowl burglary on Delford Street in Duarte, raped and murdered a mother and also killed her child. There was little doubt that Harris was the suspect, but apparently there was not enough evidence to charge him with the crime. Several years later, when fleeing from the police in pursuit he failed to make the turn where Duarte Road curves and becomes Highland Avenue, crashed, and was killed. He was simply a very bad person, who resided in the area of Buena Vista Avenue and Three Ranch Road. His sister, Denise (pseudonym), was a nice person and a classmate of mine. In my life I have run across several people who are just bad and evil. Gene Harris was one of those people.

CASA JUNARA RESTAURANT

When sixteen, one of my jobs was busboy at the Casa Junara Restaurant located in Monrovia on the southeast corner of Foothill Boulevard and Fifth Street. Nothing really stands out in my mind about the job. Nice people, nice food—and it put money in my gas tank.

CANYON CITY AUTO BODY

My brother was an automotive insurance adjuster who had many contacts with auto body shops because he gave them repair business. So it was not much trouble to get his little brother—me—a job at a couple of them. The first was with Canyon City Auto Body in Azusa, which was located in a cul-de-sac on Angelino just north of Foothill (it is now a tract of townhomes). My job consisted of sanding and masking bodywork, and driving the tow truck. I really enjoyed driving that tow truck, and picked up and dropped off cars all over the valley. I experienced a funny situation one day when a fire truck was chasing me. I'd forgot to undo the parking brake on a car I was towing, and so much smoke was pouring out of the brakes they thought it was on fire.

CITY OF HOPE MEDICAL CENTER

Having a mom in a key position in the personnel office served me well. While in high school I spent one summer working in the dietary department at City of Hope, primarily in the supply section. I received and dispersed all kinds of food, vegetables, dairy products, etc. I recall one instance where a chef got mad and punched me, which really made my mom angry. But I convinced her to forget it and let me handle the situation, as the fellow knew he'd screwed up and had apologized. Interestingly, a few years later when I was a policeman working Central Division I ran across this same fellow. He had fallen on hard times and was living in one of the flophouses on east Sixth Street; we chatted amicably but I never ran across him again after that one encounter. Having a mom who worked at the hospital, a dad who was a patient, and living in two houses immediately adjacent to the hospital, I was pretty familiar with the City of Hope and viewed it then and now as a wonderful institution.

"KEITH, WHY CAN'T YOU BE MORE LIKE JOHN BENSON?"

John Benson (pseudonym) was one of my best pals in high school. He was pretty much a "goodie two-shoes" type of guy who always did his homework and never got into trouble. My parents liked John, felt he was a good influence on me, and on several occasions—especially because of homework—suggested that I should be more like John.

But we pretty much lost contact when I joined the military, and I did not see him for about another ten years. Although I did not graduate, when in my late twenties my Duarte High School classmates invited me to participate in the ten-year reunion, and I actually sat on the committee. One of my tasks was to try to locate some of our old classmates.

Finding John Benson came as quite a surprise when I traced him to a pool hall on Huntington Drive where he worked. There I encountered a very different person than I had known: by then John had to have weighed over 400 pounds, was covered with tattoos, and had very long and scraggly hair and beard. Nevertheless, we were glad to see each other. But neither of us had turned out as we expected—I was a police sergeant at the time. John figured me for a cop before recognizing me as an old friend, saying that he was initially concerned because he was anticipating being arrested on an illegal weapons charge, and thought that was why a cop had come into the pool hall. He explained that he'd had some other run-ins with the law, including a criminal record for pimping and pandering (prostitution-related offenses). When I told my mom what had become of John, she felt as disappointed as I did.

QUITTING HIGH SCHOOL

To say that I was a lousy student at Duarte High School would be an understatement. I completed two years of mainly "Ds" and "Fs," with occasional higher grades in woodshop and physical education. Equally as bad, my attendance was terrible. Today, my kids do more homework in a week than I did during both years of high school.

I started my junior year in September of 1961, but knew that I was going into the Marine Corps on my birthday on November 12th. I am not sure why I even bothered to start my junior year, because I quit school around the first part of October. Again my brother, the claims adjuster, helped me get full-time job working for a very nice man whose name was "Smitty," at the Monarch Auto Body Shop on Myrtle Avenue in Monrovia. My duties consisted primarily of sanding and masking just-repaired cars in preparation for painting. I worked for Smitty right up to my shipping date for USMC recruit training.

Chapter Six
MY MARRIAGES & CHILDREN

Marriage to Barbara Beck

During my assignment as an undercover officer in the Public Disorder Intelligence Division (discussed in the "Law Enforcement" section of these memoirs), I would call into the office several times a week to provide information, obtain information, and talk to my supervisor. One of the individuals that I frequently spoke to, because she answered the phone, was clerk typist Barbara Beck. She seemed like a nice gal and after several conversations it was clear that a mutual interest had begun to develop. My supervisor, Sergeant Joe Ward, set up a meeting and introduced us. We hit it off right away and developed a very nice friendship, which blossomed into a loving relationship, which ultimately resulted in our marriage on April 11, 1970. Joe Ward was our best man. Barbara and I had just about ten good years. But then we started drifting apart, resulting in a formal separation in June of 1980, and a divorce in 1984. This marriage yielded three children: Jake, Stacy, and Zak. Jim, Barbara's son from a previous marriage whom I'd adopted, was a troublesome teenager but still in the picture at the time.

Even though the marriage did not last, the friendship continued to grow. We had a very amicable divorce and I don't think we ever argued about anything. After a couple years of separation we realized that it was time to get a divorce, so we met for lunch, and between the time we ordered and when the food was served we'd worked out all the details! In addition to the amount of child support agreed on, I often looked for the opportunity to send a few more bucks, and there was never a time when I was not there for her or for the children in any way. When we split up it was agreed that we would both have custody of all the kids, referred to as "joint custody," but that Jake would usually live with me and Stacy and Zak would usually be with her. To this day Barbara and her husband, Paul, a great guy, are two of our best friends.

Marriage to Cathy Trischuk

In October 1983 I was promoted to the rank of captain 2 (there were three levels of captain, one through three), and given command of the Communications Division. What were they thinking? To put an eligible bachelor in charge of almost 500 women, many of whom were single, many of whom like to play around, and all of them who sought— if they were not already happily married—a fellow with a good income! Actually, I demonstrated a great deal of restraint and, although my eyes did a great deal of roaming, I did not mess with any of my subordinates until I was just about ready to leave that assignment. I was particularly attracted to Cathy Trischuk, a dispatcher (the civil service classification was "police service representative"). Cathy had a fun personality, was a very nice person, and was one of those people who was always organizing her fellow employees for fun events. Although it turns out I was mistaken in thinking she was unattached, she was actually involved with a sheriff's lieutenant. Just before I transferred out to Wilshire division Cathy and I started sneaking around and did some dating, and became full-time companions after I left communications. Our relationship continued to blossom, and on September 24, 1988 we were married in the Newport Harbor home of two dear friends, Paul and Isabel Greenwald. Notwithstanding a few little issues here and there, and the types of minor squabbles that all married couples have, it has been a great marriage. I'm very thankful to have such a wonderful wife.

James Christopher Bushey

Jim was born on August 9, 1963, being Barbara's son from a previous marriage. His name at birth, from his biological father, was DeBorrello. Shortly after our marriage, I adopted Jim. We had a good relationship up until about the time he hit junior high school, and then a wild streak seemed to take over. As time went on he became very independent and not inclined to follow our rules; then he started smoking marijuana. When Barbara and I separated, I ended up with custody of him! Fortunately, it did not last long as his mother felt I couldn't control him. So Jim moved in with her. But that did not last very long, either. When only about fifteen, he ran away and we did not see him for several years. He re-emerged with some behaviors that caused us to believe he was headed in a positive direction, including having joined the National Guard and going off to boot camp. It is a shame that he was not able to remain on active duty, as he just picked up his old anti-social ways again when he finished his initial military training. From that point until today, he drifts in and out of our lives occasionally. While his values are different from mine, he has found religion and seems to be living a law-abiding existence with his wife in the San Diego area. Because of seeing the world through different lenses, we don't talk very much. But I continue to wish Jim and his wife well.

Jacob Anthony Bushey

My first son, Jacob Anthony Bushey, was born on May 8, 1972 at Kaiser Hospital in Fontana. His first name is from my paternal grandfather; his middle name was one his maternal grandmother always hoped would be used in the family. When just one month old Jake developed pyloric stenosis, which is a blockage of the large intestine commonly found in first-born sons, and had to have emergency surgery to correct. He and I have always been close, still are, and my love for him is unconditional. He is mentioned prominently throughout these memoirs.

Jake married a wonderful woman, Anna Bermudez, a registered nurse, and they have given me two of the greatest grandchildren a man could ask for. My first grandchild, Alyssa Mary Bushey, was born July 31, 1999, and is about to enter her teenage years. She is as smart as she is pretty, and that is pretty smart. On June 5, 2008, my grandson, Matthew Jacob Bushey, was born. That little pistol is more fun than a barrel of monkeys, and a good pal.

Stacy Ann Bushey

My beautiful and wonderful daughter, Stacy Ann Bushey, was born on August 31, 1973, also at Kaiser Hospital in Fontana. She screwed up my bird hunting by being born on opening day of dove season, but she was worth it. I usually managed to go out for opening day when I was active as a hunter, so there were typically cold stares from her mother but also some accommodation, such as celebrating her arrival with gifts from me the night before. My daughter is one of the most wonderful gals that a dad could ever hope for, and I am the most fortunate guy on earth to have her as my daughter. She remained with her mom most of the time when Barbara and I separated and divorced, and her stepfather Paul seems to adore her as much as I do. If she ever has a big church wedding, Paul and I have agreed to both walk down the aisle with her!

Stacy is one of those people who is always there when needed by loved ones and animals (reptiles, too). She was my mom's precious granddaughter and spent an enormous amount of time with her, right up until she passed away, always bringing joy into my mother's heart. Stacy was equally loving to my Aunt Dot and Uncle Matt, who went into the same nursing home as my mom, with no request or errand being a burden. Stacy was married to an okay fellow but it did not work out, so she is now single and living in Costa Mesa, where she also works in a most responsible position at a wholesale lighting company. Stacy is very much like her mother in that she is unbelievably hardworking and competent, and ends up being indispensible wherever she works. Stacy is beautiful, smart, well-educated and has a fun and goofy streak that will become obvious throughout the pages of these memoirs.

ZACHARY DAVID BUSHEY

My wonderful and fun son Zak was born on August 17, 1978. Like the rest, he too was born at Kaiser Hospital in Fontana. By the time we realized that Barbara was pregnant again we were starting to have problems in our marriage, and the pregnancy was not good news. We actually discussed aborting the pregnancy. Now the thought that we even considered such a course causes me to be unsteady. Zak is the most fun kid, and now adult, on the face of the earth. He is witty and well-liked by everyone with whom he comes into contact. Today he is a realtor and a very prominent member of the Glendora business community, as well as active in his homeowners' association.

I know it cannot be the case, but I absolutely cannot remember a time as a kid when Zak did anything wrong! I continually said that he is the only kid I ever knew who never needed to be disciplined. Given the twinkle in his eye and his mischievous nature, I am reasonably confident that he pulled stuff just like other kids. But he managed to not get caught, and by doing so was able to create an angelic persona that is probably not all that merited.

On October 21, 2006, Zak married a beautiful girl, Antoinette "Toni" Robles. They have a great marriage and live in a beautiful home in Glendora. On September 2, 2010 they gave us a beautiful little granddaughter, Addison Claire Bushey. That little gal takes my breath away, and I just do not believe it would be possible to find a cuter little girl than Addie. She is now walking, and watching the emergence of her cute little personality is beyond fun and wonderful.

Daniel Bustamante

Our first and oldest foster child, Daniel Bustamante, was born on November 26, 1976. He has one sibling, an older brother Roberto ("Bobby") Bourbois. I was the only father that either of these boys ever knew, and they spent a great deal of time in our home as I was somewhat of a "big brother" to them. As described elsewhere in detail, their mother unexpectedly passed away when Dan was just starting high school, and we immediately became his legal guardians. When their mother died, Bobby was in the Marine Corps and did well before receiving an honorable discharge. He then joined the LAPD and got married to a nice gal, Julia. While sad and complicated, Bobby and his family are no longer close to, or even in contact with, the rest of us.

Danny has been an absolute joy, and remains a close member of the family. Several years ago he married a local girl from Azusa and they had a couple of great kids, but the marriage did not survive. Dan gave us a couple of the greatest grandkids you could ask for! Nathan Daniel Bustamante was born on September 29, 2001 and Serena Marie Bustamante was born on January 9, 2004. As these memoirs are about to go to print, Danny and his kids are spending a great deal more time with Cathy and me, and we are very pleased that such is the case.

Spencer Anderson

Spencer Anderson came to us out of the blue. He was born on September 6, 1993. Due to our having been the foster parents and legal guardians of Dan Bustamante, even though Dan had been out and on his own for a while we still retained our foster home certification. One day in November of 2001 a social worker from the Department of Children & Family Services (DCFS) called, and asked Cathy if we would take a "little boy who just needs to be safe." Cathy said yes; then she told me. We took in Spencer, got him into scouting, arranged for tutoring to bring him up to grade level, nurtured him, and worked with his mother (who had a long history of substance abuse) to help her get clean (we went to her Alcoholics Anonymous graduation, etc.), all to help get him back into a clean and safe environment.

Spencer returned home after about a year. But within three months his mom had crashed and burned again. Unfortunately, DCFS completely dropped the ball, and even with additional reports of neglect and the kid being in jeopardy, the agency did nothing. In fact, we were discredited as obsessed former foster parents when we tried to raise troublesome issues that we knew to be true.

Then one evening in September 2006 we got a call out of the blue from a DCFS social worker, who said that a little boy had just been taken into protective custody because his mother had a massive drug overdose and was not expected to survive. We didn't know who the kid was. But within two hours Spencer was back in our home, with us as his legal guardians, and he remains with us to this day. He is now eighteen years old and a freshman at Citrus College. We anticipate that he will remain in our home. Spencer is like a son to us, and we love him.

Matthew Saxton

Matthew Peter Saxton was born on October 18, 1994. In December 2003, Cathy and I took him and his brother, Daniel, in as foster sons. They previously lived in a group home, Five Acres, in Altadena. Because of inappropriate behavior, Daniel was removed from our home several years ago.

We are now legal guardians to Matt; he is like a son, and someone I also love. To say that Matt is not a great student is being charitable, but he is trying; he's a nice kid with a super personality, and works hard to be helpful and responsive. Just about the time I was going to give up on him academically, I watched him manipulate a computer and my complicated portable phone and computer, and he really knows what he is doing. Matt is smarter than meets the eye, and I am waiting for his brilliance to come to the surface.

Danielle Marie Bushey

A dormant little volcano came into our home on March 31, 2006, in the form of then Dannielle Marie Avila, age 4½. She was born on October 5, 2001 and had been living in the home of the paternal grand-mother of her two older step-siblings. Unfortunately, the grandmother treated Danielle (we later dropped one "n" from her name) poorly, ap-parently because of bad blood between her son (in prison serving a life sentence) and Danielle's biological father (also in prison at the time, and now again). She came to us in the "Fost-Adopt" program; that is, a foster child eligible for adoption. She was very subdued and deathly frightened of men, because of the especially poor treatment she received at the hands of the grandmother's boyfriend. I will never forget the first meal she had with us, as she stripped virtually every morsel off the chicken wings on her plate. We later learned that her primary meals had been obtained at the childcare program in which she was enrolled. We also learned that after two years in her home the grandmother called the Department of Children & Family Services and told them to come and pick up Danielle, and when the social worker arrived the grandmother put Danielle in the car without so much as a kiss or best wishes, then turned and walked away!

We really liked the little gal, but it was not our original intent to adopt her. We gave her plenty of nurturing and love. Eventually, after a month of being standoffish, Danielle and I developed a nice relationship, which was a far cry from the early days where a little kiss from me on the back of her head resulted in hysteria. It didn't take too long for a family to pop up, meet Danielle, and want to adopt her. I thought the family was nice enough, but Cathy did not think too much of them—by this time no one was good enough for Cathy's little girl. A temporary problem but a permanent solution arose in the form of Danielle's biological mom who had just been released from jail and wanted Danielle back to live with her, her mom, and two younger step-siblings. Danielle immediately went from the "Fost-Adopt" program to just being a foster child in our home until the mother completed the number of things she needed to do to get Danielle back. Instead, the mother did none of those things, went back to jail on new charges, and Danielle was once again eligible for adoption. By now, the little gal was a permanent fixture in our home and in our hearts, and the thought of leaving the only loving home and family she had ever known was not an option. There were a couple of minor glitches. But after some administrative attention, home visits, and ultimately the support of her biological parents, the little gal, now a full-blown erupting volcano, became Danielle Marie Bushey.

Little Danielle did not exactly come into our home by accident. I whispered in the ear of our social worker and friend, Kim Mittleman, that a little girl might find a warm welcome as a foster child in our home, because I knew that Cathy would like to nurture a girl. I did not realize that the foster situation would turn into an adoption, but was not at all disappointed. Two of my biological children, Stacy and Zak, show her love and treat her just like a little sister, and she adores both of them unconditionally. She also adores our oldest foster son, Danny, who reciprocates her love and attention.

As I write this entry, Danielle is ten and I am sixty-seven. Adopting her was not the smartest thing that I have ever done, but I listened to my heart and not my mind. I am honored to be her dad.

CHAPTER SEVEN
MARINE CORPS-ENLISTED

Note: The reader is reminded that even though my life went down several parallel paths simultaneously, these memoirs are only able to describe one path at a time. Consequently, there will be some comments pertaining to situations to which the reader has not yet been introduced. Indulgence is appreciated!

RECRUITING TRAINING

PREPARING FOR BOOT CAMP

Realistically, because of my obsessive interest in the military I had been preparing for the Marine Corps since I was a small child. My brother went into the Corps in 1950, when I was about six years old, and I have been enthusiastic about the military ever since then. My greatest joys were going to surplus stores, of which there were many because so much surplus was available after World War II. For about three months before my 17th birthday, I studied everything I could find about the Marine Corps. I had the *Guidebook For Marines*, and knew it cold. I knew the General Orders, Field Sanitation & Hygiene, History & Traditions, all the field pack configurations, First Aid, Rank Structure, etc., etc. My brother borrowed an M-1 Garand rifle from someone, and taught me to identify its every part and to field strip it blindfolded! When I went into the Marine Corps on my 17th birthday, like I always knew that I would, I really knew my stuff.

"SWEEP THE DECKS"

Along with scores of other young men, I went through enlistment processing at the Armed Forces Induction Center located at 1031 South

Broadway Street in downtown Los Angeles. Interestingly, the building was then and later owned by Jack Needleman, a businessman I got to know and with whom I developed a friendship many years later when I was commanding officer of Central Area. I originally enlisted for four years, but before being sworn in I learned that I could go in for three years if my written score was high enough. So I approached the clerical sergeant and asked if I could change my contract to three years. He was indignant and said I scored high enough, but that he would have to type a form over. So I apologized and told him four was fine (boy, did I kick myself three years later, when all my friends were getting out—but four years worked out for the best). Anyway, the sergeant got nice again. Then we were sworn in, and the sergeant immediately started screaming at me, threw me a broom, and told me to "sweep the deck!" So much for my new "friend," the sergeant, and welcome to the Marine Corps! At that time I was assigned my enlisted serial number: 1989579.

A Unique Welcome at the Bus Station

Along with about a dozen other young men I was put on a Greyhound bus by the folks at the Armed Forces Processing Station in Los Angeles, with San Diego as our destination. On our arrival in San Diego we were met by a couple of stern and mean Marine staff sergeants (should I have expected anything else?). They herded us into the back of a camper shell on a USMC truck and, once inside, started whacking at us with swagger sticks! There were no injuries, but I think we all wondered why these guys had to hit us. We were driven straight to the Recruit Receiving Barracks. Like generations of new jarheads before us, we lined up and stood on the "yellow footprints," and went through the initial process of clothing and necessities issuance, showers, temporary berthing assignments. Then we were assembled into recruit platoons and introductions (if you can call screaming at us an "introduction") to our drill instructors.

Puking on The Grinder

My first Marine Corps breakfast was most memorable. In those days just about everyone smoked, including the majority of my fellow recruits in Platoon 290 and all of the drill instructors. We were marched to a chow hall and told, in very harsh terms, that we had very few minutes to go through the line, eat our chow, and be back on the Grinder (massive parade ground) in formation. The drill instructor said that the "smoking lamp would be lit" for one cigarette after chow, but only if every recruit was back in the minimal time allotted. After that very short time all but one recruit was in the formation, and he was about 30 seconds late. Consequently, that one late recruit was the only person allowed to have a cigarette, but had to simultaneously smoke a cigarette from each of the smokers in the platoon. Every recruit who smoked gave the late recruit a cigarette, the whole group of cigarettes was placed in his mouth and lit, and then a bucket was placed over his head. Then the drill instructor ordered the poor fellow to "smoke, smoke, smoke, inhale more, inhale more, etc." Finally the kid puked his guts out, with the bucket still over his head. What a pathetic sight it was, and something I can still easily visualize. I don't think I have ever visited MCRD in the 50 years since I was in boot camp, without looking at about the exact spot where that incident occurred and thinking about our first USMC breakfast.

Candy Bar in the Palm Tree

Sweets of any sort were not available in boot camp, where every minute of the 16-to-18-hour day was scheduled. About halfway through boot camp my platoon (Platoon 290) got the weeklong night duty to completely clean (including sweeping and swabbing the decks) the two-story headquarters of the Second Recruit Training Battalion. On the first night I saw there was a candy machine, but we were threatened with horrible things if we even looked at that machine, let alone got anything out of it. Nevertheless, the next night I took a dime (from my locker box) with me and, when no one was looking, bought a Mounds candy bar. I concealed it and when we returned to our Quonset hut after "taps," I snuck into a darkened area and took one heavenly bite; boy did it taste good! I then wrapped it up, crawled up a palm tree, and hid my treasure. I made it last for three or four days; each night I climbed back up that tree and took another bite. I would have been in big trouble had my sin been detected.

Every time I visit the Marine Corps Recruit Depot, I look over to where that tree and my Quonset hut were, and reflect on that Mounds bar. The tree and Quonset hut are long gone, but I can still pretty much identify the exact site.

Marine Corps Brainwashing—For Duty and Honor

For someone who has not experienced Marine Corps recruit training, this situation may seem hard to believe. But it is absolutely true, and the actions of all concerned are pretty typical given the circumstances.

Miller was a squad leader. Shapiro was in that squad, and Miller's best friend. When tasked with doing a "field day" (obsessive cleaning) on the battalion headquarters building, Miller observed Shapiro buying a candy bar from the vending machine, which was pretty much a mortal sin (though, as indicated in the previous paragraph, I didn't get caught when I committed the same sin). This situation tore Miller apart because he knew he had no alternative but to report the actions of his best friend, knowing full well that the consequences for Shapiro would be harsh. Shapiro understood that as well, and did not fault or criticize Miller for what he had to do. Without exception, all the other recruits present also accepted that Miller had no alternative. These actions were the consequence of the industrial-grade dose of duty and honor that recruits receive during basic training. If Miller had remained silent the drill instructors would never have known about Shapiro's transgression, but Miller was doing exactly what was expected of him. Anything less was not an option. It is this type of training and commitment that set Marines apart from others. As I recall, Shapiro's penalty involved multiple laps around the several-mile grinder carrying a field marching pack full of rocks. We all felt he got off easy. But I was glad I didn't get caught for doing the same thing!

Does Anyone Other than Bushey Know the Answer?

The obsession I had with all the military services, but primarily the Marine Corps, started paying off the day I entered boot camp. Without exaggerating, I knew everything! While obviously 100 percent focused on all that we were taught, I could have slept through just about every class and still "aced" any exam given. This is not to say that boot camp was a cakewalk, because it was truly tough—unbelievably physically demanding, harsh treatment by the drill instructors (it was an appropriate role they were playing, and I understood that), hand-to-hand combat and other physical skills far beyond physical conditioning, hours of "snapping in" and firing the M-1 rifle, homesickness, etc. Boot camp is intended to be a difficult experience, and it was. But it was less so for me because I knew so much, knew what to expect in terms of treatment, and would rather have been at MCRD than Disneyland.

The Tragic Overload of a Recruit

This was a sad situation that I watched unfold over a period of a couple of weeks. One of the recruits from Chicago, Private Kaskowitz (pseudonym) became psychologically overloaded with the stress of boot camp. Marine Corps recruit training is tough, with an overabundance of yelling, demands for near-impossible performance, considerable multi-tasking, and stress. Poor Kaskowitz just couldn't handle it and was often in some type of a haze; the harder the drill instructors pushed, the more he bogged down. I will never forget the situation when we were being taught to use our new ink stencil kits in marking all our uniforms with our names. Kaskowitz and most of his uniform items were covered with permanent black ink in all the wrong places, with some of his uniforms completely ruined by the ink. I can still see that confused young man sitting there in the midst of his mistakes and all the inky mess. Shortly thereafter, in the middle of one night, Kaskowitz dove head-first off his top bunk onto the concrete floor in what I assumed was a suicide attempt. He was rushed to the hospital with what certainly appeared to be severe head trauma. We never saw him again. At the time, we all thought that Kaskowitz was just a useless "shitbird." But I now look back and see a young man who, through no fault of his own, absolutely did not have the ability to perform the difficult and unique tasks associated with recruit training.

Enroute and Arrival at Rifle Range

From the establishment of the Marine Corps Recruit Depot in 1919 until 1964, all marksmanship training was conducted at the Camp Matthews rifle range in the hills east of La Jolla, in what was a remote area. The camp was named in honor of one of the Marine Corps' most famous shooters, Brigadier General Calvin B. Matthews. The recruits spent the 6th, 7th and 8th weeks of boot camp at Camp Matthews. To get there, we were transported in "cattle cars" (military transport vehicles) to a swampy area north of the recruit depot, and then marched through about 10 miles of remote terrain to get to Camp Matthews. When the marksmanship phase of boot camp was over, we were returned to the Recruit Depot by reversing the process. The "swampy area" is now known as Mission Bay, and I doubt that there is a single vacant lot along what in 1961 was remote terrain.

Everly Brothers at Camp Matthews

Don and Phil Everly were in boot camp the same time I was there. They were in a series (four platoons) a week or so behind my platoon, but we had some joint training. I will never forget either Christmas Day 1961 or New Year's Day 1962 (it was one of those), when all of the recruits at the Camp Matthews Rifle Range were taken off the "snapping in" field for an hour or so, taken into a large Butler Hut (kinda like a Quonset Hut on steroids), and treated to a performance by the Everly Brothers. Don and Phil, recruits just like the rest of us (they were reserves, to be released from active duty after six months, followed by six years in the reserves), sang a bunch of their popular tunes (they were BIG, BIG entertainers with a number of top songs). There was no music, just their singing. It was quite a treat. But back to "snapping in" after about an hour. Years later, when we became close friends, Phil Everly told me that it was a memorable experience for him and Don.

I also remember seeing them on visiting day, shortly before all of us graduated. Some very pretty girls visited them. That was okay with me, because I was in heaven consuming the cola, fried chicken, and chocolate cake my mom had brought down. That meal, after weeks of being deprived of what I really liked to eat, was about as close to heaven as a person could get.

Phil Everly and I later became close friends. When I took over as the commanding officer of Communications Division, two of the police service representatives (dispatchers) were Patti Arnold and Cathy Trischuk (now Cathy Bushey), and they were the best of friends. One day, after Cathy and I were married, she told me that Patti was dating Phil Everly, and I told her we had been in boot camp together. At first she did not believe me. So I wrote a note for Patti to give to Phil, which referred to their singing in the Butler Hut at Camp Matthews. When he got the note, Phil called me right away and we had a nice conversation. After that, Cathy and I visited him and Patti (both before and after they were married) at their home in North Hollywood, had a fun weekend on Catalina, attended several of their performances (his and Don's) in Las Vegas, and a attended a few other functions with them.

Patti is Phil's third or fourth wife, and they appear to have a nice marriage. Phil and I would kid that with each wife his houses got smaller. They now live in Tennessee and the Busheys and the Everlys have somewhat slipped away from one another. Hopefully, the future will include seeing more of the families getting together.

PEEING THROUGH A TENT OPENING—BAD IDEA!

All recruits were housed in eight-men squad tents. The heads (bathrooms) were in a row of wooden structures several hundred feet away. Fortunately, young men have pretty strong bladders and do not usually have to interrupt their sleep to make head calls (like us old farts!).

However, if it was necessary the recruit had to get dressed and walk to the head, after first untying the ropes that secured the tent's door. For this reason, some recruits would just pee through the narrow opening between the tent and tent flap without untying the knots, then run their boot over the moist ground at reveille to conceal their treachery. The drill instructors knew some recruits were inclined to take this short-cut, and instructed the fire watch recruits to hit any penis they saw with the night sticks they carried. One night I awoke to the screaming of a fire watch for the sergeant of the guard; he'd seen a penis belonging to a young man who was relieving himself, and apparently given it a pretty good whack with his nightstick.

It was not my tent. But I understand the culprit was easy to locate once the tent flap was untied, as he was bent over in pain. I don't know what sanction the midnight pisser experienced, but it couldn't have been pleasant.

Guard Duty at Camp Matthews (Defining Experience)

My first round of guard duty at the Rifle Range at Camp Matthews had an impact on me that served me well throughout my life, and continues to this day. Camp Matthews is long gone, its site now occupied by the University of California, San Diego. In 1961 it was desolate and in the middle of nowhere. One night when my entire platoon had guard duty, with different people being assigned to different portions of the camp, I was assigned as the lone sentry at "Mike" Range. I had no flashlight. My instructions were to walk a given route continuously for several hours. It was pitch-black out and I was the only human in that area (along with a lot of coyotes, skunks, etc.). Part of my route was to walk inside and cover the entire length of a target shed that was probably 75 to 100 yards long. It was completely dark inside, with rows of rooms on either side of the center walkway. The whole place creaked with aging wood.

Walking through that dark and creaky shed was scary, at first. On entering the long center pathway, no light could be seen at the other end; but I had to just keep walking. After making it about halfway through the shed you could start to see faint moonlight, which was the other end of the shed. By the time that tour of duty was over, I was strutting confidently into that sea of darkness, with my confidence weighing more heavily than my fear. It was classic USMC behavior—bullshit yourself out of fear and into confidence.

Darkness has been my friend ever since that night at Camp Matthews so long ago. Throughout my Marine Corps and law enforcement experiences, I have learned to depend on ambient light, and use a flashlight only as a last resort. Part of this is driven by a continuing desire to see others without being seen myself, and recognizing that artificial light really screws up your night vision.

Staff Sergeant Jennings' Goodness was Obvious

Loved ones were permitted to visit recruits on Sundays once they reached the rifle range. My parents and brother visited me at Camp Matthews, and the visit was somewhat emotional because I was experiencing a bit of homesickness. Although phone calls normally were not permitted, for some reason I got permission to call home the night after their visit. While on the phone with my mom, I clearly had tears in my eyes. Just as I hung up, in popped one of the three drill instructors, Staff Sergeant Jennings. He got in my face and asked if I had been crying, to which I answered, "no sir, something got in my eye." He made some remark about the dust in the air and told me to get back to the platoon area, although he clearly knew I had teared up with homesickness. He was a drill instructor, and as such knew how to be harsh. But he was a very decent and wonderful man whose qualities of decency and humanity could not be masked by his "Smokey Bear" campaign hat.

I ran across Staff Sergeant Jennings a few years later in the PX at Camp Hansen on Okinawa. As I recall, he was in the 9th Motor Transport Battalion. We had a nice chat. I regret never seeing him again.

205, and One Round Left

Talk about pressure! It was important to me that I qualify as no less than a "sharpshooter," which required a score of 210 to 220, with anything above 220 being "expert." From 190 to 209 was a "marksman," with a medal that looked like and was called "the toilet seat." My brother had always qualified as a "sharpshooter" and I wanted the same medal, which was an attractive Maltese cross suspended from a bar that contained the word "Sharpshooter." I was on the 500-yard line, shooting prone, with one round remaining and a score of 205. I would need a bull's eye to get that coveted medal. I made it! That was one very happy moment.

That wonderful and coveted USMC sharpshooter medal is the award I chose to put on the front cover of these memoirs. For the vast majority of my career, ever since transitioning to the M-16, I have consistently shot expert, which is a higher award and represented by a different medal. However, because of how powerful that experience was for me in boot camp, it is the sharpshooter's award that I chose to conspicuously display.

Started to "Pass Out" on the Grinder

My platoon had a shooting award ceremony on the Grinder almost immediately after the forced march back to MCRD from Camp Matthews. For whatever reason (perhaps I had unknowingly locked my knees) I was in the process of passing out just as one of the drill instructors, Staff Sergeant Jennings, was walking past me. He immediately recognized what was happening and directed me to a nearby curb in the shade and told me to sit down. Within a couple of minutes I felt fine and, without being directed to do so, immediately returned to the formation. I think this type of behavior and spirit contributed to my selection as one of the few promotees out of boot camp.

M-1 to the M-14 to the M-16 in One Enlistment!

In boot camp we were issued the M-1 rifle, a weapon that was developed early in World War II and used during that war and also during the Korean Conflict. It was a great weapon and I knew it intimately, having learned to field-strip it blindfolded before entering the Corps. On graduation from boot camp, I kept the rifle I had been issued and carried it with me to my first duty station, H&S Company, 2nd Battalion, 1st Marine Regiment, 1st Marine Division, Camp Pendleton. In September 1962, the month before the Cuban Missile Crisis, we were issued the M-14 rifle (.308 caliber, with a 20-round magazine). Most of us complained about having lost the M-1 (obviously, we had to turn them in), but in reality the M-14 was most likely superior, especially with its expanded magazine and the ability to fire fully automatic (when issued the adapter to do so). Just before completing my first enlistment, the Marine Corps (Army, too) upgraded to the M-16 (7.62 caliber). The M-16 had several models and was used in Vietnam and other places until the late 1990s. Although there were problems with jamming in the early models (much of it no doubt related to maintaining and cleaning the weapon) the M-16 served the military well during the time it was used.

From Loser to Honor Graduate in Three Months

I was the classic "dead-end kid" when I entered the Marine Corps, having quit high school and working at an auto body shop in Monrovia.

I can't really say that I completed two years of high school, but I was there part time for those two years. Most of my grades were "D" and "F," with an occasional "C" and maybe even a "B" in something like PE! I was an okay worker at the body shop and the other places I'd worked, but certainly nothing special. I think I was basically a good person who was very polite and reasonably well liked by people, but my future was not very bright. The only real goal I had in life—and it was an obsessive goal—was to join the Marine Corps on my 17th birthday. Unfortunately, that year my birthday fell on a Sunday. However, all the paperwork had been done, my parents had signed for me in advance, and on Monday, November 13, 1961, I was sworn into the Marine Corps and started my basic training at the Marine Corps Recruit Depot in San Diego. I am fond of telling people that, although my body was born in Alhambra, my spirit and true soul were born in San Diego during the period from November 13, 1961 through February 10, 1962. Something sure as hell happened!

The proudest day in my life—nothing yet has outshined it—was my graduation from boot camp on February 10, 1962. A day or two before graduation I was told I had been selected as one of six or seven recruits to be meritoriously promoted to private first class. WOW! I will never forget marching out by the base theatre, past my mom, pop, and brother, with those wonderful PFC stripes sewn on my sleeve. As I type this, I actually began to tear up as I reflect on the significance of that event. Obviously, my family was very proud of me. I was pretty proud of myself.

God bless the Marine Corps. I am one of those lost souls who ended up with a good life, and the Marine Corps is among the major reasons why.

I still recall going into the head on the evening of graduation, as we prepared to ship out the next morning for infantry training at Camp Pendleton. I kept looking at myself in the mirror with those PFC chevrons on my collar. Boy, was I something! The next morning I learned that being a PFC was not as big a deal to some other people as it was to me.

The Left Guide

I did not know what a "left guide" was until I became one. Two or three weeks before graduation, we had the platoon photo taken. All of us were in our winter service green uniforms. The protocol was for the drill instructors and two top recruits, one of whom was the right guide, to be on the front row of bleachers, with the rest of the platoon on the rear benches. As the photographer positioned everyone, he asked to have the "left guide" seated to the right of the drill instructors, and the "right guide" (who was Edwin Hopkins) seated on their left. To my surprise, I was identified as the "left guide" and told to sit with the drill instructors on the bench. That incident was the first indication that I was doing exceptionally well. I knew I was doing well, but not that well. I still have and treasure this platoon photo. Little did any of us realize that the two recruits seated on either side of the three drill instructors would eventually become commissioned officers—me a full colonel.

In about 1978, I was a Marine captain on active duty and participating in an exercise at Fort Irwin, out by Barstow. I made a run onto the Marine Logistics Base and ran across 2nd Lieutenant Ed Hopkins. He had just been commissioned as a Limited Duty Officer in contracts administration, and we had a nice chat. When he entered the Marine Corps, he had four years prior service as a Navy corpsman (was wounded in Korea) and four additional years of service in the Air Force. At graduation, he had two rows of ribbons and jump wings. Not surprisingly, he was both the platoon and series honor man.

2ND INFANTRY TRAINING REGIMENT

In February 1962, following three months of basic training, I was transferred to the 2nd Infantry Training Regiment at Camp Pendleton, for one month of training in the tactics and equipment of the Marine Infantry Battalion. In addition to squad and platoon tactics, our weapons included the BAR (Browning Automatic Rifle), .30 caliber machine gun, flame thrower, 3.5 rocket launcher, and additional instruction in the use of hand grenades, booby traps, and explosives. Unfortunately, I was among the unlucky ones selected to spend a couple of extra weeks at the 2nd ITR, as a messman.

SPUD LOCKER CZAR

My entire series (four platoons)—about 250 new Marines—was taken via "cattle cars" to Camp Pendleton, specifically to Camp San Onofre and the Infantry Training Regiment (ITR) to start a four-week infantry-training course. At ITR some of the new Marines, including those who had been meritoriously promoted in boot camp, were given temporary ranks for the roles they would play. The temporary ranks were reflected by arm bands having their respective stripes (sergeant for squad leader, staff sergeant for platoon leader, etc.). I just knew that I would get one of those coveted temporary training ranks, and would be a top performer in infantry training. Wrong!

The entire company (formed from the four platoons) was in formation when about twenty names were called out, including mine. Those persons were directed to fall in outside the regular company formation. We fell out, and the rest of the company was marched off! This was not a good sign. Then a corporal in a cook's uniform took charge and informed us that we were on "mess duty" for two weeks. This couldn't be happening to me! The corporal told us to stow our gear in the Quonset hut behind us and get over to the mess hall. As the others complied I approached the corporal and had a conversation that, to this day, I can almost recall verbatim. Very carefully and politely I told him I thought there had probably been a mistake in assigning me to mess duty, because I was a Pfc. He give me a funny look, was silent for a moment or so, then responded: "So you are. Okay, you're in charge of the spud locker. Now put your shit away and get your ass over to the mess hall!"

I can laugh now, but I was absolutely devastated by mess duty. I was ready to start basking in the glory of my new and exalted position, hopefully get liberty and go home for the weekend, and perform as a true leader in infantry training. It was a long two weeks, with reveille at 0245 and lights out at 1000, with a few short breaks between meals. I did not get much sleep, but sure as hell peeled a lot of potatoes! After two weeks I joined "Mike" company for my four weeks of infantry training, got and wore my coveted temporary training rank (sergeant-squad leader), graduated, and went home on my ten-day boot camp leave. As of 2012, the old mess hall is now a fitness center and the little hut that was the spud locker is gone. But its foundation still exits; I occasionally visit that foundation and reflect on my experiences there.

BBs for a Trained Killer

I came home to Duarte for my boot camp leave. It was most enjoyable, especially hanging out around the high school after classes got out and letting everybody see the loser that made good. Naturally, I did the obligatory visit to the high school, strutting around in my dress green Marine Corps uniform. After a couple of days I got a little bored with what to do with myself until school let out. Then I had an idea—shoot my beloved BB gun at cans in the back yard. Unfortunately, I was out of BBs, so I drove to Reagan's Toy Store (later the space became part of the Bank of America in Duarte) to get some. I told the women behind the counter that I wanted two containers of BBs. She put them on the counter and asked for my identification, to which I proudly whipped out my Marine Corps identification card. However, after looking at it she said I was only seventeen years old (true), and the law said you could not buy BBs unless you were eighteen (also true). I replied that I was a United States Marine, a "trained killer," and felt I should be able to buy BBs! She responded with something I will never forget: "You may be a trained killer, but you are going to have to come back with your mother if you want these BBs!"

I was furious and humiliated. When I told my mom and dad about the conversation they laughed themselves silly. But at the time I failed to see the humor. I certainly see the humor now, and it is one of my favorite stories.

———

2ND BATTALION, FIRST MARINE REGIMENT (2/1)

In late March 1962, following my six weeks of infantry training and my ten-day boot camp leave, I was assigned to one of the Marine Corps' thirty or so infantry battalions, the 2nd Battalion of the 1st Marine Regiment. It was located with the other two battalions of the First Regiment at Camp San Mateo, which is one of the many smaller bases aboard Camp Pendleton. 1st Marine Regiment was one of three regiments that made up the infantry manpower of the 1st Marine Division at Camp Pendleton. The 2nd Marine Division was at Camp Lejeune in North Carolina, the 3rd Marine Division was scattered throughout Japan and on the island of Okinawa, and the 4th Marine Division was made up of reserve units throughout the continental United States, Hawaii, Alaska and Puerto Rico.

"REPORTING IN" TO MY FIRST UNIT

After boot camp leave I reported to the aforementioned battalion, where I was assigned to the Communications Platoon within the Headquarters & Service Company. It had been pre-determined that I would be assigned to the message center, no doubt because of my typing ability. Although I could only type about 8-10 words a minute (if that), mine was breakneck speed compared to others! Most of the other troops could not type at all. I slept in a bunk bed in a large open barracks, along with about 80 other Marines. The corporals and sergeants slept at one end in their own corner surrounded by wall lockers.

Ignorance With Stripes—Liberty Canceled
(Lasting Impression)

I had an experience not long after arriving at 2/1 that left a lasting impression on me, and has influenced my actions in the leadership arena for my entire life. The battalion had just returned from overseas and just about everyone was on leave. The new folks, such as me, were trickling in each day. There were few officers and staff non-commissioned officers around, and the few supervisors were buck sergeants. My boss for a week or so was a big man with a small brain and a large chip on his shoulder, and he treated the few of us who worked for him in a pretty shabby manner. The clincher was his mistaken perception that the group of us, collectively, had failed to do some menial task to his satisfaction. As a result, he canceled our weekend liberty.

This really bothered me. I was upset at not being able to go home as I'd expected, but more concerned and disappointed that someone like this was able to run rampant and mistreat the troops. He was out of control, playing out his idiosyncrasies at the expense of innocent subordinates who were completely at his mercy. Even though only seventeen, I made a commitment to myself then and there, that I would never allow someone to behave this way if I ever found myself in a position of authority. I have often reflected on that situation throughout my life as a leader, and strongly encourage others to take measures to prevent troublesome subordinates from mistreating their troops/employees.

Message Center School

A couple of months after reporting into 2/1, we new folks were sent to various schools to be trained in our assigned military occupational specialties (MOSs). Again, no doubt because I was able to type (barely), I was selected for Message Center School, which was located in the Horno Area of Camp Pendleton. This was a three-week academic course, and I graduated 7th out of about 25 Marines. Pretty good for a high school dropout!

My typing skills are worthy of brief discussion. In high school, during my occasional visits (!), included was a year or so of typing classes. Obviously, I learned something and gained some skills. My mom really pushed me to take typing classes, saying it was a skill that would always be of benefit throughout my life. Thanks mom, you were right!

I continue to see myself as a combat infantry Marine (an old beat-up and useless one at this advanced stage in my life!). But I can remember a number of times when the grunts in my battalion (those with the hard-core infantry MOSs) were crawling in mud while I was sitting in a comfortable communications center. Let there be do doubt—I spent plenty of time in the mud, but a little less because of my MOS. Thanks again, mom!

Go Fetch An ST-One and a TR-Double E—Now!

In Marine Corps communications, even to this day, each piece of "comm gear" has a two or three-letter designation, followed by two or three numbers. The field phone of that era was the EE-8, the switchboard was SB-22, the primary tactical radios were the PRC-10 and PRC-25, etc. Every piece of gear was referred to by this type of designation. New Marines in the communications field were often sent all over the base to find a couple of critical pieces of equipment, such as the ST-1 and the TR-Double E. At each place they tried unsuccessfully to fulfil their task, a more tenured Marine would send them to some other location. It usually took them a couple of hours before figuring out that those designations were for a stone and a tree! There are different types of wire used in communications, and unsuspecting young Marines would sometime be directed to locate shoreline as well!

The Grandaddy of All Hangovers!

My first hangover had to be the worst as well. I was about 17½ and assigned one night to the graveyard shift in the Message Center at Camp San Mateo. After getting off work at about 0800, and knowing it was just about impossible to sleep in the barracks with all the noise, I drove to San Clemente Beach and tried to get some sleep. It was not a good idea, because I baked in the sun and probably got dehydrated. About 1800 I joined a few of my buddies in an abandoned Quonset hut at a birthday party for one of my pals. For dinner, I had a couple of pieces of the birthday cake. Then I started drinking, and did I ever! I drank considerable quantities of whiskey, bourbon, peppermint schnapps, gin, and vodka—very stupid, but I didn't know anything about drinking and certainly did not understand the horrible consequences of mixing booze. I can still remember being drunk and driving my car back to the barracks, then lying in my bunk as the world revolved around me. When I woke up the next morning at reveille I was still drunk, but decided to go to the mess hall and get something to eat. At the mess hall all I really cared for was milk, which ultimately just curdled in my stomach. I started puking at about 1100 and kept puking for about two days! In those days, due to what I believe was a smaller than usual esophagus, vomiting was difficult and painful and usually took me down to my knees, which just made things all the worse. I went into the comm center between puking bouts to create the illusion that I was working. On Friday I had liberty, but had to invite one of my pals to come home with me because I was still too sick to even drive my car. On the way home, I still remember having to open the door and puke in the street during one stop for a signal. This had to be the mother of all hangovers!

Bravado on a Walkway in Duarte

One evening while home on liberty, I was in my "greens" (winter service alpha uniform) and walking along the walkway of the shopping center in Duarte (the only one). A group of four or five men were walking my way. It did not appear that they were inclined to move for me, and I damn sure wasn't going to move over for them. As a result, I just bumped my way through them with bravado (and stupidity!). One of them asked me to stop, said he had been a Marine, and told me I was acting in a way that would get my "ass kicked!" I pretty much kissed him off and continued on my way. The guy was right, and there is no doubt that those four or five men could have done some real damage. It was a good example of the bravado and confidence that the Corps instills in young men. Quite a change in demeanor from someone who had been a high school loser less than six months before.

Keith Passes the G.E.D. Examination!

Not long after graduating from Message Center School, I signed up to take the GED Examination (General Education Development Equivalent—accepted as a high school diploma). It was administered in an old World War II building at "Mainside" (this described most of the buildings at Camp Pendleton, as WWII had not been that long before). I passed the GED on the first try! I still don't know how I could have passed; I'd been a horrible student and seldom attended school. I guess something must have stuck! Maybe I sat next to someone who wrote big?

Barracks and Open Squad Bays

The vast majority of today's service personnel sleep in rooms with not more than three other people, and usually less. But during my enlisted era, those below the rank of staff sergeant slept in barracks with open squad bays. It was a massive room with metal racks (bunk beds), typically occupied by 60-80 men, with a large communal bathroom containing sinks and showers at one end. Privacy was non-existent. In most instances, non-commissioned officers (corporals and sergeants) would have single racks in a corner of the squad bay that was separated from the lance corporals and below by wall lockers. While I would certainly have liked to have had a small room, I must say in retrospect that the open squad bays most likely contributed in a positive way to the strengthening of social skills and tolerance, which is a good thing because there really were no options. You either got along with others or horrible things occurred!

Rifle Racks in the Open Squad Bays

In today's military, all weapons, including rifles and pistols, are closely controlled and stored in a secured armory when not in actual use. This is a far cry from the way rifles and pistols were "secured" in my era. Rifles were kept in a rifle rack in the center of the open squad bay, most often individually secured with the assigned Marine's combination lock, and it was not unusual for one or two of the rifles in the rack of twenty or so to be completely unsecured. Pistols were typically stored in an armory, but it was not unusual for them to occasionally be in the wall locker of the Marine to whom they'd been issued. While I am sure it occurred, I do not personally recall the theft of an individual weapon during that era. Unlike today, it was also a common practice in those days for Marines to retain the same weapon whenever they changed commands. It meant taking it with them, with security precautions, as they traveled to their new command. When I graduated from recruit training, I took my M-1 Garand with me to my first duty station, and kept it until issued the M-14 in September of 1962.

While unheard of today, I actually took my rifle on liberty one time. As a PFC, I put my M-1 in my car when I went home one weekend, along with rounds I had retained from my recent qualification. Accompanied by one of my civilian pals, I took the rifle to the Fish Canyon Shooting Range above the city of Duarte and did some shooting. It was not an authorized thing to do, but the sanction would not have been much had my activities come to someone's attention. Just a different era.

Lance Corporal Anderson's "Stretching Exercises"

The tendency of virile young men to occasionally find relief for their sexual urges in a self-imposed way is one of life's realities that is seldom discussed. However, when such a desire reaches crisis proportions during the middle of the night while in bed in a barracks, the only option is to seek relief in a way that might be obvious to some of the other 60-80 young men in that intimate open squad bay, due to the old rickety and squeaky two-man racks (bunks). At one time a pretty decent fellow named George had the top bunk, while I had the bottom bunk in our two-man cozy arrangement. While I understood George's occasional spontaneous lust, his urges came on at the worst times, often when I was sleeping the soundest. The squeaking and vibrations stemming from his manual manipulations on our WWII era racks interfered with my sleep and became a sore spot in our relationship. When I raised the issue, always gently, he attributed the machinations to his "stretching" exercises. Despite my suggestions that he find other times and locations for his "stretching exercises," his disruptive one-person lust continued until his success solved the problem for both of us—he was promoted to corporal and got a single bunk behind the row of wall lockers in the coveted "NCO quarters."

I have always wished I had the ability to draw, and have been envious of those folks who draw caricatures and creative images of funny situations. Just imagine how much fun a talented cartoonist could have with a pissed-off private first class and a lust-driven lance corporal doing his "stretching exercises" in a rickety bunk bed!

As I reflect on the situation, I have to acknowledge that George was probably not the only young man to lie in a lonely bed and think about his girl back home. Had bells been attached to each of the racks, at about midnight the squad bay would probably have sounded like the Washington Cathedral at high noon on Easter Sunday!

"Halt, Who Goes There?"—As I Bounced Down the Hill!

This was both funny, and a very critical lesson as well. My battalion was involved in a field exercise in the Case Springs area of Camp Pendleton. Another PFC, "Alf" Anderson (great guy, actually from Sweden) and I were assigned a critical post for 50 percent command post security, which meant that one of us always had to be awake and vigilant to prevent a penetration by the "opposing forces." During one of my tours it was pretty cold so I decided to drape my sleeping bag over my shoulders, then I decided to sit down, then I decided to just lay down and listen—and while not intentional, I fell asleep. The next thing I knew I was being dragged down the hill by the very opposing forces I was supposed to be alert for. I still recall yelling out "Halt Who Goes There!" as I was being dragged down that hill in my sleeping bag! We appropriately got reamed for not remaining alert, and were both required to stay awake for the rest of the night. That was a good lesson, and I don't believe I ever fell asleep again when assigned to perimeter security.

Teletype Machines—Useless in the Field

My primary military occupational specialty (MOS) was message center man. In an infantry battalion, the Message Center is an absolute key to the command element and the entity involving all incoming and outgoing message traffic. The key piece of equipment was the teletype machine, which worked reasonably well in a garrison/fixed location, but was a pain in the ass in the field. Because of frequent redeployments and the numerous components that made up the field teletype systems, these systems were just more trouble than they were worth in the field. During fast-moving operations involving numerous field relocations we often found excuses to use runners and other means of passing message traffic. Thank goodness our military folks now have such great equipment, as opposed to the WWII and Korea vintage stuff that was the mainstay during my enlisted days.

Corporal Mangan Gets a "Hot Foot"

After a hard night of drinking one of the "old salts" in the battalion, Corporal Mangan, frequently slipped into a storage area and went to sleep during the day. One afternoon, a couple of his "old salt" buddies rigged up a contraption of cardboard and matchbooks, carefully and quietly attached it to one of his boots, ignited it, and stood back to watch the action. The device erupted into flames and essentially cooked the boot it was attached to. The boot obviously got very hot, and eventually the very hot boot started burning his foot. He flew off the table he had been sleeping on, yelling and screaming every profanity imaginable, "hotfooting" it around the communications warehouse. Mangan was in a blind rage, as there was no way to quickly remove the hot laced-up combat boot from his foot. His buddies were rolling in the aisles. It was an ugly—but very funny—spectacle. I was a new kid and it was not in my best interests to laugh. But it was hard not to!

PFC Bushey and the Rendezvous Ballroom

What a great place! This historic structure, built in 1928 and then re-built in 1935 after it first burned down, was a place where all the big bands played in the late 1920s, '30s, '40s and '50s. It was a gigantic structure that stretched from one block to another right on the beach-side sand in Balboa. By the 1960s, all the "Surf Music" giants (Beach Boys, Jan and Dean, etc.) were playing there, along with scores of other groups and individuals representing the music of that era. Looking snappy in my tropical USMC uniform, I went there several times on liberty and really enjoyed the music and the girls. Unfortunately, as a "wet-behind-the-ears" and somewhat immature (with respect to the opposite sex) seventeen-year old, I lacked the skills to fully take advantage of the many opportunities that existed. Still, I had a great time. This wonderful landmark, then located directly behind the gift shop on the main drag on the Balboa Peninsula, burned to the ground in 1966. What a terrible loss for generations of young people who had such good times and today retain such wonderful memories.

Pupu Uele and the Trunk Full of Brass

One of the staff sergeants in the Communications Platoon was Pupu Uele, a big Samoan who was the wire section chief. He was a not very smart, but kind man, and his Samoan accent was very strong. He was not very officious, got along pretty well with the lower-ranking guys, and was the only staff sergeant I recall who was addressed by his first name by those beneath him.

One day the whole base was shut down for a search of every inch of Camp Pendleton. As I recall, a case of hand grenades has been stolen and an understandably strong effort was underway to find and retrieve them before they left the base. The search was to include personal vehicles as well, which presented a problem for me because I had a trunk-full of empty M-1 brass shell casings I'd taken from a trash can on a nearby rifle range. My brother was a reloading enthusiast and I'd got them for him. Even though empty and discarded, this brass was not to be taken from the ranges.

All of us with our own vehicles were directed to stand by our cars and be prepared for the big search. My car was a white 1952 Ford Crestline Victoria with "tuck and roll" upholstery and a bongo drum in the rear window. A group of staff non-commissioned officers was walking our way, and Staff Sergeant Uele was among them. I quickly approached Pupu and said I had some brass in my trunk, did not want to get in trouble, and asked that he be the one to inspect my car. He replied. "for five dollar!" I quickly agreed. When he approached my car and I opened the truck, he saw all the brass and said, "holy shit, ten dollar!" Again, I quickly accepted his offer! I later passed him the ten dollars when no one was looking.

THE CANTEEN CUP CAPER

This is the first of several stories related to Robert Neman (pseudonym), one of the young Marines I served with. I have been unsuccessful in trying to think of something nice to say about this guy. He was rude, arrogant, insulting, and successfully specialized in pissing people off. He continually did and said stupid things, and had no friends that I was aware of. He was squirrely and slight, and I doubt that he could have fought his way out of a paper bag. Every time I see the cartoon of the mouse giving the finger to the elephant, I think of Neman. Get the picture?

One day we had a major inspection, conducted as I recall by the commanding general of the 1st Marine Division. This was a very big deal that everyone had been working weeks in preparation for. One of the components was the "junk on the bunk" inspection, where every Marine had all of his gear laid out in excruciating order, just right, folds measured to the micro-inch, everything shined, pressed, cleaned, etc., etc. Even the socks and skivvies had to be perfectly marked with each person's name, folded precisely, and organized as if there was a little platoon of socks lying at attention on the bunk. It took hours to assemble these works of art and many people, myself included, had a number of clothing items that we used only for these inspections.

When the inspection party (made up of all of the ranking officers in the chain of command) approached Neman, who like the rest of us was standing at attention at the foot of his rack (metal bunk bed), the general stated, pretty much just going through the motions: "Looks good Marine, got all your gear?" Neman responded: "No, Sir!" The whole entourage came to a stop, everyone looked kinda confused, and the general stated that it looked like everything was laid out on his bunk. Neman said that he was missing his canteen cup. The general replied with something to the effect: "Son, it is right there," and pointed to a canteen cup on Neman's rack. Neman responded. "No sir, that cup belongs to a friend of mine in the first battalion because mine was missing!"

If the looks of the officers in the chain of command and the sergeant major could have killed, Neman would have died then and there! This behavior was unnecessary and beyond stupid. But it was classic Bob Neman—doing stupid things and pissing people off.

68

I did not care for Bob Neman, but felt that this incident was terribly cruel. It is an indication of how sick and vindictive some people can be under the guise of humor. At the time, it was a Saturday and Neman was on duty in the battalion communication center. Occasional teletype traffic was trickling in from higher commands; the battalion was the end of the line for messages.

A couple of our colleagues created a phony message, allegedly from the Red Cross, advising that Neman's parents had been killed in an automobile accident and asking that he be notified! Neman watched the bogus message come over the wire and understandably became very upset. I thought then that our colleagues' behavior was really sick, and still feel that way.

This is an indication of how sick and cruel some Marines can be with their humor.

"I AM GOING TO TRANSFER TO THE AIR FORCE!"

Bob Neman was continually complaining about the Marine Corps, and to this day I can still hear him say: "I wish I had joined the Motherf---ing Air Force!" He was always saying this, especially when upset about something, which was most of the time. A few of us, including me, cooked up a remedy to this problem.

We created a very credible appearing—but completely false—Marine Corps order that announced alleged transfer opportunities to the Air Force. The bogus order described MOS (specialty) imbalances among the military services and listed the criteria by which Marines could transfer to the Air Force. We created an extensive list of requirements, and ensured that Neman met every one of them. The order directed any interested Marine to contact his first sergeant. We then posted the phony notice on the company bulletin board. One of the guys then ran into the barracks and told Neman that his dream had been answered, that he could now transfer to the Air Force, and told him of the order posted on the bulletin board. In typical Neman form, he said his colleague was full of it, and arrogantly stormed out. Still, the temptation was too much and we knew that Neman would make a beeline to the bulletin board to see if there really was such an order. It was there!

Neman immediately entered the Company Office and asked to see the company first sergeant, who happened to be there. Neman, in his typical arrogant demeanor, told the first sergeant that he wanted an immediate transfer to the Air Force pursuant to the posted order (which we took off the bulletin as he entered the company office!). The shit hit the fan with the first sergeant yelling and screaming, and Neman insisting that there was such an order. They both ended up outside the Company Office. The order that Neman insisted existed was not there, and the yelling and screaming by the first sergeant got even worse, with Neman limping back to the barracks with smoke coming out his rear end! This incident did not improve Neman's already-bad disposition. At the time, I thought that this was pretty funny; today I think it is ever funnier!

Slaughter Alley

The stretch of highway that stretched through Camp Pendleton, adjacent to the ocean between the cities of Oceanside and San Clemente, had the well-deserved nickname of "Slaughter Alley." At the time, it was two lanes in each direction, which were separated by nothing more than a double yellow line. There were frequent head-on collusions, often involving servicemen and usually caused by someone who was either intoxicated or fatigued. The mayhem resulting from two cars colliding at high speed was absolutely awful, with gory posters containing such images routinely posted around Camp Pendleton. Thank goodness that this stretch of Interstate 5 is now a divided highway. Portions of the old "Slaughter Alley" are still clearly visible, with a considerable section just south of San Clemente now being a recreational vehicle parking area for the San Clemente State Park beaches, and another section serving as a parking area for cars just outside the Las Pulgas Gate at Camp Pendleton.

Emergency Blood Donation— "Need a Note from Your Parents!"

One morning one of our corpsman ran through the company area frantically calling out the names of a bunch of Marines who were to report to the first sergeant. I was one of those names. It seems that there had been a terrible traffic accident in Oceanside and there was an immediate need for blood of a certain type. This is when I first learned that my blood type, "O" negative, was highly-sought for donations. There were 10 or 15 of us, and we were rushed in a military truck to a civilian hospital in Oceanside. We were ushered inside, but a snag immediately developed for me because I was only seventeen years old and my parents were not available to give permission for me to donate blood! The efforts of the sergeant in charge to explain that I now belonged to the government and no longer to my parents, and that he was in charge of me, fell on deaf ears. The fact that somebody's life was on the line was secondary to a rule that said parental permission was required for a donor under the age of 18, and nobody at that hospital had the common sense to apply reality to the situation. PFC Bushey gave no blood that day.

Poop and the Coffee Table

This is really sick! One of the Marines in my unit had a unique week-end job in Laguna Beach: defecating on the top of a glass coffee table while a prosperous sicko lay beneath the table watching the action! Obviously, all of his buddies (including me) expressed our reservations about this behavior. He responded that he had to poop anyway, and why not make good money by directing his deposits where a generous person could enjoy them. I guess he and his "friend" must have been pretty pleased with the relationship, because the Marine always had a few bucks in his pocket while the rest of us were usually broke. I think it is fair to say that all the rest of us held two thoughts in common: outrage at this outrageous behavior, and envy that the prosperous sicko had not met one of us first! Postscript: I ran into my pal, the "depositor," about twenty years later. At the time he was a newly commissioned lieutenant, having received a limited-duty commission after many years as a staff non-commissioned officer. I wish I'd remembered to remind him of his poopathons in Laguna Beach.

Cigarettes for Pop—Ship's Stores

My dad was a smoker until the day he died. In fact, the three packs a day that he smoked, which irritated the growth from tonsils removal when he was in the Army in 1919 and resulted in throat cancer, not to mention emphysema, contributed to the debilitating illnesses that caused him to take his own life in 1963. Between graduation from boot camp in early 1962 until my first deployment to the Orient in mid-1963 (with time out for the Cuban Missile Crisis and my deployment to Guantanamo Bay), I participated in a number of amphibious exercises involving several days on troop ships. Ship's stores sold stuff at really cheap prices, with no taxes to boot, once the ship was beyond the three-mile territorial limits of the United States. I always bought a couple of cartons of cigarettes for my dad, at 10 cents a pack ($2 per carton) and took them home to him on my next weekend off. Ships stores were not exactly supermarkets, but consisted of a steel cage about the size of two or three phone booths. About all you could get were cigarettes, candy, Zippo lighters with that ship's name on it, and Chanel #5 perfume. For whatever reason, every ship's store that I can recall had an assortment of Chanel #5 perfume, and that is what the girlfriends of Marines and sailors got from their boyfriends in the 1960s!

THE CUBAN MISSILE CRISIS

On October 19, 1962, a Friday, I entered the Company Office to get my liberty card to start a long weekend I had earned. As I approached the duty non-commissioned officer, the first sergeant walked over, removed the box of liberty cards, announced that the base had been shut down and that the battalion was "mounting out!" My outfit, the Second Battalion of the First Marine Regiment, was the "Ready Battalion Landing Team" for the West Coast for October, with field transport packs made up and secured on the backs of our racks (other services would call them "bunks"), and the ability to immediately deploy anywhere in the world should a crisis erupt, supposedly on four-hour notice.

I thought this was a practice drill, as we were having practice "mount outs" quite often, and it was usually more of a logistics drill to see if we could get all of the equipment in embarkation boxes within a given period of time. I just knew that "ENDEX" (the end of the exercise) would sound anytime, but it did not occur. All day and into the night we prepared gear, organized weapons, turned the keys of our personal vehicles over to a representative from the military police, and performed related tasks. All phones were shut down and no one was permitted to call off-base. One of the guys snuck off the base and went into San Clemente to bring back some of our pals who often went on their own form of liberty by crawling out through a hole in the fence surrounding the base. This shit was starting to look serious! But what is going on in the world where a Marine battalion is immediately needed? The Berlin Airlift was over; Lebanon had settled down; the "Bay of Pigs" had run its tortured course. What's going on now?

We staged on the San Mateo Grinder all night, and as the sun came up we boarded cattle cars for the short trip to the El Toro Marine Corps Air Station, just south of Santa Ana (no longer in existence). As we approached the tarmac, there were U.S. Air Force C-35 jet military transport aircraft (Boeing 707s) lined up as far as I could see! Now it was

72

really looking serious. But we still thought it was an exerise (the young troops, anyway—the leadership knew it was the real deal). The battalion, with tons of weapons, ammo, and equipment boarded the aircraft and took off. Obviously, the rumors ran rampant; where the hell are we going? About an hour into the flight, a young Air Force crewmember came on the intercom and announced that our destination was Guantanamo Bay, Cuba!

This was the international situation where history records that the United States and the Soviet Union stood on the brink of a nuclear war, because of the detected presence of Soviet nuclear missiles in Cuba that were aimed at the United States and the demand of President John F. Kennedy that the missiles be dismantled. American forces were deployed and ready for ground, air, and sea combat, and quarantine was imposed in the waters around Cuba. Ultimately, Soviet Premier Nikita Khrushchev ordered the missiles removed, and the two countries moved back from the brink of a global holocaust. By this time thousands of soldiers, sailors, airmen and Marines had deployed to the Caribbean and were ready to engage in armed combat of every type. My battalion was one of the very few that was actually on the ground in Guantanamo. In mid-December, we returned to the United States on a WWII troop transport, the USS *Bexar* APA 237 (named after a county in Texas). We passed through the Panama Canal and returned to Camp Pendleton just before Christmas 1962.

Much later, by watching a history movie, I learned that Kennedy gave up something as well, an agreement to remove the United States missiles in Turkey that were aimed at the Soviet Union. Even with the concession of the missiles, I thought that President Kennedy did a good job.

I Still Dislike Fidel Castro—Just a Little Less

I was exited about the prospect of going into combat—but please not this weekend. Through the girlfriend of one of my buddies, I had a date set up with a drop-dead beautiful girl whom I had been wooing since we were both high school freshman, and it was all set (or so I thought) for Saturday night. Unfortunately, that was the night I arrived in Cuba! All of us harbored an intense dislike of Fidel Castro, but my scorn for him was even worse because he deprived me of a date I had long sought.

When I got back to the States, my friend informed me that despite the efforts of his girlfriend, the date was never confirmed. A number of years later I learned that the girl had been in a long-time secret relationship with one of the Duarte High football coaches, and that I never had the slightest chance of a relationship with her. The Cuban Missile Crisis did not cost me a date with that gal after all. I still dislike Fidel Castro, just a little less than before.

This Beer Does Not Taste Right!

On arrival in Guantanamo Bay at the onset of the Cuban Missile Crisis, my company was briefly staged on an asphalt grinder outside the enlisted club. We all sat there for an hour, or so, and were permitted to have beer. As I drank my beer, it tasted a little odd, but I kept drinking it anyway. As we were told to board the trucks for transit to the base perimeter, I took one last long swallow on my beer to finish it off. That is when I realized that other Marines had mistaken my bottle for an ashtray! About half the ashes and cigarette butts went down my throat. Not a pleasant experience!

Mosquitoes & Hysteria (Defining Experience in My Life)

The flight from California to Cuba took about five hours, and the planes landed at the airfield on the leeward side of the base. It was hotter than hell, about 109 degrees in the shade (and there wasn't any). The humidity had to be close to 100 percent and was so thick you could cut it with a knife. This was the first time in my life, but far from the last, experiencing heat and humidity so stifling as to be near paralyzing. But it was a reality I later experienced in many of the other "garden spots" I was sent while a Marine. We were issued live ammunition and rushed, via trucks, to the jungles on the other side of the base, but still within the base, where Navy Seabees were deployed along the fenceline (miles and miles long) in an effort to minimize the infiltration of Cuban Army soldiers.

The battalion entered and set up operations in what had to be one of the worst places on earth. The nastiest jungle imaginable with stale water everywhere (it rained on-and-off all the time), more critters of every type than I had ever seen, unbelievably thick foliage and mosquitoes—millions of hungry and pissed-off mosquitoes! Due to our rapid deployment there were many things that none of us had brought. There was no mosquito repellant or mosquito nets, nor was there any likelihood of obtaining such items within the next day or so!

This was initially, for a few minutes, the absolute worst time in my life up until then. All of us were sustaining non-stop multiple mosquito bites on every exposed part of our bodies, which meant face, neck, arms, and hands. I was swatting and swatting and swatting, and naturally my efforts were making no difference; the hand I was swatting with had just as many mosquitoes clinging to it as the arm I was trying to get the mosquitoes off.

I was starting to panic and literally was on the verge of hysteria. Then something in my mind snapped. I settled down, became calm, and recall saying as if it were yesterday, "fuck it, help yourself, there's enough blood for all of us!" This was among the most significant events in my life, a necessary mindset that proved essential in Cuba and all the other places where Marines go. I was pleased and proud of myself, and knew that something very special had just happened in those last few minutes.

COMMANDANT VISITS THE TROOPS IN THE FIELD

Within several days of arriving in Cuba, General David M. Shoup, then Commandant of the Marine Corps, visited our field command post. I was among the gaggle of Marines who gathered around him as he said whatever he said, probably something about being proud of us, upholding the traditions of the Corps, importance of the mission, etc. My great recollection is what I thought then, and continue to think now, of the foolish appearance of his uniform. He wore utilities, but over each breast pocket was a red patch with gold lettering and gold trim. One patch indicated USMC (or Marines?) and the other SHOUP (or CMC?). I thought it was unnecessarily flashy and not very Marine Corps. At the time I was a private first class. I could not have imagined that the next time I would have a conversation with a commandant in the field I would be a full colonel and the primary briefer.

BUSHEY REPORTS TO THE SERGEANT MAJOR—"YOU ARE ONLY 17!"

A few days after arriving in Cuba I was out stringing comm wire when another Marine chased me down and said I was to immediately report to the battalion sergeant major! He was equal to The Lord in rank pecking order, and I was apprehensive of why he called for PFC Bushey. When I got to his office (sitting behind an embarkation box in a tent), he informed me that I should not have been allowed to deploy to Cuba, because I was only 17 years old and Marine Corps orders prohibited anyone from serving in a combat zone until they had reach the ripe old age of 18. He told me to get my gear, as I was being returned the

United States immediately. I did not think Cuba was a good place, and like everyone else I was frightened, as by then we knew of the potential missile holocaust. But the thought of being jerked out of my platoon and away from my fellow Marines and being removed because of my age was devastating.

That day I came as close as I ever had to begging. I told the sergeant major that I joined the Marine Corps to serve my county, to fight, and to die if necessary. I told him that I would feel disgraced if removed, and talked about my training, my skills, and how my departure would create a loss in my section (that was a bit of an exaggeration!). I pleaded with him to not send me home. I reminded him that I was only two or three weeks away from turning eighteen.

I don't recall his exact words, but the sergeant major replied with something pretty close to the following: "Son, I am a sergeant major in the United States Marine Corps and my job is to ensure that orders are carried out. Two days or two weeks make no difference. The bottom line is that you cannot be in a combat zone as a 17 year old—period!" He paused, appeared to be reflecting, then continued: "Right now, however, I am up to my ass in alligators and am having trouble getting all this shit on my plate out of the way. Your issue is pretty close to the bottom of the stack and will probably take two or three weeks before I can get to it. Get your ass back to your platoon for the time being!" He then looked me right in the eyes with somewhat of a mischievous twinkle in his, and a slight smile on his wrinkled face. I thanked him profusely; he nodded slightly and went back to work. I never heard another word about the issue and turned eighteen a couple of weeks later.

I later learned that he also joined the Marine Corps as soon as he turned seventeen, and had seen extensive combat in several World War II Pacific campaigns before turning eighteen.

WEAPON MISFIRES IN GUANTANAMO—THANK GOD!

This was a very bad situation that had the very real potential to not only be a fork in my road, but could easily have been the *end* of my road had it not been for an inexplicable weapon malfunction. In a logic which, even after all these years, continues to escape me, my brother convinced my parents to purchase and send a handgun to me in Cuba. But the damn thing was a single-shot .22 caliber derringer. I think it is likely that my brother wanted one, so he convinced my mom to buy the matched set; he got one, and the other was mailed in a plain package to me in Cuba, with a few loose bullets. When I opened the package and read the letter, I also placed a round in the chamber. At that moment one of my buddies, clearly not rocket-scientist material, grabbed it, proclaimed it to be a toy, cocked the hammer, and pointed right at me! I pleaded with him to put it down and insisted that it was loaded and that it was not a toy, at which time he pulled the trigger! Thank God, it did not fire. It turned out to be a manufacturing defect, where the mainspring was not strong enough to cause the rimfire cartridge to fire. I could not believe that I was still alive and had been so lucky; somebody had to be watching over me that day. I can only imagine the consequences had I sustained a fatal wound: my parents and brother would have experienced a degree of sadness and guilt that I believe would have triggered the beginning of the end to their lives.

Don't Let Dorman Kill the Lieutenant!

On arrival of my battalion in Cuba, the communications platoon got a new commander, 2nd Lieutenant Paul G. Davens (pseudonym). He was an okay person, but very gung-ho and clearly in love with himself. Because of the remnants of a very recently-removed conspicuous officer candidate school patch, it was clear that he had not been an officer very long. But he acted like an old salt who knew everything there was to know about the Corps and the art of leadership. In truth, he was lean on both counts. Worse, he wore a Ruger .357 old Western-style revolver in a custom holster, as opposed to the issued .45 semi-automatic pistols, and sported a large handlebar moustache. I am aware that he later developed into a fine officer, but he was pretty much a laughable dork as our boss in Cuba. One of the truly old-time Marines in our platoon was a "retread" corporal whose name was Bennie Dorman (pseudonym), who had previously seen combat in Korea and who had returned to the Corps after a few-year stint in CivDiv (we sometimes called civilian life "civilian division"). Dorman had no use for Davens. One night when drunk he actually threatened to kill the lieutenant, which most of us saw as just the stupid remarks of a drunk and nothing to be taken seriously. Lieutenant Davens did take the remark seriously and directed the communications chief, SSgt Aretakis (RIP) to assign a man to guard him while he slept in his hammock in the jungle. I still recall the guidance that Aretakis gave to the men that kept vigil over the sleeping lieutenant: "Don't let Dorman kill the lieutenant!"

While attending the Command & Staff College at Quantico when

I was a lieutenant colonel in the early 1990s, I ran across an article in a professional journal written by Colonel Paul G. Davens. I managed to locate him. At the time he was finishing his career as the top Marine at a Navy-Marine Corps ROTC unit at an eastern university. He was very gracious and we had a nice chat, and it was clear that he had long overcome his not untypical, newly-commissioned foolish behavior, and had gone on to a very successful Marine Corps career. We reminisced about our service in Cuba, but having to guard him from Corporal Dorman was not among the issues we discussed.

TORN HANDS AND COMM WIRE

Although my military specialty was message center, I spent a great deal of my time in Cuba working as a field wireman. We laid miles and miles of comm wire, which was necessary in order to have communications between the various units, and especially out to the isolated observation and listening posts along the fence line. Unfortunately, Cuban soldiers had a little trick up their sleeves that caused a lot of havoc. They would infiltrate our lines (we did repel a lot of them, however), find the wire lines that we had laid to the observation and listening posts, cut the wire, and then insert pins through the cut portion on the side that went to the outposts.

These pins were intended to tear open the hands of the Marines who traced the wires in order to find the malfunction, and that is exactly what happened to me. I was working my way through the jungle with the wire in the web of my hand, and searching for the likely cut portion, when I hit one of the sabotaged portions, and cut the hell out of my hand. I wrapped the hand in something, then continued with the wire in the web of my other hand, and shortly tore up that one as well (I was a slow learner!). After that, we put rags around the wire to protect our hands, and ultimately got thick leather gloves, which really did the trick. The scars in the webs of my hands have gotten smaller over the years, but are still visible.

WILLIE PETE AND THE COKE BREAK

The nature of military conflict has changed over the decades, and Coca-Cola has become among the necessary supply items that must be provided! After having strung a spool of wire from a command post to a listening post, I took a "Coke break." The Marine who was manning the post was a pal of mine and had several Cokes in a container. While we should have been inside the observation post, which was hole dug into the side of a hill and covered with sandbags, we instead were languishing outside, on the roof, shooting the bull and drinking our Cokes.

Our pleasant evening was interrupted by the firing, in our direction, of a flare gun by a Cuban soldier, which splattered white phosphorus (known as "willie pete") all over the bunker. The other Marine got the worst of it, and was hit on the neck and part of his face beneath an ear. I got a chuck of it on the fleshy part of my right elbow. It was very painful and burned like hell. A corpsman later treated both of us, but there is not much you can do other than keep clean and as protected a possible. It took months for my elbow to finally heal, and my diminishing scar now just looks like a dirty elbow!

"My Scorpion is Bigger than Yours!"

A field Marine cannot survive unless he overcomes the natural fear that most of us have for bugs, reptiles, spiders, and the like. You certainly don't have to like them, but you need to have some tolerance and not go crazy when they are encountered, including when they crawl on you. It goes with the territory. In Cuba, and many other "garden spots" that I have visited, you absolutely had to shake all the critters out of your boots and clothes before putting them on. We used to have good-natured contests in the morning to see whose boots yielded the largest scorpion!

Thanksgiving Dinner—Turkey and Gnats!

Except for occasional forays into the main part of the base to get a hamburger or hot dog, the three meals we ate daily were "C-Rations." Every now and then it was okay, but everyday for weeks on end got pretty rough—I got to the point where I was ready to eat cardboard and gargle warm spit as an alternative! We all looked forward to the "hot meal" that was promised for Thanksgiving. Unfortunately, there was a problem: the millions of gnats that wanted to share our meal with us!

The turkey and all the trimmings were brought out into the jungle in vat cans, and all the Marines lined up with our metal mess kits. The gnats were everywhere, and there was nothing that could be done to get rid of them. They were on the food in the vat cans, and immediately covered the chow the instant it was dished into in our mess kits. The food appeared black from the thousands of bugs on top of that food. We had two choices—walk away hungry or eat the bugs as part of the food. Once you got over the psychological hurdle of eating bugs, it wasn't so bad; if fact, you couldn't even taste them. It would've been nice to have received toothpicks to gets the gnats out of our teeth, though.

"The Exhibition" and Whorehouse in Panama City

Once the Cuban Missile Crisis was over, my battalion was sent back to Camp Pendleton on several World War II era troop ships. I was on the USS *Bexar* APA237, and all things considered it was not a bad journey. After all, we were going to be home for Christmas! We transited the Panama Canal, which was quite an interesting experience that took about eight hours, and then tied up on the Rodman side of the canal for a day and evening of liberty in Panama City.

A few of my buddies and I had been told of a "must see" location known as "The Exhibition," where bizarre sexual behavior was rampant. So off we went to find this mysterious place. Our information was accurate: it was truly bizarre! It was a giant, two-story barn-type of a structure with catwalks around both floors, which afforded the visitor an opportunity to see unspeakable debauchery. Every one of the twenty or so stalls, which the observer could lean into for closer looks, had a woman doing something with an item, person, or animal! I was more scared than fascinated, because I thought we should not be there and might be arrested by the military police. Sure enough, not long after our arrival a military police car came charging up the dirt road and I just knew we were in big trouble. Wrong! The military police officers just joined the tour around the catwalk!

My little group then decided to visit a whorehouse, as a couple of the fellows sought some intimate feminine companionship. After a truly memorable cab ride that I was mistakenly convinced would end in a fiery crash, we ended up at a cathouse. The structure was a very large room with beds lining all the walls, each bed surrounded by a white hospital-like curtain that could be closed for some minor degree of privacy; a woman was seated on each bed. The two horny Marines walked around the room, each picked a woman, paid the roving proprietor, went to the respective bed, pulled the curtain shut, and did whatever they did! I doubt that I have ever been considered a prude. But this pay-as-you-go affection, with some pretty shady ladies in a most unwholesome environment, just was not for me. So I hung around until my buddies were finished, and then we all went back to Central Panama City and got drunk.

In many instances—and I suspect that this was one of those instances—I continually reflected on my high school classmates back home, and what they were doing in comparison to what I was doing. They were still in the first semester of their senior year in high school, still picking their zits and whacking off behind the soda shop, and I had just completed my first combat tour of duty as a United States Marine! Very cool!

Smelly Peas on the High Seas

Pulling out of the Panama Canal Zone aboard the USS *Bexar*, my life of leisure doing nothing on the ship ran out when I was assigned to mess duty for the remainder of the voyage back to the United States. Fortunately, I have never experienced seasickness, but thought that it might have happened then. Though I never puked, the very rough seas and greasy spaghetti caused me to come close. One afternoon I was working in the ship's galley with a person who had well-deserved reputation as a shitbird, when he took off one boot and sock and actually stirred a giant vat of peas with his dirty and very smelly foot! The ability to take showers (30 seconds under a salt-water faucet after waiting several hours) was pretty much non-existent. We were all really ripe, and Kurth's (pseudonym) actions were beyond sickening. Since the chow was horrible anyway and Navy cooks (who didn't care about the Marines) were in charge, reporting Kurth's actions never occurred to me. In fact, his sweat and toe jam may have added some much-needed flavor to the vat of peas! I skipped the peas at chow that evening.

My Battalion Lands at White Beach—On Cargo Nets

The Cuban Missile Crisis struck me as a pretty big deal, and I expected a welcome home that would involve bands, speeches, and scores of accolades. That was not to be. In hindsight, my expectations were not very practical because of the hundreds of thousands of American service personnel who played a role. Unlike my outfit, which was one of the very few actually on the island and in contact with Cuban military forces, most of the other units stayed afloat offshore in support roles. The big welcome home that some of us expected never materialized. Our ship dropped anchor off the coast of Camp Pendleton, we climbed down nets over the side, and went ashore in assault landing crafts (LCVPs). But I did make it home for Christmas, and the holidays were pleasant.

My Car had been Trashed at Camp Pendleton!

When the word came down for my unit to "mount out" for what became the Cuban Missile Crisis, the entire base went into lockdown and contact with the outside world ceased. All Marines with personal vehicles had to surrender their keys and vehicles to military policemen for storage during deployment. While I was in Cuba my dad went to the base to retrieve my car, but it would not start. Also, my car was full of stuff that somebody had obviously scrounged from empty offices and storerooms, including a bunch of blank discharge certificates. Someone had obviously used the car while I was deployed. That "someone" failed to keep water in the radiator, resulting in the engine seizing up. Dad arranged to have the car towed home, and helped pay for the repairs.

David Bushey Passes Away

I got early liberty on Friday, January 18, 1963, and drove home. While I was in Cuba, my parents had moved from 1956 Cinco Robles Drive to 1636 Cotter Avenue, both in Duarte and very close to one another. When I got home dad asked me to take him to the El Monte bus station, because he needed to go into downtown Los Angeles. I drove him to the bus station and dropped him off. It was the last time I ever saw him alive.

What I didn't know was that he had been particularly despondent over his deteriorating physical condition, and that my mother sensed that he was potentially on the verge of suicide. He had been ill for many years. His throat cancer had been treated unsuccessfully with radiation, then radical surgery, after which he contracted tuberculosis due to his weakened resistance. Dad also had emphysema. Because of his refusal to consent to additional surgery on his throat, as he just did not feel he could tolerate any more, the City of Hope released him as a patient. It meant the end of legitimate pain medication (this is as I understood the situation at the time). As a result, he made regular trips to downtown Los Angeles, where he bought seconals from street peddlers to deal with his pain. He ate very little because everything had a metallic taste, and subsisted primarily on broth. Finally, he was in bed almost all the time. He was a very sick man. I completely understand his frustrations and the desire to end his life.

When my mom came home from work that day she inquired about the whereabouts of dad, then became very quiet when I told her that he had gone downtown. She did not share her concerns with me, but mom was fearful that he had left to take his life. She was right. The following morning a sheriff's unit came to our home. Mom immediately became hysterical; she knew what he had come to tell us. Dad had gone into Los Angeles, bought a bunch of pills, took a bus back to Duarte, bought a quart of beer, checked into a motel on Huntington Drive, and washed the pills down with the beer. The motel was built around a giant oak tree. The motel is long gone, but the oak tree still stands. I think about my dad every time I drive past that old oak, now surrounded by condominiums, just east of Highland Avenue on the south side of Huntington Drive.

I called my unit and was given emergency leave, and pop was laid to rest at Rose Hills Memorial Park several days later.

The Grandaddy of Chicken-Shit Traffic Citations

A couple of hours after dad's death notification I decided to drive over to the Temple City sheriff's station, hopefully to get a copy of the death report and to learn the details of my dad's death. While southbound on Buena Vista Avenue approaching Duarte Road, I apparently rolled through a stop sign and was pulled over by a deputy sheriff. He asked for identification and I gave him both my driver's license and my military identification card. He recognized the name and asked if I was related to the man who had taken his own life up on Huntington Drive. The officer had been at the scene. I replied that the deceased was my dad and that I was enroute to the Temple City station to get a copy of the report. He said I should talk to the watch commander. The bastard then issued me a citation for the stop sign!

I drove to the Temple City station and had a brief meeting with a very nice sergeant who was the watch commander. The sergeant inquired as to why I came to see him. I told him it was suggested by the deputy who had just given me a ticket. About that time, the deputy who had cited me walked into the station. The sergeant told him to hang on for a minute, then turning to me extended his condolences and said the report would not be ready for several days. He then indicated for the deputy to follow him out of the lobby area. His body language told me he was surprised over the ticket; he should have canceled it. I was not happy to get the ticket, but it was not until later that I learned just how terribly inappropriate the issuance really was.

An Unexpected Act of Kindness by the First Sergeant

I returned to my unit at Camp Pendleton the day after dad's funeral services. I went to the company officer to sign in and close out my leave. I had been given telephonic approval for the leave, which is the military equivalent of vacation time, and needed to complete the processing. The first sergeant was somehow involved in the processing and obviously knew about my situation. That wonderful man tore up the leave papers, which meant that I did not have to use up my leave time for the absence. I don't even recall him saying anything, but he probably muttered a condolence.

The Marine Corps is a unique place. While acknowledging that it has its share of jerks, it also yields some of the most wonderful people on the face of the earth. The sergeant's simple act of compassion, with few or no words exchanged, absolutely no fanfare, and consummated in about a minute, was among the things that set the standard for my subsequent leadership as a non-commissioned officer and as a commissioned officer. This first sergeant was a decorated WWII veteran, like most of the top enlisted leadership during my first enlistment, who by now has most likely made the transition into eternal life. I hope things are going well for him up there, and that he has satisfaction for the positive impact his actions had on lives such as mine.

Drunken Marine Goes Crazy in the Comm Center

The communications platoon had the usual cast of unique characters. One of them was a big bully from the coal mines of Pennsylvania, "Rat" Ratajac (pseudonym). He was dumb and mean, and even dumber and meaner when he had been drinking. Like most jerks, he did stupid things, and the folks who dealt with his behavior were his superiors. He did not care for them, especially the two staff sergeants whose desks were in the communications center.

Late one night when I was on duty, "Rat" stormed into the comm center in a drunken rage; my pleas for him to leave were met with a threat to kick my ass. He approached the desk of one of the two sergeants, opened the middle drawer, and urinated in it! He then went to the desk of the other sergeant, which had a carousel of smoking pipes on top of it, and commenced to subject each pipe stem to some indignities that I will leave to the imagination! He then stumbled out and went back to the barracks.

Holy shit, now what do I do? Reporting him was not much of an option, as it would have been hazardous to my health. I spent the rest of the night trying to undo his damage. I carefully drained and cleaned out the drawer; it wasn't easy or pleasant. I still remember drying the upside-down drawer over the heater and carefully cleansing all the items inside. I threw a few things away, liked urine soaked papers, and was hoping they would not be missed. I cleaned the pipes as best I could, but

84

certainly would not have wanted to smoke one!

I was successful in covering up this foolish and gross incident. I thought that "Rat" would brag about the things he did to the two sergeants. But I never heard a word, or even a visual acknowledgement from him, when he and I interacted. I came to believe that the dumb bastard did not even recall the incident. I sure did, but wished that I hadn't! This was one of those times when I asked myself if I should have stayed in high school, as it would have been my junior year. I did learn a lesson from this incident: if you smoke pipes, never leave them where they are accessible to someone who may not care for you!

Captain A J Squared-Away—Not!

While his last name escapes me, in my platoon we had a total shitbird whose first and middle names started with the letters A and J, and like every one else with those initials, he was referred to as "AJ." He was incompetent and arrogant, and those were his good qualities. We used to marvel at how "AJ" even got through boot camp. After a year or so in the Corps, he was still a buck private, and that was hard to do! Since he was the antithesis of being squared away, we kiddingly referred to him as "Private A J Squared Away." One Monday morning a sergeant from the base brig (military jail) showed up to clean out AJ's locker. It seems that AJ was discovered walking around San Clemente wearing captain's bars on his collar. In addition to violating every sacred rule in the Marine Corps, this idiot pulled his little stunt in the community where all of us routinely went on liberty, so it was a virtual certainty that several people recognized who he really was. Over and above facial recognition, Marine captains have a demeanor that AJ could never replicate. I occasionally think of ol' AJ and wonder what became of him. It was not likely to be anything good.

Hitchhiking to and from Camp Pendleton

It is rare to see folks hitchhiking these days, but that was not always the case. During my service as an enlisted Marine, hitchhiking was very common, especially among servicemen. I was fortunate in having a car after boot camp, and kept that 1952 Ford Victoria up until just a couple of months before deploying to the Orient. In preparation for deployment I sold it to another Marine for a reasonable price, but that left me without a set of wheels for my last few weeks in the States. During this time, I pretty much hitchhiked to and from the base to my home on the weekends. I never had any problems to speak of, as people were almost always kind to men in uniform. When returning to the base on Sunday afternoons, my mom or dad would typically drive me to a major street from which I could start hitchhiking back to Camp Pendleton. The one area of concern and caution was around Laguna Beach, because of the many homosexual men who tried to convince hitchhiking servicemen to take a diversion for inappropriate activities. I was hit on a couple of times, but it was always polite and subtle and never got at all nasty when I made it clear that I was not interested. But I appreciated the rides!

My Senior Prom

Had I not dropped out of high school, I might have graduated in June of 1963 with the rest of my classmates. They did graduate and I was invited to attend what would have been my senior prom. I showed up in my Marine dress uniform with a pretty girl on my arm, a medal on my chest (sharpshooter), a stripe on my sleeve, and a very confident demeanor. Plus, I'd got my GED over a year before! All of the guys were sweating the draft, which affected just about all eligible males in those days. But I already had half of my military service behind me. As a person who had previously been seen as most likely to fail, this was a very satisfying event for me.

"Lock-On" Training and Deployment to the Orient

During the late 1950s and into the mid-1960s, the Marine Corps had a concept known as "transplacement" battalions. The West Coast battalions, following approximately 18 months in the United States, rotated to the 3rd Marine Division in the Orient for a 13-month tour of duty. During the stateside portion of the rotation, the old-timers transfered out and the new folks transfered in. As the battalions passed each other in the Pacific, they exchanged designations and took on the identity of the other. My battalion, 2nd Battalion, 1st Marine Regiment, 1st Marine Division, became the 3rd Battalion, 9th Marine Regiment, 3rd Marine Division. We were then known as "3/9."

However, before training the battalion went through an extensive six-week training package, known as "Lock On" training. It was very heavy in combat and field activities, and intended to sharpen the battalion's ability to immediately deploy into a combat situation. All leaves had already been taken, but as someone who lived in Southern California I still managed to get home for most weekends until we actually shipped out.

Note: All of the aforementioned Marine Corps activities occurred during what would have been my junior and senior high school years, had I not dropped out and entered the military on my 17th birthday. As I look back, this was really some unique stuff (dangerous, lewd, crude and otherwise most interesting) for a high school kid!

THIRD BATTALION, NINTH MARINE REGIMENT (3/9)

In July of 1963, after having served a very eventful year and a half or so in 2/1, I became a member of the 3rd Battalion of the 9th Marine Regiment of the 3rd Marine Division. My entire previous battalion (2/1) shipped overseas and was redesignated as 3/9, with that unit returning to the United States and being redesignated as one of the battalions of the 1st Marine Division at Camp Pendleton. Although the base of operations for 3/9 was Camp Hanson on the island of Okinawa, where the division headquarters was located, all of the battalions of the 3rd Division deployed frequently around the Orient.

SETTING SAIL FOR THE ORIENT

The battalion departed San Diego for the Orient on the USS *Patrick*, a large dependent and troop ship, one of several that moved constantly to and from the Orient moving troops and dependents. We departed from the exact pier where mom, pop, and I had watched my brother Larry depart for Korea some ten years earlier. I insisted that mom and Larry not come to San Diego to watch the ship leave; instead we said our goodbyes in Duarte during my last liberty. I recalled the emotions of watching my brother's ship, the USS *Mann*, the same type of vessel, depart San Diego Bay and disappear into the evening sunset, and did not want me or my family to go through that again. The voyage took about two weeks, and included one-day stops in Hawaii and Guam.

COKE AND THE HALF-ORDER OF COLESLAW

The ship pulled into Pearl Harbor, and we all got a nice look at the then-new *Arizona* War Memorial, which had just been completed. Payday was still several days away and I was just about broke. I hitchhiked to Waikiki Beach and went to the sands by the military facility, Fort DeRussy, which at that time was nothing more than a hut where you could buy refreshments and borrow floats and bathing suits. I borrowed a bathing suit, swam for a while, then blew my entire wad of seventy-five cents on a Coke and a half-order of coleslaw. I was told there was a dance that evening at the USO in downtown Honolulu. It sounded good, so I walked over there.

While in Hawaii I took a bunch of photos. One of the rolls of film was in color, which in those days were incredibly expensive (at least on my pay!) to develop. Ultimately I threw the roll away. How stupid!

"Servicemen Welcome, No Uniforms Allowed"

I got to the USO (United Service Organization) early. It was still daylight, but that was not the problem. On the marquee in front of the building, the letters read (this is exact; I will never forget what it said): "DANCE TONIGHT, SERVICEMEN WELCOME, NO UNIFORMS ALLOWED." I was in my tropical uniform ("trops") and had no other clothes, as in those days it was prohibited for servicemen to wear civilian clothes on a naval vessel. Out of luck, I hitchhiked back to the ship. The situation really irritated me, and left a bad taste in my mouth for USOs for a number of years. Later I came to realize that this poor practice, obviously intended to keep the number of service personnel attending the dance at a manageable level, was the rare exception. The USO is a great organization.

This prohibition of civilian clothes on naval vessels is why every port had "locker clubs," where sailors and seagoing Marines could keep civilian clothes. It was the norm for personnel to have a locker with "civvies" in every port they regularly visited. These clubs usually included lounges, tailor shops, and gift shops. They were almost always in a part of town that also had a fair share of tattoo parlors and burlesque shows.

Unique Barometric Pressure and the "Jewelry Box" Smell

We arrived at Naha Harbor, Okinawa, late in the afternoon, and were bused almost to the other end of the island. Camp Hansen was named for a World War II Medal of Honor recipient from the Battle of Okinawa. I still remember my fascination with the atmospheric conditions: pretty skies, high, rapidly-moving clouds, and a most pleasant pressure in the air. I still remember that the inside of our open barracks had the same odor as the Japanese jewelry boxes I had seen in my life, including a couple that my brother had sent to our mother years earlier. Funny, the things you remember. Each structure was two cement barracks, each capable of housing about sixty Marines, joined by a common head (bathroom) in the center.

During the day, a number of Okinawan nationals spent time in the barracks spit-shining our shoes and laundering our clothes. As I recall, I paid $5 per payday for the complete maintenance of all my uniforms and daily spit-shining of my shoes and boots. We did not make much money, but this was still a great deal.

NAVY SHIPS OF MY ENLISTED ERA—WORLD WAR II VINTAGE

Without exception, every amphibious troop ship that I served on in the 1960s was a veteran of World War II. They had all seen a great deal of combat at the landings of Guadalcanal, Tarawa, Iwo Jima, Saipan, Guam, Okinawa, etc. For our amphibious exercises we crawled over the same sides and rode in the same small landing craft that carried many brave men ashore, and returned so many of their remains back to the ships. Some of the ships were the USS *Bayfield* APA33, USS *Bexar* APA237, USS *Henrico* APA45, USS *Clymer* APA27, USS *Union* AKA106, USS *Princeton* LPH5, and the USS *Cabildo* LSD16. Boy, if only those ships could talk. None of them exist any more, as the last few decades have seen a tremendous building program for the "Gator Navy."

WAR DEBRIS LITTERED THE HARBOR IN GUAM

The ship made a brief visit to Guam between Hawaii and Okinawa. As we entered the harbor there were still scores of beached landing craft, all rusty and battered, left over from the American landings at Guam in 1944. I was struck by the stifling temperature and humidity, and gained a new appreciation for the American forces who had made the landings and fought on Guam in World War II, as the campaign was at almost the identical time of the year as my brief visit. I spent my few hours of liberty walking around the abandoned Japanese airfield adjacent to the built-up base areas, reflecting on the historic nature of the island. At that time, there were at least two Japanese soldiers, left over from World War II still living in the jungle, who refused to believe the war was over!

WOMEN IN THE MEN'S HEAD

On my first day at Camp Hansen, I was in the head sitting on the pot doing what I do best, when an Okinawan woman walked in and sat right next to me! Marine Corps heads are typically not places for people who like privacy—this one had a long row of toilets with no dividers—but having a female share the facilities was a new experience for me. I was horrified, tried to look away, and got out of there as fast as I could.

By the end of my first tour in the Orient, these types of encounters usually resulted in casual conversations. The Marine Corps is not a place for people who cannot overcome inhibitions, and those who join the Corps with inhibitions usually leave without them.

The Great Fudge Disaster

After a few months overseas I got a real hankering for chocolate fudge. So I wrote home and asked my mom to whip up a batch, wrap it good, and send it to me. Now, this was never a quick turnaround. All mail went by ship, so it took at least three weeks for a letter to get home and another three weeks to get a response. The box of fudge arrived about six weeks after I asked her to send it. On the day it arrived we were all gathered around for mail call, and I opened the box the minute it was given to me. Big mistake! Within seconds, all the fudge was gone by the numerous hands that reached into the box! I was devastated. I wrote another letter home telling mom what had occurred, and asked her to send another box. When the next box arrived about another six weeks later, I took the package without saying anything to anyone. I stashed the box in my wall locker and never took a piece out unless I was sure that no one was looking! I think the box lasted me two or three days.

Burning Butts on the High Seas

This was really funny. We were aboard a troop ship; I think it was the USS *Henrico* APA45, going someplace that I don't recall. The head, like the heads on most troop ships, had a long trough with a series of wooden slats to sit on, as the toilet for bowel movements. Seawater moved constantly from one end of the trough to the other, washing away the human waste. One day someone devised an incendiary device that looked something like a hot dog container, but more sturdy, with higher sides, and filled it with wadded up tissue paper. This unknown person ignited his creation, set it adrift at one end of the trough, and ran like hell, disappearing into the annals of history. As the device made its way in the current down the trough it passed under each Marine seated, all of whom had their pants down to their ankles, burning their butts! The yelling and screaming and profanities could be heard for some distance. This was horrible, just horrible; I wish I had thought of it! The suspect absolutely would have been beaten within an inch of his life had his identity been discovered.

My Second (and Last!) Industrial Grade Hangover

The horrible hangover that I experienced at Camp San Mateo a year or two prior should have taught me a lesson. And it did—just not enough of a lesson. A few of us spent one night bar-hopping in Kin Village, just outside the Camp Hansen gate on Okinawa. As I recall I was cautious enough not to drink different types of alcohol, and also not to eat exotic food while drinking. But I sure as hell did something wrong. I still recall the spectacle I created for the officer-of-the-day and the sergeant-of-the-guard as I vomited in pain on the back steps of the barracks. In my younger days there was some type of a restriction in my esophagus that made vomiting very painful, literally taking me to my knees, and that is what was occurring. Although almost fifty years ago I can still see those two fellows watching my painful performance, shaking their heads in amusement.

Horrible Racism on Okinawa

I witnessed and experienced much worse racism in the military than in civilian life, and it was at its worse on Okinawa. While Marines of all ethnicities seemed to get along okay while on duty and on the base, off-duty and off the base it was a much different story. The dividing lines between the bars that catered to whites and blacks might just as well have been painted on the ground; they were that discernible. Hispanics were considered to be white. While there were a few bars that were somewhat transient and open to all, most of the bars were territorial with respect to units and race. While a black walking into a white bar might have been unpleasant, a white walking into a black bar may well have been fatal. While I was on the island, a white military police officer had to literally shoot his way out of a military police sub-station at a place called "the Four Corners," which was part of the city of Koza. I recall a black Marine who was in my platoon and with whom I thought I had a good relationship. But I was mistaken; the hostility he exhibited to me and some of my pals when we encountered him and a group of his pals out in Kin Village was really ugly. At times the situation was so bad that we had to wear our tropical uniforms with a tie when out in the village, the thought being that Marines were less likely to fight if it meant messing up their uniform. Plus, anyone who returned to the base with a messed-up uniform could be easily recognized as a combatant. During particularly difficult times, there were actually Marine observers with radios on key rooftops, able to report problems to the roving staff non-commissioned officer "courtesy patrols" that patrolled the village.

Violent Death Behind the Command Post

One morning a group of shirtless men descended on my battalion. They were military police criminal investigators who had removed their utility jackets so the folks they were interviewing were not aware of their rank. Some of the investigators were likely to be of lesser rank than some of the people they would be interviewing, and military protocol was for rank to not be a factor in criminal interviews. It seemed that a murder victim had been found in the reservoir behind the battalion command post, and an attempt was underway to investigate the circumstances. I do recall that the death was clearly believed to have been racially motivated. But I do not recall the ethnicity of the victim, and never learned any of the details or whether the crime was ever solved. My perception was that the black racists were the more likely to commit acts of violence, but that there were a few "good ol' boys" from the south who would not have given a second thought to following in the footsteps of some of their white racist KKK kinfolk. Camp Hansen could be a pretty dangerous place at times.

Despicable Behavior by a Small Number of Jerks

The vast majority of the Marines I served with were decent and honorable men, and they treated the Okinawan people with dignity, respect, and goodwill. Unfortunately, there were a few real jerks, and their foolish behavior could be at all-time highs when encountering burial tombs while on field exercises. It was common in the case of deaths of Okinawans to place sake, an alcoholic drink, in the tombs with the deceased. Occasionally, some idiot Marine would break into a tomb then take and drink the sake. This conduct was absolutely despicable and added validity to the island's detractors who criticized the American military.

Death of President Kennedy

November 22, 1963 was a tragic day for all Americans, and for the world. This is the day President John F. Kennedy was assassinated in Dallas by that despicable little weasel, Lee Harvey Oswald. I learned of the president's death when I fell-in for formation in the battalion's open area at about 0530. Unlike the highly emotional scenes in the United

States, I saw no crying or breakdowns, but the following days were sad and solemn. All military forces went on "high alert" just in case it was an act orchestrated by a foreign power; however, the forces stood down after several days.

This was a bad time for me, for another reason. I had been officially invited to the christening of the USS *J.C. England*, DLG-22. The ship was named after the son of my godparents, Sam and Thelma England, who had perished on the battleship *Oklahoma* during the December 7, 1941 Japanese attack on Pearl Harbor. I thought there was a chance, and there may have been, that I could have been given TAD orders (temporary additional orders) for Long Beach to attend as official guest. But I'll never know whether I had a chance, because the 30-day period of mourning for the president put a damper on everything, including the ship's christening, which became a quick and quiet affair.

Postscript: In early 1991, on temporary orders to mainland Japan with a stopover in Okinawa, I went back to Camp Hansen. Standing on the exact spot where I had been standing when informed of President Kennedy's death, just outside the battalion headquarters, was among the several places I visited that day on my memorable walk down "memory lane."

My Burning Butt in the Hot Box in Koza

As a young Marine on the island of Okinawa, I decided to get one of those massages I had heard so much about. I went into the city of Koza and found a massage parlor, where the price for the complete massage and accompanying services (not sexual!) was $1.82. The first thing I was instructed to do was disrobe and get into a steam box, after which I would be washed from head to toe by a pretty girl, then given a massage. There was a glitch however, that came to light when the gal locked me into the hot box and apparently forgot about me! After about 15 minutes I was really in misery,. My rear end was on those hot wooden planks and burning like hell. I did the best I could to get my butt off the planks inside the box by putting my neck up against the back of the box for support, but I was in real misery until the gal finally came back and let me out of that damn box. I went back a few more times, but afterward always made the girl remain nearby when I was in the hot box.

I never availed myself of the "additional services." But some of the gals provided an array of sexual services in addition to the massages. I was saving myself, but in hindsight I am not sure what I was saving myself for!

Very Kind and Considerate Japanese People

I will never forget, nor will I cease to be grateful for the very nice and helpful way that the Japanese and Okinawans treated me when I was a young Marine. At the time it seemed to me like World War II had been in the distant past. But as I look back and reflect on how time flies by, it really had not been that long ago: perhaps eighteen years. Okinawa was not part of Japan at that time, but the two were later reunited into one country—Japan. But in both countries some traumatic remnants of the war were still in evidence, such as pock-marked structures.

I still recall one particular act of kindness. While stationed at Camp Fuji on mainland Japan, I was at a train station in Gotemba and clearly experiencing consternation at trying to figure out how to get to Yuko-suka. A bilingual Japanese man recognized my plight. He found a man who was going to the first of the several towns where I would need to switch trains, and handed me off to that man, who handed me off to another at another station, and so on until I reached Yokosuka—and none other than the first man spoke English. I never forgot this and other acts of kindness, and have always sought to be just as helpful and gracious to Japanese people visiting Los Angeles.

I returned to both Okinawa and mainland Japan in 1991. While just about everyone I encountered on the street were cordial, the widespread exceptional warmth of the old days was gone.

Prostitution in the Orient

During my entire time in the Corps there was always an abundance of prostitutes wherever Marines could be found. While I was in the 3rd Marine Division, the greatest concentrations were found on Okinawa and in the Philippines. In reflecting on that era, I don't recall blatant prostitution on mainland Japan, but am certain that it also existed there. My time in Korea was spent out in the boondocks, in the middle of a freezing winter, but I am sure even there prostitutes could be found. Prostitution was not encouraged or discouraged, not seen as bad or good; it was just an absolute reality of overseas military life. It was just as common for a Marine to say he was going to "get laid" as it was to be going to a movie or to get a meal in town.

The "going rate" for the services of a prostitute during that era was $2 for a "short time" and $5 for an "over-nighter." These "flat rates" were pretty much standard throughout all of the countries in the Pacific that I visited. But the real winners were the NCOs—because they could afford *both* a meal and getting laid. My battalion never got to Australia, but I suspect that prostitution would have been very limited in that country.

I was among the very few Marines who actually got some degree of lecturing on prostitutes, because of my occasional duties as a cryptographer, access to classified materials, and my security clearance. There were instances where female spies, acting on behalf of the Soviet Union, would compromise American servicemen with sexual escapades, and then blackmail them to gain classified information. This was a real problem for service personnel in Europe, and especially in Germany; but realistically not so much for a low-level person such as myself, in an infantry battalion where our classified material was relatively low level.

As I said previously, I never availed myself of the services of a prostitute. I cannot say that my abstinence was based on morality; I was just never interested in assembly-line affection.

Venereal Disease Worked to My Advantage

Military regulations are such that the self-reporting of venereal disease is encouraged, so that immediate and appropriate medical attention can be provided. A Marine cannot be disciplined as long as he immediately reports his condition. Our company commander decided, however, that he would not promote anyone who had VD, and this worked out great for me. In late 1963, 57 percent of the men in H&S Company reportedly were being treated for some form of VD. A number of those folks were senior to me and likely to be promoted ahead of me—except for their delicate conditions. I ended up being promoted sooner than would otherwise have occurred because of all the amorous Marines in my outfit! Part of my military success is attributed to VD!

I Finally Made Lance Corporal

When I made PFC right out of boot camp, I just knew I would make lance corporal in record time as well. I was wrong! I got to add the crossed rifles under my single stripe—the insignia of a lance corporal—in November 1963.

At the time we were undergoing cold weather training at Camp Fuji, which was on the island of Hokkaido beneath the famous long-dormant volcano. It was to be another sixteen or so months before I was promoted again. Although I was in an infantry battalion where promotions were pretty good, I was not classified as an infantryman but rather a communicator. But the fastest rank generally went to those Marines in the infantry companies, as opposed to the Headquarters & Service Company where I was assigned. It was a thrill to write home and put that coveted "LCpl" on my return address, and I can still recall the first time I answered the phone in the Communications Center with my new rank.

"Blood Stripes" and Disabled Arms

For decades there was a unique Marine Corps tradition of "pinning the stripes" on newly promoted Marines. The newly promoted man would walk through a column of other Marines of either the same or higher rank of the new promotee, and each of the folks on either side of the column would slug the new promotee on the arm where the stripes would go. At the end of the column, the new promotee would turn around and walk back through the column so that everyone had the opportunity to "pin the stripes" on both of the new promotee's arms.

Let there be no doubt, these were not polite taps on the arm, but in most cases slugs as hard as the senior men could hit! When I made lance corporal, there were about 20 or 30 folks in the two columns, and each one hit me twice. After this promotion ritual, the arms of the new promotee were typically black and blue for several days, and pretty much useless for a day or so.

About a year and a half later while stationed at the Marine Corps Air Station at El Toro (since deactivated and torn down), I went through the same ritual when I made corporal. But then the column of "well-wishers was slightly smaller, because there were fewer people my rank or above in the communications center where I was assigned. One additional "treat" that I did not experience was the tradition in some units of also "pinning the blood stripe" (the red stripe on the trouser legs of the dress blue uniform for non-commissioned officers), where the same two columns got to slug each newly promoted non-commissioned officer on the upper leg between the waist and the knees. In those ceremonies it was not unusual for the new promotee to actually have trouble walking for a brief period of time. Again, folks did not "pull their punches," but typically struck with all the force they could muster.

Stupid Kids and Classified Materials

Late one night during a detail to destroy classified materials, I was among a couple of other young Marines who were still acting like high school idiots—except we had some expensive toys to play with.

For reasons that I no longer recall, while at Camp Hanson we destroyed our classified materials by incineration at White Beach at night. One evening I and two other young Marines, in a large USMC van full of classified materials to be destroyed, decided to have some fun by driving the van all over White Beach, including maneuvers pretty close to the waterline. Unfortunately, with a van full of classified materials, we got badly stuck in the muck. And the tide was rising! With an incredible stroke of good luck, I found an Army unit nearby that had a tank retriever (tow truck on steroids!), and the soldier was nice enough to extricate the van from the mess we were in.

We quickly performed our destruction duties and got back to the base. I was sweating bullets over this issue, certain that I and the other two kids would be severely disciplined if our foolish behavior came to light. Doing stupid stuff is bad enough, but doing stupid stuff when in possession of classified materials is pretty serious. This was among the lessons I learned that contributed to my maturity. Had I not found the soldier with the tank retriever, this could have been a pretty nasty "fork in my road!"

Great Sleep in the Back of a Bouncing Truck

I have just about always had trouble staying awake as a passenger in a vehicle. This was not always a bad thing, because I have usually been able to sleep like a baby in the back of a bouncing truck while lying on equipment! Reflecting on my military experience in the field, which was pretty extensive, I usually slept just fine as long as I was warm and dry. It was not always easy, but I usually managed to achieve it. I mastered the art of staying warm by always creating an outer shell made up of either a poncho or a shelter half. During that era, each Marine in the field carried one-half of a tent (referred to as a shelter, thus a shelter half). Circumstances permitting, I also removed my outer clothing and boots. The nightmare for me was trying to sleep in a foxhole with several inches of water in the bottom.

Really Cold Showers

I will never forget the cold showers at Camp Fuji! On a daily basis we bathed out of our helmets, using water we heated in large drums. However, before going on liberty on weekends we really needed a complete shower. If there ever was hot water, it was always gone by the time peons like me got to the showers. It was during winter and really cold, and the water came from nearby streams. I will always remember others and me dashing in, screaming profanities, quickly soaping down, and rinsing off. It was not a pleasant experience, but we got most of the big chunks of dirt off.

A Very Kind Gunny at Camp Fuji

While at Camp Fuji my mom sent me an audiotape, thinking that I had ready access to a tape recorder. But it was a reel, and required a recorder that was not easily found. Someone said that the H&S company gunny, Gunnery Sergeant L. Faulkner, had such a device. So I went to GySgt Faulkner, and he could not have been nicer. He did have a recorder, took me in his tent, set it up where all I had to do was hit the start key, then left so I could be alone as I listened to my mom. What a wonderful and gracious man and his act of kindness, and I've never forgotten. It was another incident that reflected the type of behavior I have tried to emulate. Gunny Faulkner will always be one of my heroes.

Almost thirty years later, as a lieutenant colonel and commanding officer of 3rd ANGLICO, I invited a close friend and former Marine, Jack Claven, to be my guest at our Marine Corps birthday ball. He asked if he could bring his dear friend to the ball, a retired Marine who had saved Jack's life by carrying him to safety on Iwo Jima. Certainly, I said; it would be an honor. Cathy and I drove to Jack's house in Glendora to get him, his wife Alice, and his friend. Jack's friend turned out to be Retired Gunnery Sergeant Faulkner, whom I immediately recognized! What a thrill and a most enjoyable evening it was. The gunny had retired in Barstow, where he'd spent many years as a volunteer armorer for the Barstow Police Department. He and Jack have both made that transition to eternal life, and I have every confidence that heaven is a better place because of the presence of those two wonderful men and Marines.

Snuggled Like a Bug in a Rug at Camp Fuji

In the big scheme of things, I cannot imagine this issue will be of much value to the reader. But it is one of those things that, for whatever reason, I sometimes think about.

Camp Fuji, at the base of the dormant volcano Mount Fuji, was a very cold place between November and January, which was the time period when I first arrived there. There were no buildings at the upper base camp where my unit was assigned, so we slept in large tents alongside all of our equipment. There was not much to do most evenings, except gamble, and as a result most of us "hit the sack" pretty early. I don't think I have ever had better sleep in my life. We slept on cots, using our ponchos and shelter halves to create a seal around the cotton sleeping bags (though down-filled, they were not adequate for the low temperatures, but the seals we created made them very toasty). I still remember snuggling and thinking about all of the things that eighteen-year-old kids think about, probably like all the other kids in that tent who were wedged between weapons and communications equipment.

THE FINGERPRINT EXPERT

In preparation for deployment to the Orient, I thought I would do something that would help prepare me for a career in law enforcement. I enrolled in an extensive correspondence course through the Institute of Applied Science in Chicago, on fingerprinting, classifications, and related topics. I spent literally scores of hours on my lessons, finally completed the course, and got my diploma as a fingerprint classification expert after returning to the United States. Other than occasionally using my knowledge to determine the primary fingerprint classification of a person whose identity was in question and comparing it with the files in Records and Identifications Division, this specialized education was never of value to me as a police officer. It was, however, of tremendous value at the time, as it kept me busy and out of the bars while overseas!

BAR FIGHT IN SASEBO

During a port call in Sasebo (Japan), I went bar-hopping with my good pal John Kraus. As we were sitting in the bar enjoying a cold beer, a drunken sailor came up, announced it was a Navy bar, and ordered us to leave. I humored him, saying that we were all Americans, and asked that we be able to finish our beers before leaving. He said okay, and staggered off. A few minutes later I heard a thump and saw something fly past my face. The sailor had delivered a sucker-punch to the side of John's head, and it was his glasses that sailed past me! John was as blind as a bat without his glasses, and dropped to the floor to find them.

Pissed, I took off after the drunk sailor. He ran out what he mistakenly thought was an exit door, but which was an internal door that went inside the back of the bar. He quickly ran back out, but in so doing swung the bamboo door open so hard that it was penetrated by the edge of the bar. At this point, three or four Japanese men (you never saw them in bars that catered to Americans) emerged from the back and started to kick the crap out of the sailor! Now the game had changed and the Japanese men were beating the American sailor, who was clearly a drunken jerk but still an American. I jumped into the fray and started pulling the Japanese off the sailor, who ultimately broke free and fled out the front door. The Japanese men disappeared into the back, John found his glasses, and we went back to our beer.

A few minutes later I heard a commotion outside the bar. Soon two shore patrolmen, a Marine sergeant and a Navy petty officer, came into the bar. It seems the drunken sailor was rounding up a bunch of other drunk sailors to return to the bar and kick my butt for kicking his, apparently confusing me with the group of Japanese men who jumped him. The matter was quickly sorted out. The group that the squid (sailor) had assembled to do a number on me was dispersed, we all shook hands, and the matter was over. But I remain grateful that the shore patrol intercepted the Navy crowd before it reached me!

THE TYPEWRITER CRISIS AT CAMP HANSEN

This was truly a crisis for me, and I thought I was going to be in big trouble. On New Year's night, just before ringing in 1964, I had the all-night duty at the Communication Center in Camp Hansen on Okinawa. Our typewriter was not working, so I went across the hallway and borrowed the special typewriter used by the S-3 Section (Operations & Training). It was a unique typewriter with a long carriage, used for typing stencils. I carried it over and placed it on a counter, and began typing letters home while seated on a stool. I inadvertently leaned back too far and started to fall, but broke my backward fall by putting a foot up to the counter. My foot caught the typewriter, and sent the heavy machine flying across the room! When it landed, it broke into several pieces. I was horrified beyond description and knew that the S-3 chief, a crusty old and mean gunny sergeant, would really make it hard on me. It was clear I could not fix the typewriter.

One of the Marines in my platoon, however, Richard Garlock, had been a typewriter repairman in civilian life. I could hardly wait for daylight to arrive so I could drag him over to battalion headquarters to hopefully fix the damaged typewriter. It was now New Year's Day. Dick was like everyone else and wanted to sleep in, but apparently he saw the horror in my eyes and reluctantly accompanied me back to see what he could do with the broken typewriter. He took one look and announced that it was destroyed. Even with replacement parts, which he obviously had no access to, it was a goner! I begged him to try to at least reassemble it, to conceal my actions. He agreed, and managed to get it so it looked okay. But the carriage would not even move.

The following day was a work day. I was in the building when the S-3 folks came to work. The clerk immediately went to the typewriter, found that it would not work, and complained to the gunny. The gunny said something about it being a worthless piece of crap and told the clerk to have it sent to supply to be replaced. That was it! To say that I was relieved is an understatement.

The South China Sea and Forty Below Zero

My battalion was "afloat" and participating in an exercise along the Korean coast in the middle of winter, which included an amphibious landing from the South China Sea. I couldn't believe my good luck, for I was given duty aboard the ship, the USS *Bayfield* APA33 (which had been the command ship for the WWII Normandy landing on June 6, 1944!). My job consisted of receiving and decoding classified message traffic, and taking classified material ashore as a courier. Life aboard a troop ship when all the Marines were aboard was pretty lousy: long lines for everything, mediocre chow and crowded, stuffy quarters. On the other hand, when the troops were ashore, being aboard was the best: the sailors broke out the best food, no lines for anything, and generally a relaxed environment. As someone who was always in the dirt on field exercises, I couldn't believe my good luck on this particular operation!

About the second day of my great duty, a classified message needed to be taken ashore. My job was to make a quick run to and from the beach and be back in paradise within an hour of so. Wrong! It was colder than hell, about 40 degrees below, and we all had heavy cold winter gear. But I saw no need to don all that specialized clothing for a quick trip ashore; my landing boat would be met by another classified courier to take my pouch, and I would quickly return to the ship. All I wore was my field jacket with the nylon liner, which was a big mistake! I climbed down the cargo net into a "peter boat" (LCVP small landing craft), experienced about a ten-minute trip to the beach, handed over the classified pouch, and was soon on the way back to the ship. Then the problems developed. The seas had picked up and were becoming so rough that the landing craft could not pull up alongside the ship, nor could it return to the beach without the real possibility of breaching (being flung sideways)!

By this time, I was freezing my ass off! After about four hours of bobbing around like a cork, the landing craft was able to pull into the well deck of the USS *Cabildo* LSD16 (landing ship dock, where the entire rear of the ship was open to facilitate small craft entering and departing). After starting to thaw out, a very considerate sailor took me to the ship's galley where a cook made the best ham sandwich I have ever eaten, and then pointed out a berthing area with vacant bunks where I crashed for the night. By the next morning the seas had settled down, and I caught a shuttle back to the USS *Bayfield*. Needless to say, I learned a very valuable lesson: when in doubt, wear all the cold weather gear!

Unwanted Butt Buddy on the USS *Cabildo*

During my brief unintended stay on the USS *Cabildo*, the kind sailor I described in the previous paragraph warned me about an unidentified serial sodomist who was loose on the ship. On several occasions he had jumped into a sailor's bunk in a crowed berthing area, clamped his hand over the unwilling victim's mouth, placed a knife to his throat, and committed sodomy. In the berthing area I selected a bunk pretty close to a hatch (door) that was adjacent to a lighted passageway. While I normally sought a bunk in an area as dark as possible, I made an exception that night. I was not about to permit my cute little 18-year-old USMC rear end to be violated by a perverted squid.

My Vietnam Service (Not Much!)

In early 1964 I was one of several communicators from my battalion who were loaned to the 9th Marines Regimental Headquarters, the higher headquarters for the three infantry battalions of which my outfit was one. This headquarters had dual designation, and was also known as the 9th Marine Amphibious Force (9th MAF), with support responsibilities for any necessary deployment into the emerging global hot spot known as Vietnam. This loan was considered a pretty good deal, primarily because of the exceptionally good chow in the regimental mess hall. For some reason, the only Marines in the mess hall were the actual cooks; all of the other duties, from cooking helpers to clean-up personnel, were performed by Okinawan contract personnel. Before being "loaned to regiment," I was among the many Marines who tried to sneak unsuccessfully into this mess hall from time to time. But I actually got to eat there when on formal loan to the 9th Marines/9th MAF.

From time to time, as a classified message courier, I shuttled classified material to and from the Danang Air Base in Vietnam, always on

C-130 aircraft out of the Futuma Marine Corps Air Station located just north of the Okinawa capital city of Naha. I spent a few nights on several occasions in a transient hut at Danang, but then went right back to Okinawa. During this era, there were occasional rocket attacks on the base, and ground combat was occurring, but the engaged Marines were exclusively performing as advisors to the South Vietnamese military.

These brief visits give me the right to say I served in Vietnam and that I am a Vietnam veteran. But, obviously, my service was next to nothing. Because my trips to Vietnam were prior to March of 1965, I do not even rate the Vietnam Service Medal; instead, I added another star to the Armed Forces Expeditionary Medal that I received, along with the Marine Corps Expeditionary Medal that I received for service during the Cuban Missile Crisis.

3RD BATTALION, 9TH MARINES "MOUNTS OUT"

Vietnam was starting to heat up, but the increasing role of the United States was still pretty much in a support and advisory status. My battalion, as part of the 9th Marine Amphibious Force, was in a constant state of readiness for deployment. In one instance, the battalion received the order to "mount-out" for deployment to Vietnam, had packed up all the gear and was enroute to Kadena Air Force Base, when the order was rescinded.

Exactly one month after the mount-out order, which had the precedence of a FLASH (immediate emergency) message, the communications center copy of this now-obsolete classified message was taken by PFC John Kraus to the S&C (secret & confidential) files custodian, Sergeant Parmalee, for destruction. Sergeant Parmalee saw the flash designation and the day of the month, and immediately went into a panic, thinking it was a brand new message to "mount out!" He rushed to the commanding officer, Lieutenant Colonel W.F. Lane, with what he mistakenly thought was the new emergency message. Colonel Lane was apparently influenced by the haste and excitement of Sergeant Parmalee and, also assuming it was a new secret emergency mount-out, initiated the mobilization of the whole battalion! Everyone again went into a high-speed wobble, packing gear, loading trucks, drawing weapons and all the other things associated with emergency mobilization. After about half-an-hour the colonel apparently figured out what had occurred, I assume because other related messages were not coming down from higher headquarters, and canceled everything. The shit kinda hit the fan over this caper, and everybody pointed at everyone else for the misunderstanding. The colonel said his haste was based on Parmalee's excitement, and Parmalee said his haste was driven by the excited manner in which Kraus delivered the message to him. That was an absolute lie; Kraus just made a routine drop-off of obsolete messages. As the matter died down Kraus was unfairly seen as the culprit, but all the key people pretty much just dropped the matter. For months afterward, we all joked about the day when Kraus mounted-out the battalion.

Mom's Pearl Earrings

One day right after payday I took the bus from Camp Hansen to Koza to buy my mom a set of pearl earrings from the Noritake Pearl Company, the top pearl jewelry outfit on the island. But first I made my bi-monthly pilgrimage to the pawnshop outside the gate to get my electric razor out of hock, as I often pawned it a few days before getting paid! Then I got on the bus for the long ride to Koza where I bought mom a very nice set of earrings, and took the bus back, exiting at the front gate to Camp Hansen. As the bus disappeared down the dirt highway, I realized I had left the bag with the earrings on the bus! I did something like slap my head in disgust, at which time I dropped the bag containing my electric razor, and watched it come out of the bag and break into several pieces! I then bent over to pick up what was left of my ruined razor, and in so doing ripped open the seat of my pants! Individually, these were three troubling events, but collectively they were kind of funny. As irritated as I was, I couldn't help but laugh.

Caught Sleeping on Watch—Kinda

Staying awake all night in a communications center can be pretty tough. This is especially difficult when you can't really get much sleep during the day because of the constant noise and music and yelling in the barracks. One of the little ploys that I (and probably millions of others) used to catnap was to sit at a desk with a book in front of me and my head resting in my hands, so it would appear that I was awake and reading the book. I was using this ploy during the wee small hours of one of my shifts in the Communications Center at Camp Hansen on Okinawa when I became aware of someone standing in front of the desk where I was "reading." Though my hazy eyes I could see that person was wearing gabardine trousers, which meant he was an officer. Thinking pretty quickly, I chuckled as if I had just read something funny, then looked up straight into the eyes of the lieutenant who was the officer of the day! I said something such as "good morning, sir, can I help you?" I will never forget the skeptical look on his face when he said something to the effect that I must be a very slow reader, because he had apparently been standing in front of me for quite some time before I looked up. I don't recall whatever response I provided before he left. But I was quite certain that he knew I had been sleeping and just chose not to make an issue out of it. Thanks, lieutenant!

LIEUTENANT SEITZ INSPECTS THE CRYPTO VAULT—SO HE THOUGHT!

Okinawa is a terribly hot and humid place during certain months, and can be down-right miserable. The crypto vault and the colonel's office were the only air-conditioned rooms in the entire battalion, the former because of sensitive cryptographic machines.

As one of the battalion's very few crypto specialists (in addition to my other duties), I was among the very few people who had access to this air-conditioned paradise. One evening I was in the crypto vault when the officer-of-the-day, First Lieutenant Seitz, pounded on the door. Demanding access, he mistakenly thought he had temporary access because he had the duty that evening. I diplomatically told him he did not have access, and urged him to review the access list posted on the door, a short list that did not identify his position. He clearly did not like my answer, and started quizzing me on just what I was doing in there, because it was after hours. Clearly he was mad, because I was a comfortable lance corporal and he was an uncomfortable lieutenant. He went so far as to suggest that I was in there just relaxing, reading, and enjoying the air conditioning! He demanded to know precisely what I was doing, and told me to be specific about the tasks I was performing.

I politely told him my duties were classified and that I was prohibited from divulging the information he demanded. He left in a huff, and I went back to relaxing, writing letters, and reading my book in that air-conditioned room.

"KEEP EATING, YOU WILL!"

Sick calls on troop ships reflect mass medical care at its worst. It usually consists of one or two enlisted Navy corpsmen, sometimes with the ship's physician, working in a tiny cubicle, tending to scores of Marines who are standing in a line that snakes throughout several adjacent passageways. The illnesses ranged from dripping male genitals to seasickness to open wounds, and everything in between. A percentage of the Marines are typically shitbirds seeking a medical slip to get out of a working party. My friend, Larry, was concerned that he had not gone to the bathroom since the ship left port, and thought it best to bring his condition to the attention of a doctor. He was in luck. After waiting an hour or so in line, he found himself in the presence of the ship's doctor. Larry explained that seven days had passed since his last bowel movement, and he felt he needed to have one. Without laying a hand on Larry, no blood pressure exam or anything, the doctor said: "Keep eating, you will... NEXT!" He kept eating, and he did.

―――――

Marine Corps Air Station, El Toro
Station Communications

In June 1964, after just under a year with 3/9, I was transferred to the Marine Corps Air Station, El Toro, just outside Santa Ana, California. El Toro was the location of the 3rd Marine Air Wing. I was assigned to the Base Communications Center.

Humanitarian Transfer to MCAS El Toro

I actually rotated back to the United States a couple months earlier than scheduled. My brother had written a letter to the commandant of the Marine Corps, requesting that I receive a humanitarian transfer to the El Toro Air Station in order to be closer to my grieving mother in the aftermath of dad's suicide. Frankly, he exaggerated the situation. A transfer to El Toro would be (was!) nice, but it was not really essential. Anyway, one morning on Okinawa, completely by surprise, I was told to pack my gear and get to the port of Naha to board a ship that was leaving that afternoon! I dropped a quick note to my mom that I was coming home. But the letter and I were on the same ship! The first she knew was when I called her from Pearl Harbor and said I would be home in about a week. There was no time to write and tell the various girls with whom I'd been corresponding that I was on my way home.

My 1958 Corvette

My big goal was to have a Corvette, and my wonderful mom helped me achieve that goal. While overseas I put just about all my money into an allotment to hopefully get a "Vette" when I returned to the States, and my mom put in considerable money as well. We had a plan, and it worked like a charm. The cost of the car would be bad enough (for a low-paid enlisted Marine, no less!), but the insurance for a teenager (even a "trained killer Marine!") would be near-prohibitive for such a high-performance vehicle. So mom bought the car and paid a year's insurance in advance while I was still 7,000 miles away and not included in the rates. It covered everyone in the household, which I then returned to! It was a 1958 in classic red with white coves on the sides. I really loved that car, and certainly experienced the social benefits of having such a cool machine. But I ended up selling it and getting a Volkswagen about a year later. It just got too expensive to maintain.

Bye Bye, Georgine

My sudden arrival back in the States came as a surprise to a lot of folks. One of them was my favorite girlfriend, Vicki, who I immediately called. She was happy that I was home (well, she said she was!). Vicki told me that her mom, whom I had known for several years, was hospitalized at the Santa Teresita Hospital in Duarte, and invited me to accompany her for a visit to her mom. We entered her mom's room, which she was sharing with another woman—the mother of one of my other girlfriends, Georgine! I had dated Georgine before going overseas, was acquainted with her mother, and had maintained a romantic correspondence with Georgine while overseas, with alleged plans to get back together when I returned! The mother, and certainly Georgine, thought I was still on Okinawa—and here I turn up hand-in-hand with another girl in Duarte. Not good! Georgine's mother never took those glaring eyes off of me from the moment I entered until the moment I left the room. That was the end of Georgine.

Vicki's mom, Vivian, remains a dear friend. In writing this entry (March 2009), I called and told her about the drama in that hospital room so many years ago. We had a good laugh. She remembered the other gal (Georgine's mom), and said that the issues of her being acquainted with me, and my infidelity, never came up.

Reporting In to Base Communications

Station Communications was part of the base's Headquarters & Headquarters Squadron, and was the communications center for all message traffic, classified and unclassified, into and out of the Marine Corps Air Station, El Toro. We processed all the messages that came and went from the various commands aboard the base. It was a critical and busy place. I was really somewhat of a fish out of water. Even through my primary MOS (military occupational specialty) was teletype operator, I had neither the skill nor the speed that was needed for that place or the pace of operations. But I was anxious to develop proficiency and do a good job. In the infantry where I had previously been assigned, the teletypes were often not used and speed was never a factor. In fact, in the "grunts" (infantry) I spent much of the time working outside of my MOS as either a field wireman or field radio operator. At El Toro, there were no foxholes but several Women Marines—both were among the new concepts for Lance Corporal Bushey!

16 Hours On and 56 Hours Off

What a deal! I could not believe my good fortune. Except when scheduled for training or a medical appointment, we worked all night every third night, and were off duty the rest of the time! The sixteen-hours shifts were tough, from 1600 in the afternoon until 0800 the next morning, but the three days off were great. I went on "comrats" (communicated rations), which allowed me to live at home and purchase my meals (not much money, but still a good deal).

"No Doze" Was No Good

The schedule where I only worked every three nights started out pretty good. But after a few months it became a real problem for my system. I was never very good at attempting to get some sleep during the day after I slept the night before, in preparation to work an all-night shift. So I typically got little or no sleep during the day prior to my sixteen-hour shift. By the end of the shift the sun had come up, I was somewhat revitalized and as a result stayed up all day. As an unintended consequence, over a period of several months I was getting about a third less sleep than I needed, and it was starting to take a toll on me. I was becoming a zombie at work! Then I discovered an over-the-counter medication called "No Doze," to help stay awake, but it made me an even more bizarre zombie. There was no chance for catnaps at work, because the volume of message traffic was very high and getting ever greater as Vietnam was really heating up. Try typing messages on a teletype machine when you are sleep-deprived and taking "No Doze!" Circumstances ultimately solved the problem when our shifts were reconfigured and the "16-56" was eliminated.

The differences between an infantry communications center and air station communications center are like night and day. In the infantry the equipment is portable, slow, often breaks, is frequently not used, and a great percentage of time is spent in the field. At an air station the pace is always high, typing speeds need to be high, the equipment is fast and automated, the environment is sterile, and there is much less tolerance for error and weak performance. I did not do well initially. My typing speed was slow and my accuracy was low, and others usually had to pick up the slack and/or correct my work. There was an initial "honeymoon" period when everyone was nice and tolerant, realizing these were new skills for me, but there reached a point when people were expecting me to become proficient and it was not happening. Then, seemingly out of the blue after I had been there four of five months, everything started going well. My skills lurched to where they needed to be, and maybe even a little beyond. Thank goodness! This was a lesson that I believe has served me well in my patience and tolerance of others in situations where difficult skills are being developed.

SHOE POLISH ACCIDENT IN THE BARRACKS

This was ugly! The commanding general was conducting a massive inspection of all aspects of his command. Included was the much-hated "junk on the bunk" where all Marines methodically and carefully and obsessively created a masterpiece of personal equipment on their racks. Although I did not live on the base, I still had to bring all of my uniforms and equipment into the squadron open barracks and put my stuff on display on an empty bunk. In taking all my stuff from my car into the barracks, which required several trips, I was also carrying a bottle of liquid heel and sole enamel for last-minute touches to my boots and shoes. On the last trip I dropped the bottle and black dye spilled all over the floor right in the middle of the barracks! Holy shit!

Everybody went crazy. We were an hour or so away from the big annual inspection, with a massive dye stain in the middle of the squad bay! I went into high gear (with no shortage of people saying some truly awful things to me) and started cleaning, sopping up, and scrubbing and scrubbing and scrubbing the cement deck (floor) with a coarse brush. After twenty or so minutes I'd got up most of the stain. But what I created was even worse. There had to have been at least twenty layers of floor wax over the cement floor, and where the dye spilled I had taken the area down to bare concrete. The result was a beautifully waxed floor in a very large squad bay with a sizable white bare spot in the middle of the giant room. Ugly is too kind a word to describe what I had caused!

During the inspection the general obviously observed my creation and commented that the twenty or so layers of wax (which had been accumulating for years, maybe as far back as World War II) should be stripped so the rest of the deck looked as nice as the white circle! On the following Thursday night, which was "field day," all lance corporals and below (I was a corporal, so wasn't required to participate in unscrewing what I had caused) had to strip the years of accumulated wax off the deck in the entire barracks so that everything matched the area I had scrubbed to the bare concrete! The hostility toward me was intense among several people—but fortunately it did not last as long as I thought it would.

From Nothing to an Immediate Row of Ribbons

Shortly after completing my third year on active duty as an enlisted Marine, I was told to report to Major R.L. Critz, commanding officer of the Headquarters & Headquarters Squadron to which the communications center was attached. I was to be awarded the Good Conduct Medal. By this time I had been overseas a couple of times and had been in a combat zone or two, but never received a campaign ribbon of any sort. It all changed this day. Apparently, in preparation for the good conduct ceremony, somebody went through my record book and determined that I should have already been awarded the Marine Corps and Armed Forces Expeditionary Medals for the Cuban Missile Crisis deployment, and an additional award of the Armed Forces Expeditionary Medal for my Vietnam deployments with the 9th Marine Expeditionary Brigade (a star that is placed on the first award). After Major Critz awarded me the Good Conduct Medal, the sergeant major handed him the two additional medals to be presented to me. Very cool! In those days when Vietnam was just starting to heat up, it was very common, in fact the norm, for career Marines who entered the Corps after Korea to only have a couple of ribbons. Typically they were the Good Conduct Medal and the National Defense Service Medal (called the "fire watch" award because just about everybody got one). When I went to work the next day, folks were surprised (and I know envious) that I had a complete row of ribbons, two of them representing expeditionary service.

The base turned solemn on a very bad day in June 1965. Late the previous evening an Air Force C-135 (military version of a civilian Boeing 707) full of Marines enroute to Vietnam, crashed shortly after take-off with the loss of all eighty-four personnel on board. The aircraft had only been airborne for a moment or so when it crashed near the top of the prominent mountain ridgeline above the base known as "Saddleback" because that is what it resembles. The next few days were very hectic as the remains were brought down and placed in a hangar, and hundreds of messages were generated. I had the unpleasant duty of generating messages to the relatives of the deceased men. Each was to be delivered personally to their homes by a Marine officer, telling of the tragedy and initiating transportation arrangements for the remains. As distasteful as my role was, it paled in comparision to the Marines who had the horrible task of trying to identify the bodies and, worse yet, of personally notifying the families.

The Pilots Were Fortunate to Have Died?

I did not observe any of what I am about to describe. However, I knew everything about the situation, as I was the communications specialist who sent and received all of the message traffic. For whatever reason, this duty could only be performed by a non-commissioned officer (NCO)—and that was me.

Two Marine officers, the pilot and the co-pilot, decided to take their wives and a civilian couple on a RON (remain overnight) flight in their CH-46 Sea Knight helicopter. To say that flying unauthorized passengers constituted a mortal sin is an understatement. This constituted extreme misconduct, and any penalty for such actions would be determined by a courts-martial, with prison time and a dishonorable separation very likely the result. The two pilots, with their enlisted crew chief, took off from the Marine Corps Air Facility at Tustin (part of El Toro, where all helicopter squadrons were located and under the same Marine Air Wing [MAW] command, but about five miles away form the main base) and landed somewhere around Lancaster, where they picked up their wives and the civilian couple (husband and wife). Their flight plan was to the Marine Corps Cold Weather Training Base just outside of the city of Bridgeport, about 9,000 feet high in the Sierra Nevada Mountains. Their scheme was to drop off their unauthorized passengers just short of the base in a clearing close to a campground, proceed to and park the helicopter at the Marine Base, and spend the evening with their wives and the other couple.

However, there was a big problem. The helicopter crashed in the High Sierra and everyone, including all of the unauthorized passengers, was killed. At Marine headquarters in Washington the shit hit the fan and splattered all the way back to El Toro, and then into the helicopter squadron and the group to which the dead pilots had been assigned. All of the next-of-kin notifications were sensitive and difficult. But that was nothing compared to the shit storm that was about to hit the 3rd Marine Air Wing, the Marine Air Group, and the Squadron (which as I recall was HMM367).

The JAG (Judge Advocate General—military lawyers) descended on the place. Everything was up for scrutiny, from levels of supervision, command actions, training, guidance, to accountability at every level and on every issue, etc. I don't know the final outcome or the final toll in ruined or damaged careers, but knowing the Marine Corps' practice of rolling heads when something big goes sideways, I suspect a bunch of careers were placed in jeopardy.

At the time of the incident just about everyone said the pilots were fortunate to have died, because their fate had they survived would have been dismal. This is a good topic for discussion on issues such as suicide, where death might seem preferable to worldly consequences. Let there be no doubt—life would have been pretty tough, at least for a couple of years, had these pilots survived. But they could have gotten through it. Certainly their USMC careers would have been over, with less than honorable discharges and possibly with some brig time. But they would still have had decades of life after that.

In my more senior years, I have found it is the rare exception, rather than the rule, where people do not get back on their feet subsequent to horribly nasty situations. Suicides are truly a permanent solution to a temporary problem. While there were no suicides associated with this tragic incident, it seemed like a good opportunity to express my thoughts on the issue.

A Successful Enlistment—Why?

This particular entry has roots that go back to 1965. For some reason that I do not now recall, one of the sergeants I worked for, Jerry Jaworski, took me aside one day and told me that I was not like most of the other Marines who worked for him. I had more "going for me" than the others, he said, and he did not want me to be negatively impacted by some of the less-stellar Marines with whom we both served.

With the benefit of clarity that stems from decades of hindsight, and in far more articulate terms than I could have used at the time, I would like to address Sergeant Jaworski's comments. While self-serving to say, it is true that I had a very successful four-year enlistment in the Marine Corps, and left active duty with some pretty decent life skills.

As I look back and reflect on what I did well, I would have to give the following reasons:

I was not a rocket scientist, nor did I have extraordinary skills. But I always did my best. While not always volunteering for additional tasks, I did my best and did not gripe when they were given to me.

I did not avail myself of the service of prostitutes, whether overseas or in the States. Notwithstanding a few beers now and then, I did not hang out in bars. I spent most of my free time (and there is plenty of it for Marines when not in the field) in relatively wholesome ways such as judo lessons, correspondence courses, and organized base activities. I very seldom stayed out late, and even though liberty usually expired at midnight while overseas, I was usually in the rack when the lights went out at 2200 hours. As a result, unlike many others I was not a zombie the next day for lack of sleep.

While there were many people whom I liked and respected, I always kept my own counsel and did not fall under the spell of any one person or group of people. While there were certainly superiors who I did not think highly of, I showed them respect and did not engage in behaviors (like many others) that caused them to recognize my reservations about them. I wrote letters home and to friends, and left the Corps with some reasonable writing skills far beyond what I had entered with. I worked on my education, and although the extensive correspondence course I took (fingerprinting and criminal identification) yielded skills that I never used, it did keep me out of bars and bordellos and occupied in a wholesome way. Finally, I went out of my way to get along with just about everyone.

Released From Active Duty

My scheduled date to be released from active duty on completion of four years of active service was November 12, 1965. It was also my twenty-first birthday. However, because I had been accepted as a student at Citrus College I was approved for an early release from active, to occur on August 20, 1965.

A couple of bad things happened on Friday, September 13, 1965

("Friday the 13th!") First, the Watts Riots began. Second—and even worse for me personally due to the escalating war in Vietnam and the need for military personnel—the Secretary of Defense extended all enlistments by four months, and also canceled all "school cuts" effective the day mine was supposed to occur!

I went into a state of rage and depression; the Corps had been a great experience, but I wanted out and to start college and my law enforcement career. My remaining active service went from about seven days to seven months! I even went to the chaplain. He didn't offer any help, but I think he gave me a small camouflaged Bible!

After three or four days, however, the extension order was modified to permit the release from active duty those Marines who had already been approved for an educational early release.

On August 20, 1965 Corporal Bushey became Mr. Bushey, and I drove out the front gate of the Marine Corps Air Station, El Toro. Because it was required, I reported to the nearest reserve center to update my address for recall, as I still had a two-year reserve obligation (no meetings were required). I went to the artillery battery in Pico Rivera and checked in, but declined the opportunity to join that outfit as communications chief. As I left active duty, the best way to describe my attitude is that I would not have taken a million dollars for my experiences, nor would I have paid a dime to do them over.

At the time, had someone told me that I would eventually return to the Marine Corps—especially as a commissioned officer—I would have suggested they take a drug test.

Chapter Eight

POST-USMC & CIVILIAN JOBS

Just Waiting to Turn 21 Years of Age

Because I had been accepted into college the Marine Corps granted me an "early out," and I was released from active duty just before the beginning of the fall semester in 1965. For a while it hadn't appeared that I would get the early release, as the Marine Corps extended all enlistments for four months as it was really ramping up for Vietnam. But it was ultimately determined that since I had already been accepted at a college I would be released.

I stayed pretty busy with school, which started three or so weeks after I got out of the Corps, and with a couple of jobs.

City of Hope Medical Center

My full-time job was working in the Cardiac Research Section of the City of Hope Medical Center as a research assistant and animal attendant. I worked for a great married couple who were also both very talented research scientists. There was much experimentation done on animals, primarily dogs, and it was my job to tend to the animals to ensure they were healthy and properly cared for. I even assisted in the surgical procedures involving the animals. It was very interesting and worthwhile work. The animals were treated extremely well and never suffered at all. Several years later, an animal rights group broke into the animal research center, stole all the animals, and did thousands of dollars worth of damage.

It was my honor and privilege to be a part of such professional and humane research, which no doubt contributed greatly to the body of medical knowledge that saved so many lives. Later, as a cop, I dealt with some animal rights zealots and found them to be strange and troubling people.

I was in a four-wheel drive club that originally had intended to be a search and rescue team (but it never happened). For that reason, I took several first-aid courses in Pasadena: basic, advanced, and instructor. The instructor for all these courses was the owner of an ambulance service in Pasadena, Karl Gilcrest (pseudonym). Karl had just bought the ambulance and sick room supply business from an old institution in Pasadena, which had originally been a mortuary and ambulance service (in that era, most ambulances were affiliated with a mortuary).

Karl was a very decent guy. He offered me a part-time job as an ambulance attendant, which I immediately accepted. Although Pasadena had its own ambulance service, Karl's outfit was one of two companies that provided city backup. Most of our work was transporting elderly and non-emergency patients, but we did get our share of emergency calls, as well. I really enjoyed the job, except for the sick room supply side—especially when I had to wrestle very heavy and big oxygen cylinders up three flights of stairs, for an emphysema patient who was waiting impatiently with cigarette in hand!

Because of his mannerisms it was obvious to me that Karl was homosexual. Nevertheless, he was pretty much the first person I had a friendship with who was gay. He was a very decent and caring man, and someone with whom I had a great relationship up until his death in about 2002. Interestingly, Karl met and married a wonderful woman who had a son, and Karl functioned as a great dad and husband right up until his death. I am certain that his wife, who also became a nice friend, was aware of his orientation. But they made it work, and it worked well for both of them and their son.

Rest in peace, my good friend.

116

Chapter Nine
MARINE CORPS-COMMISSIONED

Unique Path to Commissioned Service

With each year after I had left active duty and joined the LAPD, the Marine Corps was slowly pulling me back! As I watched the news and all that was occurring in Vietnam, with emphasis on the actions of Marines, I became more and more nostalgic.

Then one day, while working as an undercover policeman at Cal State LA, I found myself standing next to a fellow in the registration line. Because of his demeanor, I instantly recognized him as either a policeman or a Marine. Turned out, he was both! Tom Vetter was a Mustang (former enlisted) first lieutenant in the Marine Corps Reserve and a deputy with the Los Angeles County Sheriff's Department. He initially thought I was the left-wing radical who I appeared to be, but after a little careful verbal sparring I told him I was a former Marine and an undercover cop. We became fast friends. Our chance meeting turned out to be an extremely important fork in my road.

He was the assistant leader of the 14th Counterintelligence Team (USMCR), and very much interested in and in need of the type of information I was gathering in my police undercover assignment. Because of our friendship, and because I had enormous investigative latitude, I initiated several investigations in directions of critical interest to the Marine Corps. Those resulted in the arrests of several servicemen who were stealing items from warehouses in San Diego, as well as in the prevention of some other crimes and in the curtailment of some subversive and un-American activities.

The FBI and the active-duty counterintelligence folks were amazed and very curious as to just how a reserve counterintelligence team was able to develop such quality and comprehensive intelligence. As a con-

117

sequence, I was invited to apply for a direct reserve commission as an investigations officer!

I applied immediately, completed more forms, and wrote more statements than I thought possible. A couple of months after all my paperwork hit Headquarters, U.S. Marine Corps, I got a call from the office of the commandant of the Marine Corps informing me that my application had been approved. It asked that I write a letter requesting my commission be held in abeyance pending completion of my police undercover assignment. The Marine Corps really liked the intelligence I was developing and wanted it to continue, but did not want to be in the position of having a Marine intelligence officer investigating civilians subversives. This made sense, and I wrote the letter asking for my commission to be held in abeyance.

As I recall, I submitted my application for commissioning in early 1969 and, had the abeyance issue not arisen, would have been commissioned in approximately mid-1969 while the Vietnam War was going strong. I requested the abeyance be lifted in June 1970 when my undercover assignment was over, and received my orders to report for commissioning in August 1970. U.S. participation in the war was being dramatically scaled back due to "Vietnamization," which stemmed from the actions of President Nixon to turn the prosecution of the war over to the South Vietnamese Armed Forces. Sadly, it turned out to be a disaster, resulting in the fall of the South Vietnamese government in 1975.

The New Second Lieutenant

On a summer day in August 1970, accompanied by my new wife, Barbara, I reported to the Marine Corps Officer Selection Office at the Military Induction Center, 1031 South Broadway Street, Los Angeles, and was sworn in as a second lieutenant of Marines! This was the same building where approximately nine years before I'd been sworn in as a private, on my seventeenth birthday. The passion and possibility of returning to Vietnam for a real tour of duty had pretty much diminished along with the diminishing role of our government.

It was a very proud day, but came nowhere close to the pride I'd felt when I graduated from boot camp as a meritorious private first class! Damn—I never thought I would make corporal, and now I was a genuine commissioned officer! My new serial number (officers had different numbers, which began with the number zero) was 0115390.

Note: Two years later each person's social security number became his or her service number, and service-specific serial numbers ceased to exist.

Officer Candidate School—Waived

Because of the unique nature of my commission as a "specialist officer," and because of my prior enlisted service as a non-commissioned officer, I did not have to attend Officer Candidate School (OCS)! This was the type of strange commission that could only occur in the middle of a chaotic situation (when approved in 1969, such was the state of our military forces). Then people end up with all kinds of commissions (though the majority of them are temporary), with the recipients eventually reverting back to enlisted grade. Even though my commission was of a specialized nature, it was unrestricted and permanent! To this day, I still think there may have been a mistake, and that it was not intended to be unrestricted. But I'm certainly glad that it was!

Officer's Basic School

Although OCS was waived, it was expected that I would attend the Officer's Basic Course at Quantico, or as an alternative enroll and successfully complete the very extensive and laborious basic school correspondence course. Since I was newly married and had just made sergeant on the LAPD and was doing well in my career, I really did not want to take a six-month leave of absence from the police department to attend the regular basic school course. So I enrolled in the correspondence course.

When the first batch of materials arrived, I couldn't believe the size of the gigantic box, and the number of books! Anyway, I started the course and completed a few lessons, then decided to ask if this course might be held in abeyance until I had more time to devote to it. I sent a nice letter asking that the course be put on hold, and got a nice letter of response saying that my studies were being placed in abeyance and requesting that I notify them as soon as I was able to restart the course.

That was in 1971, and I still have not asked to restart the course! Throughout my Marine Corps career there was a belief and expectation that I had completed this course and, while never being dishonest in what I said, I just let my various superiors believe I had completed this course just like every other officer. Realistically, my failure to take this course did create somewhat of a void in my knowledge of some things. But I was a pretty quick study and hastily read up in those areas when issues arose, and did just fine.

As I was promoted, the selection boards apparently never went back that far in my records. Everybody pretty much automatically attends OCS and the basic school, and it is not something that even requires examination. Had the selection boards realized I never completed the basic school, it is almost certain that I would not have been promoted beyond major.

Not only did I promote all the way to full colonel, but actually served as the Assistant Chief of Staff for Operations (G-3) of an Infantry Division, and was personally commended by one of the commandants (Mundy) for my ground combat skills and knowledge. I beat out and promoted beyond a great many fine officers, some of them Naval Academy graduates and all of them graduates of the basic school, despite my failure to attend the course. I kept this secret to myself until the day I retired!

———

Fourth Light Anti-Air Missile Battalion

In mid-1971, after a number of years of not being a member of a Marine Corps unit, I was joined to one of the "firing batteries": the 4th Light Anti-Air Missile Battalion. With its headquarters at Fresno, California, the mission of the battalion was completely related to the ground-to-air HAWK medium-range missile system. As I recall, there were approximately 150 personnel assigned to the Pasadena reserve center at that time.

My First Reserve Unit as an Officer

The Fourth Light Anti-Air Missile Battalion (4th LAAM) was my first reserve unit. I joined this outfit in September 1971 at the recommendation of one of my police subordinates at the Rampart Division, Officer Bud Harper. Bud was a Vietnam veteran who was then a first lieutenant in the Marine Corps Reserve assigned to this outfit. I was in "Charlie" Company, located in Pasadena, assigned as the platoon commander of the Support Platoon. The mission of 4th LAAMBn was to train and be prepared to deploy the ground-to-air HAWK Missile System. To attain proficiency and obtain the military occupational specialty for this field required about a year-long school at Ft. Bliss in Texas. Realistically, it was a skill I would not attain and that is why I was in the service platoon (motor transport, supply, communications, etc.). It was not my intent to stay in this unit for very long, and I didn't. It was a pleasant few months, especially having the opportunity to spend time with Bud Harper, who has become a dear and lifetime friend.

One negative to it was the fairly high number of lousy Marines in the unit, who had joined the reserves to beat the draft. By that time the draft had turned into a lottery, and far fewer persons were being drafted. But those folks who previously joined to beat the draft still had a six-year reserve obligation. This was the beginning of a difficult period for the Corps, regular and reserve, as the transition to the all-volunteer military occurred. We had about ten or fifteen turds who resisted military haircuts, had lousy attitudes, and who spent most of their time trying to weasel out of their assigned tasks.

14th Counter-Intelligence Team

In January 1972, after having spent only about four months in the 4th LAAM Battalion, I transferred into the 14th Counter-Intelligence Team. It was an entity of the 4th Marine Division, and co-located with the 4th Tank Battalion on the site of the historic WWII base, Camp Elliott, just across Highway 395 from Naval Air Station, Miramar, north of San Diego. The mission of the team was to train and be able to deploy a team of trained counterintelligence personnel, all either officers or non-commissioned officers. The mission was using both active and passive measures to deny the enemy valuable information about the friendly situation, and also countering hostile espionage, subversion, and terrorism. The team was small, consisting of a total of approximately 15 persons.

Transferring and Working Within My Military Occupational SpecialITY

I transferred to the 14th Counter-Intelligence Team (14th CIT) in early 1972. The unit was housed in the back of a WWII warehouse on the old Camp Elliott Marine Base near San Diego. I enjoyed the unit, which was small, but did not particularly care for the politics of the team. When I first got there, the team was led by Major Fred Tschop. When he moved on the next senior man, Captain Bill Addison (pseudonym), became the team chief, and immediately got rid of my good friend and mentor, then-First Lieutenant Tom Vetter.

This was problematic, because Bill was a captain on the Los Angeles Sheriff's Department and Tom was transitioning from sergeant to lieutenant in the same department. Bill was not in good graces with the sheriff at the time, Peter Pitchess, so he took a leave of absence and went to Vietnam for a tour. On returning, Tom helped Addison get into the 14th CIT, knowing full well that he was bringing in a person senior to him who would probably end up as the Team OIC. But Tom felt it was the right thing to do. Addison was just too political, and spent an enormous amount of time hob-nobbing with the high-ranking Marine officials assigned to the higher headquarters.

Addison then gave Tom Vetter—the one who had brought him into the team—his walking papers! I remained in 14th CIT for a couple of years, and for the most part enjoyed the assignment. I made first lieu-tenant in late 1972 or early 1973.

"Slow Down Jack, This is God Speaking to You!"

As a young adult I had a series of International Scout four-wheel drive vehicles, all of them full of radios, a winch, rescue equipment and—most of all—a very loud industrial public address (PA) system. About 4:30 on a Saturday morning while enroute to my Marine Corps drill in San Diego, along a pitch-dark stretch of Interstate 5 somewhere south of Oceanside, I was presented with a wonderful opportunity to have some fun. There were only two cars on the road, mine and the one ahead of me, which I recognized as being driven by a fellow Marine who was also on his way to our drill. As we went around a curve, I turned my lights off, accelerated and got into his right-rear blind spot, where even if looking in my direction he could not see me because of the darkness. I then turned on my public address system and said some-thing like, "Slow down, Jack!" He was clearly startled. His brake lights went on, and he actually swerved a bit. It was hilarious watching him try to figure out where the voice was coming from, and I was naturally adjusting my speed and location so as to not be seen by him. A few mo-ments later, I spoke to him again and said something about being God and watching over him. I finally put my lights back on, got alongside him, and said "good morning" over the PA. We had a good laugh out of this, and it was always fun listening to Jack as he told the story to others. I had a great deal of fun with that PA system!

Fleet Intelligence Center—Atlantic

This was a most interesting and, at the time, highly classified expe-rience. The 14th CIT was assigned to the Fleet Intelligence Center at the Naval Base in Norfolk, Virginia. We spent two weeks assembling, coordinating, matching, and evaluating data pertaining to military activities in various nations. What I remember most is that damn Tom Vetter: he worked all day, took a couple-hour nap after work, then went bar-hopping until 0400, slept until about 0630, and started the process all over again! I kept up with him for about two days, threw in the towel and reverted back to the real me—a nice meal after work, a little TV, then eight hours of sleep.

Installation Intelligence School—Fort Meade

This was a fairly interesting school, and helped us to sharpen the skills we used in doing physical security inspections of military facilities (for classified materials, spots of vulnerability, suspicious activities, etc.). On arrival we were placed in an old WWII barracks, where dividers had been added to allegedly be "suitable" for officers. No air conditioning, and the windows had been painted shut! August in Maryland is incredibly hot and humid, and this was just plain miserable. I had an acquaintance nearby, a badge collector, who hooked me up with a fan. After prying open a couple of windows in my cubicle (tearing the hell out of the wooden frame), and directing the fan strategically, it was almost bearable.

Reestablishing My Roots in Pennsylvania

As a Marine officer I made quite a few trips to the Washington, DC area, and later as the LAPD liaison on Capitol Hill, as well. During one of my first trips I took a day off and drove to York, Pennsylvania, to see if I could find any Busheys. Boy, did I! The name was all over the place! Despite the name, I could not find anybody to talk to, but left my business card in a "Bushey mailbox." I got a letter from Evelyn Bushey Miller, who identified herself as the unofficial Bushey family historian, asking me to tell her more about my heritage. Several days after sending her the information she requested, I got a nice letter back from her that started out with, "Welcome back into the family!" As it turned out, her part of the family had lost contact with my part of the family when my dad and his brothers moved to California after World War I. Evelyn was thrilled to have heard from me. That contact has resulted in several trips to the York, East Berlin, and Gettysburg area, including participating in a couple of Bushey family reunions.

Among my most memorable events have been several visits to my dad's old home, located at 134 East 5th Street in North York, which was built by my grandfather Jacob Bushey. Different residents over the years have graciously allowed me to walk through the house, go down into the basement, and spend time on the porch. The house has been modified a bit, but is largely the same as when my dad and his family lived there. The meadow immediately below the house is still there, and still a place where kids play, including (I'm sure) the same low rocks that protrude here and there in that meadow. I have also visited, but not entered, another house at 809 West Princess Street, in York, where the family lived and where my grandfather operated his construction business. I never tire of visiting that area and reflecting on my heritage.

CRAZY MARINES AND PERPLEXED CHP OFFICERS

In 1972, on an extremely foggy morning while Tom Vetter and I were carpooling to San Diego for our Marine Corps drill meeting, I lost control of my small Toyota while trying unsuccessfully make a last-moment transition from one freeway to another. We left the pavement, went over a small curb, and bounced about forty feet down an ice plant-covered incline. Two California Highway Patrol officers arrived on scene almost immediately. As one of the officers yelled down to inquire if we were okay, Tom flashed his sheriff's badge and yelled something to the effect, "I am a sheriff, this man just groped me, and that is why we crashed!" I immediately flashed my badge and yelled that I was an LAPD officer, and that the crash was caused because the sheriff grabbed me in an inappropriate manner! The two CHP officers just shook their heads, laughed, and announced they were "out of here," or some similar term. As they departed, we asked them to send us a tow truck. Tom and I seldom fail to discuss this incident when we get together, and the scene the CHP officers encountered that foggy morning.

"GENTLEMEN, JOIN ME AT THE BAR"

During my early years in the Marine Corps, both as an enlisted Marine and as an officer, social drinking was a major pastime—to the point of being *de facto* required in many instances. As a second lieutenant, an invitation by your boss to "join him at the bar" or "join me at the club" might just as well have been a direct order. At the end of the day, the last thing I wanted to do was go sit at a bar with an alcoholic captain or major, so he would have a captive audience for his bullshit stories. I tried to avoid this crap as often as I could. But in one instance I was "counseled" by a captain that I was expected to join him and a major for after-hour

124

libations, and that a failure to do so could create a negative perception that could affect my fitness report! Nobody was happier than I when heavy social drinking went through a transition from near mandatory to near-career ending.

Fred Jones Brings Me a Navy Nurse

Fred Jones (pseudonym) was among a small group of officers with special skills in the field of installation security; he and the rest of us received occasional orders to conduct physical security evaluations (PSEs) at different Marine Corps commands. We were at the Naval Air Station in Alameda (California) inspecting the Marine Reserve CH-46 and A-4 squadrons when the following unique incident occurred. After chow, as had become our practice, I retired to my quarters and Fred, an absolute Marine Corps legend for his sexual escapades, headed for the Officer's Club for a night of booze and debauchery! At some point in the middle of the night I was awakened by someone who was fondling me! It was a drunk Navy nurse who Fred had enticed to visit me in my rack! It was very thoughtful of Fred, but I was more interested in sleep than the slobbering drunken nurse, so I chased her off.

Jackie Larsen Goes Crazy

Retired Marine Master Sergeant Dennis Larsen (pseudonym), also a retired police motorcycle officer, is truly an unforgettable character. Men love him because he is so funny and entertaining; women hate him because he is sex-crazed and cheats on any female who has the poor judgment to hook up with him. This incident occurred during a weekend drill of the 14th CIT, while Dennis was a staff sergeant. Some of us had taken our wives, and were staying in the Sands Motel just outside the Miramar Naval Air Station gate. As usual, Dennis and another Marine, Staff Sergeant Roger Garza (pseudonym), were down there by themselves and had a couple of honeys in their motel room.

I was awakened in the middle of the night by a phone call from Jackie, Dennis' wife. She demanded to know where Dennis was. I told her I didn't know. She then asked me to give him a message if I should happen to see him, to which I replied "of course." About as near as I can recall, the message went like this: "Tell Dennis I have his service revolver, and that I am on my way down there to kill him and the bimbo he is with! Then I will kill myself!" I encouraged her not to do anything rash, but said I would pass on the message if I saw him. She hung up, and I immediately called his room. When he answered I could hear the tinkling of glasses and feminine giggling. I gave him Jackie's message, to which he replied, "Oh f--k!" There was then an intercept from the motel operator with an emergency call for his room. It was obviously Jackie, so I quickly said "bye, Dennis." Within a minute, there were skidding sounds from the parking lot, indicating the high-speed departure of a vehicle.

We got the whole story the following morning. Jackie got through to Dennis and accused him of infidelity, and of course he denied everything and professed his love for her and no one else. Jackie called him a liar, and with his police service revolver she started shooting up the detailed military models and artifacts in his den. She was shouting profanities at him over the phone, describing the possessions of his that she was blasting away, and he was hearing it all. A very panic-stricken Dennis Larsen, rushing home in an attempt to save his marriage and possessions, was driving the car that abruptly left the Sands Motel.

Note: Jackie Larsen later committed suicide. I do not know if they were still married at the time.

Roger Garza Meets "A Real Woman" in New Orleans

Members of the counterintelligence team were attending a weekend of training in New Orleans, so a few of us went to the French Quarter to see the sights and to have a beer. One of the other Marines was Staff Sergeant Roger Garza (pseudonym), who in civilian life was a Sheriff's deputy. As we entered this one bar a truly pathetic creature, dressed as a female but obviously an ugly man, rushed toward Roger and screamed: "Mr. Garza, Mr. Garza, I am a real woman now!" I looked at Roger and he was grinning! Turns out this person, who had just undergone a sex change, had been an inmate in the county jail when Roger was previously assigned there. "She" adored Roger because of his compassion in getting prompt medical attention for this person, whose artificial breasts had been knocked out of alignment during a jail fight some years earlier!

It did not take us long to get out of there.

————

3rd Air-Naval Gunfire Liaison Company (ANGLICO)

In April of 1984, after having spent over two years on the 14th Counter-Intelligence Team, I transferred to the 3D Air-Naval Gunfire

126

Liaison Company (ANGLICO) in Long Beach, California. 3D AN-GLICO is a subordinate unit of the 4th Marine Division. The mission of all ANGLICO companies is to provide continuous training to personnel of either the U.S. Army or allied military organizations, who are skilled in assisting other military organizations (beyond the USMC) in calling in Marine close air support (CAS) and naval gunfire (NGF). In addition to the men in the platoons who possess these skills, normally filled by commissioned officers, the company has personnel in support roles as well (motor transport, clerical, communications, parachute riggers, etc). Since airborne insertion is a major method of entering theatres of operations, especially when in support of U.S. Army airborne divisions, the majority of the personnel who call in CAS and NGF are airborne-qualified.

As I recall, there were about 250 men in the company at the time. ANGLICO is one of two company-sized organizations in the Marine Corps that is commanded by a lieutenant colonel, the other being force recon. At that time, the unit was located in an old, turn-of-the-century schoolhouse and compound under the Vincent Thomas Bridge in Wilmington.

Most Likely Hired by Mistake!

I was very pleased to have been joined to 3D ANGLICO. However, I was hired based on the mistaken belief that I was a qualified administrative officer, which was not accurate. There were a lot of short-cuts taken during the Vietnam War, and I was one of them. Although commissioned because of my skills and knowledge in the area of counter-intelligence, I could not be formally assigned that military occupational specialty (0210) because it was a "hard MOS" that could not be assigned without attending a six-month formal school. Instead, I was commissioned as an investigations officer (0170). An administrative officer typically has an MOS in the 01-series. When I applied for 3D ANGLICO, they took one look at my MOS and mistakenly concluded I had the ability to perform the skills in the vacant administrative billet that desperately needed to be filled.

After several months of completely screwing up the admin office, the mistake was recognized and I transferred to one of the operational platoons. This was a very fortunate, mistaken fork in my many roads!

Prior to attending parachute school, I first had to successfully pass a very rigorous physical examination to ensure that I was qualified for the rigors of jump training. This physical was conducted at the Armed Forces Examining Station in Los Angeles, where most of those being examined were new enlistees. The doctor was a crusty old fart who was marginally pleasant. He looked in my first ear and announced that I had a big build-up of wax. He then threw what I assumed was a big plug of wax, larger than I could have imagined, into the trash container, where it landed with a clearly audible thump. He repeated the process and made the same comment on the second ear, concluding with another plug of wax and another audible thump. I was astonished at such a buildup of wax, and that the debris from my ear would make such a loud thump, especially because I try to keep my ears clean.

It wasn't until just a year or so ago that a light went off in my brain-housing group and I realized that nothing that came out of my ear could have landed with such a loud thump. That crusty old fart had pulled a good one on me, and it lasted about forty years.

Could Jump, but not Walk at Fort Benning

On joining the unit, I started getting myself in physical condition for jump school. I finally got my orders to report to the Airborne Course at Fort Benning, Georgia, a three-week school that went from early June to July 3rd, 1974. It was very hot and humid in Georgia, but I truly enjoyed the training. The physical aspects were pretty tough, and of the roughly 650 who took the qualifying physical fitness test, only about 425 passed the test and continued with the training! In addition to the regular attendees, such as Marines, Navy Seals, and soldiers assigned to airborne duty, there were large numbers of Annapolis midshipmen and West Point cadets, as well as NROTC students attending as part of their summer training. The first week was fitness training, the second week was practicing from towers and other training devices, and the third week was the actual jumping, to achieve the five qualifying jumps necessary to be awarded the coveted airborne badge.

On Monday of "Jump Week," my first and second actual jumps went just fine. During my third jump on Tuesday, I sprained my ankle a bit. On my fourth jump on Tuesday, I really aggravated my ankle and could hardly walk. The Army "black hat" first sergeant called me aside and inquired about my injury; I downplayed the matter and said I would be fine the next day. In no uncertain words, he said he believed my injury was probably more serious than I was describing, and directed me to report to him the next morning for evaluation before I would be permitted to make my final qualifying jump. Truthfully, I was really hurting and was afraid I would have to be dropped (one day and one jump short of graduation!).

Another Marine officer, 2nd Lt Dave Jacobson, had just graduated from Annapolis, where he had been on the gymnastics team. I had befriended him and taken him under my wing on starting the course and, boy, did he reciprocate in a big way. Dave had the answer. He told me of a midshipman who had competed successfully in a gymnastics meet with two broken ankles. He was going to use the same treatment on me. That night, we soaked my foot in ice for as long as I could take it (very painful!), repeating this several times. I got up a couple of hours early the next morning and held my foot under very hot water for about half-an-hour. Then Dave wrapped my foot so tight that I could hardly feel it.

We walked the couple of miles to Lawson Field, where we were to draw our equipment and board the aircraft for our final jump. Walking was difficult at first. But it became easier as we walked, and pretty soon I was doing great, with not the slightest limp! Once there, I reported as directed to the first sergeant for evaluation. He couldn't believe the jumping-jacks I performed, commented that my recovery was miraculous, then good-naturedly chased me off when I commented that Marines heal faster than soldiers. Anyway, we went up for the last and fifth jump and it was great—not a pain or a glitch. After the jump we went to some bleachers, were awarded our wings, and returned to our quarters to pack our gear.

When I removed my boot and the wrapping I couldn't walk without assistance! I had to be helped out of my quarters to the waiting transportation. In boarding the commercial flight home I had a virtual black band of broken capillaries stretching horizontally around my foot, and could not walk normally for almost a month! Thank you, Lieutenant Jacobson!

Where Did All the Kids Go?

This situation could have been beyond horrible. Early in my tenure with 3D ANGLICO, I held the additional responsibility of recruiting officer. I took this job seriously and actually orchestrated several large outings of recruiting prospects and poolees (sworn-in to the USMC but awaiting orders to basic training) to Camp Pendleton. It was a great recruiting event, as we let the kids actually stand adjacent to the drop zone as the parachutists descended. We had thirty or forty kids on a drop zone. I left for just a few minutes to grab several cases of C-rations, but when I returned all the kids were gone, and I hadn't passed any vehicles on the road. When I asked where the kids were, one of the Marines pointed to a pair of CH-46 helicopters disappearing over the horizon! This violated every military regulation and federal law that ever existed, and was a very bad thing. For whatever reason someone thought it was okay, and told the helicopter pilots that transporting the youngsters via military aircraft had been authorized. Thank God, there was not an accident. The end of my military career would probably have been among the lesser consequences of dead or injured kids.

"What the Hell is a Utility Pass?"

This is the kind of mischief that can occur when people understand the system, especially a Mustang officer. In the early 1970s it was a mortal sin to wear one's utility uniform off-base. It was common for people to drive to a base in civilian clothes, then pull off into the bushes and change to the utility uniform. Although my primary duty was that of an airborne fire support coordination officer, I had the additional duty of being the command's recruiting officer. As such, I spent a considerable amount of time working with recruiters and coordinating visits to Camp Pendleton by recruiting prospects.

I had an idea to address the constant switching back and forth from utilities to civilian clothes: Create a "Utility Pass." In my LAPD assignment I worked in an office that had a machine that could make letterheads and identification cards, so I had my secretary make up a very official-looking card with a massive Marine Corps emblem in the background. It read across the top: UNITED STATES MARINE CORPS UTILITY PASS. She made up several of these for me and my two enlisted assistants, with all kinds of verbiage and other information typically found on such things as identification cards and driver's licenses. To give myself a little cover in case things went sideways, and to create a scintilla of legitimacy, I took the three passes to my commanding officer for his signature in the space that was provided. He said he had never heard of such a thing. I confessed to just making them up. But he thought it was a good idea, and signed them.

My two enlisted assistants (also LAPD officers), Emmett Badar and Chuck Hawley, and I used them for a couple of years. Finally, one afternoon when departing Camp Pendleton we were stopped as always by the gate guard, and told we could not depart in the utility uniform. As always, we displayed our utility passes and he waved us through the gate. But as we were driving away the sergeant of the guard ran out of the guard shack and yelled at the gate guard to not let us leave in utilities. The guard yelled back that it was okay, because we had utility passes. As we pulled farther away and approached the highway, the last thing we heard was the sergeant of the guard yelling: "What the hell is a utility pass?"

I still see Emmett and Chuck from time to time, and we always reminisce and laugh over our utility passes.

An Unsurvivable Malfunction—So I Thought

During one of the five mandatory final jumps at Fort Benning, I observed a parachute malfunction that I did not think anyone could survive. While on the ground gathering my chute after landing, I heard the "black hats" (instructors) yelling through megaphones at one of the other jumpers that he was going to be okay, and to get his feet and knees together. I looked up and couldn't believe my eyes—a soldier had experienced a double malfunction with his reserve and main chutes, both tangled together in what was referred to as a "cigarette roll." He was descending at a very high rate of speed, passing the other descending jumpers as if they were sitting still. I knew he was a dead man, and felt the verbalization from the "black hats" was intended to let him think that he had a chance—it beats knowing that you are going to die. Not wanting to see the death, I turned my face away just before he hit the ground. But I sure felt the impact when he hit. Obviously, people rushed to him, just in case there was anything that could be done. About five minutes later, the guy was on his feet and shaking out his chutes! For all of us on the drop zone that day, this was an unbelievably vivid lesson that a well-executed parachute landing fall (PLF) can mean the difference between life and death. As I write this entry, I am sixty-seven years old and experiencing the aches and pains that stem from an active life. That guy had to have experienced some back trauma that would eventually be troublesome!

Gold Wings and a Bloody Chest

All parachutists from all branches of the military go through one military jump school, run by the Army at Fort Benning, Georgia. On completion each graduate is awarded silver basic parachutist wings. An additional five jumps, while in an authorized jump billet and representing some additional skills (night jump and equipment jump), are required before a Marine is awarded the Navy-Marine Corps Parachutist Insignia, which is gold in color and similar to pilot's wings. For years, an absolute ritual and rite of passage was for the senior jumpers, without regard to rank, to "pin" the wings on a new jumper's chest by vigorously slamming the wings, with no clutches on the rear pins, into the victim's chest! With each hard slam into his chest, and as blood clearly becomes apparent, the new jumper typically yells "U-Rah" to demonstrate toughness and glee at finally getting his "blood wings!" It was also common for jumpers to put their bloody undershirts in frames and display them in their workspaces. This practice was officially prohibited, I think, in the late 1970s. But it realistically continued, only in somewhat of a covert manner, for another several years.

Subsequent to a big scandal over "blood wings" in the mid-1990s, the then-commandant of the Marine Corps, General Krulak, issued a edict not only strongly prohibiting the practice but also proclaiming that it had never been a tradition or accepted practice. At the time of his assertion that "blood winging" had never been a Corps tradition, I was a colonel and working for a general who, when he was a captain and I was a lieutenant, had been among the many senior jumpers who slammed wings into my chest! I was and continue to be troubled by General Krulak's inaccurate remarks; he was a good man, but knowingly declaring that a past reality was not a reality detracted from his credibility. At least with me.

Spectators Go Wild at El Toro Parachute Jump

My "Cherry Jump" (first jump after jump school) was beyond memorable. We jumped at an air show held at the Marine Corps Air Station in El Toro, California, which has since been deactivated and no longer exists. We jumped from an R4D (which was very old, the military version of the DC3, also known as the C-17D and a World War II workhorse). One of the other jumpers had a malfunction with his main chute and had to deploy his reserve. With his razor-sharp K-Bar knife he cut away part of the tangled main. The truly amazing factor was that we were jumping from about 1,200 feet, and had a descent time of only about 60 seconds!! The crowd went wild with applause, and I cannot imagine that jumper didn't have to change his underwear afterward. This kind of stuff, so I thought, only happens in the movies, and the cutting away of static lines in such a short time just did not seem possible.

But it happened, and I was among the witnesses. This jump was personally painful for me because I landed on the concrete runway instead of the intended grassy area, and as with a few other jumpers ended up limping for a few days.

A Catering Truck of Marine Field Gear!

In preparation for a big inspection—as I recall a "CG" (Commanding General's inspection)—the commanding officer ordered an inventory to ensure that all personnel had all of their 782 Gear (web and related gear for field activities). The results were horrible! Scores of Marines were missing one or more items. Even though most of the missing items were not of a critical nature, they were required and their absence would cause the unit to fail a major portion of the inspection. The procedure for replacement was a "missing gear statement" from each Marine, a statement of endorsement and a recommendation from an investigating officer (loss through negligence or at no fault of the Marine), then submission of the package up through the chain of command—a real pain and administrative burden. As was not unusual, the commanding officer, Lieutenant Colonel Howard Rast, turned to me for an expedited solution (actually, I may have initiated a recommended solution).

I contacted a military surplus store in Los Angeles that had all the items in serviceable condition, negotiated reasonable prices, and had them bring a truck full of all the needed items to the next drill. At the beginning of the drill, every Marine who had missing gear, on being paid (this was before direct deposit) was shuttled across the freeway to the Long Beach Naval Station to cash their drill check. Then they were shuttled back to the unit where, based on the inventory sheet I had developed, they purchased their missing item(s) from the surplus vendor. Within four hours, our unit went from missing scores of items to each Marine having 100 percent of his gear! Not a very conventional operation, possibly never done before (in such an organized manner), and maybe even of borderline legality, but it worked. I put a great premium on this type of creativity, and am proud of my role in activities of this nature. You can make an enlisted man into an officer, but that lance corporal mentality is still there!

Not in Long Binh, or in Long Beach!

When hired into 3D ANGLICO, the commanding officer mistakenly thought I was an administrative officer because my military occupational specialty was 0170, and he desperately needed someone with those skills. I should have corrected him and explained that my specialty was 'investigations officer," which was also in the 01-series, the administrative series. But I knew I probably wouldn't have been able to get into the unit otherwise, so I decided to see if I could BS my way as an admin officer! All went okay until we had an inspection from one of the higher headquarters. The rules say that pistol and rifle qualification scores have to be typed on the appropriate page in each Marine's record book. I thought this was stupid, because it meant literally disassembling each folder to remove the weapons qualification page in order to type the scores in the designated space. I directed the clerks to cease the practice of removing and typing on the pages, and gave the direction that it was okay to neatly write the scores in ink. Then I would validate the scores with my signature, saving a ton of time.

When the big inspection occurred, the inspector was a Mustang captain who had spent his entire career as an admin weenie, and who did not think much of my shortcut. He exclaimed that "we didn't do that in Long Binh (Vietnam) and we are not going to do that in Long Beach!" After this inspection, the commanding officer—who by this time kinda liked me—permitted me to transfer to one of the operational brigade platoons.

Two Corporals Meet Again—As Gunny and a Captain

In the mid-1970s I made a trip to the Marine Corps Supply Center in Barstow, California. I went to the Supply Section to see about getting the newly-released camouflage utility uniforms issued to my personnel. I lingered at the counter as the supply sergeant was chatting with another gunnery sergeant, then noticed that the gunny had a tattoo I had seen before. He was Doug Bowden, whom I'd worked with at the El Toro Station Communications Center in 1965, where we were both corporals. He and I had been good pals because he was living with a gal, Linda, who like me was from Duarte, and we often car-pooled to and from the base.

He was shocked that I'd become a captain, and we had a great visit. He had married Linda and they were living on the base. I went back a month or so later and the three of us had dinner and a nice visit. But our friendship had a sad ending, when Linda committed suicide a couple of years after Doug retired. Doug had a drinking problem, which the Marine Corps kept from getting too bad. But once he retired Doug had no need to be sober on a regular basis, and he soon followed Linda in taking his own life.

Major Brady Parker

Major Brady Parker (pseudonym) was truly a unique personality—one of those folks you would probably want to have at your side in combat, but problematic and troublesome the rest of the time. He had a motto: "always marry an ugly woman and she will never leave you!" He married an ugly woman, had a beautiful daughter, and then the ugly woman took the beautiful daughter and left him! When I first met Brady, he noticed that the zipper catch on my brand new leather flight jacket (a very hard-to-get and prestigious item) was broken, and he volunteered to take it and get it fixed. The next time I saw him, it was a year later—he was wearing it, and it was worn to hell!

Then he decided to apply for LAPD. I had my wife make a great dinner for his arrival and overnight stay before his oral interview the next day, and he did not arrive until almost midnight! When he did arrive, before hitting the sack he asked if we had a cigarette. We had a very large bowl full of C-Ration cigarette packages arrayed in a decorative manner, and Barbara told him to help himself. After he left the next morning, we discovered that he had taken every one of the packages (probably 50-60 of them).

The last I heard of Brady was when he snatched his daughter from the front yard of his former wife's home and disappeared. I have often wondered what became of old Brady. It could not have been a happy ending.

Scrounging Equipment at Fort Irwin, and Major Mendoza

As a captain I was the officer-in-charge of an ANGLICO Detachment to Fort Irwin in support of an Army exercise, BRAVESHIELD XVIII. At this time, circa 1977, 3D ANGLICO was in pretty sad shape. Much of our equipment, especially the motor vehicles, was deadlined (out of service) for lack of replacement parts, and we couldn't use the radios because the budget wasn't adequate to acquire a necessary supply of batteries. My scrounging and innovative skills really paid off, with respect to what I was able to scrounge during the exercise—a trait that was further enhanced because the Army actually "writes off" materials as expendable during such an exercise!

This practice is contrary to the Marine Corps, which has strict accountability for everything. I scrounged so much stuff that we had to have an additional large truck (6X6) come to Fort Irwin to help us get all the goodies back home. Among the things I scrounged for the unit were: a pallet of radio batteries, enough canvas to replace the worn and torn canvas on all of our trucks and Jeeps, spare rear-ends and transmissions beyond what we needed, a score of cots, and dozens and dozens of the most-often-used motor vehicle maintenance parts. Additionally, I had a badly damaged Jeep towed to Fort Irwin, where it was completely repaired by the 7th Infantry Division field repair facility!

I was proud of what I had done for the unit. But the inspector-instructor, Major Tony Mendoza (pseudonym), was not. I kept getting the word that he was telling others I had acted inappropriately and unethically in my massive acquisitions, which was not exactly true. I knew my stuff, and how to get things done without violating the rules (at least not too many of the rules!) My commanding officer, Lieutenant Colonel Howard Rast, and the assistant inspector-instructor, Dave Zimmerman, both thought that I had done well.

I finally got tired of the back-channel back-stabbing by Mendoza, and asked for an audience with him in the presence of both Rast and Zimmerman. At the meeting I threw down the gauntlet and said I wanted to tell him everything that I'd done, how I did it and why I did it, and at the end I wanted him to either stand up and thank me or call the Naval Investigative Service and initiate an investigation into my actions. At the end of my presentation, he stood up and thanked me! Mendoza was a decent enough fellow, but somewhat of a "Nervous Nellie."

Not just because they backed me, but for many reasons related to their behavior in this matter, Howard Rast and Dave Zimmerman were two of the finest Marines I had the good fortune to serve with.

Lieutenant Hopkins? Captain Bushey?

In the late 1970s I made several trips to the Barstow Marine Corps Supply Center, to provide training to the military police personnel there. The MP chief, a gunnery sergeant, was a pal and I was doing it as a favor to him. Early one morning I was having a cup of coffee with some of the guys when a familiar-looking second lieutenant came into the Quonset hut. It was a fellow I had gone through boot camp with, Ed Hopkins! As a recruit, he had eight years of prior military service, four each in the Navy and Air Force. In the former he'd been a corpsman with the Marine Corps during the Korean War. Not surprisingly, he was both the platoon and company honor man. In our recruit graduation photo, he as the right guide was seated on one side of the drill instructors, and I as the left guide sat on their other side. I was not surprised that Ed was commissioned as a limited duty officer (some type of logistics specialty). I think he was surprised that I was a captain. But we had a great visit that morning, and also got together for lunch again a few weeks later. I regret that I have lost contact with Ed, as he is not in any of the typical USMC databases. I hope he is doing well.

Major Mendoza and the Hovering Huey at Big Bear

For one of the weekend drills, I led a detachment of parachutists to Big Bear for joint parachute operations. We conducted the drill in conjunction with an Army reserve special forces unit that provided Huey helicopters and parachutes. It was a great opportunity, as the Army folks brought scores of extra packed chutes, and all of us got in quite a few jumps. Major Mendoza (pseudonym), a regular Marine assigned to the unit, came along and brought his girlfriend. At the time I owned a two-story house right alongside the airport at Big Bear, having a large upstairs bedroom with one entire wall being a large open window with no shades or curtains. Since it would not have been right for me to sleep in my house while the troops slept in the bush, I stayed with the troops at night and let Mendoza and his honey use my home. Early the next morning we coaxed one of the pilots to fly over to my house and hover right outside the large upstairs bedroom window, where Mendoza and his honey were sleeping. The pilot keep us in stitches with his version of Mendoza's antics in covering himself and his girlfriend, shaking his fist, and moving his lips in what had to be some truly offensive profanities.

Chocolate Mountains Gunnery Range—A Real Garden Spot!

The Marine Corps has some real garden spots for training, and one of them is the truly humble mountain range known as the Chocolate Mountains, located midway between Yuma, Arizona and El Centro, California. It has been used as a military gunnery range since World War II, with decades of ordnance being dropped as part of the aerial bombing practice.

During the middle of one summer in the late 1970s, I was part of a detachment that spent two weeks on a barren mountaintop there. We were serving as forward observers in coordinating close air support and bombing missions for Navy and Marine Corps pilots flying out of the Marine Corps Air Stations at Yuma and El Toro (California), as well as others flying from aircraft carriers off the coast of California. It was hotter than hell, and a constant battle to stay hydrated. Evenings, we camped along the All-American Canal at the base of the mountain and spent quite a bit of time in the water as refuge from even the night heat.

We later learned that some folks close to the Mexican border had illegally dumped raw sewage into the canal—and that those things floating by that *looked like* turds apparently *were* turds!

Bad Conduct Discharge and Humiliation for a Malingerer

Lieutenant Colonel Bill Toole is a great Marine and a no-nonsense individual who was the commanding officer of 3D ANGLICO when this incident occurred. There were several Marine reservists who were less than worthless, and who stopped coming to the weekend drills. We processed several of these men for discharges. But when their bad-conduct discharges arrived, we had trouble getting them to come to the reserve center so we could process them out of the Corps. Toole had an idea, and he tried it on a turd I will call Private Worthless. We had one of the low-ranking clerks call Worthless on the phone, tell him there were a couple of old drill paychecks waiting for him, and to drop by and pick them up. Worthless was as stupid as he was useless, and so he came by.

While in the office waiting for his "checks," Toole had the entire outfit of several hundred men (and a few women) fall into formation. Worthless was lured outside, at which time Lt.Col. Toole ordered Worthless to "front and center" in front of the entire formation. Lt.Col. Toole then read the discharge out loud to all assembled, ordered the entire outfit to "about-face" (so everybody was facing away from Worthless), then loudly ordered Worthless to leave the compound, stating that he gave the about-face order so that good Marines would not have to look at him.

In his gang-banger attire of baggy tan pants and oversized flannel shirt, Worthless just slithered away. This action was clearly outside the norm of acceptable command behavior. But we all thought it was just fine. Bill Toole, who this day remains a dear friend and fellow member of the Devil Pups board of directors, was a bit unorthodox at times, but in my judgment always in good and appropriate ways.

I've Just Torched Camp Pendleton!

These twenty or so minutes of fright and despair had to have taken a year off my life! During a training exercise at Camp Pendleton I was the senior man on a CH-46 helicopter that was transporting a bunch of Marines to the Case Springs area of Camp Pendleton, located high in the Cleveland National Forest. As the helicopter descended to a landing, I authorized the "popping of smoke" with a colored smoke grenade, to assist the pilot in evaluating the winds. The smoke grenade immediately started a grass fire, and the high winds pushed the flames clearly beyond our ability to control or extinguish them.

I just knew that the inferno would spread throughout the base, potentially spreading into the adjacent civilian communities (Fallbrook, San Clemente, etc.), that my career was over, and my "careless" actions could well result in enormous liability for both the Marine Corps and me. I immediately contacted "Long Rifle" (range control), gave a situation report, direction of the flames, and requested the dispatch of fire apparatus. I evacuated all of our people and sat there sweating bullets as I awaited the arrival of the fire fighting assets.

After about forty-five minutes, with no fire apparatus anywhere in sight, I re-contacted range control to ensure that the assets were enroute—and was told there would be no response. When I asked why there would be no response, range control advised me something to the effect that such fires occur all the time, that they are permitted to just burn themselves out, and to not be concerned! That was among the sweetest radio transmissions I ever received.

"Slippery Little Bugger" in Virginia

This was a funny situation involving a Southern Belle who was as pretty as a picture and as dumb as a rock. Four or five of us Marine officers were having dinner at a restaurant in rural Virginia, and one of my colleagues was trying to make time with this very pretty gal.

After clearly indicating she was not interested, she suddenly took notice of the nickname embroidered on his shirt, which was different from his first name. Her face lit up like a Christmas tree and, in a Southern accent you could cut with a knife, she exclaimed, almost verbatim: "Why, you slippery little bugger—you're an intelligence officer, you can't fool me. Of course I will go out with you!" He then took her hand and they walked off to whatever destiny was to be theirs. We all looked at each other in amazement, as we were not in the intelligence field and had no idea what caused this gal to arrive at her conclusion. But for the sake of our colleague we were glad she thought that was the case!

4th Forward Area Air Defense Battalion

In April 1978, after four years in 3D ANGLICO, I transferred to the 4th Forward Area Air Defense Battalion in Pasadena. This was primarily a "ground" unit, but was under the command of the 4th Marine Air Wing. The mission was to train and, if necessary, deploy Marines who were trained in the employment of the REDEYE Ground-to-Air Missile System. As I recall, there were about 200 Marines assigned to the unit, of all ranks.

Transferring to Pasadena

During this era there was a rule that an officer could only remain in a reserve unit for three years, with the possibility of a one-year extension. He then had to go elsewhere. I had been in 3D ANGLICO for about four years and it was time to move on. My good pal, then-Major Bud Harper, with whom I served on the LAPD, invited me to join the 4th Forward Area Air Defense Battalion (FAAD), as his executive officer for the battery he commanded at the Reserve Center in Pasadena. My old pal Tom Vetter was also at the Pasadena Reserve Center. But, as he was in a HAWK missile battery, he encouraged me to transfer to Pasadena as well. I'd really liked ANGLICO, and enjoyed jumping (parachutist). But my tour was over, and Pasadena was pretty close to my home. I remained in Pasadena for about four years and, although overall I enjoyed every command I was ever part of, FAAD was not among my favorite assignments.

A "Good Old Boy" Outfit

More so than any other outfit I was part of, for the most part the Marines at the reserve unit in Pasadena spent their entire careers in Pasadena. It was truly a family-type of outfit, with many close friendships formed among the officers and staff non-commissioned officers. In my judgment this was not a healthy situation, as it occasionally led to decisions based on tenure and friendships as opposed to competency and other military considerations. The following situations illustrate my concerns.

Staff Sergeant Jones (not his real name) was a very nice man who spent his entire career in Pasadena. But as a platoon sergeant he was an absolute failure, unable to perform the most rudimentary tasks in personnel and equipment accountability. Very gentle and soft-spoken, he also had no credibility with the troops. I "encouraged" him to transfer to another unit, in hopes he could gain the skills elsewhere that he'd failed to develop in Pasadena. My actions in causing him to move on were not well received by some of the other, more senior people.

Gunnery Sergeant Lawson (not his real name) was also a nice and decent man who had spent his entire career in Pasadena. He was the battery gunnery sergeant, but pretty much scatter-brained in much of what he did. In civilian life he was a security guard who had never even developed the skills to operate a motor vehicle, and instead depended on buses to get around. Without suggesting that being a security guard is a bad thing, or the inability to drive a car is a bad thing, each represents life activities that are pretty much inconsistent with the demeanor and activities of a senior Marine staff non-commissioned officer. He eventually moved on to another unit, and I can only hope there was an improvement in his personal skills.

Chief Warrant Officer Tom Ramirez (pseudonym) had been in Pasadena since his return from Vietnam as a corporal. He was the longtime commander of the service platoon (comm., motor transport, supply, etc.). I felt he should attend the three-week school to learn the RED-EYE missile system. There he would gain critical skills that might be necessary if we were to be activated and a need arise in the firing battery, a contingency that made perfectly good sense. It could also be easily accomplished. But he fought me tooth and nail, and never did attend the short and simple course that would have greatly expanded his skills and value to the Marine Corps. He is a fine Marine, liked the job he did, and did it well, especially the latitude he enjoyed with a variety of summer training opportunities, but the Corps and the unit would have been much better served had he expanded his range of skills. He badly resented my unsuccessful efforts to send him to the REDEYE course.

WHINING NURSE SHUTS DOWN SCHOOL IN ALABAMA

In the late 1970s I was among the Marine officers selected to attend the reserve course at the Air Force's Air Command & Staff College in Montgomery, Alabama. All in all, it was a great course. Most of the instructors were Vietnam fighter and bomber jocks who really knew their stuff. I actually drove to and from Alabama, and took my son Jake with me. He farted around the quarters during the day, and rode his bicycle

(I took it in the van) around the base. During the time I was also very active as an amateur radio operator ("ham") and worked a lot of high frequency stuff.

One day a very troubling event occurred. The day consisted primarily of listening to really good presentations in an auditorium, then breaking up into small groups, going into seminar rooms, and discussing the details of the presentation we had just heard. Included among probably 300 officers from all branches were about a dozen Air Force nurses. In the middle of a really good presentation, it became obvious that someone at the side of the stage was motioning for the speaker to step to the side. He did, then disappeared. The lights came on, and a full colonel stepped to the microphone and apologized for the alleged inappropriate remark the presenter, an Air Force major, had just made! None of us could think of anything inappropriate or off-color the major said, but the whole show came to a stop because of a complaint made by one of the nurses.

We were all asked to make statements about what we'd heard. I think most of the folks, like me, could remember nothing having been said that was inappropriate. I don't know how the matter turned out, but it struck me as a pretty sorry state of affairs when one person with a questionable objection can bring an entire auditorium to a halt. I think it was an unfortunate overreaction on the part of the colonel.

Keith and Jake Visit Streator, Illinois

Streator was among the cities that my mom had lived in as a young girl, and a place I'd heard a lot about as I was growing up, from both my mom and my grandfather. Having driven to the Air Force Staff & Command College in Alabama, Jake and I decided to drive back home on a path that took us through Streator. On arrival there, I looked in the telephone book and found the name of a lady who was a niece of my grandfather, Arch Hood. She was very nice and gracious, and showed us around the town. While much had changed, I found a few places where I know my grandfather was prominent, including the local Masonic Lodge. Unfortunately, due to the closing of a large company, which in many Midwestern towns was a big part of the community's lifeblood, the city was in decline. My mom, with whom I spoke on the phone when we got there, could not remember where the house she'd lived in was located. She did recall the park she played in as a little girl, and we went there for a few minutes of reflection. We did not really know our shirttail relative very well, and as time went on we lost contact with the nice lady who hosted us that enjoyable day.

MEDITERRANEAN CRUISE

Shortly after joining FAAD I was the officer-in-charge of our participation in an amphibious exercise in Sardinia, as part of the 34th Marine Amphibious Unit (MAU). The detachment flew commercial to Cherry Point, then on a military C-141 to Barcelona, Spain, where we boarded the USS *Inchon* (LSD-12) and spent two weeks with an infantry battalion out of Camp Lejeune, North Carolina. We had a day of liberty in Barcelona, another day in Toulon (France), then conducted an amphibious exercise in two Sardinian coastal cities. Then another day in Madrid (where we were not allowed to leave the Air Force base), followed by the flight back to Cherry Point, and home. I served as the battalion's S-3 alpha (operations section), and pretty much enjoyed the experience. The people in Spain were in the main nice and friendly, while just about everyone I encountered in France, including those at the police station I visited, were arrogant jerks. My experience in France validated all the bad things I'd heard about the arrogance of the French people in general; as such, I have no desire to ever again visit France. I know that the majority of the French people must be cordial and decent, but my experiences there were not very positive.

FOND AND GRATEFUL THOUGHTS FOR A DISABLED VEHICLE

It's funny, the things we remember and some of the thoughts we had. I was a real fan of the Scout 4x4 vehicles that were produced in the 1960s and '70s by the International Harvester Corporation. In fact, I had three of them over the years. Because of a fondness for the earlier models, around 1978 I bought a used 1966 model as my third Scout. It served me very well on a number of trips, especially in the backcountry during my periods working for the Department of Fish & Game. But sometime around 1981, while enroute home from my USMCR reserve meeting in Pasadena, the engine blew up! It was ugly, with horrible sounds, smoke, and an instantly dead engine. Nevertheless, I was able to coast gracefully to the side of the freeway as my old Scout took its last breath and expired right in front of an emergency callbox! Honestly, my consternation over my predicament was far exceeded by my appreciation for a vehicle that had served me well right up until the very end.

We had a slug in the unit who claimed that he needed to be discharged from the Marine Corps because he was a Jehovah's Witness and therefore a conscientious objector (CO). I was assigned to investigate the validity of his claim and to make a recommendation regarding his application for a CO discharge. My irritation at this idiot caused my vindictiveness (and creativity) to go into high gear. I went to a Jehovah's Witness church in Pasadena (not the location where he allegedly attended services), obtained basic written material about the church, and developed a high-quality, fifty-word, multiple-choice test on that religion. For the date of the interview with him and his attorney, I also asked two pastors from the church to come to the reserve center, interview the idiot, and give me their assessment as to the genuine nature of his conscientious objector claim. He and his attorney were stunned at the process I'd assembled, especially the test; yet he had no choice but to follow my orders and instruction. Despite the very simple and basic nature of the questions, he blew the majority of them. After his interview with the two pastors, the one who appeared to be in charge made the following statement to the assembled group: "We do believe that he is sincere as a conscientious objector. But he has a long way to go before he will ever be a Jehovah's Witness!" It was my pleasure to recommend denial of his request, and to certify that in my judgment his claim was bogus. Fortunately, my boss ignored my vindictiveness, rejected my recommendation, and processed the idiot out of the Marine Corps. My boss was right in ridding the Corps of that worthless person.

THE ALCOHOLIC INSPECTOR–INSTRUCTOR MOVES IN

About a year after my assignment to Pasadena, Major Ron Arnold (pseudonym), a regular Marine officer, was assigned to Pasadena as the inspector-instructor. Ron drank more than he should have, and was always strapped for money, no doubt because of a recent divorce and child support payments. Ron quietly moved into a storeroom at the reserve center, which was a big no-no because he was drawing pay for quarters. He got caught by the battalion commander, and was told to vacate the room immediately or face disciplinary action. He and I chatted and agreed that he could move into a vacant room at my home in Azusa for a reasonable monthly sum.

This was not a very good deal, as he never paid me a cent! He took advantage of me because of his position and because his actions were likely to have a favorable impact on my Marine Corps career, including selection of the next commanding officer (who he made clear was going to be me). So I just kept my mouth shut, and he lived rent-free for about three years, all the while drawing a pretty good stipend each month for his housing allowance. Ron was never in particularly good graces with higher headquarters. and about four months before the commanding officer's tour was over and the new reserve commanding officer was to be selected (thought to be me), Arnold was transferred. It was clear that the new inspector-instructor came in with marching orders to clear certain things up, and that he quite understandably did not think fondly of Ron Arnold. But it was good that Ron was finally gone, as I too had my reservations about his personal and professional qualities. It did not work in my best interests, though, because Ron's advocacy for me did not sit well with his replacement. I was tainted by our association, and although the clear and likely choice, I was not selected as the new commanding officer when the incumbent's tour expired.

This was one of life's unfair learning experiences. I had no choice but to tolerate the leech as he took advantage of me for a couple of years, then I was tainted and suffered professionally because of our association! Yet I must say that in the end I came out ahead. Had I been selected as the commanding officer of the unit, I most likely would have remained in the anti-air field and not traveled the military path that was to be mine as a field-grade officer. The path that resulted was far better than the path I unsuccessfully sought in Pasadena.

A Hooker Takes My Picture in Barcelona

This was funny. In Spain, I was fascinated at the ornate nature of an old hotel that had been used as Nazi headquarters in Barcelona during World War II. I was in the process of taking a picture of it when a woman, obviously a prostitute, asked if I would like her to take a picture of me standing in front of this historic location. I appreciated and accepted her offer. As I was having my picture taken by the hooker, another lieutenant from LAPD and his wife, on vacation, came around the corner and saw me standing there and obviously associating with a prostitute. He smiled, and kept on walking. For years after that, my denials that I was doing anything beyond having my photo taken fell on deaf ears with that fellow.

This was really funny! I have long had the ability to make extemporaneous presentations in a way that makes it appear what I am saying is being read from a document. This has served me well on numerous occasions, especially when making public and military appearances. It has also enabled me to have a great deal of fun over the years, particularly grossing out the Navy chief petty officer who was the unit's senior corpsman.

A minor directive of some sort dealing with random urine testing for drugs had just come out, and I saw the opportunity for some fun. I took it to the chief. Feigning disbelief, I read "verbatim" the new rules for the role of Navy corpsmen in obtaining urine samples. The rules included the mandatory physical handling of each Marine's private parts, to ensure there was no hidden small tube containing someone else's "clean" urine that a drug abuser could substitute for his own during a drug test. The chief got very upset. With the veins popping out on his neck and his face red, he launched into a tirade about how he had now heard everything, and how he would retire before being forced to manhandle (pun intended) the genitals of the Marines in the unit. We all got a big kick out of this, especially because of the chief's near-violent reaction. It took him quite a while to settle down and to see the humor in my actions.

"CRUISE CONTROL" IS NOT "AUTOMATIC PILOT!"

When I first arrived at Fort Bliss for summer training, there was a big buzz going around the base about the foolish actions of some well-heeled foreign students. Fort Bliss is a major facility for training military students from allied countries in a variety of different skills; so much so, that there is actually a German Luftwaffe command right there in the middle of the west Texas desert.

Among the many foreign students there were fairly large numbers of military personnel from the oil-rich Middle Eastern countries with whom we were friendly; most of them came to the United States with quite a bit of money. It seems that one of these rocket scientists went out and bought a new van, then crashed it (incurring some deaths and injuries) when he walked to the rear of the moving vehicle after placing it on "auto pilot!" My understanding is that the difference between "cruise control" and "auto pilot" actually became a briefing topic in the "welcome aboard" package for new foreign students.

I became critically ill and my life was in danger in this instance. While on active duty at Fort Bliss, Texas I did not feel good. I went to the Beaumont Army Hospital, and in a short period of time it was established that I was a very sick person. In fact, a couple of specialists were brought in to examine me (it was in the evening), and the possibilities ranged from leukemia to mononucleosis. Additional blood was drawn and I was directed to return to my quarters, get into bed, and call the next morning for the results of the additional tests. When I called the next morning the doctor said I was okay, and that I just had a case of the "Texas Crud" and would be fine in a day or so. I was scheduled to drive back to California that day, and had Jake with me, but the doctor said it would be fine and that I was fit for the trip. I really felt horrible. But if the doctor said I was okay, I guessed I was okay.

It was a difficult trip back to Los Angeles. I felt so terrible, that on several occasions I actually had to stop the car and lie down alongside the highway. When I got home my entire body was vibrating and it was clear that something was very wrong. I called the inspector-instructor at the reserve unit, and he sent a driver to fetch me and take me to the Long Beach Naval Hospital. I was rushed into the emergency room, where my symptoms included urinating blood. I was in sad shape.

It turns out I had advanced mononucleosis, that my spleen was the size of a football because my condition had not been caught in time, and the mono had developed into hepatitis! I was put into isolation and spent two weeks in that hospital. For the next YEAR I could still feel the effects of my illness, experiencing very serious fatigue during the first couple of months. The naval medical personnel contacted the Beaumont Army Medical Center in El Paso for a summary of my treatment, but were told there was no record of my ever having been there! I wrote a personal letter to the very nice Army physician who initially had treated me and who called in the specialists. But I never received a reply.

Wing vs. Division

This is as good a place as any to discuss my perception of being assigned to the Marine Air Wing versus the Marine Division (ground forces). I have always seen myself as a ground/infantry type of Marine, and have preferred to be assigned to "division" as opposed to "wing." Without suggesting one is better than the other, there are big differences. Basically, the wing exists for one reason, and that is to fly aircraft and perform other aviation related tasks. Almost without exception, the folks calling the shots in the wing are naval aviators (pilots) and those who are not pilots are, to some extent (in my judgment) second-class citizens. It was always subtle, but always a factor. I had some great experiences in my wing assignments, but always felt more comfortable when assigned to a Marine division (ground).

The Missing Physical Examination

I did something, or failed to do something, in Pasadena, that did not set well with the new inspector-instructor, Major Phil Norton. In the Marine Corps Reserve, captains could always find a paid billet. But sometimes it got a little tough (or so I thought at the time) for a major to find a paid billet. It was not unusual for people to delay the mandatory physical examination that always preceded the formal promotion, in order to intentionally delay the promotion. But I really stretched the issue. For almost two years after having been selected for major, I failed to take the physical. Finally I got a blast from Headquarters Marine Corps to take my physical *or else* (I don't know what "else" might have been, but it would not have been nice!). I made major just before transferring from Pasadena, and my failure to take the physical in a timelier manner was among the issues that Major Norton found troubling. Captain was a great rank, and those who held the rank were often referred to as "skipper." But it was somewhat of a sad day when I pinned on the gold oak leaves of a major.

Not Selected as the New Commanding Officer

Although there are no guarantees, there was an expectation at the time I became the executive officer of 4th FAAD that I would become the next commanding officer. But it was not to be. At the time, the next commanding officer was basically the person who was supported by the inspector-instructor; the wing commander, who made the appointment, almost always honored his recommendation. While I believe I did a good job and was the most worthy and deserving for the position, I did not have the support of the "old guard," several staff non-commissioned and warrant officers who had spent just about their entire careers in Pasadena. Those folks embarked on an anti-Bushey lobbying effort with the inspector-instructor, and had an obvious influence in me not getting that command. Other factors that influenced my non-selection, in my judgment, was my failure to take the promotion physical in a timely manner (not a big thing if that was the only issue); but likely the key factor was my perceived closeness to the previous troublesome inspector-instructor, Ron Arnold.

A subsequent return to the Pasadena Marine Corps Reserve Unit was not in the cards. About six or seven years later, while wrapping up my tour as the commanding officer of 3D ANGLICO, I met the then-inspector-instructor of the 4th Forward Area Air Defense Battery in Pasadena at a social function. His name was Major Kim Stalnaker, and he seemed like a verty solid and competent fellow. We chatted quite a bit. Knowing that I was wrapping up a successful command tour, he initiated a conversation about me potentially returning to Pasadena and assuming command of 4th FAAD. I told him of my past with Pasadena, how I had not been selected previously, and my disdain for the good old boy system that existed.

Major Stalnaker had exactly the same concerns. But he pretty much assured me that any heartburn was long past, and encouraged me to apply. I did apply. My package went to the commanding officer of the Marine Air Control Group at Glencoe, Illinois, the higher headquarters where the selection, subject to ratification by the Wing commanding general, was really made.

Then Major Stalnaker called me, mad as hell, and said that another person was being selected. The group commanding officer really had not given him much of a reason. So I called the group commanding officer myself, and got jacked around with no real answer other than he had someone in mind whom he felt was a better selection. That "someone" turned out to be a pilot from the east coast, who someone else in the Glencoe chain of command wanted to take good care of!

That type of nonsense occurred more than it should have. I was a tenured commander with the proper military occupational specialty, who lived about twelve miles from the unit. But they selected someone who had never worked in the field, and had to commute a couple thousand miles for the reserve drill meetings! It was also a reflection of the preferential treatment often shown to pilots over non-pilots in the air wing, and one of the big reasons that I preferred the "ground side of the house."

In hindsight, I am very fortunate not to have been selected, as it created another "fork in my road" that turned out much better.

Marine Air Support Squadron Four

In March, 1983, after five years in Pasadena, I transferred to Marine Air Support Squadron Four (MASS-4) at El Toro. There I started the process to become a fully-qualified air support control officer.

Transferring to MCAS El Toro

When it became clear that I was not going to get the top job in Pasadena, I made application to join Marine Air Support Squadron Four (MASS-4), a subordinate unit of Marine Air Group Forty-Six (MAG-46) of the 4th Marine Air Wing (3rd MAW), at the Marine Corps Air Station at El Toro, California. I knew a bunch of the Marines there and was immediately accepted, which was a good thing because I was still smarting from the Pasadena rejection. The mission of MASS-4 was to train Marines to use the equipment and exercise the skills to manage Marine aircraft during the conduct of combat operations. These skills included taking control of tactical aircraft and coordinating the hand-off to forward observers, getting helo-borne troops into and out of drop zones, managing and deploying aircraft on strip-alerts, and related tasks. I would rather have been with a division (ground) outfit, but this assignment was available and the wing had far more major billets than did the ground division.

My First Exercise with MASS-4

I am a reasonably quick study, with an adequate degree of intelligence. Within a month of joining MASS-4, I found myself as the officer-in-charge of the MASS detachment in support of a combined arms exercise (CAX) at the Marine Air-Ground Combat Center, Twenty-Nine Palms, California. Within a day or so, I was functioning in the Direct Air Support Center (DASC) as the Senior Air Director (SAD), performing the critical job of coordinating the control of numerous actual aircraft in a very sensitive operation.

I spent a good portion of my career as a Marine officer getting assignments because of a perception that I possessed skills that I really did not possess, and then doing whatever was necessary to acquire those skills. This exercise was a good example of that trait.

WALKER SPY SCANDAL AND THE LOSS OF MY MOS!

A massive scandal surfaced in the mid-1980s. A Navy warrant officer and his seaman son, John and Michael Walker, had been stealing extremely sensitive classified material and selling it to the Soviets. These two, especially the father, were in sensitive communications-security assignments, and used their access to betray our nation. One of the fallouts was stripping hundreds of Navy and Marine personnel, including me, of their military occupational specialties in the intelligence field if the holder of that MOS was no longer working in an intelligence assignment.

My primary MOS was 0202—Intelligence Officer—but I had not worked in that field since my tenure in the 14th Counterintelligence Team. By this time I had been selected for promotion to lieutenant colonel, but had no MOS! This was not good. I needed a new military occupational specialty.

AIR SUPPORT CONTROL SCHOOL

The Air Support Control School, as part of the Communications Schools at Twenty-Nine Palms, developed a two-week course for Air Support Control officers. By the time this course came along, I had been in the air support control field with MASS-4 for a couple of years. I took the course and pretty much sailed through it. I submitted my request to Headquarters, Marine Corps, and was assigned the primary MOS of 7208—Air Support Control Officer. I would have preferred a non-aviation MOS, but my MOS never assisted or hindered me in any of my aspirations, and it really did not make any difference. Besides, when I made full colonel, I was given the new MOS of 9906—unrestricted ground colonel!

CAPTAIN, THAT HAPPENS TO BE YOUR DRIVER!

The air support control "coyote" (subject matter advisor and exercise evaluator) at the Marine Air-Ground Combat Center at Twenty-Nine Palms, Tony Broome (pseudonym) was a real dipshit. He was a very hyper and immature individual, and difficult to work with. Technically, he was savvy. But in terms of the real world, how to deal with people and leadership issues, he was very weak. He was prone to "flame out" at even minor discrepancies, and was actually a disruptive influence when monitoring activities in the Direct Air Support Center (DASC).

One very hot afternoon he outdid himself in looking foolish. A Marine was very inappropriately tampering with a rattlesnake on OP (Observation Post) Crampton. He quickly grabbed the tail of the snake and started spinning it around until the reptile's head connected with a rock, which killed the snake. Broome started yelling about the troublesome behavior of this Marine and the fact that we were supposed to be protecting wildlife, and demanded to know the unit that the Marine who killed the snake was assigned to. The Marine sheepishly reminded Broome that he was his (Broome's) driver! Those of us who did not care for Broome got quite a kick from this situation.

The "Short Term" Relationship in El Centro

In the early 1980s we were serving our two weeks of active duty training at the Naval Auxiliary Airfield, El Centro, California. A fellow officer was somewhat of a strange personality. Among the members of the squadron taking part in the training was Roger Loomis (pseudonym), a Mustang (former enlisted) who never stopped acting like a lance corporal. After hours, Roger spent a lot of time at the Officers Club. About mid-way through the two weeks he was trying his best to make time with a gal who was also spending a lot of time at the O-Club. Roger was very persistent. She finally told him straight out that she was not interested in a short-term relationship, to which he replied: "Hey, I'll be here until Friday!"

Weenie Waver Waves at the Wrong People

During one of my many trips to the Marine Corps Base at Quantico, Virginia to attend a professional development school, I was riding on a bus full of cops who were also Marine Corps Reservists. We were students at the FBI-USMC Law Enforcement Course, conducted at the FBI Academy located on the base. While northbound on Interstate 95 enroute to the Army's Aberdeen Proving Grounds for a day of orientation with various automatic weapons, a convertible pulled alongside the bus. The driver, a lone male, was smiling at us as he masturbated! We all alternated between red-hot anger and uncontrollable laughter, as there was nothing we could do. We couldn't even get a license number because of the position of the car in relation to the bus. After a few minutes, he veered off the freeway and disappeared. I suspect he would really have been pleased, had he known he was exposing himself to several dozen cops.

In March 1984 I was one of about twenty Reserve Marines, all of whom were civilian peace officers, on active duty at Headquarters, Marine Corps. We were part of a group there to study and make recommendations pertaining to the then-fairly recent bombing at the Marine Barracks in Lebanon. In fact, the head of my task team was Lieutenant Colonel Oliver North, who later gained much fame for his part in a White House scandal.

Jake also accompanied me on this trip. One evening, Jake badgered me into taking him for a walk around the White House perimeter. We ended up witnessing the unsuccessful efforts of a deranged man to jump the fence and assassinate then-President Ronald Reagan. He had a shotgun under his coat, which he pulled out when the uniformed Secret Service officers, who had been watching him, chose to approach him. They shot him in the arm and took him into custody. Jake and I became real celebrities for a day or so, and Jake was eventually the key witness in the trial held several months later in Washington.

This incident resulted in our meeting key uniformed Secret Service personnel and enjoying a number of nice after-hours visits to the White House. The episode later paid off on my many LAPD trips to Washington, where I hosted a number of after-hours visits to the White House during my ultimately successful lobbying efforts to secure additional radio channels for public safety.

A GREAT LANDING OF AN F-4 PHANTOM—WELL, ALMOST

One Saturday morning while I was at my desk at MASS-4, chaos started to reign, and a bunch of sirens were activated.

It seems that an F-4 had lined up for a perfect landing, descended with maximum proficiency and performance, and flared perfectly. Unfortunately, however, the pilot had forgot to lower the landing gear (wheels)! I was among the looky-loos who descended on the site. The damaged plane sat flat on the ground, with weeds embedded in just about all ground-level surfaces.

The pilot and the bombardier-navigator (also known as the radar intercept officer—RIO) had some pretty long faces, and with good justification. They knew their flying days were immediately over, and that their time in the Marine Corps was not going to be much longer, either. That poor plane remained in the headquarters hanger of MAG-46 (Marine Air Group 46), which was the higher headquarters to all the reserve squadrons, including mine, for several months, with the weeds still sticking out of the front apertures.

The Phantom was in the process of being phased out, as F-18s were starting to trickle to the reserves, and the damaged plane was ultimately scrapped rather than repaired. I did not run into the pilot or the RIO after that, but knew their flying days were over and that whatever was left of their USMC careers was sure to be menial. Certainly, there was an investigation and a subsequent board of inquiry. But there is not much of a defense for failure to lower the landing gear on a million-dollar airplane!

FEMALE STAFF SERGEANT—FRATERNIZATION OR RESTRAINT?

During the time I held the rank of major during my tour in MASS 4, I met and struck up a very nice platonic relationship with a full-time ("regular") female staff sergeant. It was clear to both of us that we would like to have a relationship that went beyond platonic. However, the Marine Corps not only frowned on fraternization between officers and enlisted, but actually court-martialed some officers and drummed them out of the Marine Corps for nothing other than having a romantic relationship with a female enlisted Marine.

Barbara (the female staff sergeant) went out of her way to assure me that she had the ability to be very discreet, and that she was anxious for us to become romantically involved. This was tough for me because I was single and not seeing anyone at that particular time, and Barbara had no shortage of qualities that I found attractive. She was a photo-journalist in the base public affairs office, and there was no way that we would ever be in the same chain of command. But even being on separate continents would not have been acceptable, as long as she was an enlisted Marine.

In the end, however, restraint won out over passion and our relationship did not go beyond the platonic stage. Barbara was a nice gal with a lot to offer, but I had too much to lose by crossing that forbidden line. I continue to remain strong in my belief that the Marine Corps anti-fraternization policy is a bit too strict, and should not apply in some situations involving different commands when no workplace conflict is involved. I hate to sound like a romantic, and I clearly recognize there is often more lust than love involved in fraternization, but there are times when the chemistry between two people is so strong that they are meant to be together. For that reason, I believe some flexibility on the issue is appropriate.

As I reflect on the above situation, I feel very sorry for Barbara and other women in the same position. For me, it was just a potential opportunity that never came to fruition. For Barbara, it was a continuing saga of heartache and disappointments. Her world was virtually a whopper pond of men, many of whom were single. But a good portion of those men who were of intellectual and social interest were off-limits because they were commissioned and she was enlisted. Although very smart, well-educated, and with previous journalism experience before entering the military, she fell short of the baccalaureate degree needed for commissioning. I suspect that she left the Corps. It certainly would have been understandable.

The End of My Tour at MASS-4

My tour in MASS-4 was drawing to an end. Again, I was the heir apparent to be the new commanding officer when fate again intervened. In reorganization, it was decided that MASS-4 would be downgraded from squadron to detachment status. This was bad for me personally, because a squadron is commanded by a lieutenant colonel (which I was about to be) and a major commands a detachment, which is what the unit was about to be downgraded to. It was clear that I was on the verge of being promoted out of a job, and certainly would not be the next commanding officer.

Because of the 3D ANGLICO selection several months later this redesignation was a blessing in disguise for me, as I would not have competed for 3D ANGLICO had I got the MASS-4 commanding officer's position.

––––––

Mobilization Training Unit CA-49

In October 1988, after approximately five years in MASS 4, I transferred into the Mobilization Training Unit CA-49. This was truly a "holding pattern" until something better came along.

My First (and ONLY) Unpaid Billet

Mobilization Training Units (MTUs) are somewhat of an organizational boneyard for senior officers who cannot find a paid billet, or who for whatever reason(s) choose not to serve in the more demanding paid billet status. These are unpaid assignments where points are awarded for weekend drill participation, but that's it. Realistically, very little is expected other than showing up, allegedly participating in some continuing military education, and sometimes doing minor projects.

A few of the folks in this outfit, which was commanded by a civilian airline pilot, Colonel "Birdie" Bertrand, volunteered to help develop the new command museum at El Toro. I needed a holding pattern until something else came along, and "Birdie" joined me to his MTU.

For the several months that I was there, I spent most of my time back at MASS-4 in a quasi-command position, as the imminent transition from squadron to detachment status had not yet occurred.

―――――

3RD AIR-NAVAL GUNFIRE LIAISON COMPANY (ANGLICO)

In July 1989, after several months in the Mobilization Training Unit at El Toro, I assumed command of 3D ANGLICO. Since my previous tour in this unit, it had relocated to a nice, new reserve center at the Long Beach Naval Station. This unit is absolutely one of the most coveted commands in the Marine Corps Reserve, and ranked right alongside (and maybe even a cut above) being assigned as a battalion commander. The two organizational companies in the Marine Corps, reserve and regular, that are commanded by a lieutenant colonel are ANGLICO and Force Reconnaissance. The key mission is to provide Marine forward observers to either the U.S. Army or allied military forces to coordinate the acquisition of Naval Gunfire or Marine Close Air Support. Most of the key operation billets, including the entire command staff, were airborne-designated (parachutist). There was no job in the Marine Corps that I would rather have had than to command 3D ANGLICO, and having held that position remains the highlight of my Marine Corps career.

THE COMMAND OFFICER INTERVIEW FOR 3D ANGLICO

The command tour of then-Lieutenant Colonel Mike Kromm was drawing to a close, and the process to select a new commanding officer from well over a dozen "high-speed, low-drag" lieutenant colonels was underway. The process consisted of the outgoing commanding officer, Kromm, and the inspector-instructor, Lieutenant Colonel Joe Scott, interviewing all the candidates and making a recommendation to the commanding general of the 4th Marine Division, Major General Walter

Boomer. But the process started out as a sham; it rapidly became clear that they had a favorite candidate and were not taking the other applicants seriously.

When I appeared as scheduled for my interview with Kromm and Scott, they were not there. The first sergeant advised me they were enroute back from Camp Pendleton, were running late, and asked that I await their return for my interview. A few minutes later another applicant, with whom I was acquainted, also showed up for his interview, and was also asked to wait. After about an hour, Kromm and Scott showed up and announced that they were going to interview both of us together! Those two did all the talking and painted a dismal picture of the demands on the commanding officer, in the process pretty much attempting to downplay the position and discourage our interest.

Finally, Joe Scott said the interview was over, adding, "I'll be honest with you, we'll just send all the names to division and do not know how the selection will be made!" Furious, I tore into both Kromm and Scott (diplomatically, but with no room for misunderstanding). I told them they were not being honest, that they knew exactly how the process worked, that they obviously had a favorite candidate in mind, that the process was a sham, that they were letting down "the Boomer" (implying I had some relationship with the commanding general—which I did not), and that they should be ashamed of themselves for not performing their duties in a professional and ethical manner. I told them I had spent hours preparing for the interview and was conversant on every critical issue facing the unit, but that none of those issues had even been mentioned.

I stood up, dropped my resume in front of them, and told them to give me a call if they decided to get serious about their responsibilities! Kromm tried to explain that the typical interview was not really necessary because they had our resumes. But I reminded him that as a businessman (insurance, as I recall) he would not have hired an office worker without more of an interview than had occurred in this instance. Then I walked out.

I told a friend, Chief Warrant Officer Scotty Ernce at division headquarters, about the "interview," and I believe he related to General Boomer what had occurred. I think this probably caused the commanding general to pay close attention to the process. The general did not know me; but if this was the case, it certainly did me no harm, and made the process a cleaner one. I know that my stock was good with Scotty, and suspect his stock was good with General Boomer. That alone may well have been a factor that influenced my ultimate selection.

The next day I got a call from Joe Scott, who invited me back for an interview with him. I was truly prepared for the interview, and encouraged him to invite his entire staff to listen to my thoughts and presentation—I could feel our meeting went very well. Then Kromm and I met downtown for a prolonged discussion and lunch, and again I felt it had gone well.

A month or so later, while attending the Command & Staff College at Quantico, I was notified that I had been selected as the new commanding officer of 3D ANGLICO! I was walking on air, and the envy of most of the other students for having been selected for one of the most coveted commands in the Marine Corps Reserve.

Joe Scott and I went on to be great friends. But I never asked, and he never volunteered, the name of the person who he and Kromm were pushing for the position. I think it might have been Kroom's executive officer, a Marine pilot with silver jump wings from NROTC. But he declined my strong suggestion, when I became the commanding officer, that he return to active jump status. I replaced him with Wes May as my executive officer. The pilot (I forget his name) was gracious in leaving.

Lieutenant Colonel Bushey
Featured in *Leatherneck* Magazine

For some unknown reason, the staff at *Leatherneck* magazine selected me as a Marine Corps success story. Someone thought that going from a private and a high school dropout to a lieutenant colonel commanding 3D ANGLICO was worth writing about. I was flattered to be selected for this honor, and pleased at the article. It appeared in the March 1990 edition. As a humorous footnote, the staff writer wanted to include a photo of my kids. But, except for Zak, Jake and Stacy were angry (I do not recall about what) when I brought them together for the photos, and the displeasure was obvious on their faces. So the photo could not be used!

The Commanding Officer's Crash Landing at Camp Pendleton

I had not been active as a parachutist since my first tour in ANGLICO, which had ended eleven years prior. Obviously, I was rusty in this critical area. So, in preparation for my first jump as unit commanding officer, Gunnery Sergeants Frank Brown and Scotty Anderson came to my home in Azusa, brought main and reserve parachutes, suited me up, and had me do a bunch of parachute landing falls (PLFs) off the back of a pickup truck onto my lawn.

After a month or two as the commanding officer, we had a C-141 jump over the Tank Park drop zone (DZ) at Camp Pendleton. Per custom, I was the first jumper out of the aircraft, and loved the jump and descent. But I really crashed and burned while landing! I did not do a very good PLF, landed wrong, and hit hard. I managed to hobble for the final formation, but had trouble walking for a few days afterward.

I finally healed, or so I thought; but now, in my mid-60s, I have some aches and pains, and know that my poor landing that day did damage that was masked by youth and fitness. I had an MRI done on my back and hips a couple of years ago, and several injuries are apparent. But those are just some of the things that go with an active life, and I would not trade my experiences for anything. I did not seek medical attention at the time, for fear that it would jeopardize my command assignment.

Most of the men I know and served with are like old rodeo riders. We have a few aches and pains, decreased mobility, hurting at times, but smile at the thought of the incidents that caused these injuries. These problems are likely to get worse with additional age, but that is just the way things are. I will hobble with pride!

Jumping into an Inkwell!

Night parachute operations are inherently dangerous, but reflect very necessary training for Marine parachutists. In combat situations, the likelihood of being able to pick and choose the drop zone location and time of the jump is non-existent.

One of my more memorable night jumps was into the "Tank Park" drop zone at Camp Pendleton. It was completely dark, with not much moonlight, but with some ambient light from the city of Oceanside approximately ten miles to the south. We were jumping from a C-130 Hercules four-engine transport. To reduce the likelihood of colliding with another jumper, we all had chemical glowsticks attached to our parachute harnesses.

As the commanding officer I was the first person out of the aircraft, and standing on the lowered ramp with all the noise and wind, and looking down into what I thought of as an inkwell, were not among the more enjoyable things that I have done. While waiting for the word to "go" I asked myself "What the f—k am I doing this for, when I could be sitting at home in my easy chair?" Then another thought occurred to me: What a privilege that I am still in the arena, being a United

States Marine, doing exciting things, while all of my childhood buddies were sitting in their easy chairs, drinking beer, and getting fat! The final thought was very motivating, and when I got the word to "go," I had a big smile on my face.

Approaching the ground in a parachute when it is dark is truly an exciting experience! While you can get some idea of when you are about to hit the ground by watching the horizon, you usually have no idea about what you are about to land on until it happens, hopefully in an open area, but not always. My landing in this operation was fine, but three of my men were seriously injured during the landing. The most seriously hurt was Major Fritz Bystrum, a great fellow and an attorney in Los Angeles when not a Marine. All three were hospitalized, with Fritz needing several surgeries due to a severe leg injury.

Preparing Men for Combat

I took my job very seriously, because of the importance of the mission and the likelihood that there would not be much time for training in the event of mobilization for an actual, real-world deployment. This has always been a driving force with me. But it has not always served me well, such as in Pasadena, where it sometimes appeared that the primary consideration was keeping people (even those with questionable skills) alive in the USMCR.

I truly like, covet, and respect the social and fraternal side of the Marine Corps, but the primary issue must be readiness to be immediately deployed for combat operations. Too many people fail to have this as their priority.

In August of 1990 my executive officer, Lieutenant Colonel Wes May and his family, were vacationing with me and my family at our home in Big Bear. On a Saturday morning, August 5, a news bulletin announced that Iraqi forces had just invaded Kuwait. Wes and I looked at each other with special recognition, as we were aware that such an incident involving these counties was among the situations that would trigger the activation of 3D ANGLICO.

If possible to do so, back at the base we further enhanced our training and readiness activities. We knew that we would be activated; we just did not know when the activation would occur.

LIAISON OFFICER TO THE 5TH DIVISION—
JAPANESE SELF-DEFENSE FORCE

One brigade platoon was activated and deployed to Camp Lejeune in North Carolina. The rest of 3D ANGLICO, with me at the helm, was awaiting orders as well. It was obvious that allied forces would eventually invade Kuwait and chase the Iraqis back into Iraq, but not until the troop build-up was complete. It was not complete at the time that 3D ANGLICO was tasked with providing a small detachment to the Third Marine Expeditionary Force (III MEF) to support a joint US-Japanese exercise, Yama Sakura, at Camp Chotise on the island of Hokkaido in Japan. I felt it would be a fun trip, and that as a lieutenant colonel I would be able to just kick back and enjoy the trip—boy, was I wrong!

We first went to Okinawa and joined the III MEF Marines, who were also assigned to the exercise, then flew in a C-130 to Camp Chotose. When the two staffs, American and Japanese, met for a social function with plenty of sake before the exercise began, the Japanese commander made it very clear that he expected the Marine staff officer assigned to his staff as liaison officer be among the best, brightest, and most knowledgeable members of the III MEF staff.

As I was trying to speculate as who this super person would be, Major General Henry "Hank" Stackpole, the commanding general of III MEF, announced that they had carefully selected such a person—and he was Lieutenant Colonel Bushey! I spent the next week or so with the Japanese and did a decent job; again, I got in there, did my best, and things went well.

This trip afforded me the opportunity to spend a few days on Okinawa, where I had not been since I was a lance corporal in 1964! I took a bunch of walks down memory lanes and truly enjoyed the visit. I went to my old squad bay, workspaces, recreational areas, mess halls, and the grinder where I was standing when told of President Kennedy's assassination. For a while, it appeared that 3D ANGLICO was going to be attached to III MEF for a one-year tour, and that I would be designated as the executive officer of the 3rd Surveillance, Reconnaissance and Intelligence Group (SRIG). When I visited the commanding officer of 3rd SRIG, I went into the same building where I used to buff the floors when the facility was headquarters of the 9th Marine Amphibious Force! That assignment, which for some complicated reasons would have been very desirable, did not come to pass. I am so grateful that I had the opportunity to visit a location that had been so prominent dur-

161

ing my teenage years.

Note: There is quite a story involving General Stackpole. When a captain in Vietnam, he was gravely wounded and thought to be dead. While personnel, including a Navy chaplain, were doing triage and separating the wounded from the deceased Marines, the chaplain thought he detected a slight sign of life in Captain Hank Stackpole's body. Stackpole was removed from the deceased holding area and given immediate medical attention. Obviously, he survived and went on to a distinguished career, ultimately retiring as a lieutenant general. The Navy chaplain who detected his signs of life and who is responsible for Stackpole's survival is Commander (now retired) Victor Krulak, Jr., oldest son of retired Lieutenant General Victor "Brute" Krulak, USMC, one of the true legends of the Marine Corps.

"Make Sure There's a Charlie Available for the Old Man!"

During my first tour in 3D ANGLICO, we used the standard T-10 parachute. It had no steering capability other than climbing the risers while descending in an attempt, usually unsuccessful, to cause the chute to drift in the desired direction. When I returned to 3D ANGLICO we had a new and improved parachute, the MC1-1 "Bravo," which was essentially a T-10 modified to permit some control by the installation of two toggles that the jumper could pull to partially collapse portions of the canopy, thus controlling downward drift. Clearly, the "Bravo" was a real improvement over the T-10. However, like the T-10, the typical decent speed of the "Bravo" was 16 to 22 feet per second, which means you screamed-in pretty fast. While at 3D ANGLICO, we took delivery of several MC1-1 "Charlies," which, because the material in the canopy was woven more densely, had a much slower typical descent speed of 8 to 12 feet per second.

With my aging body having been beaten pretty badly and regularly with hard landings, I fell in love with the relatively soft landings provided when using the new chutes. Toward the end of my tour, the parachute riggers made sure that there was always a "Charlie" available for the "old man" (me)!

Called Up for the First Gulf War

In early December 1990, one brigade platoon (slightly less than one-third of 3D ANGLICO) was activated for the Gulf War. The rest of us knew it was just a matter of time before the entire unit was activated. Unfortunately, in my judgment, we were not activated as soon as we should have been. In preparation for activation I made several trips to New Orleans (Division Headquarters) for consultations, but it was not happening.

I finally lobbied hard with our commanding general, Major General Cooper (Boomer had pinned on his third star, and was now commanding general of I MEF in the Southwest Asia theater, commanding all Marine ground forces in preparation for combat operations) and my direct boss, the G-3, Colonel Sexton, to get us activated. It worked, but we were not activated until the third day of the four-day war! Hostilities ceased just as we arrived at Camp Pendleton. My advanced party, the 2nd Brigade Platoon, which had been activated, did a great job and destroyed 230 Iraqi vehicles at a place called Al Wafra, for which I as their commanding officer also received accolades. I was green with envy at my troops who'd made it in combat, and wish the entire unit could have been engaged as well. My disappointment, and that of just about all of my men who did not get into combat, was very strong.

The War of Retention on Active Duty!

Now I had a new battle on my hands: keeping my troops on active duty for at least ninety days to ensure their eligibility for a whole array of veteran's benefits. Within a week or so of the end to the ground war in Kuwait/Iraq, efforts got underway to start releasing reserves back into civilian life. This was really a pain, because a number of my folks had made some pretty big sacrifices for activation (relinquished child custody, worked with employers for long-term replacements, etc.), and now it looked like a short evolution. While some of my people were anxious to return to civilian life, most of them preferred to stay on active duty for a while, and maybe even deploy as part of the occupation. Also, General Stackpole's desire for us to serve for a year on Okinawa was still potentially viable at that point.

Camp Pendleton—Del Mar Area

As long as we were going to be at Camp Pendleton for a few months, I decided to see how much critical training and how many critical administrative requirements we could achieve. I had to have set some type of a record for what one unit could accomplish in three months!

I've always been pretty savvy in knowing the system and in getting things done in spite of the bureaucracy, and those skills really paid off in this endeavor. The following were accomplished during the ninety-six days we were on active duty: Every Marine received the annual physical, forty-nine additional Marines completed jump school, approximately two dozen additional Marines obtained military driver's licenses, approximately two dozen of my communications personnel obtained technician level amateur radio licenses (I brought in outside volunteer instructors), Landing Force Training Command—Pacific (Coronado) developed and provided to several dozen Marines a one-week course on frequency propagation and the construction of field expedient high frequency radio antennas, all Marines completed the yearly marksmanship qualification with their designated weapon, all basic parachutists made the necessary additional jumps and received the Navy-Marine Corps Parachutist Badge, all Marines who required dental work had that work performed, every service record book (enlisted) and qualifications jacket (officer) was audited and updated, a detachment completed the Mountain Warfare training course at Bridgeport (California), and a great deal of additional individual training was accomplished.

All of these activities placed the unit in a superb position, and essentially cleared the decks of those issues that would interfere with training for at least the next twelve to eighteen months. These accomplishments, along with the superb combat performance of my advanced party in Iraq, contributed to me being awarded the Meritorious Service Medal, receiving a phenomenal fitness report from Lieutenant General Boomer, and no doubt contributed to my selection to full colonel several months later.

THE "PHANTOM POOPER!"

If I live to be 100, I will never understand why some people (fortunately very few) get satisfaction from surreptitiously defecating in a conspicuous location, with the obvious intent to gross-out other people. I encountered this syndrome another time or two during my Marine Corps career. In this instance, the suspect deposited a big pile of fecal matter in the middle of the floor in the barracks head (large common bathroom). Sergeant Major Trumbich got to the bottom of the matter and established conclusively (but not legally) that the suspect was a well-respected master sergeant who always had an odd side. But this was quite a surprise. He had applied for the warrant officer program, and I was in the process of creating an enthusiastic endorsement at the time of this incident; yet, obviously, I did not provide the endorsement. He knew that we knew, but couldn't prove it to a legal standard. He also knew that I withdrew the endorsement, and why. It was suggested that he seek counseling, but he denied the incident, yet did not protest very strongly. There were no overt consequences, but he was watched pretty closely after this. He was a profane and earthly fellow who probably did not view this as seriously as did others. He remained in the unit after my command tour was over, eventually retiring from the Marine Corps Reserve.

Police Motorcycle in the Garage

Gunnery Sergeant William "Willie" Sampson was among the number of Los Angeles Police officers who served under me as reservists in 3D ANGLICO. He was a Valley Traffic Division motorcycle officer whose seniority resulted in him being issued a brand-new motorcycle not long before being activated for the Gulf War. When Willie told me he would have the exact same motorcycle when he returned to the department, I commented that it would have about a year of additional mileage from being used by some other officer while he was gone. But he said that was not the case. When I asked incredulously if the department would just put it in storage for him, he cryptically replied that he'd never turned it in and that it was sitting in his garage at home! He explained that this was done with the tacit approval of his supervisors! As a long-time LAPD command officer, I knew this was contrary to every rule, law and practice of the LAPD, and was both shocked and amused. I just kept Bill's secret to myself and chuckled every time I thought about the issue.

Dusty Detective Car at the Ranges of Camp Pendleton

On a couple of occasions while on remote ranges back in the hills of Camp Pendleton, I noticed what appeared to be an unmarked police vehicle, with Minnesota license plates, driving on the dirt roads. It was dirty and dusty, with much caked mud in the fender wells. It had several antennas, including a big whip antenna on the rear, and suppressed emergency lights.

Turns out that it was the duty vehicle of a Minnesota police detective. When called to active duty, he drove his police car to Camp Pendleton and used it during the mobilization! Unbelievable!

The Commanding Officer's Rear-View Mirror!

Subsequent to the Gulf War, 3D ANGLICO was given a place of special prominence in the annual Torrance Armed Forces Parade. However, there was a problem, at least for me. The formation configuration required by the parade officials was one massive platoon as opposed to several platoons in line. That meant we had to have something like fifteen men across and twenty-five men deep. The commanding officer was to be centered in front of his command, about fifteen feet in front of the formation. The company gunnery sergeant was to be off to the side and calling cadence, but there was no way that I would be able to hear him. The likelihood of me looking stupid and being out of step was certain. However, I had an idea; develop a rear-view mirror for my helmet so that I could see my men and stay in step with them. I bought a dental mirror, painted it Marine green, and attached it to my helmet. It worked like a charm and I remained in step during the entire parade. I still have my "rear view mirror" and occasionally glance at it with funny and fond memories.

Accolades for 3D ANGLICO and Lieutenant Colonel Bushey

I consider myself to be very fortunate to have had such a successful command tour as commanding officer of the one of the Marine Corps' most elite, challenging, and important commands. From the day I took over, until the day I turned over command to Wes May, it was great! We accomplished so much, went so many places, had such rewarding experiences, and when called to active duty did a superb job. The roughly one-third of the unit who saw combat, my advanced party, distinguished themselves and destroyed approximately 230 Iraqi vehicles (and a bunch of Iraqis!)

Like every command experience, it was the men who worked for me that made it all happen. But as the person at the helm I ended my command tour with many accolades, and was awarded the Meritorious Service Medal.

Surprise Award to Marine at West Los Angeles Roll Call

Staff Sergeant R.J. Cottle was among the Los Angeles police officers under my command at 3D ANGLICO. He was a great Marine and a great cop, who was awarded the Navy Commendation Medal with the Combat "V" for combat service in my 2nd Brigade Platoon in Kuwait. The citation contained terms such as "minimizing potential hostile consequences" and "neutralizing the threat," which were Marine Corps speak for doing a great job and killing a bunch of Iraqi soldiers. The award did not reach my desk before we were released from active duty, so I decided to give it to him at the West Los Angles Police Division where he was assigned. The command staff and a great many of his fellow police officers were present, and the local police booster association provided refreshments. It was a great honor for me to present the medal to a very surprised young man.

I would run across "R.J." from time to time, and felt very proud of him. He ultimately went to Metropolitan Division and became a well-respected member of the SWAT team. He remained in the Marine Corps Reserve and attained the rank of sergeant major. He was mobilized several times for combat service in Iraq and Afganistan. In 2009, while in Afganistan, Sergeant Major R.J. Cottle was killed in action. God bless you, sergeant major.

Parachute Jumps—Final Tally and Long-Term Consequences

Between my two tours of duty in 3D ANGLICO I completed somewhere around sixty parachute jumps. The fixed-wing aircraft I jumped from included the C-130 Hercules, C-141 Starliner, C-123 Boxcar, OV-10 Bronco, and C17D Skytrain. The helicopters I jumped from included the CH53 Sea Stallion, CH46 Sky Knight, and OH-1 Huey. There may have been another aircraft or two that I do not recall. I have never been a "feather merchant" (lightweight person), but rather have always been stocky. Consequently, I have always descended pretty fast, even after my parachute canopy opened. For the T-10 and MC1-1B chutes, the advertised descent was (generally) from 16 to 20 feet per second, and for the later MC1-1C chutes, the descent was (again, generally) a wonderful 8 to 12 feet per second.

A good number of my landings could better be described as crash landings, where the term "crash & burn" was most appropriate. I streamed in fast and landed hard a number of times, but always managed to walk away, notwithstanding a few days of limping around. Now, as I approach the "Big 70," the physical residuals of all of these jump injuries, which seemed minor at the time because of a younger and more forgiving body, are taking a certain toll. I find myself limping around once in a while, and experience pain that I swear I can almost attribute to certain hard landings! No sweat, I can handle it. If given the opportunity to roll the clock back, and not have been a jumper in 3D ANGLICO, I would decline the offer. I worked hard for these aches and pains and experience them with pride (and an occasional grimace!)

Change of Command—Truly a Sad Day

My two-year tour as the commanding officer came to an end in July of 1991. The commanding general of the Fourth Marine Division had selected my executive officer, Lieutenant Colonel Wesley May, to succeed me as commanding officer of 3D ANGLICO. It would have been impossible to find a better man for the job, as Wes was and is a superb human being, a great friend, and a fine Marine. Like me, Wes was a former enlisted Marine who had received a commission during the Vietnam War. Relinquishing command was a painful process, as I had found so much personal and professional satisfaction as the commanding officer of that wonderful unit. Wes and I had a little bit of fun when I passed the pole with the unit's colors to him as part of the ceremony: as he started to pull it toward him, I gently resisted and tried to pull it back toward me, resulting in big smiles on both of our faces. The truth is that I was pretty much devastated.

As I drove home after the change of command ceremony, I actually felt somewhat lost. The previous two years had been among the busiest and most rewarding of my life, and all of a sudden I went from full steam ahead to almost a dead stop.

I was pretty much uncertain about what the future held for me in the Marine Corps. But I felt guardedly optimistic. I knew I had done an exemplary job as commanding officer, and I knew that everybody else recognized that as well, including the commanding general and the staff of the division in New Orleans. Although I personally did not get into combat with my advance party, I received strong accolades for the training and leadership I'd provided, and was given a share of the credit for the superb actions of my men in combat during the first Gulf War. It was also recognized that the degree of training and accomplishments my unit experienced during the period of active duty were nothing short of extraordinary.

The G-3 of the division, Colonel Merrill Saxton, a great guy and a strong supporter (and recipient of a Navy Cross from the Vietnam War), had assured me that I would be welcome to join the staff of the division in New Orleans. Nevertheless, it was a time when I felt somewhat lost. Fortunately, I didn't stay lost for very long, and in fact soon did join the staff of the 4th Marine Division.

MEDAL FOR TOP SOTO—15 YEARS LATE!

Master Sergeant Richard Soto is one of those wonderful men who works very hard, even now after retirement, to keep the spirit of his Marine Corps service alive. Like most master sergeants, he was referred to as "Top" Soto. Just about every year he hosts a reunion at his home, a great and enjoyable event for all of us who had the honor of serving in

3D ANGLICO.

During one of these gatherings at his house, probably around 2009, I casually asked him about the award I knew he had to have received at the time of his retirement. It is common to reward someone at the end of their career with either a Meritorious Service Medal or a Navy-Marine Corps Commendation Medal, to recognize superior service.

I could tell he was hurt when he answered my question, saying that he'd never received a medal. I believe I demonstrated some indignation, to which he replied: "Forget it, colonel, just leave it alone!" That conversation triggered an absolute resolve on my part to make sure that he got a medal! I did not realize how long the process was going to take, or just how difficult it was going to be. Since he had been retired more than five years, Marine Corps regulations stipulate that the medal recommendation had to come through a member of Congress. After having put together a pretty comprehensive package recommending the award of a Meritorious Service Medal, I processed the package through the office of then-Representative Jane Harman. Her office passed it on to the Marine Corps Congressional Liaison Officer, who then forwarded the entire package to Headquarters Marine Corps.

Between the various award boards convened both at Headquarters Marine Corps and the Secretary of the Navy, it took over two years of rewrites, soliciting additional endorsements, resubmitting to various boards, and every other imaginable delay. Finally, the Secretary of the Navy Commendations Board recommended, and Headquarters Marine Corps concurred, awarding Master Sergeant Soto the Navy-Marine Corps Commendation Medal.

Top Soto was unaware that this effort was under underway, but his wife was continually apprised and worked with me on the project. When the medal was sent to me I set up a surprise ceremony at 3D ANGLICO. I told Top Soto that I was receiving a medal, and wanted him present because of all the support he'd provided me when I was the commanding officer.

Top Soto's wife and I got hold of as many of our old associates as possible. At the end of a drill on a Sunday afternoon in August, 2011 while we were all assembled and Soto thought I was about to be called up, instead we called up Top Soto. Retired Colonel Wesley May, Soto's wife and I all participated in pinning the medal on his chest as the citation was being read. He was surprised, and I know, deeply appreciative. We all then retired to Soto's house, where his wife had prepared a surprise celebration and buffet dinner. It was a lot of work and a lot of effort, but was something I just had to do for a man who had served the Marine Corps, and me personally, so well and for so long.

––––––

4th Marine Division Staff

In the late summer of 1991, I transferred to the staff of the 4th Marine Division in New Orleans, Louisiana. At that time, I was part of a very small "battle staff" of seasoned personnel, who the commanding general could dispatch to large exercises to perform the role of a division headquarters.

Transferring to the "Big Easy"

My stock was pretty good with the commanding general and staff of the Marine Reserve Forces headquarters in New Orleans. A reorganization was underway and a true "battle staff" made up of solid reservists, as opposed to the then-existing administrative staff made up of regular personnel, would soon be assembled.

Within a month or so, I was assigned and doing my weekend drills in New Orleans. I was assigned as the Division's Operations Officer working for the G-3, a reserve colonel and employee of the State Children's Services from El Paso, Texas, Jim Preston. Jim is a great fellow and, to this day, a dear friend. Our families have visited and vacationed together, and Cathy and Jeanne are close, as well. One of our bonds was our commitment to foster kids: Jim and Jeanne had adopted three foster kids! We worked well together on several exercises and other activities.

An interesting thing about this assignment was that I had to travel to and from New Orleans for reserve drill weekends, at my own expense! Drill travel is something each reservist pays on his or her own, as the rules pretty much assume that reservists drill at a unit close to their homes, and the drill pay is assumed to have an adequate built-in allowance for this consideration. For high-ranking folks like myself, this was a price we had to pay for the honor of the positions we held. The result was that I devoted my drill pay to airline travel. However, when called to active duty for training, special meetings, conferences, or investigations—in New Orleans (NOLA) or anywhere else—orders were issued and travel costs were paid for by the government.

Professional Military Education (PME)

Although I did not attend Officers Candidate School (OSC) or the Basic School (TBS), I attended just about everything else! During my Marine Corps career as an officer I attended several intelligence courses, just about every amphibious course offered at the Naval Amphibious School at Coronado, Air Support Control School at Twentynine Palms, Air Force Command & Staff in Alabama, the Parachute Course in Georgia, Amphibious Warfare School in Quantico, Marine Corps Command & Staff College also in Quantico, Armed Forces Staff College in Virginia, and the Naval War College in Rhode Island. Many of these were the abbreviated reserve versions, involving several in-residence sessions and correspondence. There were also lesser courses and schools too numerous to mention. Certainly, this PME contributed to my successful career.

Sleazy Cabbie with Porn for the Passengers

This is not the typical chamber of commerce business practice, but not real surprising, given the unique culture of the greater New Orleans area and the devil-may-care attitude of many of the folks who live there. One day I hailed a cab to take me from my hotel in Metairie to the airport. After learning my destination, the cab driver handed me a very large three-ring binder, then hit the gas and took off for my destination. The binder was full of pictures of naked women, pages and pages of them, in every conceivable position and representing every conceivable ethnicity. While not embarrassed or offended (I was long past those hang-ups!), this was not the reading material I would have selected. But I politely scanned the pages (with perhaps a pause or two!) before handing the binder back to him. This was obviously a technique he used with male passengers to get good tips. Because of his ingenuity, I recall being a bit more generous with the tip than usual.

Visit to Lieutenant General Chesty Puller's Tomb

Chesty Puller is among the giants of the Marine Corps. His service stemmed from World War One, the Banana Wars, pre-war China, World War Two, and Korea. He retired in 1956, the recipient of five Navy Crosses. Books have been written about this great Marine. During one of my many trips to the Marine Base at Quantico, I decided to make a pilgrimage to his final resting place, in Saluda, Virginia. On top of his tomb was resting a freshly-starched camouflage USMC cover (hat) and three connected shiny silver stars, denoting the rank of lieutenant general. It was clear that some Marine provided daily maintenance to Chesty's tomb. It was my honor and privilege to pay that visit and show my respects for one of my heroes.

PLANK HOLDER IN THE NEW 4TH DIVISION STAFF

When I first transferred to New Orleans, I was assigned to the Headquarters of the Marine Reserve Forces to serve in various capacities, but primarily to be part of a battle staff that would be assembled for exercises. After a year or so in New Orleans, Marine Forces Reserve (MARFORRES) was reorganized to actually create both a 4th Division staff and a 4th Air Wing staff. We got a general and a bunch of dedicated billets, and some solid focus. At the time I became the deputy assistant G-3 (I was still a lieutenant colonel) working for Colonel Joe Sawyer, a good fellow and an attorney from Alabama. While Joe did a fine job and became a good friend, I was saddened that my good pal Jim Preston did not get the G-3 position.

In the musical chairs that occurred, a couple of years later I became the G-3 "actual" (assistant chief of staff, operations), then later the inspector general (assistant chief of staff, readiness G-7). Frankly, we were a pretty flexible group of senior officers, all with a ton of experience, including command time. When tasks or exercises arose we would often pick the person, notwithstanding his or her present billet, who was either the most qualified or available, or both. Because there were so few of us, this flexibility was truly a necessity.

PROMOTED TO COLONEL

As someone who doubted he would ever make corporal, making full colonel was quite a humbling event. I was given a date when the ceremony was to be held, on a weekend, and took Cathy with me to New Orleans that month. After the ceremony, conducted in the office of the commanding general (but not a big extravaganza), Colonel Jim and Jeanne Preston joined us for a fun lunch in the French Quarter. I still couldn't believe that I actually had eagles on my collar!

SITTING IN A BOX OF KITTY LITTER UNDER A SUNLAMP

During all of my Marine Corps service, I have spent a considerable amount of time at the Marine Corps Air Ground Combat Center at Twentynine Palms, California. It is a very big place, consisting of close to 1,000 square miles of the California desert. Although there is a built-up portion of the base with many buildings, schools, bowling alley, gym, headquarters, etc., etc., 99 percent of the base is raw desert. The base started out as an Army Air Corps glider training facility during World War II, was dormant for a while, then was given to the Marine Corps in the late 1950s. When I joined the staff of the 4th Marine Division, I started seeing a lot more of "The Stumps," as the base is sometimes called. I probably participated in a least a dozen (maybe more) two-week Combined Arms Exercises (CAX) in the 1990s. Working and practicing combat skills in 120-degree heat while wearing full combat gear, including a flak vest and helmet, is a real character builder. I could think of places I would rather have been, but few that were as well suited for training realistic to the future threats facing our nation.

COKES FOR THE ROAD GUARDS

I never forgot where I came from. As an officer I believe that I was always kind and considerate to the troops, with the exception of those instances when I dealt with troublesome and disciplinary issues. I don't think I ever returned a salute without providing a smile and a "thank you." I had then, and continue to have, enormous warmth and respect for enlisted Marines. Without understanding my emotions, even as I type this paragraph, my eyes are tearing up with emotion.

Something I really liked to do, and did it often and almost obsessively, was take ice-cold Cokes to the troops out in the middle of the desert at the Marine Corps Air Ground Combat Center (MCAGCC) at Twentynine Palms. Our exercises (and I participated in many) were usually in the middle of the summer when the temperature was 120 degrees in the shade, and there wasn't any! So I found frequent excuses (at my rank, I really didn't need an excuse!) to leave the field and go mainside (a good meal, PX, fart around, or whatever). When returning to the field I would often first go to the Oasis Café and get a dozen or so large Cokes with ice, then give them to the road guards and other young Marines manning isolated posts under the blazing sun.

The appreciation was evident on the faces of the Marines when I handed the Cokes out the window, but most looked a bit puzzled as well—having a full colonel emerge out of nowhere with a Coke for a junior enlisted man was not a common occurrence! God bless those wonderful young men. I am grateful that I had the honor to lead and support them.

A very key and critical issue in the conduct of combat operations is the ability to have secure communications. This is accomplished by using special equipment to encrypt radio transmissions.

Unfortunately, during my entire time in the Marine Corps this was easier said than done, as the equipment was pretty complicated and prone to failure. I realize there are those who would disagree with this assessment, but from my perspective in the trenches, encryption just did not work out. As I reflect on this reality, I don't think I ever participated in an exercise where we didn't plan to encrypt, but never once did it ever come to pass. In the fog of training and with the challenges that go along with complicated activities, all the effort that would have gone into encryption would have measurably detracted from all the other things we needed to accomplish.

Fortunately, things have changed, and encryption is not now the hassle it used to be. Thank goodness for that, as it is a critical area and the last thing combat Marines need is for the bad guys to be listening to our radio transmissions.

Foolish Behavior Necessitated Dangerous Med-Evac in High Winds

Marines are not immune from stupid and immature behavior, and sometimes people do things so foolish as to endanger the lives of others. I was witness to the potential catastrophic consequences of such behavior one very dark summer evening at the top of OP Crampton at the Marine Corps Base at Twentynine Palms.

It was an extremely windy night, and we were on an outcropping several thousand feet above the desert floor. A young lance corporal decided that he would kill a rattlesnake by squirting lighter fluid on it, with the dispenser acting like a flamethrower. First of all, this was just stupid and immature. We did not need to screw with the snakes; ignore them, and generally speaking they will ignore you. Second, he failed to realize that he was spraying lighter fluid into the wind, igniting it as it left the container. He ended up spraying burning lighter fluid all over himself and sustaining some very serious burns over a good portion of his body, much of it exposed because it was so hot (middle of the summer) and his clothing was minimal.

Realistically, the only way to get him off the OP and to medical treatment was via helicopter. But to do so in the dark with the horrific winds was very dangerous. Nevertheless, the two pilots on call that night at the main part of the base for emergency med-evacs decided to try to get him off that mountain. We were all so pissed at the kid we were damn near ready to let him die, yet obviously we didn't take that approach. After several efforts, the Huey helicopter (UH-1) managed to touch down, load him on board, and transport him to the base hospital. I know he did not die, but beyond that I don't know what his fate was. He was badly burned and I am sure he required a considerable amount of prolonged medical care.

COMMENDED BY THE COMMANDANT OF THE MARINE CORPS

One of the professional highlights of my Marine Corps career was being personally and warmly commended by General Mundy, the Commandant of the Marine Corps (CMC), for my performance as the Assistant Chief of Staff (G-3) during a Combined Arms Exercise (CAX) at the MCAGCC, Twentynine Palms. I was the fellow who planned and orchestrated the activities of scores of aircraft, armored vehicles, and hundreds of men in a very successful and realistic amphibious combat exercise.

Not bad for someone who once doubted he would ever go beyond private first class!

A DIFFERENT KIND OF INSPECTOR GENERAL

As I completed my tour as the assistant chief of staff, G-3, Brigadier General Fred Lopez, a long-time friend and the new commanding general of the 4th Marine Division, asked if I was interested in becoming the Inspector General of the 4th Marine Division. The official title was Assistant Chief of Staff, G-7 (Readiness). I told General Lopez that I would be honored to assume that position.

However, I diplomatically indicated a condition that I felt was essential if I was to take on the position: that a deficient report by me or my personnel would not result in adverse action against the commanding officer of the inspected unit, unless there was intentional misconduct, fraud, or clearly negligent performance. I also needed the ability to mobilize "assist" teams to help a unit get up to acceptable performance, before finalizing my inspection report. In the past, it was not unusual for the previous commanding general of Marine Forces Reserve to order the relief of a commanding officer, based on deficient inspection results. But it was my opinion that some of those reliefs were unnecessary and inappropriate. General Lopez shook my hand and said he saw things in exactly the same light. I became the inspector general.

In the approximately two years that I held this position, my section conducted scores of various types of inspections, including MORDTs (Mobilization Organizational Readiness Deployment Tests), which were unannounced and greatly feared. My biggest challenge was making sure that the personnel who constituted my inspection team manpower (most of whom were in various reserve staff groups throughout the nation) deferred to my leadership and direction. These were good people, mostly senior field-grade officers including several full colonels, who were used to performing inspections and having the final say in the results, as opposed to now falling under the cognizance of the commanding general of the 4th Marine Division, which meant working for me. There were a few spirited discussions. But, using a combination of goodwill, persuasion, education, and just a tad bit of authority, I got things under control and pretty much smoothed out among all the inspectors.

During my tenure, not one commanding officer was relieved because of inspection results. It was the norm, rather than the exception, for me to put my people in assist mode, as opposed to inspection mode, immediately upon arrival. Also, it was common for me to call headquarters and get approval for "man-days" authorization, the military equivalent of overtime for the unit, to bring in some personnel to assist in resolving a problem area discovered during the inspection period. I was proud to say that my inspection reflected the state of the unit at the time the team departed, not at the time it arrived. Needless to say, I was well thought of throughout the division for compassion and common sense. My previous experience as an enlisted Marine absolutely contributed to my approach in these types of activities.

Painful Investigation of a Fellow Colonel

This was nasty and painful. During a two-week period at Twentynine Palms in a large tent out in the middle of the desert, one of my fellow colonels (who was known as a very religious man and a non-drinker) did something that ended his promising career. He got drunk with a bunch of enlisted Marines, switched collar insignias with a sergeant, participated in singing truly raunchy songs, hoisted a female nurse (lieutenant) in the air and paraded around the tent while holding her in his arms— against her will and despite her protests. She made a formal complaint, and it was given to me to investigate.

It was what it was, and despite my efforts to be as helpful as I could

176

to his defense attorney, he was forced into retirement. Fortunately, he was allowed to retire as a full colonel, but probably six or so years before mandatory retirement. He had been the executive officer of an aviation squadron during the First Gulf War, had just been elevated to the presidency of a very significant military support organization, and there was a very good chance—prior to this incident—that he would have been among the very few reserve colonels to actually promote to the rank of brigadier general.

The pain I felt for him was somewhat minimized, as I was aware of and had been troubled by a "dark side" of him that some others had not seen. About a year before, to keep from being embarrassed over a relatively minor issue, he flat-out lied to a general by saying he had made a notification to a major on an issue, when in fact I was absolutely aware that he had not made the notification. At the time, and in the presence of the general, I diplomatically corrected him. He responded—incorrectly—that it was I who was wrong. His actions had the potential, had I not intervened, to be damaging to the major's career. I was very troubled by this behavior, which was especially puzzling because of the overt way he wore his Christianity on his sleeve. I believe he was morally corrupt, with variable ethics, and that his forced retirement was in the Corps' best interests.

TROUBLING INFORMATION ABOUT A GENERAL (SELECT)

I still don't know the whole story on this situation. There was a fellow colonel on the staff, who in civilian life was married and an attorney in the Midwest. His closest associate was the colonel who was forced into retirement over the escapade that involved manhandling the Navy nurse while drunk.

This particular colonel was among several of us who were in the zone for consideration for promotion to brigadier general. As a fairly junior colonel I knew I was not really competitive for the selection board; the colonel in question was competitive, along with several others. There was very clearly a growing sense of anticipation about this particular colonel's potential selection, but it was really puzzling to me and others. He continually discussed the issue with passion. The later-disgraced colonel, who was a key player in an influential Marine Corps reserve association, discussed the matter as if it was likely that this colonel would be selected. Finally, the commanding general and the assistant division commanding general—both fine gentlemen and great Marines—also discussed this same colonel to the exclusion of the other colonels, with the same sense of anticipation. It was obvious that things were happening behind the scenes, and that most likely these two generals had been pushing—again behind the scenes—the selection board to select this particular colonel for promotion.

Well, it happened. The selection board results were announced, and he was one of about four reserve colonels (from a total of probably four hundred reserve colonels) selected for promotion to brigadier general. It was no surprise. But I was at a loss about how this had occurred, as it was inconsistent with the fairness and procedures as I understood the process to be. Now I think I have figured it out—politics at the highest levels plays a major role in general officer promotions.

I had real reservations about this guy, and at one time I even considered sharing some of my observations with one of the two generals who later became a real sponsor of his. He was incredibly bright and knowledgeable about the Corps, and complex operational strategies and processes, but seemed weak in essential character traits. I felt that he was reckless and immature, and that he had a sense of inappropriate entitlement based on his rank. First, he drove his automobile like a teenager, frequently gunning the engine and racing around corners on two wheels—not the kind of behavior you associate with a mature adult. Second, I had a very strong sense that he was engaged in extramarital affairs that had the potential to blow up in his face and be an embarrassment to the Corps. It was a matter that first came to my attention based on rather cryptic comments made by not-too-happy-with-him Navy nurses, when I investigated the disgraced colonel. Finally, when people did nice things for him he barely acknowledged their actions. This was a matter that really hit me when I shipped an entire box of antique Marine Corps uniforms to him for his collection, and never even got a "thank you." I had the sense that he felt he could pretty much do as he pleased, and that some of the rules that pertained to the rest of us did not apply to him.

A couple of other issues, in hindsight, should probably have derailed this fellow's promotion. I believe it occurred after selection but before pinning on his star. On at least one occasion one of the two generals became aware that this colonel was focusing inappropriate attention on a female major, and quietly told him to knock it off. Also, it was fairly common knowledge that he—and again, the later disgraced colonel—had engaged in some type of troubling behavior while on a deployment to Korea, but it never became an official matter.

Subsequent to his promotion to brigadier general, he became the commanding general of a reserve command on the East Coast. Within about a year all of these weak character traits exploded in his face, and he did in fact bring discredit to the Marine Corps. As a commanding general, he became engaged in a sexual relationship with the wife of a Marine sergeant (violating the wife of an enlisted Marine is beyond a mortal sin in the USMC!) When confronted with the issue, he lied to his boss, a lieutenant general. There were other problems with his behavior and actions, as well, as his true character deficiencies came to the surface, but they paled in comparison to his actions with the wife of an enlisted man. He was relieved of command, demoted back to colonel, and forced to retire from the Marine Corps. Then authorities in his state charged him with state tax evasion, convicted him, and put him on criminal probation. It is unfortunate that he cast the Corps in such an unpleasant light.

I continue to feel pain for the two generals, who I know really went to bat to get this guy promoted to brigadier general. Both are truly wonderful men who I respect greatly, and I have every confidence that they truly believed him to be the best, brightest, and most deserving. While the opportunity is not likely to arise, and if it did the pain would probably prevent a candid discussion on this issue, I would really like to hear the whole story on this man from one of those generals who influenced his promotion. Knowing they orchestrated the promotion of a person who brought such discredit on the Corps, and that in so doing prevented the promotion to general of a more deserving person, has to be very painful for these gentlemen. Like me, both of these generals have been retired for over ten years.

I have asked myself several times if I should have shared my reservations about this colonel, who was a colleague and potential competitive officer, with one or both of the two generals who were clearly his sponsors. On one hand, the information would certainly have been of value. However, the information may well have been poorly received and seen as biased because it was coming from a disgruntled promotional candidate. Also, for someone to step outside the box and be this candid with a general about another high-ranking officer would have been outside the norm of acceptable interaction. It was also very clear that these two generals really liked this guy. So in all likelihood, the only victim from such a candid discussion would probably have been me!

As I teach leadership, and mentor high-ranking law enforcement officials, I frequently think of this situation as I consider the dilemma of how to select those people one chooses to intensely mentor and push ahead in various organizations. This experience has influenced me in arriving at a couple of additional criteria to be applied in determining whether someone is worthy of being pushed up professionally. First, does he or she have credibility with their peers? This fellow looked good to his superiors, but not to his peers. Second, is he or she someone who routinely does thoughtful things for others when there is not likely to be any personal payoff? Again, this fellow would have flunked this test big time; everything was for and about him.

EXONERATING AN INNOCENT COLONEL

As the inspector general it was my responsibility, circumstances permitting, to personally conduct sensitive investigations involving fellow colonels. A regular Marine female gunnery sergeant assigned to a regimental inspector-instructor staff within the 4th Division, filed a formal complaint of sexual harassment against the regimental commanding officer and a male gunnery sergeant. She alleged direct harassment by her gunnery sergeant colleague in the administrative section, and biased treatment because of her gender and ethnicity (she was a minority) by the regimental commanding officer. The colonel who was the focus of the allegations had just received orders to a coveted assignment at the Pentagon; obviously, those orders were placed in abeyance pending the outcome of my investigation. I was assigned to personally conduct the investigation, and had to make several trips to regimental headquarters during the inquiry.

It did not take long to realize that her accusations were totally without merit, and that she was the one who had acted inappropriately in a variety of situations. Then, when she started to experience the very predictable consequences of her poor performance and behavior, she attempted to turn herself into the victim. This was not the first time I encountered this type of troublesome behavior during my police and military careers. Some of the actions that triggered the consequences she found troubling included not showing up for work as scheduled, deficient performance in the conduct of critical administrative tasks, inappropriate use of a government credit card, and failing to take the physical fitness tests as directed and required. However, based on the sensitive nature of the sexual harassment charge and the potential likelihood that my investigation would be closely scrutinized, I was determined to ensure that it was the most comprehensive investigation ever seen by the Judge Advocate

General (JAG) in the Marine Forces Reserve (MARFORRES), which was higher headquarters over the 4th Marine Division.

My investigation not only completely disproved her allegations, but also uncovered additional problematic actions on her part. The scores of interviews I conducted made clear that her conduct and performance were totally substandard and unacceptable for a person of her rank, and that she lacked the knowledge required of her position. Among a variety of uncomplimentary actions was my discovery that she had falsified a note from a physician in order to be excused from physical activities! My report and investigative findings were as solid as could be, and were cited by the JAG as comprehensive and irrefutable. In addition to finding her allegations without merit, I made several recommendations pertaining to her including additional training, closer supervision, and an evaluation of her physical fitness for continued military service.

Not surprisingly, she tried to torpedo my investigation. As a prominent member of the Women Marines Association (WMA), she went directly to a female general who had a reputation for taking special interest in women's issues, and who some thought was unrealistically sympathetic to gender allegations (I do not know if this was accurate). This female general obviously went straight to my general. A copy of my investigation (about four inches thick!) ended up on his desk, with numerous yellow sticky notes scattered throughout its pages.

My commanding general had just replaced the former general. Known as very political, he was someone—in my judgment—who would not have hesitated to sacrifice me if he could advance his standing with this particular female general. Somewhat boldly, but diplomatically, I entered his office. While pointing to my investigation, I feigned surprise that he had a copy (it had previously been approved by the outgoing commanding general and forwarded to the JAG), and asked if he had any questions. He said he had no questions, and that was almost the end of the issue. But the new commanding general had brought with him a new chief of staff, a colonel who was the same ethnicity as the female gunnery sergeant. During transitional discussions, this colonel commented that any investigation as thick as the one I had conducted most assuredly had to be a "cover-up" of some sort. I cannot think of a time when I came closer to knocking a fellow Marine officer on his ass!

The "hold" on the proposed reassignment of the regimental commanding officer was lifted and he did receive his new, coveted assignment at the Pentagon. I never did follow up to determine the fate of the female gunnery sergeant. But I am quite certain that her allegations, which I proved to be without merit, and the new issues about her that stemmed from my findings, did no good for her career.

Disappointed With the New Commanding General

I chose to leave the 4th Division staff when a newly promoted general, whom I thought poorly of, became the commanding general. In my judgment, this fellow reflected the epitome of troubling general officer politics. When he was initially promoted there was wide-spread disappointment and outrage, as it was painfully clear that his promotion had been based on politics, favoritism and Beltway intrigue, as opposed to performance and merit.

Just about his entire career as a senior officer had been spent in a staff group assignment, not out in the commands and trenches like the rest of us. He had been a senior aide to a United States senator and had superb contacts at the highest levels of government. I am certain that he took and/or orchestrated actions that benefitted the Marine Corps. But, like just about everyone else, I felt that promotion to general officer over much more qualified and deserving colonels should not have been his reward. It was well known that he had a superb relationship with the commandant and other senior general officers. These high-level contacts were obvious during his tenure as a general officer, continued right up to his retirement extravaganza, and fueled cynicism of the general officer promotion process. I remain surprised that the top leadership of the Corps was not more sensitive to the impression this troubling issue created in the minds of many.

I was displeased when he was assigned as my commanding general. At the time I was the inspector general, and one of his several key staff officers. Without any conflict or rancor, I was not impressed with his demeanor during the single weekend drill in which we served together, and decided that I did not want to serve as one of his top people. I contacted the commanding general of the I MEF Augmentation Command Element (MACE) at Camp Pendleton, who had previously offered me an assignment, and arranged for transfer to that command.

I must confess that my impression of this person was likely tainted by my disdain for the process that caused him to be promoted. While far from the most worthy and deserving, I am sure that he was basically a good person and an honorable Marine.

A terrible tragedy occurred along the Rio Grande river in the community of Redford, Texas. Four Marines had been loaned to JTF-6 (Joint Task Force) out of El Paso, and were deployed in a alleged concealed "hide site" to watch for narcotic smugglers, when they shot and killed an 18-year-old man who was herding his goats.

The subsequent investigations, which became very controversial because of the involvement of ethnic and immigrants rights groups, revealed the matter to be an unfortunate and unintentional tragedy. The young man saw the Marines, who were dressed in bizarre camouflage outfits, out in the area where he herded his goats, and he fired a couple of .22 rounds in their direction. In self-defense, one of the Marines fired back and killed the lad. Headquarters contacted me—at the time the marshal of San Bernardino County—to go on active duty and lead the investigation, which I was certainly capable of doing. However, it was then decided to add a Marine lawyer (JAG) and his assistant (also a lawyer) to the team.

Before it was over, a two-star general who was also a lawyer (and a great guy, notwithstanding some disagreements), was put in charge of the team. In my judgment, the effort became a bureaucratic cluster fornication! Politics took precedence over the practical, and form became more important than substance. The key attorney (a nice guy), who was a lieutenant colonel, spent literally hours each day on the phone talking with attorneys at Headquarters Marine Corps. Every step we took was discussed and vetted by a distant group of attorneys. The final straw for me occurred on the ground at the shooting site, when we most likely found the shell casings from the rifle the kid had used to fire on the Marines. When the Presidio County Sheriff's Department declined to get involved and book the shell casings as evidence, the combined legal troika decided that the casings should remain where they were on the ground. My pleas to photograph them in place, then carefully gather and send them to the Texas Department of Public Safety, fell on deaf ears. Before it was over, the lieutenant colonel insisted on rewriting even my interview notes for consistency with his writing style.

I found a way of disengaging from the investigation a bit prematurely. This experience was one among several that convinced me of the inappropriateness of having a lawyer lead an investigation. They were all good people with good intentions, but the process should have been led by an experienced and talented investigator, with significant legal support. This matter was largely resolved through tighter rules governing military participation with federal law enforcement authorities, strengthened training, and a monetary settlement to the family of the victim.

———

I MEF Augmentation Command Element

In mid-1997, after approximately six years on the staff of the 4th Marine Division, I transferred to the Augmentation Command Element of the 1st Marine Expeditionary Force at Camp Pendleton, as the head of the Operations Group. This outfit was essentially a manpower and training entity for senior officers and senior enlisted personnel, with the mission of preparing senior personnel for key positions to augment deployment with the I MEF. In additional to potential activation at some point, there were always exercises and other events where some degree of augmentation was necessary, and the folks in this outfit got quite a lot of experience with their active duty counterparts.

My Last Marine Corps Assignment

My last assignment in the Marine Corps was Head, Operations Group, I MACE at Camp Del Mar. I enjoyed this assignment, and felt that I made a real and positive difference in attracting and preparing some outstanding folks for augmentation when needed. It was close to home, at the beach, and I had the opportunity to work with some fine people. My last commanding general was Brigadier General Frank Quinlan, a friend and great guy who treated me very well.

I actually submitted my retirement papers in July 1998, which was several months before the date that I had to retire. I did this for unselfish reasons. We were starting to ramp-up for a critical exercise in Korea, and my mandatory retirement date in mid-1999 pretty much coincided with the end of that exercise. It seemed a waste to invest all that training and preparation expertise in a person who was on the very brink of retirement. Also, it was hard to build up my typical enthusiastic head-of-steam over this particular deployment, as I knew the effort would be wasted and it would be my swan song. As a result, I applied for retirement effective the same month that the extensive planning process was due to commence. There was another reason, as well: I wanted to go out "on top," while all was well. I was still badly stinging from the poor manner in which I'd been treated when retiring from another organization that I loved, the Los Angeles Police Department.

So I felt it was the right time to go—when all was well and positive.

Retirement From the Marine Corps

It was my desire to have a low-key retirement ceremony, one that involved all ranks from private to general, in a somewhat casual setting where I would be given the opportunity to share my thoughts with all of my fellow Marines. Given my rank and service, I was entitled to a very formal ceremony—including a parade—where the entire unit would "pass in review" in honor of the retiree. While I may have been a colonel, I still recalled what a pain it was for all the troops to rehearse and be involved in parade practice in preparation for such an event. Had I exercised this option, the drill weekend would have been dominated by practice and preparation for my retirement ceremony. I wanted no part of such formality.

Instead, I asked only to be given the opportunity, in a "school circle" setting (informally gathered around me in a shady area), to address all the Marines. I wanted my family present, as well. I specifically requested that the uniform of the day (again my call) be the utility uniform (the most casual). Finally, I asked that everyone of every rank be my guest at the Officer's Club, after my remarks, for beverages and heavy hors d'oeuvres.

General Quinlin honored my desires, and it was a great experience. I spoke to all the troops about the Corps, about the honor of serving, the need for every person to be proficient in their occupational fields, and strongly encouraged all to remain in the reserves. Cathy and my adult children were present. After my remarks, we all retired to the Officer's Club for a most enjoyable and casual event.

Afterward, Cathy and I drove home and there, for the last time, I took off my Marine uniform.

Post-USMC Retirement Thoughts & Actions

Prior to the early 1970s, just about every physically-fit young man served in the military. Except for different types of deferments (married with kids, full-time college student, or juice with someone at the local draft board), young men either enlisted in the service branch of their choice or were drafted for two years into the Army. While I am extremely pro-military, I also recognize that the military, while a very good thing, is not the only way to serve your country or to gain exceptional skills. Thus I am not the least bit critical of those who did not serve, except for intentional draft dodgers when the draft was in effect.

The military has yielded some of the very finest men I have ever had the honor to associate with. However, it has also produced some of the biggest jerks I have ever known. Bottom line, is that I think the military is of tremendous value in the acquisition of unique skills and perspectives. But I also clearly realize that these same qualities can also be acquired in other ways.

With respect to the women who have served: Ladies, you are truly extraordinary and, generally speaking, you have acquired superb skills and perspectives that your sisters will never know.

———

Return to the Corps and Orders to Iraq

We all remember the events of September 11, 2001, when our world forever changed. On that day, three American commercial airliners were hijacked by Muslim extremists and deliberately crashed into the "twin towers" of the World Trade Center in New York City and the Pentagon in Washington. Another plane, apparently targeted for the White House or the U.S. Capitol building, crashed into a Pennsylvania field after several heroic Americans aboard fought back against the terrorists who had seized the aircraft. Immediately, many reservists were called up for a variety of duties, and the Marines invaded Iraq. To say that I was itching to get into the fight was an understatement; I wanted very badly to return to the Corps and do my part.

However, there was a timing issue. First, I needed to complete my retirement process from the San Bernardino County Sheriff's Department. I was in a parallel law enforcement career by this time, along with my Marine Corps career. It was all but certain that the county would grant me disability retirement because of a right hand that never completely recovered from carpel tunnel surgery. But to return to active military duty and head for combat before that county process had run its course, would certainly invalidate my disability claim, even though the Marine Corps indicated that the limitations on one hand would not disqualify me for active duty.

I was in the pipeline to rotate into Camp Fallujah and head up a unique intelligence gathering function, and had been approved/selected by then-Major General Amos of the 2nd Marine Division (named as Commandant of the Marine Corps in 2010). My retirement was approved in May of 2005, and I was slated to report to Camp Pendleton no later than July first. I had my orders in hand, purchased new uniforms, was receiving daily message briefings from the headquarters unit in Iraq of which I would part, and had coordinated my report date with the Mobilization Unit (commanded by my good friend, Colonel Harry Williams).

Then, about two weeks before reporting, I got an e-mail from Iraq stating that Headquarters, U. S. Marine Corps, had denied my request for active duty. The Marine Corps, just before I was due to report, rescinded the waiver policy for any retiree who had reached the age of sixty, my age at the time.

I was devastated then, and remain broken-hearted, at my inability to serve my country this one last time.

I remain grateful that Cathy, although reluctantly, had finally agreed to support my return to the Marine Corps. The burden of our foster kids would have been hers alone, and she took it like a trooper. One benefit for her would have been a few months of not having to listen to me snore at night! I worked very hard to get myself back into acceptable physical shape, including the use of a personal trainer at a gym. I also spent a great deal of time getting myself back up to par regarding professional military education. Although age had taken its toll, I was back within the umbrella of acceptable physical and professional skills at the time the waiver rule was rescinded. I am stilled pissed about the last-minute cancellation of my orders to combat duty in Iraq.

(Left) My father, David Bushey, as a private in "B" Company, 1st Gas Regiment (mustard gas!) at Edgewood Arsenal, Maryland. 1919.

(Below) Dinner party, 1944. From left to right: My Uncle Keith Hood (mom's brother), his wife Ilene, my Aunt Dot (mom's sister) my mother and dad, Mary and David Bushey. Mom was pregnant with me at the time.

(Above) My older brother, Larry, mom and me. At home in San Gabriel, circa 1947.

(Left) Laurence D. Bushey at the Field Music School, Marine Corps Recruit Depot, San Diego. 1951.

(Right) Pfc. Laurence David Bushey, USMC, stands at left in this photo taken at the San Francisco Naval Shipyard. Photo appeared on the cover of Leatherneck *magazine, July 1951.*

(Top left) Keith and Mary Bushey, Balboa Fun Zone. Circa 1952.

(Above) Keith Bushey in 1952, shortly before getting kicked out of the Cub Scouts.

Left: Keith Bushey, age sixteen. Duarte High School, 1961.

USMC Infantry training photo.
March 1962.

Pfc. Keith Bushey at Camp
Pendleton, California. 1962.

(Left and below) Marines Pfc. Bushey outside the Message Center, Guantanamo Bay,
during the Cuban Missile Crisis. 1962.

Pfc. Bushey (white shirt) clowns around with some buddies while aboard a troopship bound for Korea, circa 1963.

Pfc. Keith D. Bushey takes five in the Communications Center at Camp Hansen, Okinawa. 1963.

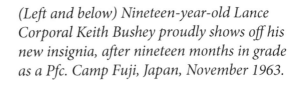

(Left and below) Nineteen-year-old Lance Corporal Keith Bushey proudly shows off his new insignia, after nineteen months in grade as a Pfc. Camp Fuji, Japan, November 1963.

Lance Corporal Bushey (center) administers haircuts to his pals aboard a troopship somewhere in the Pacific, circa 1964.

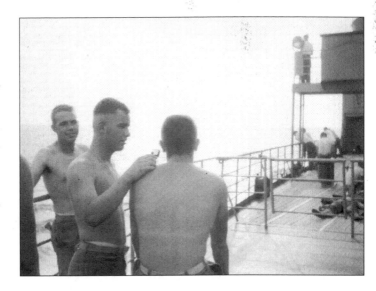

(Above) Mary Bushey at our home in Duarte, 1963.

(Right) Keith Bushey during assignment to the LAPD's Jail Division, 1967.

(Below) Driving the "Paddy Wagon" hauling drunks to jail. LAPD Central Division, 1966.

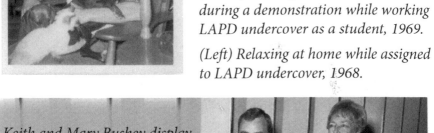

(Above) Keith speaks to the media during a demonstration while working LAPD undercover as a student, 1969.

(Left) Relaxing at home while assigned to LAPD undercover, 1968.

Keith and Mary Bushey display Keith's badge collection at an LAPD recruiting event, 1967.

LAPD Chief Edward Davis promotes Keith D. Bushey to sergeant, 1970.

1Lt Bushey, USMC Jump School graduation, Ft. Benning, 1973.

Naval Amphibious Base, Coronado, CA, 1974.

Lt. Keith D. Bushey, LAPD Rampart Division, 1979.

(Right) Stacy, Keith, Zak and Jake Bushey. Photo taken at the LAPD, Los Angeles. 1984.

Below: LAPD Capitol Hill representative Keith Bushey visits the Oval Office in the White House, Washington, DC. 1985.

(Above) Captain Keith Bushey, Los Angeles Police Department, 1985.

(Above) Zak Bushey enjoys the view from the hills overlooking the San Gabriel Valley, 1987.

(Right) Stacy and Major Keith Bushey at the Marine Corps Ball, 1987.

(Below) Keith and Cathy Bushey at the Police Memorial Run, 1989.

(Right) Cathy and Keith Bushey, 1988.

(Below) Lt. Col. Keith Bushey, USMC, commanding officer of 3D ANGLICO, prepares to exit a C-141 over Camp Pendleton, California. 1989.

(Below) Mary Bushey joins Keith as he prepares for a parachute operation. 3D ANGLICO Family Day, 1990.

(Left) Stacy Ann Bushey, 1991.

(Below) Jake Bushey, in his LAPD Academy graduation portrait, 1995.

(Bottom left) Jake Bushey with Los Angeles Police Department Chief Daryl Gates. Circa 1992.

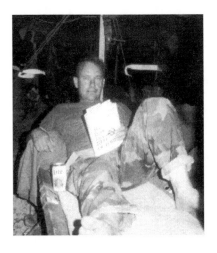

(Above left) Col. Keith Bushey gets some sack time at the Marine Corps Air-Ground Combat Center, Twentynine Palms, California. Circa 1996.

(Above right) Captain "Andy" Anderson and Marshal Keith Bushey at the Nevada Police Games, 1997. (The medals are perhaps more a reflection of the fewer participants in our age class, than our superb performance.)

(Above) Colonel Keith Bushey, USMC, 1996.

(Above) Deputy Chief Keith Bushey, San Bernardino County Sheriff's Department, 2004.

(Above) Alyssa, Jake, Anna and Matthew Bushey, 2012.

(Above) Keith's brother Larry Bushey's son Tommy and daughter, Nancy, pose at the beach with Uncle Keith, 2012.

(Left) Larry's youngest son, Bill Bushey, circa 1988. Bill is a California Highway Patrol officer today.

Danielle Marie Bushey, 2009.

(Above) Toni, Zak and Addison ("Addie") Bushey, 2012.

(Above) The Busheys' foster son, Dan Bustamante, with his daughter Serena and son Nathan. The trio joined Grandpa Keith Bushey at the Huntington Beach pier, in summer 2012.

(Right) Cathy and Keith Bushey, 2001.

Deputy game wardens Keith Bushey (left) and Jack Herman patrolling in the Angeles National Forest, circa 1981.

Deputy Chief Keith Bushey "cheating death" in Copper Canyon on the Colorado River while with the San Bernardino County Sheriff's Department, 2004.

(Left) The Busheys attended a luau at Old Lahaina, Maui, Hawaii, in February 2003. Left to right: Zak, Keith, Spencer Anderson, Cathy and Stacy.

The Bushey clan at home with some of their toys, summer 2012. Left to right: Spencer, Danielle, Cathy, Keith, Will and Matthew.

The photograph above shows a portion of the Bushey family's law enforcement badge museum, 2012. On display are some 5,000 badges!

CHAPTER TEN

BECOMING A COP

Note: Once again, the reader is reminded that even though my life went down several parallel paths simultaneously, these memoirs are only able to describe one path at a time. Consequently, there will be some comments pertaining to situations to which the reader has not yet been introduced. Continued indulgence is appreciated.

APPLICATIONS TO OTHER LAW ENFORCEMENT AGENCIES

Like just about any other young man who ever wanted to be a cop, I looked at and applied to several different agencies before starting with the Los Angeles County Sheriff's Department, then moving over to the Los Angeles Police Department. A few of these departments are worthy of mention:

My brother was a policeman in the desert town of Blythe during the summer of 1965, when I was just about to get off USMC active duty. We both thought it would be nice if I went to work there, too. So I went to Blythe, met the chief (Hugh Ingram), who was very pleasant and supportive. He gave me the written test in his office and I did well. However, before hiring me he had to get the city council's okay to hire the relative of an existing city employee, because of a nepotism rule. Before the city council even took up the issue, my brother resigned to take the position of assistant city manager in Desert Hot Springs. Thank goodness, it didn't work out! I was much better off where I ended up, in Los Angeles.

While I still had just a year or so left in the Corps, I knew I wanted to be a cop, and was madly in love with a Mormon gal from Utah who worked with my mom at the City of Hope. I just knew that we would end up getting married, have a bunch of little Mormon children, and live in Utah. Accordingly, I sent a letter to the police chief in Ogden

208

(her home town) inquiring about employment there as a cop. The chief replied that the minimum hiring age for that department was 25 years old, and to contact him in a few years if I was still interested! Guess it was a maturity rule. The job did not work out, and neither did the gal I was madly in love with. I recently learned that she still lives in Utah, is in her late 60s, but that she never did marry. I hope I didn't ruin her for someone else!

The city of Arcadia also seemed like a good place to be a cop. It sits right in the middle of the San Gabriel Valley, the old stomping grounds from my youth. I applied, passed the written, and then flunked the oral. I don't know why, but it was also probably a good thing. Nevertheless, some twenty-five years later I was contacted by a search firm and encouraged to apply for the Arcadia P.D. chief's position! I chose not to apply for it, but had some fun with the headhunter when I told him I had previously been found unacceptable as an officer there. As luck would have it, one of my high school pals, Dave Hinig, went to Arcadia and eventually became chief. Dave is a great guy, and did a fine job as the chief before retiring. Dave continues to take interim police chief positions from time to time.

When my brother went to Desert Hot Springs as the assistant city manager (he lasted about two weeks, if that), I gave up on Blythe and applied with the Coachella Police Department, which is kind of a suburb of Indio. I got a nice letter back from the chief, with an invitation to come to the station, meet him, and take the written test. But in the envelope with the nice letter from the chief was a note from a disgruntled officer that said; "This place is a mess; if you know what is good for you, you should join the Riverside Sheriff's Department." He even signed it with his badge and number! He must have been on his way out the door, as that was a pretty gutsy thing to do. I kept the note for years, and probably still have it in one of my boxes out in the garage. Anyway, before I got the chance to go to Coachella to take the test, my brother had left Desert Hot Springs.

West Covina was close to home and also seemed like a good place to be a cop. When I went to the police station, which as I recall was in a residence being used as a temporary facility, I was immediately measured to ensure that I was 5' 8" in height. I was about a quarter-inch too short. There went my career with the West Covina Police Department.

Chapter Eleven
LOS ANGELES COUNTY SHERIFF'S DEPARTMENT

Joining the Los Angeles County Sheriff's Department—Strategy

I was just a tad bit too short to be a cop. Both the Los Angeles County Sheriff's Department and the Los Angeles Police Department required applicants to be at least 5' 8" in height. However, I was about a quarter-inch shorter than that. I devised a plan that I thought might resolve that problem. First, I would become a reserve deputy sheriff, and have my height measured by a more lenient reserve physician. I could then use that physical examination when I transitioned (hopefully) to become a regular deputy sheriff. It worked! However, I did not stay with the Sheriff's Department.

Sheriff's Reserve Class #11

Just after turning twenty-one years of age in November of 1965, and while enrolled as a first-semester student at Citrus College, I applied to be a sheriff's reserve deputy out of the Temple City Station (the same station where I had been detained and booked for burglary as a teenager).

Everything went well, including being measured at the required 5' 8" height by a very nice (and lenient!) physician who was also a reserve deputy sheriff. The academy, even though a reserve academy, was actually pretty tough, being run much like Marine Corps boot camp. I did fine there, but some folks who lacked a military background did not. It included a lot of memory work and the hated and constant "switchee-changee" exercises, where we had to change from our PT uniforms into our training uniforms then back into our PT uniforms quite often, in a very hurried and frantic process. It was also tough physically, especially the runs up and down the long driveway between the Academy and Eastern Avenue.

Running Up and Down a Steep Canyon

A particularly challenging running route was up and down a steep trail from the Academy to the bottom of the canyon to its immediate east. That canyon is now home to the Long Beach Freeway and several industrial complexes.

"Off-the-Street Program"

I applied and was transitioning to the "off the street program," to become a regular deputy, and got past the height issue as planned. I was first assigned to Biscaluz Center, then detailed to the gatehouse outside the Sybil Brand Institute for Women. My job was to check the weapons of the officers from many agencies who were going in and out of the secure building, as weapons could not be taken into the jail.

While transitioning from reserve to regular status, I got some disappointing news: I would not be starting the next regular class of the sheriff's academy, after all. This was near-devastating, as I was mentally and physically prepared and wanted to get started with my career. Although treated okay, we "off-the-streeters" were pretty much second-class citizens, and even had to turn in our badges at the end of our shifts. Even if I had started the next academy class, about two weeks away, I would have spent four months in the academy and about another four or five years at the jail, as the department had not yet established correctional or custody officer positions. It would have been quite a while before I would see the inside of a patrol car, but it was a wait I was prepared to accept. However, I felt very irritated by the delay before being able to start the academy.

Adios, Sheriff's Department!

The Los Angeles Police Department permitted interested parties to apply for employment when they reached their nineteenth birthday, and a couple of years prior I had done just that. In early 1964 while on leave from the Marine Corps, I took the written, oral, and physical agility tests. A couple months prior to my twenty-first birthday the LAPD started my background check, but at the time I was still inclined to stay with the sheriff's department. That is, until the academy delay fiasco. At the height of my irritation I went home and found my certification from the LAPD in the mail. I was scheduled to start the academy in about two weeks—and that was it. I resigned from the sheriff's department. In less than four months, I had completed the LAPD academy and was patrolling the streets. I have never regretted my decision to go with the LAPD.

While somewhat impulsive at the time, the decision to leave the sheriff's department and go with the LAPD was a huge decision that had an effect on most of the rest of my life. My big issue was just wanting to get into the field and start doing cop things, which is certainly what occurred. While the estimated jail tour when I made the switch was something like three or four years, the sheriff's department created the class of "correction officer" not long after that, and the jail time for new deputies dropped dramatically (as I recall). I had a very high opinion of the L.A. County Sheriff's Department at that time, and that high opinion exists to this day, with some of my very best friends being active and retired members of that great department.

Chapter Twelve
LOS ANGELES POLICE DEPARTMENT

Too Short to be a Cop

The height limit for the LAPD was 5' 8"—and I wasn't! On a good day I could not break 5' 7¾". To hopefully pass the physical, I went to an osteopath in El Monte immediately before the medical exam, and got stretched! He actually put me on a rack, attached leather straps to my feet, and pulled on my body while manipulating my spine. The result was that I was 5' 8½" when I left his office. I lay down in the back of my mom's car while she drove me straight to the Central Receiving Hospital (now the site of the new Rampart Station). The first thing the doctor did was measure my height. But I was once again 5' 7¾", as I had shrunk back down! Nevertheless, the doc wrote 5' 7¾" in pencil, continued the physical, and I passed! A year later, when taking my annual physical as a policeman, I saw the original paperwork and noted that the doctor had changed his pencil markings to 5' 8". I remain so grateful for the actions of that man, and wish I had a way of thanking him. This was truly a critical fork in one of my many roads.

The Police Academy
Recruit Training

I started the LAPD Academy on January 31, 1966, and graduated three months later. I did well there. I think about 110 recruits started and about 86 graduated. I placed number 7.

I worked hard to excel in all areas. I think I was among the top academically, I shot reasonably well, and was in about the top 25 percent in physical fitness. I would've liked to have been one of the top three graduating recruits, but I really couldn't complain at my standing. The academy was demanding, yet I don't believe I was ever in jeopardy of failing anything. The long runs up the hills were pretty tough, but I was in good shape and never even came close to dropping out of formation. In those days, all recruits rode along with regular officers one weekend day each week, after the fifth week of training. All of my ride-alongs were in Central, and that division was my first assignment out of the academy. I ended up as the regular partner with several of the folks I worked with on the weekends out of the academy.

Thirty Percent Attrition—Foolish Self-Fulfilling Prophesy

Even today, some forty-five years after I joined the LAPD, I get sick at the thought of all the wonderful men who washed out of the academy because of an absolute belief and expectation, which became a *de facto* requirement, that about 30% of recruits would prove to be unsuitable and would be washed out of the academy. In hindsight, because I and everyone else pretty much accepted such foolishness as reality, this was a really horrible practice. I recall a conversation (that I am now ashamed of) where I argued with the department's first psychologist, Marty Riser, because I thought he was mistaken in his criticism of this foolish self-fulfilling prophesy. In hindsight, it was so terribly wrong and unfair. To some extent, I think the academy now takes a few inappropriate chances with candidates of questionable suitability, but for the most part LAPD hires fine young men and women.

My Very First Radio Call

On my first ride-along out of the academy (we had, as I recall, three before we graduated), I was assigned to Central Unit 1A87, working with Officer Val Valdez, a good guy I also worked with after graduation from the academy. After fueling up at Parker Center, Val said to "clear" us. I picked up the microphone and said: "One adam eighty-seven clear." The immediate response was three beeps on the radio, and "roger, one adam eighty seven, shots fired, officer down—Lemoyne Street, handle code three!"

At that point I experienced something that inevitably comes with the territory of being a Los Angeles policeman: head thrown back from the rapid acceleration of a high-performance engine, red lights flashing, siren screaming! At every rank, that was the way LAPD did business. It was quite a ride for thirty-one years, and I never lost the exhilaration of responding to "hot" calls. We ran straight into the situations that others ran away from, and I loved every minute of it. Our call that night turned out to be a big nothing, a kid with a BB gun and a cop who slipped and fell while trying to take cover from what he mistakenly thought was a genuine weapon.

Who is This, Ensign Pulver?

One night, on one of my weekend assignments out of the academy, wearing my brand-new uniform and high-and-tight haircut, my partner and I arrested a middle-aged woman for driving under the influence. She was really drunk, and really a mess. She obviously had lived a pretty hard life, reeked of booze and cheap perfume, and had several layers of make-up over a hard face. He handcuffed her and placed her in the back seat of the police unit, with me seated next to her. She looked at me through terribly bloodshot eyes and in a raspy voice, said: "Who the fuck is this, Ensign Pulver?"

A Looky-Loo Needs a New Paint Job

On another weekend assignment while still in the Police Academy, I was working unit 3T5 with Officer Cliff Nutting, a great guy who later became a good friend and a subordinate. 3T5 was a traffic unit working primarily in the University Division (later changed to Southwest Division). We got a call regarding a CPI (City Property Involved) traffic accident. On arrival at the scene we learned that a drunk driver had backed over the motorcycles of two officers, Larry Binkley and Jerome Brackley. The officers had a few scratches, but nothing serious. The sight of the suspect's car, raised up because it was sitting on top of two police motorcycles, was causing quite a back-up of spectators.

I was directing traffic and trying to clear the congestion. But one person was really going slow, not obeying my commands to move on promptly, and it was clear that his attitude toward the police was not that positive. I finally tapped the hood of his car with my flashlight, and a terrible thing occurred: a big spider-web appeared in the paint of his hood! In that era, some people had massive layers of metallic paint on their cars. This was obviously one of them, and I had just ruined his paint job. I was horrified, but said nothing, and he didn't notice what had occurred. I just kept my mouth shut and never heard a word about what happened that night.

For the first couple months of recruit training I carpooled to and from the academy with another recruit, and it was quite an experience. Mike Carter (pseudonym) had an overactive imagination and a brain about the size of a pea. Although married to a lovely girl and the father of two beautiful children, he was cheating with another woman. Mike asked me to go to her house in Temple City and tell her he was called out of town on a trip and would not be seeing her for a while, as part of his strategy to break off the relationship. Foolishly, I agreed. When I went to the house, I was greated by a woman who had to be at least ten years older than Mike, and not all that attractive. When I passed on Mike's message, she replied by commenting that he seemed to have changed "since his assignment as a vice lieutenant, especially after having recently sustained a wound in the shoot-out with armed suspects!" I don't recall my response to her comments, but I probably nodded in agreement as I left.

A couple of days later when on our way home at the end of the day, Mike got into a verbal altercation with a motorist he'd cut off, and used his badge to pull the guy over. He then played a very "heavy" tough-cop role, and gave the guy a bad time and a real tongue-lashing. That was it for me. Beyond being disgusted by this idiot, I was concerned that his actions would get us both fired. So I went to my squad advisor and reported the incident with the motorist (not mentioning the woman in Temple City). Mike was called in to the academy office but apparently talked his way out of any formal discipline, which was fine with me. I just wanted to cover my rear end and stay away from my troublesome fellow recruit.

Mike made it through the academy and was assigned to Hollenbeck. But things did not go well for him. While I don't know the details, he was not well thought of and got in some type of trouble, but apparently completed his probation. He then transferred to Jail Division, where he sustained some type of injury and ended up on light duty. Eventually Mike left the department, but I am not aware if it was a termination or medical retirement. I know that he died sometime in the late 1960s or early 1970s, but again am not aware of the circumstances. I do vividly recall his lovely red-headed wife and those beautiful children, and reflect what a shame it was that he was such an idiot.

By the time I graduated from the Police Academy I was dating a little gal, Janet, a clerk in the Records & Identification Division (R&I). She was the niece of Officer Arleigh McCree, one hell of a fine cop who had just been awarded the Medal of Valor. Arleigh had about two years on the job and worked a south end division, I believe 77th Street.

Janet and I attended my graduation party at the academy. That night, Arleigh came by, took me aside, gave me six semi-wadcutter bullets, and told me to put them in my off-duty, two-inch revolver. He explained they weren't authorized, but that no one would say anything if I used them in a "good shooting." Despite his assurances that no problems would develop, I liked my job too much to potentially put it in jeopardy by intentionally violating the rules. Although Janet and I did not last much longer, I remained friends with Arleigh until his on-duty death in North Hollywood in 1987. He was a member of the bomb squad and was killed instantly with another bomb squad member, Ron Ball, when a bomb they were attempting to defuse detonated.

CENTRAL DIVISION

In May 1966, following three months at the Police Academy, I was assigned to Central Patrol Division. The division was located on the first floor of the Police Administration Building at 150 N. Los Angeles Street (later renamed "Parker Center"). At that time, the division's boundries were the Los Angeles River on the north and east, the Santa Monica Freeway on the south, and Hoover Street on the west. The division also included all of the Silver Lake District.

During my tenure in Central the Rampart Station was opened, and Central's western boundry was reduced significantly, with the Harbor Freeway being as far west as we went. Elysian Park, Echo Park, and the Silver Lake district all went to the new Rampart station. To the best of my recollection, there were probably around 250 persons of all ranks assigned to Central at the time I transferred in. A number of those people transferred to Rampart when that division opened, about half-way through my tour of duty.

When I was a new policeman, if there was any serious effort to place probationary officers with more professional senior personnel, it was not obvious to me! Central Division in 1966 had some of the best folks I have ever dealt with—but also some of the worst cops you could imagine, and a bunch in between. I know, because during my time as a probationary officer I worked the gamut, from great to good to okay to awful.

While I cannot imagine there wasn't some discussion about whom to best place new officers with, it could not have been a solid consideration. The preferences of the senior officers, and those likely to complain the least, struck me as being more compelling. Prior to the "Jacobs Plan" in 1970, when all the various pay grades were developed within the basic civil service ranks, the only uniform difference among officers was the number of hash marks on the sleeve. All policeman had slick sleeves, as there were no advanced pay grades in those days. Today, there are sleeve insignias for many non-supervisory pay-grades within the civil service rank of police officer, including two stripes for training officers and two stripes with a star for senior lead officers.

When I was a policeman (before the title was changed to police officer), there was no extra pay or any other incentive for working with and training a new officer. While there were several folks who truly took the time to help me develop (Jim Conners, "Val" Valdez and Stan Williams), most of what I picked up was through osmosis, and trial and error. Remember, it was the era when new cops in some other departments actually went out and worked the streets as the second person, while waiting for their academy class to begin! As a highly-motivated Marine Corps veteran, I had the smarts and discipline to pretty much thrive. But there were those who could not cut it, and were terminated on probation.

The Psycho With a Sword in Pershing Square

As a fairly new officer, I was assigned one evening with Officer Ron Kiser to Unit 1A87. In the late afternoon, we received an all-units radio call to respond to Pershing Square, where a man with a sword was threatening people. On arrival we observed a deranged man standing in the fountain and swinging a sword around, and learned that he had taken swings at several people before entering the water-filled fountain. I asked Ron how we should proceed. He told me it was not "we," but rather just "me!" Ron said it was the junior officer's responsibility to go into the fountain, disarm the suspect, cuff him, and take him to the police car.

And that's what I did.

The "Bubbles" Initiation

In the mid- to late 1960s, every probationary officer assigned to Central Division met "Bubbles"—in a very startling and inappropriate way.

Bubbles was among the pathetic creatures who lived on Skid Row, and existed by "turning tricks" (prostitution). She was overweight, with breasts that were quite sizable. Like most street-walking prostitutes she hated vice officers, but liked patrol officers, as the latter were the folks who dealt with barbaric pimps. When new officers came to Central, Bubbles was always pleased to work with the senior officers by grossing out the new officers. Her typical introduction was to walk over to the probationary officer's side of the car and flip both breasts inside the police car, right into the face of the probationer!

The supervisors, for the most part, were in on these shenanigans. Today, we most appropriately recoil in disgust at this type of inappropriate misconduct. But that type of humor was fairly common when I first became a cop.

Cleaning Up Skid Row!

The optimism of youth is truly a good thing! As a brand-new Los Angeles policeman I was assigned to the downtown Skid Row district. Although I didn't verbalize it openly, I just knew that my hard work and professionalism would result in a better and safer downtown Los Angeles. I just knew I would have a positive influence on all of the drugs, the hypes (heroin addicts) and the crime, and would be successful in putting criminals in jail and keeping them there. Boy, was I wrong!

I worked just as hard and exercised just as much professionalism as can be imagined, but the social factors, as well as the flaws in our justice system, were then and are now great impediments to success. I came to realize that the only real solution would be economic, in terms of redevelopment.

Twenty-seven years after becoming a new policeman in Central Division, I returned to the same division as commanding officer, and truly enjoyed being back in that very challenging environment. I became heavily involved with the various civic organizations, as well as the many social and homeless organizations—and with all of those organizarions' competing priorities.

During my tenure as the commanding officer of Central Area, I became more convinced than ever that the only real answer would be found in tearing down the old and dilapidated buildings and replacing them with new construction, both residential and commercial. Today, I'm so pleased to see all that has occurred over the last several years, including the conversion of old buildings into residential lofts and the emergence of many nice restaurants, high-end grocery stores, coffee houses and other businesses that are truly contributing to the vitality of downtown Los Angeles. I never lost my enthusiasm for playing a role in making downtown a better place. But I came to realize that all the hard work in the world by policemen pales in comparison to the impact of redevelopment. Now downtown Los Angeles is becoming a pretty nice place!

Transvestite Nurse in Surgery

When still a fairly new officer, my partner and I responded to a robbery and shooting that had just occurred at the large old hotel located on the southeast corner of 5th & Main (it is still there and still looks the same after more than forty years). Upon arrival, we learned that a robbery had occurred and the suspect had been shot by the clerk, but still managed to escape. I do not recall the details, but somehow we determined that the wounded suspect was in a bungalow near Rampart and Bellevue (which was still within Central Division at that time). We went to the location, made entry, and encountered a unique situation.

The wounded suspect was laid out on the kitchen table and being operated on by a transvestite, dressed in a starched nurse's uniform, white nylon stalkings and all, who was attempting to remove the bullet!

Mom Would Wait Up to Hear of My Shift Experiences

The only difference between being a cop and going to Disneyland was that being a LA cop was more fun! Like most new cops, I was very enthusiastic about the job and everything that went along with it. I shared the Duarte home with my mom for about my first four years on the department. My wonderful mother, Mary Bushey, was every bit the proud mom, and often waited up for me to come home and share the shift's experiences with her.

Depression at Having to Take Days Off

Being a cop in Central had to be more fun than being a pedophile at Coney Island. It was usually eight hours (or more) of non-stop blood, guts, death, destruction, fights, and donuts. I would gladly have given up some of my days off because the job was so much fun, exciting, and interesting. In most instances, certain sadness came upon me as I completed my last shift before days off. I believe my attitude was fairly typical of other new officers during that era.

A Perplexing Question Regarding Use of Force

At the time of this writing I have been a cop of some sort for about 45 years, and discuss this perplexing question in just about all of the presentations I make to law enforcement groups throughout the United States (and occasionally Canada). First, it is a reality that cops routinely deal with about the worst things our society has to offer: terrible people, terrible crimes, blood, guts, devastation, deprivation and heartache. The second reality that most cops will tell you is that being a law enforcement officer, despite all the above issues, and more, is the best job in the world! When cops are unhappy, it is almost always because of internal issues, and not because of issues in the field. Go figure.

Station Call—2500 Ivanhoe Drive

Not long after graduating from the academy, I spent a deployment period working Unit 1A1 with Officer Jim Connors. I do not recall the name of the third man in the car, but Jim was a great guy and a great teacher. Also, he was married to a pretty policewoman, Olivia, and going by the Business Office Division (BOD) with him to visit his wife was always a pleasant experience.

The Silverlake district was part of 1A1's area, and each night we were required to make several station calls (drive by to ensure that everything was okay) to the residence of William H. Parker, our chief of police. In all of those scores of visits, I never once saw either Chief Parker or his wife, Helen, at the house. In fact, I only saw him personally once, in the elevator at the Police Administration building. When I graduated from the academy he was off on sick leave. He had not returned back to work very long before he died of a heart attack on the evening of July 16, 1966, at the Statler-Hilton Hotel, 7th & Figueroa Streets. Although I was working that evening, I was not aware of Chief Parker's death until the end of our watch.

"I'm Sorry, I Meant Shit!"

This was so funny. As a new cop I took my mom to court with me on several occasions. One time, before my case was called, we listened to a case where a woman had been charged with child abuse for maintaining an unfit home. One of the witnesses was a next-door neighbor of the defendant, and the neighbor had just described the condition of the home under direct examination, including a comment that "there was crap all over the place." When cross-examination began the defense attorney almost immediately asked, in a very innocent and seemingly sincere manner, what the witness meant by saying there was "crap all over the place." The witness responded by saying: "I'm sorry, I meant shit!" Everybody in the courtroom, including the judge, broke out into considerable laughter.

Half-Hour Waits for 10 Seconds of Information

Today's database inquiries, such as criminal history and warrant information, are often measured in seconds. In the 1960s, these inquiries typically took about twenty minutes, or longer. The request would go from the car to the communications dispatcher, forwarded to the person who was manning the pneumatic tubes, transmitted to Records & Identifications Division where record clerks manually searched the files, then the process was repeated in reverse for whatever information was (or was not) found. It often took so long that officers were sometimes tempted to cut folks loose instead of waiting for the returns. But the occasional "Code 6 Charles" (suspected wanted on a felony warrant) was enough to cause most cops to just cool their heels and wait for the return.

Visit to Every Sheriff's Department in California

As a young boy I collected law enforcement badges. But I really started some serious collecting when I actually became a cop. Within my first year or so with the LAPD, I decided to drive to every sheriff's department in California in pursuit of a badge! I took a long string of days off and did just that. Almost without exception I was met with goodwill and had enjoyable visits, as just about everyone I spoke with knew somebody and thought well of the LAPD. I was successful in getting an old badge from almost all of the departments. Equally as important, I made a bunch of nice friends.

On my trip throughout California in an effort to get a badge from each sheriff's department, I went to the old courthouse in Woodland where the Yolo County Sheriff's Office was located. When I asked to see the sheriff, a crusty old deputy asked why I wanted to see the old man. I told him I wanted to try to get a badge, but the deputy told me the sheriff was a jerk and wouldn't give me the sweat off his you-know-whats. I told the deputy I wanted to try anyway, so he told me to go into the sheriff's inner office. The deputy was right: the sheriff was a jerk and quickly dismissed both me and my request. Back in the outer office, the crusty, old deputy said that he'd told me so. Then he handed me a badge, saying he'd taken it out of the sheriff's safe while I was talking with the sheriff, and to forget where it came from! In my collecting endeavors, things similar to this have happened on several occasions.

THE BADGE FOR MY COLLECTION WAS STILL WARM!

Among the many locations I visited in pursuit of acquiring badges for my collection was the Los Angeles Housing Department, as that organization had a small police department. I went to headquarters and was told that I would have to talk to the executive director, but would have to wait in the outer office until the meeting he was conducting was over. As I waited, it became clear that something bad was happening in his office. Hostile words were being exchanged, and the two secretaries whose desks were in the outer office kept exchanging nervous glances at each other. After a few minutes, an obviously distraught man stormed out of the director's office and left the building.

A secretary told the director I wanted to talk to him, and I was immediately invited into his office and warmly received. When I asked the director if it might be possible to acquire a badge for my collection, his response was another question: "Did you see the guy that just left my office?" When I replied in the affirmative, he stated, "I just fired the guy. Here, you can have his badge!" My glee at getting a nice badge for my collection was mixed with sadness for the fellow who had just lost his job. As time went on in my collecting endeavors, I acquired a number of badges whose previous owners had left their departments under unhappy circumstances.

Astonished at the Trust of My Game Warden Cousin

During one of my trips to Northern California I visited my cousin, Russ Bushey, Jr., who was the resident game warden in the town of Burney, in Shasta County.

I spent a couple of days with him and his family, and rode along with him on patrol. Every time he went home Russ parked his marked Fish & Game unit in the alley behind his house, removed his police equipment belt containing his revolver, then left it on the seat of his unlocked and unattended vehicle while he went into his house. Not only was the vehicle unlocked, but the windows were even left down! I couldn't believe this was happening, as anyone could have reached in and removed his weapon. In discussing it with Russ, he said that he lived in a town where people trusted each other, and where the kids had a healthy respect for firearms and could be depended on to not tamper with his gun or the car. I still thought he was crazy! Russ was a great fellow, about thirty years my senior, who ultimately had a massive heart attack and died while on patrol on the Pit River.

Public Intoxication and the "Sundance Decision"

During my entire time in Central, public drunkenness was viewed as a criminal offense. Without exaggeration, the officers in Central Division had to have made well in excess of 100 public drunkenness arrests (647f of the Penal Code) every day. It was a vicious cycle of arrests by officers on the beat, the "B" wagons ("Paddy Wagons" for drunks) making arrests, a few hours spent in the drunk tank, then being released on their own recognizance with a court date—and the process started all over again.

This all ended in the mid-1970s when a court decision ("Sundance") ruled that serial public intoxication was an illness that required treatment and not a criminal charge. It also mandated revisions in the way drunks were dealt with. This turned out to be a positive factor in dealing with this impossible problem, with much of the support for homeless alcoholics being provided by private groups.

Looking back, we really spun our wheels and wasted a great deal of time and effort, both for the courts and for us, prior to "Sundance."

Infidelity Translates to Termination

There have always been men (women, too) who like to cheat on their spouses. But there was a time on the LAPD when it was really not a very good idea. Under Chief Parker, it was a firing offense. Every rap sheet (the monthly disciplinary summary) contained the names of officers who had been fired for "maintaining an inappropriate relationship with a female not his wife." I don't recall when this issue pretty much ceased to be seen in a disciplinary light, and was treated as more of a personal issue. Since Chief Gates had a reputation as a bit of a player and a ladies man, it is understandable that this type of conduct became less of an issue as he approached the top of the department. In discussing this matter with a person who was a captain during the Parker era, my friend explained that adultery wasn't actually much of an issue unless extraordinary circumstances arose to make it an issue.

TRUE CONTENTMENT: IRONING AND BOOBS

On a radio call for some issue that I don't recall, I encountered a unique person. While I was interviewing a young couple in a rooming house, a tall and gangly man was also present in the room, ironing a stack of clothes and injecting himself into our conversation. He was truly ugly, with long stringy hair. He couldn't wait to tell me that he was actually a woman and had boobs, and then opened his loose flannel shirt to show me his new man-made breasts!

It turned out that he was the young couple's "maid," and did all their household chores in return for room and board. Before leaving the couple told me that their "maid" did a great job, and thoroughly enjoyed performing tasks typically performed by women. In my career I encountered a number of people like this fellow, who had subjected themselves to various degrees of body modifcation, and have often wondered what became of some of them. In his case, if he later decided to remain male he could have had his breasts removed. But some of the folks I encountered took surgical measures that were clearly not reversible.

COOPER'S DONUT STANDS

For many years, there were a great many "lean-to" donut stands located throughout the downtown area. Most were aluminum attachments to buildings that offered, as I recall, four options: coffee, Cokes, glazed donuts, or plain cake donuts. The items were free for cops, and just about all the folks manning these 24-hour businesses were ex-cons or ex-substance abusers. The headquarters was on the northwest corner of 6th Street and Towne Avenue, where all the donuts were made. Cooper's Donut Stands were an essential parts of every cop's shifts.

My Favorite Places—Then and Now!

These memoirs would not be complete without mentioning two of my favorite places to eat: "Phillipe's" and "The Pantry." These historic places have both been around for a long time—Phillipe's since the turn of the century, and The Pantry since the mid-1920s. I have never had a bad meal at either place, and believe me, I have had many meals at both.

We Can Drive Up the Hill or Use the Siren
—But Not Both!

In the 1960s we had mechanical "growler" sirens on the roofs of our black-and-while police cars. When activated, which was actually pretty rare, they drew a great deal of current from the car battery. I will never forget a unique experience when responding to a code 3 call (red lights and siren) in the Echo Park area. After going up and down a couple of hills enroute to the location of the call, the police car started slowing down and obviously could not make it up the last hill to the call. We actually had to shut down the siren, coast a ways back down the hill, and take another run at the hill with the siren turned off. Then we made it up the hill.

On a related note, I recall that the "mechanical brake" on many of those sirens malfunctioned, causing a low moaning noise to come out of the siren at higher speeds when the siren turbine was churning with the wind. To counter the problem, we would make plugs out of field inter-view cards and place them in the siren to eliminate the noise.

Horror at the Top of Baxter Street

The very top of Baxter Street between Silverlake Drive and Glen-dale Boulevard has long been a location where old cops like to scare new cops during ride-alongs. As you crest the top of the hill, from Glendale Boulevard all you can see is the Silverlake Reservoir several hundred yards below. It is so steep, you cannot initially see the street—just the reservoir.

As a new cop, I had the hell scared out of me with this little time-honored ritual, and left my stomach at the top of that hill. For the rest of my career, I relished scaring the hell out of countless others. My last victim was Assistant Sheriff Ron Bieberdorf, when he and I and a few other San Bernardino County folks visited the Police Academy for lunch. I just couldn't resist a detour to Baxter Street!

"Kid, Learn to Relieve Yourself on City Time"

As a new policeman, I worked with a number of interesting characters, and Officer Bob Nett (pseudonym) certainly fell into that category. He was a decent and affable fellow, but pretty much an old burned-out cop, like many that I worked with in that era who did just enough to get by. He was a "morning watch copper," who spent as much time as he could "in the hole" sleeping instead of working. Like clockwork, we would go to the Police Administration Building (later named Parker Center) every morning around 0300 so he could have his bowel movement. He continually told me that I should regulate my body so I could do as he did, and have my primary bowel movements on "city time."

As he took care of his business, I was usually waiting in the adjacent locker room. When Bob was about finished he would yell out, "I am transferring another lieutenant to the harbor" just before flushing the toilet. He was referring to the city's sewage plant close to the Harbor Division. Quite a character!

Deceived by Smart Crooks Who Cleaned Out Pelta Furs

Some forty-five years later, I'm still troubled by this incident. In the wee small hours one morning, a series of radio calls came out indicating that shots were being fired on the upper floors of a commercial building in the garment district. As units were responding, an additional call came out indicating even more problems, and an explosion at the building. Understandably, just about every available unit rushed to the location. Because of the potential danger of shots being fired and an explosion, all officers exercised a great deal of care, which took a certain amount of time, being very cautious in entering and going to the upper floors of a vacant structure where the incident was allegedly occurring.

After about an hour and a half it was clear that no problem was at that location, and we cleared the scene. While all the officers were deployed at this phony shooting location, a series of other calls came out indicating silent burglar alarms at a number of other locations. One of them was Pelta Furs, which as I recall was on West 7th Street. During that era there was no shortage of silent burglar alarms, but most of them were false alarms. Well, the silent burglar alarm call to Pelta Furs was not phony! As all the officers were dealing with the bogus shooting call in the garment district, burglars were cleaning out valuable fur coats and related garments from the high-end fur company. It became clear that the call to the garment district was a diversion to draw the officers away from where a very serious burglary was being committed. Plain and simple, the bad guys outfoxed the police in this instance. I don't believe this burglary was ever solved, either.

A number of years later as a captain in the Wilshire district, a similar call came out much like the one I had been part of so many years before in Central. I thought it might be possible that another diversion of this nature was taking place, and notified Communications Division via landline to be very sensitive to silent burglar alarms at other high-end retail establishments during that time. As it turned out, it was not the case. But I never stopped feeling a little bit of pain and humiliation from that diversion so many years prior, and have remained sensitive to the potential for future diversions of that nature. I think probably the greatest question, realistically, is why more crooks have not used the same diversion technique. I'm glad they haven't!

CARELESSNESS AT A LIQUOR STORE ON BEVERLY BOULEVARD

For a cop, carelessness can be fatal. One night I did something really stupid, but somebody was watching over me and what could have been a problem did not develop into one. In the small hours of the morning, when working 1A51 with Officer Rick Manrique, we received a silent burglary alarm to a liquor store on Beverly Boulevard. Most of us, inappropriately, sometimes acted pretty lackadaisical about such calls, because the overwhelming number of them were false alarms. Rick took the rear and I took the front. Contrary to common sense and everything I had been taught, I walked up and tried the front door by jiggling it. Almost immediately, I looked in and saw a burglar stuffing cartons of cigarettes into a gunnysack. Fortunately, we made the arrest without any difficulties, but there could well have been a much unhappier ending had the suspect been armed. This was a good lesson that I never forgot.

MASTURBATING IN THE MASHED POTATOES—LAST MEAL THERE!

Among the tasks often performed at roll calls by the watch commander is "reading off" significant entries from the previous day's "Daily Occurrence Sheet." This helps keep officers informed of crime trends and other activities of interest.

One day, the watch commander read an entry about the cook in a restaurant frequented by officers, who had been arrested for masturbating in the mashed potatoes! This was very troubling for us to hear, and especially so for those who considered the place to be their regular "eating spot." I am not aware of any cop who again ate there during the rest of my time in Central Division. This was really a shame, because it is a well-established location with quite an interesting history, and a place where my parents occasionally took me when I was a little boy. Later, as the captain of Central Area, the long-time owner and I became friends, and in recent years I've taken my kids there. However, this place was at the top of our psychological "off-limits" list in 1966!

Great "In Progress" Burglary Arrest but Two Unhappy Old-Timers!

For a month or so while still somewhat of an embryonic policeman in Central Division, I spent time assigned to Unit 1A79. It was on the south end of the division, in an industrial area where virtually all the businesses were closed at night. The graveyard shift was especially desolate, which was just fine with my two "old-timer" partners, Harvey and Bruce. Both of these fellows had well-deserved reputations for doing very little work and getting quite a bit of sleep while on duty. These two chaps, really nice guys but burned out as cops, would park their police car in a darkened industrial area and sleep between radio calls, which were few and far between because nothing much ever happened in their assigned area. Their favorite "hole" was a small parking area with no illumination, at the end of a long driveway.

About three o'clock on a very quiet morning, Harvey had briefly exited the warm police car to relieve himself when he heard some muffled pounding and chiseling noises. Walking a short distance to see what the noise was, he observed two burglars burrowing into the back wall of a closed business! He quickly returned to the car, woke up Bruce, and the officers arrested the burglary suspects. It was really a great arrest, as these suspects had been capering in this industrial area for some time. Their arrest even cleared a bunch of other crimes. But everyone from the watch commander down realized that the only way these two guys would ever make an observation arrest of this nature, was if the suspects were capering near the officers' sleeping hole! For Harvey and Bruce, the exhilaration of a great arrest was tempered by their need to find a new place to sleep, where a diligent sergeant could not find them. Most sergeants, however, pretty much deferred to their senior status and left them alone, and I'm confident there were several sergeants who also "hit the hole."

"No More Free Donuts for Cops"

When I was a young cop in Central, there was a high-end donut and sandwich shop on the southeast corner of 5ᵗʰ & Hill Streets. Everything was free for cops, so it was a popular location with officers on all of the watches. One day, there appeared a massive sign in the window that read: "No More Free Donuts For Cops." Turned out the owner had been arrested for drunk driving. Oh well, it was good while it lasted.

Rotten Partner, Pretty Girls, and Tacos

As a new officer, I spent one deployment period assigned to 1A33. My two other partners (day) were Tommy Rogers (pseudonym) and Stan Williams (the three officers rotate so that two are always working each shift). Williams was a great guy who worked hard to train me well, but Rogers was an absolute idiot.

One summer afternoon while working with Rogers, he spotted a couple of pretty Mexican girls (neither spoke English) sitting on a bus bench. After managing to lure them into the police car, he drove to the taco stand on the east side of Echo Park Avenue just north of Sunset Boulevard (it's still there) and bought a big bag of tacos and four Cokes. Rogers then drove to a small canyon adjacent to Dodger Stadium (now part of the ballpark's parking area). Taking some of the tacos and two Cokes, he took one of the girls by the hand and disappeared into the bushes, telling me to do as I pleased with the other one! The girl left behind and I just looked at each other and ate the tacos. A few minutes later Rogers and his honey emerged from the bushes. It was obvious that a sexual encounter had occurred. He then drove back to the bus stop where he'd picked up the girls, and dropped them off.

That rotten bastard violated everything that I believed in and stood for. However, as a probationary officer there was realistically nothing I could do about it. I later learned that he'd previously taken a six-month suspension for similar conduct with a street-walking prostitute in 77ᵗʰ Division a couple of years before. Later, he was a detective when I was his commanding officer in Central Area. I had him watched like a hawk, and I made it clear to him that I had not forgotten his despicable behavior so many years earlier.

Cell Extractions in 1966

Cell extractions have evolved into a real science of late, with officers using advanced tactics and specialized equipment for the task. When I was new to the profession, the cell-extraction device was a probationary officer! This was pretty much a rite of passage, and the inability to extract a combative suspect from a cell, absent truly aggravating circumstances, placed any new officer in jeopardy of failing the probationary period.

MALCOMB BEATY KILLED AT YORK AND NORTH FIGUEROA

Malcolm Beaty and I sat next to each other all through the academy and became friends. Out of the academy, he was assigned to Highland Park Division. Late one night, Malcolm was riding as passenger officer in a car driven by Officer Brown (pseudonym), who had a reputation as a "hot dog" and reckless driver. They got into a pursuit, Brown lost control, and the unit smashed into a utility pole at York and North Figueroa. Beatty was gravely injured in the accident.

He lingered at Central Receiving Hospital for about a week before succumbing to his injuries. I still recall seeing him at Central Receiving, and literally being able to look into his head because of the enormous injury. This was my first LAPD friend killed on the job, but unfortunately not the last, and it was pretty hard on me. For a while I actually considered leaving the department, but in hindsight I wasn't really serious about moving on to another profession.

The utility pole still stands, on the east side of Figueroa just north of York. It is recognizable, as the steel skirt placed around the lower portion of the pole to reinforce it after the accident is still there.

VICK'S VAPO-RUB & CIGARS—

ESSENTIAL EQUIPMENT FOR RIPE BODIES

Dealing with dead bodies was an everyday occurrence in Central Division. From victims to suspects to winos, and everything in between, death was a routine occurrence. You got used to death, but never to the horrible stench of decomposing corpses. It was not uncommon for the police to be called about someone who had not been seen for several days, because of an unpleasant smell coming from a room in one of the scores of fleabag hotels. Within a short time of arriving at Central, I began keeping a small container of Vick's Vapo-Rub in my gear, which I'd put a wad of on my upper lip to block out the stench of decomposing human tissue.

While working an "L Car" (one-man unit) in Central, I saw one of the weirdest things I have ever witnessed. I got a call to "see the woman" in an upstairs unit of an old rat-trap rooming house. When I contacted the PR (person reporting), she reported that a man in a downstairs unit was operating some type of machinery all hours of the day and night, that the whole structure would shake, and she wanted it to stop. She did not know what kind of machinery he was operating.

I went downstairs, knocked on the door and was met by a man who was really sleazy—yellow teeth, thick dirty glasses, several days' growth of beard, dirty white dress shirt with big yellow perspiration stains under the arms, etc. Somehow, I ended up inside the unit (in those days we usually walked in without being invited, yet sensitive to officer safety), and saw something really strange. Mounted upside-down on the ceiling above the pull-down bed was a sewing machine! It had a long plastic pipe contraption jury-rigged to the portion of the machine that went up and down as it was operated, that extended all the way down to the bed, with a grommet-type thing at the bottom. An electrical cord snaked down the wall to the pillow, behind which was the treadle for activating the machine.

This guy had a homemade masturbation device that hung down and attached to his penis, and was activated by pressing his head back against the pillow! I was astounded, made some comment about making sure he didn't put it on zigzag, and suggested he find a quieter way to find self-affection.

Only in Los Angeles!

Pursuit in a Paddy Wagon—Bad Idea!

During the scores of presentations I make to law enforcement executives, I continually remind them that among the most difficult challenges we face is managing the twenty-one and twenty-two-year-old officer who acts his or her age! While we wish it wasn't true, the reality is that many of these young officers still have some growing up to do, and behave in immature manners at times. Unfortunately, much of my wisdom in this area is based on reflecting upon some of the foolish things I did as a young officer. My pursuit in a paddy wagon, which we called "B-Wagons," is an example of what can happen when impulsiveness and immaturity come together.

I was behind the wheel, patrolling Skid Row in the B-Wagon with another young officer, when a patrol unit went in pursuit of a fleeing vehicle. With more initiative than brains, we took off at a pretty good rate of speed and joined the pursuit! There was absolutely no need for our services, and the large B-Wagon, full of drunks in the back, was certainly not suitable for high-speed driving. I still recall (with great embarrassment) the noise from the drunks bouncing off the walls as we raced around corners, and their yelling at us to "knock it off!" The drunks in the back were smarter than the officers in the front. The only thing worse than a unit occupied by an immature officer is a unit that is occupied by two of them!

SECRET MESSAGE TO JUDGES

When I was a new officer it was common, in the case of a violators who were jerks, to place a unique symbol on the court copy of traffic citations. We would put a dot surrounded by a circle in a conspicuous location to indicate that the violator was an asshole! Realistically, I don't know to what extent the various judges paid attention to these unique *ex-parte* communications, but I'm confident there were some particularly pro-police judges who did. This practice was prohibited long ago!

"THE FLARE AND THE BURNING PICKUP!"

Los Angeles was the last city to turn traffic enforcement on the freeways over to the California Highway Patrol, which finally occurred in 1968. Prior to that transfer, we had scores of police officers assigned to the freeways for traffic enforcement. While on the morning watch (midnight shift), my partner and I were assigned to assist a traffic unit on the Santa Monica Freeway, somewhere around Central Avenue. Specifically, our job was to route traffic off the freeway because of a serious accident that was being investigated. I was at one off-ramp, and my partner with our vehicle, was at another. I had laid out a flare pattern when a fellow in a pickup truck, obviously drunk, drove right through the flares and proceeded in the direction of the serious accident, which was a mile or so down the freeway. I had to jump aside to keep from being struck.

I was so angry that I picked up a lighted flare and threw it at the truck, with the flare landing in the bed of the pickup. Almost immediately, the bed of the pick-up erupted in flames! I surmise that the back of the truck was full of oily rags, or something similar. There was nothing I could do, as my partner had the car and we didn't have portable radios at the time. My last recollection is of the pickup disappearing from sight with the rear bed in flames! The truck exited before reaching the accident, because none of the other officers saw the burning truck. Lucky for me, nothing was ever said about the incident.

"Turn Around, Asshole!"

Main Street in downtown was a real cesspool when I was a young officer. Bars, pawn shops, tattoo parlors, burlesque shows and porno theaters were the prominent businesses. Main Street was frequented by sickos, kids looking for a thrill, straying husbands, blatant homosexuals, prostitutes, and servicemen on liberty.

One of the trouble spots was the Optic Theatre, located at 533 South Main (long gone). Drunken servicemen would frequently go in there to sleep off their binges. Street vultures would target these servicemen, sit next to them, ensure they were passed out, and steal their wallets. Sometimes the vultures would actually use a razor blade to slit open their victim's pocket and remove the wallet. The MO was always the same: take the wallet, go into the bathroom, remove the cash, and throw the wallet in the trash can, because outside the theatre they were always being stopped and questioned for any number of reasons, and did not want to be caught with the wallet of a victim.

I really enjoyed working the detail, by dressing the way a serviceman would look on liberty (spit-shined oxfords, civilian clothes, etc.). Inside the theatre I would lay prostrate in a seat with my wallet pocket (and wallet) visible, waiting to be the victim of a robbery. It never took long!

One night, I put a large note in the bait wallet that read in big letters: "TURN AROUND, ASSHOLE!" Sure enough, it was promptly taken by a suspect who immediately went into the men's room, opened the wallet to remove any cash, saw the note, and turned around to see us standing there! He went to jail, and the wallet—without the note—was booked as evidence. These idiots were so predictable.

The "Victim" in Drunk Roles

Working as the victim in drunk roles was so much fun that I would have done it while on vacation for no pay! As the decoy I would lay at the entrance to an alley wearing spit-shined military shoes, clutching a ditty bag with military insignia on it (concealing a gun in my hand in case things really went bad), and pretending to be passed out.

The MO was always the same: the bad guy would shake the passed-out victim, try to figure out if he might be a cop, take the wallet out of his pocket, and flee into the bowels of the alley. My partner was hidden in those alley bowels, and would jump out; the suspect would turn around and see me now on my feet, and the fight was on. There was usually a foot pursuit, and always a fight. No one ever got away from me. For a former Marine full of testosterone, nothing could have been more fun! My few scrapes and bruises were nothing, compared to the scrapes and bruises on the robbery suspects.

Taking Home a Wino—Not a Good Idea!

Officer Bill Morgan was one of my very first regular partners. Together, we worked unit 1A29 in the Skid Row district out of Central Division. Bill was a fun and decent man, but—at least in this instance—he had a heart that was just a little too big.

Ol' Roy was one of the hundreds of down-and-out winos we regularly dealt with, and generally a pleasant man. Bill decided to invite Roy to live in the Morgans' garage in El Monte, where he would be housed and fed in exchange for doing yard work and odd jobs around the house. But the arrangement started out pretty rocky, because Roy mostly wanted to sit in the garage and drink his wine. Things hit bottom after about two weeks, when Roy ransacked Bill's house and stole everything not nailed down, including Bill's coveted coin collection. Bill was understandably livid, and had all the officers out searching for Roy.

To the best of my knowledge Roy was never seen again, causing the rest of us to speculate that either he'd skipped town and kept going ...or that Bill found him.

Sap Gloves and Drunken Indians

When I was a policeman in Central Division, the area around 3rd & Main was a major hangout for Native Americans. They would go there to drink and socialize, and we got frequent calls to the bars, particularly on the northwest corner. In those days, saps (blackjacks) were authorized, as were "sap gloves." I carried a large beavertail sap known as the "Gonzalez 245," and wore sap gloves with eight ounces of powdered lead in each knuckle, equipment items that came in particularly handy when walking a beat or assigned to the "B" Wagon (paddy wagon). I will never forget an arrest in that intersection when I ended up in a fight with several drunk Indians. It was no contest: between their unsteadiness and my tools, I easily prevailed. A bunch of Indians went to jail that night. To this day, I never drive by that intersection without reflecting on that fight.

Although "saps" were authorized, they were supposed to be a spring-loaded thing that we called the "Mickey Mouse Agitator." My sap was named after its maker, a sheriff's deputy, and bore the same numbers of "assault with a deadly weapon" in the Penal Code. I wanted to get the larger one, known as the "187" (code for murder), but it was too fat to fit into the sap pocket of my uniform trousers!

Saps and sap gloves are a thing of the past. Mine are in a display case in my office at home.

"The Name is Captain Ladheim!"

Early one morning when my partner, Harvey Duncan, and I were going end-of-watch, we encountered one of his classmates and old acquaintances, Captain Jerry Ladheim (pseudonym), in the hallway of Parker Center (it was then known as the Police Administration Building, and Chief Parker was still alive).

Harvey greeted his old friend by saying, "Hi, Lad, how's it going?" Ladheim replied: "Officer Duncan, my name is Captain Ladheim!" What an idiot! I felt bad for Harvey, because I know he must have felt humiliated. Ladheim was later forced into retirement when he was the commanding officer of Foothill Division. The officer working horse patrol in Hansen Dam caught Ladheim and his secretary doing the evil deed in his unmarked car. It could not have happened to a nicer guy!

For my entire career, and regardless of my rank or position, I insisted that my old friends and partners call me by my first name when not in a formal setting.

Big Resistance to Seat Belts!

We could put a man on the moon, by the late 1960s. But society hadn't yet realized how seat belts could save so many lives. So, when the wearing of seat belts became mandatory in police vehicles, just about all of us were very resistant. We argued that they impaired our rapid exit from the cars, such as at the end of pursuits or when spotting a fugitive walking down the street. Such a delay would usually result in suspects getting away.

In retrospect, all the excuses were foolish. The big issue was probably just one of resisting change. Given all the traffic carnage that cops have seen, I think a person would have to look awfully hard to find a cop who doesn't wear seat belts these days.

Dozing While Driving—A Big Wake-up Call

There was a time when I occasionally had trouble staying awake while driving. Obviously, this could have been quite a problem. Fortunately, it was always momentary, and I never had an accident.

My real wake-up call occurred one night when a date and I, along with a good pal and his wife, were returning from movie. I dozed off for just a moment; while out of it, my car drifted from the northbound to the southbound lanes of a busy street that had a raised center median. The drifting occurred at the exact moment we passed through a large intersection! It is amazing that I did not collide with the center divider.

This was my real wake-up call. From that moment, forty-some years ago, I pull over if I start to feel the slightest bit weary to the point that dozing-off might be possible.

Suspect Urinates on Officer

A suspect made a very serious mistake during a plainclothes drunk role investigation during my tenure in Central Division.

He had devised a pretty unique way of determining whether or not the drunken person, his intended victim in a street robbery, was a decoy policeman. Before committing the robbery, he would urinate on the prostrate form. This technique apparently worked pretty well for a while, and gave him some peace of mind that his victims were not cops. That is, until he ran across a victim who was a cop!

It was not a good night for that suspect.

Horrible Self-Mutilation by a Pretty Girl

One morning, I got a call to meet the ambulance unit at the YWCA, which at the time was on 6th Street by the Harbor Freeway. What a horrible and tragic situation greeted me!

A young and attractive woman, who appeared to be in her early 20s, had scores of deep, self-inflicted cuts all over her body, from her face to her feet. She had taken a razor blade and just started slashing. Just about all the wounds were long, deep, and laid wide-open. Virtually every wound would require, at the very least, extensive stitches. I still recall the stoic look on her face as she was being wheeled out on the stretcher.

It is likely that she survived, but I can only imagine the plastic surgery that was required, if even possible, to mitigate the many scars that she ended up with.

It would have been interesting to know why she did what she did.

Right Place at the Right Time, for a Badge Collector

For a law enforcement badge collector, which I had been since just a boy, being assigned to Central Division in 1966 was truly the right place at the right time. Located within Central Division were three badge companies, and all of them were generous to young Officer Bushey. The manager of the badge department of Los Angeles Stamp & Stationery, formed originally in 1885 as the Los Angeles Rubber Stamp Company, gave me a bunch of old stuff and permitted me to order anything I wanted. Leo Rovin of Entenmann Badge Company, who later became a co-owner, sold me a handful of used, turned-in badges at $1.00 each during my weekly visits to the company on 18th Street. Finally, a company long known primarily for military insignia, Wolf-Brown (located downtown on Broadway,) had a few law enforcement badges that they gave to me.

Within a couple of years L.A. Stamp & Stationery went out of business, Entenmann had some legal issues with badges and discontinued being my source for old stuff, and Wolf-Brown shut down their Los Angeles operation. As a new cop, I probably started with about twenty badges. When my eighteen-month (or so) tour in Central Division was over, I probably had around 500 badges in my collection!

Badge Bonanza From My Uncle Russ Bushey

My Uncle, Russ Bushey, was one of my dad's older brothers. Subsequent to World War I all of the brothers came to California. Russ settled in the Modoc County small township of Canby, where he had a nice ranch. However, his primary career was with the California Department of Fish & Game. Prior to his retirement in about 1960, he was the top wildlife official for all of the far-northern part of the state. I still recall that he just about always wore a uniform, even when on vacation. When not working, as I recall, it was the regular uniform (green pants and jacket, khaki shirt, black tie), but without a badge or patches.

During a visit to our home in Duarte in the late 1960s after my dad's death, I told Russ I was a badge collector and inquired as to whether he had any old badges lying around. He said he thought he did, and if he could find them he would mail them to me. Boy, did he! A couple weeks later I got a box of beautiful and rare old Fish & Game badges, plus an old tin star from Inyo County that dated from when he had been dual-commissioned at one time.

To this day, all of Uncle Russ' badges remain among the finest in my collection and are prominently displayed in my personal badge museum.

MY PAL—EL MONTE POLICE CHIEF ORVAL DAVIS

I was a new badge collector, but until I met Chief Orval Davis of the El Monte Police Department I wasn't aware of anyone else who had the same hobby. It turns out that there were a few of us, but very few. We just didn't know each other.

I think I learned of Chief Davis' badge collecting through an article in the paper. When I paid him a visit he was incredibly gracious and generous. During our several-year friendship before he retired, we gave each other extra badges that we would acquire. He had an absolute killer collection from the County of Los Angeles that he'd got from his good pal, James Pascoe, who had been in sheriff's personnel. Pascoe literally had the keys to the vault, and access to all of the old badges that had been accumulated over the years. Included among the great stuff in Orval's collection was the duty badge worn by the legendary Sheriff Eugene Biscaluz from the 1920s to the late 1940s. There were tons of other great stuff. Orval took his collection seriously, and really worked at it. He got badges from all of the IACP, state, and local meetings and conventions that he attended. When he got a badge he always clipped off the pin, drilled a couple of small holes, and mounted it onto one of his many plaques.

After Orval's death in the mid-1970s, I remained friendly and helpful with his widow, Faye. It was my pleasure to help with some of the chores and minor maintenance at their home in Temple City. While I would have been anxious to get my hands on his collection after his death, I was not about to act like a ghoul and attempt to take advantage of his widow. Other than casually letting Faye know that I was always available, if she decided to dispose of the collection and could use some sound advice, the issue was otherwise never discussed.

Some forty years later, long after Fay's passing, my dear friend Ray Sherrard bought the entire Orval Davis collection from their estate. In turn, I got about half of the 2,500 or so badges from Ray, including all the ones I had been salivating about all those years, including Sheriff Biscaluz' badge and original Series 1 through 5 LAPD badges.

I hope my pal Orval is looking down, and knows that I have endeavored to be a worthy steward of his collection (at least half of it!).

Walking a Beat and Looking Stupid

The long-term foot beat officers were almost exclusively "old timers," and they were pretty good at what they did. Most of those fellows would walk with their nightsticks in their hands, twirling them as they walked down the sidewalk.

Sometimes the newer officers, like me, would attempt to twirl our batons. But we usually dropped them and ended up looking stupid. I can still hear the loud and sickening sound of hard wood bouncing on the sidewalk, and attracting the attention of just about everyone.

Cockroach on the Chili-Cheeseburger

There was, and still is, a well-known open-air hamburger stand that stays open twenty-four hours a day. As burger joints go, this was a darn good one, and most of the cops would occasionally go there. I particularly liked (and still do!) their chili-cheeseburgers, and have eaten scores of them over the hood of a police car.

One night, while I stood in line behind an obnoxious drunk, I observed a troubling sight: the fellow making the burgers scooped a cockroach off the floor with his spatula, and put in on the drunk's hamburger! With a proud look on his face the cook caught my eye, and I too thought it was kind of funny because the drunk was acting like a real jerk. However, I also realized that a cop could easily and unknowingly suffer the same fate by some burger-flipper who was pissed about a ticket, or whatever.

In the decades since that incident, whenever in a police uniform I have always watched the preparation of my food at that location. Frankly, in my forty-some years as a cop, I suspect I have eaten meals where some pissed-off, anti-police cook has spit in or otherwise tampered with my food.

Wish it wasn't so, but it has probably occurred several times.

"Dead Body" Calls Came Out With the Sunrise

The heyday of nice movie theatres along Main Street was long gone, but the theatres were still there. During the 1960s, these theatres were very much run-down. Now they just showed grainy "B" grade movies to perverts looking for a place to play with themselves, an occasional drunk serviceman, and winos that sought shelter from the elements. They all shut down about six in the morning, and whoever was left, usually just the winos, were ushered out for whatever marginal cleaning that took place.

It was also very common for winos to die in those theatres, and DB (dead body) calls came out, to one or more of the theatres, just about every morning at around closing time. Perhaps it was just my imagination, but the musty odor in all those theatres also seemed to carry the smell of death. These were pretty pathetic places to be, with sticky floors and sticky arm rests as remnants from you know what. Ugh!

Suicide Jumpers Made Quite an Impact!

It was not unusual for persons to commit suicide downtown, by jumping off the roofs of the scores of high-rise buildings. During that era, most of Los Angeles' tall buildings were no more than about twenty stories tall.

One of the first of such calls that I responded to was at the Cecil Hotel in the 600 block of South Main Street. It was a place that my dad favored, when staying downtown before he died; he used to rave about the chili in the hotel's restaurant. I still recalled being puzzled at the bodies of the first couple of "jumpers" I saw, because of what appeared to be numerous open cuts on their bodies. I soon learned that the wounds were not cuts, but places where the pressure from the impact had forced internal tissue from the body to burst out in what appeared to be large incisions. Obviously, the bodily damage was not just these pressure wounds, but also frequent head trauma that occurred not unlike when a melon was dropped from a few feet.

I suspect that most of these human tragedies could have been averted if the victims had someone to work through their problems with. As I grow older, I have truly come to recognize that suicides are most often very permanent solutions to temporary problems.

Hitting the "Holes" (Note Plural)

As a new policeman, I did not know of any officer who did not occasionally pull into a secluded area and take a nap when assigned to the morning watch (graveyard shift). It was just a matter of degree. I will never forget one of my first experiences when an "old timer," Max Reynolds, first took me to "the hole." I was terrified! I just knew that a sergeant would catch us, and I would be terminated on probation. It was a large parking lot in the industrial area around 22nd and Maple, accessible only through a long driveway. Max pulled in and immediately went to sleep. I sat at attention and was petrified. For the next few minutes, as cars approach us in the driveway, I would shake Max and tell him it might be a sergeant. He didn't even open his eyes. By the time we finally got a radio call and had to leave, the parking lot was filled with police cars of every type, and from several divisions!

I especially remember one hole that was in the middle of an abandoned industrial complex, about where Piper Tech is now located. We drove several hundred yards through the weeds and into the back of an old warehouse. When we got a call and had to leave, we pulled on a chain to open a garage door, and easily exited right out onto Macy Street. We shared that location with a bunch of homeless men who we could hear moving around in the building while we tried to get some sleep!

Two of my favorite "hole" stories involve the same guys, Ron Grey and Gary Seeget. They were truly a couple of fun partners, both of whom later became subordinates. In one instance, they awoke one morning to find their unit surrounded by other parked cars! Another time they had backed into a recess between loading platforms adjacent to train tracks. When they awoke, they noticed they were blocked by a freight train, and had to ask the engineer to move the whole train so they could get back to the station at end-of-watch!

MET RETIRED HISTORIC DETECTIVE LIEUTENANT AT CAL STATE, LA

One evening while attending a book fair at Cal State LA, I met a long-retired LAPD detective lieutenant named Jesse Kimbrough. He was accompanied by a granddaughter, as he was getting up there in years, having joined the LAPD in 1916 and retired in 1939.

Jesse was the author of a novel called *Defender of the Angels*, about the trials and tribulations of a black police officer in the early part of the 20th century. He autographed, then gave me a copy of his book, which is absolutely fascinating. I still have the book, and have re-read it several times.

During the course of my historical research I have become familiar with this interesting man, and the problems and racism that minority officers confronted during that early era. I am very glad to have met him.

SHOOTING AT A BURGLAR, AND A SUSPENSION

In the wee small hours on the morning watch, Heath Haggerty and I got a radio call about a rape in progress at the Time Motel on Sunset

Boulevard, in the vicinity of Reservoir Street. There had been a series of hot-prowl burglaries in that area, and the description of our suspect matched the description in the other burglaries. As Heath and I arrived and deployed, I saw the suspect who matched the exact description put out by Communications, as he was running out of the motel complex. I immediately started chasing him and yelled to Heath, who also started running after the guy. I was yelling, "stop, or I'll shoot!"

The suspect ran through a gate into a backyard, and slammed the gate shut behind him, which locked. He was clearly getting away. So Heath cranked off one round, and I immediately followed suit with a round of my own. We did not hit him with our gunfire, but he must have thought we were getting pretty serious, because he stopped. He was good for that attempted rape and the other burglaries, and went to jail.

Later, Heath said he fired because I was yelling "stop or I'll shoot," and I fired because he fired! It was determined that, although the suspect was in fact the bad guy, we did not have adequate justification at that time and from just the radio transmission, to use deadly force. We each were awarded two relinquished days off for poor tactics.

Chief Parker's Purgatory—Worked Well for Me!

Chief William H. Parker did not like Officer Michael B. Hannon! Hannon was an anti-war, anti-police brutality activist who while off-duty participated in related activities. In 1965, he was given a six-month suspension for conduct unbecoming an officer (CUBO), because of his participation in a demonstration.

Parker did not want Hannon serving in the public eye, and fashioned quite a unique assignment for him on his return to duty. In that era, a policeman was assigned full-time to the Office of the City Treasurer for security. For years the position was held by an old-timer and coin collector, whose days were pretty much spent at a desk behind the counter, going through rolls and rolls of coins looking for gems for his collection. Parker decided that Hannon was going to be put in that position. But first he had a security box, which was close to soundproof and had one-way glass, made just for him! It was very secure, you could see out but nobody could see in, the door could only be locked from the inside, and there was a button to push in the event of a robbery. That was it.

What Parker failed to recognize is that he did a real favor for Hannon, who was a law school student at night and now had a place he could study for eight hours a day! Within a year Hannon had passed the bar, resigned from the department, and Parker was dead. The old-timer returned to the City Treasury, but had to do his coin collecting and screening inside the Hannon Memorial Security Booth.

During the summer of 1967 I asked to work the booth for a month while the old-timer went on vacation. I spent the entire shift, every day, doing homework for a very aggressive summer school program that I'd signed up for—worked pretty good for me! The booth is long-gone now, and today the city hall security folks perform those duties in the Office of the City Treasurer.

You Can't be Allison; She's in Canada!

I had a date with a gal from Arcadia whose name was Allison. We met at Citrus College. I thought, apparently mistakenly, that a mutual attraction existed between us. When I called Allison for a second date, she told me she wasn't available because of an imminent family trip to Canada. While on duty that weekend, however, I spotted Allison in her car with a few other girls in the area around Olvera Street. I activated my red lights and pulled her over. As I approached her driver's door she recognized me and exhibited a combination of relief and embarrassment. Obviously, she called me by name.

Of course, I made some wise-ass remark that she looked like someone I knew, but couldn't be that person because my acquaintance was in Canada. I don't recall exactly what she said, but she made some excuse about a deferred or canceled trip, and hoped to see me again. I don't know if she was truly interested in seeing me again, because I never gave her another call. I just wanted her to know that I knew she had been dishonest with me.

Death at the Mixer Bar

Failing to obey the commands of a police officer, especially during a felony situation, can be pretty hazardous to a suspect's health.

One early morning my partner and I got a call to back-up another unit for a "459 in progress" (burglary) at the Mixer Bar, on the east side of the Silverlake District. Officer Heath Haggerty took the rear and my partner and I took the front. Soon it was obvious that one of the two suspects had tried to leave by the back door, and there had encountered Haggerty. I heard two or three commands for the suspect to put his hands where Heath could see them. Then I heard a shot.

At about that same time I caught the other suspect as he tried to slip out the front door. As I walked my suspect past the dead body of his fellow crime partner, the thought occurred to me that he should not have

244

kept his hands concealed from Haggerty. Haggerty had been a Navy gunner's mate during World War II and a Marine during the Korean War, and clearly was not someone to play games with. While attending Heath's funeral at the Riverside National Cemetery in about 2009, I reflected on that and other incidents involving this colorful, no-nonsense officer.

Pants-less Men Chasing Thieves

Then, as always, it was common for horny men to engage the services of a prostitute. Often the woman had a male accomplice hiding in a closet, waiting for the right moment to grab and run off with the man's pants. Most of their male victims slithered away in silence and humiliation. But a few of them took after the pants thief (with his wallet still in the pocket) in a foot pursuit. These crimes typically occurred in the fleabag hotels, many of which were in the immediate area where LAPD's Central Facilities Building is now located. I took a lot of reports for these crimes, and on several occasions ran across the pants-less victim chasing the suspects. The latter was quite a sight, but I do not recall a victim with no pants and no shoes ever catching one of the thieves. Nor do I recall having much sympathy for these "victims."

Jumped Into a Literal Bed of Thieves

One afternoon my partner, Gary Dierks, and I got a call to the Wolfer Printing Company, a very old company located in a very old building on Skid Row. The person in the printing shop said there were some men on the roof doing something suspicious, maybe shooting heroin, who most likely had got onto the roof by jumping a couple of feet from the adjacent fleabag hotel.

We went up to the roof and found a couple of bank bags full of small bills and change! We also noticed that one of the windows of the adjacent hotel was open, and speculated that whoever had been on the roof had come from that room. Gary jumped across the small gap between the buildings and disappeared behind the window curtain.

He immediately started screaming for me, so I also jumped into the room, landing smack onto a bed that was full of money. We had interrupted a group of three gamblers dividing up their proceeds on the bed, and they had scattered like cockroaches. Gary and I managed to catch two of the three suspects in the room, but one got away—temporarily. Somehow, we identified the vehicle the third suspect had been driving. We then took the celluloid out of the distributor, staked out his car, and arrested him an hour or so later when he slithered back to get his vehicle. The money was booked and everybody went to jail. I don't recall what we charged them with.

Pursuit into Pasadena—"Did You Want Me?"

This was quite a memorable pursuit. It started around 11th and Francisco, when a driver failed to yield after a minor traffic accident with a police unit, and extended all the way into downtown Pasadena. As the suspect exited the Pasadena Freeway and went north on Arroyo Parkway, a Pasadena Police unit shined his spotlight into the vehicle being pursued, blinding the suspect. The suspect's vehicle went up a curb and hurled a complete block from Colorado to the next street to the north, finally coming to rest on top of a phone booth in an upper parking lot. As we ran to the suspect's destroyed and crushed vehicle, I thought the suspect was probably dead. We were wrong! When we shined our flashlights into the car's interior the unscathed suspect stated: "Did you want me?" That was 1966, and I suspect he was not still unscathed by the time he was booked!

Traffic Unit Pushed to the Pursuit Termination Point

The aforementioned pursuit met the criteria for handling by an Accident Investigation Division (AID) traffic unit. Clearly, it would be a complex traffic investigation, not something any non-traffic unit would want anything to do with.

It would be near-impossible to describe the measures that patrol units would take to avoid handling traffic accident investigations. This situation said it all. When the engine of the assigned AID unit blew up during the pursuit, a patrol unit then pushed the traffic unit all the way into Pasadena to handle the investigation!

"Trigger Treat" and Metropolitan Division Stakeouts

Halloween 1966 is memorable, not for what I did or personally saw, but because of a situation involving typical warped police humor.

During that era it was fairly common for Metropolitan Division officers to be assigned to stakeout duties at locations where armed robberies often occurred, and to shoot the robbers when weapons were produced. Liquor stores were favorite locations. There the officers would often conceal themselves behind advertisements while sitting atop walk-in coolers. Verbal commands were not typically given; when the crook produced a weapon it was assumed he was prepared to use it, and he was blown right back out the door with a blast from a police shotgun.

One such incident occurred on Halloween. This time, the suspect survived. A teletype went out to other agencies, indicating the description of the suspect and his *modus operandi* as possible aids in identifying other crimes the same suspect may have committed. But the author of the teletype couldn't resist adding a statement the suspect made later in the hospital: He walked in the liquor store, produced a weapon, heard the words "trigger treat," and several hours afterward woke up in the hospital!

Working in a Patrol Car—But Unable to Walk!

In my early young adult years, I was very much interested in search and rescue activities and wanted to join the Los Angeles County Sheriff's Search & Rescue team. But I was ineligible because all members had to be sworn in as reserve sheriff's deputies, and that department had a policy prohibiting peace officers from other agencies also being sworn in as a deputy sheriff.

As an alternative, I joined the Civil Air Patrol and became a member of a ground search and rescue unit. One afternoon while on an actual mission working with air units, my team responded to an observation of a crashed airplane just above the Rim of the World Drive near Lake Arrowhead. While I was climbing a fairly steep shale incline, a group of CAP cadets ran up the same incline and started a small rockslide. A fairly substantial boulder struck my knee and knocked me down, and another struck me in the head. I was genuinely injured and was taken to the hospital, where my head was sewn up. The X-rays and examination revealed a bruised, but unbroken knee. In retrospect, my team did not have the training or skills for dangerous or complicated rescues; our good intentions were not enough. The unsupervised kids were doing exactly what kids are inclined to do, so I really had no one to blame for my injuries but myself.

I literally could not walk without using some type of support for about a week, but still went to work! I was off probation (barely) and assigned to an "A" car (two men) on the graveyard shift in Central Division. By this time I had made an personal commitment with myself to never call in sick again (during my entire LAPD career I took one sick day, as a probationer). So I went to work. I had trouble just getting into the roll-call room, and after that getting to my assigned unit. With the cooperation of my partner, we were not very pro-active for several days, and when it was necessary to exit the vehicle I propped myself up between the frame and the open door. We were lucky nothing big happened during the several days of my recovery.

Pretty Girl Failed to Appreciate My Humor

One day, when working an "L" car (no partner), I received a radio call about a possible "DB" (dead body) in an alley behind a downtown office building. On arrival at the scene I was met by a pretty young gal, who excitedly told me there was someone on the ground behind a trash dumpster and she thought he might be deceased. I checked, and sure enough there was a deceased homeless man lying on the ground, with no evidence of foul play that I could see. It was just another of the many similar deaths we dealt with all the time.

Being a wise-ass, I returned to the girl and said something to the effect of: "Okay, why did you do it? Tell me all about it." Believing that I actually perceived her to be a suspect, she got really upset, turned pale and started stammering. At that point I told her I was just kidding, and that it appeared to be a natural death. She then got very angry, her face went from pale to red, and she started berating me for having morbid fun at the expense of a dead person when I should be feeling sad, etc. Obviously, she was right. I initially thought about giving her a call at some point for lunch, or whatever, but after her reaction to my inappropriate humor I felt that such a call would not be well received.

Wino Physician with a Broken Arm

Of the virtually hundreds of homeless winos that I arrested or have otherwise dealt with, a few stand out in my mind. Among the most memorable was a pathetic person with dirt and grime literally ground into his skin, who had a folded certificate in his inner jacket pocket. It was his doctor of medicine (MD) diploma. We arrested him, like thousands of others, for 647f PC, public drunkenness. Due to his complaint about something wrong with his arm, we first took him for medical treatment. His arm had been broken and untreated for some time! The physician and the nurse at Central Jail were just as stunned as my partner and I at how a man could slip so far, from prominence to skid row. I don't recall much of the conversation, but seem to remember that a divorce played a major role in starting his downfall. (I suspect alcohol was a factor as well?)

Danny Sanchez (pseudonym) was among the more unique of the many interesting partners I worked with. He was an okay guy and an okay partner, but with what I felt was a slightly warped personality.

I only worked with him when I was a new cop, and as I look back it seems that new cops were the only people he was assigned with; I suspect the more senior officers asked to not have to work with him. One night Danny and I were working 1B1 (the "B" wagon, for picking up drunks), and I was driving. While going down an alley he screamed for me to stop, then jumped out of the vehicle with a camera in his hand. He took a picture of something on the ground and said, "That was a great one." When I asked what it was, he said it was a truly unique pile of shit! This guy, I am sure just to gross people out, would take pictures of various piles of crap, and kept them in a scrapbook on a coffee table at his home in Alhambra. The last time I saw him has to be twenty years ago. By that time he was an airport cop in the Midwest, back visiting his old stomping grounds in Los Angeles.

THE WATCH COMMANDER DISAPPEARED—FOREVER!

Lieutenant Ed Cunningham (pseudonym) was hyper, but for the most part a decent guy, at least to me. He was seen as somewhat of a squirrel by most of the old-timers. Although I was not on his watch, he was always encouraging me to leave the morning watch (graveyard shift) and work for him on the PM (evening) shift. While he never did or said anything that was the least bit inappropriate, I did note that I was among several young officers he went out of his way to chat with. At the time, however, I felt it was due to our initiative and aggressiveness. One Saturday morning there was an anti-war demonstration at Parker Center. A bunch of normally off-duty folks, me included, had been called in, and Lieutenant Cunningham was the field commander. The demonstration went off without a glitch, and Lieutenant Cunningham invited everyone to go to Echo Park for a brief celebration. But I had to miss the event due to conflicting plans.

That was the last time I saw the lieutenant. The next day we learned that Lieutenant Cunningham had tried to grope a vice officer (obviously someone he did not recognize as a fellow cop) in the men's room at Echo Park. When confronted with the charges and the evidence, he chose to resign.

In the early 2000s, when I was the marshal of San Bernardino County, I got a call out of the blue from Lieutenant Cunningham's widow! Why she called me, and why I was even on her radar screen, was beyond me. She was living in Lancaster, and said that her husband had died several months prior. She went on to tell me that her husband had been framed in the termination, and should never have been forced to resign. My initial impression was that she was trying to lay the groundwork to potentially get a spousal pension, but I ultimately came to believe that she was just working to cleanse her late husband's reputation. She did not sound drunk. After our conversation, I did not hear from her again. I am a good friend with the man who was the captain of the Central Division at that time. He knew all about what occurred—Cunningham did what he was accused of doing.

Burglary at the Car Wash Yields Multiple Arrests— Quota Achieved!

One of my many partners was a very energetic officer named John Gelsen. We worked together for a couple of months on unit 1A29, trying very hard to "produce impressive statistics." One night we caught a person breaking into a car wash on East 7th Street. The suspect had kicked in a door and the entry point was highly visible to anyone walking down the street.

You guessed it! After contacting the owner, John and I hid our unit in a nearby alley and went "code 5" on the car wash. We were confident that other idiots would see the opening and enter the establishment, which would produce additional felony arrests for us. By the time the owner arrived to secure the premises, we had a half-dozen or so additional suspects in custody for burglary! Our "stats" were pretty impressive for that night, but in hindsight we were just spinning our wheels and clogging the system. In that part of the city, after hours, everybody was either a suspect or a victim, with tonight's victim being tomorrow's suspect.

John was a pretty decent guy and a fun partner. As a detective, he died of a heart attack at work several years later. By the way, there was no "quota" other than what we sought to achieve.

Rejected by the "Dating Game"

For some reason I do not now recall, I was called and given an audition to appear on the then-popular television show, "The Dating Game." When I got to the studio the men were seated on one side of a partition and the women on the other. The gals would ask the guys questions, then both would be evaluated based on their questions and the answers.

I still recall the only question I was asked (and my answer): "Number 7, you took me on a date to a nice restrauant, we had a great meal, and when the time came to pay the check you discovered you didn't have enough money to pay the bill. What would you do?" I replied to the gal behind the partition who had asked the question, "I would explain that I needed to use the restroom, and ask you to meet me at the car. Then I'd go into the restroom, climb out the window, and meet you at the car!"

At that point the moderator said: "We thank and excuse you, Number 7!" When leaving the studio, I ended up in the elevator with the gal who asked me the question. She'd also been given her walking papers. I asked her out, she accepted, and a week or so later we did have a nice dinner (and I did not, nor would I have ever, really crawled out the bathroom window). Our date was a real shocker for me, however, because she lived in Sepulveda. I had never before (even though I'd been on the LAPD for a year, or so) seen the enormity of the San Fernando Valley. She was a nice gal, but too "GU" (geographically undesirable) for me.

THE ULTIMATE REJECTION BY A GIRL I DATED

As a new cop (and later as a single old cop, as well!), I was active in dating, and by all measures pretty successful in my friendships. However, there was an occasional glitch, and "Linda" was one of them. She was the friend of a good friend's wife, so we double-dated one evening and had a nice time. The first date led to a second, and soon we double-dated with another good pal, John, whose mother was the famous movie star, Dorothy Lamar.

The four of us end up at John's house in North Hollywood, and at the end of the evening I took Linda back to her home in the Lakewood area. The next morning John called with quite a story: Linda had returned to his apartment a couple of hours after she and I were there! She was apparently "star-struck" by his second-generation celebrity status, and went back to put the make on him, staying until dawn.

My emotions, in a span of about ten seconds, went from disbelief to anger to indifference. Screw her! Even more unbelievable were her extensive efforts to make up with me, obviously because she didn't have any luck with John. I'll bet I received a card a day for about three weeks, with apologies and pleas to get back together. I finally called her, saying that her actions were not something I was inclined to forget, and to stop bothering me.

John is a great guy. I last saw him around 2010, when I encouraged him to come and get the .45 semi-automatic pistol that his father, long deceased, had carried on numerous missions as a bomber pilot during World War II. John had swapped it to me in the late 1960s. But, as I grew older, I realized that he should really have his dad's gun back. It was my pleasure to reunite the son with his dad's pistol, no strings attached or swap necessary.

Drunken Officer Shoots His Way Out of the "B-Wagon"

Since the beginning of time, off-duty officers will occasionally gather for a few beers after a work shift, sometimes at a remote location in the division where they work. While these types of gatherings are strongly discouraged these days, they were frequent realities in years past. It also was not uncommon for some on-duty officers, if not tied-up on calls, to drop by for a Coke and to just say "hi."

One such activity, which took place late one night in a multi-story parking structure downtown, really went sideways. The several on-duty officers who dropped by included a sergeant and the "B-Wagon" officers (for transporting large numbers of drunks). When a few drunk off-duty cops placed another drunk off-duty cop (who still had a firearm in his possession) in the back of the "B-Wagon" and locked him in, he took exception to their action by trying to shoot his way out! Obviously, he damaged the vehicle with a number of bullet holes, and the matter became the subject of an investigation. Those disciplined included the sergeant who was still on probation and lucky to somehow keep his stripes.

George Washington Carver Medal
for Commitment to Diversity

A retired woman sheriff's executive is probably still shaking her head over this one. I had a friend in the 1960s who was not very sensitive to racial issues (an understatement). At the time, he was a security chief of a Los Angeles County facility. No long after we met, I was given a box of old ceremonial and sports medals, one of which was the "George Washington Carver Medal." My friend was opposed to everything George Washington Carver stood for, which gave me an evil idea. I had the medal mounted in a frame with a bogus certificate commending my pal for his commitment to racial equality, and sent it to him in the mail. He immediately figured out that it was from me.

Not long afterward, his department came under critical review. A black female sheriff's lieutenant was detailed to his department to do an audit, including a review of his behavior and leadership skills. He later told me that when she out-and-out accused him of being a racist (a pretty easy conclusion for her to arrive at), he brought out the medal and certificate I'd jokingly sent him and showed it to her to prove he wasn't a racist. He said she appeared dumbfounded, shook her head, and walked away. She later promoted to a fairly high rank in the Sheriff's Department and I became somewhat acquainted with her. But I never had the inclination to tell her the truth about my pal's coveted award.

STACK OF GAMEWELL BOXES—HELP YOURSELF!

While working an "L Car" out of Central I somehow learned that the Gamewell boxes, which had been taken off of Bunker Hill, were stacked at a city yard near San Fernando Road and Figueroa Street. I thought it would be neat to get one and use it at home to keep my revolver in. I found the yard, and a stack of old Gamewell boxes that was taller than I was. The fellow in charge told me to help myself and take all I wanted! I took two, one for myself and another for a pal. For years I have lamented my failure to truly help myself! The one I took for myself remains in use, in my home, for weapons and other valuable items.

STAFF SERGEANT WOLFMULE ON MAIN STREET

While on active duty in the Marine Corps and stationed on Okinawa, there was a a Native American staff sergeant who I did not particularly care for. We were in the same company, but he was in the Flames (flame throwers) Platoon and I was in the Communications Platoon. I never had any direct dealings with him. Nevertheless, I saw him as a jerk and avoided dealing with him.

Later, as a cop, my partner and I got a call regarding a "390-415" (drunk disturbing the peace) at 3rd and Main, where the bars catered to Native Americans. There I again came face-to-face with Staff Sergeant Wolfmule (pseudonym). He kind of recognized me through his bloodshot eyes. He had engaged in behavior that was clearly worthy of going to jail, but I dusted him off and turned him over to a couple of his pals, who assured me they would take care of him. I was not about to put a fellow Marine in jail for that type of minor offense, even a Marine I didn't particularly care for.

You owe me, Wolfmule!

This was fun, and kind of cool. I have always had a particular interest in electronics and radios, and occasionally hung out at the police radio shop. One of my buddies, a radio technician, made a "lie detector" for me. It consisted of a low-wattage bulb attached to a simple wire, which would light up when placed close to a police car antenna when the microphone was "keyed."

We had fun using them as "lie detectors" when questioning dumb people!

Purchased and Carried Personal Shotgun

Shotguns were not available to uniformed patrol officers until the late 1960s. The shotguns in Property Division were reserved for Metropolitan and specialized detective divisions, primarily for stakeouts. I am aware that some uniformed officers, primarily supervisors, had them during the 1965 Watts Riots, but they were not available to patrol when I went on the department.

Not long after I became a cop, an incident took place that I believe involved an assault on a Sparklett's Water truck driver. It ignited some minor disturbances, which many feared would trigger another massive riot, but fortunately that did not occur. Like many other officers, after this incident I purchased and carried my own personal shotgun in the trunk of my patrol car. I still recall going to the police credit union and taking out a loan for about $76, then purchasing the gun from the F. Morton Pitt Police Supply Company. The gun I purchased was similar to those the department ultimately adopted—an Ithica "deer slayer." I realize this story must seem impossible by today's standards, but it was perfectly acceptable and a common practice when I was a new cop.

Loan to the Central Vice Unit

Toward the end of my tour in Central Division, I spent a month on loan to the Vice Unit. We worked prostitutes, but mostly conducted lewd conduct investigations in public bathrooms.

Lewd conduct was a big problem at the time, as normal people who just wanted to relieve themselves were often subjected to sickening behavior. Verbal overtures were often accompanied by smiles while suspects held and pointed their genitals at someone with whom they hoped to have a sexual encounter. "Glory holes" were often installed in the partitions between stalls, and it was pretty startling for an unsuspecting man seated on a toilet to see a penis emerge through the hole in the partition! We staked-out where there were screened observation rooms, and also personally operated the suspects, with arrests being made when the verbiage reached the legal threshold for a penal code violation.

There were some pretty sad stories that went along with these arrests. While most of the arrestees were folks with not much to lose, it was unfortunately not unheard-of to arrest someone who would very clearly lose everything in his life because of the mandatory reporting requirements. One arrest that I recall to this day was a schoolteacher with a beautiful wife and beautiful little twin daughters. Certainly he lost his job, and probably his family, as well. While recognizing that human sexuality comes in many forms, it is pretty difficult for me to understand how lust could be satisfied in a smelly public bathroom!

Catching Whores Because of Holes in the Doors

A unique way of establishing acts of prostitution came to an end during my time in Central. For the life of me, I do not recall what law (or lack of a law) permitted us to do it. But some officers, primarily vice officers, carried small corkscrew devices used to bore holes in doors to investigate acts of prostitution they believed were taking place. Every wooden door in every fleabag hotel was full of small holes, some new and many patched up, all the result of police investigations. The corkscrews were also pretty handy in making a small hole in the taillight of a car you wanted to follow, as the emanating white light was visible from a considerable distance. My corkscrew is displayed prominently, along with my massive blackjack and sap gloves, in a display case at my home museum.

Disciplinary Bail Schedule—1966

Among the many things within the LAPD that have changed over the years are the disciplinary standards.

Back in the day, the names of all officers being disciplined were included on the summary that went out to the entire department. Also during that era, it was most common to be penalized by relinquishing regular days off, as opposed to suspension days. As an example, when I was penalized with two RDOs (regular days off) I did not lose any salary, but received seven as opposed to nine days off that 30-day deployment period. As there was no prohibition from taking accrued compensatory overtime off, I still had adequate time off.

Every "rap sheet" listed one or more officers who were terminated for having a romantic relationship with a person "other than his wife." I believe that adultery was more of an issue of discretion than propriety; if it didn't become an issue, it was not a matter of concern. While falsification of a report was pretty serious, I don't recall what the average penalty was. For "false and misleading statements" (for instance, lying during the course of a personnel investigation), the average penalty range was two to four RDOs.

As I recall, there were not too many instances where officers were disciplined for excessive force. Perhaps we were gentler then, or people were less inclined to make complaints, or supervisors were less inclined to take complaints. Maybe all these issues contributed to the relatively small number of disciplines for use-of-force violations.

Consequences for Unauthorized Ammunition

There were rules in the 1960s and early 1970s pertaining to authorized and unauthorized ammunition, but the rules were often ignored. It was not uncommon for officers to carry the popular (but unauthorized) semi-hollow point wad-cutter bullets, or anything else they wanted to carry. Officers could also carry their own revolvers, including .357s, but the .357 ammunition was not authorized. While I always followed these particular rules (there were others where I wasn't as diligent!), many officers carried whatever they felt like carrying, because there were seldom adverse consequences.

Before inspections, supervisors would often remind people to ensure the ammunition shown was authorized. In officer-involved shootings, the type of ammunition was not among the questions asked. In autopsies, the coroner gave the bullet removed from a body to a detective who did not care and was not about to raise the issue. Like many things during that era, possession and use of unauthorized ammunition was against the rules, but it was never an issue unless something extraordinary occurred to make it an issue.

That was just the way it was when I was a new cop.

Wearing the Uniform Hat

Except for officers performing traffic functions, where the hat was white and helpful for visibility, officers always hated wearing the uniform hat and looked for every opportunity to avoid wearing it.

From the time I joined the department until wearing of the hat became optional in the 1980s, wearing them became a ritualistic game both for officers and supervisors. The majority of officers did not wear them in the absence of a supervisor, and when a supervisor came on scene one of the officers would return to the car and fetch both officers' hats! Typically, a supervisor would not say anything as long as they were retrieved and worn while the supervisor was present.

Oh Yeah, Payson Got a Violation, All Right!

Not surprisingly, new cops keep track of how their Police Academy classmates are doing in their new assignments. One of my classmates, Payson, didn't do too well.

On a one-night loan to vice for a lewd-conduct task force, he was sent into a public bathroom known for its notoriously lewd conduct violations. As instructed, when he got a violation, he signaled the other officers to close in and assist in arresting the suspect. But his senior partners were surprised to learn that the only two people in the room were Payson and his suspect—there was no second suspect who the first suspect would have propositioned for illicit sex.

When he was quizzed about what had occurred, Payson proudly declared that he had a solid violation: He had permitted the suspect to perform oral copulation on him! I don't know the details, but not long afterward Pason ceased to be a Los Angeles policeman.

Summer Deaths in a Railroad Tank Car

It is hard to imagine anything worse than this. While I was still working in Central, the putrefied remains of several illegal aliens were discovered in a railroad tank car. They had apparently slipped into the tank car to sneak further inland from the border. Somehow the top latch closed, and they were trapped and had to have experienced what must have been horrible deaths.

On being discovered in the middle of the summer, they had been in the tank for several weeks. The coroner's employee who had to remove their remains truly earned his wages that day!

Flirting on the Gamewell—Big Mistake

During what turned out be one of my last days assigned to Central Patrol Division, I had a need to call the Jail Division. I used the Gamewell call box system to do so and the girl at the other end, who was assigned to Jail Division as a clerk, sounded really nice. I flirted with her for quite a while and finally suggested that maybe she and I should get together and go to the beach, as it was still a nice time of the year. She thought it was a good idea, and we made plans to meet up in near future.

Later that night I snuck into the jail to see what she looked like, and I really did not like what I saw! She was not my type, and I realized that she was not someone who I would be likely to call for a date. Unfortunately, the next day I received notice that I was being transferred into Jail Division! During my three-month assignment at the jail, I worked very hard to avoid her, and was able to do so. I'm sure I must have hurt her feelings, and for that I am sorry. It was a great lesson for me. I don't think I ever again flirted with some gal over the phone, at least not seriously, until I at least knew what she looked like!

JAIL DIVISION

In October 1967, after approximately eighteen great months in Central Division, I "wheeled" into Jail Division.

The jail was then housed within the Police Administration Building complex, downtown at 150 N. Los Angeles Street. In that era all officers, for their second assignment, went to either the Jail or the Parking & Intersection Control divisions, which was known as "being on the wheel." Once a three-month tour in one of those two divisions was completed, an officer was considered to be "off the wheel," and could conceivably remain in the next division for the remainder of his career.

As I recall, there were probably around 100 persons, of all ranks, assigned to the Jail Division at the time.

CAPTAIN EARL SANSING INTERVENES FOR OFFICER BUSHEY

That October, I was on the transfer from Central Division to the Parking & Intersection Control Division. This was a real problem for me, because I was attending Citrus College full-time during the day and PIC was strictly a day watch assignment, directing traffic at key intersections in downtown Los Angeles on a split shift.

So I went to Personnel Division and pled my case to the commanding officer, Captain Earl Sansing. He said he would see what he could do. That wonderful man got on the phone and called all the other officers who had received transfers to the Jail, until he found one who was willing to swap with me! He then called me personally at home with the good news. For the rest of my career, I worshipped the ground that Earl Sansing walked on, and have sought to be just as kind and considerate with those young officers who have sought my assistance.

"Willing to Have"—That's All?

A month or so into my assignment at Jail Division, I received my transfer rating report from Central Division.

I was devastated. Overall, the report was good, and I believe it reflected my performance, which frankly was good. I was aware that I was seen as one of the more capable and promising young officers, because I had been told this by a number of my supervisors.

However, the rating report had a series of boxes to be checked to indicate the desirability of the officer to serve in that assignment again. They were: Particularly Desire, Glad to Have, Willing to Have, Prefer Not to Have, and Particularly Desire Not to Have. On my rating, the box "willing to have" had been checked. I couldn't believe this was accurate, and felt certain I should have at least rated a "glad to have." I could not let this mistake (as I saw it) become part of my record, so I made an appointment and met with the captain of the Central Division, Larry Walton. When I expressed my consternation, he said, "let's take a walk." He took me upstairs to Personnel Division, asked for my personnel package, flipped to that evaluation (which was right on top), scratched out the category that gave me the heartburn, and put a great big check mark on "Glad To Have!" I was very grateful, and Larry Walton earned a top spot on my good-guy list.

To this day, Larry Walton and his wife Beverly are dear friends. We have visited their ranch in Utopia, Texas, and they have been at our home. I really did not have contact with him after that incident until about 1992, when he visited the commanding officer of Central Area (me!) to see if there was any interest for a real quality Central reunion. What a wonderful opportunity to reconnect with such a wonderful man. I rolled out the red carpet, and we had the best reunion ever, with plenty of support from his old division and the young kid he had taken such good care of years before.

The actions of Larry Walton, by changing that mark on my evaluation in the manner he did, was a lesson that absolutely had a positive impact on my career leadership and people skills.

Uncharacteristic Compassion to Unusual Persons

We received quite a few female imposters, commonly known as "drag queens," in the Jail. Most were prostitutes who acted like real jerks and were repugnant to deal with. We would get the occasional drag queen who was polite, who did not behave in a bizarre manner, who was horribly humiliated, and who was in a state of panic because he was soon to be seen in female attire by the person (most often a relative) in the public waiting room who had just paid bail to get him released.

While I was just as homophobic as the other officers of the era, that awkward situation, for both the arrestee and the person posting the bail, touched some compassionate part of me. Unlike some of my fellow officers who enjoyed observing the pain and humiliation during these situations, I would often make male attire available from the stash of old clothes we maintained for the homeless we had to delouse, etc. As I look back, I suspect that enabling some of those folks to shed their female attire before being reunited with their families was a big fork in the road of their lives.

Joey Hernandez Brings Happiness to Other Prisoners

As I recall, this slightly-built, feminine-acting and appearing transvestite was named Joey Hernandez. With all the Joey Hernandezes in the world, I won't worry about using a pseudonym. Joey was a streetwalking male transvestite prostitute who really enjoyed his occupation. He was a regular in Central Division, which at that time extended west all the way to Hoover. Joey always had a good attitude when he and whomever he was "servicing" were taken into custody, which was quite often. There was no doubt that he truly enjoyed all the things that he experienced, and the things he did to and for his male customers; he might just as well have worn a "welcome" sign on each of his bodily orifices! He was a "regular" when I worked Central patrol and vice, and again a regular after I transferred into Jail Division.

While today's jails segregate people for every possible category, in 1967 all males were housed in the same large dormitory-type tank, the only exception being psychos or really high-powered felonies. When Joey came into the jail, always dressed as a woman, he was just put in the big cellblock with 40 or 50 other male prisoners. As I reflect on those times, I now realize that some of the constant yelling must have been Joey squealing with delight and his fellow inmates moaning with pleasure. Except for medical emergencies, when inmates reported a problem in the back of the large holding tanks, we paid very little attention to what was otherwise occurring in the back of those tanks.

By today's standards, that type of inattention would be unthinkable, but it was the norm in that era.

Transsexual Determined to be "Mutilated Male"

Things have changed in the last half-century or so. Back then, homosexuality was pretty much a dirty word, and transsexuals were close to unheard-of. While there was no shortage of "drag queens," those who had undergone some degree of surgical intervention to transform themselves into the opposite gender were rare.

Today's understanding and acceptance did not exist in society, let alone in the jails, in the late 1960s. This reality is best illustrated by a situation that I witnessed during my tour in Jail Division, where a surgically altered individual whose male genitals had been removed and a vagina constructed, was determined to be a "mutilated male." He/she was then placed into the male section of the Jail. Very different times! Such placement today could easily result in a federal investigation for violation of civil rights.

My First and Last (Serious) Motorcycle Crash

Like many new cops, I had to have a motorcycle! How could I truly be cool without such a manly machine? I bought a Honda 305 Scrambler, good for both the street and the dirt.

One morning about 0800, while enroute from my LAPD graveyard shift to Citrus College for a mid-term exam, I crashed. While making the transition from the eastbound San Bernardino Freeway to northbound Rivergrade Road (now the 605 Freeway), I was traveling behind a gravel truck that was leaking some sand. When I hit the curve a bit faster than I should have, my bike hit the low guardrail and I went airborne. Fortunately, I landed about half-way down the 45-degree embankment, which broke much of my fall.

I was very briefly knocked unconscious, but regained consciousnesses just as two CHP officers were coming down the embankment. I jumped up (painfully!), told them I was a cop, was uninjured (not exactly accurate), and did not desire an accident report. After a handshake or two, they left. I then bent my handlebars back around and was able to drive, more like an automotive limp with my damaged motorcycle, to Citrus College where I took my exam.

After school I went to the Santa Teresita Hospital for treatment and X-rays. Nothing was broken, but a few bandages were applied to a pretty badly scraped-up leg. I then drove the motorcycle to the local dealer, George Dye Honda in Duarte, and told him to fix it and then sell it. In addition to frequent factors beyond the control of even careful riders, I possessed too little maturity and too much testosterone. I was wise to get rid of that bike before killing myself.

No More of Sweeney's Health Food Farts

I spent most of my three months in Jail Division on the morning watch (graveyard shift) assigned to the Misdemeanor Section. Somewhat like patrol, there were three of us, with the expectation that two of us would always be on duty for each shift. The senior officer, an "old-timer" (probably in his late 30s!), was a fun and decent guy whose last name was Sweeney. I have long forgotten what his first name was. Sweeney truly fell into the category of "health food nut," as everything he ate was something organic. He made and brought his lunch each day, an assortment of things that looked like turdballs rolled in sesame seeds and similar foul-looking delicacies. Sweeney also rode his bike to and from work each day—from Huntington Beach!

As seemed to be the case with many of my fellow officers, he took great pride in being able to produce some truly horrible farts on a frequent basis, and I can attest that health-food farts are among the worst. When I transferred out of the Jail I missed working with my pal Sweeney, but I didn't miss his horribly awful-smelling health-food farts.

Administrative Detective Division

In January 1968, after having completed the obligatory three-month tour in the Jail Division, I was specifically selected for and transferred into the newly-created Automated Field Interview Unit. It was part of the Administrative Detective Division of the Detective Bureau.

The role of this new unit was to automate the daily influx of field interview cards completed by field personnel, and to be able to use that new data base as a tool to identify crime suspects. There were two policemen, two clerk typists, and several police student workers assigned to this unit, which was located on the 7th floor of the Police Administration Building.

Selected for the Automated Field Interview Unit

As I was wrapping up my three-month tour in Jail Division, I was asked to contact Sergeant "Swede" Johnson in the Administrative Unit of the Detective Bureau (known then as "Administrative Detectives").

We met, and Johnson told me he was developing a unit to automate field interview cards (FIs). He'd heard that I was a bright and capable young officer, and would I be interested in becoming one of the two officers in the unit?

What a compliment and opportunity it was, for someone with so little time! I immediately accepted. I was the night watch officer, had a clerk typist who worked for me, and our job was to take the hundreds of FI cards that came in from all over the city, code them, send them to a keypunch operator, and file them for retrieval by sorting machines. Obviously, this was before computers, but it was really state of the art at that time. If a crime was committed and there was a vehicle involved, the only description was the ethnicity of the driver, the color of the vehicle, and perhaps one or two numbers of the license plate, we would pull various drawers, put stuff in the sorters, and initiate a series of searches. It was a great tool that resulted in many arrests and the solving of thousands of crimes over the years. It continues to exist, but with modern technology. I was honored to have been a part of it in my early years.

HISTORICAL ARCHIEVES THROWN OUT!

During my nine or so months in the Automated Field Interview Unit, where I worked on the 7th floor of the Police Administration Building, I was given permission by Captain Clifford Shannon of the Public Affairs Division to be the volunteer historian of the Department's Archives. The archives were located in a fairly small room to the immediate southwest of the elevators, in the same south corridor as Public Affairs. I spent quite a bit of time looking at all the items from the department's past, organizing and categorizing them, etc.

One day I went to the archives, unlocked the door, and to my amazement found a new office with a couple of women seated behind desks, typing! I asked what had happened to the archives, and the gals told me to take up my concerns with Lieutenant Herron. I immediately chased down Lieutenant Jack Herron, voiced my concerns, and asked what happened to all of the historic items. It was clear that Herron did not care much about me or the archives. In a very short conversation, he said that Public Affairs needed the room and that he'd had all the historic items sent to a warehouse on Jackson Street!

I rushed to the Jackson Street warehouse, which is long-gone but which then sat between the present "tinker-toy" parking structure and Alameda Street. At the time it was the garage for police motorcycles, the radio shop, and a storage facility. In the corner, on several pallets, were all the historic crown jewels; photos, guns, badges, uniforms, night sticks, etc., etc. There was no security for the pallets, and the usual hosts of warehouse-type folks were all over the place. I couldn't believe what had happened, and feared that some artifacts had already been taken. I was wrong, as I think I got there in time, but will never know for sure.

Unsure of what to do, I called Supply Division to see if the many items could be safely stored. I was very lucky in that I spoke to a wonderful man, Lieutenant Bob May, who immediately grasped the significance of what had occurred. Lieutenant May told me to stand guard over the items. A truck would immediately be dispatched to gather up all the items, and in the meantime he would find a safe location. He was true to his word: a truck was there within minutes, and all of the historic items were taken to a large cell at the recently-closed City Jail on Avenue 19. The items remained in that cell for probably close to thirty years, until turned over to Richard Kalk when the LAPD Historical Society got its first storage structure.

Bob May is one of my heroes, as he literally saved the department's crown jewels. Among my many regrets in life is that I did not stay in contact with him. Several years ago, when I was still with the San Bernardino County Sheriff's Department, I learned that he had passed away. I was unable to attend his funeral services, as I attended the services for Retired Deputy Chief John McAllister, which were held the same day and time. I did, however, send a letter to Bob's family, in which I recounted how he saved the department's historic items. Bob May was a department hero for another reason as well: in the 1950s, he and his partner caught the infamous "Red Light Bandit," Caryl Chessman, who was found guilty of numerous assaults and rape, sentenced to death, and ultimately executed sometime around 1970.

I am now, and for some time have been, a member of the Board of Directors of the Los Angeles Police Historical Society. A couple of years ago, my son Jake told me of a fellow sergeant whose dad was retired Lieutenant Jack Herron! I sent Lieutenant Herron a nice note and encouraged him to join the Historical Society via the payroll deduction program, mentioning that it was the least he could do! I reminded him that I saved all the stuff that he basically threw away (might as well have, as all of it would have been gone in a day or two due to pilferage). I never heard back from him!

Department Position Papers
on Just About Everything of Contemporary Interest

I still recall the Public Affairs Section had a file of position papers that outlined the official department position on just about every subject imaginable. Specifically, I recall the following: Semi-automatic pistols were inferior to revolvers, and would never be suitable for police work; chemical compliance sprays, such as MACE, were ineffective and would never be used by the department; women were not suitable for conventional police duties, just juvenile work; dogs were not suitable for police duties, etc. Funny how things change!

Traded a Payroll Deduction for a Submachine Gun!

Officer Norm Conn was a wonderful man, and pretty much "Mr. American Legion" in the LAPD. From his office in Public Affairs, Norm coordinated the many (at that time) department American Legion activities including a band, motor drill team, and LAPD Post 361.

While visiting with him one afternoon (we both worked on the 7th floor and were fellow veterans) he was sorting through all kinds of World War II memorabilia brought back after the war by officers who had been mobilized for military service. One time there had apparently been a big display where all this neat stuff had been shown, but it was now being boxed up and, as I recall, taken to the Patriotic Hall museum. One of the things sitting there was a fully-automatic, 9mm British Owens submachine gun, with a large capacity magazine. I asked Norm what he was going to do with it, as it was sitting off to one side. When he said he had no plans for it, I said I thought it was pretty neat and would not mind having it. He said he would give it to me in return for my signature on a payroll deduct card, which would enroll me as a member of American Legion Post 361! I signed the card and then and there became the proud owner of a submachine gun. Later, in a trade with a deputy sheriff, I acquired another fully-automatic weapon, a U.S. M-2 carbine. I realize that by today's standards my possession of these fully automatic weapons is near-impossible to imagine, but in those days there were plenty of these types of guns around. While they were not legal, it was really no big deal and could be half-ass justified for a cop.

About five years later, while on loan from Rampart to Internal Affairs, an officer was under investigation and facing likely termination for several acts of misconduct including the possession of a fully-automatic weapon. It turned out that massive federal firearms legislation in the late 1960s really tightened the laws, with big penalties, related to fully-automatic weapons. Within just a couple of days of becoming aware of these realities, my two fully-automatic weapons hit the ocean floor somewhere between Long Beach and Catalina Island.

A Very Nice & Kind Man—Sergeant Ben Staffer

From very early in my career with the Los Angeles Police Department, I was interested and fascinated with the history of the city, the department, and crime. As a young cop in about 1967, I went to the Records & Identification Division and asked the watch commander, Sergeant Ben Staffer, if I could go down to the mezzanine where all the old records were kept, and pull some of the interesting packages. He not only gave me permission to browse around, but also took the time to show me how to find some of the stuff I was looking for.

This experience caused Ben and me to become life-long friends, as I was so impressed with his goodwill and kindness. Also, he was a World War II Marine who had participated in the landings at Saipan, Roi Namur and Iwo Jima as a member of "Charlie" Company of the 4th Tank Battalion, 4th Marine Division. We became hunting partners, and Ben came to be like an uncle to my sons as the years went by. On his retirement, Ben became one of my volunteer monitors when I was the commanding officer of Communications Division.

When Ben died in the mid-1990s his wife, Jane, asked me to give an impromptu eulogy at his services, which were graveside only at Rose Hills in Whittier. What an honor it was, to have the opportunity to tell all present how much I loved and respected that very decent and kind man. Rest in peace, my dear friend.

Officer Bushey Needs to Mature

I only got one rating report while assigned to "Auto FIs," and it was not a very good one. Sergeant "Swede" Johnson wrote it. Basically, it described me as a good cop, a hard worker, and someone who did a good job. However, there was a very stinging and negative comment that I needed to mature as an officer. Unfortunately, it was an accurate comment. I worked on the evening shift and was in charge of two people, a clerk typist and a student worker. I screwed off quite a bit, often taking off to deal with personal business or whatever.

In addition to this comment, the day watch officer, Dan Lang, who also had seniority over me, took me aside and told me the same thing in no uncertain words. I needed this message, and in hindsight appreciate his candor. I believe I did in fact mature because of the honesty of Swede Johnson and Dan Lang. Dan went on to be a lieutenant before he retired, and certainly could have gone higher had he chosen to do so.

————

Intelligence Division

In October 1968, after approximately nine months in the Automated Field Interview Unit, I transferred into the "Specials Unit" of Intelligence Division as an undercover operator. The purpose of this unit was to investigate and gather data on organizations and individuals believed to be involved in subversive and un-American activities. In earlier years, this unit was known as the "Red Squad." The assignment turned out to be quite an experience.

Introduction to Police Intelligence

My path into Intelligence Division was unique, and pretty much accidental. One day I ran across Officer Bill Lesner, who had done my background check when I applied for the department. He was a nice fellow, who recalled my background and visiting my home during the background investigation.

Bill told me he was working the "Specials Unit" of Intelligence Division, where his job was to investigate subversive and un-American activities. He explained that it was a very "hush-hush" assignment and said the unit was located at the old Georgia Street Receiving Hospital facility. His comments really got my attention, as I was attending California State College–Los Angeles as a full-time student during the day, and always running across activities that I believed were subversive and un-American.

He suggested that I drop him a note, or better yet fill out an Intelligence Report, Form 3.19, if I saw anything that fell into this category. I saw plenty, and started sending quite a few 3.19s to Bill Lesner dealing with the Communist Party (CPUSA), Socialist Workers Party (SWP), Progressive Labor Party (PLP), and Students for a Democratic Society (SDS).

I was certainly proud to be a cop. But I kept that fact to myself at school, and was seen pretty much as just another returning Vietnam veteran attending school on the GI Bill (which in fact I was). I started dropping in on meetings, got on mailing lists, met a few folks, and reported things of potential interest to the Specials Unit. I would get periodic calls from Bill Lesner and others, asking for elaboration on this or that point, or to provide additional information on a certain person(s), etc. I was happy to help, and saw my actions as just being a good and loyal American. I had no thoughts about transferring into the unit, and knew nothing about anyone being in an undercover assignment.

You Are Doing More Than the Rest of the Division Combined!

One day, out of the blue, I got a phone call from the Administrative Sergeant, Stan Smith, who explained that I could not be granted overtime for my activities. I responded that I'd never even considered requesting compensation, but rather saw my actions as those of a patriotic American.

Stan explained that this was not the issue. What he was really asking, was would I consider transferring into the Specials Unit of Intelligence Division, and working full-time as an undercover agent! He explained that the unit was getting more good intelligence from me alone than was being produced by everyone else in the Intelligence Division combined! I immediately said I was interested. Stan replied that the captain would initiate a request to the chief of police to authorize me to go undercover.

Undercover—Deep Undercover!

A day or two later, Sergeant Smith called and said my undercover assignment was approved. Effective on a certain date, I would be assigned to the Specials Unit of Intelligence Division as the first undercover officer to be assigned primarily to a college campus. When I inquired about any training I would need, he replied "just keep doing what you're doing." There was no training program.

I was told to not carry a badge or identification, that I was exempted from monthly weapons qualification, and told to stay completely away from police facilities. All my records were purged or cleansed to remove any indication that I was a cop, including the modification of my college records by a Cal State College administrator who worked closely with the department. I did not even get a paycheck, but received my salary in cash every two weeks at a Taco Bell on Valley Boulevard in Alhambra. The cash was in the bag when I got my order! I was given "cold" (untraceable—not in the system) Colorado license plates for my car, as part of my cover story of being from the "Four Corners area of Colorado," and periodic gas money. I was assigned the designation of

"S-255," which I was to place on my reports and give as my identifier when I called the office.

Such an assignment would be much more difficult to coordinate today than it was when I went undercover in 1968. Since I had used my actual name on mailing lists, I pretty much had to stick with it. There was no Internet or all the other ways of learning about a person that exist today. For the two years that I was undercover, I supposedly worked as an ambulance driver for White's Mortuary in Azusa, a cover story made possible with the cooperation of Mr. White. This gave me an explanation for having some money and routine absences. At the time, I lived at home with my mom in Duarte. I had a telephone at home that we referred to as the "asshole phone," to be used only for my undercover activities (it was locked in an old police callbox, so it would not be accidentally answered if I wasn't home).

Rigid Political Views and Lean Female Pickings

The undercover assignment was hard on my social life. First, with long hair and a beard I had an appearance that was not acceptable to any girl who had my values, and had to be very careful about to whom I revealed my true identity as a policeman. While I did okay, the reservoir of females with whom I could socialize was smaller than I would have liked. Secondly, I was a staunch Republican and frankly not attracted to any female who was a Democrat. In hindsight it was pretty stupid, but it reflected the reality of my rigid mindset in those days.

Difference Between Hippies and Radicals

Most of the people I associated with while undercover probably looked like hippies. But many were hard core-radical socialists who were much different from hippies. The biggest distinction was the absolute absence of drugs of any type among the socialist radicals. Drugs were seen as counter-revolutionary and, believe it or not, were felt by some of my pals to be a capitalist plot to "control the masses." The other big distinction was primary goal and focus: radicals were very disciplined, and never took their eye off the primary goal of pursuing the transition to a socialist society.

Hippies, for the most part, kinda oozed in various directions that were out of the mainstream, and were opposed and willing to demonstrate against most government policies or programs. Let there be no doubt, there were hoards of hippies in all of the organizations and demonstrations. But they were pawns in the games of the radicals, who were the behind-the-scenes organizers.

TYPICAL DAY WHILE UNDERCOVER

The best way I can describe my undercover work hours would be "day on and stay on!" My job was to be with the radical organizers, and involved in their activities. There were a few days that I had to myself, but not too many. A typical day would be attending one to three meetings during the day, another meeting at night, then up to the wee hours of the morning running a mimeograph machine whipping out posters or flyers, etc. The one time of the day that I could usually be free and slip away was early to mid-morning, because the bad guys were usually not morning people.

I was very diligent, as I was always worried that the meeting I missed may have been the key meeting that I really needed to attend. Many of the activities I attended and participated in were garbage, but they were necessary to establish and maintain my credibility—and, again, there was sometimes no way of knowing when something important would happen. Conspiracies are a good example. To establish one, it was critical to follow it from cradle to grave, especially identifying all of the players, and that is what I tried very hard to do. Being in the Intelligence Division, we never made arrests. But it was critical to gain and pass accurate information to other department entities, especially the Criminal Conspiracy Section, which did conduct investigations and make arrests in certain instances.

There were days when I had very little to do, but just being present with the targets of my investigations and doing nothing was often a necessity. For the most part, the folks I investigated lived, slept and ate together. I could disappear from time to time, but my days were often 18 to 20 hours.

My saving grace was the cover story I had for employment: I was (allegedly) an ambulance attendant working out of a mortuary (most ambulances originated from one during that era) out in the far-eastern end of the San Gabriel Valley. So I usually had a reasonable excuse to slip away. The owner of the mortuary was on-board, and very helpful to the police department, to the point of having a phone listed to the mortuary ring in my home. Decent meals never occurred when I was with my fellow radicals, but only when I found time to slip away.

Successful at Resisting
Feminine Opportunities

Having a radical girlfriend would have been the worst thing I could have done! Women not only tend to be possessive, but they have great intuition. My occasional disappearing acts back into the normal world, a day here and a day or so there, would have been very much noticed by a girlfriend. The sex would have been free, but the price would have been too high.

I had a couple of gals from the normal world who knew that I was an undercover cop. From time to time I would take one of them to radical events and introduce her as the girl I was dating (but never both at the same time!) This ruse pretty much gave me the cover I needed to not get involved with a number of very accessible female radicals.

Not a Good Assignment
for a Married Person

The department made a serious mistake in placing another officer, who was married and had children, in an undercover assignment similar to mine. In my judgment he did not do a very good job, but his poor performance was completely understandable. Wives have this little hang-up about wanting their husbands home with some reasonable degree of regularity, and as such family life is completely inconsistent with the undercover investigatory procedures.

There were times when it was "day-on-and-stay-on" (often around the clock for several days at a time), when I might have to leave on a moment's notice for some distant location, but that just did not work for my fellow undercover officer. He was in a unique location, but often was not on top of fast-moving events, which resulted in critical information that did not always reach the department when it was needed. He asked, and I covered for him as much as I could, but there were organizations he was in that I did not have access to, and the department was just out of luck.

Like me, he went to school and got a bunch of units, but his contributions were marginal. He is a good guy and we remained close friends as each of us moved up in the department after our undercover tours were over. A married person should never be placed in an assignment of the nature that I was in.

Anatomy of a Subversive-Inspired Violent Confrontation and Demonstrations

A basic core belief of the several organizations that advocated the overthrow of the United States government, was to take whatever actions were necessary to cause the people to rise and up and confront the "imperialist and capitalist individuals and organizations" that ran the government.

To this end, the dominant socialist organization, with its true organizational affiliation concealed, would play a role in maneuvering a dupe into a role of leadership, then encourage the dupe to lead that organization in demonstrations that often involved civil disobedience. The dupe and others in positions of leadership (and still others with the biggest mouths) often went to jail, but not the socialist(s) wielding the influence behind the scenes. It was an era when the police, confronted with civil disobedience and rocks and bottles, were often more than happy to respond in kind. This scenario played itself out hundreds of times during the turbulent 1960s. The role and influence of the various socialist organizations were most often what I would call "persuasively subtle," giving support and encouragement for civil disobedience while avoiding direct suggestions for illegal behavior.

My Role in Preventing Violent Confrontations and Demonstrations

I am very proud of the role that I often played in preventing riots and unnecessary police response. There were a number of times when the folks I was investigating would plan to try to stir something up, try to get the police to respond and over-react, and essentially orchestrate a big demonstration and mass arrests.

On a number of occasions I advised the office (Intelligence Division) to encourage the concerned police divisions to not over-react, and to keep the cops out of sight. I have every confidence that while undercover I was able to play a pivotal role in preventing a number of potentially violent demonstrations.

Working for a Thief

Shortly after going undercover, I was assigned to work under the supervision of a policeman who was functioning as an investigator (the department did not have the civil service rank of investigator or detective until several years later). Ray (pseudonym) struck me as an okay guy, but not very energetic and not having the passion I felt he should have for the important job the division was doing.

One day, I was about to leave on an out-of-state trip, hitchhiking and bumming rides with other radicals. I requested a few bucks from Ray for expenses, which were provided in the form of "secret service funds." Ray explained that the division was temporarily out of those funds, but he would have the money waiting for me when I returned. I had requested about $50, as I recall, and at his direction I signed a form acknowledging receipt of the money.

A couple of weeks later when I met with him and asked for the money, Ray said that I'd already been paid, and showed me the signed receipt as proof! It was an out-and-out lie! I asked to have a meeting set up with a supervisor, Sergeant Jack Davis. He was a great guy, but clearly in a bind, and chose to believe Ray, who apparently had badmouthed me for fiscal carelessness (and who knows what else). Because I was so deep undercover and met solely with my handler—who at the time was Ray—I was at a real disadvantage in prevailing with my concerns. As a result, due to what was described by Ray as a "personality conflict," I was assigned to another handler. Obviously, it was a good thing.

Unfortunately, though, when Jack did my rating, I received a negative comment for something like not managing my secret service funds as well as I should have. Jack Davis and I went on to become great friends over the years. I'm not sure whether he actually believed my allegation that Ray stole the money. Ray is among those who long-ago retired. I hope he is able to read these memoirs—and realize that I have never forgotten that he is a thief.

A Gutsy Student Body President

During one particularly boisterous anti-war demonstration, I mistakenly thought that I was about to watch the student body president get his butt kicked. As a group of approximately ten to fifteen demonstrators made a move to tear down the American flag, the student body president confronted them and made it clear that they would have to go through him to get at the flagpole. There were several tense moments and some harsh words exchanged, but the group eventually broke up and drifted off. I was not close enough to hear what was said, but the kid clearly stood his ground and earned my respect.

That spunky kid's name was Steve Cooley, and he went on to become the district attorney of Los Angeles County.

The true mark of success for someone who plans a demonstration is to get the police to respond in a massive way. The LAPD did just this on many occasions when I was a new officer. Frankly, young cops like this stuff and like putting idiots in jail, and this reality sometimes drove unnecessary responses.

I learned a long time ago, and for years have practiced what I learned, that the best response is an absolute minimal response. If there is a real potential for trouble, stage your officers in a concealed location where they are out of sight but can rapidly reach the scene if necessary. Have a unit, low profile with no helmets visible, down the street, to interact with the demonstrators should dialog be necessary, and to keep a continuous watch on what is occurring. It is important to have mature leadership that will not overact to taunts and shouting. This tactic very often works well, and seldom do the concealed officers have to respond to the scene.

"The Truth Hurts" (Defining Experience in My Life)

In December 1968 I was nominated by my fellow SDS radicals to attend the SDS annual convention in Ann Arbor, Michigan. I was to go with two other radicals, both members of the Socialist Worker's Party. We drove in an old jalopy all the way.

I think it was our second night on the road. We were in Tucumcari, New Mexico, telling jokes when one of the other guys made a comment about some joke I'd made: "That's a good one, did you hear it when you were on patrol?" My heart stopped! I thought he must have realized that I was a cop and was playing with my mind. We later pulled over alongside the road to get some rest. But I remained awake and near panic, thinking that if I went to sleep one of the two might kill me and dump my body in the pasture we were parked next to.

The next day we were driving through Oklahoma City. Out of the blue one of the other two looked in my direction and made some comment about "fucking sneaky cops." I was already on edge and very paranoid, and perceived his remark as another comment about their realization that I was a cop.

Later that day I was driving while we were on Route 66 in southern Missouri. We were passing the time with some stupid word game, where one person would describe something and the others would try to see who could first identify what was being described. I don't recall the description, but one of them replied "an undercover cop!"

That did it for me. I was near-frantic, and anxious to bring the matter to the surface and hopefully convince these two that I wasn't a cop. I hit the brakes very hard and skidded to a stop on the gravel roadside, grabbed the one who made the comment by the shirt and told him I was going to "kick his ass" if he didn't stop playing stupid mind games based on the belief that I was a cop. Both became very apologetic, and said that I was just tired and being unnecessarily paranoid. One said the Tucumcari remark referred to me being on patrol in Vietnam when I was a Marine, the Oklahoma City remark was based on seeing a traffic cop behind a billboard, and the remark that set me off was completely innocent and unrelated to me in any way. We all calmed down and continued to the conference.

This incident was one of the biggest lessons in my life, and truly a defining experience. What I learned is that the truth hurts, and it is a natural tendency for people to really get upset when confronted with a painful reality. My paranoia was out of control and resulted in an outburst that was most inappropriate. Thank goodness, neither of my two "pals" was smart enough to see my behavior as a danger sign that I might have had something to be paranoid about—and figure out that I really was an undercover cop.

THE *ANARCHISTS COOKBOOK* AND THE UNIVERSITY OF MICHIGAN

When it was voted that I would be one of the three people to attend the SDS Conference in Ann Arbor, everybody passed the hat to dig up some money to support our attendance.

I think we ended up with about thirty dollars. This was a very good thing, as it enabled me to be legitimately involved in the highest levels of the Students for a Democratic Society, and gain information that was helpful to not only the Los Angeles Police Department but also to the FBI, which received a copy all my investigative reports. In company with two other SDS members, who were actually members of the Socialist Workers Party, we spent several days driving across the country. On our arrival in Ann Arbor, Michigan, we slept on the floor of a flophouse used by SDS members in that part of the country. I attended meeting after meeting on every warped subject you can imagine, including a workshop on making modifications to the *Anarchist's Cookbook*, in reality a bomb-making guide for radicals.

It was really quite a trip. On the return journey to Los Angeles, I told my two buddies that I had a friend in Missouri who I was going to stop and visit with, which I did. My friend was a retired Los Angeles policeman named Fred Cook. We had a pretty nice visit, and fortunately his family was able to tolerate my long hair and beard. As I reflect on this and other activities while I was undercover, I cannot help but think about the big issue that people make out of officer safety these days. I was a couple of thousand miles away from the nearest backup, with no badge, no gun, and no way to contact anybody other than a collect call to the Intelligence Division every few days. It was an experience, and a lonely one at that!

As I write these memoirs in 2012, President Obama continues to be criticized for his association with a college professor named Bill Ayers. I do not specifically recall Ayers' activities at the Michigan SDS Convention in 1968, but I recall very well the vitriolic and anti-American activities of his wife, Bernadine Dohrn, who ultimately became a wanted fugitive on the FBI's list of the Ten Most Wanted in the United States. President Obama is richly deserving of intense criticism for having anything to do with these folks who, at least at one time, strongly advocated actions highly adverse to our nation.

"I Am Going to Kick Your Ass!"

"Holy Shit, is it You?"

Not long after going undercover, I was part of a large group of idiots who were at the Century Plaza Hotel protesting the Vietnam War.

A "tactical alert" had been called, and several hundred uniformed officers were formed in a skirmish line keeping us demonstrators away from the building. Directly in front of me in the skirmish line stood a friend and classmate from the academy, Bob Manlove. However, with my long hair and beard he did not recognize me. The demonstrators were getting pretty loud and robust and it didn't appear it would be very long before the police started using force to push the demonstrators back while declaring an unlawful assembly. Bob looked right at me and said that he was close to "kicking my ass," or something to that effect. But he froze in place when I replied that he should not treat one of his academy classmates that way! I then said "Bushey," to which he replied something like, "holy shit!" He instantly figured that I was undercover.

Not long afterward, the event was declared to be an unlawful assembly and a few folks got thumped and went to jail. Bobby and I exchanged knowing glances when I backed off before the action started.

My way of preparing for mid-term and final examinations was to go to the college at about 2:00 am, find a vacant classroom, and cram right up until exam time. Probably not a great study habit, but it must have worked for me. I was always on the dean's list, and typically maintained a grade point average above about 3.6.

I frequently did something else while in those classrooms: I created fairly extensive but easy-to-understand diagrams of subversive organizations and "front groups" on the blackboards, then wrote "please save" around the bracket containing what I had written. These messages outlined the relationship of anti-American organizations (such as the Communist Party and the Socialist Workers Party) with seemingly innocent organizations (such as the Students for a Democratic Society and the Student Mobilization Committee), which were largely subversive "front groups" that recruited unknowing and innocent students. Placing the word "save" within brackets on the blackboard was a technique used by the instructors who wanted information retained in that room for additional discussion.

I hope my mischief assisted in educating some folks.

Meeting in the Bushes With Deputy Chief Edward Davis

At the time I went undercover, I had already been a student at Cal State LA for several months. But I was known by a number of folks (just about all of whom were cops or criminal justice professors) as an LAPD officer.

One instructor with whom I had a nice relationship was then-LAPD Deputy Chief Edward M. Davis. Because I saw him on a fairly regular basis on campus, we chatted when I went undercover and he was aware of my status and investigative activities. For several months, until he was named chief of police and stopped teaching at Cal State, he and I would periodically meet in the bushes on the east side of North Hall (later named Martin Luther King Hall). I would give him a first-hand update of my activities and the information that I was gathering. I truly liked Ed Davis and felt that he was among our better police chiefs. After retiring, he ran unsuccessfully for governor, but was later elected and served for quite a while as a state senator. He retired to the Morro Bay area and on one occasion hosted my son Jake in his home when Jake was doing independent historical research.

Not long after going undercover I was at Valley College (Fulton & Burbank), where I met a couple of pretty bad hombres who were actively plotting the assassination of a highway patrol officer as part of their effort to "trigger the revolution." Along with a very reliable citizen who was working with me (his identifier was S-257), I worked our way into this small cell. We made a number of overt acts toward the conspiracy, including acquiring radio frequencies, maps of the terrain and exact roads where the ambush was being planned in remote Mono County, CHP shift schedules, etc. Since a copy of all my reports went to the FBI, they were aware of the activity.

While done carelessly but not intentionally, two FBI agents who knew just enough to be dangerous actually went to the house on Hart Street in North Hollywood where the two primary suspects lived, and attempted to question them based on "rumors that reached the FBI!" This was terrible, as only four people I was aware of knew what was occurring: the two suspects and my non-sworn partner and I.

To their great credit, the FBI agents realized their mistake and immediately contacted Intelligence Division. I was notified right away. I was due to go to the Hart Street house later that day for a meeting, but was genuinely afraid of getting shot, as these two were very bad actors. Instead, I called and raised hell with them, saying the same FBI agents had gone to my pad! I said that other than Bill and myself, they were the only ones who knew what we had been discussing, and that one of them had to be an informant. They told me to settle down, saying they'd also been visited by the FBI and suspected that it was either Bill or I who was responsible. While I believe my actions created just enough doubt to take the heat off us, we were never able to get back into the confidence of the two suspects. But I do believe they stayed on the radar screen of several local, state, and federal agencies for quite some time.

The Communists and Socialists Hated Each Other More than Capitalism!

One of the biggest enemies facing the various subversive and un-American organizations was their oftentimes fierce hatred for one another!

The three primary subversive organizations were the Communist Party USA (CPUSA-Marxist Leninist), the Socialist Workers Party (SWP-Trotskyites), and the Progressive Labor Party (PLP-Maoists).

Each of these anti-American outfits had a number of "front groups" whose leadership actually came from those three organizations. Generally speaking, the key members of these various parties had deep ideological beliefs that their particular brand of socialism was right and the other brands were wrong, and tended to be very vocal and emotional in both what they advocated and what they felt was wrong. For instance, it was not unusual for the SWP and the PLP to refer to members of the CPUSA as "right wing reactionaries!"

It was also fairly common, in fact almost the norm, for members of SWP and PLP to have originally been members of CPUSA, but found it wasn't radical enough for them. Basically, the CPUSA was the most moderate, the SWP in the middle, and the PLP the most radical. All of them were anti-American and strongly advocated the overthrow of capitalism. It was just a matter of strategy to achieve their objective.

SDS CONFERENCE IN AUSTIN, TEXAS

Among my more memorable activities while undercover was attending the SDS annual conference, during the summer of 1969, at the University of Texas in Austin.

I found a unique way to get to Texas: I offered to drive a new motor home from its place of manufacture in El Monte to the dealership in Houston where it had been ordered. I was given enough money for gas and told where to deliver the motor home. After picking up the motor home from the company, a couple of SDS radicals from Cal State Los Angeles joined me for the trip to Texas. The several days and nights of meetings were pretty much taken up by the typical radical gatherings, with me slipping off from time to time and having a real meal. After the conference I delivered the motor home to the dealership and, although I told my colleagues that I was going to hitchhike home, I actually caught a flight back to Los Angeles.

At one point during the conference a number of us went to Johnson City to demonstrate outside of President Johnson's ranch. We were not well received! Instead, we were taken into custody by the local sheriff, held at the station for several hours, then told to leave that area and never return. A copy of the Los Angeles *Free Press*, a pretty radical publication for that era, was in the car we were all riding in. For a while it appeared that we were going to be arrested and charged with possession of pornographic material. They didn't have to tell me twice not to return!

One situation that I remember very vividly was the absolute hatred

I felt for one of the well-known male radicals. There was a time at the conference when I could have easily ended his life without experiencing any consequences. I cannot say that I didn't give the issue some thought, but in the end I obviously chose to not take that horrific action. I think one of the reasons I remember it so well, is that I was frightened to even possess those thoughts.

The hatred that an undercover officer has the potential to develop, especially in such an instance as this when we're talking about somebody who was aggressively seeking ways to damage the United States, is among the reasons why people should not remain undercover for excessive periods of time.

Nasty Waitress in Fort Stockton

Young men with long hair and beards were really not very well received anywhere in the late 1960s, with the exception of places like San Francisco.

Around midnight, while on our trip through Texas with the two radicals, we stopped for a meal at a restaurant in Fort Stockton. There I learned just how poorly Texans perceived young men with long hair and beards. From the moment we entered the diner—as I recall we were the only customers—the waitress met us with a great deal of hostility. When she brought menus to our table, she literally threw them at us. She was very rude and nasty when we ordered our food. When one of the other fellows ordered a cheeseburger, she asked if he wanted cheese on it; when he stated he wanted a *cheeseburger*, she told him not to get smart with her. When she brought the utensils to our table, she dropped them into the middle like pick-up sticks.

It was a really hostile environment. After bringing our food to the table, she remained a short distance away, literally glaring at us. When we finished our meal she walked over and in a strong Texas accent asked a question that I will never forget: "Why do y'all look like shit?" Interestingly, just as we started to leave she softened up and engaged us in conversation, confiding that she had a son who was involved in using narcotics!

More Reception than was Anticipated
at the Embassy Auditorium

My fellow members of the Students for a Democratic Society were impressed with my willingness to head up the reception and registration

280

functions for a weekend SDS conference to be held at the Embassy Auditorium in downtown Los Angeles. I set up the reception area, where all who were registering were visible via telephoto lens from an Intelligence Division observation post on the second floor of an old hotel across the street from the auditorium. I then obtained a bunch of large "Hello My Name Is...." paper clothing labels. As I registered each person, I wrote their name and organization (i.e., Berkeley SDS) in large neat letters, while they unknowingly had their picture taken by my pals across the street. Then I reached over and put the label on their shirts. How cool was that—perfect mug shots with identifying information! In terms of creativity, this was one of my finest hours!

Paralyisis in East Los Angeles and an Empty Office on a Friday Afternoon

One Friday morning several of the radical student organizations, with the Students for a Democratic Society (SDS) in the lead, came up with a unique way to protest the college's actions in denying tenure to a radical professor: by completely blocking the eastbound lanes of the San Bernardino freeway (Interstate 10) during the evening rush hour!

Realizing the havoc that several hundred students running around and sitting on the freeway could do to a Friday afternoon rush-hour, I immediately contacted the office with that information. Throughout the day I managed to slip away on several occasions to provide updates on the planned activities, routes, strategy, those involved, and related information. I also strongly suggested that our Scientific Investigation Division be contacted to take photos and video of the incident for potential prosecution. My assumption, which I felt was reasonable, was that the LAPD was poised to deal with what was about to occur.

At about 4:00 p.m. the sit-in began. About 100 students converged on the freeway, which stopped all eastbound traffic. Some were sitting in the roadway; others were running around carrying protest signs. Of course, the freeway came to a dead stop, with hundreds of cars backed up all the way into the downtown Los Angeles interchange. What a mess!

The only thing missing was the police! Not only was no one from Intelligence Division present, but that division apparently had failed to notify the area division (Hollenbeck) or the California Highway Patrol. After about twenty minutes, a lone Highway Patrol motocycle officer stumbled into the mess, and with the help of several other CHP officers he'd called for assistance, got all the idiots off the freeway (me included).

Those twenty minutes resulted in several subsequent hours of chaos.

On Monday when I called the office and asked why nothing had been done the previous Friday, I was reminded that nothing gets done on Friday afternoons in that division! In a division where unsupervised people had take-home cars with radios, who officially began and ended their work shifts at home (and saw Fridays as essentially work half-days), I guess I shouldn't have been surprised. But I certainly was disappointed.

For the sake of anyone reading this who might be critical of this troubling lack of command effectiveness, let me say that I've seen nothing similar to this incident over the subsequent four decades. Almost without exception, those with take-home vehicles have a genuine need to do so, and start and end their shifts in the workplace—not in their home driveways.

Long Hair and Beards not Well-Received in Modoc County

While undercover, I took some vacation time and drove all the way up to Modoc County to visit my relatives, who lived outside of the town of Alturas in the tiny community of Canby. Bill McClennan (pseudonym), a close friend who was volunteering as an undercover operator with the LAPD and who also had long hair and a beard, accompanied me. My dad's brother Russ and his wife Flo had a very nice ranch on the Pit River.

I knew that Aunt Flo, whom I hadn't seen for several years, played cards with her friends at a little establishment of some type in Canby. When I walked in, however, she recognized but barely acknowledged me. Flo did not like my appearance, cop or not.

A day or so later when Bill and I visited the café in the Niles Hotel in Alturas, a couple of tough old broads at the counter started talking about "kicking our hippie asses." Obviously speaking loud enough for our benefit, they were offended by our long hair and beards. But they didn't know we were undercover LAPD.

It was really a fun couple of days. At night, I would drive through Russ' and Flo's fields in my 4x4 Scout, shining the spotlight on scores of deer. Among the things I did during the day was hike up to a cave where bootleggers had made and stored booze during Prohibition, and explore around their ranch and outbuildings.

I have not been to Modoc County in about thirty-five years, because it is so far from home. I regret not visiting for so long. Russ and Flo both passed away many years ago; but one of their sons, Bob, still lives and farms on the property. Rest in peace, Russ and Flo.

282

MISSING STEEL RODS UNDER THE SAND AT VENICE BEACH

I was among the many radicals who planned to incite a police riot at Venice Beach on July 4, 1969. It was the intention of the SDS to stimulate a large demonstration, in hopes of getting the LAPD to overreact. At approximately 11:00 p.m. on July 3, I was among the radicals who buried a bunch of steel rebar rods in the sand, with the thought that the demonstrators could dig them up the next day for the intended battle with the police. It took about an hour to bury all the rods (probably 50 or 60), then we all went home. About an hour after we left, obviously based on the information I provided to Intelligence Division, a bunch of Metro officers went to the beach and dug up every one of the rods! It was really funny, watching my radical buddies search for rods in the sand the next day!

July 4 turned out to be a nice day, with no problems whatsoever. On that day my role was first-aid person, complete with a white helmet bearing a Red Cross and a knapsack full of bandages. At one point the captain of the Venice Division, Bob Sillings, who certainly did not know I was an undercover police officer, approached me in a very friendly way and said he hoped that my skills as a first-aid person would not be necessary. I responded that I hoped he was right. It was all I could do to refrain from telling him I was also a Los Angeles police officer. I had long hair and a beard, and looked pretty radical.

Several years later when I was in the Manuals & Orders Unit as a sergeant, I developed a nice relationship with Capt. Sillings during his tenure as commanding officer of the Property Division. He was a really great guy. But he had somehow irritated somebody, which is why he was assigned to Property Division. However, it worked well for me, because he would occasionally slip me law enforcement badges that had previously been booked into evidence, which were slated to be destroyed! He and I discussed and laughed about our earlier encounter at Venice Beach. Several years later, Bob Sillings became afflicted with a horrible degenerative disease that slowly caused him to be incapacitated; it was painful watching him deteriorate and go from a limp to a cane, then finally into a wheelchair, before he stopped coming to work altogether.

The Venice Beach demonstration and the actions of the SDS radicals in attempting to stimulate violence was actually pretty typical of most big demonstrations during the era. The leadership, or at least a portion of the leadership, for the radical groups typically came from either the Communist Party USA, the Socialist Workers party, or the progressive

Labor Party. These socialist radicals disguised their true identity, instead posing as liberals and radical students. The rank-and-file of most of the antiwar organizations was made up primarily of liberal college students and other people who did not want to go into the military. Despite the strong efforts of the radical leadership to subtly lead the rank-and-file into violent actions, when push came to shove the rank-and-file—again, mostly students and people who just opposed the war—chose not to engage in violent or otherwise illegal activity.

NUCLEAR-TIPPED ARTILLERY SHELLS

After one of many anti-war demonstrations, several of us "anti-war veterans" got together to plan additional subversive activities. One of the guys identified himself as an Army first lieutenant, recently released from active duty, whose specialty was the maintenance of nuclear-tipped artillery shells!

While I did not know much about artillery, I knew from other things he said that it was likely he had been an Army officer, and what he said with respect to nuclear rounds seemed to make sense. He volunteered to help create a leaflet, something like a mini *Anarchist's Cookbook*, describing these nuclear artillery shells. We all agreed that it would be among the things on our agenda for the future. Obviously, I wrote a detailed report about our conversation, but never heard anything more or saw the fellow again. I imagine there was a follow-up by the FBI. But, as was often the case, and probably appropriately so, I did not receive follow-up on some of the information I passed on, unless it was something I actually needed to know.

CUTTING SUGAR CANE IN CUBA—ALMOST!

During my tenure undercover, Fidel Castro created a program where American college students could go to Cuba at different times of the year and cut sugarcane. This was seen as a way of permitting American antiwar radicals to demonstrate their solidarity with the working people of Cuba.

The Socialist Workers Party solicited me to go to Cuba for one of these sugar-cutting visits, which as I recall was to last about six weeks. Intelligence Division took the matter under consideration, but it was ultimately determined that my going to Cuba would not be a good idea. I concurred with that decision, as I didn't have any great desire to spend twelve hours a day, seven days a week, in the hot sun cutting sugarcane! Over and above the distasteful physical issues, I can only imagine what my fate would have been had I been identified as an undercover cop while in Cuba!

Bob Kosta Decided to Go Home!

This was a troubling situation that could have had enormous adverse consequences. In about 1969, UCLA administration approved the request of an alleged "minority children's improvement organization" to use a classroom/meeting room complex on campus during the summer recess.

After securing the rooms, the group denied access to UCLA officials! UCLA apparently conveyed its dismay to the LAPD, and I was asked by my supervisors if I could possibly gain entry to the complex to determine what was occurring there. The complex was on about the 7th or 8th story of what I recall was a student residential building.

When my overt efforts as an SDS leader failed because I was a "white honky motherf-----," I decided to try to slip in under the cover of darkness. It was decided that Bob Kosta (pseudonym), a martial arts expert who was assigned as an investigator in the Intelligence Division (not undercover), would provide cover in the bushes alongside the escape path I had chosen. He would intercept and "stop" anyone who might chase me, in the event I was caught in my nocturnal investigation. A guard was posted in the lobby; however, when his rounds took him outside I managed to take the elevator to the floor in question.

It was the middle of the night, and I couldn't gain entry to the complex. I had no choice but to take the elevator down, and hope that either the guard wasn't there or wouldn't pay attention to me. But immediately on exiting the elevator, the guard was standing right there! He tried to grab me, but I broke loose and took off running toward the exit path where Kosta was waiting to stop anyone who chased me. As I ran down the path, it became clear that Kosta was not there! I later learned that after a period of time he felt everything was okay, and went home!

That guard chased me all over UCLA before I was finally able to get away from him. This incident occurred over forty years ago, and I still get pissed every time I think about Kosta's laziness and selfishness in leaving me in a very difficult situation.

S-255 Meets S-264

One afternoon a fellow SDS member said he wanted me to meet another anti-war former Marine, whose name was Ted. That is when I learned I was not the only undercover LAPD officer investigating subversive and un-American activities on college campuses. At one time, Ted and I had been patrol car partners in Central Division! He was a former Marine, and we got along pretty well. Ted's "secret agent" identifier was S-264.

Obviously, we did not let on that we knew each other. But we were able to assist one another on occasion, and exchange helpful information. Ted retired as a captain and is now a practicing attorney.

Sickening Actions of an Anti-War Actress

Among the troubling actions stemming from the anti-Vietnam War movement was the widely publicized and troublesome behavior of a well-known female entertainer, including her anti-American actions when visiting North Vietnamese troops in Hanoi. While undercover, I had the opportunity to witness an absolutely disgusting situation involving her and another woman at a political rally in MacArthur Park.

The other woman had a little girl, probably about four of five years old. The girl walked several feet away then approached and said hello to two uniformed police officers. As the officers crouched down and started talking to the little girl, the well-known entertainer walked over, grabbed the child by the arm, pulled her away, and pointed to the officers and said "bad, bad!"

My hatred for that ......person grew even stronger than it had previously been, if such was possible.

"Keith Bushey is a Cop!"

One day I received information, and I really don't remember the source, that Irving Hirshbaum (pseudonym) of the Peace Action Council (PAC) was going to "out" me as an undercover police officer at a meeting of the PAC that evening! As can be imagined, this was very upsetting news. However, I believed it was likely he didn't have information that I was a police officer, but rather was looking for the opportunity to discredit me because he and I were in rival organizations. I was aligned with the Socialist Workers Party and he was aligned with the Communist Party USA, rival organizations that were both trying to play a behind-the-scenes leadership role in the Students for a Democratic Society (SDS).

I considered not going to the meeting, but felt that failing to show up would be seen an indication that there was some truth to what he intended to say. So I went to the meeting that night. Sure enough, a few minutes into the meeting Irving stood up and stated he had confidential information that I was an undercover cop. I jumped to my feet and gave a speech to the assembled group, which was probably somewhere around 150 people. I said the only thing worse than "red-baiting" was "cop-baiting," and that irresponsible comments such as those made by Hirshbaum were terribly divisive, false, and counter-revolutionary. I indicated that I wanted no part of an organization that would tolerate that type of reckless behavior, and walked out. It turned out that a large number of those present believed me, agreed with what I said, and walked out, as well! If there was ever a time where a real line of bullshit came in handy, this was the time!

There was a troubling side to this situation. Two sergeants, my handlers in Intelligence Division, also came to the location and positioned themselves outside and down the block. If the situation had turned real ugly and I was in any danger, they were going to rescue me. After I stormed out, I tried to contact them, and discovered that they had both gone home! Unfortunately, I had come to expect that type of lackadaisical behavior from some of the investigators assigned to that division. It is a good thing for me that real problems didn't develop. These two sergeants were good guys, but I really did not appreciate their premature departure.

"Come on Greenlee—Screw Me on the Table"

This is a good example of the truly despicable behavior on the part of some of the radicals I associated with while undercover.

During one of the instances when a group of radicals (me included!) ran roughshod over the campus and intruded on classes and meetings, we found ourselves in the conference room of the college president, whose name was Greenlee. This man struck me as a reasonable and decent person, who was just trying to strike a balance between free speech rights and appropriate behavior on campus. At one point, while issuing our "demands" for whatever the hell we were demanding, one of my female SDS associates, who was actually somewhat attractive (if she had not been such a jerk), got in President Greenlee's face and suggested that "you can fuck me right now on the conference table."

I was particularly irritated. But obviously I couldn't show it, because although these idiots said crap like that all the time, the academic setting with a restrained educator just struck me as "over the top," even for these jerks. President Greenlee politely declined her offer. But I can only imagine what was going through his mind (perhaps a good spanking for a spoiled little brat!)

The flow of information from me to the FBI was immediate, with no redaction, and of a very high quality. The flow from the FBI to other agencies was not quite the same.

The bureau works very well with other agencies these days, but things didn't work quite so well during the J. Edgar Hoover era. While I am sure there must have been some exceptions, the FBI tended to hoard information. When it was passed on, it was not always done in a timely manner and often there was significant redacting.

While undercover, I remained a member of the Marine Corps Reserve (although not active because of my appearance), and had friends in the Marine Corps intelligence community. Because of my reputation among fellow radicals as an anti-war Vietnam veteran I was a well-placed in the anti-war community, and was active in "GIs and Vietnam Vets Against the War in Vietnam." Spending time in the anti-war military community was completely consistent with my LAPD assignment.

On several occasions early in my undercover tenure, I received and passed on information to the FBI. In turn, the bureau should have provided it to either the Marine Corps or the Navy. But in only one instance was it passed on, and even then it was distorted and too late to be of any realistic value. As a result, with the permission of my supervisors, I provided information on military subversion not only to the bureau, but also directly to Marine Corps Counter-Intelligence.

To say the Marine Corps was estatic is an understatement, because of the information pertaining to the Corps. The Marine Corps became a helpful provider of information to the Navy and Coast Guard, which those services deeply appreciated. My liaison to the Marine Corps contributed to my being commissioned as a second lieutenant in 1970.

THE "KEITH BUSHEY MEMORIAL GUARD SHACK"

I became aware of a group of anti-war sailors, who were stealing building equipment, materials and supplies from a number of WWII-era warehouses located across Interstate 15 from the Miramar Naval Air Station. They then used the pilfered goods to assist with creating anti-war "coffee houses" intended for servicemen and -women on liberty to visit. I was able to identify the sailors involved and pinpoint the location where the thefts were occurring, and passed the information to military intelligence. Obviously, I had to be very careful, to minimize the possibility that I could be determined to be the source of the information given to the military authorities.

I don't know how those sailors were dealt with, but they almost immediately disappeared off the anti-war radar screen. As a consequence of their thefts the Navy built an elevated guard shack, which was manned by sentries for several years. Within the Marine counterintelligence community, this sentry tower was kiddingly referred to as the "Keith Bushey Memorial Guard Shack!" The elevated structure remained standing above those old warehouses long after it was no longer manned. I always reminisce about this investigation as I drive past its location during trips to San Diego.

FOILED SAILOR'S PLAN TO DISABLE AIRCRAFT CARRIER

While visiting a "coffee house" in San Diego that was a refuge for anti-war military personnel, I met a big-mouthed sailor who was bragging about his ability and intentions to sabotage the powerplant of the aircraft carrier on which he was assigned. Because his seaman's stripes were red in color, I knew he was a "snipe" (engine room sailor), and as he described what he intended to do (put ball bearings in sensitive parts of the propulsion system), he seemed to know what he was talking about (at least to this layman). Obviously, I passed this info immediately, before even writing the report. All I know is that I never saw him again, and his ship steamed out of port without any problems that I was aware of. This is another of those situations where I have absolutely no doubt that my report triggered immediate actions, yet never found out what those actions were. But the fact that the "snipe" all but immediately disappeared would suggest something happened.

HOSTILE RECEPTION FOR RADICALS AT CAMP PENDLETON

I was among the former servicemen taking part in a covert effort by the "Student Mobilization Committee to End the War in Vietnam" (a "front" group for one of the socialist organzations). Our task was to sneak aboard Camp Pendleton on a Saturday and distribute anti-war leaflets in various barracks, telling of an upcoming demonstration.

Obviously, I had given Marine Counterintelligence a "heads up" regarding our incursion, and agents from the Naval Investigative Service (NIS) had a reception committee awaiting our arrival (because Marine counterintelligence could not deal with civilians). Unfortunately, the NIS folks had not given very good guidance to the Marine military policemen at the gate, because it was a real cluster. I was in the first car to approach the gate when at least three MPs jumped out, each of whom instructed the driver of the car to do something different (one said pull to the right, another said pull to the left, and still another said to continue forward!).

Even in the midst of all that was occurring, I had to chuckle at the confusion. The whole group of us (15 or 20) were detained for about an hour, interviewed, photographed, and sent on our way with a stern warning to not return. Of course, there was much speculation as to how the Marine Corps knew we were coming. But it never focused on me.

Got a Great Grade from Radical Former Priest

Franz Fontaine (pseudonym) was a visiting professor in South American studies on a one-year fellowship at Cal State LA. He was also a former priest, supposedly "defrocked," who had left Guatemala under troubling circumstances. My understanding is that he provided support to the anti-government guerrilla forces and was removed from that country with the assistance of the U.S. government. Two things were very clear: He thought very little of the United States government, and was in great sympathy with the anti-governmental forces in many, if not all, of the South and Central American counties.

To be fair, history has shown that some of the governments in that region being supported by the United States during that era were brutal and corrupt. So there certainly was some merit to his concerns. However, there was no balance in any of his presentations, or in the books he had us read. He was a very pleasant and gracious man, which in my judgment made it all the worse, because impressionable students were easily swayed and influenced by the distorted anti-American things he said.

As a course requirement each student had to write a term paper on the situation (I do not recall the details) in one of the South or Central American counties. I wrote a scathing anti-American paper presenting all kinds of uncorroborated speculation as facts, something that would and should have been rejected as horrible research by any other professor. Fontaine gave me an "A+" with all kinds of complimentary notes jotted throughout the paper.

He was not retained beyond the one year at the college. I believe he remained in Los Angeles and stayed active in far-left wing politics. Personally, I liked the guy; I just wished he had been more balanced. While I suspect the answer was yes, I do not know if he was aligned with any of the prominent subversive organizations.

Because of my status with the Socialist Workers Party, and someone within that organization who had infiltrated the Students for a Democratic Society, I was one hot number and a hero with the FBI. A copy of every report I wrote, and they were done well and plentiful, went to the bureau. While I have been told in later years that there were undercover FBI agents in the SWP, I don't believe it. I was undercover during the J. Edgar Hoover era and, unless I am badly mistaken and the LAPD was continuously lied to, I was the primary Southern California SWP source of information for the FBI.

In 1968 the bureau had a hiring campaign, and opened up new agent positions to college graduates who had investigative experience with local or state law enforcement agencies. An agent who was familiar with my activities and performance recruited me to become an FBI agent.

I started the hiring process and was well into it before finally yielding to the pleas of my mother not to do so. Mom realized that I would have to relocate, most likely to the East Coast, and did not want me to move away. When processing, I told the recruiting agent that I was poor at math and feared I might have a problem with that part of the entrance examination. But he informed me that "I had already successfully taken the entrance examination!" Guess they really wanted me.

Interestingly, a few years later just about the entire FBI squad out of the New York City Division was indicted for "dirty tricks," etc., during the course of investigations. It had been looking into the SWP. I think I probably would have been part of it, had I become an agent. I did then and still do have the highest regard for the bureau (notwithstanding a glitch here and there), but I probably made the right decision to remain with the LAPD.

ALL BY MYSELF FOR THE SERGEANT'S EXAMINATION IN THE BASEMENT OF CITY HALL

Because of my covert status, I could not be seen where my presence might be associated with law enforcement. Additionally, my superiors were sensitive to the potential careless actions of another member of the department, who might recognize me as a cop and say something that would blow my cover. Because of this, I was not able to take my sergeant's examination at the high school, where hundreds of other officers would assemble for the test.

Instead, at 7 o'clock on the Saturday morning of the exam, in a prearranged fashion I was met on a streetcorner downtown by a Personnel Department employee. He picked me up in his private vehicle, and we then drove to the underground parking facility at City Hall. He took me to a private room, laid out the test materials, face down, and we waited until exactly 8:00 am when the exam started for the hundreds of others taking the test. I was then told to pick up my exam and get started.

Except for a bathroom break, it was just him and me in that room. At exactly noon, when all the other candidates were told to close their booklets, he instructed me to close mine. He then took all of my materials, drove me back to where he had picked me up, dropped me off, and wished me luck.

Before the exam, I was aware it would be one-on-one with just a personnel employee, and kinda hoped to get a little extra time if I needed it. No way! This guy was stoic, taciturn, and all business. Turns out I got a very high grade, anyway.

Those "Out Now" Pins Made for a Nice Weekend in San Francisco

I was a master at finding some justification to be somewhere on short notice. On occasion I would be told of a meeting that was taking place somewhere, often a good distance away, and informed that the department or the FBI really needed someone at that meeting. Could I possibly find a way to attend? I never failed! As time went on, I pretty much knew radicals just about everywhere, and would do some strategizing and fast-talking that would cause me to land where the office wanted me to be.

One such effort involved the planning cell for a massive demonstration at Golden Gate Park in San Francisco. Going to the demonstration was easy—but working my way into the planning cell the night before, on about fours hours' notice, involved some creativity. I had just got married to Barbara, who was a secretary in Intelligence Division, so I hopped on a flight to San Francisco and took her with me.

I ended up at the meeting where the office wanted me to be, and passed on information that I believe was relayed (and hopefully helpful) to the San Francisco Police Department. At the meeting, each key participant was asked to be responsible for selling something like 500 big anti-war pins that read: "Out Now" (for out of Vietnam). The price was $1 each, and we were to turn in the money at the end of the demonstration. Barbara joined me at the demonstration and we sold several hundred of the pins, but—would you believe?—I forgot to turn in the money! There was no real accounting, each key participant just grabbed a big bag of the pins when they left the planning meeting, and I just kinda forgot that I took one of those bags. The pins paid for her flight, two nights in a great hotel, a nice dinner at the top of the Mark Hopkins Hotel ("Top of the Mark"), and other expenses.

I realize I have just copped-out to embezzlement. But the statutes have run, and I remain thankful for the really nice weekend that was provided by those idiots!

Three Undercover Agents Pumping Each Other for Information!

After surfacing from my undercover assignment, I was shown a very amusing photograph. Taken with a telephoto lens, it showed me having an intense conversation with two other radicals; obviously, I was in the process of surreptitiously soliciting information. It did not strike me as anything out of the ordinary until I was told that the other two folks were also undercover cops! One was an LAPD cop who I did not know, and the other a sheriff's undercover intelligence officer. We were all surreptitiously pumping each other for information. This was pretty funny, but not really that surprising, as we were not permitted to know the identity of other undercover operatives.

My Oral Interview for Sergeant

Since the oral examinations were given in a downtown business building and there would never be more than just a couple candidates at any time in the waiting room, I took my oral interview just like everybody else (except for coming up the back stairs as opposed to the lobby elevators). Luck was with me that day! One of the three captains (John Demarest) was a World War II Marine officer who was also a "Mustang," in that he had been enlisted before being commissioned.

John liked me because I had been a Marine. He loved me when I mentioned that I had been approved and was awaiting my swearing-in as a Marine second lieutenant. Another of the captains (Frank Beeson) was kind of a wise-ass, and asked me an "off the wall" question that by chance I just happened to have the answer to. He reeled back in his chair, and said "I don't have any more questions for this young man!"

I do not recall who the third captain was, but overall the interview went very well. Because of my undercover assignment I was a bit of a novelty, and right in the thick of all of society's social issues that were driving the department crazy (massive demonstrations, etc.) Turns out that I got a very good score for the degree of seniority I possessed, with just four years of total service on the police department.

GETTING MY SERGEANT'S BADGE—"WHO THE HELL IS 45.5?"

Promotional competition in the LAPD was a blood sport when I was coming up in the organization. Candidates really slugged it out for the highest written and oral scores, and the serious candidates knew and followed each other's performance like hawks. I did well, and ended up on a portion of the eligible list with a bunch of guys who were well aware of one another.

On the day of promotion I slipped up the back stairs of Parker Center and into Personnel Division, where I was among four or five policemen who were also promoting to sergeant. A couple were above me, and a couple were below me on the eligible list. As I recall, those present had the numbers 43, 44, 45, and 46. They were really puzzled when someone they didn't know and whose name didn't show up on the eligible list was there to get promoted right in the midst of the rest of them.

They were further puzzled when it was announced for number 45.5 to come forward for processing. Because of my undercover status, the police and personnel departments had worked out a process where I was given a numerical score but not placed on the regular lineal list. I scored between number 45 and number 46, thus was designated "45.5."

I was assigned sergeant's badge number 526, and was now Sergeant S-255 of Intelligence Division!

GIVEN THE OPPORTUNITY TO REMAIN UNDERCOVER

When promoted to sergeant, I was given the opportunity to remain undercover indefinitely. The leadership of the department hoped I would make that choice, but it was pretty clear that I wanted to surface and return to the mainstream of the department. I needed once again to be a full-time decent person. As I have said many times, I wouldn't trade my undercover experiences for a million dollars—and I wouldn't give a nickel to do them over again.

MARY BUSHEY GOES WILD AT THE UCLA NROTC GRADUATION

This was just too funny! My last official undercover function was to participate as one of the anti-war demonstrators at the NROTC Graduation at UCLA in June of 1970. The guest speakers were Governor Ronald Reagan and actor John Wayne. My new wife, Barbara, and my mom attended the function! About half-way through the ceremony, all of the idiots/demonstrators stood up and attempted to disrupt the event by running up and down the aisles shouting obscenities and anti-war slogans. It was a big mistake! Many people in the audience, which was almost exclusively politically conservative and pro-military, moved into the aisles and confronted the demonstrators, and a few punches were thrown. One idiot/demonstrator, who was standing pretty close to my wife and my mother, was knocked down and his glasses went flying. My wife and mom rushed over and stomped on his glasses! Good for them!

DEVELOPED UNDERCOVER OPERATIONS MANUAL

I was given no training whatsoever when I went undercover, but was just told to keep doing what I was doing, in gathering information. While undercover I did some things well, and also made some serious mistakes. I continually made notes on things that I learned, mistakes to be avoided, strategies that I developed, and tricks that I mastered, all with the intent of sharing this information with future undercover officers. After surfacing from undercover, I remained in the division for about six weeks, which had recently been renamed Public Disorder Intelligence Division (PDID). During that time I reduced virtually all of my notes to a rough draft of a training manual, which was then used in the training and orientation of new undercover officers (UCs).

AN UGLY EXIT INTERVIEW WITH THE COMMANDING OFFICER

I was then, and remain today, very proud of my undercover assignment. I know clearly that I made a difference, by identifying hardcore criminals and terrorists (not a term used then, but certainly applicable), by giving law enforcement agencies a "heads-up" on pending criminal acts and demonstrations, in preventing violence, by aiding various agencies to recognize that a number of those who appeared to be engaged in criminal behavior were just idealistic students with honorable intentions, and in preventing acts of sabotage against military installations and naval vessels.

Unfortunately, despite all the good, widespread problems existed within the division, as well. While I truly liked and got along reasonably well with the investigators, I was troubled by an overall complacent attitude that occasionally placed me and other undercover officers (UCs) at risk, and which occasionally resulted in undercover folks being blamed for the mistakes of their handlers. Out of loyalty to the department and the divison, and for the concern of the safety of the other UCs, on my last day in the division I asked to have a chat with the captain, John

Townsend (pseudonym).

Without naming names, speaking in generalities and in a constructive vein, I referred to my experiences and overall impressions during my couple of years undercover. I suggested it might be helpful to occasionally task the lieutenants to meet separately with the UCs without the presence of their handlers, to solicit their thoughts and suggestions and to inquire about recommendations they might have to enhance their effectiveness. A couple of lieutenants I really respected, Jack Briggs and Terry Hannon, knew how to supervise in a positive way and could easily have tightened up the ship if directed to do so by the captain.

I mentioned that on several occasions during the course of my assignment I'd found myself in physical danger because my "back-ups" had gone end of watch without notifying me; that the department had been surprised by demostrations I'd reported the details about because someone wanted to go home on time, which resulted in unnecessary tactical alerts and wasted manpower; and that I'd actually had money stolen from me by an investigator who pocketed the secret service fund after having me sign a blank request chit.

After hearing me out, the captain leaned back in his chair and said something I can recall almost verbatim: "You know, I've been with this department for over twenty-five years, but this is the first time a boot sergeant has ever come into my office and told me how to run my division. I guess this must be a new trend for the department!" I quickly stood up, reiterated that I'd just been trying to be helpful and constructive, apologized for taking up his time—and left.

This assignment, and the complacency of some people, made a lasting impact on me about how even the best people sometimes become dysfunctional when left to their own devices, are assumed to be "top-notch" without justification, and not adequately supervised. The painful lessons I learned from PDID were a factor in the subsequent success I went on to experience as a leader.

During the late 1970s and early 1980s, the department's intelligence gathering practices were under full-blown attack by the ACLU and related organizations and interests. This was a sad and troubling state of affairs for me, because the division had done so much good in preparing for and preventing violence. The allegations dealt with violations of people's rights, etc., which largely were not true. In the 1980s, as a captain, I appeared before a department board of inquiry led by one of my heroes, then-Commander Larry Cramer. The actions of the Public Disorder Intelligence Division during my tenure were being examined.

At that time I was the first UC who had become a command officer. It was thought that my perspective would be particularly insighful and helpful, and I hope it was. While I stood tall for the extraordinarily good work and effectiveness of the LAPD's intelligence gathering practices, I was equally candid about my concerns—including my conversation with Captain Townsend, and his reaction.

Donating my Undercover Files to the University of Southern California

While undercover, I kept duplicate copies of just about every leaflet, handout, brochure, news articles from campus publications, and scores of other items that I acquired while undercover.

I always thought that I might someday write a book about my experiences. Eventually, however, I lost my passion to do it. After decades of this material sitting in a safe in my garage, I decided to donate it to an institution where it would always be available for researchers. The first institution that I contacted, the University of Southern California, jumped on the opportunity to acquire the material. After some "cleansing" to redact a few names here and there, I turned it over. It is now part of the university's Special Collections Library. Before donating it, the university signed an agreement to accept legal liability for any potential litigation related to the contents of what I had donated.

In a way, the memoirs you are now reading are part of the book I never wrote about my undercover experiences. Some of the more interesting stories are reflected in these pages.

RAMPART DIVISION

Rampart Division was opened in mid-1966, and took in portions of what had been Central and Hollywood Divisions. The boundries were roughly Normandie Street on the west, the Los Angeles River on the north and east, and the Santa Monica Freeway on the south. As I recall, there were approximately 250 persons assigned to Rampart at that time, which included both patrol and detectives.

"You Don't Want to Work Rampart!"

I had it in my head that I wanted to work Rampart Division. Because of my undercover assignment, I was pretty much given the opportunity to pick my division, and that is where I wanted to go. During my time in Central, part of what ultimately became Rampart was in Central, and I just liked that part of the city.

A couple of folks told me the Rampart captain was a real jerk, and that I would not like working for him. I took the position that captains come and go, but the division was stationary. He wouldn't be there forever, and I didn't want to lose a chance to work where I desired because of someone who might not be there much longer, anyway. Rampart it was. I did not have a problem with the captain and, as I thought might happen, he transferred elsewhere within a couple of months or so. I never regretted my decision to work Rampart.

The Phony Landslide that Really Occurred

As I was a brand-new sergeant and somewhat "wet behind the ears," two of the more senior sergeants would occasionally "screw" with me. One rainy Sunday morning I assumed duties as the day watch commander. My two senior pals, Gene Schreiner and Kenny Baker, both "morning watchers" and about to go home, advised me that it appeared a landslide was likely where a portion of Elysian Park extended over the eastbound lane of the Interstate 5 Freeway where it transitioned to the southbound Interstate 110 Freeway.

This location had been a problem in the past, so the information was troubling and required my immediate action. Although their story was bogus (they had received no such information), I put extraordinary effort into dealing with the problem, getting a city engineer to respond and evaluate the hillside and putting barriers in place where the mud was likely to come down. Guess what? The hillside started sliding, it was addressed immediately, and I ended up with a commendation for my quick action!

Bomb in the Ladies' Room

My two senior sergeant pals were beside themselves with amazement over my good fortune at having been commended for the landslide situation, when it was intended by them to be a joke.

So they hatched another scheme that *really* backfired. They made a phony bomb, planted it in the women's bathroom, and told an orderly that the room needed servicing. The results were predictable. The orderly found the bomb and immediately came running to me, the day watch commander. The phony explosive device looked authentic, containing

298

old flares resembling dynamite (the lettering indicating they were flares had worn off). They were attached to an alarm clock with what appeared to be explosive primacord, and the whole thing was then stuffed into a paper bag under a couch.

My first though was "Baker and Schreiner!" But I couldn't afford to take a chance. This was the Vietnam War era, with a great deal of civil disobedience, and there had been legitimate bombs recently placed in the federal building and the county Hall of Justice. I immediately started the evacuation, but before calling communications I announced to the assembled group in the watch commander's office that if it was a joke, it was time to speak up.

Except for the two pranksters, others also believed the bomb was real, so I made the call. Within minutes there were fire trucks racing up the street, a helicopter overhead, and the last of the occupants was streaming out of the building. The joke quickly unraveled when investigators from Internal Affairs Division descended on the station to conduct an investigation. Baker and Schreiner each got a ten-day suspension, and their watch commander, who mistakenly acknowledged that he "heard something about playing a joke on Bushey," got a four-day suspension.

Now the real heartache for Baker and Schreiner: I was again commended for my professional behavior, in dealing with the potential explosive device at the station! These two fellows became good friends, and never stopped telling people that jokes played on me were not a good idea. Truth be known, is that I too love pranks—but it's important to not let them get out of hand.

The Shootout at Rampart Station

My assignment as a sergeant in Rampart Division, from the summer of 1970 until mid-1973, was during a very divisive time in our nation. The Vietnam War was scaling down, but radical groups were still active and had engaged in the bombing of public buildings throughout the country. As a result, the LAPD actually had officers assigned to "station security" duties at all its facilities. Rampart Division had an officer assigned to both the upper and lower levels of the station, twenty-four hours a day.

One morning the officer on the upper deck, Tom Wilson (pseudoynm), called for help, screaming that he was receiving fire from a sniper in a car in front of the station and that he was returning fire, as well. Naturally, all hell broke loose. The investigation clearly revealed shots fired by Tom, but could find absolutely no indication that shots had been fired at him or the station. He said the shots must have been high, and passed over the facility. Tom was a unique individual who had a penchant for questionable behavior (which is why he, even though fairly senior, was assigned to station security!) The unproven evaluation of the incident was that he had greatly over-reacted to a car backfire or some similar innocent action.

Within a very few years, Tom left the department. As I recall, he obtained a medical retirement. He had also been in additional trouble (he was always in trouble!) and probably would have been terminated had the retirement not occurred. He died an early death a few years after that, from some ailment that I do not recall.

"Shooting" at the Front Desk

This was a prank that could have had tragic consequences, but fortunately it was well-planned and executed to keep it under control.

Sergeant Leland ("Lee") Helms was a wonderful, gentle, and habitually nervous man who was the frequent target of jokes. Toward the end of his career he worked exclusively inside as the "station sergeant," mostly doing miscellaneous chores around the station such as working on the deployment schedule and approving reports. He typically did not wear a police equipment belt (his gun, handcuffs, etc., were kept in his locker), which was most significant to the prank.

The key conspirators in the prank were two officers, Gary Seeget and Don Bender (RIP), and watch commander Ray Rolon. It was a relatively quiet weeknight. Throughout the early evening the two officers feigned hostility with one another, with much hollering back and forth (when there were no citizens in the lobby). Lee kept trying to calm down the two officers, but his efforts to bring about peace never lasted for more than a few minutes. Later that evening Ray went to the break room at the other end of the station, supposedly to eat, but actually to be close enough to keep the prank from getting out of control. Several minutes after Rolon had departed amid the continued yelling back and forth between Seeget and Benter, Seeget fired a blank round from the shotgun that was kept at the desk (he removed the powder and slugs, leaving just the primer, but the blast was loud). He then entered the office where Lee was sitting and said something to the effect that he was sorry for what he just did, but he'd lost control of himself and just couldn't take it any longer. Seeget then walked back into the jail area.

Lee just about had a heart attack (it's amazing that he didn't), and displayed an array of emotions including disbelief, fear, anger, and hyperventilation. He feared a continuation of the "violence," being convinced that Benter was dead and Seeget had now barricaded himself in the jail area.

About that time Ray Rolon wisely and immediately appeared. But he let the prank go on just a bit longer, because it was apparently so much fun watching Lee's behavior. When he was told it had been a prank, Lee didn't think it was very funny. But everybody else did.

Interestingly, years later when I was with the San Bernadino County Sheriff's Department, I learned that a similar prank in Big Bear involving the country fire department did result in a fire captain actually having a heart attack (fortunately, not fatal).

Exploding Transformers and a Bouncing Toyota

In the early morning of February 9, 1971 I was driving on the Hollywood Freeway and getting ready to exit at the Benton Way off-ramp. But it seemed that something was very wrong with my Toyota Corolla—it was bouncing all over the place!

Then I noticed a series of exploding transformers alongside the freeway. The problem wasn't with my car—it was the 1971 Sylmar earthquake! I reached the station within a minute or so, and found the officer assigned to station security was pretty shaken-up. I was immediately loaned to the Department of Building & Safety, and assigned to accompany a building inspector who was passing judgment on whether a number of damaged buildings could remain occupied or had to be evacuated and "red-tagged."

This was among Los Angeles' worst earthquakes, resulting in over forty fatalities, 1,000 injuries and hundreds of demolished homes. It took the city many months to recover from this tragedy.

Sergeant Smith Bounces Off the Awning
on Bonnie Brae Street

One Sunday evening (don't know why I recall it was a Sunday!), the watch commander, Sergeant Tom Bauman, had me call the station Code 2 (come immediately). He explained that Sergeant Bill Smith (pseudonym), who was off duty and had a well-earned reputation for doing stupid shit, had just ruined the awning over the entrance to an apartment building on Bonnie Brae, while escaping from the manager who caught him inappropriately visiting a female tenant.

As I recall, the manager was somewhat of a "fuddy duddy" who did not look fondly on males visiting his unmarried female tenants. Bill was seen exiting the gal's apartment, and ran when he saw the manager coming up the stairs. Bill climbed out a front window onto the awning that covered the entryway to the building, and immediately fell through the fabric. The manager knew that Bill was a cop (the idiot would sometimes visit while on duty and in uniform). He immediately called the station to complain about Bill and the ruined awning. I managed to calm down the manager, in part because I insisted that Bill would pay for the awning. Bill was married and the awning was fairly expensive—but he managed to come up with the money to replace it.

At a Rampart reunion in Laughlin a couple of years back, I ran across Bill Smith, who had a nice new wife on his arm. He became visibly upset when, like everybody else who attends these gatherings, I started to mention things involving him so many years ago. I got the message, real fast, that he did not want his wife to know about many of his past antics. Given some of the truly foolish things he did, even more than the rest of us, I somewhat understand! Bill always had a mischievous twinkle in his eye, and in Laughlin I noticed it was still there!

But Sarge, He Said He Didn't Do It!

Officer Hankerson (pseudonym) was a very nice and extremely intelligent probationary officer—but pretty lean in the area of common sense.

One day, his training officer came to me. He was livid. The two officers had responded to the "burglary in progress" of a phone booth and, although they did not observe the crime in progress, the suspect was caught exiting a phone booth that had just been burglarized, had a crowbar in his hand, and a pocket full of dimes (many dimes!)

The senior officer handcuffed the suspect, then returned to the police car to put out a "code 4" (no further assistance needed), as the suspect was in custody. When he returned to the phone booth, the suspect was uncuffed and walking away! The senior officer grabbed the suspect, recuffed him, put him into the back of the unit, and severely chastised Hankerson.

The probationary officer's explanation for cutting the suspect loose was, "He said he didn't do it!" Somehow, the young officer made his probation, then served twenty-some years in lackluster assignments (mostly working the desk, etc.) before retiring several years ago.

Until about the mid-1980s, domestic disputes were handled much different than they are today. Now, any indication of one person striking a spouse or domestic partner results in mandatory arrest. But prior to the mid-1980s, domestic disputes almost never resulted in an arrest, or even a report. It was typical to either chase the man away with instructions to not return until the next day, or to instruct the woman to stay elsewhere with friends or relatives.

I can still recall one particularly noteworthy dispute, when furniture was literally flying out an upstairs window when my partner and I arrived. In Joseph Wambaugh's book, *The New Centurions*, he describes the situation where an old-salt cop had the warring spouses put their hands jointly on a penal code or a badge, then declared them to be legally divorced. While I never saw it happen, I don't doubt that someone may have done it!

That is just the way it was several decades ago.

Declined to Apply with PSA for Pilot Training

I was surprised and flattered by a potential employment overture that came my way in 1971, when approached by a Pacific Southwest Airways (PSA) executive who asked if I was interested in becoming an airline pilot!

I know that by today's standards it would be unthinkable for someone with a mere private pilot's license to possibly be considered for airline flight training. But those were different times. The airlines were rapidly expanding, but the supply of viable pilot applicants was far less than what was needed due to the demands of the Vietnam War. The military draft was in full force, and just about every physically qualified young man either had been or would be drafted, not to mention the tens of thousands already serving in the military. There were plenty of military aviators, but a larger percentage than usual was remaining on active duty because of the war.

Certainly, I had nowhere near the skills needed to fly a commercial airliner. But my combination of a pilot's license, bachelor's degree, excellent health, solid background (police sergeant), and having fulfilled my military obligation caused me to be an attractive candidate for commercial flight training with PSA. Interestingly, shortly afterward there was a glut of pilots as the Vietnam War scaled down. Within about five years the airlines were laying off pilots because of a downturn in that part of the economy!

I am glad I did not pursue that opportunity.

"Chief's Office—What do You Want, Asshole?"

This was a pretty funny situation, but also one the officer richly deserved the four days for which he was suspended. Bob Martino (pseudonym) was a supervisory pain in the ass, and prone to push the envelope as far as he could. He liked to "bait" supervisors, and I was among his victims when I was still wet-behind-the-ears as a new sergeant.

On this particular day Martino was working the desk. While engaged in a heated telephonic discussion with a citizen, he actually called the citizen an "asshole." It was clear that Martino was responding to a citizen's insistence to call the chief of police over his unhappiness with him. He then gave the citizen a number to call, which was just another number in the rotary phone on the desk where Martino was sitting. After about thirty seconds, the other line rang. Martino answered, saying: "Chief's Office—What do you want, asshole?"

I did not use formal discipline very often in those days, but in the case of Martino's actions in this matter I made an exception. Martino later resigned under a cloud, when it was discovered that he was using data from crimes as leads for his off-duty burglar alarm company.

FBI Tries to "Steal" Bank Robber

One morning a lone, armed suspect robbed the Bank of America at Sunset and Echo Park. He was then seen fleeing the scene southbound on Echo Park Avenue. I was among the units that saturated the area and, with the help of a citizen who pointed out where the suspect had gone, we located and arrested him inside the dwelling at 1000 Echo Park Avenue. (Why do I remember that exact address? Hell, I don't know!)

We were inside the dwelling with the cuffed suspect and all the evidence, including a handgun and the stolen money. But then two FBI agents came in, and announced they would take the suspect and evidence because bank robbery was a federal crime. I told the agents that my officers had made the arrest, and they would be transporting the suspect to Rampart Station. Any issues they cared to pursue could be dealt with at that time.

The FBI men did not like it. They tried to con the suspect out of us, but failed. I really could not fault their efforts, as it was during the era of J. Edgar Hoover and such an arrest would have been a real feather in their hat. However, my officers were justifiably proud of their arrest. The last thing I was going to do was let a couple of feds run off with our suspect!

Suspects Jumped the Wall—Big Mistake!

One afternoon during my assignment as officer-in-charge of the Special Problems Unit, two of my officers requested that I respond to their location in about the 1500 block of West Sixth Street. They had been chasing a couple of individuals who appeared suspicious.

The two suspects had jumped a wall that was about four feet high on one side—but had a drop of approximately thirty feet on the other side! The officers explained that they ran after the suspects but didn't jump the wall. When they looked down, they saw both suspects lying on the ground and moaning in pain! That's when they called me. But for some reason they didn't call an ambulance.

On arrival I immediately followed them to the back of the premises where the wall was located, and we looked down where they said the suspects had fallen. Nobody was there! Apparently the two suspects had crawled away.

Oh well, we all cleared the scene. But we never did find out what happened to the pair of suspects who tried to outrun my officers. There have been many procedural changes in the Los Angeles Police Department since this incident in the early 1970s—a situation like this clearly would be handled much differently today!

Fellow Sergeant Took "Dirty Harry" a Bit too Seriously!

One of my closest pals, and a great cop, was now-deceased retired Sergeant Larry Manderschied. We served together at Rampart as sergeants in the early 1970s, and he worked for me at Rampart in the later 1970s when I was a lieutenant.

During our young and foolish days, Larry did something that was really foolish. After seeing the first "Dirty Harry" movie, Larry wanted to have a .44 Magnum handgun. He bought one, and had a uniform holster made that looked just like the duty holsters we all wore, but obviously a bit bigger. On occasion Larry actually carried the .44 on his side in that LAPD look-alike holster!

Larry was a pretty daring and colorful guy, especially during those years. After retiring from the LAPD, he went to work for the Los Angeles Community College Police Department, and later became a deputy when that organization was absorbed into the L.A. Sheriff's Department. That wonderful man succumbed to cancer in about 2002. Rest in peace, Larry.

SUICIDE JUMPER CHANGES HIS MIND—TOO LATE!

The Mayflower Hotel is located just west of the Harbor Freeway on 7th Street. It is a very nice hotel today, and was clearly majestic when first built. But like many of LA's historic landmarks, the Mayflower endured a few rough years in the 1960s and 1970s before redevelopment began in earnest.

One afternoon, Officer Gary Lyons received a call to the Mayflower because a man on the roof was despondent and threatening to jump off the fourteen-story structure. When Gary got to the top of the building, the man flung himself over the side, but held onto the rope from the flagpole located at the edge of the roof. Gary was successful in talking the man out of taking his own life, but now a serious problem arose. As Gary was helping the man back up, the old rope started to unbraid. It ultimately broke completely.

The sight of the anguished look on the man's face as he fell to his death was something that bothered Gary for a long time. Today I drive past the Mayflower Hotel from time to time, and always glance up at that flagpole. I hope they replaced the rope.

OUR GUNS WERE "NEUTERED!"

The department finally had enough of accidental discharges, where cocked weapons fired when the officers tripped during foot pursuits. Admittedly, because of greater accuracy with a cocked weapon, it was very common for officers to put their weapons in the single-action mode when there was a chance that a shooting might occur.

An accidental discharge while running with a cocked revolver was almost predictable. Because of this, the department embarked on a program to retrain officers to only fire their revolvers in double-action mode. LAPD then mandated that every service revolver be modified, at the academy, so that it could not be cocked in a single-action manner. This new policy was unpopular with just about everyone, but it did greatly curtail the number of accidental discharges. The training was pretty good, and I think just about everyone became fairly proficient in double-action shooting.

The department started the process of transitioning to semi-automatic pistols in the early 1980s, and revolvers are now a complete thing of the past with the Los Angeles Police Department.

Nature of Police Behavior in the 1970s

Joseph Wambaugh is a friend. He was also a great cop, and is a superb writer. Certainly without intending to do so, Joe's novels have the potential to create an impression in the minds of readers that the majority of cops in the eras he writes about were pretty warped and unique characters. That isn't exactly the case. While the officers in his books are fictional characters, there absolutely were cops who exhibited the types of behaviors found in his books. Too, just about 100 percent of the cops were pretty calloused characters who were seldom surprised by the things they saw and experienced on a daily basis. Most, however, were also loving husbands, great dads, loyal sons, contributing members of their communities, non-alcoholics, and all-around good and decent people. Again, Joe Wambaugh and the other writers do not suggest otherwise, but a little positive reinforcement of the police officers' personal qualities is helpful after reading some of the best novels that are out there.

"Hello Kent, Remember Me?"

This story actually began in 1966, when Kent Urban (pseudonym) managed to get away from me in a vehicular pursuit. He had a "souped-up" 1962 Ford that just plain outran my black-and-white when I tried to stop him for speeding. Although I did not get his license number, one of my fellow Central officers knew exactly who he was and passed on the info to me. He also told me that Kent was gloating over having gotten away from me. That pissed me off. Fortunately, Kent Urban made the mistake of having a unique name that I did not forget.

Fast-forward seven years. By 1973 I was the officer-in-charge of the Rampart Special Problems Unit (SPU). My troops and I were arresting a great many "hype-burglars" (heroin addicts who steal to support their habits), and worked hard to identify the folks who were buying their stolen property.

Several of these suspects had the name of my old "buddy" Kent Urban and his phone number written on slips of paper in their wallets, which immediately got my attention. In doing a little poking around, I learned that Urban was a major receiver of stolen automotive parts, that stolen Porsche vehicles and parts were his specialty, and further that the garage of his house on Oceanview Street was full of stolen automotive property!

Knowing and proving are two different things. So I directed all of my officers to drive past the Oceanview address during every trip to and from the station. In doing so, hopefully one of them would see the garage door open and confirm what we had been told of its contents, as "the eyes cannot commit a trespass." After a couple of days of loose surveillance, one of my units got me on the tactical channel and said the garage door was open and that a large quantity of automotive parts was conspicuously visible. Kent Urban was conversing with some folks in the driveway.

I gave the word to "move in," and we really hit pay dirt. The open garage was full of stolen parts, and many of them actually had serial numbers. The two people Urban was chatting with were hypes who were selling him stuff. They immediately rolled over on him and cooperated with the investigation. We called Burglary-Auto Division, and a couple of detectives who specialized in commercial auto theft responded right away. It was a pleasure to finally arrest Kent Urban. At the time I asked him if he remembered me, and the night in '66 when he got away from me in that pursuit. I don't recall exactly what he said—but his attitude was pretty poor!

"Kent's Tied Up Now, Can I Take a Message?"

We spent a great deal of time in the home and garage of Kent Urban. Just itemizing all of the stolen items was a big job in itself. We were assisted by detectives from the Burglary-Auto Division, who were most helpful in pointing out hidden serial number locations on some of the parts.

While still at the scene, I answered a call that came in on Urban's phone. When the caller asked to speak to Kent, I indicated that he was "tied up," which was somewhat true because he was in handcuffs. The caller asked who I was and I said "Keith," also true. The caller seemed to recognize my name as someone who was part of their circle of friends and said something to the effect of "oh, hi Keith!" I responded in kind and asked if I could take a message for Kent. His response was pretty interesting. The caller said the Porsche he had spoken to Kent about was back in the parking lot of a shopping center in the Valley, and that he was going to "get it now." Could Kent bring over the stuff they needed to strip it?

I told the caller that I'd have Kent call him right back and asked for his phone number. The caller said Kent had the phone number. But I said the place was a mess—which was true because we were tearing it apart looking for stuff—and that to be on the safe side to give the number to me again, which he did.

Within a couple minutes of giving this information to the team from Burglary-Auto Division, they had determined the address of that phone and were on their way to the San Fernando Valley. I got a callback within an hour from the Burglary-Auto detectives, who told me they were sitting down the street from the caller's house when he pulled into his driveway with the Porsche he had just stolen from the shopping center! This was a very good day for me and the LAPD, but a very bad day for Kent Urban. I don't know the ultimate outcome of the charges, but the evidence was so strong that I suspect he took some type of a plea and avoided a trial.

Avoiding a No-Win Neighbor Dispute and Plenty of Poop!

To a great extent, cops are in a fishbowl twenty-four hours a day, even when off-duty. If there is ever a neighbor dispute, the fact that one of the parties is a cop always becomes an issue, and it is common for the non-cop neighbor to call the station and try to make trouble for the off-duty officer.

This is never good, and among the reasons why I have always been pretty tolerant of neighbors. However, my tolerance was severely tested in the early 1970s while I was a sergeant at Rampart. An idiot neighbor's dog continually, daily and almost on schedule, would come over and leave a big pile of poop on our front lawn; how that much poop came out of such a little dog still amazes me!

Rather than confront the neighbor, who had all the earmarks of a confrontational person, I decided to send a bunch of poop back to where it came from. I got a heavy-duty clear plastic bag, filled it to the brim with dog poop, attached the poop-filled bag to the dog's collar with a note (saying something to the effect of, "Here is some of your dog poop back!"), then chased the dog out of my yard. The only glitch was that the dog apparently liked the nice way I treated him while attaching the poop-filled bag to his collar, and was reluctant to leave!

We never saw the dog again. I still chuckle at the sight of that little dog dragging that big bag of poop down the street!

Late one evening, two of my officers responded to a domestic dispute on Mountain View Street, just north of Temple. The officers were Bert DiMauro and Dale Bourgois. As the officers approached the house, a suspect inside fired a high-powered rifle. The bullet struck Bourgois in the thigh and took out a pretty good chunk of his leg; his wound was serious.

Within a short time the suspect was dead. I then proceeded to Dale's house (somewhere in the suburbs) to notify his wife and take her to the hospital where he was being treated. But I was concerned that if I went to the front door and knocked, she would freak out at the sight of a uniformed sergeant standing there, thinking (logically) that her husband was dead. So I came up with a better strategy. I parked my police car in front of the darkened house and went to the next door neighbor's home, where I explained what had happened to the neighbors and made arrangements for them to watch the Bourgois children while I took Dale's wife to the hospital.

I then called Dale's wife from the neighbor's home, explained that Dale was okay (he was actually seriously wounded) and that he had asked me to call her. She immediately challenged me, saying it couldn't be true because a notification like that would always be made in person and not over the phone. I acknowledged her statement, but said I was afraid that she would faint if I went to the door. I then told her I was next door with the neighbors and to look out her front window and she would see my police car. The neighbors and I then went to the Bourgois house and I took her to the hospital to be with her husband. It worked like a charm, and she did not become an emotional basket case. Dale recovered from his wound and continued with his career.

LELAND HELMS TURNS WHITE

A fellow patrol sergeant, long since deceased, had a habit of always responding (if he was not tied up elsewhere) to dead body calls.

One morning when that sergeant and I were on duty, a dead body call came out on Columbia Street. Knowing my fellow patrol sergeant was likely to respond, I hurried to the location with the intention of having some fun. Two officers were already there. It was a natural death, with the deceased lying on a bed in a back room. With the morbid concurrence of the two officers, I quickly grabbed the sheet off the deceased, curled myself into a ball in a chair in the front room, and pulled it over me.

Predictably, the patrol sergeant arrived shortly after. He inquired as to the circumstances of the death. The other officers told him it was a pretty difficult situation, and encouraged him to examine the deceased himself. As the sergeant pulled the sheet off me, I let out a bloodcurdling scream and lurched toward him. He immediately stumbled backward, smashed into a wall, then started screaming at me that the situation really wasn't very funny. The officers and I thought it was very funny, and the more we laughed the madder he became.

I still think it was funny. This is an example of the type of gallows humor that officers frequently engage in, but that someone who's not a police officer may well find to be offensive.

RAMPART IMMIGRATION

After a couple years as a uniformed patrol sergeant, I became the officer-in-charge of the Rampart Special Problems Unit (SPU). At the time there was a lot of heartburn within the police department about the rampant illegal immigration from South and Central America, as well as Mexico, along with a belief that much of our daytime burglary problem was the result of unemployed illegal aliens. I believe it was true.

As a consequence, each Friday was reserved for illegal alien sweeps by my SPU. I let each of my four two-man teams go end-of-watch after each of the four units had scooped up and delivered forty illegal aliens to the U.S. Immigration Service, which was then located in the basement of the federal building at 300 North Los Angeles Street. Just about every unit completed their part of the sweep before noon.

It was really just a big game, in some respects. I imagine that some of the folks we scooped up had families who were left behind in LA, although most probably were sending the money they earned to their families south of the border. Neverthless, I don't recall any of the illegals ever really getting upset at being arrested. The border was a sieve. Most of them were probably back within days, after enjoying a visit with their families.

LIEUTENANT PETE DELGADO RETURNS TO LOS ANGELES

A part of Los Angeles' dark history walked into Rampart Station one morning while I was the watch commander. He was elderly, stooped over, walked with a cane, and identified himself as Pete Delgado. He also said that he was an old-time LAPD lieutenant from the 1930s. As luck would have it, he came to the one person in a thousand who knew exactly who he was, because of my interest in the department's history.

Pete had been the "bag man" for Mayor Frank Shaw, who was recalled in 1938! In that era, Delgado disappeared with a large amount of cash and went to Mexico. He was a fugitive for many years. But by the time he came to the station, I am sure that all of those who could have testified against him were dead. He knew that, too, and I doubt he would have returned for a visit any sooner. We had a very nice chat, during which it became clear that he had done exactly what he'd been accused of.

At the time of his visit he owned a resort in Chihuahua, Mexico, which he invited me to come down and stay at as his guest. I am sorry that I never had the opportunity to take him up on his offer. I'm sure I would have enjoyed spending time with him and learning more of that troubled era in Los Angeles politics.

Hundreds of Dildos Standing at Attention in Azusa

Dave Houts, an Azusa policeman, was one of my closest pals during this era. I had taken him on ride-alongs on a couple of occasions, so I accepted his invitation for me to go on a ride-along with him. He was well aware of the weird stuff that commonly occurred in the lives of LAPD officers, and assured me that there was equally bizarre activity in Azusa. But Dave insisted on showing, rather than telling me about, that activity.

From the Azusa Police Station we drove to a building in the industrial part of the city. We pulled our unit up against the wall, then stood on the vehicle's hood to look into some fairly high windows. I couldn't believe my eyes! The place was full of row after row of erect dildos, in every conceivable shape, size, and color! There had to be hundreds of those unique devices. I guess this company must have been one of the nation's top providers of artificial male genitals.

The dildo company is long-gone. But the building is still there, and now occupied by a wonderful man and good friend who sells various types of flags. I occasionally rib him about the activities of one of the former tenants!

Portable Blimp for the Houts Family

This is another fun story about my good pal, Dave Houts, the Azusa policeman. He and his wife, Patricia, were very close with Barbara and me, and both families had small kids. We did a lot of things together and even took vacations together.

However, Dave had a bad habit of spending money he didn't have, and felt that as long as he could still put charges on his credit card, all was good. One day, just to be funny, I ginned up a phony letterhead from the "Dawson Dirigible Company," then on that letterhead sent a letter to his house advising him that the blimp he ordered on credit, which was "perfect for a family of four such as his," had been approved. Furthermore, efforts were being made to extend his credit so that he could also acquire a blimp docking mechanism for his backyard.

My little plan backfired! Patricia received the letter while Dave was at work, became hysterical, called the station in a blind rage and raised hell with him! He immediately figured that I was the culprit, and stability was restored. Sorry, Pat.

Search for Sex Offender and Arizona Highway Patrol Death

Patrol cops hear literally scores of wanted-persons radio transmissions, just about every day. While all are taken seriously, and officers try to keep their eyes open for the described suspects and vehicles, every once in a while one of those transmissions really resonates and the officer(s) puts a great deal of special effort into finding and arresting the suspect. I had one of those experiences during the early morning hours of February 5, 1971.

Broadcasts were coming out about every fifteen minutes, including a vehicle description, to be on the lookout for a suspect named Bertram Greenberg, who had raped and murdered a thirteen-year-old girl. I took this broadcast more seriously than most and spent a great deal of time and effort in an unsuccessful attempt to find Greenberg. As it turned out, while we were still looking for him in Los Angeles, he was well on his way eastbound on Interstate 40.

Later that day, during separate traffic stops just minutes apart, he shot and killed two Arizona Highway Patrol officers, James Keeton and Don Becksted. It is believed that Becksted wasn't aware that Keeton had been shot just minutes before. Later that same day, Greenberg was shot and killed in a shootout with the police in New Mexico. Like most cops, I was sad for several reasons, not the least of which was because he killed a couple of cops. Had we got him in Los Angeles, those two Arizona officers would not have lost their lives.

In 2007, as part of the district attorney's delegation to Washington, D.C. for Police Week, Cathy and I were in a café with a group of other cops and delegates. While standing in line, I noticed the woman behind me had a name badge identifying her as part of a police survivor's group. Her name was "Becksted." I had never forgotten that name because of the Greenberg incident. I asked if she was the widow of the Arizona Highway Patrol officer from 1971, and she replied in the affirmative. We had a very nice chat, each of us describing our roles in that terrible tragedy. We exchanged information and parted with hugs. I remain active in police circles, including survivor groups, and hope that our paths cross again.

"Sarge, an Old Man Wants to Give You Some Badges"

Talk about luck and timing! One day when on patrol as a sergeant in Rampart, a unit asked me to meet them at 2nd and Kenmore. On arrival, they told me they had just spoken to an elderly man who identified himself as a retired policeman, and that he had badges he wanted to give to the right person before he died!

As a badge collector and someone who is near-obsessed with the history of the LAPD, I was extremely interested and responded immediately to the nearby residence where the man lived. What a wonderful visit and a wonderful man! He was retired Detective Inspector Francis T. Hawtrey, who retired from the department in 1940. He had been very prominent during the 1920s and 1930s, and can be found in just about all of the LAPD publications from that era. He was also the key person in developing the two-way radio system for the department. He and his wife, Alice, were very gracious hosts. He gave me the series five gold badge he had carried, and his old gold retirement badge, as well. He explained that he was supposed to have turned in his duty badge when his retirement badge was being issued in 1940, and had put it on the counter, but took it back and slipped in his pocket when the girl at the counter turned her back.

As I am working on this entry for my memoirs, I just glanced up at both of those badges, which I truly treasure as part of my extensive badge collection.

The Impossible Pursuit

I was not present when this occurred, but it is too precious a story to let die with the participants. Officers Lou Graham and Norman Bonneau were two of my best men, and Sergeant Tom Proctor was a fellow supervisor and a good pal. One night, in an alley, the officers spotted a "duck" (abandoned stolen vehicle) that was listed on the hot sheet of

314

outstanding stolen vehicles.

For whatever crazy reason the officers, both who had twinkles in their eyes and mischievous natures, decided to place themselves in pursuit of that car! They did a few broadcasts of where they were allegedly pursuing the car and, when they could hear other sirens getting close, announced that the suspects had abandoned the car in the alley (where it had been parked all along) and that the suspects were GOA (gone on arrival). The tow truck and Sergeant Proctor arrived at about the same time and, as the officers were basking in the glory of the supervisor's compliments about the professional broadcasting of the pursuit, the tow truck driver was becoming increasingly insistent in trying to get one of the officers away from the sergeant's conversation. When one of the officers did step aside, somewhat irritated at the interruption, the tow truck driver whispered in his ear that the vehicle's engine was missing!

Oh my God, how funny! The officers kept their mouths shut and no one was ever the wiser. In those days, there were not pursuit summaries and the many other requirements that exist today. I did not learn of this situation until about a year or so ago, when Lou Graham, long retired and now director of security for the Universal Hilton, told me the story shortly after Norm's death.

Sergeant J. J. Kelly and His Auto Body Shop

Sergeant J. J. Kelly was a handy guy to have around if you had a minor accident with your police car. He had a body shop in Rampart Division, and performed a number of minor repairs for his pals who otherwise would have gotten in hot water for backing into posts, scraping against a wall and related transgressions. Old J.J. was a decent and fun man to have as a friend.

Volkswagen Turned Into a Police Car!

Oh my God, this was funny! A fellow sergeant and a great guy, Sam Guluzzo, had a VW Bug that he drove to and from work each day.

One day shortly after he arrived at work, a couple of his fellow sergeants, including J. J. Kelly who owned the previously-mentioned body shop in Rampart, snatched Sam's car and took it to the body shop. Throughout the day, the VW was painted and transformed into a black-and-white police bug, complete with siren, red lights, antennas, spotlight, LAPD door decals and whatever else could be found! To say that Sam was surprised is an understatement. What a fun joke!! Sam passed away a few years ago, but I'm told that he coveted his VW police bug until the day he died, and understand the car is still around somewhere.

SICK AS A DOG WITH UNKNOWN ILLNESS

I have always been healthy and, as earlier mentioned, I just did not call in sick. If I were really hurting, which was seldom, I would take an accumulated overtime day off.

In this particular instance, I was just starting a two-week vacation when I got really sick. The symptoms were extreme weakness, chills, and profuse sweating. Within a period of about a week and a half, I lost something like seventeen pounds. I was *really* sick. Finally, Barbara took me to the emergency room at the Kaiser Hospital in Fontana. After a wait and a few tests, the on-duty physician came into the treatment room, proclaimed there was nothing medically wrong with me, and asked me: "What is the real problem, young man?"

I was so pissed, I could have punched the guy. His bedside manners were horrible, he clearly remained skeptical after I assured him that my only concerns were physical. Finally, he gave me some type of medication. After a couple of weeks, I started feeling better, but remained weak for quite a while.

To this day, I don't know what caused the illness; I guess a virus of some sort. Fortunately, that was the only bad experience I've had with Kaiser in over forty years with them being the primary health care provider for my family and me. I am a real cheerleader for the Kaiser Health Plan, and over the years have learned how to navigate their bureaucracy pretty well.

THE AIRLINE STEWARDESS HOOKER

While in Rampart as a sergeant, I spent a couple of months on loan to the vice unit. One night I was partnered with Jerry DeRosa, a great guy and someone who previously had been among my subordinates in patrol. Jerry's claim to fame was having been the first unit on the scene of the slaughter at the home of actress Sharon Tate, where she and several others were slain and butchered by the Charles Manson Clan.

Jerry and I were "poaching" in Hollywood for prostitutes, as the pickings were better than in Rampart, and in those days it wasn't a big deal to grab hookers out of other divisions. We snatched a guy off the street who had just been "serviced" by a gal we recognized as a prostitute, and he was armed with a .45 semi-automatic pistol. He explained that he was a businessman from Long Beach and always carried his gun when visiting prostitutes, as he was afraid (with much justification) of being robbed by a potential pimp of the gal he was "visiting." He seemed like a pretty decent sort and pleaded with us to cut him loose and forget the gun.

We made him an offer he couldn't refuse! It was clear that all of his liaisons were telephone appointments (or "outcalls") as opposed to the "street-walking" variety. We said we would cut him loose and forget the gun if he would grease the skids for us to make liaison (and arrest!) three outcall prostitutes. He agreed and made three calls to three gals and stiffed us in with all three. We made appointments with all three, got violations, and arrested all three. One of the prostitutes—the third gal—was particularly interesting.

The third gal lived in a luxury apartment on Kings Road in Beverly Hills (we poached out of the city as well). Jerry "was up," as it his turn to make the call and the arrest. After he called and made an immediate appointment to be "serviced," we proceeded to the location. He knocked on the door and she let him in while I remained concealed outside in the hallway. The procedure was for him to get the violation, then open the door and I would enter.

I waited and waited and waited, and finally after about a half-hour I knocked on the door. Jerry opened the door and let me in, and introduced me to the gal as if she was a personal friend! I was obviously puzzled by the situation and asked him, in a whisper, if he ever got a violation. He replied that he got the violation within moments of entering, but was enjoying his conversation with her and forgot I was even outside! This gal was drop-dead beautiful, in a very provocative night-gown, had given him a glass of wine and imported chocolates when he entered, and was truly captivating.

Turns out she was a Western Airlines stewardess who was a high-class hooker on the side. She was most cooperative and a pleasure to deal with. We let her change clothes and took her to Parker Center (then known as the Police Administration Building, PAB) for booking. At Jerry's insistence, we did not follow protocol and notify the apartment manager of the arrest. Although I was in charge I chose not to push the issue. This was my first experience with a high-class call girl, as just about all the prostitutes I had previously dealt with were pathetic hypes.

Probationary Officer Kills a Mirror at Rampart Station!

This is probably a good example of the expression: "the difference between men and boys is the cost of their toys." One afternoon, just before PM roll call began, a shot rang out in the men's room behind the roll call room. We all ran in and found just one person, a very embarrassed probationary police officer with a gun in his hand and a hole in the mirror! He tried to give us some cock-and-bull story about how the weapon accidently went off as he was reattaching the keeper straps on his Sam Brown duty belt, but we all knew better. He was playing quick-draw and admiring his new police image in the mirror, and that is how the accidental discharge occurred. I do not recall the consequences that he experienced for this stupidity, but he probably received a day or two suspension.

Female Impersonators Made a Very Big Mistake

Things have changed a great deal in the last forty or fifty years, including medical protocols. There was one situation where, as I recall, two female impersonators were arrested for a drug-related offense. They were handcuffed to the bench outside of the Detective Bureau. The arresting officer believed that one (or both?) had intentionally swallowed drugs when the officers approached them on the street, and had called an ambulance to the station. This was before the advent of paramedics; medical crews then were ambulance attendants with advanced first-aid training. One of them, maybe both, denied ingesting anything and declined medical treatment, which would have meant a trip to the hospital for stomach-pumping.

Within about twenty minutes after the RA unit departed, one of them died while still handcuffed to the bench. There was no fanfare associated with the incident, like there would be today—just a death report and covered body awaiting the coroner's arrival.

Deceived by Industrial Polluters in Frogtown

Although it occurred many years ago, I am still troubled by this incident. On patrol in the wee small hours of the morning, I came across a tanker truck that was obviously depositing something into the drainage system. The metal street grating had been set off to one side, and the truck's large hose was inserted into the opening in the street. I initiated a conversation with the two men, who immediately told me they had a permit to dump their waste into the sewer system, and they produced a permit from the Los Angeles County Health Department.

Knowing very little about the issue, I assumed the permit was valid and left the men to their dumping activity. Later I found out the permit was for the operation of a waste company, and certainly didn't permit dumping waste directly into the sewer system. Plain and simple: I didn't know the difference, and had been deceived. I later learned that the fee to legitimately dispose of some substances ran into the thousands of dollars. Goodness only knows what they were dumping into the public sewer system.

Those two are probably still laughing at the dumb cop who did not know what they were up to, and permitted them to continue their criminal activity.

My Pal at the Hall of Justice—Badges!

Prior to the late 1950s when Peter J. Pitchess replaced the legendary Eugene W. Biscaluz as the sheriff of Los Angeles County, that department had given out thousands of honorary, special, auxiliary, etc., badges for decades. Just about every celebrity, politician and otherwise prominent individual had a gold badge, often custom-made of precious metals and gemstones. Most were engraved on back, indicating the names of who presented and who received the badge.

When Pitchess took office, he initiated a massive effort to retrieve all those badges. While thousands of them were not retrieved, other thousands were picked up, then put into locked filing cabinets in a room on an upper floor of the Hall of Justice.

Among the top aides to Sheriff Pitchess was a friend of mine, who took me to the room and permitted me to help myself (within reason). Unfortunately, the high-ranking sheriff's officials who'd had access to that room over the previous fifteen years or so since the badges had been picked up, had already pilfered most of the really precious and beautiful badges. However, I ended up with about a dozen fairly nice badges, including several that have the names of prominent people engraved on the reverse.

Not Selected for Internal Affairs

During about my third year as a patrol sergeant, I went "on loan" to Internal Affairs Division (IAD) for a couple of months. These loans were necessary for people who wanted to be reassigned to IAD, to give the leadership of that division the opportunity to evaluate those who wanted to transfer in. During my two-month loan, I worked on a very sensitive investigation. It involved allegations made by a former detective, who was then serving time in federal prison, for narcotics trafficking.

In an effort to be transferred to a federal prison closer to California, he was cooperating with the authorities and allegedly providing information about other rogue cops. The investigation really didn't go anywhere, as the former cop was obviously not telling the truth.

At the conclusion of my loan, I was told I had done a good job and could expect to shortly be transferred into IAD as a regular investigator. A couple of months after returning to patrol I went to my captain, and asked him to call the captain at IAD to inquire when the transfer would occur. A short time later my captain called me into his office and gave me the bad news: the captain at IAD had opted not to select me for the reassignment. No reason was given. Obviously, I was very disappointed.

About three years later my stock with IAD had obviously improved, as I was offered a position in IAD as the assistant advocate. The unit now had a new captain. However, it was determined (accurately) that I would soon be promoted to lieutenant, and it wouldn't make sense for me to assume a position of that importance for what was likely to be a brief period.

An assignment to IAD was a very coveted move, perceived as close to essential for a sergeant to promote to lieutenant. Somehow, I made it anyway. Fortunately, internal investigative experience can also be obtained at the divisional level, and as a pretty decent writer I got plenty of it.

This is one of the many examples in my life, where the painful closing of one door opened up a much better door. My subsequent assignment as the officer-in-charge of the Manuals & Orders Unit, in Management Services Division, turned out to be of much greater promotional value, and gave me experiences that have served me well throughout my entire professional life.

What the Hell! Is a Squirrel Being Sodomized, or What?

During one of my loans to Rampart Vice as a supervisor, I confused the hell out of my boss with respect to conflicting hand signals. My good friend (and boss at the time), then-Lieutenant Jim Chambers, and I were working a public restroom in Elysian Park, as the result of numerous lewd conduct complaints.

We were "working supervisors," and made arrests just like the men who worked for us (during that era, women did not work these types of operational assignments, except as decoys in "sting" operations).

I was doing the "operating," and Jim was a couple hundred feet way in the bushes as my back-up. When I got the violation, I stepped out of the bathroom and mistakenly gave Jim the wrong hand signal (which I immediately corrected with what I thought was the correct one), to join me in making the arrest. I guess my conflicting signals pretty much confused Jim. He later told me he wasn't able to determine whether I had a violation, and if I did, whether it was for lewd conduct or a park visitor sodomizing a squirrel!

Jim is a great guy, and was a tremendous supporter of me during most of my career. At one time or another I worked under him in every supervisory and command rank that he held. Jim now lives in Oregon, and I regret that we've not been able to visit for many years.

HOOKER AT THE CAVE—"I LIKE YOU!"

While assigned to the Rampart Vice Unit, I was a supervisor on the PM watch. One night my partner, Jerry DeRosa, and I were working a 3.18 (formal complaint of vice activities) involving an alleged prostitute at The Cave, a bar on Sunset Boulevard north of Alvarado. It actually looked like a cave built into the side of the hill.

The suspect was a very worn-out gal with red hair and a few missing teeth, who would hustle the customers for drinks then sell her diminished attributes. Jerry and I decided that I would try to "work" the gal, and he would be my cover in the background.

What a night! I spent at least a couple of hours buying her drinks and dancing before the place closed. At closing, I still did not have a violation. So I suggested that I take her home (thinking I could still get a violation).

We got into the car, where Jerry had already concealed himself in the trunk, and drove to where she directed me, somewhere in the Echo Park area. I parked the car and she got out. When I remained seated, she asked if I was coming in with her. I replied that I wanted to make sure that she and I would really have a nice experience (or something to that effect, being careful not to use words that would constitute entrapment). She replied that we were certainly going to have sex. I said I didn't have much money (as I needed a dollar amount to establish the violation).

She responded that "she liked me," and I would not have to pay! I roared away from her standing at the curb, with Jerry laughing like a hyena, clearly audible, coming from the trunk!

One afternoon as a vice sergeant, my partner and I were investigating a report of prostitution in the residential neighborhood just east of Los Angeles City College. We staked out on the house in question and observed a steady stream of men going in and out, at about fifteen-minute intervals, which was a pretty good indication of potential prostitution activity. We snuck around the house, using the bushes for concealment, and looked in the windows.

As we did this, we heard police radio transmissions coming from within the residence! We found the window to the room where the activity was coming from, and made a most unique observation. A woman was providing oral affection to a male customer while watching the then-popular television show, "Adam-12"! The activity was well organized, as she had her customer in a position that gave her an unobstructed view of the television screen, and a virtual work station with a large supply of mouthwash and paper towels. This was truly a convergence of best business practices, police support, and love!

I guess it must not have been a problem for her customers—but listening to police calls doesn't strike me as something that would stimulate an amorous mindset.

STRIPPERS IN ROLL CALLS

Boy, times have really changed! Today, any hint of sexual activities in the workplace results in lawsuits and discipline. But this was not always the case.

For probably the first twenty years of my career with the LAPD, it was fairly common for co-workers to get together and kick in enough money to hire a stripper to come into roll call for birthdays and other special occasions. As the commanding officer of Communications Division, where most of the employees were women, it was common for them to bring in male strippers for such events. It was good, clean fun, and the strippers never went all the way.

One of my favorites occurred in Communications Division. The male stripper was dressed as a police sergeant. When he started giving roll call training and people questioned the accuracy of whatever he was saying, he began removing his police uniform to the song "The Stripper"!

The gals went wild, and it was a real fun event.

Like most cops, I have had several instances of finding a sick or injured person during a "welfare check," and it is always nice to be able to help someone in such circumstances. One instance continues to stand out in my mind.

A very elderly woman who resided on Bellevue Street had not been seen for several days. The air was busy with radio calls, so I went ahead and "rogered" that I would handle this non-priority incident and meet with a neighbor who was concerned about the woman.

I looked in her windows but couldn't see anything, nor was there any response to my knocking on the door. I went to the rear of the house and observed a very high, small window that most likely was a bathroom. I had to get up and stand on some object to reach the window, but it was closed and covered with blinds so I couldn't see in.

However, when I tapped on the window, in response someone tapped back! I immediately forced entry through the front door and went to the bathroom. On the floor, dehydrated, hungry and in a pathetic state, lay a sweet little old lady who was essentially paralyzed because of a fall and a broken hip. I was pleased to find her, but she was *really* pleased to see me. We chatted a bit while waiting for the ambulance to arrive. These types of incidents make routine days, better days.

A Sniper Misses His Mark (Thankfully!)

The first time I was ambushed occurred while responding to a 415 (disturbing the peace) call on Douglas Street, just east of Glendale Boulevard. There had also been a report of "shots fired," which caused me and several other officers to approach the location on foot.

As I recall, it was close to midnight. As we moved along the row of houses we started taking gunfire, and could hear the rounds impacting around us. Obviously, we took cover, and continued a tactical approach. We never did learn who the shooter(s) was, and cannot say they knew they were shooting at the police, as gang members were always shooting at each other in the area. The experience certainly validated the wisdom of moving in the shadows and taking advantage of the dark. To this day, I strongly subscribe to the cop's absolute reality that "darkness is my friend."

Making the "Laser Lady" Happy

This crazy woman was truly a legend for a number of years with the LAPD. She would often call, initially sound very intelligent, then beg and demand that the police department do something to protect her from the bombarding laser transmissions from outer space! Trying to reason with her, or just hanging up on her, were not realistic options. She would quickly call back, either to Rampart Station (she was a resident of Rampart) or to Communications Division.

Finally, we all realized that it was just easier, and even kind of fun, to humor her. So we would typically launch a complicated charade when she called—by placing our hands over our mouths to create "microphone" and similar sounds, then someone would fan papers to create a bogus helicopter sound, another voice would direct the helicopter to respond to her house and "lower the laser shield," along with a series of additional bogus radio transmissions.

At the end of our charade she would thank us sincerely and profusely, and hang up. In another week or two she would call again, and we would repeat our theatrical performance. Years later, when going through my personnel file, I found a letter of commendation this crazy lady had sent to the chief, outlining my actions in "lowering the laser shield."

So much for carefully reviewing commendation letters!

Ducks in the Wall Lockers

Cops can be just as cruel as they can be creative. On several occasions, disliked personnel (in one particularly notorious case, a supervisor) had ducks from MacArthur Park put inside their wall lockers. The ducks did not squeal, but just sat there and crapped all over everything.

Glad I never went sideways with the folks who liked to do this stuff. It was not a pleasant experience when the victim came back to work and opened his locker.

Commander Kirby Inspects Rampart Station

Commander Carroll Kirby (RIP) was a very bright individual, who had a well-deserved reputation for being hyper. He was a nice and decent man, but his hyperactivity often led to actions that others saw as foolish.

In the early 1970s he was the commanding officer of the Inspection & Control function out of the office of the Chief of Police, with the responsibility to conduct audits and make inspections over important

324

functions. One night during the time I was a uniformed sergeant, Kirby literally stormed into the Rampart watch commander's office. He announced that he had penetrated that station's security system, and that if he had been a bomber all of us would be dead (this was the era of bombings by radical groups, when we actually had officers working "station security" around the clock).

He went on to describe how he had jumped the fence behind the station, crawled between cars, dashed around the parking aisle when the officer was not looking, darted into the carwash enclosure, and sneaked into the building. The watch commander, Vern Dossey, immediately called the officer who was working station security in the downstairs portion of the facility and told him he was not doing his job. Someone had managed to sneak past him and get into the building!

The officer responded that the only person he had seen in the last few minutes was Commander Kirby! The officer was watching Kirby the whole time, and doubtless wondering why a staff officer was acting so strangely! Too funny!

Management Services Division

In April 1973, after approximately three years in Rampart Division, I successfully competed for an advanced pay grade position of "Sergeant II," and assumed the duties as officer-in-charge of the Manuals & Orders Unit in Management Services Division (MSD). This division was the primary entity within the department for writing, modifying, and maintaining information pertaining to department-wide policies, procedures, and legal issues. As I recall, there were probably somewhere around forty personnel assigned to the Management Services Division during that era.

Selected for Manuals & Orders—A BIG Fork in My Road

After three or so years in patrol, including vice and the special problems unit, I was ready to try something else. I was feeling somewhat discouraged because of my failure to be selected for a permanent assignment in Internal Affairs. So I applied for one of the most coveted sergeant positions in the department, as the officer-in-charge of the Manuals and Orders Unit.

This unit, with nine policemen/orders writers and a sergeant, was responsible for maintaining the department's manual, doing all special orders, and basically being on top of all the department's critical directives. Many of the department's top officers had held previous assignments to "M&O," and it was seen as a great career opportunity. The person who was to make the selection, more so than others in the process, was newly-promoted Lieutenant Andy Blakley. The fact that Andy took an immediate liking to me was among the best things that happened in my life and in my career. Even though I did not do particularly well on the department's English exam (a hard-core requirement), Andy believed in me and talked the captain, Bill Brown, into selecting me for the job.

It turned out that I did a truly great job, put out a great product, selected some of the department's best and brightest for staff positions, and put myself on a very successful promotional track (with a few bumps in the road). But this assignment really established a promotional mind-set for me. Andy Blakley and I become life-long friends. I had the honor to give the eulogy at his funeral. To this day I remain close to his widow, Louise, and endeavor to be helpful when problems arise in her life. Andy was a WWII P-38 pilot and one of the most wonderful men I have ever known.

God bless you, Andy! Thank you for all you did for me.

SELECTING THE BEST AND THE BRIGHTEST

Notwithstanding a few mistakes in the M&O assignment, there is one thing I did that was really a good thing, and something that served the department very well for years to come. Although there was a time when Manuals & Orders was an assignment that involved the best and brightest young officers, that was not the case when I took over. My predecessor was a good fellow, but pretty much just an "old-timer" without a great deal of energy who somehow got the officer-in-charge position. For the most part, the officers he had selected for the unit were equally as unspectacular.

I immediately decided that I would only select officers for orders-writer positions who were truly the best, brightest, and most deserving. I obtained rosters of academy classes for officers who had somewhere between four and seven years, pulled the personnel files of those who had graduated at the top of their classes, and invited those who had stellar records in the field to apply for vacancies as they arose. Most of those folks did pretty well, including Deputy Chief Ron Bergmann, Deputy Chief Carlo Cudio, Deputy Chief Bob Gil, Commander Dan Koenig (later as a civilian Dan became the executive director of the Police Commission), Captain Alan Deal, Captain Nick Salicos, and a bunch of lieutenants. All of my policemen promoted and left as sergeants. I am proud to have left a legacy of excellence, and in playing a key role in developing a number of folks who went on to positions of senior leadership.

My Second Pal at the Hall of Justice—More Badges!

Unbeknownst to my other pal at the Hall of Justice, I became friends with a sheriff's official who had found a different stash of badges from those I'd previously seen on one of the upper floors. He took me to an old building that had steel mesh covering all the doors and windows, at the county purchasing complex just south of Lincoln Park.

On entering, I could not believe my eyes: several rooms were filled with box after box after box of old badges dating from about 1900 through the 1930s! Unlike the other badges, which were of a precious nature, most of these had been stamped-out by the hundreds. There were thousands of special, auxiliary, and reserve deputy sheriffs, constables, marshals, and everything in-between. Many of the badges actually had the name of the community in which the bearers had worked.

What a find, and he had permission from somebody to pretty much help himself! He delegated the "help yourself" invitation to me, and I did just that. Unfortunately, I later became aware that he was at the top of the shit list and in the sights of a higher ranking sheriff's official who was looking for an excuse to fire him. As a result, I returned most of the badges I got from that building to him, as I did not want to get in hot water over the way they were obtained.

However, I should have kept them, because the potential problems I feared never did become a reality. Over the span of the next few decades, in one way or another, I reacquired most of those badges anyway. I never drive past Lincoln Park without glancing over to the spot where that long-since torn down building used to stand.

The Smoking Typewriter

There was a time when I was the officer-in-charge of the Manuals & Orders Unit, when I occasionally smoked cigars. In those days, there was no prohibition against smoking inside of buildings, and large numbers of smokers worked in the offices in Parker Center.

The senior clerk-typist in the unit, a great little lady named Annie Fujioka, used to occasionally give me a hard time over the smell of the cigar smoke. Consistent with the non-stop jokes we were always playing on one another within the unit, I had an idea. I got a long piece of surgical tubing and snaked it along the wall about twenty feet from my desk up inside Annie's typewriter. Then, for the next couple of days, whenever I smoked a cigar I would blow an occasional puff into the tube, which put the smoke and odor right into her typewriter! Annie came in one morning and said her husband, Eddie, had complained that she was starting to smell like a stale cigar! I confessed my sin, and removed the tube.

TAMPERING WITH THE
FBI NATIONAL ACADEMY SELECTION PROCESS

The Federal Bureau of Investigation annually hosts several three-month, in-residence law enforcement executive training courses for officers from police and sheriff departments throughout the country. Known as the FBI National Academy, it is very coveted training and an honor to attend.

LAPD typically sends four to six officers per year, allegedly selecting them through a management-development advisory committee. The committee, consisting of several captains, actually exists, and the captains on the committee work long and hard to select and recommend to the chief of police which applicants should attend. The applicants also work long and hard to put together a very structured application package. I was acquainted with a great lady, Judy Jacobs, a secretary whose duties included supporting the selection committee. As a favor to me (top secret at the time), she closely watched my application as it worked its way through the process, as I badly wanted to attend the course. It was held at the FBI Academy, in Quantico, Virginia.

One day Judy called and gave me great news: I'd been selected as a primary candidate to attend the FBI National Academy. I was thrilled beyond description, and actually began the process of arranging for a place for my family to stay in rural Maryland while I attended the three-month course.

Several days later the official list came out from the Office of the Chief of Police. My name was not mentioned, not even as an alternate! I was heartbroken, and learned from Judy that one of the assistant chiefs had replaced my name with someone he preferred to attend the course. I was livid, but could not appeal or complain without violating the trust that Judy had placed in me by telling me what occurred. A year later, it happened again: the committee selected me, but my name was switched with that of an assistant chief's aide, in one of the sixth floor personality contests.

When I became a commander and took over the Personnel Group, I was sad to see that the foolish nonsense I experienced, with respect to the FBI National Academy (other things too!), continued to be the case. Sergeants and lieutenants jump through a bunch of hoops to apply, the committee meets and works in good faith to select the most qualified and deserving candidates to attend the course, then certain deputy and assistant chiefs disregarded everything to send their favorite people. Equally disgusting was the notice that announced the "selection of those to attend," implying that the process took place as described in the Manual of the Los Angeles Police Department.

When the Cat (Sergeant) is Away, the Mice (Policemen) Will Play

One day during my time as the OIC of M&O, I had to leave early for a doctor's appointment. After walking all the way to my car in the industrial area east of Parker Center, I realized that I had left something I needed in my desk. While walking back to the police building, I ran into my entire crew of subordinates, who figured that since I was gone they would slip out as well. I wasn't pleased, but it seems we all had a pretty good laugh over the incident. The office ended up being empty that afternoon.

Searching for the Pieces of My Revolver

I suspect that I am not the only man to have left his revolver on the clothes hook of an inside commode door. It happened in the seventh floor men's room of Parker Center, when I worked the Manuals & Orders Unit of Management Services Division. I had nine of the most creative and mischievous officers on the department working for me, including the one who found my gun within seconds of me exiting that bathroom. These guys disassembled the gun completely and hid its different parts all over the division, then developed rhymes I had to understand in order to figure out where each part was hidden. Although the damn search consumed the better part of that day, and was a real pain in the butt, it was all in good fun. That was the last time I left my gun in a stall!

Captain Jack Eberhardt—A Fun and Decent Man

Captain Jack Eberhardt was on the "shit list" of Chief of Police Edward M. Davis. As the commanding officer of Public Affairs, he apparently had dropped the ball during the organization, planning and ticket sales for the Annual Police-Celebrity Golf Tournament.

Jack had hoped to be promoted to captain III and be given command of a geographic area, but instead he remained a captain II and was put in the Management Services Division. He was a bit abrasive and didn't think much of the upper staff, but was a fun and delightful man to work for. We played jokes on him and he reciprocated by playing jokes on us, as well.

Jack was finally let out of purgatory and given command of the West Los Angeles Area, which was a captain III position, from which he ultimately retired. I stayed in touch with "Captain Jack" over the years, and while with the San Bernardino County Sheriff's Department met him for lunch one day. At lunch, he gave me a rough copy of the memoirs he was writing, which he hoped to complete after his long-planned vacation to China. We planned to have another lunch, at The Pantry Café in downtown Los Angeles, on his return.

Unfortunately, that wonderful man died of a heart attack while in China. Because of my fondness for that fun and decent man, I continue to make and provide copies of his almost-completed memoirs to other "old-timers" from the department. I think he would like that. Jack was a bit of an "acquired taste," but I feel fortunate to be among those folks who acquired that taste. Rest in peace, Captain Jack.

A UNIQUE LIE DETECTOR!

This was really funny! Dragging a pencil eraser across a blank piece of paper will leave an invisible residue that cigarette ashes adhere to.

I just about always kept handy a blank sheet of paper with the eraser residue on it, having something like "liar" or "asshole" spelled out on it. On suitable occasions when I thought someone was vulnerable, I would subject my victim to either the "lie detector" or "personality test," which consisted of having them sit on one of my specially-prepared blank pieces of paper that appeared to have been randomly taken from a nearby ream of blank sheets.

While they sat on the paper, I would ask whatever question I thought suitable. Then I'd remove the paper and subject it to the "development process," which consisted of emptying a tray of ashes (in those days, smoking occurred in all workplaces) onto the paper and tilting the paper back and forth until the ashes adhered to the erasure residue. Now the word, previously invisible to the naked eye, was spelled out. Imagine their surprise! This is a really great trick that I thoroughly enjoyed playing on unsuspecting victims.

I worked and studied hard in my efforts to promote to the rank of lieutenant. Amazingly, shortly after taking over as the OIC of Manuals & Orders, I got an extremely high score on the first oral lieutenant's exam I took. Unfortunately, I had put no effort into the written exam, and did not have the final score needed to make lieutenant during the course of the two-year list. In that era, promotions were based strictly on the combined scores from the written and oral examinations, plus a small amount for seniority. Once the process was over, you had a place on the list and would be promoted when your number came up—assuming there were vacancies and promotions during the two-year life of the list.

I studied hard for the list that became effective in 1976, including taking a full month of vacation time to cram for the written portion of the test. I did well and came out number 21 out of the several hundred sergeants who took the exam. Before being promoted, I attended the three-week lieutenant's school conducted at the Valley Services Facility in Van Nuys. Except for an acrimonious relationship with one other sergeant, Mike Carson (pseudonym), I truly enjoyed the training and the relationships.

In July 1976, after several months of nail-biting due to an ultimately unsuccessful proposal within the City Council to eliminate eighteen lieutenant positions (community relations lieutenants from the geographic areas), I was promoted to lieutenant. Going to Personnel Division and being issued my lieutenant's badge (number 90) and identification card were among my happiest professional experiences.

Unfortunately, I did not stay happy for very long.

GETTING THE RUNAROUND ON MY ASSIGNMENT

As a new lieutenant, I was assigned to Rampart Field Services Division. I could not wait to assume my new duties as a watch commander in my old division! When I reported in to the Field Services captain, John Madell, he said that I was not actually going to work at Rampart, but was only shown there on paper until additional decisions regarding lieutenant assignments were finalized. I was advised to call Commander Ritter in the "back room" of the Office of Operations for further guidance. I called Ritter, and he advised me that the matter of my assigned division had not yet been finalized, but that I was being assigned, possibly temporarily, to Hollywood Area. I was a bit puzzled by this runaround, but still a pretty happy guy.

Hollywood Support Division

Hollywood Area consisted of two primary divisions: Field Services Division (patrol) and Support Division (detectives, traffic, and miscellaneous). It covered a large area, with boundries that roughly included Normandie to the east, the Golden State Freeway to the north, Mulholland Drive to the west, and Third Street to the south. As I recall, there were about 450 personnel then assigned to Hollywood Area. At the time, the division was housed in a 1920s-era building immediately north of its present location. My boss in the Hollywood Support Division was Captain Ed Chitwood.

Captain Harry Hanson Did Not Want Me in Hollywood

What should have been one of the happiest periods in my life turned into one of the worst. I reported in to Captain Harry Hanson (pseudonym), the Commanding Officer of Hollywood Area. Shortly after entering his office and sitting down, I told him how pleased I was to be in Hollywood and that I was anxious to do a good job. While I don't recall exactly what he said, he made it clear that he was not pleased to have me at Hollywood, I would only be there on loan for a short while, and I should not get too comfortable! He said I would be working in the Hollywood Support Division for Captain Ed Chitwood. I was beyond devastated and heartbroken. All of a sudden I was a leper—a lieutenant who was being shunned by several divisions.

It was either this day or the next that I got a call from Officer Dan Koenig, one of my men in the Manuals & Orders Unit I'd just left. Dan informed me that he had been in the "back room" of the Office of Operations and overheard a conversation about me. It seems that the single sergeant I had a conflict with in Lieutenant's School, Mike Carson (pseudonym), who worked for Commander Ritter, had convinced the commander (also the coordinator of lieutenant assignments) that I was a real jerk. This unflattering assessment obviously found its way into conversations with several others, and was the reason I was basically being rejected for a couple of assignments. Although there was no shortage of folks who thought I was a decent guy, that reality was not obvious to me at the time. I was crushed and in a despondent state for several weeks.

I am aware that I did a GREAT job in the approximately six-week period I was in Hollywood Support. There had just been a major scandal involving several officers who had been sexually involved with female explorer scouts, and I was the person who wrote all of the detailed and sensitive letters of transmittal for the disciplinary reports. I was also the person who did the planning and provided security oversight and coordination for a visit of the Israeli Philharmonic to the Hollywood Bowl.

After about four weeks into the loan, I was approached by the commanding officer of the Hollywood Operations Division, Captain Frank Isabel (RIP), and asked if I would like to work for him as a patrol team leader. I said I would like it very much, but I had already been told by Captain Hanson, the area commander, that I would not be staying at Hollywood. Captain Isabel responded that he was the captain of the Operations Division, and felt the decision was his to make. A couple of hours after our conversation, Captain Isabel came to me and said that I was right: Captain Hanson had made it very clear that I would be leaving Hollywood. At the time, neither Hanson nor I realized that I would be returning to Hollywood four years later as a captain.

COMMUNICATIONS DIVISION

In late of August of 1976, following my distinguished six weeks or so in Hollywood, I was transferred to Communications Division. This was the twenty-four-hour nerve center for the police department, where telephone calls from citizens were converted to radio calls for officers, and where just about all dispatching took place. This division also had a small satellite office in Van Nuys to handle the same activities, but exclusively to the San Fernando Valley. As I recall, the total number of persons assigned to the division was approximately eighty, most of whom were policemen handling the complaint board (answering phones) and dispatchers handling the radio frequencies.

ONE PLEASANT MONTH

After my short stint in Hollywood, in September 1976 I was given my permanent assignment as the graveyard shift commander in Communications Division. There I was warmly received by a very nice and gracious man, Captain Del Wheaton (RIP). That was nice, as I was at a point of desperation where I needed a friendly face.

On the graveyard shift I had two sergeants, Ray Schaeffer and Ed Jurman, both decent men. The deployment was such that two of us were always expected to be present on a shift. Ray was pretty much the brains of the outfit, and did a real fine job. Ed owned an automotive repair shop in the Rampart area, and spent a good portion of his duty shifts sleeping in the camper of his pickup truck outside the back door of the Communications Center. I was somewhat of a beaten dog and did not have the energy or inclination to take on the historic practice of occasional marginal supervision by the sworn supervisors in that division.

HOLLENBECK FIELD OPERATIONS DIVISION

In late September 1976, after only one month in Commuications Division, I transferred into the Hollenbeck Field Services Division as a team leader. The station was located at 2111 East 1ˢᵗ Street, and my boss was Captain Jim Chambers. The boundries of the division at the time were roughly the Los Angeles River on the west, Indiana Street on the east, City Terrace on the North, and Olympic Boulevard on the south. As I recall, there were approximately 225 persons then assigned to the Hollenbeck area, including both the field operations and support divisions.

BACK INTO THE MAINSTREAM AND OUT OF PURGATORY!

A couple of weeks after reporting in to Communications Division, I got a call from a long-time friend and supporter, Captain Jim Chambers. Jim had actually been one of my sergeants when I was a new policeman, and we had remained friends over the years. He was the commanding officer of the Hollenbeck Field Services Division, and asked if I would like to go to work for him in Hollenbeck as a team leader. Obviously, I was thrilled and started to potentially see a light at the end of the leper tunnel that I felt I had been placed in. Jim was aware of the way I had been jacked around, and made it clear that he did not agree with the few folks who had their reservations about me. In October of 1976 I began my two years in Hollenbeck.

TAKING OVER A TROUBLED TEAM IN HOLLENBECK

Within Hollenbeck Area, Captain Rudy DeLeon was the Area Commanding Officer, Captain Jim Chambers commanded the Operations Division and Captain Doug Watson commanded the Support Division.

The Operations (Patrol) Division consisted of three teams, each led by a lieutenant. I was assigned as team leader for Team Two, which placed me as the top cop for the Boyle Heights portion of the division, responsible for patrol and detective operations roughly between Valley Boulevard and Soto Streets. Some of the notable locations were General Hospital, White Memorial Hospital, the Pico-Aliso Housing Projects, the Ramona Gardens Housing Projects, and more gang-related streets of violence than I thought existed.

In addition to an overwhelming number of fine officers, I also had on my team about a dozen troublesome police officers who had previously got in hot water, but who Captain DeLeon had given another chance. Rudy became a wonderful friend and remained so until his passing in 2010 (I attended his funeral). He had a big heart and was a sucker for a sob story. Not infrequently did he go to an officer's disciplinary hearing and testify that the officer, some of whom were facing possible termination, should be given another chance and was welcome to come to work for him in Hollenbeck!

The lieutenant I had replaced in Hollenbeck was somewhat of an alcoholic and absentee landlord. The wayward officers who came to Hollenbeck usually ended up on Team Two, because the lieutenant either had not been around to object, or wasn't paying attention to these critical personnel issues—and because the fine lieutenants who led Team One (Bob Taylor) and Team Three (Rod Fick) strenuously objected to having these troublesome officers assigned to their teams.

Getting some of these folks to do their job was tough, and before I transferred out two of these slugs were fired for creating reports, citations and field interview cards on non-existent persons, to appear that they were actually working. While I have enjoyed every assignment I've ever held, this was an assignment I enjoyed a bit less than the others!

Great Partners—Bob Taylor and Rod Fick

I was fortunate to have two great men as fellow team leaders. Lieutenants Bob Taylor and Rodell Fick were great guys and great leaders who always went out of their way to be team players in some of the challenges that we all faced. Bob had Team 1 (between Valley Boulevard and the Pasadena Freeway) and Rod had Team 3 (between Soto and Indiana Streets).

These fine gents set the standard for cooperation and unselfishness. There were times when I was in a manpower crunch, and either Bob or Rod immediately bailed me out; it was my pleasure to do the same for them. Rod retired and went to Corona as a captain, retired from there and is now an attorney. Bob, who remains a close friend, went to USC as an assistant chief, retired from there to become the Los Angeles County Ombudsman, then the Chief of the Los Angeles County Probation Department, from which he retired. Today, Bob and I serve together on the Police Historical Society, where he is the 2012 chairman.

Explorers on Stakeout Reduce Burglaries to Officers' Cars

When Hollenbeck Station was built, inadequate thought had been given to employee parking. As a result, a good percentage of the personnel at Hollenbeck had to park on adjacent streets, or a block or so away in a church parking lot. Unfortunately, it was very common for police employees to have their cars vandalized and broken into.

As the team leader for Boyle Heights, where the station was located, addressing this issue was my responsibility. I had always been pro-Explorer Scouts, and saw this as an opportunity to get the kids involved in a surveillance capacity. It worked out great. I had the Explorer captain create a schedule for the kids to be deployed on rooftops, with guidance to contact the nearest patrol unit if they saw suspicious activity, and before long we'd arrested a number of local suspects who had been breaking into our cars. Supervision was particularly easy, because all of the kids were on stakeout locations within a hundred yards or so of the station. I created a surveillance ribbon for the Explorers' uniforms, with stars to be added for each arrest the bearer of the ribbon was responsible for. Some of our kids ended up with more stars than the Chairman of the Joint Chiefs of Staff!

Scuba Diver in Hollenbeck Station

This was so funny. One of my men, Joe Alba, was a fun guy, a good cop, and a good sport. Fortunately, he could take a joke. Joe was among the volunteer members of the LAPD's Underwater Dive Team, had his own extensive SCUBA equipment, and was available twenty-four hours a day regardless of his regular assignment, to respond to emergency callouts where SCUBA skills were necessary.

About 3 a.m. one night, several officers hatched a plot to have some fun with Joe. They called him, saying his skills were immediately needed for a possible body recovery in Hollenbeck Park and that he was to immediately respond to the station in full SCUBA regalia, for further transportation with the detectives to the location where the body was believed to be. Of course, there was no such incident; these guys were

336

just screwing with Joe. About half an hour later, Joe came walking in the front door of the station, outfitted in his wet suit complete with swim fins and SCUBA tank! What a sight, with laughter that did not subside until the sun came up. Thank goodness, Joe had a sense of humor!

Joe could dish it out pretty well himself. Because he had a fair complexion and a slight build, one time he was made up very professionally as a female at one of the local studios to act as a potential victim for a purse-snatching operation. He really looked good! That night, all dolled up, he approached the desk officer and started acting very provocatively, including challenging the officer's masculinity and making a series of shocking remarks.

It took several minutes before a very embarrassed and uncomfortable desk officer finally figured out that the hot chick with the foul mouth was actually Joe Alba! No group of people has more fun or is more creative with their humor than cops.

FRANTIC VACATION AND A MASTER'S DEGREE

I received my bachelor's degree in 1969 and by 1971 had completed all of the course work for the Master of Science degree. For several years afterward I gathered a great deal of information for my thesis, but did not get around to writing it. In mid-1977 I got a call from my advisor at Cal State LA, who advised that the seven-year window for thesis submission was about to close for me, and that all of my work toward the master's degree would be invalid if I didn't get my thesis in within a couple of months.

I requested and received an immediate vacation from the LAPD, and spent the next month sequestered in my home office pounding out my thesis on an old typewriter. After that another couple of weeks were devoted to having it typed by a professional, then submissions, kickbacks and more submissions. Finally, toward the end of the summer, I was awarded my Master of Science degree in Public Administration. As with my bachelor's degree, I wasn't interested in participating in a commencement exercise, so I had the diploma mailed to me.

HORRIBLY BLOODY CRIME SCENE—NOT REALLY

Boy, I got this one wrong! One afternoon, one of my units called me to the scene of a horribly brutal homicide—except it wasn't a crime at all. There was blood everywhere in the apartment, giving rise to the likelihood of a violent struggle. My detectives also responded, and after a while I cleared the scene so the investigators could do their magic.

Later that day, one of my detectives informed me that what I thought was a terribly brutal homicide and violent struggle was actually a natural death! It turned out that the deceased had a serious medical condition (an understatement!) where his lungs had filled up with blood, or something to that effect. He regurgitated large quanties of blood while apparently thrashing around the room before he collapsed and died. I had never seen this before, nor have I since.

EXCESSIVE FORCE IN HOLLENBECK

This situation caused me some sleepless nights. One night, I was the Area Duty Officer (ADO) and was patrolling around Hollenbeck in an unmarked unit. A motor officer requested help at the intersection of First and State Streets, and I was the first person to arrive. The officer had pulled over a drunk driver, who then put his car in reverse and backed over the police motorcycle. The officer just barely avoided serious injury.

The officer was very upset, and I had to intervene to keep him from using unnecessary force on the drunk driver. Apparently, prior to my arrival the officer had used more force than was necessary, and his actions had been observed by a number of citizens who were emerging from a church across the street. About an hour later, while at the station, a crowd of people came to the station and demanded to see the officer in charge to report the inappropriate actions of the officer.

As the lieutenant on duty, I was the senior person in charge. When the crowd saw me they became even more agitated, saying that I knew the officer was out of control because I had pulled him off the suspect. Several people in the crowd demanded that a disciplinary report be made, accusing the officer of excessive force. But I held firm in my belief that his actions were necessary and not outside the bounds of propriety. Frankly, I was really pushing the envelope, as the officer probably did need to be disciplined. But I chose not to go down that path because of the circumstances of the arrest.

Several members of this crowd later went to Parker Center and initiated the complaint that I refused to take. Fortunately, after several weeks the investigation came back classified as "not sustained," which meant there was no real resolution. To my great relief, the situation did not come back to haunt me. The latitude I exercised in this matter has not existed within the LAPD for a great many years.

For my entire life up until this incident, I could not drink coffee—or at least didn't think I could drink coffee. I loved the smell of it, both brewing and the grounds, but got nauseous when it touched my lips.

As a young Marine, I recall being on an exercise in Korea when it was 40 degrees below zero and the only thing warm was coffee. I held a canteen cup of warm coffee inside my field jacket to get warm, but just could not drink it. For my first ten or so years on the department, especially on the morning watch, I would drink Coke because I couldn't tolerate coffee. Believe me, I wanted to be able to drink it, but couldn't.

One day, as a police lieutenant, I was attending a department training seminar at USC. The instructor was Deputy Chief Lewis Reiter. I had worked all night, was having trouble staying awake, and certainly didn't want to doze off in the presence of someone who potentially had influence over my future. I decided to get a cup of coffee, fill it with cream and sugar, and sip on it, figuring the unpleasantness would hopefully keep me awake. I found that I liked it, and by the end of the day was drinking it black! I am grateful that I finally started drinking coffee, and wish I had started much earlier. Now I enjoy coffee in the morning, or after a special meal.

A note about Lewis Reiter: After his retirement from the LAPD, he became an expert witness in use-of-force issues, including the representation of plaintiffs suing law enforcement agencies. I feel that he went to the "dark side." I was especially indignant of his public criticism of Chief Daryl Gates' approach in evaluating uses of force, while Reiter had been chairman of the use-of-force committee under Gates. While certainly not privy to all the conversations he might have had with Chief Gates during that era, I appeared before that board on many occasions while it was chaired by Reiter, but I did not perceive the problems he later described.

A LOVING WIFE VISITS HER HUSBAND AT HOLLENBECK STATION

One evening when I was the Area Duty Officer (ADO) at Hollenbeck Division, my friend and academy classmate, Officer Ira Beetley (pseudonym), was working the desk. Ira was (and is) a good guy and a pretty nice friend; however, fidelity to his many wives was not a strong point with him. He was a real player who constantly cheated on his various wives.

This evening, his wife at the time came to the station and brought him dinner. I was truly impressed as she spread out a red-and-white checkered tablecloth on a table in the break room, then brought out fried chicken and all the fixings! But when Ira went to the men's room to wash his hands, she immediately went into the report writing room to see what days off he'd been assigned that month, as she apparently (and correctly!) suspected he was actually off some days he told her he'd been working—and most likely with another woman. What she saw was obviously upsetting, as she started yelling and screaming and berating him, which caused quite a scene and disturbance inside the police station. I think there was more violence inside the station than on the mean streets outside, that night!

I still see Ira occasionally, and was even invited to his last wedding. He retired from the LAPD many years ago, even before me, and now works as a field law enforcement liaison for a police equipment company. We visited often when I was with the San Bernardino County Sheriff's Department, as he lives in that county and then had dealings with the department. He is a nice and fun pal, who I think is now dedicated to just one wife.

Don't Say It, Lieutenant—Don't Friggin' Say It!

This is one of my favorite stories! As a lieutenant in Hollenbeck on one PM shift, I was the Area Duty Officer (ADO). I went to roll call to offer two hours of paid overtime to any officer who wanted to put in two additional hours after work—from midnight until 0200—to work a detail to apprehend drunk drivers. Drunk driving was a real problem in the division at that time (still is a big problem).

One of my troops, Richard Santiago, went off on a verbal tangent about how the department was just harassing the Mexicans, and how drinking and driving were historic realities that we really should not bother with. A couple of guys signed up for the detail, but Richard was not one of them. Later that evening, close to midnight, there was a gigantic crash in front of the police station. A drunk driver had smashed into and totaled Richard Santiago's prized possession, a completely-restored classic vehicle! Richard was immediately called to the station, and was devastated when he saw the remnants of his car. When we ran into each other in the hallway, he screamed at me: "Don't say it, lieutenant—don't friggin' say it!"

I still see Richard from time to time. We have a nice friendship, and I never tire of telling this story. In early 2009 I ran across Richard's son, a police officer in Northeast Area, who did not know of this incident! It was again my pleasure to repeat the story!

Ambushed in Pico Aliso

On New Year's Eve, while patrolling in the Pico Aliso Housing Projects, I started taking gunfire. I could hear the rounds impacting around me, and thought that one round hit my unit (it didn't, but probably hit the nearby trash dumpster). Having no idea where the gunfire was coming from, I accelerated and got the hell out of there. This is among the reasons we started pulling in units, or had them park under freeway overpasses or other safe areas, around midnight in neighborhoods where gunfire is rampant on New Year's Eve.

A Big Pay Raise and a New Pickup—Oops!

My wife, Barbara, agreed that it was time for me to get a new car. She had got her Ford Pinto station wagon, and now it was my turn to get a pickup truck. We were waiting until after the pay increase that all police employees were to receive on July 1, to determine what type of monthly payment we could handle.

In early August my paycheck reflected the raise, and it was substantial, so I went out and bought an almost brand-new full-sized pickup. Unfortunately, I failed to recognize that a good part of the additional pay was the result of IOD (injured on duty) pay, where no taxes were withheld from my paycheck because of the four days I'd been off-duty with pneumonia. As it turned out, my overly-optimistic financial forecast was so bad that I actually felt it necessary to turn around and sell the truck, because making the payments would have been too difficult.

Barbara said we could try to keep it, but I felt it was best to not do so. Tragically, I sold it to an El Monte police lieutenant, Hal Kelso, who died in that truck a couple of years later when he went off the road and over a cliff during a trip to his home in Big Bear.

Lieutenant Bushey's "Trojan Horse"

When old Hollenbeck officers get together, this situation invariably comes up for reminiscing.

My creativity, frustration, and military background came together to address the problem of gang members pelting my personnel with rocks and bottles during traffic stops in the Ramona Gardens Housing Project. I borrowed officers from other divisions and put together a really great and fun operation. A local trucking firm loaned me a big truck that had a covered rear portion that I filled with cops. My intent was to have a patrol unit conspicuously stop the truck for a "traffic violation" right in the middle of the projects, where the rocks and bottle attacks most often originated.

The "staged" traffic stop had the predictable results. The unit hit the siren once, which stimulated an almost instantaneous gathering of gang members with their rocks and bottles. I let the situation gather a bit of steam while I radio-directed a number of motorcycle officers to coast in and seal off the likely avenues of escape. At the appropriate moment I gave the word, and about forty officers jumped from the truck and engaged the gang members. A bunch of shitheads went to jail that night!

Rocks and bottles in Ramona Gardens ceased to be a problem, at least during the rest of my tour in Hollenbeck. Like many other unique activities, this operation triggered a cartoon. Drawn by Officer Marco Tenario, it shows me in an Admiral Dewey hat, striking a Napoleonic pose, wearing a parachute and tumbling from the back of the truck, with a long saber with a wheel on the bottom touching the ground.

STAKEOUT AT LANCASTER & EVERGREEN—HOLY S--T!

Like many other unbelievable situations, I start this story with the admonition that you can't make this stuff up! I was doing my best to provide protection for a young woman who found the courage to renounce her affiliation with a gang and actually testified about the criminal activities of one of its members. Because her elderly father lived in the house, she refused our offer to be housed in a safe location. It was so bad, that at night you could literally look through bullet holes in the house and see light from the rear yard. She slept in the bathtub to avoid being hit by gunfire from drive-by shootings, and had erected a safe enclosure within the house for her dad.

One night, I put a couple of officers in a unmarked van just a couple of houses away. I also had a marked chase unit hidden in a back driveway about a block away, with the thought of apprehending any drive-by shooters. We hadn't planned on the possibility of a local turd trying to break into the surveilance van, but that is exactly what occurred. A lone suspect pried open a rear window and pretty much had about half his body inside the van, when one of the two officers grabbed his upper torso to make an arrest for auto burglary. At almost that exact moment, a car full of gang members pulled a drive-by and opened fire on the house!

The van, with the auto burglary suspect hanging out of the window being held by one of the officers, took off after the drive-by vehicle, and was immediately joined by the black-and-white patrol car. Apparently not aware that the van contained armed officers, the gang members shot at the van, which evoked a very predictable barrage of gunfire from the patrol unit. Nobody died, but the occupants of the drive-by vehicle all suffered police gunshot wounds.

I still recall the stoic resignation of Lieutenant Chuck Higbee, the head of the Officer-Involved Shooting Team out of Robbery Homicide Division, as I explained what had occurred and took him on a tour of the shooting scene that was several hundred yards long.

DETECTIVE SNELSON RECEIVES
UNITED AIRLINES AWARD FOR EXCELLENCE

Karl and Shirley Snelson were both detectives at Hollenbeck Division when I was there. Karl was on my team, and although a great guy and fine detective, he was a bit stoic and radiated somewhat of a negative attitude.

One day the devil made me have some fun with him. Among the many awards and medallions I acquired from a trophy shop that went out of business were several big and heavy medallions from a major airline. Clearly, at one time they had to have been presented for something pretty meritorious, but were long obsolete by the time they came my way.

Being the owner of an engraving machine, I engraved Karl's name on one of them, then sent it to him in a padded envelope via the U.S. Mail. He went crazy, trying to figure out what the award was all about, and spent several hours on the phone talking to God knows how many people, in an effort to get to the bottom of the matter. I had clued Shirley in on the prank, and we finally fessed up to my mischief. As I recall, Karl was not as amused as I was.

MOJO PUNCHES OUT PABLO AND LOSES HIS JOB

Raymond "Mojo" Montano (pseudonym) was a personable and effective member of my team, with a real passion for policing. Unfortunately, he also had a passion for a young woman named Virginia.

Mojo came to Hollenbeck under a big cloud, and just barely avoided being fired at the time for developing a romantic and sexual relationship with a student while he was in Juvenile Division and assigned to the "Student Role in Government" program at the high school she attended. When Virginia became pregnant, Mojo divorced his wife (they had children, as well) and married her, which saved him from termination.

While on my team, he was a hard worker who became especially observant for drunk drivers just before his shift ended, and frequently got a couple hours' of cash overtime at the end of his regularly-assigned work hours. Of course, he badly needed the money because he was supporting his former wife and kids as well as his new wife and child. Mojo was insanely jealous of Virginia, and with good reason, because she was quite a player. She knew how to push his buttons and did so frequently, resulting in a series of disciplinary actions. The last occurred while he was on duty and in uniform and in his police vehicle, when he drove to a downtown retail shoe store and cold-cocked the man with whom Virginia was having an affair at the time. This incident was the final straw, and Mojo was terminated.

After being terminated from LAPD, he became a housing authority officer, then apparently moved on to several other small agencies. Some twenty-five years later I ran across Mojo, when he was an applicant for the chief of a police department I was serving as coordinator of the selection process. At the time of the selection process, he was the chief of a very small department in a rural part of the state. Although he did not make the cut for the chief's position, I was pleased to see that he had kept the faith and was able to pull his life together and remain in the profession he loved.

An interesting thing occurred during his two departmental disciplinary boards of rights while I was his boss. Mojo was in the Army Reserve and his commanding officer was a friend of mine. We testified before panels and saved his job during the first board, but were not able to do much good for the shoe store punch-out that got him fired. After the board, my Army buddy told me he had real reservations about Mojo and only testified on his behalf because of our friendship.

My reply was equally truthful. I told him that I'd also developed serious reservations about Mojo's fitness to remain a cop, but had testified because of our friendship, as I thought my Army buddy was an aggressive supporter of Mojo! Had it not been for our mistaken beliefs that we were doing what the other one wanted, Mojo might well have been terminated earlier!

Thank Goodness for Father John Santillia—Oops!

For years, Father John Santillia (pseudonym) was someone we could often depend on to assist with troubled young men. He was the prominent and long-serving priest at a local parish, and someone who was well thought-of throughout Hollenbeck and the East Los Angeles communities.

Thirty years later, during the horrific scandal involving the Catholic Church over protecting pedophile priests, Father Santillia was identified as one of the priests in the Los Angeles Diocese who had been accused of molesting young boys. This certainly brought about a sinking feeling on my part. But I received no details other than the general shocking news, and was never contacted as part of any investigation.

Morally Rearmed by Drunk Commander!

During my assignment in Hollenbeck, the department was still reeling from the effects of the Hollywood Explorer sex scandal, where several officers were fired for being sexually involved with female Explorer Scouts.

The chief of police, Edward Davis, decreed that every department employee would be "morally rearmed" by a staff officer (commander or above). During an evening watch roll call, Commander Frank Beeson (RIP) morally rearmed me and the other officers on duty, with his inspirational discussion and guidance.

Unfortunately, Commander Beeson, who had quite a reputation as a drinker, was under the influence of alcohol and accompanied by his girlfriend at the time of his visit. I have long joked about having been morally rearmed by a drunken commander as, somehow, I don't think this is what Chief Davis had in mind! Frank Beeson, who passed on a number of years ago, was a decent fellow, but he did have a very widely recognized problem with the bottle.

"Lieutenant Bushey, Are You Crazy?"

I'm glad that then-Deputy Chief Bob Vernon didn't hold a grudge, because I really irritated him early in our relationship. In 1977, six officers from the Hollenbeck and Rampart divisions formed an off-duty party group called "Six Pack Productions." The officers, including Ron Aguilar, Richard Santiago, Phil Burrell, and Larry Garcia, arranged for the locations and put on some really enjoyable parties at a number of venues. Chief Vernon, who had some pretty high moral standards, expressed outrage at the existence of these events, and perceived, with some justification, that they were wild affairs involving married officers who were cheating on their wives.

One afternoon, Chief Vernon called Hollenbeck Station and wanted the six officers and me (because I was the team leader over the Holiday Inn on Mission Avenue where an event was planned for the following Friday night) to come to the station immediately for an emergency meeting. When we all met, the chief said flat-out that he wanted the event to be cancelled, and did not want any more of these parties to occur.

As diplomatically as they could, with Aguilar as the spokesman, they made it clear the party was an off-duty affair, not the chief's business, and that it was not going to be canceled. At one point I said that perhaps the party should not be interfered with, because cops were going to party anyway, and at least they were all in one place. Now a very exasperated Chief Vernon asked me if I was crazy!

Realizing that the party was not going to be canceled, the chief made it very clear that any problems at the party would be considered as serious misconduct. He stated that he would personally attend the resulting disciplinary hearing, testify that he had encouraged cancellation of the party, and the officers refused to cooperate; such an appearance would almost automatically ensure severe penalties.

While the party was nevertheless held, the officers really worked hard to ensure there were no troubling incidents. While Chief Vernon's actions might be criticized by some who feel that officers' off-duty actions are of no business to the department, I think he acted appropriately. After all, any big problems would have been described publically as "involving LAPD personnel," and the chief's concerns and actions did cause the promoters to work hard to keep problems from occurring. I remain good friends with some of these officers, and when we get together the issue of "Six-Pack Productions" and "Lieutenant Bushey, are you crazy?" are often laughed about.

Horrible Tragedy: Police Shooting of a Hostage

This was a very sad day, and definitely a low point in my career. One day the angry husband of a receptionist went to her place of work, a medical office, to confront the physician that was apparently having an affair with his wife.

The office was on North Broadway. It had secure windows and a secure interior, where no one could enter the physician's workspaces and treatment rooms without being buzzed-in by the receptionist. The doctor saw the angry husband approach the building, saw that he was armed with a rifle, and called the police. The husband's demand to be admitted to the physician's workspaces was denied by a man who was the of-

346

fice manager. The armed suspect demanded the keys to the doctor's car, which were quickly provided through an opening. Then the suspect took the office manager hostage, got into the back seat, and forced the office manager to drive off. The first police unit arrived just as the doctor's car (with the hostage driving) pulled out of the parking lot, and the suspect opened fire on the police unit. The police unit radioed that they were in pursuit and were being fired on, and pretty soon it grew into a massive pursuit.

The first unit was aware that the driver was a hostage. However, when the passenger officer in that first unit was struck by a round, that unit peeled off enroute to the hospital, and the information about the driver being a hostage was not passed on to the remaining units in the pursuit. After several miles and many rounds being fired, the doctor's vehicle collided with another car at the intersection of Sunset and Figueroa. Two of my officers bravely ran to the car, while receiving a hail of bullets from the suspect, and shot both the suspect and the driver to death!

It took a while to sort out all that had occurred, and all of us were devastated that we'd killed a hostage. When the detectives responded to the doctor's office to start the process of piecing together all that had occurred, they were met by the wife and young daughter of the deceased hostage. They had gone to the office to take the now-deceased office manager to lunch for his 37th birthday.

Captain Bushey of the Idaho State Police!

A good friend and former fellow Rampart patrol sergeant, Tom Proctor, had retired and was working for the Idaho Commission on Peace Officer Standards and Training. He was a longtime and very active member of the Church of Latter Day Saints (Mormon). One day he called me, and said that he was a finalist for the superintendent of the Idaho State Police. He asked if I would be willing to work for him, on a part-time basis, if he got the position.

Tom was a great motivational leader, but pretty lean on the administrative side of things, and that is why he reached out to me. I told him that I would help him in any way possible. A few days later he called and said, "We got the job!" Knowing my interest in badges, he immediately sent me a badge and identification card making me an ISP captain! For the next several months, I would fly up for a few days at a time and assisted in supervisory training, audits, forms and procedures development, and related tasks.

Tom had only been in office for a few months when a new governor was elected, and was among the many folks replaced. I have some interesting stories from my short tenure in Idaho, and all things considered it was a real learning experience and overall enjoyable.

Selected for Air Support Division as a Pilot—"On Hold"

Having obtained my private pilot's license in 1969, and with a few hours under my belt (honestly, not many), I applied for the opening for a lieutenant-pilot in Air Support Division in 1977.

I am all but certain that I was the person who was going to be placed in that position. But the position was placed "on hold" pending the results of a statewide election, where Proposition 13 was going before the voters. This was a very controversial measure which, if passed by the voters, would restrict property taxes to no more than one percent of the property's assessed evaluation. If it passed it would result in a decease in funding for many things and was sure to tighten the fiscal belt for public agencies, including the police.

The lieutenant opening in Air Support Division was for one of the three watch commanders, in a division that in addition to the captain also had a lieutenant assistant commanding officer. In the event that Proposition 13 passed, the plan was to go from three conventional watches (shifts) to two overlapping mid-watches, and to leave vacant the lieutenant's position I had applied for. Well, Proposition 13 passed, and the position that I believe I was slated to fill was eliminated. It was clear that my future in the LAPD would be on the ground.

New Chief and the End of "Team Policing"

In late 1978 Chief Ed Davis retired, and Daryl Gates was appointed as his replacement. One of Chief Gates' first acts was to eliminate "team policing." As unfortunate as it was (I was a real advocate of this concept), it just was not working in Los Angeles due to inadequate personnel. The concept was to have officers assigned long-term to neighborhoods and to keep them in those neighborhoods.

Unfortunately, due to crossover rates caused by too many radio calls and too few units, it was near-impossible to keep officers in their assigned districts. As a consequence, many things became dysfunctional, especially the relationships between team leaders who wanted their personnel kept in their districts, and the watch commanders who were trying to get calls answered within a reasonable period of time.

Several months later as a watch commander at Rampart, managing my personnel and the radio calls was a breeze compared to all the problems we had with team policing. I still believe in team policing, but only if adequate personnel and equipment are available to make it work. Given fiscal realities and the enormous resources that team policing would require in Los Angeles, I don't think it will ever completely occur beyond philosophical efforts.

————

CENTRAL TRAFFIC DIVISION

Central Traffic Division was among the largest division commands in the city, with responsibility for all traffic accidents, motorcyle enforcement and traffic control in the metropolitan part of the city, known as the Central Bureau. As I recall, the number of assigned personnel was somewhere around 350 persons, including uniformed traffic investigation officers, uniformed traffic enforcement motorcycle officers, uniformed civilian traffic control officers, accident follow-up detectives, and an assortment of support personnel. The division was located within the Central Facilities Building at the corner of 5th and Wall Streets.

ASKED TO GO ON "ON LOAN" TO CENTRAL TRAFFIC DIVISION

In late October 1978 the commanding officer of Central Bureau, then-Deputy Chief Bob Vernon, sent out a memo soliciting ideas on how to address the growing issue of traffic accidents and deaths involving Hispanic aliens. I guess I was in an intellectually fertile mood when the memo arrived, and I wrote a comprehensive report, with recommendations on the subject.

Chief Vernon called and thanked me for my response and ideas. He then asked if I would be interested in going on loan to the Central Traffic Division in order to implement my recommendations and also to assist the captain, a great fellow named Al Schlocker, who was at the time overwhelmed with administrative projects and disciplinary investigations. Since team policing had just been discontinued by new Chief Gates, I was in the process of transitioning to the conventional role of a watch commander, which was fine. But since I no longer had a dedicated team or piece of turf to call my own, I agreed to go the traffic division for a few months.

I very seriously took my responsibilities to develop a traffic safety education program for Hispanic aliens. In concert with Dr. Martin Riser of our Behavior Sciences Section, and artists within the department, I developed a series of posters and billboards directed specifically at Hispanic aliens, and they were really good. I worked with Pacific Outdoor Advertising and got billboards dedicated throughout the city, with very attractive and powerful posters placed at conspicuous (and problem) locations. We also had special posters made, which we placed at or near locations where deaths and serious injuries involving Hispanic aliens had occurred.

I suspect my efforts did some good and saved a few lives, but the continuous unabated flow of illegal aliens from Mexico and South and Central America was overwhelming. At one point, and I suspect the percentages are still about the same, approximately half of all traffic accidents in parts of the city involved at least one unlicensed illegal alien driving a car that was not insured and with very confusing registration. I am afraid that it required more than Lieutenant Bushey's efforts to solve this problem.

"The Old Broad Deserved the Black Eye!"

From almost my first moment as the temporary assistant commanding officer of Central Traffic Division, Captain Al Schlocker was appreciative of my loan to him. Among my other duties, he gave me a bunch of disciplinary reports (known as "Cover Letters") to write, summarizing the allegation(s) and recommending whatever discipline might be appropriate.

At the time Al and I were not well acquainted, but I had the impression that he had a sense of humor and I wanted to give him a good taste of mine. One of the disciplinary cases involved a motor officer who had a nasty former mother-in-law, who alleged that the officer had hit her and given her a black eye. As I recall, this was not the case; the allegation was bogus, with the officer's estranged wife and vicious mother-in-law trying to get his visitation rights denied.

The very detailed letter I wrote, which reflected the division's "Administrative Insight," was an articulate and logical description of a horrid woman whose single goal in life was to ruin the officer's career. It described her ability to drive a normally restrained person to the breaking point, concluding with "the old bitch deserved the black eye." I then took this case and buried it into the stack of many others that were going to the captain for his review.

Later that afternoon there was a howl of laughter that could be heard throughout the entire building! Al Schlocker had found my planted little joke. He had a great sense of humor, and I thoroughly enjoyed the several months we worked together.

Going to Bat for "Eddie Haskell"

The character known as Eddie Haskell in the "Leave it to Beaver" TV series later became Officer Ken Osmond of the LAPD. I met him when I was his lieutenant in the Central Traffic Division and he was a motorcycle officer. He approached me about the possibility of a six-month leave of absence to go on the road with the old cast from "Leave it to Beaver." I wasn't particularly optimistic, because the department really frowned on leaves of absence for that long. Nevertheless, I wrote a compelling request, got a few endorsements, and it was approved. But the road show with the old cast never materialized, so he didn't take the leave of absence.

A year of so later, Ken was in a shooting and took a round in the chest, but his protective vest saved him. Not long after that he retired, but I don't recall the details.

Grandma in a Rug—Stolen with the Car!

This was a tragedy with a very humorous side to it. It shouldn't be funny, but it was (at least to me!).

One of my officers, Martin Gomez (pseudonym) approached me with a story and solicited my opinion as to what, if anything, he should do. Several days before, his parents and some other relatives traveled in the family station wagon to Mexico, for what was likely to be their last visit to Marty's very ill grandmother, who was not expected to live much longer.

During the visit, the grandmother did in fact pass away. The family wanted to bring her remains to the United States for burial, but realized it would be difficult to navigate the bureauacy and pay off the predictable bribes to crooked Mexican officials. So, they decided to wrap Granny in a rug, tie the rug to the roof of the car, and hopefully pass through the customs checkpoint without being inspected.

They made it through the checkpoint without any problems, and stopped for lunch in San Diego. But when they came out of the restaurant, they discovered their car had been stolen! They were horrified, as Granny was still wrapped in the rug on the roof. They had no option but to report the car as stolen. It was ultimately recovered, but without Granny or the rug!

The last time I spoke to Marty was several years ago, and the family still does not know what happened to Granny! While our conversation was long and somewhat complicated, I finally recommended to Marty just to keep his mouth shut about the incident!

Note: I am aware that a situation involving a deceased person wrapped in a rug was depicted in a Chevy Chase movie. But I am under the strong impression that the situation described actually occurred. The officer came into my office, was obviously in distress over the issue, and sought assistance on how best to deal with the situation. Maybe it was this incident that led to the scene in the movie?

———

Rampart Patrol Division

In January 1979, after my three-month loan to the Central Traffic Division, I went back "home" to Rampart Division. Except for the fact that the Silver Lake community had been placed into the Hollywood area, the boundries were much as they had been when I served there as a sergeant several years back. As I recall, the personnel strength at this time was about 350 persons of all ranks.

Personally Requested by the Rampart Patrol Captain

After a couple of months in the Central Traffic Division I got a call from Captain Rick Batson at Rampart Patrol Division. He said some very flattering things about me, and hoped that I would accept his offer to return to Rampart as a watch commander. I was enjoying Central Traffic, but traffic wasn't my passion. I had planned to return to conventional patrol at some point, and gratefully accepted Rick's offer. It was a great tour of duty, and among the most enjoyable assignments in my long LAPD career.

Punk Rock Concert and Mexican Wedding

Looking back on my career, this is one of my favorite incidents, largely because it turned out well because of my actions.

At the beginning of a PM shift while I was the watch commander, I became aware of a potentially problematic situation at the large Elks

352

Lodge building on Parkview Avenue, immediately south of Sixth Street. There were two seemingly incompatible functions taking place: a Mexican wedding on the ground floor and a punk rock concert on the second floor. Not good!

I was also advised that there were several off-duty officers working security at the location. A couple of hours into the shift, after receiving several calls from the off-duty officers describing all the conflict occurring in the building, I requested a tactical alert and had responding units from the surrounding divisions stage on a nearby rooftop parking structure.

Units were rolling in hot and heavy. But before I could get them all in place and organized, the off-duty officers put out a "help call." I immediately assembled a heavy squad, with Sergeant Grady Dublin in charge, and had them double-time with batons at parade rest into the fray, with orders to get to the off-duty officers and protect them until the rest of us could get there.

Within about ten minutes, all of us were there and the rock concert was shut down. It went very well and my good friend and assistant watch commander, Sergeant Ken Espiau, wrote a quality, extensive report on all that occurred. His report was instrumental in preventing a city payout for the claims that were filed. I was flattered at the positive characterization of my leadership.

A few years later a good pal, who had been among the men in the first squad that responded, offered to let me hear a tape recording he had made as the squad ran up the massive stairway to confront the rowdy punk rockers. He reminded me that any statute of limitations had long passed and the incident fell into a historic category! Before playing the recording, he said the voice was of a punk rocker who was attempting to throw urine onto the officers, and that in response one of the officers literally threw him over the balcony.

The recording went something like this: " You can't do thaa-a-a.......!" I suspect such tactics wouldn't set well by today's standards, but neither can I say I was upset by what I heard. Any idiot who tries to throw urine on a police officer does so at significant personal risk!

LOOKING OUT FOR TROUBLED OFFICERS

While I would not tolerate any serious misconduct, I often found ways other than the disciplinary system to deal with good cops who had fallen on hard times involving situations such as divorces or alcoholism.

I had a few guys on my watch who shared an enormous mutual respect and fondness. We often worked behind the scenes in a harmonious conspiracy to solve problems without formal departmental involvement. I cannot say this was appropriate, but in hindsight it seemed to be effective at the time. Now, over thirty years later, I am honored to always be invited (not everyone is!) to the Rampart gatherings at Laughlin every year. I really love these guys.

Great Trip to Mexico—Sad at Our Inability to do it Again

I was in a group of officers from Rampart who planned and went on a great and fun trip to San Felipe, Mexico, during the 1980 spring break. Jake went with me. We loaded our two, three-wheel Honda all-terrain vehicles (ATVs) into my old International Scout, and off we went.

We had a great week of fun on the beach, took long ATV rides, and romped and laughed and ate with all the other Rampart folks who went. I was really looking forward to another such trip, but it just did not materialize. For a number of years I have been hoping that Baja California would become less dangerous, but with the drug cartels and all the murders, it has just gotten worse. In the past few years, the violence has been awful, literally including massacres and decapitated heads stuck on fence posts. As a cop, I think I would be in even more jeopardy than the average person.

In 2010, Cathy and I took all the kids on a four-day Mexican Riviera cruise from Los Angeles to Ensenada and back. We spent several hours in the very conspicuous areas of Ensenada close to the ship, and had a fun time. After some chow and a little bit of shopping, we returned to the ship. I remain sad that Mexican trips and vacations are no longer practical for my family and me.

Clerk "Fingers" the Suspect on Vermont Avenue

An unlucky crook made a very bad decision one evening. When he tried to climb into the take-out order window of a fast-food restaurant across from Los Angeles City College, a female employee bit off a portion of the suspect's finger!

When we got there, most of the suspect was gone, but the gal gave us the part of his finger he'd left behind. Like just about all crimes, patrol officers did the initial report, and the Rampart detectives did investigation and the follow-up. I don't recall hearing if the suspect was ever identified or arrested.

Mace Solves a Homeless Problem at Denny's!

Two of my "rocket scientists" (also known as immature cops) were taking code 7 (meal break) at a Denny's restaurant one evening, when the waitress asked them to assist her. There was a smelly homeless guy several booths away who did not want to leave after having been asked to do so.

Without even standing up, one of my officers removed his chemical MACE from the holder on his duty belt, held it at a high angle, and sent a stream of the liquid tear gas right into the face of the homeless guy! One of the other patrons did not think much of this foolishness, and called the station. As I recall, this little stunt resulted in a several-day suspension for both officers.

Mace in the Windshield Wiper Reservoir

Cops are pretty creative. I got wind of a unique prank that my officers were playing on one another, and most likely also on unsuspecting troublesome citizens.

They would put MACE, a liquid incapacitating substance used to subdue combative suspects, in the police vehicle's windshield wiper solution reservoir, then turn the small nozzle away from the glass and point it at a right angle. This allowed them to shoot the chemical tear gas at anyone on the sidewalk, or into the window of an adjacent vehicle.

I jumped on the sergeants pretty hard to have the troops knock this stuff off. While I am sure there had to have been some disgruntled citizens, no one ever came forward and complained.

Coordinating Three Unrelated Homicide Scenes Simultaneously

Rampart was a very busy place when I served there as a watch commander. I think I set a record one evening, when I coordinated three unrelated homicide scenes simultaneously! That place really went wild on frequent occasions.

"Shut Up Jack—Just Eat It!"

A bunch of us Rampart folks went to Holtville (California, in Imperial County) for opening day of dove season one year. One of the dozen or so of us attending was a great guy and good pal, Jack Herman. Jack is a demanding customer in eating establishments, with a well-deserved reputation for sending food back if he feels it isn't adequately cooked, or prepared, or whatever. It was a common occurrence.

I decided to have some fun at Jack's expense. So I tipped the waitress pretty handsomely to put a plate of food that had been sitting in the kitchen for several hours in front of Jack when the food was delivered to our table. I told her to serve him last, and when he started to object just to say, "Sir, that is what you ordered," and rush away before she started laughing.

In advance, I implored Jack to behave himself and not to humiliate us with his typical practice of complaining about the food; to just shut up, eat, and enjoy the meal. He assured me he would do just that.

It worked just as planned! When the waitress put the plate in front of Jack, he was visibly upset and said, "What's this?" She replied: "Sir, that is what you ordered," and rushed off. I pointed at Jack, reminding him to behave himself and to eat his food without complaint. After he spent several moments chewing with some difficulty on what appeared to be mummified ravioli, we all broke up in uncontrollable laughter.

Jack took it pretty well—and then the waitress brought out his real meal.

RAW CHICKEN FOR KEITH BUSHEY

Jack Herman got back at me, in a very public way, for the stale ravioli he ate in Holtville. A year or so later, as a captain I was among the guests at the reception for his wedding.

Our food was delivered to each setting under a beautiful silver-plate cover. When the waiter removed the cover from my setting, a large raw chicken was sitting on my plate! Jack was lying in wait with a camera, and quickly snapped the picture of my surprised expression. Nice payback, Jack!

MUMMIFIED BODY SEVERAL FEET FROM MILLIONS OF PEOPLE

As the watch commander, I was curious when a "dead body" call came out from the median of the Hollywood Freeway, just east of Vermont.

On arriving, I was confronted with quite a sight—a mummified man! Apparently, several months before a homeless individual had lay down in some high grass, and died. He was literally lying within ten feet of thousands of cars daily which, in both directions, passed his temporary resting place. When the change of seasons caused the grass to wilt, he was found. In reflecting on this situation, I don't recall (if I ever knew) why he didn't deteriorate like most bodies, but he was pretty much mummified. Maybe it was all the alcohol in his body?

Baxter Decides to Walk a Beat

Police departments are just like society—made up of all types of different and unique individuals. One of the most unusual, but a good guy, was Jim Baxter (RIP). Jim was among my subordinates when I was a watch commander in Rampart Division.

Late one afternoon Officer Jerry Dible, another great guy, approached me in the watch commander's office. Jerry said that he had just seen Jim Baxter walking briskly westbound on Sunset Boulevard. When he asked what he was doing, Jim replied there were no vehicles available, so he'd decided to walk everywhere on that shift in order to handle his calls!

Jerry explained that Jim was very agitated at the absence of available patrol cars (there was often a wait at the change of watch), and that Jim had declined Jerry's offer for a ride back to the station! By checking the radio log, I knew where Jim was heading (his next radio call), so I sent a sergeant to pick him up and bring him to the station.

The sergeant found and brought Baxter to the station. But as it was really ugly because of Jim's agitation, I actually had Behavioral Sciences (BSS) send an on-call psychologist to the station to evaluate the situation. The psychologist turned out to be a very dear friend, Dr. Nels Klyver.

As it turned out, I had probably overreacted in asking BSS to respond. Jim was just being himself, sending out a strong message about being disappointed at having to wait so long for an available police car at change of watch. Jim was just being Jim, and all things considered, he was a pretty lovable character!

As I write this entry in June of 2012, I do so with great sadness. Jim Baxter passed away last month, in Texas.

Give the Lady's Body a Break!

People who have not worked in Los Angeles may find this hard to believe, but those of us who served on the LAPD will see this as just another Saturday night—unique, but not an unheard-of situation.

An elderly woman was struck and killed by a hit-and-run driver on Hoover Street. There is a slight rise in the terrain, thus somewhat less visibility for cars traveling in both directions, and it is a very dangerous place for a pedestrian to cross the street at night.

Because of the rampant intoxicated driving in that neighborhood, most of them illegal aliens, it was logical to assume that a drunk driver killed her. Seeing what had happened, her neighbor (a retired fireman) rushed out in the street to help her, at which time he was also struck by a second vehicle and seriously injured. Then her body was again run over by a hit-and-run driver who was most certainly also intoxicated.

I was among the first units to arrive on the grisly scene, and immediately put out a very conspicuous flare pattern. Within moments another drunk driver burst through the flare pattern, drove over the already mutilated remains of the woman, and kept going! We caught and arrested the third drunk driver, but never did identify the first two suspects who'd driven over the poor lady. This is just one of the hundreds of experiences that cause me to refer to my thirty-one years with the LAPD as an incredible ride in the fast lane of law enforcement.

Watch Commanders Belong in the Field

While I liked some assignments better than others, I enjoyed—to some extent—every job I had on the LAPD. The sole exception was my brief and humiliating stint in the "staff inspector" position made especially for me by Chief Willie Williams and his unethical disciples.

I think the position I most enjoyed was as the morning watch commander of the Rampart Patrol Division, a position I held for most of 1979 and 1980 until my promotion to captain in July of the latter year. I was really living the dream and enjoying the best of both worlds—being the guy in charge and doing police work as well.

Unlike most watch commanders, I spent the majority of my time in the field! I would start out the shift with roll call, after which I would do the "heavy" administrative lifting (typically the deployment/line-up for the next day), and then turn the office over to one of my sergeants. Morning watch roll call was at 2300 hours. I usually managed to get into the field before 0100 hours, and typically "stayed out" until about 0600 hours. In late 1979 the captains list came out. I knew I was likely to be promoted in mid-1980, and that when it occurred my days in the field would be pretty much over. I made the best of it, and thoroughly enjoyed my last few months in the field.

Streamlight Flashlight Prevented a Shooting

In the late 1970s the flashlight industry really took off, and very high-power rechargeable flashlights started coming onto the market.

The day that I purchased one of these flashlights, the Streamlight SL-20, it kept me out of a shooting—and saved the life of the suspect!

During the evening hours, when I was the watch commander but still liked to go out into the field, I was eastbound on 3rd Street just north of the Harbor Freeway when a person ran out into the street and waved me down. An off-duty police officer, he pointed to a man walking westbound on the sidewalk, who was allegedly armed with a pistol.

The situation couldn't have come at a worse time, as an "officer needs help" call had just come out. Everyone, me included, was enroute to that call, and the radio frequency was tied up with chatter. But I immediately exited my vehicle and drew my weapon, with my new Streamlight in my left hand. Taking as much cover I could, I approached the suspect from behind, identified myself, and told him to freeze. He immediately swung around with a pistol in his hand, and started to raise it in my direction.

I immediately hit him with the beam of my new 20,000-candle-power flashlight, and he dropped the weapon. It turns out the gun was stolen, and he had a rap sheet as long as your arm for all kinds of offenses up to and including attempted murder. Obviously, he went to jail.

I have reflected on that situation many times. As in a number of other situations, I was completely justified in using deadly force. But I chose not to because I found an alternative. Had I shot that suspect, there would have been no problems whatsoever—he was an armed ex-convict with a long criminal record who started to raise a gun in my direction. From a philosophical standpoint, I have often wondered: would the world be a better place if I'd killed the bad guy that night?

It is certainly not my place to play God. But on the other hand, I think it is very probable that this person—once he got out of jail for the offense that night—continued his life of crime, which certainly would have involved victimizing other people and very possibly taking the lives of innocent persons. While I have never knowingly taken another person's life, notwithstanding experiences in the military where our enemies may have perished as a result of my actions, sending a bad guy to his happy hunting ground would not bother me at all.

While I really liked that flashlight, in hindsight the world might have been a better place if I hadn't purchased it until the following day!

Drunk Indian Lands on Police Car Hood

It was early, during a morning watch tour of duty while accompanied by my assistant watch commander, Sergeant Dick Roach, and with my young son Jake as a ride-along in the front seat between us. I was driving eastbound on Sunset Boulevard somewhere east of Echo Park Avenue, when we all got quite a surprise: a Native American wearing war paint and headdress and carrying a guitar, seemingly came out of nowhere and jumped on the hood of our unmarked police car! Not surprisingly, he was drunk and soon went to jail. But I don't know who was more surprised—us at his sudden appearance on the hood of our car, or him when he found out it was a police car!

The "Off-the-Record" Discussion with the Captain

A man for whom I once had enormous respect taught me a very valuable lesson one night. While I do not remember the subject, I went into his office and asked if we could discuss a personnel issue "off the record." He did an outstanding job educating me to the fact that nothing is ever "off the record," and that while handling situations in such a manner usually seems like today's solution, it inevitably becomes tomorrow's nightmare. His explanation was superb, and was instrumental in shaping my thinking and behavior with respect to handling issues the proper way.

That man was tops in my book for a long time. Unfortunately, as time went on and he rose to become a key person on Willie Williams' staff, I came to realize that he didn't always practice what he preached. He lacked either the ability or inclination, or both, to challenge and intervene when wrong things were being done. In my final dealings with him he was concentrating on his personal survival in an advanced pay grade, not in the best interests of the department. It was sad to see, and a validation of my belief that lousy leadership brings out the worst in some people.

Two Little Urchins
Who Needed a Dad

One day shortly after conducting PM watch roll call, the desk officer told me there was a woman with a baby and a young boy who was requesting a tour of the station. I was happy to oblige.

During out tour I was really taken with the little boy, whose name was Bobby (actually "Roberto"). He was outgoing, about seven years old (the same as my son Jake), and very much interested in the police department. With his mother's permission, I occasionally began taking Bobby home on the weekends to play with Jake and do the things that little boys who live in the MacArthur Park district don't have the opportunity to do. As the infant blossomed into a young boy I started taking him home as well, as he and my son Zak were also about the same age. Before long Bobby and Danny became part of our family. Around 1991, Bobby joined the Marine Corps, and in 1996 he became an LAPD officer.

In the early 90s, while Bobby was in the Marine Corps, we returned Danny to his home one Sunday afternoon. Shortly thereafter we got a call from the Rampart watch commander, who said he had a young boy at the station who had just found his mother deceased, and who insisted that he was closely associated with us. By the following morning, we were in the process of becoming Danny's legal guardians.

Danny was way behind in school, but between Cathy's tutoring and summer school he graduated when he should have from Glendora High School. While still with us he put himself through San Antonio Junior College, got his paramedic's certificate, and became a firefighter with the Crest Forest Fire District. At this writing, Danny is now a captain with the Orange County Fire Authority. Both Bobby and Danny got married and have children. But Bobby, while still an LAPD officer, has pretty much slipped out of our life. Danny got married and has a couple of great kids that Cathy and I are thrilled to have as grandchildren. Sadly, his marriage is dissolving at the time of this entry, but we get to see a great deal more of his kids.

THE DEER AND THE DEADBEAT

Glen Hargett (RIP) was a dear friend and fellow instructor at Citrus College. In fact, he was among my instructors when I first attended Citrus as a student. Glen and I became hunting buddies, and he was truly a great outdoorsman.

One day, just before he and I were about to drive to Bridgeport (California) for the opening day of deer season (which was the next morning), Glen called and asked if I would join him in hosting a third person in our hunting party. The kid was named José. He was economically disadvantaged and a participant in a funded economic opportunity program for indigent minority kids at Citrus. I said fine, so Glen bought the kid a hunting license and loaned him a rifle.

On the approximately eight-hour drive to the area to go hunting, all José wanted to talk about was the disparity between the "haves" and the "have nots," and about his participation in Hispanic rights organizations. On the trip, both going and coming, José made no contribution toward gas, meals or snacks; Glen and I paid for everything.

After arriving in Bridgeport and parking the vehicle, we hiked about four or five miles to a meadow where Glen felt we might get a deer. He was right: it was José who, with a lucky shot, killed a buck. Unfortunately, José was "grossed out" during the process of gutting the animal, so that task fell to Glen and me. Then, because of José's "bad back," Glen and I were the ones who carried the deer out of the wilderness to the car.

On the trip back home, with breaks for gas and restaurants but with no contribution from the big eater, José, again we had to listen to his nonsense as well as move the deer carcass around to avoid having the ticks from the deceased animal jump onto us. When we got back to the Covina area we dropped the animal off at a meat locker, and Glen and I split the fee for butchering and packing. We had decided that the meat would be divided between the three of us. José was to pick up the meat when the butchering was done, then provide our shares to Glen and me.

That was the last time we saw either the deer or that flake José—he kept all the venison for himself. Talk about an entitlement mentality! My thoughts about José are far from fond, and Glen never again suggested talking another person like him along on our hunting trips.

Two Poisoned Sandwiches

One evening, I backed up one of my units that had responded to a "homicide in progress." When I got there, the officers, Gary Seeget and Bill Morstad, were inside the dwelling (turned out to be a family dispute). But their car was left standing in the middle of the street, as they had "bailed out" and rushed into the house due to the nature of the call. So I decided to put their car in neutral (you could do that with cars during that era) and push it to the curb.

When I got into their car I noticed a paper bag between the seats that had a great smell. It was two beef dip sandwiches! I couldn't resist, so I unwrapped and took a big bite out of each one, then carefully re-wrapped the sandwiches and replaced them in the bag. Later, Seeget ran into me at the station. He told me that fate had intervened that evening, and had potentially kept him from contracting some horrible disease.

Gary went on to tell me how he and Bill had bought two sandwiches, but got the hot call before they were able to eat them. They had to throw their coffee out the window when rushing to the call, but finally returned to the sandwich shop to get fresh coffee before eating their sandwiches. Back at the sandwich shop they were met by the excited owner, who explained that he had mistakenly given them tainted meat and was afraid they would get sick. He said the owner was very relieved to learn that the "tainted sandwiches" had not been eaten, and gave the police officers two fresh sandwiches.

Gary's efforts to get back at me didn't work! I pled ignorance, and told him that it was indeed his lucky day. Those guys knew I was the suspect. But we still laugh about it when our retired lives cross paths.

ANGELIC WOMAN DEAD OF HEROIN OVERDOSE

While the faces of the hundreds of deceased persons I've seen have pretty much faded from memory, there are a few that are burned into my consciousness. The beautiful woman who died of a heroin overdose at 1731 North Glendale Boulevard was one of those.

One evening while I was a lieutenant, I got a call to meet one of my units regarding a death investigation in a motel room on Glendale Boulevard just north of Alvarado. On arrival, I was greeted with a very tragic and highly unusual sight—a beautiful young woman who could have been a double for Mary Poppins. She was dead of a heroin overdose. She was also drop-dead (no pun intended) beautiful and very wholesome appearing, with immaculate hair and manicured nails.

At the scene was the man who had called the police, a very distraught family friend who feared the worst and had been searching for her. He explained that several years earlier she had been a heroin junkie, but had pulled her life together, married a great fellow who adored her, had a couple of great little kids, and lived in a nice house in Glendale. The friend explained that there were continuing concerns about the potential for her to return to her old stomping grounds, and to heroin.

Sadly, that is exactly what happened. Although I did not follow up with the autopsy report, it appeared likely that her first fix when returning to that environment was "too hot," and resulted in her death. I still drive past that location from time to time, and never fail to glance over at the corner window of the second-floor room where that beautiful woman died.

SEEGET'S REAR END EXPLODES

If a panel of behavioral scientists were to evaluate this situation and conclude that all involved, both witnesses and involved parties, are somewhat psychologically warped, I would not disagree. But it is what it is, and reflects the type of activities and humor that have always been a part of my life.

Gary Seeget was a long-time friend, one of my senior partners when I was a probationary officer, and later a subordinate when I was both a sergeant and a lieutenant. His lifetime legacy will be his farts, which were truly horrible and something he seemed always able to produce whenever he choose to do so, which was quite often. His nickname was "The Green Mist."

I was the watch commander one night, when his ability to produce a fart on command went horribly wrong—resulting in a portion of his rectum being pushed out his anus! It was an ugly situation, and he was obviously in horrible pain. Gary was placed on his stomach on the back seat of a police car and rushed to Queen of Angels Hospital for emergency medical treatment.

Gary clearly deserved the pain he experienced that night, especially because of all the horrible farts he had subjected the rest of us to over the years. But he was a lovable old fart (pun intended) who we were all fond of, and he got our sympathy that night. Subsequent to the repair job on his rear end, his workplace farts resumed. But now they were more carefully delivered, and no longer on the previous "on call" basis.

The Female Supervisor Could Not Seem to Lose Weight

This is one of the few incidents in these memoirs that I knew of but did not personally witness. Nonetheless, it is such a precious story that it needs to be written down somewhere—and apparently this book is the place.

Not long after I left Rampart Divison, a female supervisor transfered in. By all accounts she was a very nice person, but understandably lacking in the full range of skills that most of her colleagues possessed because women were just then moving into the street operational ranks of policing. Like many of us, she was constantly fighting the "battle of the bulge," and working to keep her weight under control—made obvious by the yogurt and orange that were nightly placed on her desk.

Her devious male collagues noticed this, and seized the opportunity to have some long-term fun with her. On several occasions they took her freshly-cleaned uniforms from the cleaner's rack, and had them taken in just a bit! At a recent reunion of Rampart alumni, these scoundrels were still chuckling at her frustration with uniforms that always fit too tight!

Rampart was Just a Great Tour of Duty

My tour of duty as a watch commander in Rampart Patrol Division was about as good as it gets. Everything just seemed to fit. My skills, personality and attitude were in sync with the captains, my peers, and my subordinates.

364

Now, thirty some years later, our old Rampart crowd stills meets for lunch once a month and makes annual trips to Laughlin, Nevada. I am very flattered to always be invited. It's also good to hear the nice things those men (and a couple of women—there were not many in those days) have to say about me. That crowd has no use whatsoever for some of the previous lieutenants and above, and do not mince any words in making it clear that "assholes are not welcome" (the actual term used in the e-mails and literature!) at our luncheons and annual gathering.

Jake Spent a Number of Nights in the Jail

Barbara and I separated in early 1980 and ultimately divorced in 1984. While not pleasant, it was civil, and as time went on we became each other's greatest advocates and very close friends, a situation that exists to this day.

When she moved out, it was agreed that we would have dual custody of the kids. But Jake would usually be with me, while Stacy and Zak would usually be with her. Toward the end of my tour as a lieutenant and morning watch commander at Rampart, and after school let out in June of 1980, I started taking Jake to work with me.

While there, I would put him to sleep in the jail. He not only loved it, but frequently conned me into letting him ride around with me at night. I admit, it was not the right thing to do. Nevertheless, it was only for a couple of weeks and Jake was well known and fondly thought of as sort of a "mascot" around the station. He enjoyed the experience, and today we both look back with fondness on that couple of weeks.

"Walking Small" Nightstick for the Watch Commander

On my last night as watch commander in Rampart, the wonderful troops I'd had the honor to supervise gave me a going-away and congratulatory gift—a massive hand-carved nightstick! It measures about three feet long and four inches in diameter, with "Walking Small" in giant letters.

I was truly touched by their thoughtful gesture and told all assembled that it would always be conspicuously displayed in my office, where it has been. It was a fun topic of conversation throughout all of my LAPD assignments, and as a marshal and sheriff's chief deputy as well. As I type this entry it remains on display in my home office. There is another story behind this gift that, even though it goes back over thirty years, I elected to not put in writing. However, all my old troops from

Rampaert know the story, and frequently remind me about what occurred with this nightstick.

Promoted to Captain

I had previously taken the captain's examination, and came out number 11 on the eligibility list. In that era, promotions were based entirely
on the candidate's cumulative final score on the written and oral examinations, with another factor added for seniority in the previous rank. The
process preceded the rule of three whole scores that is now used.

I was truly a "dark horse" in the process, because I was still a patrol
watch commander and not in a coveted lieutenant II assignment. Just
about every other lieutenant in the top 20 of so eligible candidates was
in an advanced pay grade.

In early July 1980, I was promoted to captain. While this was a difficult time because my wife Barbara and I had separated, it was also a
very happy time because of my promotion.

Getting Captain's Badge Number 44

The Rampart Area Commander, Captain Roger Guindon, was retiring the same week I was being promoted to captain. He had a nice old
badge in good condition, with a number that I really liked—44.

I asked Roger if he could earmark his badge for reassignment to me.
He was happy to do so, and within a day or so of him turning it in, it
was reassigned to me. Roger, who died several years ago, was a great guy.

But that badge had seen some horrific tragedy and sadness. Roger's
then sixteen-year-old son, Steven, was shot to death in an assassination,
which was believed to have resulted from Roger's tenacious effectiveness
as the commanding officer of Narcotics Division.

I will never forget Steven's photo in his dad's office: it had the words
"My Son" beneath the picture. Rest in peace, Roger and Steven.

Equal Opportunity Development Division

In July 1980, after about a year and a half in Rampart as a lieutenant, I went on loan to the Equal Opportunity Development Division
(EODD) as a captain. EODD was the entity within the department
responsible for investigation, policies, procedures and compliance with
city, state, and federal laws and guidelines dealing with equal opportu-

nity and affirmative action issues.

ANOTHER REQUEST FROM DEPUTY CHIEF VERNON

On the day that I was promoted to captain, I also got another call from then-Deputy Chief Vernon who, at that time, was the commanding officer of the Personnel & Training Bureau. He had called on me before for special tasks. This time, he asked if I would be willing to take on another—to go on loan as a captain to the Employee Opportunity Development Division (EODD) to lead an effort to attract women to the police department because of a federal court consent decree. I accepted the loan assignment. Officially, I was the commanding officer of the North Hollywood Patrol Division, but the Office of Operations agreed to my short-term loan to EODD.

RECRUITING WOMEN

I remain proud of the way that we really ramped up efforts to attract women to the police department as sworn officers. My partner was a great lady, Sergeant Jeannie Eisentraut, who was very dedicated and full of energy. We oversaw the development of top-notch materials, including written and broadcast. We reached out aggressively to colleges and the military, and really did achieve an increase in applications from women. We also worked hard to identify any unnecessary impediments to attracting, recruiting, processing, training, and assigning them. I was only involved in this effort for a couple of months, but like to think that I made a positive difference.

MY "UNETHICAL" RECRUITING ACTIVITIES

Although a captain, I was a junior captain, and not the commanding officer of EODD—Captain Matthew Hunt was. In subsequent years Matt and I became good friends, and to this day I have enormous respect for him. But our relationship in attracting women to the department for police officer positions was somewhat strained. We went sideways over my actions involving the military.

Using my many military contacts, and based on my understanding of how to accomplish things through the military, I put together a massive police orientation and recruiting day intended for female military personnel from a number of Southern California military bases. I even got the military to agree to use military transportation to bring the servicewomen to and from the police academy for the event.

The intent was clearly to recruit women to the police service. It was known to all the military commanders I dealt with, although we collectively agreed to conduct the activity under the umbrella of law enforcement liaison primarily for female military police personnel.

Matt was not in favor of my actions and felt that the true intent, versus the official intent (even though it was a strategy developed in concert with the military), was unethical. I disagreed with Matt, and felt disappointed at his position and characterization, but he was the boss and I had to respect and accept his guidance. The event was canceled. Although it was a cordial relationship, I pretty much lost my enthusiasm for the EODD loan, and I think Matt lost his enthusiasm for my loan, as well. I moved on to my regular assignment in North Hollywood. Although retirement has resulted in us not seeing each other very often, I consider Matt to be a good friend, and I hold him in the highest esteem.

———

North Hollywood Patrol Division

In August 1980, after a couple of months on loan to the Employee Opportunity Development Division, I assumed my duties as the commanding officer of the North Hollywood Patrol Division, within the North Hollywood Area. The other entity within the area was the detective division. As I recall, the total number of persons within the area, including both patrol and detectives, was slightly over 200.

Don't You Ever Raise that Issue Again!

Several months into my assignment at North Hollywood, I was scheduled for a "one-on-one" chat with Deputy Chief Barry Wade, who at the time was the commanding officer of the Valley Bureau. He was a solid leader, usually soft-spoken, and someone I thought well of.

After discussing the usual issues such as crime, community relations and the many issues facing North Hollywood, Chief Wade asked if there was anything else I would like to share with him before terminating our chat. I said yes, there was, and went on to tell him about the adverse impact that illegal immigration was having on crime and the quality of life in the Valley, and how it was getting worse. I suggested that the LAPD break ranks with the others who had buried their heads in the sand on this issue, start sharing these problematic realities with others, and encourage the enforcement of our immigration laws.

Chief Wade became annoyed and made it clear, telling me very directly, that I was to never raise that issue again. Obviously, I had struck a key nerve, and quickly backed off. I did not like the chief's reaction, but came to realize how terribly complicated the issue was, and the problems that arise when illegals see the LAPD as an arm of Immigration and fail to report crimes or cooperate in investigations.

Before we both retired, I had the opportunity to work for him one more time when he was the director of the Office of Administrative Services and I was the captain of Communications Division and project manager of the Emergency Command, Control, and Communications Project. Barry is a good man, and I hope our paths will cross again one of these times.

Unique Medical Treatment by a Unique Nurse

While in North Hollywood, I fell in with a group of men, three of whom were physicians and the other an attorney. They were a fun group, and their commitment to having fun really went over the top when the attorney checked into the hospital that was collectively owned by his doctor pals.

Joe, the attorney and an occasional pro-tem judge, was to have surgery to repair a hernia. After checking into the hospital but before his surgery, an attractive nurse, white nylons and all, went into his room and feigned consternation at the doctor's alleged instructions in the medical chart. She made the comment, "I guess the doctor knows best," closed the door to the room, then provided a most unique and unconventional "medical procedure" on the attorney.

The nurse was actually an outcall prostitute hired by the doctors and dressed in nurse's attire! Joe said nothing about the incident until prodded a couple of weeks later by the attorneys during lunch, as to whether or not something unique occurred before his surgery. Until this lunch Joe apparently hadn't realized it was a prank, and he was a bit hurt because he said something to the effect of "I thought she liked me!" The laughter lasted for quite a while. I know, because I was at that luncheon when the cat came out of the bag. What occurred was actually a crime, and I certainly would not have participated in the behavior—but I must confess to laughing awful hard at a very funny prank.

Officer Constance Gets Served with Divorce Papers

George Constance (pseudonym) was among the couple hundred officers who worked for me in the North Hollywood Patrol Division. He was a particularly interesting fellow, because he was not only a good cop, but also a very talented businessman who operated a company during his off-duty hours. I had a number of chats with George, and got the impression that he had a loving wife and successful marriage. However, all was apparently not well, and he found out in a most unique and calculated way.

While seated with the family at the dinner table, shoes off and relaxed, the doorbell rang. He walked out of the house onto the screened porch, and greeted the man who had just rung the doorbell. When George opened the door, the man said: "You have just been served," then walked away.

At that moment, he heard the latch close on the front door, which prevented him from going back into the house. George had just been served with divorce papers from the wife with whom he'd been sitting at the table, and was locked out of his own home. George swore it was a complete surprise. They ultimately divorced after a very contentious fight over assets.

———

Hollywood Patrol Division

In October 1981, after less than six months in North Hollywood, I was assigned as the commanding officer of the Hollywood Patrol Division, with the divisional boundries as previous described. As I recall, the personnel strength was approximately 400 persons assigned to the overall area, with the majority of them in the Patrol Division.

Since my last assignment to Hollywood, a new station had been built. It was located at 1358 Wilcox Avenue.

Specifically Selected for Hollywood Division

I had only been in North Hollywood for about six months when I was called to the West Bureau officers and informed that I was being transferred to command the Hollywood Patrol Division. The deputy chief, a good guy, said that I'd been selected because they believed I could help clean up a troubled division, and also that I could keep the area commanding officer (my new boss) out of trouble. I was very flattered. In hindsight, I realize I did not have the skills, as a very new captain, to be as effective as the others believed I could be.

I do believe that I was reasonably competent as a patrol captain, but woefully ill-equipped to do all that was expected of me. While not expected to run the entire area, I was expected to keep the captain who did have that job on-task and out of trouble.

One of the biggest lessons I learned out of the Hollywood experience is not to expect a subordinate command officer to keep a superior command officer out of trouble. In hindsight, the department came to this same realization, and the person who had been my boss, a very decent man but who had not been adequately "minding the store," was later eased into retirement.

I have always wondered, about and to some extent suspected, another reason for my transfer out of North Hollywood and into Hollywood. While I do believe there existed a high opinion of my skills, it is possible that my area captain in North Hollywood wanted me gone because of a dating relationship I had with a local businesswoman. She was a very respectable lady, and our association was honorable, but I don't think my boss liked the fact that we were dating. His consternation could have been related to a real problem with the guy I replaced, who also had a relationship with a local businesswoman. Unknown to the captain, however, her business was prostitution, and the guy was married! If this matter was a factor, it was never mentioned. But I would not be surprised to learn it was part of the overall transfer equation.

CHANGE OF COMMAND—TRANSITIONAL DISCUSSION

The department was unhappy with the fellow I was replacing. He was a very talented guy who had been an absolute superstar and destined to further organizational greatness. Probably he would have gone all the way to the rank of deputy chief had he not decided to put his energies into the business world.

Hollywood was a very active place with no shortage of challenges, both externally with crime and internally with personnel. In just the eight or so hours before our discussion, three serious things occurred: $1,100 had been stolen from the bail box in the watch commander's office; it was learned that a patrol officer was married to a local streetwalking prostitute; and a sergeant who was pending relief from duty was ambushed and shot (the wound was minor) under most suspicious circumstances.

I could easily write several pages on the critical issues that he and I should have discussed during our transition of command talk. But he spent no more than five minutes, barely skimming the surface of divisional issues, before cleaning out and leaving the office.

During our very brief transition discussion with the captain I replaced at Hollywood Patrol Division, he told me that among the "perks" of the position was having lunch once or twice a month with the director of security at Paramount Studios, Harry Hanson (pseudonym).

Harry Hanson was the same fellow who essentially had kicked me out of Hollywood four years before, when I was a new lieutenant! At that time, not only did he not want me in the Support Division where I was temporarily assigned, he denied the request of one of his subordinate captains for me to remain in the Operations Division as a team leader. This fellow went out of his way to make me miserable and feel humiliated, and it worked. Now I was supposed to be his buddy?

The security position at Paramount required a close working relationship with the leadership at the Hollywood Police Station, and certainly that was among the reasons Hanson got the job. I told the outgoing captain I had no use for Hanson, and it was a perk he could take with him. His efforts to tell me what a decent guy Hanson was fell on deaf ears!

For the next month or so I kept getting phone messages from Harry Hanson to call him. I promptly crumpled them up and threw them in the trash can. Then the area commanding officer called me into his office and encouraged me to "lighten up on Harry Hanson—after all, he is one of us and we take care of our own!" I told him that Harry Hanson had screwed me and many other people, that he did not take care of people when he was on the department, that he did not deserve our goodwill, and that I wanted nothing to do with him.

In hindsight, this was a pretty extraordinary position for a new captain to take with his boss, but it illustrates the depth of my dislike for Harry Hanson. My boss went on to say that Harry needed our help with parking issues, and I responded that he could transfer all forty or so parking officers to his area (my boss' domain), but that as long as the parking folks worked for me, Hanson was not going to get any more service than any other citizen! My boss shrugged and dropped the subject.

A week or so later, my secretary came into my office and announced that Harry Hanson was on the line, that he knew I was in the office, and was threatening to call Internal Affairs unless I took his call!

I picked up the phone and identified myself in the appropriate way, to which he stated (I remember his exact words): "Keith, Harry Hanson here, how the hell are you, great to have you in Hollywood!" I said: "How can I help you?" He replied, "Keith, I have this little parking problem…," at which time I interrupted him and said I would have Remo Cunniberti, the traffic supervisor, contact him. I then hung up.

I called in the traffic supervisor (a civilian position—he was a retired Navy chief petty officer, as I recall) and started to tell him that I had received a call from retired Captain Harry Hanson….

He interrupted me, and stated something to the effect of: "I know, I know—drop everything else and get over to Paramount and take care of the parking issues on the surrounding streets!" I responded that he was wrong, and gave him a direct order to not give Hanson any more service than we would give anyone else—no more, no less! Cunniberti's face lit up like a Christmas tree, and he responded "all right!"

Two or three months later, Hanson was gone from Paramount. I can only hope, and want badly to believe, that my actions contributed to his loss of that job. Aside from my experiences with Harry Hanson, he was widely disliked by just about all of the folks from that era who had any dealings with him. We have a bunch of legends on the LAPD, and he was one of our bad legends: a very contrary man who left a lot of unhappy people in his wake.

Note: Harry Hanson died several years ago. I gave some thought to finding his grave and urinating on it, but do not like standing in lines.

Dangling in Pink Lace Panties

I never say that I have seen it all, and this is one of the reasons why. Being a cop in Los Angeles yields some pretty bizarre stuff; being the captain of Hollywood yields even more.

One afternoon a radio call came out, "ambulance shooting," and directed the assigned police unit to a porno bookstore. On arriving, the officers discovered that a botched robbery had occurred and the proprietor had been seriously wounded (I think he subsequently died of the gunshot wound). In an adjacent room they discovered an adult male, clad only in pink lace panties, handcuffed and standing on a platform that was part of a human-size pendulum!

The officers' investigation revealed that the proprietor not only ran the bookstore, but for a fee would also handcuff you to the pendulum in any attire you desired, then whip and humiliate you. It seems the proprietor was giving the guy in the panties a dose of humiliation when the armed robber entered the location, robbed the place, shot the whipper, and fled. The fellow wearing the pink panties got quite a bit of additional humiliation from all the officers, paramedics and others who responded to the scene. He wasn't removed from the pendulum for an hour or so, as the scene was being dealt with, crime broadcasts initiated, etc!

AUTHORIZING DEADLY FORCE, AND ITS IMPACT

The LAPD SWAT Team has always been the best in the nation (San Bernardino County Sheriff's is right up there, as well!), and has done a remarkable job of avoiding deadly force in the vast majority of violent encounters. Unfortunately, however, there are instances when deadly force is the only reasonable option if further violence is to be avoided, especially in preventing injury or death to innocent persons.

In those few SWAT operations where it appears that the only reasonable option is to neutralize the suspect, a tactical plan is developed and the concurrence of the field commander is solicited. Without intending to sound dramatic, approval of these recommendations by a field commander, usually a staff or command officer, is tantamount to authorizing the taking of a human life.

I have authorized this type of recommendation on several occasions, with a multi-hostage situation and the apprehension of a cop-killer coming immediately to mind. Both resulted in the demise of the suspect. Just what is the psychological impact on a person who knowingly authorizes the taking of a human life under these circumstances? In my case, the psychological impact is absolutely none. *Hasta la vista*, baby!

FATHERLY DISCUSSION WITH NEW FEMALE OFFICERS WHO WERE MARRIED

It was clear to me that new female officers married to men who were not cops had a rough road ahead of them. Being assigned as a cop in Hollywood was like eight hours of breaking news: a very exciting and interesting place to be. I could only imagine how drab a man with a regular job could look to a new female officer, especially one working in the midst of many young and single male officers who were easily available.

During my welcome discussion with new female officers who were married, I always raised the hazard of them unintentionally minimizing the potentially-drab lives of non-cop husbands. Due to the potential for non-cop husbands to feel minimized because of their wives' exciting lives, I would tell them how important it was to go that extra mile and show interest in their husbands' lives and activities. While I did not keep statistics, I cannot think of any of those marriages that survived. My concern and efforts were far greater than my counseling effectiveness.

This incident falls into the category of stuff you cannot make up! One afternoon on a Fourth of July during my tenure as the patrol captain in Hollywood, two of my officers stopped some kids with a batch of illegal fireworks and did what many cops do—they took the fireworks for themselves!

A little later they saw two prostitutes, with whom they had a cordial informant-type relationship, driving westbound in a convertible on Sunset Boulevard. The officers thought they would have a little fun, so they lit a string of firecrackers and threw them into the prostitute's open convertible. The driver was wearing a very short mini-shirt, and the entire string of 200 firecrackers exploded between her legs!

Requesting an ambulance and a sergeant was probably among the most difficult things either of those officers ever did. The injuries were pretty bizarre, yet not life-threatening. But they certainly put the victim (or *that* part of her!) out of work for a while. There was a lawsuit and quick settlement by the city (I was gone from that command by the time it was resolved, and am not aware of the amount). The officers were up-front and contrite during the whole investigation. As I recall, the thrower got a ten-day suspension, and the other officer took five days for not intervening to prevent the fireworks throwing (he probably had encouraged the prank!)

YOU WILL NOT FIND A MARINE
ENGAGED IN THAT TYPE OF BEHAVIOR!

This was one of the low points in my assignment as commanding officer of Hollywood Patrol Division. One night I was riding with one of my sergeants, Vern Dandridge, who was also an Army Reserve officer. He delighted in telling me about the Marines he had encountered in cars, engaged in sexual activities with other males. Obviously, I told him he was full of bull.

About half-way into the shift that night, while checking out an overlook in the Hollywood Hills, we came across a parked car with its windows all steamed up. While we take no joy in tampering with a couple who are enjoying one-another's company, we typically do a quick check to ensure the gal isn't being compelled to do something against her will.

In this case we found two men, buck-naked, doing the evil deed. When we asked for identification, one of them was an active-duty Marine corporal! Humiliated and embarrassed are good terms to describe my demeanor for the rest of that shift. I did contact the corporal's commanding officer, but do not know what came of the situation. To this day, when Vern and I cross paths, he is the one that always relishes telling this story.

Robbery-Shooting at the Acapulco, and Traffic Control

On a Saturday afternoon, I went into Hollywood Station for an after-hours inspection. Jake, who was then about nine or ten and proudly wearing his Deputy Auxiliary Police (DAP) badge and khaki uniform, went with me. The watch commander, Lieutenant Randy Mancini, said he had a fairly complicated and sensitive issue he wanted to kick around, and suggested we go out in the field for a while and chat, where we would not be disturbed.

Officer Frank Pettinato, who coordinated the Explorer surveillance team, was there, and suggested that Jake could go with him and sit on a rooftop surveillance that was underway. He would be safe and out of the way there; it sounded good, so I let him go.

Mancini and I were cruising around and yakking when a code 3 call came out for any unit to responded to a robbery in progress and shots fired at the Acapulco Restaurant, at the intersection of Sunset and Orange. Since no other units were available, Randy and I "bought" the call and responded with red lights and siren.

As we approached the intersection just before the restaurant, there stood Jake in his little khaki uniform, looking very official and directing traffic away from the location! It seems that Pettinato had been enroute to the surveillance location when the hot call came out. So he responded, learned there was a shooting victim down and the suspects were gone, so he was establishing a crime scene prior to the arrival of other units. Jake was part of it. Somehow, I was not surprised. Jake often managed to worm his way into all kinds of stuff.

Steve Johnson and His Good Pal, Dallas

One evening during my assignment as the commanding officer of the Hollywood Patrol Division, my very good friend Steve scheduled a ridealong for him and two of his friends. Prior to the trio's arrival, I noticed that one of Hollywood's most notorious and ugliest transvestite prostitutes, "Dallas," was handcuffed in the jail corridor obviously awaiting to be booked on prostitution charges.

376

To say that Dallas was ugly is truly an understatement! He was over six feet tall, with flaming red hair, very large and artificial sagging breasts that were barely contained by a tiny halter top, hot pants (with a suspicious bulge!), long and ugly purplish legs (bulging veins resulting from years of heroin injections), gigantic feet in little "girlie" sandals, bright pink long toenails, and a face that looked like John Wayne in lipstick! He was one of our regular customers, never gave us any trouble, was friendly and outgoing, and said "Hi Cap" when he saw me. I immediately sensed a unique opportunity!

I told Dallas that I would soon be back in the corridor with three guests to the station, and asked if he would do me a favor—tell one of the men, whom I described and identified by the name "Steve," that he loved and missed him? Dallas said sure. Boy, did he put on a show!

A few minutes later, with Steve and his two buddies in tow, I entered the booking corridor. Dallas looked right at Steve and blurted out the following (or very close): "Steve! Oh, Steve, where have you been? I still love and miss you! What happened to our life together and the little house in the suburbs with the white picket fence that we were going to share?"

Stunned and horrified, Steve turned bright crimson, looked at me and murmured something really nasty—he knew he'd been had! I was so proud! This has been a fun story for Steve and me for many years, though even after all these years he has asked me to not put his name in this book. I reluctantly honor that request.

DISCRIMINATING LIPS

While at Hollywood, there occurred a number of internal investigations. One such investigation yielded a perspective from a prostitute that struck me as unique.

The situation involved a prolonged association between the prostitute and a Hollywood police officer, with the gal having routinely performed oral copulation on the officer. In exploring the details and nature of the relationship between the pair, the internal affairs investigator (he played the audio-tape for me) asked the prostitute to describe the nature of the relationship. Specifically, had there been hugging and kissing and genuine affection between them? She very indignantly replied that the officer was a jerk, and there was no way that her lips would ever touch his lips! Given the other location where her lips had been, it struck me that she had a pretty confused set of lips with unique priorities!

Crazy Mary was a mentally-retarded woman who had a chronological age of about thirty, but the mental age of about six. Accompanied by her dolls and baby carriage, Mary spent a good deal of time out in front of the station, almost always sitting in bizarre positions and puffing furiously on a cigarettte.

Bud was a very talented photographer whose skills and willingness to take photos for the department had led to his appointment as a special reserve officer. The position was without pay and held no real authority, but on occasion it was bestowed on those who donated their unique skills in support of the LAPD.

One day, we needed an immediate photo of something (I don't recall what it was). But SID (Scientific Investigation Division) didn't have a photographer available. So we contacted Bud, who immediately came to the station. Bud asked only that we replace the film he would use, which we were pleased to do. He took our photos, and the roll of film he provided and shot was sent to SID for processing.

Shortly afterward, however, we got a disturbing call from SID. They informed us that the roll of film contained, in addition to the photos we'd requested, a number of sickeningly pornographic images of a woman—and she was Crazy Mary. Bud was immediately terminated from the LAPD reserve program. Notwithstanding the reality that he had taken advantage of a mentally retarded person, the complexities of the situation were such that the city attorney felt a successful prosection would be unlikely.

JEANNE AND THE RED POLKA-DOT PANTIES

I was very fortunate to have a secretary, Jeanne Pettyjohn, who was also a talented stenographer. I had never previously developed or used dictation skills, but the heavy volume of administrative and disciplinary work at Hollywood compelled me to try, and I became very proficient at dictation.

One day, while dictating a very detailed and sensitive disciplinary report to Jeanne, I decided to have some fun. She was furiously and intently typing my dictation when I added a bogus allegation about a number of Hollywood officers who had been identified by a prostitute as allegedly having had sexual intercourse with her. Supposedly, each involved officer's name was written in one of the white circles on her red panties, which had been taken into evidence.

I then started "reading" the names of the officers who were identified in these white circles, and this juicy information clearly got her interest as she wrote down every one of names. After mentioning several names of some officers (if anyone would pull that kind of nonsense, it would be them), I mentioned the name of an older, very dignified and white-haired officer who worked the desk.

Jeanne looked up and screamed "NO!" Then she realized she'd been had! I am not exaggering when I say that she and I laughly loudly and hysterically for about five minutes.

Who is John Belushi?

I was sitting in my office one morning when Lieutenant Randy Mancini, a great guy and dear friend who later retired as a captain, excitedly entered. Randy told me that John Belushi had just been found dead in one of the bungalows at the Chateau Marmont Hotel on Sunset Boulevard.

My first question was "who is John Belushi?" I guess I was about the only person in the world who didn't know who he was! He had spent the night with a Canadian woman, Cathy Smith, then ultimately died of a heroin overdose. The word of his death soon got out. By early afternoon the streets around the police station were littered with news vehicles, and news personnel were swarming like locusts. The investigation was simple and straightforward—it was what it was, and it did not take long to establish Belushi's death as an accidental overdose.

This case long bothered me for another reason. The reporting of his death was all over the news before his remains were even removed from the scene, and there is no doubt that many of his friends and relatives learned of his death through media broadcasts. I found this to be very troublesome, and vowed to work even harder in high-profile deaths to ensure that families were notified by us before they heard it on the news.

Little did I realize at the time, that approximately 140 million people would one day learn of my strong feelings and actions in this matter! Later, my insistence that O.J. Simpson be immediately notified by detectives of the death of Nicole Brown-Simpson, his former wife and the mother of his children, resulted in his arrest and probable cause for the discovery of evidence at his Brentwood estate.

New officers, of both genders, typically go out of their way to be polite, cordial, and low-profile. Officer Patricia Foster (pseudonym) was definitely the exception. When reporting into Hollywood from the academy, she appeared in extremely tight shorts and a halter-top that left nothing to the imagination. She was attractive and well endowed, and knew it.

On her very first trip as a new probationary officer, when she entered the rear door to get to her locker, her appearance was clearly noticed by several male officers and supervisors. Pat looked right at the group and stated something to the effect of, "put those filthy eyes back into your filthy minds!" It caused quite a stir and a negative reaction, because it was clear that she dressed and acted in a way that invited the type of reactions she got.

Before she left the department (as related in subsequent paragraphs), I learned that she had previously failed the background for another agency, after having intentionally flashed bare breasts at window washers descending past the window of the office where she worked at the time.

After this incident, but prior to her termination, an investigation revealed that while on a trip to the Colorado River with other Hollywood officers, she left the company of her companion momentarily and flashed her breasts at a member of a white supremacy motorcycle gang. It literally incited a fight between the officer she was with and the gang member she flashed! This, of all the things involving the training officer who was aware of her likely termination, became a big investigation in itself and resulted in disciplinany action for several other officers. Pat was a real piece of work, and wherever she went she left chaos in her wake.

"Officer Foster, You are Terminated! Did You Hear That, Bob?"

As it turned out, Officer Patricia Foster had engaged in misconduct (for which she was ultimately terminated) on the night of her academy graduation.

That evening, she and another officer went to a prominent discothéque, flashed their badges and identified themselves as "vice officers" in order to get in without paying the cover charge. Foolishly, even though the graduation-night misconduct was known, she was sent to Hollywood to work, as opposed to being placed on administrative leave.

She sure left a negative mark in Hollywood. Unfortunately, before the investigation was completed on the discotheque charges, she engaged in additional disgusting behavior in Hollywood, including the fight at the Colorado River she incited because of her indecent exposure.

When the termination documents reached my desk, I had her called into my office. Before I could say anything, she asked if the matter was related to issues such as termination, work actions, deprivation of employment, etc. It sounded like she was literally quoting from the Labor Code.

When I replied that the matter did fit one of those categories, she immediately insisted that nothing further take place until her attorney was present, but he would not be available for about a week. I informed her that she was not entitled to an attorney for what was about to occur, as there was no role for an attorney to play. But I had no objection to the presence of her attorney, if she could have him respond immediately to the station.

I was acquainted with her attorney and, although we usually were on opposite sides of cases, he was a decent fellow. She called the attorney from my office and said something to the effect of, "Bob, this is it, can you come over to Hollywood Station now?" Patricia said he wanted to talk to me. When I took the phone he asked if I could put off whatever it was (he knew she was getting fired) for several days. I denied his request, but said that I would activate the speakerphone so he could hear all that was said, which he said was fine.

I remember the conversation as if it were yesterday. I said, "Bob, can you hear me?" When he said yes, I said, "Officer Foster, you are terminated. Bob, did you hear that?"

I would rather engage in a raging gun battle with only one round of ammunition than have to fire someone, but it goes with the territory and is something I have done on a number of occasions. With one exception, I have always done so with sadness and a heavy heart. But in the case of former Officer Patricia Foster, this one exception was a pleasure!

"Here is Your ID Card. Now Sign the Form!"

Several hours after firing Patricia Foster, she stormed back into my office for me to sign a form for her to receive her final paycheck. The form was also an inventory, to ensure that she turned in all of her city equipment. I noted that she indicated her identification card had been lost.

I suspected she just wanted to keep it, but I was not going to play her silly-ass game. So I told her I would not sign the form until I got the ID card back. She insisted that it was lost, a report had been made, and that I had to sign the form. When I refused, she stormed out of the office.

A few minutes later I got a call from one of the directors of the Police Protective League. He encouraged me to sign the form, saying that the league would bring legal action to compel my signature if I continued to refuse to do so. When I asked how long that process would take (I already knew it would be several weeks at the earliest), he acknowledged it would take quite a while, to which I responded that it would give former Officer Foster time to find the card!

I guess the director conveyed my remarks to Foster, because within about fifteen minutes she again stormed into my office, threw the identification card on my desk, and demanded that I sign the form. I smiled, signed the form, and never saw Foster again.

The Foster matter is a very good example of the occasional necessity to ignore legal advice, or at least to get a second opinion. This woman should never have been hired by the LAPD, but a deputy city attorney with the best of intentions, yet lacking an understanding of the potential consequences of bad advice, opined that a failure to hire her could result in the same type of civil litigation she had instigated against the previous law enforcement agency that declined to hire her. So the attorney recommended that she not be disqualified.

Further aggravating the situation was another bad decision to send her to a division to work, as opposed to placing her on administrative leave, as it was all but certain that she would be terminated for her actions on graduation night. The lack of courage, insight, and decisiveness placed a very serious problem in my lap, and created a mess that was difficult to clean up.

MICHAEL CAVASO—A GREAT COP BUT SEXUALLY PERVERTED

Mike Cavaso (pseudonym) was absolutely one of the finest cops I encountered in my 45 years in policing. Moreover, he was a delight to deal with and was the first person to step forward and accept responsibility for his involvement in troublesome actions.

Unfortunately, he was also a sexual pervert who I do not believe had the ability to avoid sexual opportunities. The first time I became aware of this was when he somehow avoided getting fired for having sex with a female Explorer scout, instead getting a six-month suspension. Then I selected him and his partner to be the field training officers for a very sensitive matter involving a troublesome female probationer (yup, Patricia Foster) who was under investigation for serious misconduct and likely to be terminated. Mike was sleeping with her within a week, and was also involved with her in a horrifically massive misconduct matter involving numerous outside agencies, in Parker, Arizona.

Later, he was charged (and apparently convicted) of having sex with a thirteen-year-old niece who was living in his home with him and his wife. Obviously, he was terminated from the department. I occasionally bring up his sad and pathetic face on the California Megan's Law Sex Offender website. What a shame.

The Ruined Date and an Angelic-Appearing Suspect

My hot date on this particularly Saturday night did not work out well, either for me or for a shooting suspect.

While my companion and I were having a nice dinner at a classy restrauant in Hollywood, I got a call regarding a barricaded suspect right down the street from where we were dining. The location was the Holiday Inn on Highland Avenue. It was a high-rise hotel with a circular restrauant on the top floor that actually revolved.

On arriving at the scene with my date in tow, I learned that a gunman on one of the upper floors had knocked out a window and shot at several people in the streets below. I learned there hadn't been any fatalities but do not recall if anyone had been hit by the suspect's gunfire.

Within minutes, we had quite a group assembled outside of the suspect's locked door. He was demanding three things: a priest, a pizza, and a newsman. We got the priest and the reporter right away, but the pizza took a few minutes.

After an hour or two of unsuccessful negotiations, additional shots were fired out the window. But we had evacuated everyone we could from the streets below. SWAT proposed, and I quickly approved, a tactical plan to have the fire department punch a hole in the wall between the suspect's room and the hallway, and to "neutralize" the suspect if he tried to respond with gunfire.

The plan worked well when the fire department opened an immediate hole in the wall. However, while the wall was being penetrated, the suspect took his own life with a single gunshot wound to his head. The scene was more surreal than most—and I have seen plenty—because the dead suspect was covered with a fine white dust from the dislodged stucco created when entry was forced into the room. Even the small flow of blood from his fatal head wound was covered with the white dust.

I am not sure what my female companion thought I had planned for us to do after dinner. I'm confident, though, that sitting in the lobby of a hotel, watching all the cops and firefighters running around with all types of guns and equipment, was not exactly what she had in mind. But she was a good sport, and it made a good story for her to share with her friends.

Jumping to Conclusions About a Dead Teenager

I remain ashamed of my actions in this matter. But it did reinforce a very important lesson: things are seldom what they appear to be.

Late one evening, one of my units went in pursuit of a speeding vehicle. The chase ended when the suspect's vehicle struck a sixteen-year-old boy riding a motorcycle, resulting in the youngster's traumatic and instantaneous death. I first went to the scene, then to the station, where I was told that one of the officers, a woman who I thought well of at the time, had allowed the dead boy's father to identify his son's mutilated remains at the scene of the accident! I was upset and indignant at the news, and was inappropriately vocal in prematurely condemning the officer's actions.

Later that morning as the reports were being completed, the officer came into my office and asked to speak to me about the matter. I invited her in and to sit down, but I suspect my demeanor was as hostile as my thoughts. She explained that the dead boy lived about a block from the incident, that his father (who had been waiting up for his son to arrive home) heard the sirens and commotion, went to the scene, and recognized the twisted wreckage of his son's motorcycle. She further explained that the circumstances were such that her actions were justified in informing the man of his son's death, as the boy's body was present and covered with a sheet. I agreed. She continued, telling me that the father had insisted on seeing his son, and that her efforts and those of others to persuade him otherwise went unheeded. He persevered, insisting that he see his boy right then and there.

Finally, she assisted the corner in arranging the remains in the coroner's vehicle in such a way that only a portion of the boy's face was visible, with most of the trauma being covered by the sheet. Reluctantly, the father was permitted to see his son.

Once she fully explained the situation, I had to agree that she had handled this difficult matter in an appropriate and compassionate manner. I apologized to my officer for having jumped to a conclusion without knowing the facts. For a number of years since, I have used this horrible event to illustrate how things are rarely as they at first seem.

384

What Stressed Me Out? Bogus Stress Claims!

Because of laxities in worker's compensation laws (since strengthened to some minor extent), the 1980s saw quite a few bogus claims for police-related stress. These claims were made possible by ambulance-chasing attorneys and unscrupulous psychologists who knew know how to play the system. As a result a number of officers, almost all of them lousy cops in my opinion, were able to get worker compensation awards and disability retirement pensions.

These situations really stressed me out! I put a great deal of effort into fighting these claims—in fact, too much effort, because it distracted me from other leadership responsibilities. I won a couple of battles, but lost all the wars: the workers' compensation rule which mandated that conflicts be resolved in favor of the applicant (something to that effect), made successfully fighting these claims futile.

My only gains occurred several years later, when I was the commanding officer of the Personnel Group. I delighted in denying CCW (carrying concealed weapons) permits, which were routinely granted to honorably retired police officers, to anyone who claimed to be psychologically disabled because of having been a cop. It still bugs me, when I think of some of the worthless former cops running around and drawing tax-free disability pensions for non-existent disabilities.

Bomb Failed to Detonate at Hollywood Palladium

Early in my tenure at Hollywood, I was among the guests invited to attend an affair at the Hollywood Palladium to benefit the Committee to Aid Homeless Armenians. The guest of honor was then-Governor George Deukmejian; the other guests included a bunch of public officials including my boss, Commander Larry Binkley, and his wife. Being single at the time, I was accompanied by a date.

Shortly after all the guests had arrived, quite a commotion and an evacuation occurred, due to the discovery of an explosive device that had been planted along the bottom of the many glass doors in the entryway to the Palladium. Fortunately, the device failed to detonate as planned. Had the device gone off at the intended time, scores of persons, including my date and me, would likely have sustained horrible injuries or even death from flying plate glass fragments.

The subsequent investigation determined that a radical Armenian group, which was in strong opposition to the moderate Armenian group sponsoring the event, had planted the device. During my several assignments in West Bureau, I had quite a bit of experience dealing with Armenian groups, and made many friends from that wonderful community. Without being judgmental—because my job was to serve all of our communities—I also came to understand the hatred that existed toward the Turks. I also learned early-on that radical Armenian groups were pretty adamant. You were either part of the problem or part of the solution, as they saw it, and they had little tolerance for some of the more moderate Armenian groups.

Cruel Executions and Off-Duty Weapons

During my active law enforcement years, I usually carried a weapon while off-duty. But not always.

This changed in the wake of a multi-victim homicide at the Bob's Big Boy on La Cienega Boulevard in West Los Angeles, in December of 1980. After robbing the restaurant, the suspects herded the half-dozen or so employees and patrons into the freezer and shot them to death. If only one of the patrons had been an armed off-duty officer, the outcome would have been much different.

Subsequent to this horrific crime, I became much more diligent about carrying a weapon while off-duty. Now, in retirement, I find myself slipping again. But I need to remind myself that the above tragedy would have had a much different outcome, even if the armed officer was retired.

Midnight Meeting with Internal Affairs

During the evening of July 4, 1981, I was at home playing with my amateur radio equipment and preparing for a midnight radio conversation that was to include King Hussein of Monaco, who was also a ham operator.

In the middle of turning a radio dial, I got a call from Al Fried, the chief investigator in Internal Affairs Divison, informing me that he and the division's commanding officer, Don Vincent, would be at my home at midnight to discuss a very sensitive issue. This could not be a good thing! King Hussein immediately fell off my radar screen.

When they arrived, I was briefed as to a growing belief that two of my morning watch officers, Ron Venegas and Jack Myers, were committing burglaries while on-duty and in uniform! This information, for me, was tantamount to a volcanic eruption in the middle of Los Angeles, and was just one of those things that is close to unmentionable.

Al and Don explained that several months earlier, in March, the FBI was told by an informant that the two officers, who were assigned to a special burglary response unit ("Code 30 Unit"), would sometimes take items for themselves after arriving and determining that a burglary had in fact occurred. The informant said he believed the officers would also sometimes break a window to activate a burglar alarm, knowing they would be the unit to get the call, then force entry and steal items.

Obviously, we hoped this information was not true. However, investigators at internal affairs had been reviewing and comparing several month's worth of records and found some disturbing coincidences that did not look good. I was advised of the continuing investigation, as the assistance of one person (me) inside the division was necessary to obtain schedules, information, days off, etc.

I was specifically told not to say anything to my boss, the area commanding officer. I thought then, and continue to think, that this admonition was a bit unfair to him. He was a very good, decent and ethical man, but he didn't work that hard and was absent too much. The concern was that he might drop a hint to one of the subjects that an investigation was occurring, thus cause anything that may have been happening to stop, thereby avoiding a major scandal and further problems for him. Such would have never occurred.

The Covert Investigation

The covert internal affairs investigation went on for several months. It was coordinated by a wonderful man and a police academy classmate, Lieutenant Rick Dinse.

For a while, it appeared nothing was happening, and the limited surveillance was not yielding much to substantiate the information from the informant. It was actually causing me some problems, because of other morning watch issues I really could not address, but did not think were linked to the informant's information.

I also felt very uncomfortable with the actions of two morning watch sergeants, Roger Gunson (pseudonym) and Joe Bellwood (pseudonym). I felt they were too close to their troops and should be moved to another watch, but was asked by Rick Dinse to not move them until the investigation had run its course. At the time, we had no reason to suspect these two sergeants were involved in any inappropriate activities, but realized that a rotation of supervisors could disrupt watch activities and make it more difficult to establish if crimes were being committed. The investigation went on and I continued to provide information as required.

December 7, 1981, became the LAPD's "Day of Infamy." Not only was it the fortieth anniversary of the Japanese attack on Pearl Harbor, but a horrible day for me as well.

In the early morning hours internal affairs investigators initiated a sting, as part of the covert investigation that had been going on for several months. The two rogue LAPD officers took the bait. The investigators, with the cooperation of the shop owner, broke a door window at a video shop so that it appeared a burglary had occurred. The suspect officers were then dispatched to investigate the burglary. The rogue officers, Jack Myers and Ron Venegas, stole a bunch of videotapes and some other items. Moments afterward, while in their patrol car and in uniform, they were stopped and arrested.

RESULT OF THE HOLLYWOOD BURGLARY SCANDAL

Before the investigation was over, several additional officers were charged and ultimately terminated, along with Myers and Venegas, for receiving items they knew were stolen by the two police burglars and for also taking items from premises during investigations.

Two of the terminated men were sergeants. The charges against them included really troublesome behaviors, although I recall some charges were later dropped and one (or both) of the supervisors received retirement benefits.

One of the police burglars, Jack Myers, was killed in a single-car traffic accident after having been relieved of duty, but while the investigation was still progressing. While there was speculation that he was murdered to keep him from implicating other officers, there was no indication that his death was anything other than a tragic accident.

BURNED BY THE MEDIA IN HOLLYWOOD

I have always tried to be good to the media and facilitate their news-gathering (within appropriate boundaries), and for the most part my experiences have been very positive.

One noteworthy exception occurred in the case of a reporter named Cynthia Smith (pseudonym). On the day the two Hollywood officers were arrested for on-duty burglaries, she was among the reporters who descended on the station and asked for my interview. As with the other reporters, I tried to be helpful. As it was a pretty tough day for me, I consented to be interviewed but asked that it not be live, and that I be given the opportunity to review the tape and do it over if I wasn't happy with the first take. My request was not unreasonable. The news truck was full of monitors where this could easily have been done.

Although she consented, when she started the interview she indicated it was "live from Hollywood Station!" She obviously was not the least bit interested in anyone or anything other than herself, and betrayed my trust. I never forgot her breach of trust and unprofessionalism, and never dealt with her again. While she will never know what she missed, her actions on that day clearly resulted in later stories she never had the opportunity to report on. I believe I had a reputation for going "that extra mile" with news folks who I respected, and it's a shame that her actions prevented her from falling into that category.

A Painful and Humiliating Transfer

There were a lot of painful consequences stemming from the Hollywood burglary scandal. Before the investigation was over, several additional officers and supervisors were implicated and ultimately terminated, primarily for receiving things they knew (or should have known) were stolen.

Appropriately, the scandal also caused the department to take a much closer look at the overall environment that enabled the place to become a problem command, as well as all the things over the years that had contributed to the situation. My boss, a good fellow but someone who did not give adequate attention to his responsibilities, was forced into retirement.

I mistakenly believed, based on vibes I had been getting, that I would be promoted to the position of captain III and would take his place as the area commanding officer.

To the contrary—a couple of months later I got a call in the evening from Deputy Chief Dan Sullivan, who apologetically told me that the next day's *Los Angeles Times* would have a lead story about the problems at Hollywood and would indicate I was being transferred as part of a "management shake-up!" A friend, Captain Smitson, was being made the area commander and I was being transferred to West Los Angeles in a lateral move as the patrol captain. The decision was made above Chief Sullivan's level, most likely by Assistant Chief Harvey, who was the director of the Officer of Operations. I was crushed, and terribly embarrassed about this situation.

During the course of the devastating phone conversation with Deputy Chief Sullivan, I mentioned that I had a fairly important meeting the following morning with other command officers. However, I felt too humiliated to even attend. The chief said he understood completely, and told me not to worry about attending the meeting. He was very gracious and, again, apologetic about the transfer.

After our conversation, I sat and stewed over the matter for a few minutes. Then I decided I'd be damned if I was going go put my tail between my legs and crawl into a corner and feel sorry for myself. I called Chief Sullivan back and told him I would attend the meeting after all, that I would be the first to arrive and the last to leave the meeting, and that I was not going to turn to shit just because things were going poorly for me. Sullivan thanked me for my position and understanding.

LETTER FROM CAPTAIN BUSHEY
TO CHIEF GATES

Reading about my transfer in the *Los Angeles Times* was pretty tough, though I'll must say I wasn't treated harshly and there was no inference that I had performed poorly or been part of the problem. In fact, I think the reporter probably went out of his way to avoid any negative inference about me.

Still, it was pretty painful. I felt the need to communicate directly with Chief Gates on this issue. So I wrote him a personal letter that I had delivered directly to his office by one of my sergeants. In it, I said I felt that I had worked hard and effectively, and that the many command problems I'd inherited were not easily solved. I recall two specific statements very clearly. In one, I suggested that "the grim reaper" had struck (the burglaries, etc.) before my efforts had begun to pay off. In the second I told him that, despite the pain I was experiencing, my commitment to my responsibilities and to the Los Angeles Police Department remained as strong as ever, and that I would do the best job possible, wherever I was assigned.

Later in the day, Chief Gates called me personally, and was what I would call "guardedly gracious." He somewhat apologized for my transfer, suggesting that it would be better for my career and that there were challenges in West Los Angeles that needed to be addressed, etc. He minced his words and said nothing I actually found comforting.

"Dad, There's a Blonde in the Front Room!"
(Defining Experience)

In terms of low points in one's professional life, this was certainly one of mine. On the second evening after my transfer, Jake came into the bedroom where I was reading and told me "there's a blonde lady in the front room who would like to talk to you."

She turned out to be another reporter from the *Los Angeles Times*, a very nice lady and an objective reporter whose name was Claire Spiegel. Despite her goodwill and charm, it represented just more pain and more public focus about my transfer.

Nevertheless, shortly after she left I experienced a powerful realization that I refer to as one of my "defining experiences"—something that had a tremendous impact on me and the way I look at things. I was standing next to the window in my bedroom, looking out at the silhouette of downtown Los Angeles and believing my career was over, when some internal voice made it clear to me that from that moment forward I should derive my greatest satisfaction from just knowing I had done the best job I could!

It was a very powerful and wonderful moment, during which I truly accepted the reality that sometimes you do everything you can, but things sometimes don't work out, and that reality and politics are often strong and uncontrollable factors. This continues to be among the key considerations in my life, and is something I often share with others.

Letter from Chief Gates About My Transfer

Father Mort Ward, an Episcopal priest, was among my many friends who were indignant over my transfer and who felt I had not been treated fairly. Without my knowledge, Mort sent a personal letter of protest to Chief Gates, in which he expressed his consternation. Mort got a nice letter back from Gates that explained I had done a good job. But the chief felt, though it was unfair to me, that he needed to put a whole new management team in place, as a signal to the community that the department was truly addressing the many problems within that command.

I was pleased to see the letter, and wished the chief had called me after the transfer and told me the same things personally. Realistically, such a call might have been premature, pending the completion of a command review, especially considering the ultimate findings that were overall complimentary of my performance.

Good question. Maybe yes and maybe no. Among my greatest detractors was Assistant Chief Harvey. Perhaps he should have given more consideration to the fact that the burglaries had been occurring for years before I went to Hollywood as the second-in-command, and that it was he who had permitted the area commanding officer to long remain in that position despite reservations about his performance.

Being candid about my performance, and notwithstanding the fact that I worked my tail off, I had quite a bit of room to grow in the development of my command leadership skills, especially in the area of delegation. By failing to delegate and mentor appropriately, I allowed myself to be overwhelmed and consumed with more than I could handle.

Despite my shortcomings, I was probably among the strongest patrol captains, but clearly in one of the most difficult and challenging command assignments. If the situation were to be repeated and I had my way, based on what I know today, my preference would be to have remained as the patrol captain and be mentored by a strong new area commanding officer.

WEST LOS ANGELES PATROL DIVISION

In April 1982, after just under a year and a half at Hollywood, I was reassigned as the commanding officer of the West Los Angeles Patrol Division. While not one of the department's "hot" divisions, it was among the largest and most important. The station was located at 1663 Butler Avenue. It took in most of the "West Side" of Los Angeles and included West Los Angeles, Westwood, Brentwood, Bel Air, Pacific Palisades and Century City. As I recall, the total strength of the entire West Los Angeles Area, including both the patrol and detective divisions, was approximately 250 persons.

IMMEDIATE AND LONG-TERM ACTING AREA COMMANDING OFFICER

For a good portion of my tour at West Los Angeles Division, where I was the patrol commanding officer, I actually served as the acting area commanding officer. It was a captain III billet.

When I got there, the area commanding officer, Jerry Bova, went off on vacation for several weeks and was then given a new assignment.

Bova was replaced by Bob Jones, whose arrival was delayed by a couple of months because of built-up vacation time. Then Jones retired and used up a bunch of vacation time before being replaced, and the replacement, John Wilbanks, also had much vacation time to "burn" before actually starting his duties. I spent a good portion of the year and a half I was assigned to this division as the "top cop" (Area Commanding Officer) for West Los Angeles.

Uncomfortable in the Midst of Wealth

I look back on my tenure as commanding officer of the West Los Angeles Patrol Division with pride and fond thoughts. But it was somewhat awkward to be assigned there. First, it was a long drive from my home in Azusa. In fact, during busy commute times, I could never make the drive to or from work without at least one "pit stop!" As someone who always tried to respond to critical after-hours situations, I also did a great deal of driving.

The other awkward situation probably arose because of a certain degree of insecurity on my part. I felt uncomfortable in my daily interactions with people who were far more prosperous than me! I didn't resent the wealth of others, but perhaps felt just a bit of envy. This insecurity was no doubt also influenced by the fact that I was still in the early stages of a marital separation that was going to result in a divorce, that my house was on the market, that it would not sell unless I chose to almost give it away, and that I was struggling a bit to make ends meet. (I ultimately retained the house when I bought out my former wife.)

There was, however, a related advantage to all of the prosperity in West Los Angeles: there were many great receptions after work where the heavy hors d'oeuvres substituted for dinner!

Intelligence Lieutenant: "You Don't Have a Need to Know!"

Not long after my assignment as commanding officer of the West Los Angeles Patrol Division, I found myself as the field commander for the visit of President Ronald Reagan to Los Angeles. Specifically, my area of concern would be the president's activities in and around the Century Plaza Hotel, where he was staying.

A massive demonstration was planned for the afternoon before the president departed. The several thousand demonstrators' stated intention was to march onto and disrupt the hotel. While the Secret Service was deployed in immediate proximity to the president, I was responsible for keeping those several thousand potentially-hostile people away from him. My command post was in an upper hotel room, where I could see most of what was occurring. A number of persons, including Lieutenant J. I. Shillman (pseudonym) from the Public Disorder Intelligence Division (PDID), were part of my command post cadre. The organization leading the demonstration was one that the Police Department already had under active investigation, and its leaders had been previously identified.

At one point I became concerned that the demonstration's leadership might attempt to incite violence. Because of my concerns, I turned to Shillman and asked him to tell me about the backgrounds and previous actions of those leading the demonstration. As someone who had previously been undercover in organizations that disrupted such events, I knew the value of this information, and that it was available. But he refused to share the information he possessed, saying I did not have authorization or a need to know!

I replied that I was a captain in the Los Angeles Police Department, that I was the field commander, that I was burdened with the responsibility of protecting the president of the United States, that I was currently at that moment dealing with a potential threat to the president of the United States, and I needed the information! He still refused! I told him that having an Intelligence Division and gathering information is useless, unless we get it when we need it—and I was hard-pressed to think of a more worthy need than to aid in protecting the president of the United States!

My comments fell on deaf ears. What an idiot! I promptly expressed my concerns up the chain of command; others expressed concern as well, and stated the problem would be fixed. I don't know if Shillman was reprimanded or not over this situation. Nevertheless, I somehow doubt he ceased his troublesome behavior, as people don't really change much once set in their ways.

It was an era when PDID wasn't effective in evaluating its own performance. A couple of years later, because of concerns over weak leadership and a command that was potentially out of control, a board of inquiry was convened to explore the actions of that division. As one who had once been assigned there, but was now a command officer, I was invited. I welcomed the opportunity to share my perspective, and hope my testimony was of value.

Long-retired Assistant Chief Wesley Harvey was not one of my supporters. A number of years earlier, when I'd been a sergeant competing to be a lieutenant, Harvey was a commander in my chain of command and had a favorable opinion of me. In the wake of the Hollywood burglary scandal, however, Chief Harvey lost confidence in and did not think very well of me. He most certainly played a role in my transfer out of Hollywood Division and into West Los Angeles Division.

Shortly after arriving at West Los Angeles Division, I found myself the field commander of all of the LAPD forces deployed in support of then-President Ronald Reagan's visit to Century City. My command post was on an upper floor suite of the Century Plaza Hotel. Quite frankly, I knew my stuff and did a fine job as field commander.

My boss at the time was Deputy Chief Dan Sullivan, who was always pretty much a supporter and felt that I'd got a raw deal in being transferred from Hollywood to West Los Angeles. His boss was Chief Harvey, and Dan was well aware that Harvey was not among my supporters (to say the least). There were a lot of moving parts to the command post, and my performance was superb. At the end of the operation, Chief Sullivan came up to me and said, "I wish Chief Harvey had been here to see your performance!" I appreciated his comment, because I was at a point in my career where bad news had been coming more frequently than good news. I guess one of the things I can say in my defense is that I was not the only person Harvey didn't care for, and was in good company with an awful lot of other people.

It is very typical for high-ranking LAPD people to have well-attended retirement functions. In the case of Wes Harvey, I'm not sure it would have been very well attended. This struck me as sad, as I was among the folks who once held a very high opinion of him, and was saddened to have been among those who went sideways with him.

Not too long after this episode, Assistant Chief Wes Harvey retired from the police department. He was apparently an unhappy person, and his departure seemed to be on the spur of the moment. There was no goodbye and no fanfare; he was just gone. To my knowledge, he has chosen not to participate in various LAPD retired functions and associations, and to this day, almost 30 years later, he apparently remains distant from his former colleagues whenever they run into him. It is behavior that those who worked hard for him and served him well must certainly find disappointing.

As the acting area commanding officer, I was in charge of the West L.A. Vice Unit, among other entities. We ran a joint investigation with the Administrative Vice Division that was unbelievable.

A noted madam, Alice Jones (pseudonym), was active in supplying prosperous men with pretty gals. One of our investigations resulted in information that she had put together a chartered flight of blonde prostitutes for a weeklong trip and visit to the Middle East, where wealthy Arab men were able to overdose on pretty blonde women. This was quite a contrast to my vice operator days, when all the "fallen" women I encountered were truly pathetic creatures.

Sleazy Cop, Phony Nanny, and Stolen Property

While a captain at West LA, I ran into a very troubling situation. Initially I didn't know how to address it, or even where to start.

I had an officer who cheated on his wife with a woman who later turned out to be a parolee. He even took the woman home to his wife to be the nanny for his children! After a while, he took the phony "nanny" to one of the businesses on his beat and urged the owner to give his "relative" a job.

It came to a head one day when his wife found out the gal was giving her attention to more than just the kids, and the businessman learned that the officer's "relative" had been stealing him blind.

When I walked into the station I was apprised of the situation, and that the wife had a gun and was on her way to the station to kill her police officer husband! Also, the businessman had complained to the local chamber of commerce and inquired about how to file a claim for the stolen property with the city attorney, declaring that the officer was responsible. At least three calls on this issue were waiting for me as I walked in the door!

I went across the street to West Bureau to discuss the issue with Deputy Chief Ron Frankel, a great boss and a dear friend. I told him I really needed some advice on this one. He proceeded to dissect the situation in a way that made clear the courses of action that needed to be taken. I was impressed and appreciative, and told Ron it was obvious to me why he was a deputy chief. He laughed, and said something I will never forget: "I'm not smart, just old. I've been around so long that I've made every mistake imaginable, and have stumbled across the right answers through the process of elimination!"

Ron was (and is!) a very wise man. His expression is something I have consistently repeated to others in my command activities and leadership teachings.

Insubordinate to an Assistant Chief

My ill-will with the commanding officer of Personnel Division, who I will just refer to as "Bill," got pretty heated in the early part of 1983. I was very unhappy with several officers who claimed to be disabled due to on-duty injuries, and displeased with what I perceived to be a lack of adequate effort on the part of Personnel Division to deal with the officers involved.

I was fortunate to recruit a retired businessman with significant human resources experience, as a "specialist reserve police officer." I wanted him to investigate the bogus claims and create documentation that countered the claims that were being made. The retired businessman, "Marshall," did a great job.

But the captain of personnel truly resented my actions. Bill had the background unit dig deeper into Marshall's past than was done when he became a specialist reserve, and found that Marshall had been disbarred as an attorney in the early 1960s for co-mingling clients' funds with his own, a fact I was not aware of. Despite my fondness for Marshall and appreciation for all he had done, I had to concur that the disbarment was tanamount to a felony conviction. Thus, he was not suitable to continue as a reserve officer, even in the "specialist" category that was reserved for specific non-enforcement duties in which an individual had expertise.

When Bill called, he gleefully directed me to immediately terminate Marshall, a directive he had the right to order because of his status as the head of personnel. However, I had a problem: Marshall was then in Cedars-Sinai Hospital in the final stage of dying of cancer, and I was not about to fire a man on his deathbed. I made that clear to Bill. Bill made it equally clear that he was ordering me to immediately advise Marshall that he was terminated, and to retrieve the department's identification card (specialist reserve officers do not carry badges). I asked for Bill's understanding, and committed to retrieving the card as soon as Marshall passed, which was imminent. But that stubborn fellow captain reiterated his directive. I just plain refused to fire a dying man.

A short time later I got a call from Assistant Chief Dotson, who was Bill's boss, and was given the order to go to the hospital, fire Marshall, and retrieve his ID card. While cordial, I told the chief I couldn't do that, and explained why. Dotson quizzed me on the severity of Marshall's condition. I'm confident that Bill told him it was a sham and I just did not want to fire my friend. I don't know if Dotson accepted what I said, or just didn't want to get in a battle over the issue. He mumbled something about getting the card as soon as I could, and hung up. Within a week Marshall was dead, and I attended the services of my good friend. While getting the ID card from his widow I made no mention of the termination, only that I was retrieving the department's property per protocol.

My Good Pal—Ted Knight

Ted Knight was a well-known TV personality who came across as a fun and decent man. He lived in Pacific Palisades and I was the captain over that portion of the city. I met him at several functions, and came to know him as a friend. He was a great fellow whose off-camera persona was exactly how he appeared before the cameras. Ted was just a really nice person who was an absolute delight to spend time with, and a privilege to be able to call a friend. Unlike far too many of today's entertainment personalities, there was nothing pretentious or phony about this wonderful man. I was saddened at his passing several years ago.

Art Isabelle Plays "Verbal Chicken" in Pacific Palisades

This situation has to be at the top of the list of strange behavior. Since the late 1970s I had been a part-time instructor at Citrus College (discussed in a later chapter), and each semester I usually had either a transvestite or transsexual among my many guest speakers. These folks were sent on my request from an outfit known as CHIC (Cross-dressers Homosapien Intersocial Club). One of the cross-dressers who repeatedly came to my classes was a wealthy financial guru from Pacific Palisades. He would drive all the way to Glendora, rent a room, get all dolled up, then make his appearance in my class. He was good at what he did, and was popular with the students who interacted with him.

For his sixtieth birthday, he strongly encouraged me to attend a party at his home. Since I figured I owed him for all his trips to the school on my behalf, I agreed to attend. He lived in a massive house in a very high-end neighborhood, with actor Chevy Chase as one of his neighbors. I was one of about fifty persons at his party, which included many of his family members and business associates.

After dinner he asked all his guests to assemble at the bottom of a massive circular stairway, while he stood several steps above the rest

398

of us. He then announced that he would call out names and ask those called to describe how they met him and the nature of their interactions with him. I was certain I wouldn't be called on, because the only way I knew him was as "Rita," dressed in frilly feminine attire.

I was wrong—I was the first person he called on to step up and provide the information he'd requested! Holy shit! What was I to say? And what was this guy doing? It struck me as almost tantamount to playing "Russian Roulette" with his guests. Did he want me to "out him?" If so, he didn't get his wish. I said that I met him during the course of my duties as commanding officer of the West Los Angeles Police Division, immediately recognized extraordinary talents and an ability to share unique perspectives with others, and because of those attributes I invited and remained grateful for his many appearances as a guest speaker at the college where I taught. Glad I am good at extemporaneous speaking!

He beamed, and thanked me for my kind words; if it was a form of Russian roulette, he hit an empty cylinder with me. Interestingly, he invited his teenage daughter to come to one of his presentations as "Rita," which she did. That struck me as a little too much information for a unique father to share with a teenage daughter.

CAPTAIN BUSHEY AND SUSAN ANTON

What a great prank on me! One morning as I entered my outer office, my adjutant, Sergeant Wally Graves, informed me that "the boys" had been considering my social life as a bachelor. They had decided I was an okay guy, but that I needed a tall, good-looking blonde to set me straight in life. As the conversation progressed, Wally said that they had even identified such a woman for me: actress Susan Anton. I don't recall my response, but I certainly didn't argue with the selection, as Susan Anton was (and probably still is) a beautiful lady.

Wally said the boys had actually acquired Susan Anton for me—and that she was attired in a negligee and waiting for me in my office! I entered my office and there she was, the real Susan Anton, in the flesh!

She had been detained for drunk driving, being distraught following a disagreement with another person, who if I recall accurately was fellow actor Dudley Moore. As she had the appearance of a person who had been drinking and was very upset, she was being detained in my office. It was private, and the officers were being sensitive to her situation.

I merely nodded and backed out of my office. She was later released. Cops seldom miss the opportunity to have some fun with one another, and this was a great example of it.

―――

COMMUNICATIONS DIVISION

In October 1983, after approximately a year and a half at West Los Angeles, I took over as the commanding officer of the Communications Division. I took over the same week the division was physically moved from its much smaller and antiquated spaces in Parker Center to the new communications center, located on the fourth sub-level of City Hall East.

At that time there were approximately 500 persons assigned to the division, the majority being in the newly-created job classification of "police service representative." It was the new job description for police dispatchers.

There were also approximately 125 sworn personnel serving in the division, as well.

CHIEF GATES SAID THAT BUSHEY HAS A "CB" LICENSE!

Shortly after taking over Communications Division, I was having a chat with my boss, mentor and good friend, Commander Larry Binkley. He had obviously supported me for the promotion and assignment. Larry said that Chief Daryl Gates concurred, and felt that I was the right person for the job because "Bushey has a CB License!"

Imagine, placing a forty-million-dollar command and control project, with roughly five hundred personnel, in the hands of a person because he has a license to operate a low-power citizen band radio! Actually, I didn't have a CB license. But it was known that I had an amateur ("ham") radio license, and even had a ham radio in my assigned take-home car.

I think history will reveal that I did a pretty decent job in the new assignment. If so, my performance was based on many qualities beyond merely having an amateur radio license.

MANAGING 400 MENSTRUAL CYCLES

I detested a certain comment and always asked others not to make it, as it was inappropriate and offensive. As the commanding officer of communications division, where roughly eighty percent of my approximately 500 subordinates were women, it was not unusual for someone to refer to me, or introduce me, as the captain who had to deal with several hundred menstrual cycles a month. It was always the women who made this comment!

I used to cringe every time I heard it, as it was far from politically correct. It also had the potential to offend someone, although I don't think anyone could credibly argue that this natural occurrence wasn't an occasional factor in the behavior of some of my more challenging employees!

Having this many female subordinates, and all the drama that went with it, was truly a unique experience—not good or bad, right or wrong, strong or weak, but a unique experience. In hindsight, the skills that were required and the challenges I encountered were greater than any assignment I had before or since the interesting years I spent as the commanding officer of Communications Division.

Millie, Tamales, and the New Captain

The pettiness and foolishness of troublesome females became very obvious shortly after my assumption of command of the Communications Division.

Rosa, the mother of Bobby and Danny, the two little boys who became my unofficial little brothers from Rampart Division, had made a gigantic pot of homemade tamales, dozens of them, for me to give to the personnel of the division. I carried the large pot across the dispatch floor to the elevator, then down to the break room, and put them out for my employees to enjoy.

One of the police service representatives, Millie Gilders (pseudonym), advised me that she wanted to make a disciplinary complaint against me for carrying food onto the dispatch floor! It turned out she had been counseled by a supervisor for eating food at her position, and if she got in trouble then I should get in trouble, too!

Petty is too charitable a word to describe her actions. I advised her that I had carefully evaluated the matter and determined that transporting the tamales across the floor was the most appropriate course of action in that instance. I decided to forgive myself, and to allow my employees to enjoy the tamales! In my four and one-half years in this command, I witnessed similar foolishness on a fairly regular basis.

There was no shortage of drama in Communications Division! About the worst I can remember involved a motorcycle officer named Jack Elliott (pseudonym), who was married to a police service representative named Judy. Jack also was romantically involved with a another police service representative, whose name was Linda.

Jack left and divorced Judy for Linda, and it became a pretty nasty affair. Both ladies were on the day shift, as they both had considerable seniority and it was not in my ability to transfer either or both of them to other shifts. They had their own sets of friends. Not only were these two bitter enemies, but their friends divided into camps and they became bitter enemies, as well.

One day Jack took the easy way out: he was killed in an on-duty motorcycle accident! It turns out that he may have been in the process of leaving Linda and going back to Judy (depends on whose version you care to believe), but the potential rearrangement was not consummated prior to his untimely and tragic death.

Now things really got nasty! I cannot even tell you how many hours I spent talking to these two ladies, individually of course, dealing with the fallout from all that had occurred. To this day, each of the women insists that she is the legitimate grieving widow of Jack, and both participate in memorial activities as the wife of an officer who died in the line of duty. I'm fond of saying that when my time comes I don't know whether I'm going north or south—but the first thing I'm going to do is look for Jack and kick his ass for leaving me with the mess he created!

MY "RED LIGHT" OBSESSION

There was a red light posted conspicuously in the communications center. When the red light was on, it indicated there were 911 calls that had not yet been answered.

It's fair to say that I was obsessed with this red light. All I could think about was the calls that hadn't yet been answered might well have involved a house on fire with someone trapped inside, a baby not breathing, a violent crime in progress, or some other type of immediate emergency situation. Most of the personnel in the dispatch center were pretty cavalier about that red light, and didn't worry too much about it because they had been dealing with it for many years. To me it was a very big thing, and my obsession with keeping that red light out as much as possible drove a great many of my actions.

I had an idea that worked out very well, and to this day it exists as one of the procedures in Communications Division.

When the new dispatch center was developed, we had one heck of a problem obtaining equipment capable of managing incoming calls, and being able to route them where we wanted them to go in the dispatch center. Once we had the ability to route calls to the positions we chose, we still had a big problem. All incoming calls would go into a single queue, and as operators became available the next incoming call would go to that queue. I had a real problem with it, because it wasn't unusual to have a lot of unanswered calls in the queue, some of which were unquestionably emergency calls. By just doing the math, I knew we didn't have enough operators to immediately handle each incoming call.

Accordingly, I came up with the idea of developing a two-tier system, by which every call would go to a small group of operators. They would immediately screen each call to determine whether or not it was an emergency, immediately handle those that were emergencies, and transfer the others into a queue to be handled on a non-emergency basis.

My vision was that the majority of calls, even though they came in on a 911 line, were actually of a non-emergency nature. These calls could be quickly passed through the first tier (emergency calls only), then be answered by the next available operator in the second tier (for calls that had been screened and were determined to be of non-emergency nature).

I faced enormous criticism from the senior police service representatives, who insisted the workload on the second tier would be greatly increased, and that the people on the first year would have little to do other than quickly screening and transferring calls.

Had it been a democracy, it would have been one vote for (mine) and about thirty against. But I felt very strongly about the modification, stuck to my guns and had the system modified to accomplish the two-tier system. It worked great! We still had some emergency calls that experienced delays in answering, but the delay was much less than it had been previously. Ever since then, the department has been quickly screening all incoming calls, immediately handling those that are emergencies, and sending those determined to be nonemergency to the second tier. I am proud of having developed this efficient system.

I continue to be proud of another procedure that I developed, which also continues to be used to this day.

For a crime in progress with a suspect's description, it generally takes somewhere around two or three minutes for the operator to get all of the information from the caller and then put the broadcast out over the frequency. This is a real problem, because a suspect who is departing the scene, even if driving under the speed limit, can travel a good distance in a minute or two.

I was of the belief that a tremendous number of suspects were not captured, at least in part, because of the time it took to get the information from the caller and put that information out over the air. Accordingly, I developed (again with great opposition from the senior police service representatives, and a number of the nonsupervisory personnel as well) the "hot shot" broadcast procedure.

When a caller came on the line to report a crime in progress (or one that had just been committed), our new procedure had the operator quickly get very basic information, put the caller on hold, activate the radio transmitter and put out a call to all units that a robbery was in progress (or whatever the incident was) at a particular location, adding the vehicle description and direction of travel if available. The operator would then go back to the caller for the detailed information.

I really liked this system. It enabled the units to be immediately notified that a crime was occurring so they could start in that direction, while allowing the operator to continue gathering additional information such as a detailed description of the suspects. The procedure remains applicable to this day, but I'm saddened it may not be used to the extent that it should be. Apparently, the little bit of extra effort required is a bit too much for some dispatchers.

CHAT WITH ASSISTANT CHIEF IANNONE
ABOUT THE BURGLARY SCANDAL

In 1984, not long after my assignment to Communications Division, I competed in the promotional process for the rank of commander. I know I did well on the written portion. But I got a horrible score on the oral interview portion of the examination, conducted by the three assistant chiefs.

As it was the promotional ritual on the LAPD at that time, afterward I made appointments to talk to those who had sat on my 1984 oral interview for commander, to see how I could have improved, etc.

When I sat down with Assistant Chief Marvin Iannone, it was a pleasant meeting. But he got right to the heart of my lousy grade: I'd been the captain at Hollywood when the burglary scandal went down. I quickly but politely reminded him that he was the chief of that bureau for a good portion of the seven years that the two principals, Myers and Venegas, were committing the burglaries. I had only been there about five months when it was learned the thefts were occurring!

He responded that, had he been there a little longer, he probably would have been able to detect and deal with the situation. I responded that if I had been there sooner, I believe I too would have been able to detect and deal with the situation! To his credit, he said that he believed I probably would have been able to, and that perhaps my low score was unfair. Chief Iannone told me straight-out that he would give me a much better score the next time I took an oral interview for commander. He was true to his word, when a couple of years later I received a score from him in the mid-90s. Unfortunately, because the number of commander billets had been reduced from 24 to 17, there were no promotions made during the entire life of the next two or three commander lists (all of which I did well on).

During the 1984 oral examination for commander, Assistant Chiefs Wes Harvey and Marvin Iannone each gave me the identical score of 79, which is the worst score I ever received, before or since. Assistant Chief Robert Vernon gave me (if I recall correctly) a score of 91, which was respectable given my relative lack of seniority as a captain. While the candidates are not supposed to know who gave each individual score, only the total, I could see each score and recognized the initials when I went to the Personnel Department for the written feedback review after the scores were posted.

CHIEF GATES STOMPS ON MY STAR!

Despite my lousy written scores from two of the three assistant chiefs who sat on my oral examinations for commander, I still got an overall high score and came out number 5 on the list of eligibles. This was because I really did well on the written examination. This overall score on the list was very respectable and, under most circumstances, would have enabled my promotion during the two-year life of the eligibility list. However, in a budget-cutting move, the city's chief administrative office (CAO) recommended reducing the number of commander positions from twenty-four to seventeen. If adopted, it would have put me twelve positions away from promoting versus five positions away. If adopted, it would mean no promotions for several years, as the department would have to attrite down to the recommended number.

Most of us felt, I believe accurately, that Chief Gates could have done some wheeling and dealing to retain at least some if not all of the commander positions that were recommended for elimination. However, when Gates went before the council he ranted and raved about how screwed-up the recommendation was, then threw the CAO's report on the floor and stomped on it. I just knew that he was stomping my promotion and others right into the ground. I was correct. His little temper tantrum was not well received by the council or the mayor, and all seventeen positions were eliminated.

Jogging in Elysian Park

Throughout my LAPD career, I often jogged in Elysian Park. Nearby, the Police Academy was a great place to shower and get a bite after a run.

As both a sergeant and lieutenant I had spurts of a running routine, but it really got into high gear when I took over as commanding officer of the Communications Division. From that assignment through my retirement, I typically ran at the Academy-Elysian Park at noontime. I had a few regular running partners from time to time, including Commander Tom Windham (who went on to be the chief of police in Fort Worth and died of cancer while in office) and Dr. Nels Klyver (forced out as the head of Behavioral Science by Bernard Parks). But for the most part I ran by myself. These were good times in terms of fitness, eating healthy, and enjoying my noon break.

Promoted to Captain III—A Nice Surprise

In late 1984, I got a surprise promotion to captain III and also a big pay increase.

As the commanding officer of the West Los Angeles patrol division, I held the civil service rank of captain and the pay grade of captain I. When I transferred to the Communications Division, which was a specialized division, I was upgraded to captain II. In communications, I was given additional responsibility as program manager of the Emergency Command Control and Communication System (ECCCS). Ultimately I was made the LAPD representative on Capitol Hill, primarily in pursuit of additional radio spectrum. Although there had been talk about upgrading me to captain III, I didn't sense it was of a serious nature then, but something that would be nice at some future time.

It happened that my immediate supervisor and very good friend and supporter, Commander Larry Binkley, and my bureau commanding officer, Deputy Chief Clyde Cronkite, had taken the matter seriously and processed a request through the office of the city administrative officer for my promotion to the top level of captain. I was sitting at my desk one day when the new transfer came out, and read that I was now a captain III. Obviously, I felt very pleased. It hadn't been that long before that I thought my career was at a dead-end because of the Hollywood burglary scandal, but it turned out that I made captain III before any of my contemporaries. I took a lot of satisfaction in that promotion.

Tell the Superintendent to Keep the Gun!

One of the young police officers assigned to Communications Division went home to Chicago on his vacation. He took his service revolver with him, and made the mistake of having it in his possession when his visited his parents in a city housing project. Because of frequent violence, the Chicago Police Department paid a great deal of attention to visitors. Their attention resulted in the detention of my young officer and confiscation of his LAPD weapon. Fortunately, he wasn't also arrested.

On learning what had occurred, I contacted the Chicago precinct captain to coordinate return of the firearm. He was nice, but said the matter had to be handled through the Office of the Superintendent. I ultimately was put in contact with a deputy superintendent who told me that Chief Gates would have to personally contact the superintendent (their title for police chief) to get the gun back.

I thought this request by Chicago's top cop was petty and unnecessary, and nothing more than a desire to see Chief Gates eat some crow. I diplomatically stated my feelings to the deputy superintendent, who somewhat smugly said that it would have to occur for the gun to be returned. I spoke personally to Chief Gates, who immediately agreed with my assessment of the situation. He told me to tell the cops in Chicago to keep the gun.

When I called the deputy superintendent to convey Chief Gates' message, he immediately exclaimed that the superintendent was still waiting for the call from Chief Gates. I replied that it would be a long wait, that Gates had no intention of calling the superintendent, and for them to just keep the gun! I really enjoyed that phone call!

There was growing anger and indignation among some women in communications over what was perceived as the intentional spreading of human waste throughout one of the women's bathrooms. While I never visited the "scene of the crimes," I guess they were nasty and disgusting.

These horrific incidents would occur every week or so. The matter actually went on for over a month, with the efforts to identify the suspects being referred to by the supervisors as the "poopatrator investigation." It was obviously a pretty big deal among some of our employees.

Eventually, the suspect was determined to be a very nice and embarrassed woman, who had a serious problem with spontaneous aggressive bowels. Why the biological waste was spread over as many places in the bathroom as described was something I did not know, and did not care to know. I am unaware what was worked out with the woman to prevent re-occurrences, but to my knowledge the troublesome incidents stopped.

Robber Picks the Wrong Victim— an Armed Police Dispatcher

One morning I received a call that one of my employees had been in an off-duty shooting and killed a robbery suspect. I received a number of these calls over the years. But this one was different—the employee was a female police service representative who was illegally carrying a concealed weapon!

I immediately responded to the scene at the home of my employee, Toni Gomez (pseudonym). She was there and was doing well, but the dead suspect on her porch wasn't. It was pretty cut-and-dried: she arrived home from work and was standing on her porch in the process of entering her home, when the suspect assaulted and tried to rob her of her purse. During the struggle she produced a loaded pistol and killed the suspect.

It looked good to me, and I was proud of her. The potential glitch was the possibility of major discipline for illegally carrying a concealed firearm. Although she was not likely to be prosecuted due to an inability to criminally prove that she'd carried the firearm off her property, it was clear she had been carrying, and it could pretty easily be determined administratively.

My boss and friend, Commander Larry Binkley, came up with a great idea that I immediately embraced: give her a quick written admonishment (the lowest form of formal discipline), which would preclude any further discipline under the double jeopardy rule, if some hue and cry ever developed for harsher punishment. There were never any further consequences, but one less criminal was prowling the streets in Los Angeles.

Tragic Loss of the Bar-Arm Control Hold

Many things have occurred that harmed the Los Angeles Police Department, but the loss of the ability of officers to used the bar-arm control hold, except as a last resort where deadly force is justified, is close to the top of that harmful list. It was a great way to immediately get control of an unruly suspect—a push on the shoulder, spin him around, and bam! the suspect was on the ground.

Without exaggeration, I am sure that I used this control hold several hundred times as a policeman, sergeant, and even as a lieutenant. Like just about everyone else, in my case there never once was a situation where subsequent medical treatment was required; people simply lacked the ability to continue to struggle. The beginning of the end occurred with the deaths of several suspects who were impervious to pain and continued to struggle. Adding to the mix were the deaths of a few folks who had greatly weakened systems due to sickle-cell anemia.

At one of Chief Gates' presentations in support of retaining this control hold, he used the word "normal" to describe the thousands of persons who had been subjected to the bar-arm control hold over the years without medical complications. But the racists and opponents immediately turned it into a racial matter by characterizing the matter as being between "blacks" and "normals"! Naturally, there were lawsuits brought by attorneys on behalf of the very few persons who, because of their unique medical conditions, died when the bar-arm was used on them. The Police Commission sided with the chief in the belief that the bar-arm control hold was necessary as a tool in the continuum of force options. But in a very rare move, the city council yielded to political pressure by special interest groups, overrode the commission, and directed that the police department could only use the bar-arm control hold in situations that merit deadly force.

In the battle to retain the bar-arm, the chief strongly urged the commission and the council to recognize that the bar-arm was the only realistically effective control hold option between very light and very heavy use of force. While officers were trained in hand and wrist locks, realistically they were impractical and useless most of the time. Gates predicted, and history validated his prediction, that the disuse of the bar-arm would necessarily result in greatly expanded use of the baton, including broken bones and injuries that would not have occurred with quick and easy application of the bar-arm control hold.

In subsequent years, a large percentage of use of force incidents involving the baton, chemical spray, and the taser would not have been necessary had the department not lost its ability to use that truly effective and overall safe technique, except for situations where deadly force was justified. There is no doubt in my mind—absolutely no doubt—that the Rodney King scandal would never have occurred, had the department not lost the ability to use the bar-arm control hold in these situations. Rodney King could have been brought under control with very little fanfare by application of this effective tactic.

The Truth Fell to the Cutting Room Floor!

This was among the many lessons I learned about the media. Channel 5 television did a series of reports on the Los Angeles Police Department. Among the statements made was that police officers who were transferred into Communication Division were often of a mediocre nature. This was absolutely untrue!

Due to equipment limitations, we had to bring about 100 police officers into the Communications Division so that somebody would always be available to answer emergency calls. At that time (mid-1980s) we were experiencing problems with inadequate switching equipment and a very high attrition rate of civilian police service representatives (dispatchers).

In response to the news report, I contacted a news anchor with Channel 5 with whom I had a good relationship. I asked him to actually come down to the Dispatch Center, with a cameraman, see the fine young men and women who were assigned there, then do a follow-up report that remedied the previously-broadcast unfair statements.

I had every expectation that he would say good things. He came down with a cameraman and took a lot of footage, including a detailed interview with me. But that night, the coverage about the Dispatch Center on channel 5 was just as bad as the previous night! I was really unhappy, and called my friend at Channel 5. He apologized profusely, explaining that the editor was the one who made the decisions and just about all the positive stuff I said had ended up on the cutting room floor! This really bothered me, especially because it maligned the fine young men and women who were down there on temporary assignment. I know it bothered those officers and their families, as well. The situation taught me a lesson that served me well in later years by ensuring, sometimes in conversation with the news editor, that the coverage include my perspective.

MAJOR SHOOTING WITH MULTIPLE VICTIMS DOWN— RADIO BROADCAST

One evening I was driving around the city, as it was my turn to be the chief's duty officer. I rolled up on a shooting and observed three victims lying on the ground. It was clear that they had been shot, and the situation was pretty chaotic.

As I was talking to the senior officer, I heard a radio broadcast going out using my call sign and describing the outstanding suspects! The crime broadcast was voiced by my young son, Jake, who was on a ride-along with me that night. He sought every possible opportunity to ride with me and was able to make his voice sound deeper than it really was. He got pretty good at operating the radio and, when necessary, putting out crime broadcasts.

AN UNBELIEVABLE DAY WITH GENERAL CURTIS LEMAY

In 1967, then-Chief Tom Reddin assembled a blue-ribbon committee to meet and make recommendations about how technology could benefit the police department.

One of the committee members was then-just retired General Curtis LeMay, former chief of staff of the United States Air Force and legendary World War II Army Air Force commander and strategic military giant.

Toward the end of my assignment in Communications Division, in 1987, the committee was invited to spend a day seeing all that had occurred in the LAPD in the twenty years since they first met. Frankly, the names of the others escape me, but for me the heavy hitter was Curtis LeMay. In a wonderful fluke, he and I spent a couple of private hours together. It was such an honor and a pleasure to talk one-on-one with such a renowned military leader, and to hear first hand the details of his decisions in bringing about the low-level daylight bombings over Germany and later the incendiary bombings over Japan. We also discussed his place on the presidential ticket with George Wallace in 1966, and how he knew they didn't have a chance. But anything he could do to harm Hubert Humphrey, with whom he had tangled when head of the Air Force, was a worthwhile effort.

He was getting up pretty well in years, requiring hearing aids in both ears and walking canes, but his mind remained very sharp. At the time he lived in the Air Force Village housing area immediately adjacent to March Air Force Base, in Riverside, California. I encouraged him to feel free to contact me if I could ever do anything to assist him in any way, and he graciously said that he would. Realistically, I knew that I would never see him again, and was most grateful for the time I was able to spend with him.

DISCIPLINE FOR CAPTAIN BUSHEY—CLEAR INSUBORDINATION!

This was back-channel bullshit at its worst, but I was not going to stand still and permit a deserving officer to get screwed. When I took over Communications Division, attrition was horrible and training was even worse.

Among my actions was successfully lobbying to gain control over the old communications center, and to convert it as a simulator to train new dispatchers. The person who made it happen, and did a wonderful job, was Officer Richard Maier, who incidentally had been a classmate. He designed and oversaw the modification of the simulator, developed the schedules and cirriculum, conducted the classes, and ultimately was awarded the department's Meritorious Service Medal for his exemplary performance and achievements. I believed that the officer in charge of the simulator should hold the advanced pay grade position of "police officer III," and was able to get the position upgraded to that level. The position was advertised and Rich was among the applicants—but, realistically, who could outshine the person who had developed the simulator, was running the simulator, and received a medal for his activities?

Unbelivably, the oral panel made up of three of my lieutenants, including one who absolutely had been "planted" in that position by my boss, selected someone else! Worse, they didn't even have Rich in the top three, where I could have legitimately selected him over the person the panel recommended! I was livid at the back-channel treachery that was occurring, where my boss was interfering with my command through another person with racist implications. The officer selected was a fine young man and with great potential, but far less worthy and deserving of the position. I intentionally tampered with the system in an inappropriate way, so that what had occurred would be obvious to all. I then selected Rich for the position, signed the upgrade recommendation, and forwarded it to my boss. Now the shit really hit the fan!

While my approval was in the mail, the back-channel communications between the "plant" lieutenant (actually a nice guy and a friend in many ways, but still a "plant" from the bureau) were in high gear. My boss did exactly what I knew he would do—he denied my signed upgrade recommendation, then disciplined me with a "Notice to Correct Deficiencies" for my inappropriate behavior.

Rich was very understanding regarding the denial of his promotion, but I absolutely insisted that he file a grievance against me for informing him of the promotion and putting his selection in writing. I knew he would ultimately prevail and be upgraded to the higher level. Rich was very reluctant to do it, because he didn't want to make more trouble for me, but I persevered and made him file the grievance.

As I knew he would, my boss rejected the grievance, but Rich (with me in the background—two can play the back-channel game!) pushed it to the next level, and an arbitrator ultimately approved his upgrade. When Rich was promoted, he went to another division, as there were no vacancies in Communications Division when he got the good news.

I have always tried to be a professional and responsive command officer. But standing by when one of my people is being screwed by someone else acting inappropriately is not something I'm inclined to tolerate. This was one of those situations where I felt I had to take an ethical stand, and was prepared to accept the consequences. While the minor discipline I received was irritating and arguably inappropriate, because it was the result of my refusal to accept the sneaky back-channel behavior of my boss, I felt that accepting the admonition and moving on was the best course of action. My guess is that my boss didn't want the matter to become widely known either, as it would have highlighted his foolishness. My decision turned out to be wise, and I continued to interact with this particular superior in other assignments.

DON'T EVER HELP TO SAVE THE PUBLIC AGAIN!

During my tenure as the commanding officer of Communications Division, I encountered one of the most foolish and downright stupid bureaucratic situations of my career.

The Los Angeles Police Department and the Los Angeles Fire Department operated on separate frequency bands, and lacked the ability to communicate with each other. However, the police department helicopters did have a unique and expensive radio that was capable of transmitting anywhere on the frequency spectrum, including the ability to communicate with city fire apparatus.

One summer afternoon a brush fire broke out in the hills at the top of Echo Park and adjacent to Elysian Park. A police helicopter was overhead and was able to determine that the responding fire apparatus was using a small and narrow street in an attempt to reach this fire in a heavy brush area. Accordingly, the police helicopter observer tuned the special radio to the frequency of the responding fire apparatus, and led the fire trucks directly to the fire, which was promptly extinguished.

Unbelievably, a high-ranking fire staff officer named Thompson (pseudonym) called his counterpart on the police department, Commander George Morrison, and made it clear that he didn't want the police department operating on fire channels! This was beyond stupid, as the utilization was highly beneficial in assisting both departments to serve the public, and in promptly arriving and putting out a potentially catastrophic brush fire.

George Morrison called me in and made it real clear that he wanted me to contact the air support folks involved, and to not permit this to occur again. I couldn't believe George was telling me this, and diplomatically exchanged some heated words with him; I also couldn't believe he would buy into that nonsense. George was not pleased with my response. It became clear that he was becoming increasingly frustrated at his inability to get through to me on this issue, and I was certainly becoming frustrated at my inability to get through to him.

In the middle of our heated conversation, his aide, a sergeant, gave me the high sign to shut up. I took his cue and departed back for my office. The sergeant called me a while later to tell me that George was having a bad day, and in a great deal of pain because of an old shoulder injury, thus his response very likely had been influenced by medication he was taking. I was glad to hear this, because George was a better man than that. I couldn't imagine that he would think it was unacceptable to use a tremendous radio capability in order to deal with a serious public safety problem. As time went on, George's injury became more acute and caused him greater pain, finally resulting in his retirement. To George's last days (he died in 2011) we remained good friends. I forgave George for the position he took while under medication, but never forgot the actions of that idiot on the fire department who told us to stay off their frequencies.

In mid-2010 I went to the deserted Parker Center and took a walk down memory lane. I walked the floors, primarily the fifth and sixth, and reflected on all the things that had occurred in the various offices. It was very sentimental to me. Like most people, I looked for some mementos to scrounge, but others had already pilfered just about everything. However, there were still a few plastic room numbers on some of the doors, including the door to what had once been George Morrison's office. I removed that plastic room number. Along with a nice letter about our friendship and my respect for George, I sent it to his son, Brian Morrison, who at the time was a sergeant in Metropolitan Division. I ran into Brian a few months later and he thanked me for the letter and the plastic sign.

Gadfly Thrown Out of Communications

During my tenure in Communications Division, there was a gadfly named Shatner (pseudonym) who published a cheesy little throwaway newspaper about happenings at the Los Angeles Civic Center. He was always writing negative things about my employees, and referred to the women who wore uniforms as "police bluebirds." Shatner continually asserted that his actions were consistent with a free press, in that he was just a newspaper reporter and publisher doing his civic responsibility by bringing the actions of public employees to the attention of the public. He was just a gadfly who published a nothing newspaper that very few people paid any attention to. I didn't care for this little man and neither did my employees.

One morning Shatner came down to the communications center and began interviewing my employees, insisting that he was exercising his rights as a legitimate newspaper reporter. I directed one of my employees (I believe she was Laura Robles) to escort him out of the building, and I told him not to come back again. He immediately called the LAPD press relations spokesperson, Commander Bill Booth, and complained about my actions.

Bill, a great guy, called to remind me that Shatner had a right to be down there (Communications Division was in the fourth sub-level of City Hall East). I told Bill the guy was a jerk, a disruptive influence who had disrespected the dispatchers, and that I did not want him down there anymore. I asked Bill if he would tell that to Mr. Shatner, which wasn't really what Bill wanted to hear, but he did support my position. Mr. Shatner never came down there again, and my employees appreciated the position I had taken.

There were a couple of months when I was in an uncomfortable position. One of the two commanders in the Support Services Bureau, which was the command to which I reported, really got on my case. He was second-guessing everything I did, criticizing me personally, and initiated an audit to determine the performance of the division and me personally. I couldn't understand why he was going to so much trouble to make my life miserable. Then I found out. He had been in a dispute within Chief Daryl Gates, and apparently felt that I had intentionally provided information that put him, the commander, in a bad position.

Several months before, as part of what was intended to be a healing process between the chief and this commander (they had feuded in the past), the commander was assigned the responsibility of conducting an audit throughout the department to determine how the command staff perceived the leadership of Chief Gates. About halfway through his audit, a couple of captains apparently complained that the commander was asking biased questions likely to result in responses critical of the chief. Chief Gates was livid at the bias assertions and directed my good friend and jogging partner, Commander Tom Windham, to interview the captains who had been interviewed by this commander to determine if bias was perceived to have occurred. I was interviewed and had no criticism whatsoever of the questions I had been asked by this commander.

As it turned out, Tom Windham did not care for the commander who did the survey. In Tom's written report to the chief, he documented some personal and candid comments I had made during our daily jogs in Elysian Park. I absolutely hadn't intended for those conversations between Tom and me to ever be reduced to writing, but Tom did just that, and things I said that were critical of the commander ended up in Tom's written report.

The dispute between this commander and Chief Gates escalated when Gates issued a reprimand to the commander. The commander then went to court and was successful in obtaining a court order for the department to give him a copy of the complete investigative report that had resulted in his reprimand. Obviously, the report contained Tom Windham's comments about what I had privately said.

Plain and simple, the commander was pissed at me because of the comments attributed to me in the report he received. Fortunately, the pissed-off commander was the second-in-command in the Bureau, while the other commander, who was actually the Bureau commanding officer, was a good friend of mine. This thing eventually blew over, and later the distraught commander and I developed a good relationship.

A MEDAL FOR ANNABELLE

The annual LAPD Devil Pups Luncheon at the Police Academy, which I had assisted another police captain and Devil Pup Board member, Frank Patchett, in organizing, created a fun opportunity to provide recognition to a special gal. The guest speaker was an active duty Marine Corps major general and astronaut, William Bolden, a good guy.

The special gal was my secretary, Annabelle Garcia, who was always doing Marine Corps stuff for me, most of it off-duty (yeah, right!) Using a real medal and citation, I created a Navy Achievement Medal for Staff Sergeant Annabelle Louise Garcia of the United States Marine Corps Reserve Auxiliary. Louise was not her name, just a fun name I gave her, nor was there an auxiliary or any protocol that she could be presented a legitimate award for.

I asked General Bolden if he would present the phony award, and he immediately agreed. At the appointed moment in the luncheon, General Bolden asked "Staff Sergeant Annabelle Louise Garcia" to come up to the podium. Annabelle squealed, "Oh shit!" It was the first time I'd ever heard her swear! When the general pinned the medal on Annabelle, he remarked that she probably-deserved the medal for "having to put up with Colonel Bushey!"

There was a lot of truth to what the general said. General Bolden retired from the Marine Corps several years ago and at the time of this entry in June, 2012, he is the administrator of the National Aeronautics and Space Administration.

THE PREGNANT MEDFLY ON HALLOWEEN

In about the mid-1980s the department started becoming more and more politically correct. As a result, people stopped bringing strippers to department events and roll calls, and became more sensitive and careful about actions and comments that could offend people and under-represented groups.

In Communications Division we just about always had a fun and spirited Halloween costume contest, with many employees coming to work wearing all types of different costumes. One of the female dispatchers came to work as a pregnant medfly—the fly whose larvae were threatening citrus crops in California at the time. Her costume included a gigantic male penis attached to the clothing on the outside of her pubic region.

I saw this and immediately broke into a cold sweat! I just knew that I would get in hot water for permitting somebody to come to work dressed this way. While I laughed and congratulated her on the unique costume, I asked her to shed it immediately. Later, I put out a memo that applauded people for their creativity, but reminded them to avoid actions that might be offensive to other people. Plain and simple, I put out that memo to cover my ass for when when the expected flak occurred. Fortunately, no one complained. I still have a picture of that gal and a copy of my memo.

Halloween brought out some unique qualities, and potential hidden secrets, in some of our employees. There were some great costumes. One that attracted a lot of attention and resulted in much conversation was a male employee who went to work on Halloween dressed as a woman. Everybody agreed that the way he walked, talked and applied makeup indicated that he must have had quite a bit of experience as a crossdresser!

A SPECIALIST AT "BAD NEWS ON FRIDAYS"

As I write these memoirs, I am recognized as one of the nation's top law enforcement leadership presenters. In addition to doing some freelancing, I also work part time for the FBI Law Enforcement Executive Development Association. Simply stated, I write and lecture on leadership issues. As I dictate this particular paragraph, I am in my motel room in Las Cruces, New Mexico, having just completed a day of lecturing to the command staff of the Dona Ana County Sheriff's Department.

Everybody has their pet peeves—one of mine is encouraging supervisors and managers to not unnecessarily deliver bad news on Fridays, or just before personnel leave on vacation. Like most things, my passion for this issue is the result of pain I endured in the past. During a good part of my tenure in Communications Division, I worked for a commander who relished giving me a harsh note on Friday afternoons. It just about always spoiled my weekends. This commander, who was actually a great friend and supporter, did the same to me during other assignments in which we served together, too. He could be pretty harsh at times, but a caring and talented manager as well. As leaders, we all have room for growth, and in my opinion this was his. While I always supported him and appreciated his support of me, this was a practice I thought wasn't all that great.

Police Service Representative Joey Pinellas is one of my heroes. At one time he worked for me in Communications Division, but later transferred out and worked as a desk officer at the North Hollywood Station.

One day, a woman walked into North Hollywood Station with a box of old, legitimate police and fire badges, saying she did not know what to do with them. Joey told her about me, and she said it would be fine to give them to me. Joey called me immediately. I dropped everything I was doing, and immediately responded to North Hollywood Station to pick up the badges. They were beauties, and remain some of the nicest ones in my collection.

Every time I see Joey I remind him of my continuing appreciation.

OLYMPIC PIN FRENZY

There were actually two major activities during the 1984 Los Angeles Police Olympics—the athletic events and pin collecting! Everybody had to have a pin from every entity, division, department, and whatever. Without exaggeration, there had to have been no fewer than 300 police division and agency pins made. Many were made up ahead of time, but others were manufactured, at great expense, in a matter of just a couple of days during the Olympics themselves.

One hundred dollars was quite a chunk of change to pay for a lapel pin in 1984, but plenty of them sold for that amount. It was amazing to see the scores of pins on the vests of my dispatchers during the Olympics, as well as the hordes of pin vendors all over the city. They were especially prevalent across from the two Olympic Villages at USC and in Westwood.

NO CONTRIBUTION—NO HATS, PINS, OR CREDENTIALS!

As the commanding officer of Communications Division during the 1984 Olympic Games, one of my responsibilities was the recruitment, processing, training, and deployment of amateur radio volunteers to fill requests for communications support at the various venues throughout the city.

Everyone was processed for the highly coveted credentials, and packages were assembled for each containing a special hat, pins, and other unique memorabilia developed just for the volunteers. The needs were for a couple of radio operators here, a couple there, but not the type of situation where I felt comfortable turning over a complete venue to a single radio club, which is exactly what one particular radio club wanted me to do. The last thing that I was about to do was to turn over some of my responsibilities to a high-maintenance group of folks who seemed to delight in drama and conflict.

When time came for deployment, all of the members of this one club threw down the gauntlet: if they couldn't all work together, they were not going to assist during the games! I was really irritated, but not about to yield to these spoiled old brats. So they played no role, and I somehow filled their spots with other amateur volunteers. After the Olympics were over, the head of that club contacted me and had the guts to ask for the credentials and goody packages they had never been issued, because they'd failed to report as agreed.

I don't think I'm usually a vindictive person. But I made an exception in their case. I sent their ID cards to them—but cut in half! I gave the items from their goody bags to the other folks who fulfilled their commitments.

LAPD Representative on Capitol Hill

As the project manager of the Emergency Command, Control, and Communications System (ECCCS), I was also responsible for pursuing the acquisition of additional radio frequencies for the department, to expand our radio and data systems. This assignment caused me to become active in California public safety communications circles and, as previously mentioned, ultimately resulted in my selection as the head of the effort within Southern California to obtain radio spectrum for other agencies as well.

These duties, which were in addition to my role as the commanding officer of Communications Division, necessitated frequent trips to Washington, DC, as well as attendance at other communications-related conferences and activities around the United States.

Thirty-Nine New Radio Frequencies

While the commanding officer of Communications Division, I became the key person in the police department in pursuit of additional radio channels to expand our communications system. During this era, I was also elected as the president of the Southern California Public Safety Communications Association. As a result, I spent a great deal of time on Capitol Hill in Washington DC, primarily lobbying members of Congress and the Federal Communications Commission to get additional radio spectrum for police and fire agencies in the greater Los Angeles area.

Realistically, the two key individuals were me and a commander from the Los Angeles County Sheriff's Department. Our efforts, which began in late 1983, resulted in an entire UHF radio channel being reallocated from the broadcast industry to public safety in early 1988. With the participation of the various public safety agencies in the greater Los Angeles area, primarily in meetings where I played a leadership role, brutal exchanges were often involved in the allocation of these new channels, and also in the relinquishing of previous channels as new ones were assigned. The Los Angeles Police Department ended up with thirty-nine new radio channels, on top of the eighteen we already possessed.

I received a lot of accolades for this accomplishment, and I know it was among the factors that contributed to my continuing upward mobility within the Los Angeles Police Department. The department's radio system has expanded greatly, and my accomplishments in tripling the number of radio channels continue to be of great value to the police department. I'm proud of the role I played in obtaining these additional radio channels, especially for the LAPD, but for the other agencies as well.

Death of a Dear Friend and Badge Collector Pal

Charles Funaro and I became good friends. I had known him very casually as a badge collector in the late 1960s, but our friendship really bloomed starting in 1980 during my brief tenure as commanding officer of the North Hollywood Patrol Division. He had a successful company that specialized in investigating aircraft accidents for insurance companies, with a very nice office in North Hollywood. We visited quite often, did some badge swapping, and I thought I got to know his family well, even using the services of his attorney son, Charles Jr., for some personal litigation.

In about 1985, when I literally was walking out the door for LAX to catch a flight to the Marine Base in Quantico, Virginia, for training, I got a disturbing call from his daughter. My friend had died of a heart attack. I was crushed, both at the loss of a dear friend and also at my inability to attend his services. I was also pretty curious about getting the call from his adult daughter, Susan, who I didn't even know existed!

I told Susan I would call her on my return from my military leave and would like to take her and her mom, Jackie, to lunch. When I returned and took the daughter and widow to lunch, I was stunned to find that Chuck had such an attractive, single and intelligent daughter, especially since I was single and unattached. I remained in contact with the family and actually dated Susan a couple of times, but things did not materialize romantically. It turned out that Susan and her father, my pal, had a very complicated relationship that I am not sure I ever really understood.

In about 2010, after years of no contact, Charles Jr. and I rekindled our friendship. This was made possible by my son, Jake, who recalled the name when he saw a Funaro in Pasadena who was an attorney. So Jake reached out and brought us back together again. In mid-2011, I was thrilled to be given the opportunity to purchase from the family the badge collection that my friend had assembled, and which had been in storage for over two decades. This also brought me closer to another Funaro brother, Mike, who I'd last seen as a youngster when he and his parents used a cabin I then owned at Big Bear. I also had a nice chat again with Susan, who now runs a bed and breakfast in Arkansas. Chuck Jr. is a great friend and someone I hope remains on my radar screen for the rest of my days.

State Police Sergeant Creates Communications Chaos

One of my several state police friends asked permission for members of that department, when the need arose, to directly contact our commications center by transmitting on an LAPD radio frequency. This made sense to me, and was consistent with my efforts, then underway, to enhance communications inter-operability among the many law enforcement agencies in Los Angeles County.

Unfortunately, among the many fine officers on that department was a sergeant who badly misused the capability that I made possible. He would do foolish things, like getting involved in unnecessary altercations with winos sleeping in alleys, then call us for assistance. The personnel in Central Division, where the sergeant spent most of his time, got very tired of responding to his calls to deal with situations that LAPD had neither the time nor inclination to address. It wasn't until I threatened to revoke the interoperability agreement, unless the radio with our channel was taken away from the troublesome sergeant, that the foolish calls stopped being made. Overall, the California State Police, with a primary responsibility to protect state personnel and property, was a good outfit. It was later absorbed into the California Highway Patrol.

Talk about the epitome of getting busted. One night around midnight, with the forbidden fruit of a subordinate female in my car, Cathy and I exchanged a loving embrace and kiss while at a freeway on-ramp stop sign several blocks north of Parker Center.

Several days later I ran into one of Chief Daryl Gates' bodyguard/drivers, Gene Arreola. He took me aside and said that he and Chief Gates, in the chief's car, were directly behind us that night, and got a big kick out of my amorous activities! I doubt that he would have been so charitable had he known the other party was one of my subordinates. This incident occurred very close to the end of my tour as the commanding officer of Communications Division, when there was no doubt that my transfer was imminent. Still, the revelation of our relationship at that time would not have been well received by the department. Chief Gates had quite a reputation as a ladies' man earlier in his career, and I suspect that he too had at one time engaged in similar activities.

Constantly Ill-at-Ease in Washington

I look back on my many trips to Washington, DC with a great deal of fondness. I had a lot of fun, met a number of wonderful people, and believe that I accomplished a great deal. However, one overriding consideration was a continuous feeling of unease because of the often-toxic political climate back in Los Angeles.

Unfortunately, my boss at the time, then-Commander Bernard Parks, was in my judgment not a very good leader. He was clearly among the smartest and hardest-working individuals I had ever met, but there was always a constant unease because of his inclination to micro-manage some of the actions of the commands that reported to him. He was extremely efficient, but in many ways not very effective. He would often focus on minutia, as opposed to things that were really important.

I was also troubled by the back-channel communications that some of my subordinates had with him by virtue of their common ethnicity. In addition, there were a number of actions he took with some unfortunate personnel selections that appeared to be driven by his commitment to affirmative action, which were made contrary to common sense and over my strong objections. I was very uneasy being away, knowing that my boss was most likely tinkering with my command. I suspect that some of my concerns were not merited, but nevertheless I was almost always ill-at-ease when working for Bernard Parks. Despite reservations over some of his actions, I worked long and hard to be loyal and responsive to him.

Murder in Progress at Twelfth & K in Washington?

On my first trip to Washington, DC as the police department's representative, I did not know the city at all, and ended up staying at a motel in a less desirable part of town. As with a great many of my trips, I took Jake with me, who was then around the age of eleven or twelve.

We were awakened in the middle of the night by subdued screams and things obviously being banged around in the next room. By this time I realized we were in a place where wild behavior might routinely occur. But I was also afraid to ignore what was occurring. The thought of not doing something, and encountering yellow tape around a crime scene the next morning, occurred to me. So I stepped into the hallway, got the room number, called the room, said I was the bell captain and wanted to ensure that everything was all right. The woman who answered the phone replied with some very colorful and contemptuous language, and reminded me (thinking I was the bell captain) that she was not to be disturbed. I told Jake to just go back to sleep.

Suspect Picks Wrong Jewelry Display Case to Smash

Things didn't go very well for a robbery suspect in Baltimore one day. I was among the many cops in the lobby of a high-end hotel. We were there to participate in an APCO (Association of Public Safety Communications Officers) Convention, when some idiot decided to do a "smash and grab" robbery of gems from a jewelry store located in the lobby. He smashed open a display counter and grabbed a bunch of items. Our only delay in reacting was due to our incredulity that something like this was occurring ten feet from where we were standing. About twenty hands grabbed the suspect simultaneously. Since nobody had handcuffs with them, we just sat on the suspect until the police arrived. I suspect that crook will take a closer look at his surroundings before trying this stunt again.

"Got Some Wine Out in Da Caar!"

On a slow afternoon while attending an APCO (Association of Public Safety Communications Officers) in Milwaukee, I went into a soul food place that specialized in barbeque.

The woman behind the counter was very much on the heavy side and had a highly visible array of gold teeth. While I was ordering, she asked what I wanted to drink. In my typical wise-ass fashion, I replied, "Ripple." When she asked what it was, I replied that it was really cheap wine. She looked at me in reflective way, and with a wink replied: "I got some in da caar!" It was a slow afternoon and I was somewhat bored, but not that bored! The food was good, I had a Coke instead of whatever was in her car. Our closer relationship never materialized!

Jogging in the Wrong Park

I learned a good lesson in Milwaukee—always ask a cop where the best place to jog is, and especially places where jogging might not be a good idea.

One afternoon while attending the conference in Milwaukee, I decided to take a long jog. There was what appeared to be a nice park along the waterfront not too far from my hotel. Before I finished my jog through the trail I'd selected, three separate men stood up alongside the trail as I approached, each displaying a smile and an erection! I was not as thrilled to see them, but they apparently were happy to see me. That park was a one-jog experience. When I later mentioned to a Milwaukee officer what happened, he thought it was funny and told me that park was notorious for gay encounters.

Wilshire Area

In March 1988, after four and a half years in Communications, I was reassigned as the commanding officer of the Wilshire Area. There I was over both the patrol and detective divisions, as well as the vice, jail, community relations, records and garage units. At the time the divisional boundaries were roughly Robertson Boulevard on the west, Santa Monica Freeway on the south, Normandie Street on the east, and Third Street on the north. As I recall, the total number of personnel in the area was approximately 350 persons of all ranks.

Off to a Good Start

While moving belongings from my old office in Communications Division to my new office in the Wilshire Area one day, I was driving in the eastern portion of Wilshire when an "all units" call came out at a tow service.

I don't recall the nature of the call, other than there was urgency to it. Since I was almost right on top of the location, I went "code 6" over the radio (out for investigation).

Because I'm not a foolish person who typically charges into situations without backup, I positioned myself so I could see what was going on and hopefully be of assistance to the responding units. But circumstances overtook my good intentions when a person yelled that the suspect was armed with a handgun. My interpretation was that some innocent person was potentially in immediate jeopardy, thereby necessitating immediate action on my part.

When I carefully approached the suspect, I observed that he was apparently passed out over a desk with the gun next to one of his hands. So I immediately rushed the suspect and took away his gun.

About that time an additional radio transmission came out advising that the suspect was armed. I replied over the radio: " Not any longer!" All the Wilshire units on the air at the time quickly became aware that they had a new area commanding officer who wasn't reluctant to do police work. However, I didn't bother broadcasting over the air the additional information that the suspect's handgun was actually a BB gun!

"OPERATION RESCUE" AND THE CELEBRITY LAWYER

In the late 1980s, the issue over abortion clinics resulted in a number of demonstrations around the country. One of the activities in the greater Los Angeles area was for anti-abortion demonstrators to surround an abortion clinic and keep people from entering the business. Often when this happened, pro-abortion forces would respond to the same location and initiate a confrontation, sometimes ending in violence.

There were three abortion clinics within the boundaries of the Wilshire Area, and I experienced tactical situations at all three of them. One was particularly noteworthy, when somebody I really didn't care for (at that time) agreed with the decision I made. At a massive demonstration at an abortion clinic on Pico Boulevard, the anti-abortion folks showed up in large numbers and were using a megaphone, which was against the city's municipal code. I directed one of my lieutenants to go over and tell the leadership of the anti-abortion forces to stop using the megaphone. As he walked over to them, I noted that leading civil rights attorney Gloria Allred had arrived, and was conferring with the people my lieutenant was about to talk to.

I just knew that Ms. Allred was going to oppose my guidance, and that I would have to deal with her. But when my lieutenant came back, he said he'd delivered the message, and that none other than Gloria Allred reinforced the wisdom of my message to the demonstrators. I couldn't believe that she and I were on the same sheet of music. Gloria is a person who really likes the limelight and who manages to get involved in a number of high-profile cases, especially those involving women's issues. I got to know Gloria a little bit in later years, because of her friendship with my friend Los Angeles County District Attorney Steve Cooley. She is actually a pretty darn nice person, but someone who truly likes the limelight.

Marketing Access to Me! A Unique Cultural Lesson

As the new commanding officer of the Wilshire Area, it didn't take long to learn two things about the Korean community. The first was that it was made up of wonderful people who were law-abiding and working hard to be good citizens. The second was unfortunately the opposite: there also was a number of crooked people in that community working hard to line their own pockets.

Within a short time of my arrival, I was descended on by a man who was reputed to be a key representative of the Korean community. He immediately began bringing people to my office to meet me, and to have their photo taken with me. But I soon realized this fellow was taking advantage of a majority of the residents, who believed that proximity to someone in power, as in Korea, had business advantages. The photos were being displayed prominently in businesses to demonstrate the alleged existence of their special influence with me! I also learned that he was encouraging Korean businessmen to join our community business group, but that he was personally pocketing a portion of the donations coming from that community.

Much to the chagrin of this Korean crook, I worked hard to develop a great number of contacts in the Korean community, as opposed to his desire to be the sole one with whom I coordinated. Finally, I started having my picture taken with everyone—men, women, children, families, businesses, schools, the clergy, and everyone else—so that the pictures with me became so common they no longer conveyed special access or influence.

I enjoyed the many friends I met in Koreatown, but I also had to be careful not to unintentionally become a pawn in a crook's game.

For reasons that will soon be obvious, I am being intentionally vague as I describe this truly unusual situation.

One of my many acquaintances held a responsible position, where his immediate response was occasionally required. One night he and a woman with whom he was having an extramarital affair spent the night in a motel in the city. In the wee small hours of the morning he received a page that his presence was essential because of a critical incident. As he left the motel room he found himself smack in the middle of a crime scene, with yellow tape, a homicide victim, and a bunch of cops! Of course, he was well known to the officers.

However, this wasn't the type of situation where people would just forget seeing him there. By the end of the day, his amorous affair and horrible luck were known throughout the department. To further aggravate the matter, his wife was also a department employee. The last I heard, they were still together—but I can only imagine the intensity of some of their discussions in the wake of his very conspicuous infidelity.

"Concerned Citizens" and Beverage Control Permits

I learned a very interesting lesson in my dealings with two "neighborhood activists." Allegedly, they were opposed to granting additional liquor licenses for the Wilshire area in which they resided, and were very aggressive in pressuring me to recommend the denial of all new requests to the Alcoholic Beverage Commission. They were forceful and articulate, and some of what they said, especially potential over-saturation of liquor stores in minority neighborhoods, made sense. However, I started to smell a rat when they put the heat on me to oppose a beer and wine permit for a restaurant known as the Souplantation, which was clearly going to be a high-end establishment in a nice neighborhood. To oppose the request could clearly result in a business that would be less financially viable because the other restaurants in the area did have such permits. Their opposition just didn't make sense.

Then I found out why: these two were pushing the Souplantation to make a sizable financial donation to their "neighborhood group" (comprised of only those two) in return for dropping its opposition to the liquor license permit application. I came close to being a pawn in their game. This one is among the many lessons I continue to pass on in my leadership training to today's law enforcement leaders.

As a longtime member of the International Police Association, it was common for me to host police officers from other countries in my home. One day I got a call from a friend, George Salyer (RIP), a captain with the U.S. Capitol Police in Washington. George asked if I could host a "fine young police cadet" from Germany for a few days, to which I immediately answered it would be a pleasure. A day or so later I picked up "Franz," the nineteen-year-old German police cadet, from the airport, and got him settled in for what I expected to be no more than several days. The next day I took him to work with me—and that was where problems started to develop.

Within just a few hours he'd asked several of the records clerks to go out with him, and actually left the station with one of them at noontime for what I later came to believe was a sexual encounter. A night or two later he took out a female friend of our family; the next night we discovered that she was covered (at least the parts of her body that were visible!) from head to toe with bruises from his teeth and lips ("hickies").

I decided he'd spent enough time with the Busheys, and that it was time for him to move on to his next destination. When I raised the issue, however, he announced that he intended to stay with us for his entire three-month "holiday" in the United States! Wrong! Within a day I had taken him back at LAX and was pleased to have him gone.

A day or so later I called my pal George and told him of my problems with the young man he'd described as a "fine young police cadet!" In his own way, and somewhat sheepishly, George acknowledged that Franz had also been a pain-in-the-ass in Washington, and hoped the kid would have learned from the "fatherly chat" George had with him. Nonsense! He just wanted the troublesome kid to be gone, and kissed him off to me. George passed away several years back, and in addition to the loss of a friend, I am also saddened I didn't get the opportunity to pay him back for the sour kraut!

MURDER OF REBECCA SCHAEFFER

July 18th of 1989 was a sad day for several hundred thousand people. A deranged young man, who had been fixated on and stalking a beautiful young actress, went to her Wilshire area home and shot her to death. The man was 19-year-old Robert Bardo. The actress was 21-year-old Rebecca Schaeffer, who had a leading role in the television series "My Sister Sam." He went to her place twice that day; first to try to talk to her and get her to sign an autograph, and then the second time when he shot her point-blank in the chest as she opened the door.

Bardo had been stalking her on and off for three years, and was able to obtain her home address through motor vehicle records. All homicides are tragic, but the senseless loss of this promising young woman hit many people very hard. Her death was one of the several tragic incidents stemming from celebrity stalking, which resulted in the strengthening of criminal laws dealing with this type of obsessive behavior. This was among several cases, out of literally hundreds, in which I took a rather personal interest. It was investigated and prosecuted by my homicide detectives, and they did a fine job.

My Shattered Image of Officer "Shirley Temple!"

Because of excessive and inappropriate utilization of the mobile digital terminals (MDTs) in police units, Communications Division would do random monthly audits. Any copies of problematic conversations would be forwarded to the concerned geographic area for "appropriate action."

One morning my patrol captain, Glenn Ackerman, came into my office with a grin on his face and a copy of an MDT transmission in his hand. One of our female officers, who struck me as a real prude with a "Shirley Temple" ambiance, had been caught in one of the random audits. Now Glenn was about to counsel her on an inappropriate transmission. She'd had an ongoing dialog with an officer in another division who she was obviously dating. During their chat session on the subject of oral affection, she'd taken the opportunity to describe her specific strengths and proclivity.

I could only imagine the humiliation she would experience when her captain had her read what she'd said on the MDT, and sign an acknowledgment of counseling on the issue. I resisted the temptation to join Glenn in his counseling session, as that would have been inappropriate and unnecessary. But I did capture the look on her face when she left Glenn's office; it was about as crimson as it could possibly have been. Glenn and I kiddingly agreed that the matter had caused us to have a new appreciation for that fine young officer.

Pagers for the Explorer Scouts

I have always been supportive of police Explorer scouts, and believe strongly that they can be used in a great number of tasks that others do not think they should be used for.

430

In the Wilshire Area, I asked for and received an allocation from the WCPC (Wilshire Community Police Counsel) to purchase pagers for the Explorer scouts, for use when there was a need to summon them to the station. I actually had used Explorer scouts for crime scene security containment, but obviously only when circumstances indicated that the kids wouldn't be in any jeopardy. This worked out great, and literally saved us hundreds of man-hours by having the Explorer scouts perform containment tasks that otherwise would have been performed by sworn police officers. I always looked for opportunities to use Explorer scouts in the performance of unique tasks, and am surprised that more police executives do not share my enthusiasm for this superb resource.

"Lips is Lips"

One afternoon, my patrol commanding officer and good friend, Captain Glenn Ackerman, came into my office, laughing uncontrollably (well, almost).

He had just walked through the booking area and observed a transvestite prostitute and his/her "trick," the male customer who had paid to be the recipient of the transvestite's oral affection. Apparently, the transvestite prostitute was even uglier than most, and Glenn inquired of the handcuffed "trick" as how he could possibly permit allowing that pitiful creature to place his/her lips on his penis.

Glenn's laughter was based on the "trick's" response: "lips is lips!"

This has been a source of great amusement for Glenn and me over many years, and we never chat or exchange correspondence (Christmas cards, etc.) without sharing that sick historic quote.

Prostitution Sting Operation and Officer "Plain Jane"

We would occasionally conduct prostitution operations by deploying undercover female officers to arrest the "Johns" who would commit the act of solicitation.

At the time, the department's percentage of female officers was still pretty small, and for that reason we would borrow female officers from other divisions for our task force operations. One night our cadre of female officers included one woman who was very nice, but not terribly attractive. As the operation got underway, it was like shooting fish in a barrel—the female officers, with the exception of "Plain Jane," were reeling in the Johns one right after the other. All of us felt horrible, as we knew how humiliated "Plain Jane" had to be. Finally, one slobbering drunk made a half-hearted innuendo toward Jane. That was enough for us: we hooked him up, transported him to the booking area, and congratulated the female officer for a great arrest. Since it was close to end of watch, we permitted the female officer to go home.

We then uncuffed the drunk who'd made the innuendo—which fell far short of a violation of the law—and sent him on his way!

Getting an Officer to His Critically Injured Wife

One morning while sitting in my office at Wilshire, I got a troubling emergency call from the Colton Police Department, which is about fifty miles east of Los Angeles in San Bernardino County. Their personnel were on the scene of a serious traffic accident in which one of the critically injured parties was the wife of one of my officers, Kevin Williams, who at the time was in the field. Laura Williams was asking that her husband be notified.

I immediately had Kevin respond to the station, then asked the watch commander at Air Support Division if it was possible to have a helicopter transport our officer to Loma Linda Medical Center, where Laura was being taken. Within a very short time Kevin was flown to the hospital. He arrived just a short time after Laura was wheeled into emergency.

Thankfully, Laura made a complete recovery. Subsequent to retiring, Kevin Williams accepted a position as a captain with a sheriff's department in Oregon. My understanding is that today all in the family are doing well.

Sergeant Roger Benson and the LAX Scandal

As the commanding officer of Wilshire Area, I was contacted by the commanding officer of West Bureau, who at that time was a commander named Kent Hinson (pseudonym). Hinson and I got off to somewhat of a rough start, but eventually we had a pretty nice relationship.

He had previously initiated an investigation into alleged timekeeping improprieties involving the personnel at the LAPD LAX substation. Hinson assigned one of my sergeants, Michael Malone (pseudonym), to conduct the investigation. Mike was an okay guy in many respects, but he was known to some people as "the claw," because he was seen as pretty harsh in his assessment of others while conducting personnel investigations.

Hinson told me he was administratively transferring two sergeants from the Airport Substation to Wilshire Area, and they were both under investigation for timekeeping improprieties. I was somewhat aware of the allegations, but didn't see them to be anywhere near as serious as Hinson and Malone. To me, it was more an issue of questionable discretion, but without evil intent. Before one of the sergeants, Roger Benson (pseudonym), reported in to Wilshire, he called me to request permission to start his 30-day vacation. I really didn't think this was a very good idea, because I don't like the thought of someone spending his vacation worrying about what's going on at work. I also believed his worry was probably more than was warranted. Nevertheless, Roger persisted in his request to go on vacation.

Before I let him take that vacation, I had him bring his wife to the phone. I told them I didn't think the matter was as serious as other people did, and I didn't want him worrying about the situation while on vacation. I made it very clear to both Roger and his wife that I expected them to pick up the phone and call me, even in the middle the night if necessary, to discuss the matter and put his mind at ease.

I realized I was pushing the envelope on this issue, discussing the disposition of an investigation before the investigation had run its course. But I had very strong negative thoughts about why the investigation was initiated, the severity of what had allegedly been discovered, and the unfortunately negative tenacity of the person conducting the investigation. Also, as Benson's commanding officer, I would be the person who recommend the disposition to the chief of police.

As I predicted, the penalty was relatively light. On a related note, from about that point on in my professional career, with all the agencies I ultimately worked for, I pushed hard for quick dispositions in disciplinary matters because I recognize that waiting for the axe to fall is most often far more painful than the matter's ultimate disposition. From time to time, once I saw which way the winds of an investigation were blowing, I would push the envelope just a tad and whisper in the officer's ear that things looked like they were going to be okay. I'm glad I did this. It probably caused a number of personnel to avoid a great number of sleepless nights!

THE FLOATING FISH OVER LOS ANGELES

As a command officer, I sat on literally hundreds of boards of rights, which were disciplinary tribunals. Having made captain in 1980, but not retiring until 1996, I had a long run as a tenured staff and command officer. Because of my seniority, I was most often chairperson of the three-man tribunals (although we had female officers by this time, very few had achieved the level of captain. I do not believe I ever had a female command officer on any board I served on).

One such board was so funny, that I had to work hard to keep from laughing during just about the entire procedure. Two morning watch officers from Newton area, while on patrol, saw a very large helium-filled fish hovering over a seafood restaurant. It was having a grand opening, but as it was the middle of the night the restaurant was closed. So the two officers removed the fish from the restaurant, tethered it to their police car and drove around the division for a while. Afterward, they took the fish to the station, tied it atop the flagpole, and stiffed a call to the watch commander (allegedly made by a reporter from the news media) asking was there really a large fish flying over Newton Street station?

The watch commander immediately went to the flagpole, saw the fish hovering over the station, untied it, and let it drift away! The $5,000 fish then drifted into the approach airspace for Los Angeles International Airport, resulting in a notice to incoming planes to avoid a flying fish.

By that time the two officers realized they'd really screwed up, and confessed their sin to the watch commander. This little stunt probably cost the city a few thousand bucks, because the fish was valuable and had to be replaced. I think we gave each of the officers a ten-day suspension. Too funny!

VISIT BY A HIGH SCHOOL PAL WITH MEDICAL PROBLEMS

Bill Quick and I were great pals in high school, and we both quit school to enter the military. Bill went into the Air Force. He was a great fellow, but seemed to be a magnet for ill health, and he received a medical discharge over a "tongue infection," whatever that was. When he visited and spent a day with me at Wilshire Station, he was on the list for a heart transplant that, unfortunately never came about; he died several months later of heart failure. After so many years of not seeing one another, I was thrilled to reconnect with Bill, and felt deeply saddened when the Grim Reaper got to him before a new heart became available.

While we visited, he related another medical condition stemming from an incident that could only have happened to someone like Bill. One night, he was a passenger riding in a travel trailer being pulled by a car, and awoke when the vehicles came to a stop. Looking out the window of the trailer (where he shouldn't have been in the first place), he

434

saw his buddy had stopped to assist a couple of women whose car had broken down. Ever the dapper and gracious ladies' man, Bill decided to see how he could help.

Unfortunately, when he opened the trailer door and stepped out, Bill fell about thirty feet—they had stopped on a bridge! The trailer was apparently just high enough for its door to clear the low bridge railing, and in the darkness Bill didn't see the danger. I don't recall the specific injuries that Bill sustained, but they were on top of all of the other ailments the poor fellow suffered from.

THE DISASSEMBLED SERGEANT'S CAR

Sergeant Al Pesanti was a great guy and a fine supervisor, and was absolutely amazing for being able to find crooks and solve crimes. He was a "shit magnet," but in a very positive sense. In addition, he was always very gracious about letting my young son, Jake, go on ride-alongs with him.

It was Al's last day in Wilshire before transferring to another division, and Jake was riding along with him when they joined a bunch of other cops for code 7 (meal break) at a local diner. While inside, a few of his buddies literally disassembled his police car! They removed the doors, hood, and trunk lid, and then videotaped him as he left the diner. The video image of him driving that skeleton of a car back to the station was priceless. Obviously, the culprits reassembled the car and everyone, especially Al, got a big kick out of the prank.

"I THINK IT'S TIME TO GO BACK TO PENNSYLVANIA!"

In the summer of 1989, two fairly elderly shirt-tail relatives came to California to achieve their dream of visiting the Crystal Cathedral in Anaheim, and listening to the Reverend Robert Shuller. John and Isabelle Hinkle stayed at our home during their visit. They were farmers from York Springs, Pennsylavnia, and pretty naive about the rest of the world. John's mother was a Bushey and part of the old Bushey clan from that part of the country. My dad and all of his brothers were from nearby York, Pennsylvania.

On a Saturday morning, I took John into the city with me. While I did an "after-hours inspection," I thought John might enjoy seeing the Wilshire Area. We first responded to a radio call of a "murder in progress," which turned out to be a nothing more than a lovers' quarrel. The woman involved was the sterotypical angry woman who had been scorned. While yelling and screaming that she was going to castrate her boyfriend with a hunting knife, she was very animated and all of her probably 400-pound body made quite a sight. I saw the opportunity for some fun, and the devil made me introduce John to her as a detective who needed to know all the details! His eyes were the size of saucers as she yelled and screamed and deposited spit (from screaming) all over John as he kept trying to back away from her. She had him backed up to a wall when I finally "rescued" him!

We then went to the station where I gave him a tour of the jail, including two nude transsexuals lying on bunks with their new boob jobs and their male genitilia dangling in a very obvious manner. After staring at the two transsexuals for several moments, he turned to me and said, "I think its time for me to go back to Pennsylvania!" This is one of my favorite stories, and was one of John's favorite stories before he and Isabelle passed away.

QUICK AND DIRTY MILITARY PARACHUTE OPERATION

I experienced a few truly hectic days that were as rewarding as they were tiring. My Marine tour as the commanding officer of 3RD AN-GLICO spanned my police assignments in Wilshire and Northeast Areas. There were a few occasions when quick and dirty parachute jumps became possible after work at the Los Alamitos Armed Forces Reserve Center, and I usually took advantage of them. I would rush from the station to the base, suit up in my military uniform, go through the pre-jump activities, and participate in a night parachute operation. Typical for the military, the evolution lasted several hours, and I usually wouldn't get home until around midnight. I didn't complain in the least, and occasionally arrived home just in time to be called out to a critical late-night homicide or some other police operation. I felt blessed to have the honor to continue to serve in the military, and to participate in such neat activities with such expensive toys!

BOWLING FOR PENNIES—CASE SOLVED!

My recollection of this matter is not as good as those of some of my former subordinates. But apparently my consternation and anger were pretty strong. My good friend and former subordinate, Paul Mock, occasionally reminds me of how irritated I was over this issue. Paul was the officer-in-charge of the Wilshire Vice Unit when one of his teams, led by a sergeant who was a great guy, did something really stupid. Acting on some information they had received, they went to a bowling alley and observed a group of older women wagering pennies as the stakes for bowling scores. Pennies! Why the officers did what they did, I will never know—but they cited the women for illegal gambling!

Thank goodness they didn't make any physical arrests. It didn't take long for the media to get wind of the officers' actions, and I got a call from press relations asking if it was true that a group of older women were cited for gambling for pennies. By all accounts, despite my fading memory, I was pretty upset when I learned what my folks had done. Supposedly, I took a big verbal chunk out of Paul's rear end. Thankfully, the media didn't make much of a deal over it, and it showed up as just a small article on one of the back pages.

"Fly High and Land Low"

This was very funny. One of the several subordinate captains who worked for me at Wilshire was John Mutz, a good man. One evening he was presiding over a community meeting where several citizens were complaining about the noise and blinding light from low-flying police helicopters.

John told the group that he would address the issue. Then he told them of a new police program involving the Air Support Division that didn't really exist, called "Fly High and Land Low!" In attempting to describe a quieter tactic to recommend to the pilots, he quickly and mistakenly came up with a term that was really a no-brainer! I still give John a good-natured hard time over this when I see him, which unfortunately is not often.

Lying Lieutenant

During my LAPD career I met a few folks who I didn't particularly care for. But I have to say that, except for this situation, I never knew a manager who was an outright liar.

During my tenure as the commanding officer of Wilshire area, I had a number of lieutenants assigned to my command. In this instance, our Vice personnel took into custody a peace officer from a state agency who had been caught in the act with a prostitute. His weapon was taken away from him. Soon it was revealed that he was the son of a very well-respected former police department staff officer, someone whom we all thought well of.

Certainly, there was no effort made to cover up anything. But with the input of the bureau commanding officer and out of courtesy to the retired staff officer, it was determined to "gently" notify the agency the retired staff officer's son worked for, and to return his gun without a lot of fanfare. I made it abundantly clear to the lieutenant to ensure that the notification was made in a sensitive manner and without drama, and to a particular person who was yet to be identified.

The lieutenant, who was just about to leave for a week-long class, apparently forgot my guidance. As a result, the detectives who normally handled weapon issues made a routine notification to the agency, with the result that a number of people immediately learned about the inappropriate behavior of the retired staff officer's son. My boss, the bureau commanding officer, was absolutely livid. He was among those who thought the world of this former staff officer, had actually spoken to him about this issue, and assured him that the matter would be handled appropriately and discreetly. The bureau commanding officer came to the station and interviewed the lieutenant and me separately, and was told by the latter that I'd never said anything to him about making a discreet notification. The lieutenant out-and-out lied, and I think the bureau commanding officer chose to accept his version of the events. This situation didn't do me any good, and I believe it contributed to my transfer to Northeast Area.

This lieutenant continued to move up in the organization until forced out several years later by a subsequent chief of police.

———

Northeast Area

In June 1990, after just under two years in Wilshire, I was reassigned as the commanding officer of the Northeast Area. I was over both the patrol and detective divisions, as well as the vice, community relations, records, and garage units. Due to the close proximity of Jail Division, there was no jail at the Northeast station. As I recall, there were approximately 250 persons assigned to the Northeast area, of all ranks. The station was located at 3353 San Fernando Road.

Assigned as the Commanding Officer of Northeast

On an afternoon in June of 1990, just as I got home from work, I got a call from Commander Jim Jones. He was the commanding officer of Operations-West Bureau, and my boss. Jim was not very happy with me for one legitimate reason, and for another reason that was not.

The legitimate criticism was based on my failure to stay on top of my overtime situation, with the consequence that a number of detectives had accrued much more overtime than I should have allowed. It was not something I'd dealt with before, and plain and simple I screwed up and deserved criticism. The other situation was unfair. It was the result of Jim having accepted the lying lieutenant's version of events with respect to the just-described weapons notification.

In transferring to Northeast I was pleased to have Commander Jim Chambers, the Central Bureau commanding officer, as my new boss. Jim was also a good man, a good friend and someone who always went out of his way to treat me well.

Interesting, a little more than three years later when I found myself a commander in the West Bureau, in the drawer of my new desk was a folder that had been maintained about me when I was the area commanding officer at Wilshire. Maintaining a folder containing notes and thoughts and documents is a good and common practice, and helpful when it comes to writing an evaluation of a command officer. I must not have been too much of a problem, as the folder was full of good and postive information.

Another factor entered into my reassignment. That was a desire on the part of several people, including a black police commissioner who was also a former assistant chief, to have a particular black captain given an area command in South-Central Los Angeles. As Wilshire Area was partially in South-Central Los Angeles, it fit the bill. There is no doubt in my mind that the bureau commanding officer's efforts to achieve this goal (not necessarily inappropriate) was also a factor in my transfer to Northeast Area. I was unhappy and felt humiliated, as Northeast was seen as a lesser challenge than Wilshire. Nevertheless, I went to Northeast and did the best job I could. My performance as the commanding officer of Northeast Area was seen by everyone as superb, and contributed to my later assignment as the commanding officer of Central Area (which was a real can of worms and seen by everyone as a challenge).

To add insult to injury, five months after I left the Wilshire Area, the new commanding officer got an award for his superb management skills in Wilshire! Backing out the approximate two-month window for processing an award recommendation, my replacement was commended for the first three months of his service in Wilshire—but it was all stuff that I had accomplished!

It is interesting that Jim Jones, a very decent and talented individual, was given the shaft at a later date by Chief Willie Williams and some of the same crowd. I hate to say this, but I'm one among many people who perceived somewhat of an ethnic organizational junta when Williams was chief, and that ethnicity was occasionally more of a factor than it should have been with Williams, and later with Bernard Parks when he was chief.

There were several people of color who should never have been promoted to higher ranks. But they were promoted over far-more-qualified and deserving non-African-American command officers. In the case of Jim Jones, he truly did a great deal of the heavy lifting at the staff and command level when Williams was first appointed chief of police, and should have been among the first people promoted to the rank of deputy chief. Yet he was never promoted. Jim tried hard to do the best job he could for new Chief Willie Williams, but it certainly didn't do Jim any good. Despite my disappointment at the role that Jim played in my transfer from Wilshire, I continue to hold him in the highest esteem and have had the opportunity to interact with him several times since he retired. Jim is married to a former deputy city attorney, Donna Weiss, and a finer and more professional lady never walked the face the earth.

The Stacy Lim Shooting

On a late Friday night I was lying in my sleeping bag in the field at Camp Pendleton on a USMC drill weekend, when my LAPD pager went off. It took me quite a while to get to a phone and contact Northeast Station.

The watch commander informed me that one of my female officers, Stacy Lim, had been in an off-duty shooting, had killed the suspect, but that she was in grave condition at the Henry Mayo Hospital in Newhall. I immediately rushed to the hospital, arriving in the small hours of the morning. Stacy was indeed in grave condition, and in surgery when we arrived.

It seems that several young thugs saw her driving her SUV in the vicinity of the Northeast police station, but didn't realize she was a police officer who had just got off duty. One of them intended to carjack her for the rims on her car, so he followed her all the way to her residence in the Newhall area. When she pulled into her driveway, the thug approached with a .357 revolver and demanded her keys. Stacy responded with a few rounds from her 9mm Baretta, and killed him. But she was critically wounded by his gunfire. Cathy (who had joined me) and I sat with Stacy's dad throughout the surgery.

Shortly after daybreak, the surgeon advised us that he had operated extensively to treat Stacy's chest wound and to stop the internal bleeding. He had done everything possible. But he said that she was now in

God's hands, and we needed to pray that the surgery had been success-ful. The next few hours would be the most critical.

Cathy and I drove home. But about the time we reached the house I got another page. The hospital advised us that the internal bleeding had started again and it didn't appear that Stacy would survive. We im-mediately returned to the hospital to be with her and her family as she slipped away. However, on our arrival back at Henry Mayo, the physi-cian said a miracle had occurred—the bleeding had stopped! This fine officer ultimately experienced a full recovery!

At the time of this writing, Stacy is a weapons and tactics instructor at the LAPD Academy and a fierce softball player! Miracles do happen.

SCARED STRAIGHT, PARENTAL MENTORING, AND RESTORATION

One of my troops at Northeast was Officer Frank DiPaola, a great and innovative guy. He and I put together a program that was absolutely superb; frankly, he deserves the lion's share of the credit.

We had an Explorer surveillance team we would put on stakeouts. They would communicate their observations of crimes in progress to a dedicated chase car, whose officers would then corroborate their obser-vations and make the arrests. We arrested many folks for breaking into cars, and many little turds and gang members for painting graffiti. With the assistance of a judge, Northeast Area was designated as a referral agency for alternate measures when criminal prosecution did not appear to be appropriate. Typically, graffiti artists would be referred to North-east, where DiPaola would coordinate their parents' participation in a parental counseling program, and the kids would be enrolled in a work release program that involved painting out graffiti! It worked great! We had a truck-full of paint and a regular route to the usual locations, plus a program where any citizen or businessperson could call and have graffiti removed almost immediately.

This was a great program, in which some kids were very likely put back on the right path, where parents experienced the consequences of not supervising their kids adequately, and where we made our commu-nity a better and more attractive place. When I transferred to Central, I took Frank with me, and he did a great job of developing the "Central Enhancement Corps," to improve conditions downtown. Unfortunately, the CEC was not as successful as it could and should have been. Anoth-er judge refused to permit the Central Police Station to be considered a referral agency, because several non-profits complained they were not getting adequate referrals.

ACTIVATED FOR THE GULF WAR

From the moment I learned that Iraqi military forces had entered Kuwait in August 1990, there was no doubt that the Marine Corps Reserve unit I then commanded, the 3D Air-Naval Gunfire Liaison Company (3D ANGLICO), would be activated. Being familiar with then-classified war plans, I was aware that 3D ANGLICO was part of an existing military contingency and would be activated for this type of situation in that part of the world.

I was frustrated we weren't activated sooner. Then I learned that the regular commanding officer of 1ST ANGLICO wanted my troops to bolster the size of his unit, but didn't want an additional ANGLICO command in theatre. Unfortunately, this was typical careerist behavior in the sometimes dog-eat-dog, competitive active duty senior officer environment. One brigade platoon was requested in late November 1990, so I plused-up (reinforced) the Second Brigade platoon and shipped them off to the Second Marine Division at Camp Lejeune (NC), to which they would be attached. Shortly after Christmas, the platoon deployed to Southwest Asia (SWA). These wonderful men did a great job when the ground war was initiated, destroying approximately 230 Iraqi armored vehicles.

The remainder of 3D ANGLICO wasn't activated until the third day of the four-day war, in late January 1991! Frankly, had it not been for my behind-the-scenes maneuvering and whining and begging, we might not have been activated at all. Despite the efforts of some to cause de-activation to occur sooner, 3D ANGLICO remained on active duty at Camp Pendleton (including the advance party that had returned from SWA) until May of 1991. The Marine Corps section in these memoirs provides additional information pertaining to this period and activities.

HORRIBLE IMAGES ON CNN

While on active duty and watching CNN, I witnessed a video of several police officers beating a downed motorist. While not knowing exactly what had occurred, it was clear that much of the force being used was overkill and unnecessary. I watched it, wondering which police department was involved, then was shocked and sickened when I learned it was my own LAPD. This incident was the now-infamous Rodney King beating. It completely changed the LAPD and everyone who was part of it, including me.

442

Back Went Out— Totally Disabled for a Few Days!

Backs can be pretty tricky, and mine is no exception. I learned a valuable lesson about how *not* to lift things, when I encountered a pregnant woman with a flat tire on the Glendale Freeway.

I was in uniform and didn't want to get dirty, but I was determined to change the tire for her. I foolishly changed the tire in the wrong manner, by lifting the old tire off and putting the new tire on while squatting. Had I put a knee on the ground, and not all the weight on my lower back, I would have been all right. But I lifted it inappropriately and really paid the price.

About two days later, while exiting the police car of an officer I was having lunch with, my back went out. I absolutely could not stand up straight! It turned out to be a muscular issue, and I was literally a hunchback for several days. For those who read this, take good care of your back and learn to lift properly. In my senior years, I find myself paying an increasingly stiff price (along with an occasional stiff back) for not taking better care of my back during a very active life.

Pinning a Medal on Staff Sergeant Cottle at His Roll Call

In his professional life, Staff Sergeant R. J. Cottle was a Los Angeles police officer assigned to the West Los Angeles Field Services Division. He also was one of my men in 3D ANGLICO who deployed to Kuwait during the First Gulf War. After distinguishing himself in combat, he was nominated for and received the Navy Commendation Medal with the combat "V" device.

I decided to surprise him by pinning the military medal on his chest at his police roll call. His captain really did a great job, getting a celebratory cake and inviting a number of officers and prominent citizens. It was a wonderful event for that wonderful man, and an absolute honor for me to read the citation and give Staff Sergeant Cottle his well-deserved medal.

Several years later, in 2011, while on his fourth deployment for the Iraq/Afghanistan War and on a leave of absence from Metropolitan Division-SWAT, Sergeant Major R. J. Cottle was killed in action.

God bless you—and *Semper Fidelis*—Sergeant Major Cottle.

The Rodney King beating triggered a firestorm within the Los Angeles Police Department. The actions of the officers in using excessive force on a suspect, Rodney King, who had led the police and CHP on a long pursuit, were not defensible. Every individual and entity who disliked the LAPD and Chief Daryl Gates saw it as their opportunity to take on the department and potentially achieve some significant changes in the way the LAPD was alleged to have done business.

At the time Chief Gates and Mayor Bradley did not have a bad relationship, as they had no relationship at all! The mayor and the chief despised each other, and didn't even talk to one another. In addition to the mayor, a number of members of the Los Angeles City Council also disliked Chief Gates and saw the Rodney King affair as a potential opportunity to force Chief Gates to retire.

When I returned from the Marine Corps, I encountered a department that was under siege by many politicians and the media. Former U.S. Secretary of State Warren Christopher had been selected to lead a study of the department, made up primarily of volunteer lawyers, and it was pretty clear that the results would be ugly. All kinds of changes were being contemplated and made with respect to uses of force and recording use of force incidents, and just about everything else imaginable. Intensive efforts were underway on the part of many people, especially the liberal politicians, to force Chief Gates to retire; the writing was on the wall and it appeared likely that he would be forced out.

This was a really ugly time, and it was clear that the department was under a microscope and under siege. Everyone was pretty much braced to anticipate what the future might hold for the department. Nothing being predicted was seen as positive.

Quality of the Christopher Report

In the wake of the 1992 riots, the city commissioned former U.S. Secretary of State Warren Christopher, who at the time was a principal in a prominent law firm, to oversee a massive investigation to determine if the department's response had been appropriate in the Rodney King incident, what when wrong with that response (plenty!), and to make recommendations for the future. This report, coordinated by scores of pro bono attorneys and others, ended up being extensive and very critical, including a recommendation that it was time for Chief Daryl Gates to retire.

A very big part of the report dealing with the riots was the section having to do with the role and actions of the military forces that had come into Los Angeles. These actions were certainly known to me, because I was the key liaison and representative to all the military units that entered the city, including the Army, Army National Guard, and the Marine Corps.

Believing that a detailed account of all that had occurred would be required, I kept meticulous files and records. But no one ever asked for them! The Christopher Report obviously contained a great deal of commentary on the military, but I was never interviewed nor were my records ever requested. My reservations about the thoroughness and objectivity of the Christopher Commission Report were further validated by one unbelievable omission—how could a report that allegedly described what occurred during riots where the military played a major role, be anywhere near accurate without accurate information from the military?

Chief Gates' Role in His Demise

The actions that forced Chief Daryl Gates out of the police department, and brought Willie Williams in from Philadelphia, have been often discussed. While I had nothing but contempt for Mayor Bradley and the commission led by Warren Christopher he set up to review the Rodney King affair, it is my opinion that Chief Gates made a sizable contribution to his own downfall. He had been the chief for about fourteen years, but had pretty much lost patience with and held in contempt those who disagreed with his positions and/or the actions of the LAPD. I have said many times that he needed a reservoir of goodwill to survive the Rodney King issue and the recommendations of the Christopher Commission. Unfortunately, that reservoir was close to empty.

Extensive Search Yields the Weakest Candidate

When I returned from active duty following my activation for the first war in the Persian Gulf, I came back to a police department that was under terrible fire. The Rodney King incident turned out to be the rallying point for everybody who disliked the police department in general, and Daryl Gates in particular. The pressure to force Gates to step down and retire was extraordinary. In my judgment, the commissioning of the Christoper Report to investigate the Rodney King incident was a political effort that was preordained to heavily slam the department and to call for the retirement of Daryl Gates. That is exactly what occurred. After months of being under siege Gates announced his retirement, which became effective shortly after the Los Angeles Riots. At some point before the riots, the Police Commission selected, and Mayor Bradley ratified, the hiring of Philadelphia Police Commissioner Willie Williams to be the chief of the Los Angeles Police Department.

In hindsight, just about everyone, including several who played a role in his selection, came to realize their decision could not have been worse! He was grossly overweight, not well-educated for the position, and really did not have as much experience as it might have seemed, having started his career as a park police officer in Philadelphia. There is little doubt in my mind that his ethnicity was a major factor in his selection, and the fact that he was seen as an out-of-town reformer from a major agency—notwithstanding the reality that the department he came from had occasionally been seen as a troubled agency, including during a period when he was at the helm.

It is impossible to exaggerate the magnitude of the negative impact that Willie Williams had on the Los Angeles Police Department, its personnel, and the community. Under the revised city charter that became effective at the time Williams was hired, a police chief was hired for one term of five years. He could receive a second term, but could not serve longer than ten years.

Willie Williams started crashing and burning within a very short time after his arrival in Los Angeles. But the city muddled through his poor performance, and all the damage it was doing, for a little over four years. At that time Williams was nudged out of the department.

The dynamics that contributed to the selection of Willie Williams were something I have occasionally seen, before and since, in promotional and police chief selection processes where I have been involved. I have witnessed first-hand assessment centers where some candidates perform well in leaderless group discussions and impromptu presentations, but prove to be very weak in writing skills and complex problem-solving exercises. While recognizing that Willie Williams was a decent man who tried his best, I honestly do not believe that he would have been competitive at even the LAPD lieutenant level in a challenging assessment center process.

Predictably, Williams raised the issue that he was being discriminated against, arguing that it was among the reasons he was not given a second term. Equally predictably, the city gave him a financial payout to get him to go away. My observations of the Williams era, and the pain that I personally endured as a result of his leadership failures, stimulated me to write a fairly extensive manuscript, "Sobering Thoughts for Municipal Officials: The Consequences of Hiring a Weak Police Chief." This manuscript was ultimately published in the monthly magazine of the International City Management Association. Additionally, I had scores of copies made and, with a cover letter, provided copies of this manuscript to literally dozens of city managers and mayors throughout the country, based on their advertisements for police chief openings. I encourage those who are reading these memoirs to also obtain and read a copy of the above manuscript. It can be found on Google, and also on my website (www.KeithBushey.com). I hope I have done all the things necessary to ensure that this manuscript, and the lessons contained within it, last longer than I do!

Welcome Home. Now Pee in the Bottle!

As reflected in the military portion of these memoirs, I was called to active duty during the first Persian Gulf War, and left on a military leave of absence from the Los Angeles Police Department. I was very pleased that Chief Gates kept my command, Northeast Area, open for me, with Patrol Captain Dan Schatz acting in the capacity of area commanding officer during my absence.

I'm not sure what I expected for my first day back at the Los Angeles Police Department, but I got quite an interesting surprise. As I walked into the station for the first time in several months, then into my office, a sergeant and a police officer from the medical liaison unit were waiting for me. While I was away, my name popped up for a random urinalysis drug test, but the test obviously couldn't be administered. Anyway, after being welcomed back by these two individuals, I was asked to pee in the bottle!

Actually, I found this to be more amusing than irritating, as there was nothing personal or targeted toward me, just bureaucracy in action!

My Gay Friend, the Police Commissioner

As the commanding officer of Northeast area, among the many communities I was responsible for was a large neighborhood having a very large percentage of gay men and women. Accordingly, I sought to develop friendships with prominent individuals from the gay community who could assist me in my liaisons and activities involving that community. I was fortunate to meet a wonderful man, Art Mattox. Art and I became very close friends, and he also became close friends with my family.

Art had tremendous credibility, and was instrumental in assisting with the inroads I was able to make into the gay community as a whole, and with many of its organizations. We introduced some real interesting initiatives. One of them included taking men who had been arrested for lewd conduct in Griffith Park, and subjecting them to a lot of training about the adverse consequences of their behavior and the negative impact their actions had on the gay community in the greater Los Angeles area. We then used them—as a condition of their probation—to assist the police department in dissuading other individuals from engaging in similar activities in the park.

My friendship with and utilization of Art caused him to pop up on the radar screen of a number of people, including Mayor Richard Riordan, who appointed him to the Los Angeles Police Commission! After his service on the police commission, Art was appointed to the city's Ethics Commission! His regular job at that time was with the Xerox Corporation; however, he ultimately went to work for the Betty Ford Center in Palm Springs, and to this day remains one of my best friends.

CONSTERNATION OVER "CODE X"

This is a matter I really didn't care for, and brought to a stop whenever I learned of it.

Some officers who cheated on their wives would have the desk officer show them "Code X." It meant that if the man's wife called, she would be told her husband was on a special assignment (such as a stakeout), but that the desk officer could contact him if necessary on the police radio. Then the desk officer would call the amorous officer at a number he'd provided, and he'd be told to contact his wife. I have never cheated on either of my wives, and this wasn't an issue of morality for me, but one of consternation in dragging the department into someone's foolish personal behavior. I repeatedly told people not to involve the department in their irresponsible behavior, and never tired of explaining how such behavior is one of the key reasons cops have such lousy reputations with women (including my daughter Stacy!)

CRIME CONTROL MEETINGS

I'm not suggesting that crime wasn't always a big issue in the LAPD. But, because of competing near-obsessive activities at all levels related to personnel issues, during my tenure there was never a department-wide practice or policy as to how crime coordination should occur. Certainly, there was always the expectation that commanding officers would coordinate crime information and enforcement, but it was done differently throughout the department.

In all three geographic areas that I commanded, I would have periodic "crime control meetings," where I would bring the detectives, senior lead officers and the community relations officer together to exchange information, thoughts and strategies. I believe it was a good process, and that it was helpful in our efforts to reduce crime and put bad guys (and gals) in jail.

When several years later Bill Bratton came to Los Angeles as the chief of police, he brought with him the "Comstat" process. In it, captains are called downtown and put on the carpet, to demonstrate their awareness of crime, to report on measures being taken to make our communities safer and to deal with criminal activity.

This struck me as a great process, and I wish it had been in place when I was with the department. I've heard some criticism, probably merited in some instances, that the theatrical expectations have become so strong that the process appears to be more important than the end product, with the humilitation of command officers apparently being the goal in some instances. Still, when done well and reasonably, it strikes me as a very good thing to ensure that command officers are giving appropriate attention to crime.

Phantom Pooper With a Badge

On my way to work one morning I got a cell phone call from my detective commanding officer, Lieutenant Raul Vega. Raul explained that the detective division was up in arms and absolutely livid because someone, obviously a gang member who wanted to retaliate against the gang coordinator, had sneaked into the station in the middle the night and defecated in Detective III Bob State's chair! Raul explained that I had a near-mutiny on my hands in the detective bureau because of this horrible security breach.

When I arrived, I examined the scene and quickly came to believe that what occurred wasn't an intrusion by a gang member for retaliation. There was a disgusting mess in Bob's chair, obviously the result of some very nervous and out-of-control bowels. I couldn't imagine some gang member staking out in the bushes and waiting for the gate to open while his bowels were rumbling, then at some opportune moment rushing in the back door and being able to coordinate the messy defecation I was looking at.

I explained to the detectives that this was clearly a "SID," a "shit in distress," and I felt it was more likely the result of a sick or drunk police employee. Soon the focus of the investigation shifted to the cot room where police officers often slept, immediately adjacent to the detective bureau. As it turned out, one of the officers who had used the room the previous night had a drinking problem. But when interviewed, he denied any knowledge of the incident. I told Raul to interview him again, and to tell him that we were going to take a biological sample of the mess and compare it with the officer. I also told Raul to inform the alcoholic officer that if he went voluntarily to the Behavioral Sciences Services Section (BSS) to seek counseling for the matter, the investigation might just go away and be forgotten. Raul came back, and told me the officer immediately went to BSS. Case closed.

Truly Horrible Days—The 1992 Los Angeles Riots

As previously mentioned, I was away on active duty with the Marine Corps when the Rodney King incident occurred. When I watched video clips of the beating on cable news, I couldn't believe it had happened in Los Angeles. Chief Gates kept my assignment as commanding officer at Northeast open for me, and my subordinate captain, Dan Schatz, ran the area in my absence. Dan is a great man and a good friend. I returned to Los Angeles in time for the riots that took place when some folks became unhappy with the "not guilty" verdicts handed down by the Superior Court in Simi Valley. Experiencing and witnessing the resulting burning and looting was horrible. Those were some of the worst days in my life.

Deputy Chief Matt Hunt
Accurately Predicted Civil Disobedience

During the Rodney King case, jury deliberations were held in the Superior Court in Simi Valley, where the fate of the four accused officers was being considered. Eventually the case was moved to Ventura County on a change of venue. There was much speculation that "not guilty" verdicts would result in civil unrest in parts of Los Angeles.

Most police officials, including me, were convinced that our city was above that type of mass criminal behavior, and there would be no rioting. Nevertheless, a meeting was called in the sixth floor conference room,

Room 618, with all bureau and area commanding officers. As I recall, only one person was convinced there would be violence. He was Deputy Chief Matt Hunt. Most of us believed that he was overreacting and was mistaken. It turned out that Matt was right, and it was the rest of us who were mistaken. The riots were horrible, and just as Matt had predicted.

Chief Gates Seizes Up

Almost as soon as the riots started, I was designated to coordinate mutual aid and military support by Chief Gates, who selected me for this task based on my military background. On the first morning of the riots (they had begun the previous afternoon) a large group of folks met in the Sheriff's Conference Room at the Hall of Justice. Sheriff Sherman Block was there with his entire staff, as was CHP Commissioner Maury Halligan with his entire staff. The commanding general of the National Guard was there with his entire staff. The county and city fire chiefs were there with their entire staffs.

Chief Gates was there with only his driver and me, as a good number of his top people had either retired or were distancing themselves from him.

I will never forget a very troublesome moment during the discussion about how best to get National Guard and mutual aid troops into the city of Los Angeles. When Sheriff Block asked for Chief Gates' opinion on the organizational configuration that had just been suggested, Chief Gates seized up in what I will call psychological paralysis. The silence was deafening. Everyone was looking at Gates in a way that was both impatient and sympathetic.

Finally, I leaned over and whispered into Chief Gates' ear that we should go ahead and agree to what was being suggested. Apparently my words jarred him back to reality. He nodded his head in agreement and said yes. Poor Gates had been under siege for months. He had been forced from office, an outsider of questionable competence was about to take over the department, half his staff was not talking to him, and he was being blamed for the fact the city was burning. It's no small wonder that he seized up!

Trauma in the Emergency Operations Center

Sheriff Block was highly critical of Chief Gates. Block's consternation with the LAPD, coupled with years of inter-department rivalry, made the Sheriff's Emergency Operations Center (EOC) a very hostile place for an LAPD captain to be. Unfortunately, I was the LAPD captain! Initially, I had to fight to even get a place to sit, then had to do battle to try to get adequate numbers of military and mutual-aid law enforcement personnel into the city of Los Angeles.

The major part of the rioting occurred in Los Angeles proper. I'll never forget the statement one Sheriff's lieutenant made in response to my request for additional personnel: "Captain, Los Angeles is just one of the 88 cities in Los Angeles County! We'll get to you when we can!" I was in a really hostile environment, and must be candid in saying that the situation probably brought out the worst in me, as well. By the end of the riots, all of our nerves were pretty frayed. I'll never forget (but wish I could!) stepping out of the EOC into the night air and seeing the smoke and fire rising from the city I loved and had always tried to serve to the best of my abilities.

This negative situation had a profound effect on me. One result was that I wrote my POST Command College ISP (Independent Study Project) on "Military Support to Civil Authorities." In it, I placed a strong emphasis on developing and maintaining good relationships with those you are likely to interact with, in advance of unusual occurrences. My successful planning and execution of operational and evacuation activities for the 2003 San Bernardino Forest fires were a direct consequence of the lessons I learned—especially the actions to avoid—in the Sheriff's EOC during the 1993 Los Angeles Riots.

Briefing Mayor Bradley

One of the most unfortunate and well-known situations that existed during the last few years of Daryl Gates' tenure as police chief, was the fact that he and Mayor Tom Bradley didn't like and didn't talk to each other.

I learned this first-hand during the riots, when I was detailed to brief the mayor on behalf of the chief. My final briefing to the mayor had been on the Friday afternoon of the riots, with one of his key aides and somewhat of a friend of mine, Phil Depoian, present. The riots were starting to abate and law enforcement was getting a pretty good handle on gaining control. I was directed by Chief Gates and Sheriff Block to tell the mayor in no uncertain terms that federalization (bringing in federal troops) was unwise and completely unnecessary.

Phil and the mayor really quizzed me on this issue, and it became clear they had seen it as a potential necessity. I left at about 3:00 pm, believing I had convinced the mayor that federalization was not necessary and, for a bunch of procedural reasons as well, it would be a bad idea.

At 4:00 pm, while I was standing next to Gates and Block, President George Bush came on national television live, and announced he was granting the request of the mayor of Los Angeles to send federal troops into the city! Block and Gates were extremely upset that their assessment had fallen on deaf ears, and that unnecessary federalization and all of the limitations on how state troops can perform when federalized, had occurred. We later learned that prominent attorney Warren Christopher, working behind the scenes, was the person who convinced Bradley to seek federalization.

"Sheriff, You Have Been Lied to by Your Staff"

The sheriff's department conducted a massive meeting of all command personnel from all law enforcement agencies a couple of weeks after the riots ended. The purpose of the meeting was to capture lessons learned and to discuss strategies for dealing with the potential of further civil unrest. When Sheriff Block took the podium, he stated (among other things) that one of the problems during the riots was caused by an LAPD captain who used his personal relationships to have a Marine Corps unit respond directly into the city of Los Angeles without being processed through the sheriff's EOC.

I had been the liaison for military mutual aid, but knew nothing of this. Then it occurred to me that Block might have been told the LAPD captain was me, which certainly would not have been accurate. While I did have reservations about some of the things that occurred in the EOC, I played by the rules and never once circumvented any process.

Later that day I dictated a letter to Sheriff Block, in which I told him that if I was the one he referred to, he had been given inaccurate information. I had one of my sergeants hand-deliver the message to his office. Sheriff Block called me right back. We were quite well acquainted, because I was Chief Gates' representative on Capitol Hill, along with Sheriff Block's representative, and I had attended meetings and strategy sessions with him.

The sheriff got right to the point. He said he'd been told that a Marine unit deployed directly into the city, and that it was I who caused it to occur because of my status as a Marine Reserve lieutenant colonel. I told the sheriff that neither allegation was true, and I minced no words telling him that he had been lied to by his staff. I also did something pretty extraordinary—I offered to take a polygraph exam to be administered by his department!

453

He essentially apologized, and said there must have been some confusion, to which I reiterated my belief that he had been outright lied to. During the riots, tempers had flared in the EOC. I thought a couple of his high-ranking personnel had acted foolishly, and had apparently chose me as a target to deflect some things that went sideways.

We ended our chat on a positive note. While I'm not certain, I think my comments set in motion a reflection on the accuracy of some of the things he had been told by his own people.

Daryl Gates' Last Days

During the several weeks following the riots, nothing much really occurred. Obviously, there was a great deal of cleaning-up done throughout the city, the prosecutions of riot-related crimes, and finger-pointing by the many politicians who came out of the woodwork once the violence had subsided.

By this time Gates' book, *CHIEF*, had arrived from the publisher, and he spent many hours in his office personally inscribing messages to the hundreds of men and women (including me) who asked him to do so.

Gates' departure from Parker Center was a dark and emotional day for the many people who lined the hallways as he left. There was fanfare at the swearing-in ceremony for Willie Williams on June 30th, but not much of it came from the police department, except for a few staff and command officers who wanted to get an early shot at sucking-up to him. Out of respect for the department and the position of police chief, the attendance from the police department was respectable. But there were far more officers present than there were smiles.

A farewell picnic for Daryl Gates took place at the Academy on June 24; it was attended by several thousand people.

Everybody Wanted Chief Williams to Succeed

There have been concerns and allegations in some circles that Chief Willie Williams was doomed to fail because of all the people who wanted him to.

This is not true. Just about everybody I dealt with at my level were strong in two beliefs: We wished he hadn't been selected as chief, but we wanted him to succeed. The department had been beaten, battered, and dragged through the political mud for over a year. If Williams failed, the department would continue to suffer. Nobody wanted that.

454

But there reached a point, and it actually didn't take too long, when it became clear that Williams did not have the skills for the job. He walked into an environment where the vast majority of people were sorry he had been selected, but they realized for better or worse that he was now the chief and we all wanted him to do well.

Central Area

In the summer of 1992, after approximately two years in Northeast area, I was reassigned as the commanding officer of Central Area. There I was over both the patrol and detective divisions, as well as the vice, community relations, records, and homeless units. Central was located in the massive Central Facilities Building, where neither a separate jail nor a garage unit was necessary. As I recall, there were approximately 350 personnel assigned to Central Area at that time, of all ranks.

Keith, I am About to Complicate Your Life

One afternoon in early 1992 I got a call from Deputy Chief Bernard Parks, who was my boss as the commanding officer of Operations-Central Bureau. He said that he was about to complicate my life, as I was being reassigned to Central Area as the Area Commanding Officer. I was truly sad to be leaving Northeast, but pleased and flattered to be given one of the most demanding commands in the LAPD.

Taking Over in the Wake of an Unpopular Captain

All things considered, I was pleased to transfer to Central. While I liked Northeast, Central Area was widely recognized as a complex and challenging command. My assignment there signaled a considerable degree of confidence in me personally.

As I was still smarting from my bullshit reassignment from Wilshire to Northeast, I really welcomed being given a task that everyone recognized was pretty tough. I took over from a very unpopular captain who had been pushed into retirement. Shortly after I arrived at Central, one of the sergeants who disliked my predecessor told me that people were so happy to see him go and for me to arrive, that "you could sit in the middle of Sixth & Main Streets at high noon and masturbate, and the troops would give you a standing ovation!" Taking over in the wake of an unpopular person is always a good thing.

While the commanding officer of Central Area, I dealt with daily tragedies. Nothing, however, is more painful in the workplace than the loss of a fellow employee.

One day while I was working in my office, the watch commander came in and informed me that one of our officers had just taken his life. The officer had gone to the roof parking lot above the station and shot himself in the head with his service weapon!

I'm ashamed that I didn't recognize his name, and only vaguely recognized his face. I hadn't been in Central that long, and was still struggling to get to know the several hundred officers I was honored to have in my command.

It turned out that this fine young man had come from a very troubled home that was largely devoid of love. Recently he'd gone into a deep depression when dumped by his first real girlfriend. She was reportedly the first person with whom he'd ever had a truly loving relationship, and it was said that he overwhelmed her with affection that unintentionally drove her away. Then he met another gal, fell madly in love, and apparently also overwhelmed her with affection and drove her away. This second rejection was what caused him to take his own life.

While I don't know the details, there was a great deal of anger from his fellow officers at the thought that his life insurance money would go to the two lousy parents whose lack of love and affection contributed to his death. Tragically, his suicide was a permanent solution to a temporary problem.

APOLOGIES TO AN ACCUSED OFFICER

The Rodney King matter, where a black parolee was beaten at the termination of a freeway pursuit in early 1991, was a terrible event for the Los Angeles Police Department and the trigger that ultimately resulted in the departure of Chief Daryl Gates and the hiring of Chief Willie Williams.

Afterward, the not-guilty verdict in state court of the four officers charged with King's beating was the triggering event for the massive Los Angeles riots that took place in 1992. Just about everybody who'd been anywhere near that pursuit was tainted. A number of officers were disciplined, which included being ordered to department trial boards to face a variety of charges.

I was the chairman of one such trial board, involving a senior officer and his female probationer. They were charged with failure to take appropriate action when they observed excessive force being applied at the termination of the pursuit. The senior officer was Joseph Napolitano, and the other officer was Ingrid Larsen. Since Larsen was a probationer, she was not entitled to a board of rights and had previously received a ten-day suspension for her alleged failure to take action. Napolitano was the only officer at this particular board (there were many other accused officers in other boards stemming from this incident). Napolitano's board took place roughly eighteen months after the incident. He had been working the desk the entire time, having been removed from the field pending his trial board.

The board was very short! By using the videotape of the incident (taken by a bystander, sold to the news media and subsequently shown thousands of times throughout the world!), the defense representative was able to definitely establish there had been no misconduct during the brief time the two officers pulled up to the incident and observed what was occurring. As the misconduct took place after they had driven off, we found Officer Napolitano not guilty. As the chairman of the board, and on behalf of the department, I apologized to Officer Napolitano for the months of anguish he had clearly experienced while waiting for the disciplinary hearing. I also indicated, all of it transcribed into the official record, that Officer Larsen had been unfairly penalized for something she had not done. I then generated a letter to the chief of police recommending that Officer Larsen's discipline be rescinded and that her suspension days be restored. My apology was picked up and printed in the *Los Angeles Times*. Officer Larsen's penalty was never rescinded and her suspension days were never restored.

Unfortunately, this was indicative of the hysteria that often surrounded well-publicized LAPD scandals. Like the Hollywood burglary scandal, and later the Raphael Perez-Rampart scandal, there were good and innocent officers, as well as guilty personnel, who ended up being disciplined and tainted during the course of the massive investigations.

Those Dreaded Phone Calls From the Chief of Staff

Not surprisingly, there were times when the chief of police, or other members of his top staff, were not pleased at the penalty recommendation from a board of rights. Their typical concern was that the recommended penalty was too light. That sometimes didn't sit well with the chief, because by city statute he had the ability to lower, but not increase, a penalty recommended by the board. In such instances, the chief of staff would usually call the chairperson of the board, indicate that the chief had concerns, and inquire about the matter and ask how the recommended penalty had been arrived at.

On the occasions when I expected such a call, I was seldom disappointed. Accordingly, I always went to great lengths to create a written rationale that fully explained the views of the board. Despite the inquiries, no one ever gave me much of a hard time about a board where I'd served as chairperson (which in later years was most of the time). But there were times when I knew the chief felt I had been too lenient. Interestingly, as I reflect back, I don't ever recall a time when someone thought I had been too harsh. I found the members of a board to typically be very knowledgeable about the cases, and they ended up having the best perspective about what had occurred and the totality of circumstances. Most people understood this reality.

STANDARD OF PROOF FOR INTERNAL POLICE DISCIPLINE

In the case of violations of criminal law, the burden of proof in court to determine guilt is "guilt beyond a reasonable doubt." For administrative hearings, including police boards of rights, the standard to determine guilt is a "preponderance of evidence," which means an officer can be found guilty if 51% of the evidence points to culpability on his or her part.

That minimal burden of preponderance never worked for me. While a command officer on the LAPD, as the marshal of San Bernardino County, and while a deputy chief on the San Bernardino County Sheriff's Department, I did not find employees guilty unless I was certain that they had committed or omitted the acts they were accused of.

My standard for cops was (and is) "guilt beyond a reasonable doubt."

REFUSAL TO PERMIT THE DEPARTMENT TO BE USED FOR RETALIATION

Divorces and break-ups can be pretty nasty. Whoever coined the term pertaining to a "woman scorned" (men too!) really knew what he (or she) was talking about. In my long career as a supervisor, manager, and executive, I have been on the receiving end of many attempts by scorned lovers, wives (particularly), and husbands to use the department as a tool to retaliate against someone because of a failed relationship. When contacted, I did not immediately shut them down or refuse to listen to the issue, as the last thing I wanted to do was kiss something off only to later learn that genuine violence was involved. Once I determined that I was part of the process of "being used" to harm a former spouse or lover, I made it real clear that the department was not going to get involved. That is what courts, attorneys, counselors, and restraining orders are for. I also recommended counseling through the Behavior Sciences Section on many occasions. Concerned, yes; involved, no.

Disappointed in Someone I'd Mentored

When I was the commanding officer of Central Area, a perceived scandal got a great deal of press. It seems that two Hollenbeck detectives, Teague and Merkel, had falsified reports in an effort to prove that a suspect was guilty of murder. If true, this was bad and serious stuff. When the alleged falsification was uncovered by a deputy district attorney, it was immediately reported to the department.

At this time, the department was still reeling from the Rodney King matter and the LA riots of 1992. Chief Willie Williams hastily called a press conference, announcing that an investigation had been launched into the actions of two "rogue detectives" (as I recall, that is the term he used—if not, it was something close, and equally derogatory), and they had been relieved from duty. At the time the investigation was initiated, I knew only what I'd read in the papers and had been told internally, and had no reason to doubt the validity of the allegations. If true, they were serious and would most likely result in criminal charges and terminations.

Then I was selected as the chairman of the board of rights for Teague and Merkel. Although somewhat unusual and arguably inappropriate, a representative of the Police Protective League, the union that represents lieutenants and below, came to me with an explosive revelation: the two detectives had done nothing wrong, and evidence to be presented at the hearing would clearly established their innocence! The PPL person not only wanted to clear the detectives, but also to spare the detectives and the department the embarrassment of a public hearing that would only put the department in further unfavorable light. When I reviewed the evidence, it became absolutely clear the detectives had done nothing wrong! The "false report" seen by the deputy district attorney was an investigative ploy used as a prop in the interrogation of the suspects, a most appropriate and legal procedure. The only issue was that it was located in the wrong section of the homicide book/investigation. This matter was easily explained.

I went to the commanding officer of the involved bureau, a deputy chief, and presented him with the evidence that the officers had done nothing wrong. I emphasized that these detectives, who had long been relieved from duty, had to be suffering terribly. I urged him to intervene with the chief of police to immediately correct this injustice and have the matter looked at in a fresh light.

The deputy chief made it clear it was a "hot potato" (my term, as I do not recall his exact expression) and that he was not about the open a can of worms. He felt the best course was to let the matter go before a board of rights. Normally, I would have agreed, but their innocence was so obvious, the detectives had to be emotional basket-cases over their public relief from duty, and the department was about to look very foolish. I was ashamed of this deputy chief, who had worked for me many years before, when I had been his mentor and supporter. Unfortunately, he was more concerned with not rocking the boat than with doing the right thing. As predicted, the board very quickly determined that the two detectives had not done anything wrong, and that the primary problems stemmed from a misinterpretation by an inexperienced deputy district attorney.

GAINING WEIGHT AT THE BUFFET DURING BAKER-TO-VEGAS

I participated in the annual police relay race known as "Baker-to-Vegas," sponsored by the Los Angeles Police Revolver & Athletic Club. The race involves scores of law enforcement agencies, fielding teams of runners that cover the 120-mile course across the Mojave Desert.

One year, my dear pal and his wife, Jim and Robin Collins, joined Cathy and me. After getting up one morning, Cathy and I went down to the buffet in the hotel to meet Jim and Robin. There we found a very upset Jim Collins, visibly despondent because he was gaining too much weight, as evidenced by the t-shirt that was clearly struggling to contain his upper body.

While chatting, Robin checked the tab on the back of Jim's collar to ensure it was the right size—and discovered it was her shirt and not his! Oh my goodness, we all laughed until we were about to wet our pants. How funny, and what a relief for a fellow who really loves those buffets!

CENTRAL ENHANCEMENT CORPS

As the commanding officer of Central Area, I was always looking for ways the department could play a role in enhancing the downtown area. I came up with something that I really liked, that really worked, that the business community loved, and which ultimately failed because of special interests that influenced the courts.

But for several months, I successfully had men and women who were arrested for minor issues in the downtown area referred to Central Division for "work release" credits. We had red vests with CENTRAL ENHANCEMENT CORPS embroidered on the back, which, along with a broom and debris pick-up device, were issued to the work release crews. Each work release individual was then assigned a specific downtown block where they would spend several hours walking around and picking up virtually every bit of trash.

It worked great and was highly touted—until several grant-funded agencies that used court referrals for their projects complained they were not getting enough workers, because so many violators were being assigned to the Central Enhancement Corps. My meeting with the presiding judge was pretty much a waste of time, as he sided with the agencies the courts had been working with. I was in the process of doing some scheming to overcome the problem with the courts, when I was promoted and left Central Area.

You Catch 'em—You Clean 'em

During my tenure as area commanding officer, Central was a "whopper pond" for criminals. You could just about walk out the station door and grab someone, with a good chance that he or she was wanted for something, in possession of drugs, or more likely, both. There were plenty of crooks to go around, and other agencies often conducted investigations and made arrests in Central.

One agency, the Metropolitan Transit Authority (MTA) Police Department, had a few officers who liked to make arrests, but didn't like to do the related reports. Instead, they merely turned their suspects over to my officers for processing and booking. Once in a while, this practice would have been acceptable. But these few MTA officers were hooking, and we were doing the booking and related reports, in far too many instances.

Accordingly, I put out the infamous (for a while) "You Catch 'em—You Clean 'em Memo" to my folks, and sent a copy to the MTA police chief, Sharon Papa. The memo was intended to be helpful, and offered tutoring to MTA personnel on our reports and procedures. But the intent was clear: we did not intend to continue writing their reports and booking their suspects.

The results were immediate. Our MTA-related workload dropped off to almost nothing. A couple of weeks after I sent the memo to the

MTA, I ran across Sharon Papa at a downtown meeting where I perceived hostility and a cold shoulder, which I attributed to her not appreciating my letter and position.

A couple of years later, in 1996, I was serving as the human resources czar for the LAPD, and again encountered Sharon Papa. I was involved in the personnel side of the absorbtion of some MTA personnel into the police department, as that agency was being disbanded and its personnel were moving into either the police or sheriff's departments. I found her to be the consummate professional, and a pleasure to deal with. Although the merger did not occur prior to my retirement, Sharon entered the LAPD at the rank of commander and quickly established herself as one of the finest staff officers on the department, where she continues to serve. I had numerous dealings with Sharon on mutual law enforcement issues during my tenure in San Bernardino County, and continue to deal with her in several peace officer associations. I feel fortunate to be able to count this exceptional lady among my friends.

Impromptu Presentation in San Marcos

My ability to ad-lib and make extemporaneous presentations is pretty much legend. This next situation contributed to that legend. It is often brought up by Rod Hoops, who went on to be sheriff of the San Bernardino County Sheriff's Department and who, as a lieutenant, was among my classmates in the California POST Command College Class 17.

An instructor named Dorothy had made a series of presentations on some subject, after which all students gathered into breakout groups to formulate their presentations on whatever the issue was. My group had written their thoughts onto butcher paper, which was mounted on an easel.

I'd been gone the entire morning, and had missed everything, returning to the classroom just as Dorothy invited a representative from my group to come forward and make its presentation. Just to have some fun with me, the leader of my group said I was the spokesperson and would make the presentation! I stood before the group, glanced at the comments on the butcher paper, and made about a fifteen-minute presentation, with much of the material pulled right out of my body from where the sun doesn't shine.

Dorothy listened intently, and at the end of the presentation complimented me on it. The entire class was aware of what occurred and were astounded. They gave me a standing ovation.

The days of folks getting promoted consistent with the total of their written and oral scores, plus the seniority factor, were long over by the time the process took place that caused me to be promoted to commander.

Now there was an assessment center, a written exercise, and an oral interview. The candidates were ranked in the order of whole scores. I was in Band Two by myself. I was the second highest candidate, with the top person being one whole score ahead of me in Band One, also by himself. As I recall, there was one person in Band Three, a couple in Band Four, etc.

I don't believe that at this point Chief Williams had started to really dislike me, but even if he had it's still likely I would have been promoted. Because of my high score and being in a top band by myself, he would not have been able to "reach" other bands to promote other people unless he first promoted me. Thus, in October 1993 I became Commander Bushey. I was beyond thrilled when notified that I was being assigned to Operations-West Bureau as the assistant bureau commanding officer. I would be working for a great fellow whom I had long liked and respected, Deputy Chief Ron Frankle.

––––––

OPERATIONS—WEST BUREAU

Operations-West Bureau was the entity that was responsible for roughly one fourth of the city for conventional patrol, detective, gang, and traffic activities. The bureau consisted of Hollywood, Wilshire, West Los Angeles, and Pacific Areas, plus West Traffic Division, the substation at the Los Angeles International Airport, and the West Side Combined Resources Against Street Hoodlums Section (CRASH). The bureau officers were on an upper floor of leased office space at 6464 West Sunset Boulevard.

WORKING FOR DEPUTY CHIEF RON FRANKLE

Ron is one of the finest men I have ever had the good fortune to associate with. He was no-nonsense with respect to his responsibilities, but in exercising those responsibilities revealed a heart as big as Los Angeles. He gave me a great deal of discretion, which I certainly did not abuse. Because of high blood pressure, he was off IOD (injured on duty sick time status) quite a bit, and during those times I functioned in his stead as the bureau commanding officer.

TEAGUE, MERKEL, AND A PISSED-OFF POLICE CHIEF

The board of rights (disciplinary hearing) for detectives Teague and Merkel took place after I had been promoted to commander. I served as the chairman. These two innocent detectives had been relieved from duty for close to a year, all because a sloppy deputy district attorney had misinterpreted a report and the police department jumped to negative conclusions without closely reviewing the matter.

It was a very short board, and both officers were quickly found not guilty of attempting to frame the suspect. As I recall, we found one of the two guilty for not placing the report in the appropriate portion of the homicide book/folder (one of the charges initiated by the department), and gave him a warning. It was the lowest penalty possible.

Both publicly, and on the record, I apologized to the two detectives on behalf of the department. I then wrote a commendation to their defense representative, Officer Tim Sands, for his work in establishing what was initially seen as a sinister conspiracy as nothing more than a simple error (something to that effect).

Within the next day or so, Detectives Teague and Merkel initiated a multi-million dollar lawsuit against Chief Willie Williams for defamation of character (etc., etc.), citing my findings to support their position! This likely was the first reason, perhaps among other reasons, why Chief Willie Williams did not care for Commander Bushey!

COMMAND COLLEGE CRUISE AND THE EARTHQUAKE

In January of 1994, Cathy and I joined several other couples from my Command College class on a graduation cruise to Mexico.

One day out of port on our seven-day Mexican Riviera cruise, we got the news that a devastating earthquake had struck Los Angeles, with massive damage resulting. It became known as the 1994 Northridge Earthquake.

I was beyond frustrated! My place was at West Bureau, dealing with the event, not 200 miles off the coast of Mexico! I got through to Ron Frankle on the ship-to-shore phone and told him I would catch the first plane out of the first port we pulled into in Mexico. But Ron made it clear—very clear—that I was to remain and enjoy the cruise, and there would be plenty left for me to do when the ship returned to Los Angeles a week later.

464

That's Ron Frankle! Even though I personally would have liked to return, I remained with Cathy and the others, and had a great time. Ron was right—there was plenty left to do when I returned, including another week or so of twelve-hour shifts.

Mentoring Investments—Good and Otherwise

With thirty-plus years on the LAPD, I was starting to reap what I had sown in terms of mentoring. However, I wasn't completely pleased with the performance of some of my former subordinates. While most of my investments, like Commander Dan Koenig, Captain Al Deal, and Deputy Chief Ron Bergmann caused me to be proud, a couple of others (who I'll not identify) lacked the personal qualities that I mistakenly thought they possessed.

The first hint was their failure to reach out and wish me well when I left the department—I dropped off their radar screen at the moment I was no longer in a position to do them any good. They were not bad people. But to some extent they forgot who helped them achieve the positions they held and, most troubling, avoided situations where their voices should have been heard. For self-serving and selfish reasons, they stayed clear of areas where more courageous persons would have gone.

Ray Sherrard's Fiftieth Birthday Party—Surprise!

Ray Sherrard has been my best friend during just about my entire adult life. We had a great time when I put together a surprise birthday party for his fiftieth! It was held at the El Encanto Restaurant in Azusa Canyon. All of his friends and all of my family attended, and we really did surprise him. To give him a little bit of a jolt, I hired a gal to come in as a stripper. She was a real hit with everyone—but was most appreciated by my young son Zak, who reminded me that he had a birthday coming up himself!

Poor Zak! He just couldn't take his tender twelve-year-old eyes off the gal's formidable breastworks.

Double Homicide on Greenleaf

All murders are horrible, but this double homicide hit pretty close to home. One of my sergeants in the West Los Angeles Area, Jack Wells, had a close acquaintance with a lady whose name was Connie Navarro. She was also the mother of rock-star guitarist, Dave Navarro.

Jack, a very decent and caring person, was a bit of a shoulder for Connie to cry on. She had been dating a New Yorker, whose last name was Ricardi, but the relationship was apparently pretty rocky. As I recall, Jack advised Connie to get out of the relationship, but it apparently didn't happen.

One day, Jack became concerned at his inability to contact Connie. So we sent someone (I don't recall if Jack was one of the initial units) to her apartment on Greenleaf Street to check on her. There we found Connie and her female roommate, Sue Jory, both dead. Ricardi had murdered them, and stuffed their bodies into a linen cabinet in the hallway.

We were able to make some quick inquiries, and learned that Ricardi lived in an apartment in Santa Monica. I was among the officers who converged on that location; unfortunately, we missed him by just a couple of minutes. He was wanted for several years, was featured on the "America's Most Wanted" TV show, and also made the FBI's Top Ten Most Wanted. Although I don't recall the details, he was captured after something like ten years on the run, convicted of the two murders, and sentenced to death. But, like just about every person on California's death row, he'll probably die of old age!

Directing Mutual Aid—
Not the Negative Reaction that I Anticipated

For many years the LAPD had a reputation, with some justification, for not working particularly well with other law enforcement agencies. The department at that time was not part of the county's law enforcement mutual aid pact. It was not so much the issue of not wanting to cooperate, but rather that the LAPD was so big and had so many resources we seldom needed outside assistance.

Very early one morning I received a call from the Pacific Division watch commander, who advised me that an officer-involved shooting involving the Culver City Police Department had occurred on our boundary. We were being asked to assist with a perimeter, but just within the Los Angeles portion of the containment area. I directed the watch commander to assemble a couple squads of officers, each led by a sergeant, and to make those squads available to work at the direction of the Culver City Police leadership, in the event that city thought such would be helpful.

While this was clearly outside the historic practices of the LAPD—especially having our officers being directed by an outside agency—it struck me as the right thing to do. As things turned out, it came as a welcome surprise to both the Pacific watch commander and the Culver City folks. All went well, our personnel played a very helpful role in capturing the suspects, and LAPD received deep gratitude from Culver City. The criticism that I felt might come from the Office of Operations or the Chief of Police never materialized. My unauthorized mutual aid was treated pretty much as a non-issue, which was a very good thing. In the LAPD of today, mutual aid is routinely provided to other agencies.

Reuniting a Woman with Her Police Sergeant Dad

A friend of a friend put a woman in contact with me who was hoping to find her biological father, whom she had never met, and whose mother had separated the child from her father at birth. She believed her father was a Los Angeles police officer.

I was able to locate her father, a sergeant, who worked right down the street from my West Bureau office at the Hollywood Station. I contacted the sergeant, assured him he was in no trouble, and asked him to come by my office. I felt understandably apprehensive, and didn't know how he would react to the information or to my potential intrusion into such a personal matter.

I told him of his daughter's efforts to locate him, and gave him the option of forgetting that I'd ever brought the matter to his attention. He became pretty emotional, saying he'd always wondered what happened to his daughter, and now he had the opportunity to find out. He was guardedly pleased and took her number, making a commitment to get in touch with her. A couple of weeks later he called and thanked me profusely, for enabling his reunion with the wonderful woman who he felt from now on would always be a very big part of his life.

Maintaining a Foster Child's Hispanic Heritage

Daniel Bustamante and his older brother, Bobby (Roberto), lived with their mother in a series of flop houses in the Rampart district. Both boys had long been a part of my life, as I'd been acting as somewhat of a "big brother" to them since Bobby was a little kid and Danny was an infant. For years I'd also been taking them to my home on occasion to play with my kids and experience a better life than they had at home.

One Sunday afternoon following our visit, Cathy and I dropped off Danny at his mom's rooming house. But a short time later we got a call from the Rampart watch commander. He had tragic news: Danny had found his mother deceased (from natural causes) and identified us as the only relatives he had. Bobby was by then in the Marine Corps, serving away from the Southern California area.

After convincing the Department of Children's & Family Services that Danny was a long-term *de facto* member of our family, we went to court and asked to be declared his legal guardians. But at the time, there was an effort to place children in homes of the same ethnicity as the child. In court the judge made it a point to remind us that Danny was of a different ethnicity, and that it was our responsibility to take measures to maintain his Hispanic cultural heritage. I replied we would do so by taking Danny to a Taco Bell restaurant once a week! We all shared a laugh over this comment.

BRENTWOOD HOMICIDE NOTIFICATION

In the early morning hours of June 13, 1994, after having just arrived home from a USMC drill in New Orleans, I got a call from Detective Ron Phillips of the Homicide Unit at the West Los Angeles Area. He informed me that he and his partner, Detective Mark Fuhrman, were at the scene of a double homicide on Bundy Drive—and one of the victims was the former wife of O. J. Simpson, the actor and one-time Heisman Trophy winner. The other victim was a male, at the time unidentified (but later ID'd as Ron Goldman). Phillips stated that the Simpson children were also present, and had apparently been upstairs asleep at the time of the murders.

Phillips and Fuhrman were experienced homicide detectives who didn't need my advice. However, I directed them to locate and notify O. J. Simpson as soon as possible, explaining that I didn't want another situation such as the Belushi overdose, when word of the death leaked out before the family was notified. I certainly did not rule out O. J. Simpson as a suspect. But the fact he was the divorced husband, as opposed to the estranged spouse, and that his children were at the scene, tilted any initial perception as the suspect away from him in my mind.

An hour or so later I got another call. This time it was from Detective Tom Lange of the Robbery Homicide Division, a friend and former Marine. Tom explained that he and his partner, Phil Vannater, had evaluated the circumstances and decided to take over the case, as it fit Robbery-Homicide's criteria for a case that required expertise and/or resources beyond those available to area detective units. This was good news, as we had plenty of homicides in West Bureau; to get out from under one of them, especially a double involving a celebrity, was fine with me.

I did inquire whether the notification I'd directed had been made, but was informed it had not yet been done. I became unequivocally direct, ordering them to immediately find Simpson and get the notification process underway so that loved ones of the victims didn't learn of the tragedy the first time from the media. Even though Lange and Vannater were not subordinates in my chain of command, I made it clear that it was an order from a staff officer on the LAPD. I was not rude or nasty, but recognized the situation was one in which a hint or suggestion wasn't adequate to ensure my guidance was taken seriously. Ours was a cordial discussion. Lange said they would take care of the notification immediately.

Around dawn I got another call, this one from another friend and subordinate, Lieutenant "Spanky" Spangler of West Los Angeles Detectives. He told me that when the detectives went to O. J. Simpson's Rockingham residence to make the death notification per my direction, they found evidence pointing to Simpson as the suspect responsible for the two murders!

The rest is history. I was later called as the final witness in that trial.

Killer of Officer Charles Heim—Approved Tactical Plan

Los Angeles Police Officer Charles Heim was shot and killed on October 22, 1994. The killer was identified, and a massive search was conducted to find the suspect. After several days, the suspect was located in a motor lodge in the Hollywood area. As the commander in West Bureau, I was among those who responded to the scene. Prior to my arrival, the suspect had fired a round at one of the officers who had surrounded the unit he was occupying. In weighing the various options, the SWAT team recommended, and as the ranking person I approved, putting a bullet in the suspect's head if we could get a shot at him and he had the gun in his hand. He made the mistake of showing us his head while holding a gun, and we had the honor of putting a bullet into his head.

One of My Pet Peeves

In all of my command assignments, in both the police and sheriff's departments, I always pushed my folks to work hard to help the victims of crimes get their property back. Certainly, I wanted bad guys arrested and convicted, but the recovery of property was also something I felt was very important (and still do!) In the rush to make an arrest and move on to the next case, and because property recovery is typically not an area of measurement of investigative effectiveness, it is not unusual for it to be overlooked. Also, there are times when there is inadequate justification for an arrest, but when legal measures can be taken to get property back.

469

I wanted officers to be tenacious in pursuing those measures. This has long been one of my pet priorities.

Homicide Victim and Shots Fired in Oakwood

The Oakwood neighborhood of Pacific Division yielded a considerable number of shootings, homicides, and other gang-related crimes. It was somewhat of a Ground Zero for drug-dealing competition between two rival gangs, the Shoreline Crips and the V13. On two occasions when I was present at homicide scenes, shots from additional violence could be heard on adjacent streets. Gang activities also caused a great deal of trouble at Venice Beach on Saturdays and Sundays during the summer, which resulted in a very heavy police presence that required loanees from other divisions, as well. Because of my position in West Bureau, I was the staff officer responsible for providing police services in these situations.

My Buddy, Steven Seagal

It is not unusual for persons of prominence to have friendly relationships with the public officials who serve their communities. During the course of my careers, primarily after I attained command level rank, I had nice relationships with a number of individuals. One of them was superstar action actor Steven Seagal, who was a resident in one of West Los Angeles Division's most expensive and prominent neighborhoods. I don't recall how we met, but he was most gracious and was my guest at several functions, including two Jack Webb dinners (annual Police Historical Society events).

At the last Jack Webb dinner, he was accompanied by a gal who was at the center of somewhat of a scandal: the babysitter who Seagal had allegedly left his wife for. The girl was supposedly only seventeen years old, although he claimed she was nineteen. I didn't know and really didn't care; it was fun having him at our table.

Although I certainly didn't overwhelm him with calls, I did phone from time to time on different issues, and always got through immediately. After retiring from the LAPD and moving on to San Bernardino County, I unsuccessfully attempted to reach him several times, but finally gave up. I was hoping to lure him to a rodeo or whatever out in my new department.

I always recognized that our friendship was based on my position and not my sterling personality, so I really had no reason to be surprised or offended when I stopped hearing from him. It was a fun relationship while it lasted.

———

PERSONNEL GROUP

In May 1995, after about a year and a half in Operations-West Bureau, I was reassigned as the commanding officer of the Personnel Group. My office was located on the fifth floor of Parker Center. In that capacity, I was over Personnel Division, Equal Opportunity Development Division, Medical Liaison Section, Officer Representation Section, Reserve Coordination Section, and the Employee Assistance Unit. As I recall, there were approximately two hundred personnel assigned throughout the group.

TRANSITION DISCUSSION

I was pleased to be taking over the Personnel Group. I've always had an interest in personnel and human resources issues, and saw my new assignment as something I thought I would enjoy.

I would have preferred to remain in the Office of Operations where the street police work was done. But I knew that wasn't in the cards, because I had just finished my tour in West Bureau. Additionally, I would be working out of Parker Center, and geographically that was about as close to home as I could get. I replaced a good man and a good friend, Commander Dan Watson, who was being moved to Operations-Central Bureau.

Dan and I had a number of helpful chats during the transition. He raised a couple of issues that I should have seen as flags of even a brighter red color than they initially appeared. First, he indicated some tampering from the chief's office with the selective certification process for hiring new officers, explaining that he occasionally got guidance, always verbal, to deviate when hiring more of a particular category (ethnicity and gender) than the consent decree provided for.

Second, he indicated that EODD (Equal Opportunity Development Division, a subordinate unit under the Personnel Group) was investigating a case involving a minority female sergeant, Kathleen Anderson (pseudonym), which had a bunch of high-level interest and political overtones. The individuals who appeared to be taking a special interest in the Anderson case included a councilwoman, a police commissioner, a prominent civil rights attorney, a prominent national minority association, and several staff officers of the same ethnicity as the sergeant.

While my ignorance was blissful at the time, I later painfully learned more about all the interest and tampering in the Anderson case.

RETIRING MOTOR OFFICER TURNS IN HIS MOTORCYCLE

One day a retiring motorcycle officer actually placed his motorcycle in the freight elevator at Parker Center, took it to the fifth floor, and parked it outside the door of Personnel Division. He then entered the office, turned in his equipment, and processed his retirement. Someone from his division had to come and get his motorcycle. I thought this was very funny, but the captain of Personnel Division, Dan Schatz, who worked for me, was really irritated. As I look back, I still think it was funny.

CATHY'S FORTIETH BIRTHDAY PARTY—SURPRISE!

In March 1996, I planned a great surprise party for my wife's fortieth birthday. I worked with the manager of the Figueroa Hotel to obtain a large room for the surprise party. Then I invited scores of people, including Phil Everly of Everly Brothers fame. Since it was a work night for Cathy, I connived with the Central commanding officer, Captain Dick Bonneau, to phony-up a vice operation where a PSR (police service representative—radio dispatcher) was necessary for operating the radios to coordinate a non-existent task force.

Cathy was taking a college course, and saw the task force assignment as kind of a kickback opportunity to get some homework done. At the carefully coordinated moment, she walked in the door of the large room with a carefree look while carrying her homework, and everyone yelled, "Surprise!" It was a fun event, and we got her good!

FINAL WITNESS IN THE O. J. SIMPSON MURDER TRIAL

My fifteen minutes of fame occurred on September 21, 1995, when I was called as the final witness in the O. J. Simpson murder trial.

On the night the murders took place, I had directed detectives to go to the Simpson home and notify him of the crimes, so that his family would learn of the tragedy from loved ones as opposed to the radio or television. Several years before, during the investigation of the drug overdose death of actor John Belushi, we failed to make the family notification before the matter hit the airways, and I didn't want it to happen again.

As it turned out, when going to Simpson's home on Rockingham in Brentwood to make the notification per my orders, the detectives discovered evidence that implicated O. J. Simpson in the murders. I was called to rebut the bogus defense assertion that our detectives were sent there under the ruse of a death noticication, but that they realty were on an evidence-hunting expedition.

This televised court appearance was watched by about 140 million persons and did propel me to a degree of fame in some circles for months afterward. That fame included numerous requests for autographs, and being recognized on streets all over the country. It also flushed out old friends who saw the testimony and contacted me. I was on the stand for about an hour and a half and was cross-examined by Johnny Cochran (who I loathed). I remain flattered at the accolades I received for my testimony and professionalism on the stand.

Called "The Head of the Conspiracy" by Prominent News Analyst

On the evening after my testimony in the Simpson case, I watched the news to see how my testimony was perceived by the various "talking heads." For the most part, the reviews were good. I am a reasonably articulate and a professional person when I work at it, and was certainly at the top of my game on the stand that day. I was cross-examined by someone who I loathed, Johnny Cochran, and got high marks for saying what I wanted to say, while frustrating the hell out of him.

One commentator described me as a ramrod-straight Daryl Gates clone and look-alike, which I took as a compliment. My favorite was from the prominent legal analyst (why anyone would ask for his opinion is beyond me!), Alan Derchowitz, who described me as the "head person who orchestrated the conspiracy to convict O. J. Simpson" (or something to the effect). Again I was flattered, that anyone could think I was that talented!

Some Black LAPD Employees Cheered at the "Not Guilty" Verdict

I still haven't come to grips with, or can I understand how many intelligent black persons, including police officers, could fail to recognize that O. J. Simpson was guilty of those murders. My favorite quote came from one of the jurors who, in discussing the people's case stated: "if they didn't have the blood and DNA, they wouldn't have had anything!"

What else do you need?

In several LAPD divisions some black employees, including police officers, celebrated the not guilty verdict. I can only assume that the pain of past discrimination occasionally masks reality.

Kept Giving New Police Officers the Badges Worn by Their Dads

I guess subtle insubordination is the best way to describe my actions in this matter. Badges are among the most cherished possessions of cops, and there is no higher honor than for a father to pass his badge on to his son if the latter also joins the force. This had been a long-standing and most appropriate practice on the LAPD.

However, a glitch arose: the awkward situation of not being able to give a female police officer her dad's badge if it carried the title of "Policeman." Consequently, the chief's office decided that, since it wasn't fair to the small number of new women officers whose dads had been cops, then we wouldn't do it for the much larger number of sons and fathers, either. How stupid was that! No female officer complained that I was aware of, and so what? We would do it for them when able to do so.

I told Personnel Division to keep providing the father's badges to the sons. But my treachery came to light not long before I retired, when a fairly prominent detective asked Chief Williams to join him in placing his old policeman's badge on his graduating son's chest. I'm not sure that Williams even understood or remembered the issue. But one of his key people, my boss, knew exactly what I had done and gave me a very dirty look. For whatever reason, my boss didn't further discuss the issue with me and I just kept giving sons their dads' badges.

Abuse of Selective Certification

Selective certification was a procedure where, with judicial approval, the police department could selectively move the hiring threshold oral scores for various ethnicities and genders based on the comparable city workforce percentages. For example, we could essentially put one race in front of another for hiring, in order to pursue the goal of a department that bore some ethnic resemblance to the city's workforce. I would be dishonest if I were to say that I liked this process, because I didn't. However, I did realize it was necessary to pursue our hiring objectives, and therefore I completely supported the process. The problem was that the chief's office occasionally tampered with the process, and violated the discretion that had been judicially provided for.

The best (or worse) example was to go beyond the discretion provided for African-American candidates, and selectively certify them well beyond the comparable workforce percentages. This was at a time when we were far below the workforce percentages in processing Hispanic applicants. The guidance always came down verbally, but when documentation was requested the answer was "just do it!"

To this day, I retain detailed notes of those troubling conversations, and the guidance I received. This is a good example of how the Williams administration would stretch and abuse already existing prerogatives to achieve desired results. I will never forget an unbelievably tortured legal opinion that caused grief for a very decent deputy city attorney, and necessitated him scurrying around Parker Center in an attempt (almost successful) to scoop up and destroy every copy that existed. The troublesome legal opinion attempted to justify accelerated additional subjective certification, on top of an already subjective interpretation based on subjectively perceived attrition rates (see what I mean by "tortured"?).

MANIPULATION OF FBI NATIONAL ACADEMY SELECTIONS

Being selected to attend the three-month FBI National Academy is one of the top honors and professional development experiences for state and local law enforcement officers. For the LAPD, a very comprehensive and credible process was used to select those to attend from the many people who submitted applications (very detailed applications!)

The applications were sent to a five-person Management Development Advisory Committee consisting of command officers. They, with the assistance of staff, obtained and compiled comprehensive data on each candidate, which included a semi-background investigation to determine internal performance and perceptions. From this very competitive process, the Management Development Advisory Committee selected both primary and alternate candidates for the dedicated LAPD spots in the upcoming FBI National Academy classes, subject to the ratification of the chief of police.

In early 1996, the committee sent me the names of the folks they had selected for the upcoming classes, and I prepared a departmental memorandum for distribution, which was then sent to my boss for his final signature. He changed all kinds of stuff, including deleting the names of some people who had been selected, adding names of people who had not been selected, and reshuffling others from primary to alternate or vice-versa! What a crock of despicable and unethical behavior

475

it was, and that's what he put out. I am sure he was just one of the folks at higher levels who tampered with and bastardized what should have been a very credible process. I later learned that one of the names added, which had not been selected by the committee, was a gal with whom one of the top staff officers had a long-standing and unique relationship.

I was disappointed, but not completely surprised at this tampering with the process. Clearly, the chief of police has the right to make adjustments. But the tampering done to the work of the committee was so extensive and subjective that it was wrong to even have a process, as it might just as well have not existed.

As a sergeant, many years prior I was twice selected by the committee, and twice taken off the recommended list, in order to send other sergeants who were aides to staff officers. This type of manipulation, where people apply in good faith and are selected by a committee acting in good faith, only to have the final process twisted like a pretzel, is wrong and unethical. I hope this abuse no longer occurs.

Inappropriate Ratifications Sought at Lower Levels

From almost Day One in Personnel Group, it became obvious to me that people in my upper chain of command were anxious to influence various things. But they would not put their questionable or inappropriate directions in writing. It was almost always a phone call, stating that the chief wanted this or that done, or not done. In a couple of instances I diplomatically asked for documentation, in the event the action was later scrutinized. I was told to "just do it."

In all these instances, I created memoranda to the record. I also came to realize that some of the guidance I received did not come from the chief of police, but rather was a reflection of what somebody else wanted to occur. They simply used the auspices of the chief to get what they wanted. Besides being a pretty poor reflection on those individuals, this is also a classic consequence of what happens when an organization has a weak person at the helm.

Loyalty on the Sixth Floor at Parker Center

There was no shortage of loyalty among the top staff on the Los Angeles Police Department. But it was a matter of to whom and to what certain people were loyal! The degree of backstabbing and self-serving behavior was sickening and obvious. If there was any reasonably persuasive effort by the top folks to educate and influence Chief Williams in a positive direction, it was never obvious to me. In my judgment, several of the top staff of the Los Angeles Police Department were not worthy of the fine men and women on the streets.

Another unique dynamic was also taking place behind the scenes— a growing loyalty on the part of many staff and command officers to Bernard Parks as opposed to Willie Williams. It was especially apparent among some minority command personnel. Many, if not most (!), of Williams' top people were engaged in back-channel relationships with Parks, and were predicting (accurately, as it turned out) that Williams would not last and that Parks would end up as the police chief.

This reality was clearly undermining Williams. But there was little doubt Williams would be leaving—it was just a matter of when.

Knew When to Shut Up, But Chose Not to!

The longer a person uses an outhouse, the less noticeable is the smell!

I think the same thing occurred with some folks on the sixth floor of Parker Center—they failed to realize when discretion slipped into inappropriate and unethical actions and behavior. Without suggesting that I was any great ethical savior, I wasn't able to go along with some of the guidance I received without questioning what was occurring. It may be that my Marine Corps training and experiences influenced my perspective and actions, as at the time I was a full Marine colonel and inspector general (over all reserve ground forces in the Continental United States, Puerto Rico, Hawaii, and Alaska).

While I tried not to be disruptive or troublesome, I guess it is pretty hard to raise certain issues and take contrary positions without irritating those who see the world through difference lenses. In many of the troublesome issues discussed in these memoirs, I did not have the ability to remain silent.

Things that Were Just Plain Wrong!

By late 1995 and early 1996, it was obvious to me that the regime of Willie Williams did not place much emphasis on honesty or ethical behavior, with respect to some personnel issues. Even though the city was under a consent decree that authorized "selective certification" (preferential treatment and hiring) of some folks in underrepresented groups (gender and ethnicity), the Williams clan insisted on (and I resisted violating the rules) hiring even more blacks, to the exclusion of whites and equally under-represented Hispanics and Asians.

Councilwoman Jackie Goldberg was on my case, because we were not promoting enough females (we couldn't: there weren't enough who were eligible!) I was also getting a great deal of back-channel chatter, in an attempt to influence me to inappropriately find discrimination in the Kathleen Anderson matter, of which my predecessor had notified me during our transition discussion.

I was really irritated when directed to ignore the list of those who had been appropriately selected by the Management Development Committee to attend the FBI National Academy, and to arbitrarily insert the names of folks who had not been selected. The directive included one woman who I later learned was the long-term paramour of the superior who orchestrated the addition of her name.

Sexual Orientation Politics at Their Worst
—a Sad Day for Citizens

By the 1990s, nobody much cared about the sexual orientation of Los Angeles police personnel. It was pretty much a non-issue, except when a gay employee who was a problem wanted to evoke that status as a crutch or an excuse for their misfortunes. As the commanding officer of Personnel Group I was aware of a lesbian officer who was badly mistreated by her domestic companion, including physical abuse, being forced to hitchhike to work, and subjected to truly awful humiliation. This officer filed a worker's compensation claim alleging physical stress and it was most appropriately denied, not because her stress wasn't real, but because it was caused by her off-duty relationship and activities and not work-related, as clearly indicated by a worker's compensation investigation. However, an activist on the city council browbeat the Personnel Department into removing any indication of her off-duty personal relationship from the claim, which was the reason for the stress! Once the true reason for the stress was removed, all that remained were the allegations against the department. Those allegations had not really been looked at closely because the true stress was so obvious, so the employee received the workers compensation award! This was yet another example, of many, where activist city officials pursue their special agendas as the expense of the citizens.

A Great Day with the Son of Chief George K. Home

My son Jake, a great historical researcher, was able to find the then-91 year-old-son of George K. Home, who served as chief of the Los

Angeles Police Department from 1919 to 1920. The son, DeForest Home (RIP), a wonderful man and retired Los Angeles attorney, lived in northern San Diego County. We shared many nice conversations, and he volunteered to drive to Los Angeles to spend the day telling us about his dad and visiting their various family homes (he drove just fine and possessed the full range of mental faculties).

What a day! We first went to DeForest's birth home in Angelino Heights. Among the things he pointed out there, was a nearby house where one of the Kaiser's spies was alleged to have resided during World War I! We then went to the house at 1018 South St. Andrews, where Chief Home resided for many years, including during the times he was moving up in the department and when serving as the police chief. At the time of our visit, the house was a small Korean Church. The minister was very cordial and permitted us to walk throughout the premises, which were largely as they had been when the Home family resided there. DeForest pointed out the closet where his dad kept the sawed-off shotgun he always maintained at the ready, the parlor where the ruling czars and mayor of Los Angeles met, the covered parking area alongside the house where the chief's car was staged with an officer-chauffeur, and the bedroom where George Home died in the late 1930s. If that house could only talk!

Attacked by Dogs and Hawks in Elysian Park

Dr. Nels Klyver, of the Behavioral Sciences Section, was among my closest pals on the LAPD. For several years we often jogged together at noontime on the many trails in the Elysian Park, starting and finishing at the Police Academy. He and I had a few rough days in 1995 when a hawk took a disliking to him, and a dog took a dislike to me! In Nels' case, he probably got a little too close to the nest where baby hawks existed, and really pissed off an adult hawk; for several days, as he passed through a certain part of a trail, the hawk actually dived on him in a very conspicuous and threatening manner. In my case, a dog from a house adjacent to one of the trails must have been attracted by my bubbly butt, and tried to get a piece of it; I got the wound cleansed at the jail dispensary and had a cordial chat with a very apologetic owner.

Multiple Homicides at Piper Tech

As bad days go, July 19th of 1995 was about as bad as it gets. I had just exited Parker Center enroute to the academy when an all-units call came out regarding a shooting in progress and victims down at the Erwin Piper Technical Center, commonly known as "Piper Tech." This is a massive, multi-story industrial building owned by the City of Los Angeles, containing numerous city entities including the Police Supply Division, Air Support Division, City Printshop, and the General Services Radio Shop where police and fire communications installation and repair are provided.

Willie Woods, a disgruntled radio technician who was upset over a poor work evaluation, went to the Radio Shop and shot and killed four supervisors. I was among the early units on the scene, and the shooter had already surrendered to the first officers to arrive. Because of my long tenure in developing the department's new communications system, I was acquainted with all four of the victims, two of whom were fairly close friends, Tony Gain and Neil Carpenter. I attended the funeral services for both men. Tony was seventy-nine years old and was the number-one employee in the city for seniority, having been with the city for fifty-three years. Willie Woods was ultimately given four life prison sentences without the possibility of parole.

Military Awards are Stupid?

I am still frosted about this situation, not just because of what someone said, but also because of what I failed to say. At one of the annual dinners of the Police Historical Society, which are black-tie events, I was wearing my LAPD command officer's dress uniform. Beneath my badge was my USMC parachutist's insignia and several rows of military awards and campaign ribbons. The wearing of military awards was not only permitted at such events, but encouraged.

At the time I was a commander. During the evening I was approached by someone who outranked me and who was in my chain of command. He looked at my military awards, smirked, and said they looked "kind of stupid!" I wanted so badly to tell him what I really thought—that he was most likely envious because of my military service and, as a person who was clearly eligible for the draft during Vietnam, just how had he managed to evade military service? I was probably smart for not saying what I thought and wanted to say, because this fellow was in a position to cause me pain, so I muttered some bland response and that was the end of it.

It is interesting to ask why some of the top people at the LAPD, including just about all who I do not care for, though of prime age for the draft before and during Vietnam, avoided service. I have heard a few lame excuses from a few of them concerning different types of deferment. But the bottom line is that they found a way to avoid the military, which I believe is consistent with their self-serving character.

COMMANDER BUSHEY DIRECTS TRAFFIC!

I typically went home by driving through Elysian Park, taking Stadium Way through the park to the small part of Academy Road that connects that part of Stadium Way to the better-traveled portion of Stadium Way (a major thoroughfare into Dodger Stadium), then to the Glendale Freeway.

On far too many occasions when a game was being played at Dodger Stadium, the assigned traffic control officer (TCO) from the city's Department of Transportation would arrive late. This would cause an enormous back-up of cars on the Academy Drive feeder to the more heavily-traveled portion of Stadium Way, because of the inability to turn left due to the constant flow of heavy traffic into the stadium. When this occurred, it was common for me to take a shortcut through the park to a major portion of Stadium Way. I would then activate my rear flashing lights, get out with my badge on my belt, and direct traffic by temporarily stopping the flow of stadium traffic, thus permitting the scores of cars that were backed up on Academy Road to turn left onto Stadium Way. People realized that I, as an LAPD officer, was "going above & beyond" to assist our citizens. The gratitude of those who had been stranded was always obvious with many "thank you" remarks and thumbs up. I would typically remain at the location and direct traffic until the tardy TCO took over the duties, usually somewhat sheepishly. People clearly knew that I was a police officer, but most likely would have been really surprised had they known I was among the top people on the department.

CHIEF WILLIAMS' STATEMENT OF SUPPORT!

My blood pressure still goes up when I think of this issue. As the commanding officer of Personnel Group, I was also the chairman of the Department's Affirmative Action Advisory Committee (AAAC). Notwithstanding the bias of my earlier days, by this time in my life I had come to truly recognize that the only thing that really counts about a person is his/her character. Today, I strongly believe I harbor no bias related to gender, ethnicity, or sexual orientation. I believe that most of the men and women of the police department who were acquainted with me would agree with this self-assessment.

Based on some criticism the department was receiving about alleged discrimination, in the wake of the troubling testimony of Detective Mark Fuhrman in the O.J. Simpson trial, the AAAC put together a statement that was intended to be read by the chief of police in a public setting. A great many officers representing the face of the LAPD would be standing behind him, reflecting a virtual sea of ethnic and gender diversity. The statement was two-pronged: the department would not tolerate any type of discrimination, and that the vast majority of the men and women of the department do not harbor any bias.

At the pre-planned event, with all of the officers standing behind him, Chief Williams came to the podium and read only one-half of the statement—that the department would not tolerate any type of discrimination. He conspicuously left out the second part, about the vast majority of the men and women of the department not harboring bias!

I was beside myself with anger and anguish, unsure whether he'd omitted the second portion of the prepared statement by accident or design. Considering the many other questionable remarks the chief had made, it might have been by accident. However, I couldn't fail to recognize it as an intentional omission, because of the potential personal advantage to him in keeping alive the perception of racism within the department. After all, he had got the job, in part because of a perception of racism, and could potentially benefit by the perception that it was still an issue requiring his attention.

I realize this second bit of speculation may seem questionable. But I suspect it appears plausible for anyone within the department at that time—this is how absurd things had become by then.

COMMITMENT TO AFFIRMATIVE ACTION

As a white male in charge of the Personnel Group, and over the Equal Opportunity Development Division (EODD), there were those who attacked me personally by insisting that I was seeking opportunities to circumvent affirmative action policies.

Nothing could have been farther from the truth. I saw affirmative action as a necessary evil, which, although occasionally unfair to some individuals, was a necessary process to move the department in a direction where the faces of the LAPD would resemble the faces of the people of Los Angeles. The ideal situation, and the one I long embraced, was to coach, mentor and encourage extraordinary men and women in under-represented groups to compete for promotion, so the desired diversity would be achieved without having to introduce excessive preferential treatment into the LAPD's promotional policies.

Unfortunately, the city was changing much faster than the public policies and the bureaucracy, and greater flexibility in hiring and promotions became necessary. I believe that the affirmative action rules and policies in place at the time, though painful and opposed by some individuals, were necessary and appropriate. Among my challenges was to hold the line on those rules and policies, and attempt to prevent the unmerited and foolish personnel actions that were put forth under the guise of affirmative action—then being called racist or sexist for my efforts.

NATURE OF DISCRIMINATION COMPLAINTS

Let there be no doubt, that some absolutely valid discrimination complaints existed. I hope that I was as worthy in my personal attention, and that of my staff, toward the conduct of comprehensive investigations and in seeking appropriate remedies for such situations.

Unfortunately, in my judgement, there was a large percentage of outright false discrimination complaints, or that were highly exaggerated, for the purpose of achieving unmerited remedies and monetary settlements. Among the most troubling were those initiated by weak or problem employees against the individuals and commands whose worst sin was attempting to improve the employee's behavior! These problems were greatly exacerbated by the corps of private attorneys anxious to take up these cases, to portray the department as the evil empire, portray the supervisors as evil, and seek monetary damages via court process. Although troublesome for the department, the ultimate losers in this disgusting process were the citizens of Los Angeles.

I believe there were many times when a minority employee who sought redress of his or her grievances, did so with honorable intent, because of the very human tendency to blame someone else for our problems. I am reminded of the two-day relinquishment of my days off for a shooting policy violation when I was a new officer; it was several years before I could be honest with myself and acknowledge I'd been wrong. I think there are times when some in under-represented groups, when they get into trouble, are slow to acknowledge personal responsibility for their actions and instead attribute the negative consequences they experience to gender, ethnicity, or sexual orientation. Sorting through situations like these, especially with the abundance of people willing to think the worst and take up the cause, special interest organizations that thrive by keeping the perception of bias alive, and attorneys standing in line to take the cases, can be a real pain for the equal employment opportunity officer.

In many of these problematic situations, employees claim they just want the problem resolved. But in actuality they are already working with an attorney. They use the department's process to merely go through the motions, and hopefully cause information to be developed that their attorneys can get under later discovery and use against the department.

This reality is a real lose-lose for the department, because the honest and good faith development of information that might suggest weakness on the part of the department, or an involved individual, is likely to be later exaggerated and used against the department.

City Personnel Department: A Truly Dysfunctional Relationship

The final say on who can be hired as a police officer rests not with the police department, but with the city's Personnel Department. In my judgment, this is a dysfunctional process that often results in questionable disqualifications. The police department is certainly knowledgeable with respect to what to look for in new officers, and to oversee the background process, but the completed investigative package goes to the Personnel Department for final approval. During my time in the Personnel Group, I encountered several situations where I strongly believed the city's disqualifications were unfair and inappropriate. I believe that at least one disqualification, of a superb reserve officer who spoke multiple languages, was intended to let me know who was the boss in hiring decisions. In several other instances, the ranting of a gay city council member resulted in disqualifing any candidates who were known to have told jokes with adverse gay connotations. While anti-gay jokes have no place in the lives or careers of mature adults, it is a pretty unrealistic bar for young persons, and especially military veterans.

With respect to the fine candidate who I believe was rejected simply to send me a message that the personnel division was in charge, I later hired him as a deputy marshal. He is now a San Bernardino County sheriff's sergeant, who is at the top of the lieutenant's eligibility list!

Almost EOW on the San Bernardino Freeway

On Easter Sunday 1996, I went into the office for a brief period for some reason I no longer recall. After the visit, I probably went to the Pantry Café, one of my favorite eating establishments, for breakfast. Enroute home I was traveling on the eastbound San Bernardino

484

Freeway in the East Los Angeles area when I observed a car stopped in the diamond (carpool) lane. The hood of the car was up, and in it were a woman and a small girl. This was clearly a dangerous situation, so I pulled in behind the vehicle and activated my emergency lights. I requested tow service and decided to remain until the tow truck arrived, as my emergency lights provided a much-needed degree of safety. As I was seated in my vehicle, I saw a truly horrible sight in my rear view mirror—a car was coming at me at a high rate of speed! I could see the driver and passenger chatting in an animated way, and the driver clearly wasn't paying attention to the roadway ahead. The vehicle bearing down on me, a Jeep Cherokee, was doing at least the speed limit and I was at a complete stop, as was the other vehicle with the mother and daughter inside immediately in front of me.

I braced myself for the end of my life and a fiery collision, when at the last moment the Cherokee swerved out of the diamond lane and into the number-one traffic lane. The move triggered a chain-reaction collision involving three other cars, with vehicles and debris spreading over all the freeway lanes. Miraculously, no one was injured. Since I was a factor in the collision, I called for a traffic unit and a supervisor to work with the Highway Patrol in the investigation. The supervisor was Lieutenant Ron Newton. Ron later told me there was no way that either I or the mother and daughter could have survived the rear-end collision that almost occurred. I am thankful the fellow in the Cherokee looked up at the last moment!

Note: In police parlance, EOW means "end of watch." It is a term sometimes used when someone dies.

Falsehoods Regarding Elimination
of the Representation Unit

When appearing before the city council on some issue, during a break I found myself engaged in a pleasant conversation with a nice person, Councilwoman Laura Chick. She was pretty much a friend. Along with Jackie Goldberg, Laura sat on a key council committee that had a significant impact on the police department. Laura commented that she was prepared to concur with the perspective of the Command Officer's Association for the elimination of the Officer's Representation Section (ORS) via de-funding by the council. She explained that two chief-level officers had visited her on the issue and, subsequent to her questioning, indicated that through their association the command officers supported the elimination. This was absolutely untrue. Not only was I a command officer active in the association, but also the ORS was under my command! There were a few folks that really disliked the ORS because of the advocacy of assigned officers in their role as representatives of other officers accused of serious misconduct. However, most folks, including me, saw it as preferable to having lawyers do the job.

A staff meeting was held a day or so later, involving all commanders and above. I raised the issue, without being specific, that there was talk in the council about eliminating the ORS, and that it would be a big mistake. Most of those present agreed with my comments. My actions apparently torpedoed the plans of certain people, and the unit was not eliminated.

MY CHAT WITH CHIEF WILLIAMS

It was obvious to me that Chief Williams did not understand the variety of issues related to the Officer's Representation Section, and that some who were not honest brokers were selectively educating him on the issue. I checked the chief's schedule, and decided to "bump into him" at the academy one morning, and take a moment to chat with him on the subject of the ORS. I did run across him, and the climate was right (I think) for the chat we had. After briefly discussing the ORS, I said I would like to give him some advice, which I thought was something that loyal subordinates should have the courage to do. I was still loyal to him at that point, although it was becoming more difficult.

I was candid in sharing my perspective that he had good intentions, but that he was making a number of serious mistakes. I attributed the mistakes, without naming any names or organizations, to the questionable advice that I believed he was getting from persons outside the department. He did not deny it. I suggested that he form a "kitchen cabinet" made up of solid folks within the department, and to vet his actions and decisions through that group.

Chief Williams replied that it was a "great idea," and thanked me for raising the issue. But my exhilaration at having influenced the chief in a positive way was short-lived. I later learned that I was among a number of people who had given him the same advice, but he didn't pay any more attention to me than he did to them. I am convinced that Willie Williams is basically a good and decent man, who lacks the totality of leadership skills to effectively manage an organization, including how to use and manage staff.

There is not a problem with the existence of special interests; the problem is the level and nature of those influences. Special interests play an important role in helping to educate decision makers and flush out the often wide variety of factors that influence important issues. Simply stated, a special interest is a person or organization advocating for a particular policy, product, position, or law.

In Los Angeles, politics is a contact sport, where the lobbyists and special interests spend big bucks to gain influence with the politicians, and where the politicians rake in thousands of dollars while insisting they are not influenced by special interest money. You don't get elected to the city council without raising a couple hundred thousand dollars, and just about every elected officials hovers very close to the ethical line.

The problem arises when those interests have the ability to exert undue influence on decision makers, and the decision makers' weak skills in being willing or able to do what is necessary to maintain some degree of balance and holistic perspective. My perspective is that Chief Williams did not have the skills to deal with the sophistication of skilled lobbyists, and that he had allegiances that weighed more heavily than was appropriate.

The "Undermining" of Chief Williams

The absolute reality that "if there is a void, it will be filled" applies to a leadership void.

I believe that Chief Williams was floundering under the magnitude of his position, and being buffeted by the force and magnitude of strong-willed individuals and organizations. Most of his key people recognized that Chief Williams was struggling, and several of them worked hard to convince him to pursue their agendas as his own. A number of the top folks had covertly aligned themselves with Bernard Parks (who Williams had demoted from assistant chief to deputy chief), and while supportive to his face were part of behind-the-scenes efforts to cause Chief Williams to fail, which wasn't a difficult task. As previously mentioned, in my opinion, the majority of the LAPD top staff felt it was just a matter of time before Parks became the chief and, to some extent, were walking a fine line between the two men. One of my good friends, a fellow commander, felt that he later suffered professionally under Parks because of his earlier efforts to help Williams to succeed; I completely believe it.

Along with my son Jake and longtime wonderful friend Ray Sherrard, I am a co-author of *The Centurion's Shield*. This is a great hardback book (also available in softcover) about the history of badges of the Los Angeles Police Department. Ray did the lion's share of the work, and Jake provided substantial assistance, with my contributions being far less. We worked hard to get this book done; as luck would have it, they were delivered right in the midst of the industrial-grade battle over my bullshit transfer to be the "Staff Inspector," and the personnel complaint against me (both are discussed in subsequent paragraphs). I just love this book, and am so proud of what Ray and Jake, with a little bit of me, accomplished. Unfortunately, I was not able to enjoy the fruits of our labor on the book, or enjoy much of anything else, during those troubling times. Once I was able to put the crap behind me, I was able to really bask in the pride of the book. To this day, I'm still basking in that pride.

CLASH WITH A COUNCILWOMAN

There is a lot to like about Jackie Goldberg. As a Marine, I truly appreciate her bulldog determination to prevail in those areas for which she has passion. The problem is that, in my judgment, she is solely focused on the final goal and has no use for the little things in between, such as reality, rules, and anything else that might interfere with the things she seeks to achieve. She and I went sideways over the issue of female promotions within the LAPD, with her being very critical of the department and with me as her focal point, because she believed that we weren't promoting adequate numbers of women. She was not swayed by hard figures that clearly demonstrated the lack of adequate numbers of women in the various feeder pools for each rank, to realistically see many promotions at the time. The department was doing fine at the sergeant and detective levels, but for lieutenant and above the pools were pretty lean because we didn't realistically start hiring women in significant numbers until the 1980s.

Unfortunately for her (and me!), I am also a bulldog, and went toe-to-toe with her on the council floor, much to the chagrin of Chief Williams who was present. Councilwoman Goldberg made it clear, on several occasions and to a number of people including Chief Williams and me, that she believed I was unsuited for the personnel position I held. After my transfer to the position of staff inspector, both she and Chief Williams went out of their way to emphasize that she played no role in my movement out of the Personnel Group. I didn't believe either of them.

Coordinating an Officer's Sex Change?

Just what I didn't need! My very good and close friend, then-Police Commissioner Art Mattox, who is gay, contacted me on behalf of an anonymous officer to inquire about the potential response of the department and its actions if the officer were to pursue a gender reassignment. This had occurred within several other agencies, and I knew that it was just a matter of time until the issue arose in Los Angeles. I assured Art that the officer's actions would be dealt with in a compassionate and professional manner, and that I would work hard to deal positively with all of the issues that would likely arise.

Art got back to me several days later, and said that the officer had chosen to remain in the originally-issued bodily cocoon, at least for the time being. With all the crap that was going on in my arena, this unique challenge was the very last thing I needed, especially under the Williams regime and its obsessive overreaction to special interest groups—there would have been no limit to the number of individuals and organizations who would have tried to get involved in such an endeavor. While I would have worked hard to handle the situation appropriately, I was relieved when it didn't materialize.

"Lets Get Our Buns in Gear"
and "the Big Weenie" Conspiracy

A couple of terms I've used over the years are "come on folks, let's get our buns in gear," and that "he (or she) is acting like a big weenie." Certainly, I never intended any sexual connotation. One day, a couple of weeks before the bottom fell out for me in Personnel Group, my secretary Kris confronted me, in a nice way, and told me she was offended at a remark I'd made the previous day when asking her to come into my office to take dictation. Apparently I said, "Get your buns in here." I felt most remorseful, and apologized to her. Although certainly it was done in a kidding and light-hearted manner, I instantly saw why she didn't appreciate the comment. She accepted my apology. I committed to not using that term again, and I didn't.

Refusal to Find Woman Sergeant
a Victim of Discrimination

The discrimination case that my predecessor, Commander Dan Watson, and I had discussed during our transition, which was under investigation by my subordinate command (EODD), finally landed on my desk. I read every word, but could not find a basis for discrimination, even after kicking it back a few times for additional information.

The sergeant described several incidents in which she felt she'd been treated harshly or differently, and implied that the treatment was because of her gender and ethnicity. My interpretation of the contents of the extensive investigation was that the sergeant, for the most part, had been experiencing the consequences of her own misconduct and weak performance. Further, I was shocked to learn that an internal investigation in which her bureau commanding officer recommended a disciplinary trial board, for several acts of alleged misconduct, had been basically withdrawn by the Office of the Chief of Police, and the charges dropped. It was something I'd never heard of happening! Finally, the two non-minority male sergeants who reported some of the troubling behavior that resulted in the recommendation for a trial board had been essentially branded as racists, and were administratively transferred out of the division where she was assigned!

There was no doubt that this situation had the potential to turn very ugly. All of the female sergeant's supporters, none of whom had seen any part of the investigation, were advocating for her to be found the victim of discrimination before the investigation was even completed. Perhaps I was naïve, but I was operating under the mistaken assumption that Sergeant Anderson was sincere in her statements up to that time; that what she sought was a resolution of the issues and elimination of the discriminatory environment she believed existed. While I was beginning to think there was an underlying plan for litigation, no legal filings had as yet taken place. Although the documentation in my judgment indicated that she was more the cause than the victim of the circumstances she found troubling, I decided to attempt a resolution through a unique process involving prominent people and a prominent organization.

Confidential Divisional Environmental Audit

The Office of the Chief of Staff had recently caused "Confidential Environmental Audits" to be conducted in two geographic areas. One of them was the area where Sergeant Anderson was assigned, and where the alleged harassment and discrimination had occurred. These audits were considered to be highly confidential, for what struck me as good and honorable reasons. The department wanted to get to the bottom of the situation, and find and fix problems if they existed. However, the department did not want its self-imposed investigations, done for good and objective internal reasons, to be something a plaintiff's attorneys could get hold of and use against the department in litigation. Based on the rumblings I'd heard from those who supported Sergeant Anderson, my assumption was that the audit for her geographic area would contain substantial indications of problems that might well influence my findings. I was given access to the audit for her geographic area; it contained no indication of harassment or discrimination where she was assigned, or while she was assigned there!

Chain of Command Supports Facilitation Process Recommendation

If ever there was an "honest broker" in Los Angeles, it was (and still is) the Museum of Tolerance. A very credible organization that embraces diversity, the museum was used by the LAPD and many other organizations for training and orientation. I approached this organization and asked if, as a favor to the LAPD, they would conduct a facilitation process in which Sergeant Anderson and the two male sergeants would participate in a process to identify and break down barriers to meaningful dialog, and to "walk a mile in each other's shoes." The Museum agreed, and we started on the mechanics and participants. The first facilitator selected was a very prominent and well-respected woman psychologist, who was the same ethnicity as Sergeant Anderson. When contacted, both male sergeants indicated a willingness to participate. My chain of command really liked this idea. I believed that they knew there was little (if any) merit to her allegations and, while lacking the spine to outright tell the chief that, did see the facilitation process as a good way to resolve the issue without putting their sorry butts on the line. In a meeting with my chain of command and the chief of police, I got the go-ahead to offer the facilitation process to Sergeant Anderson.

Complainant Refuses Facilitation Discussions

The meeting with Sergeant Anderson and her attorney did not go well. The attorney did most of the talking, saying that her client should not be further exposed to the two sergeants. She encouraged me "to do the right thing," and find that her client was the victim of discrimination. In our meeting it became clear to me that the goal was litigation, not the elimination of the problems that allegedly existed. The attorney introduced me to a new term when she said, "sometimes what you see depends on where you sit." I liked the term and the analogy, but try as I did to be as fair and objective as I know how, I could only come to the overall conclusion that Sergeant Anderson wasn't the victim of discrimination. The meeting was unproductive. Sergeant Anderson refused the facilitation process that had been assembled.

FRIENDLY CALL FROM A RETIRED WOMAN CAPTAIN

Right in the middle of the Sergeant Anderson matter, and out of the blue, I got a call from a long-retired female captain who was a very decent person and someone I considered a friend. Without threatening or attempting to intimidate me, she passed on her perception that it would be in my best interest to declare that Sergeant Anderson was the victim of discrimination, and make it my finding in my role as the department's EEO. She opined, correctly as it turned out, that to do otherwise might well be harmful to my career. It was nice to hear from her, and I know she meant well—but I didn't appreciate the actions of whoever put her up to making the call. We ended the conversation on a positive note. But it was clear to me that she perceived I wasn't going to change my mind, and that I would eventually regret my stubbornness on the issue.

SUBJECTIVITY, INTERPRETATION, AND "MY AGENDA"

In matters of harassment and discrimination there are often differing interpretations about the propriety and impact of various actions. Probably the greatest areas are the "test" someone chooses to apply, the "reasonable person standard," or the stated "perspective in the eyes of the victim." Obviously the latter is problematic, because if that perspective is accepted, anyone who is accused is guilty and everyone who alleges they have been harmed is a victim. I worked very hard to look at the Anderson matter from multiple perspectives and, within the bounds of propriety and confidentiality, solicited the perspectives of a number of others, including women and minorities. All those folks felt the vast preponderance of evidence made clear that she was not the victim of discrimination. There was an indication that some negative statements about the situation had been made to several captains by the two sergeants, but they were found to have occurred after the sergeants learned that the chief of police was dismissing the misconduct charges against her. In this whole sorry, no-win situation, I had but one agenda: to follow the evidence, to make a determination based solely on that evidence, and not be swayed by all who were trying to influence the outcome of the discrimination allegations.

Refusal to Permit My Findings to be Modified

The manual for the Los Angeles Police Department describes the duties and responsibilities of each specialized staff officer's position. For my position—commanding officer of the Personnel Group—I was in the chain of command and reported to the commanding officer of Human Resources, who reported to the director of the Office of Administrative Services, who then reported to the chief of police. However, the manual also identified the commanding officer of Personnel Group (me) as the department's Equal Employment Opportunity officer (EEO), and the chief of police as the second level of review for EEO issues. I interpreted this to mean that my EEO findings were separate from my conventional chain of command reporting requirements, and that my EEO findings went directly to the chief of police for his role as the second level of review. The third level of review was the Police Commission. When it became obvious that there were multiple perspectives on the Sergeant Anderson case, my boss directed a number of changes to my document, which reflected my findings in my role as the Department's EEO.

I politely declined (a nice way of saying refused!) to make the changes, and made it clear that if the document were going to have my signature as the EEO, then the findings would be my findings and not those of other people. I certainly didn't want to irritate my boss, but this was an issue in which I had no intention of yielding. I suggested that he should use the "military endorsement" process, by attaching to my report a separate document reflecting his disagreement or perspective. I was a bit surprised that he didn't become indignant at my suggestion, probably because it was a no-win situation and he was perfectly willing to let me commit organizational suicide by myself!

The Six-Page Blue Note to Commander Bushey

The first I learned of the six-page blue note was from my adjutant, a fine fellow and later a good friend, Sergeant Pat Findley. He told me there was a big buzz on the sixth floor (where the chief, assistant chiefs, and deputy chiefs had their offices) about a six-page blue note coming my way from the chief of police. For years, the various chiefs used a half-size sheet of blue paper, bearing the heading of the Office of the Chief of Police, to send personal notes to folks within the department. Over the years, I received a few blue notes from various chiefs, all of them complimentary, and I never heard of one beyond a single page, let along six pages!

I wasn't pleased when I received it. It was clearly intended to undermine my findings in the Sergeant Anderson matter, by challenging each of my key points with arguments that were inconsistent with the results of the EODD investigation. On the last page, Chief Williams asked if I thought a white male lieutenant would have been treated the same as Sergeant Anderson, and concluded with "Let's discuss."

"The Infamous Bushey Note to Chief Williams"

I saw exactly what was occurring. The forces aligned in support of Sergeant Anderson were seeking one of two things: either for me to change my report or, if failing in that effort, to create a final report containing findings that indicated she was the victim of discrimination.

The chief had the ability to override my findings, of course; but I was not going to permit my findings and report to be modified for the benefit of the various individuals and special interests who were pulling strings behind the scenes. Accordingly, despite the fact that he wanted to "discuss" the issue, I gave the chief and his buddies exactly what they did not want—a point-by-point written rebuttal to the six-page blue note he had sent me! I also seized the opportunity to tell the chief that I did not feel a white sergeant would have received the special attention and preferential treatment given to Sergeant Anderson, including the virtual dismissing of several counts of serious misconduct and canceling a disciplinary trial board. I indicated to the chief that I hoped my response was helpful to him in better understanding the case, and that I looked forward to the "discussion" he recommended. But I knew my response would not be well received, and I didn't look forward to our discussion. In litigation that resulted from this matter, the office of the city attorney referred to my response as "the Infamous Bushey Note to Chief Williams."

Within a day or so of providing my findings that Sergeant Anderson was not the victim of harassment or discrimination, I was under investigation! One thing just about everyone could agree on, was the "unique" personality of a woman named Roseanne (pseudonym), who was the secretary to a commander in an adjacent office. She was often nasty and rude. Of deep concern to me was the fact that two women who applied for and were selected to be my secretary later declined the position when they learned they would be in close proximity to Roseanne—she was that disliked. While I made an effort to be cordial, Roseanne was certainly aware that I was displeased over her toxic personality having cost me two great secretaries. I often discussed her behavior with her boss, a fellow commander. This commander was very close to the commander perceived to be the guardian angel of the sergeant who I refused to find to be the victim of discrimination. I continued to suspect the involvement of both of them in subsequent painful events.

One day, I was informed that Roseanne had approached an instructor at an affirmative action class, and complained that she was offended at the remark I'd made to my secretary (for which I had apologized). She also said that at one time she'd heard me use the word "vaseline" in a conversation with another colleague and that on another occasion I'd referred to someone as a "big weenie." This was exactly what Chief Williams and his pals needed to push me out of my assignment in Personnel Group. A personnel complaint was initiated, after which I was reassigned to a previously non-existent position as "staff inspector."

Deputy City Attorneys See No Misconduct

My opinion was that these allegations were bogus, in that my actions did not rise to the level of misconduct, and that my statements weren't something a reasonable person would find offensive. I consulted with a number of people, including several attorneys, two of whom were deputy city attorneys with extensive experience in personnel matters. Donna James and Bob Karmer (pseudonyms) both felt the charges were ridiculous, and certainly didn't amount to misconduct. In fact, no person outside the Willie Williams inner circle felt that misconduct had occurred. A couple of years after I left, I was told by a third city attorney, Kristy Adamson (pseudonym), who reviewed the matter after I retired, that my actions did not amount to misconduct and that the discipline against me had been withdrawn. She later learned that the discipline hadn't been withdrawn, but remained strong in her belief that my actions did not amount to misconduct.

As it turned out, five months after retiring I was advised, via letter from Internal Affairs Division, that the complaint against me had been sustained and an "official reprimand" had been placed in my retired personnel file. In the big scheme of things this was a big nothing. For me personally, however, it was a very painful experience.

Interestingly, for the next couple of years and for whatever reasons, the disciplinary investigation went in and out of my retired personnel file. It was obvious that someone was reviewing what had occurred. My guess is that one of the issues may have been about concerns of potential liability to the city, should I have chosen to take some action in court.

During the time all the crap was going down, I had personal conversations with Mayor Richard Riordan and Police Commissioner Art Mattox about the issue. Both recognized I was being screwed, and that Williams was wrong, but the reality is that the chief of police is the person who manages the department and administers discipline. My guess is that the totality of circumstances involving my dismissal was one among many factors that resulted in Williams not getting a second term as police chief.

I also continue to find great satisfaction in the fact that my former colleagues, who sold their souls for their own benefit to Chief Williams, are pretty much non-persons and are shunned from the department today. Neither ever shows up at the academy for lunch, retirement functions, etc.

Native American Doll From an Unknown Officer

To say that I was unhappy as these things were happening is an understatement. I was hurting and humiliated, and my consternation was reflected, doubtless to some extent, in my appearance (weight loss) and demeanor.

One afternoon while I was at the academy, I was approached by a police officer who I knew only by sight. He took me aside, handed me a carved animal with several smaller carvings attached at the top by a string/harness, and said he wanted me to have it. He explained that it was a Native American symbol intended to give strength and protection to warriors.

It really came to me at a good time, when I most needed it. I sincerely wish I could remember who the officer was, so I could express my appreciation for his thoughtfulness. In hindsight, his was a very profound gesture, with an origin I still don't understand. But his carved animal is prominently displayed in my office, and is a very special possession.

BERNARD PARKS SEES NOTHING TO SUSTAIN

At the time of the charges against me, the deputy chief of the Special Services Bureau, whose subordinate commands included Internal Affairs, was my old boss, Bernard Parks. He had also been a victim of the Willie Williams regime, having recently been demoted from assistant chief to deputy chief. (In a public rebuke to Williams, the city council passed a resolution that Parks would retain the salary of an assistant chief.) I discussed the matter with Parks, and he was clear in his opinion that no misconduct had taken place on my part. He felt it was a subjective matter, that my language ("lets get our buns in gear" and "acted like a big weenie") was not in itself offensive, and the fact that a person claimed she'd been offended was not adequate reason to sustain charges.

Several years later, when I was with the San Bernardino County Sheriff's Department as a deputy chief, I ran into Parks at the Baker to Vegas Relay Race. He was then Los Angeles' Chief of Police. During our chat I reminded him of our conversation, and asked him to pull my file and reclassify the matter as having not involved any misconduct. He replied that he would review the matter.

Even though I was retired, it troubled me to have a blemish in my otherwise stellar LAPD personnel file. A couple of months later I received, at the sheriff's department, a very brief "Dear Mr. Bushey" letter from Parks, stating that I had admitted to the misconduct, that he was not going to change the classification in my file, and considered the matter closed! This was terribly offensive to me. I had never admitted to misconduct, just to using the terms that he agreed did not constitue misconduct.

Bernard Parks was clearly a challenge to work for. But I gave him several years of loyalty and hard work, and saw his perfunctory response as not only wrong but a terrible insult to me personally, as someone who had worked very hard to serve him well. In hindsight, I shouldn't have been surprised at receiving the impersonal letter, as opposed to a phone call, with the determination that he chose not to change the classification. Parks' long-term practice was to deliver bad news either in writing or through another person. So much for courage and leadership.

These pages truly cannot express the unbelievable pain, anguish and humiliation I felt at being very conspicuously removed from a high-profile and important assignment and being given a do-nothing job, without a staff, with the mission to drive around the city at night. Other than "inspecting the city at night," there were no specifics involving the assignment.

When I was invited to suggest what my duties should consist of, my recommendations that I would take over the leadership of any major police incident after-hours and would also be the press relations spokesperson for the police chief at night were immediately rejected. Not surprising, the last thing the Williams crowd wanted was to have me making statements to the media.

One of the worst aspects of the humiliating transfer and the knowledge that I was under investigation (for allegedly improper comments!) was that I could not defend myself. The Kathleen Anderson discrimination complaint and investigation were confidential personnel matters, and for me to have spoken out on these issues—which I would liked to have done, to explain what was occurring to me and why—would have been a violation of city and department rules, and the state government code. The rampant untrue rumors that I was under investigation for a serious matter broke my heart, especially one from a friend who had heard that internal affairs had searched my locker pursuant to a search warrant. Certainly none of it was true. But the pain to me was severe and deep.

When I became *persona non grata* with Chief Williams and his yes-men, it was interesting to watch some of my weak-kneed fellow command officers avoid me like the plague, somewhat akin to the way that cockroaches scatter when exposed to light (however unfair this analogy may be to cockroaches).

LEGACY—PROTECTIVE LEAGUE DIRECTORS

There are no words to describe how flattered and grateful I was at the actions of the Los Angeles Police Protective League, with respect to the actions being taken against me by Chief Williams and his close associates. Shortly after being notified that I was being moved out of Personnel Group and assigned to the newly created non-position of staff inspector, I got a call from the league president, Dave Hepburn. Dave explained that the Protective League's board of directors had just come out of an executive session, where it was voted unanimously to support me in any action I chose to take against the chief of police!

Their action was HUGE, because the league represents lieutenants and below, whereas my employee group was the Command Officer's Association (COA). Dave explained that my years of fairness to their membership was such that I was considered one of the LAPD's finest command officers, and it was clear I was transferred because I'd stood up for the two sergeants whose only sin was to challenge the troubling behavior of another sergeant.

I thanked Dave and the board, but realistically couldn't think of anything the league could do for me. Among my most cherished possessions is the issue of *The Thin Blue Line* for September 1996, in which almost all of the league directors devoted a part of their editorial columns to nice comments about me. I don't believe there was a time before or since when so much space was devoted in the union's publication to favorable remarks about a staff or command officer.

CHIEF OPERATIONS OFFICER—INTER-CON SECURITY?

It didn't take long for just about everybody associated with the police department to learn that I had fallen out of grace with the chief of police and his cronies. I was contacted by a few people who raised the possibility of going to work with or for them. The most serious overture came from Police Commissioner Rick Hernandez. Rick was the son of a long-term dear friend and retired police Lieutenant, Hank Hernandez, who had developed a successful private security company known as INTER-CON.

Hank had turned over the company business to Rick, who was searching for the right person to be the company's chief operating officer. Rick reached out to me. I really thought I was going to go in that direction. But as we got down to the nitty-gritty of hammering out an employment contract, I found that the challenges were likely to be enormous, but the job security and future weren't all that secure. Although the title sounded pretty good, I realized that I would be spending a lot of time in the trenches dealing personally with security guards to ensure appropriate compliance with the firm's contracts. But in the end it just didn't interest me. Ultimately, I thanked Rick for considering me, but chose not to pursue the opportunity. Ultimately, my move to the law enforcement community in San Bernardino County could not have been a better thing for me, both personally and professionally.

A day or so after being told I was being transferred out of Personnel Group and being made the "staff inspector," I requested and was granted an audience with Chief of Police Willie Williams. I went to his office and was ushered into a room where he was meeting with his three assistant chiefs, Ron Banks, Bayan Lewis and Frank Piersol.

I told Chief Williams he was making a terrible mistake by treating me the way he was, based on exercising my best judgment in the Kathleen Anderson matter, and that any fair-minded person would have arrived at the same finding. I also said that I remained convinced, contrary to his insistence that it didn't occur, that City Councilwoman Jackie Goldberg played a role in my transfer, as she had made it clear that she didn't believe I was suited for Personnel Group. I also told him that as the chief of police he had the right to assign someone wherever he pleased, and if he wanted me to clean the trash cans in back of Parker Center, they would be the shiniest trash cans in Los Angeles! I was later asked about this meeting in the federal court trial involving the two sergeants who were unfairly transferred and branded as racists, and repeated my statement about the trash cans, which has become well-known among a lot people.

There are some things I would have liked to have said in that meeting, but didn't feel I could do so without putting my police officer son in jeopardy of second-hand retaliation, and also because I was looking at potential opportunities in other law enforcement agencies and did not want to "burn my bridges." I would liked to have told the three assistant chiefs they collectively should have been ashamed of themselves for not exerting greater effort and influence in attempting to point the chief in appropriate directions, and to strongly challenge inappropriate decisions. It was a very short meeting.

ENTIRE DISCRIMINATION FILE COPIED AND RETAINED

There is no doubt that the personnel complaint and my transfer were products of the Anderson case, in which I'd dug in my feet and refused to find discrimination. I wasn't sure what the future held with respect to this case, but since it was essentially bringing my LAPD career to an end, I felt the need to retain copies of all documents relating to the matter, including my correspondence with the chief of police. Recognizing that unethical efforts were underway to criticize my actions, I wanted to ensure I was on safe ground in retaining copies of all materials. The city attorney's office opined that, since it was my work product, and materials on which my work product was based, I was within the law (government code) to retain copies of the materials as long as they were maintained in a secure location and treated as confidential. Before leaving Personnel Group, I had the concerned investigator make and provide me copies of virtually every related document, including notes and phone messages. After just a few days in my new assignment as the "staff inspector," I was hired as the marshal of San Bernardino County.

Within a short period of time, this complete copy of the original file was safe in the marshal's main vault in San Bernardino, consistent with the advice I'd received from the office of the Los Angeles city attorney. I knew that what I was doing was smart. But at the time I didn't realize just how smart my actions were.

DISCRIMINATION FOUND—ONE-PAGE DOCUMENT

Within two weeks of my reassignment out of Personnel Group and from the position of Equal Employment Opportunity Officer, a one-page document was created by the office of the Chief of Police finding that the female sergeant whose case was the primary reason for my re-assignment was a victim of discrimination! The entire investigative file, which clearly supported my previous finding that she was not the vic-tim of discrimination, also disappeared! I didn't learn these things until well after my retirement from the LAPD. Then I had the opportunity to review additional documentation in conjunction with a lawsuit filed against the LAPD by the two sergeants who were branded as racists, and administratively transferred as a result of her allegations and the unethi-cal actions of certain members of the executive staff. As indicated in the previous paragraph, I'd made and retained a complete copy of the entire file that soon mysteriously disappeared.

AN ETHICAL PERSON'S WORST NIGHTMARE

The Anderson case had an abundance of the worst possible ingre-dients for somebody whose only agenda was doing the right thing, and who was driven solely by the evidence and objective considerations. The matter consisted of the confluence of a weak and unqualified police chief, multiple special interests, personal agendas, likely criminal behavior (the entire investigative file "disappeared"), and racial and gender politics. Realistically, just about every department has people who will go down the aforementioned paths if given the opportunity. More than anything else, the difference between departments where these issues are excessive and all-consuming, or those where the issues are dealt with in a reasonable and objective way, is the level of leadership skills of the police chief.

RETIREMENT FROM THE LOS ANGELES POLICE DEPARTMENT

Although I was humiliated, and had no immediate prospects of a responsible assignment within the Los Angeles Police Department, I was not going to retire until I felt certain the San Bernardino County Marshal's Department was all I hoped it would be. As a result, I was sworn in as the San Bernardino County marshal while on a thirty-day vacation from the LAPD. I actually drew a full salary from each department for a couple of weeks.

In mid-August 1996, with Cathy following me in my LAPD Crown Victoria, I drove to Parker Center, turned in all the equipment I was required to return, and officially retired. While I had attained a great position that most of my fellow LAPD command officers would have killed for, I was nonetheless in great emotional pain that day. Financially, I got a pretty good vacation and sick time payout, in part because I'd only taken one sick day (not counting the four "injured on duty" days I'd taken while recovering from pneumonia) in my 31 years with the LAPD.

RETIREMENT CELEBRATION AT THE ACADEMY

I allowed a retirement celebration to be held for me, only because I didn't want to ride out of the organization I loved and believed I had served so long and well, without a credible departure. It was put together by Jake and my long-term dear friends and loyal subordinates, secretary Annabelle Garcia and administrative assistant Gloria Grube.

The party was held in the Rock Garden at the Police Academy, about two months after I left the department. I said I would pay for the event, that all who came would be my guests, and that is exactly what happened. "No speeches, no gifts, just good conversation," was stated conspicuously on my retirement poster. I provided an open bar (never again!) and heavy hors d'oeuvres, with a total tab of over $5,000. It was well attended, but I was a pretty unhappy person and didn't enjoy it as much as I should have.

My longtime friend and supporter, Councilman Zev Yaroslavsky, was among those in attendance. But my lasting memories also include the presence of one of the spineless individuals above me in the chain of command, who came and drank my beer and acted as if nothing had ever happened.

Chapter Thirteen
POST-LAPD RETIREMENT THOUGHTS AND ACTIVITIES

Leadership Not Worthy of the Rank and File

In my last couple of years with the Los Angeles Police Department, I found my motivation in the faces and superb performance of the truly wonderful men and women of the department, but was ashamed at the lack of leadership at the higher levels. It was particularly troublesome to watch some unethical command officers bask in the glory of wonderful reputations that had been achieved by others. I sadly had come to recognize that some of the top leadership was not worthy of the rank and file of the department.

Special Award from the Police Protective League

Several months after I retired from the police department, one of the directors of the Police Protective League came to my office in San Bernardino. On behalf of the entire Board of Directors, he presented me with a plaque made especially for me. I was overwhelmed with emotion and gratitude. The plaque continues to be among my most cherished possessions, and will always have a prominent place in any agency office I have the honor to occupy. The plaque reads:

COMMANDER KEITH BUSHEY

*The Credit Belongs to Those Who Are Actually in the Arena,
Who Serve Valiantly, Who Know the Great Enthusiasms,
The Great Devotions, & Spend Themselves In a Worthy Cause;
Who At Best Know the Triumph of High Achievement, and Who
At the Worst, If They Fail, Fail While Daring Greatly,
So That Their Place Shall Never Be With Those Cold and
Timid Souls Who Know Neither Victory Nor Defeat.*
—*Theodore Roosevelt*

To One Who Was Always in the Arena Fighting for Our Members! Thank You From the Entire Los Angeles Police Protective League.

"Consequences of Hiring a Weak Police Chief"

Having a front-row seat to the horrifically adverse impact that Chief Willie Williams had on the Los Angeles Police Department was unbelievably painful to others and me. Notwithstanding some troubling selective recollections, he was basically a good and decent man with good intentions, but who absolutely did not have the skills for the job. I ultimately wrote an extensive article, titled "The Consequences of Hiring a Weak Police Chief." It appeared in *Public Management*, published monthly by the International City Management Association, in March 2002. For several years after it was published I often sent copies, along with a brief note, to the mayor and city manager of every major city (and some not so major, as well) that advertised an opening for the position of police chief. I remain flattered at the accolades I continue to receive for this article, and am confident that I made a contribution to the quality of some police chief selection processes.

I have had several other criminal justice professionals, whose insight and judgment I trust, act as my editors. After one of the rough draft reviews, one of my editors, then-Chief Lee Dean of the San Bernardino Police Department, provided valuable input including a comment that the article appeared to be somewhat of a catharsis for me. Lee was exactly right. His comment caused me to consciously recognize that most of the articles I wrote for publication were, to some extent, a catharsis for things I'd found to be troubling.

Plenty to Write About

Writing and having published the article on the consequences of hiring a weak police chief was just one of several topics that stemmed primarily from my service, observations, and experiences on the Los Angeles Police Department.

Other published articles stemming from my LAPD years included: "The Unproductive Police Executive" (*Police Chief*), "Helpful Hints for New Command Officers" (*Police Chief*), "Ignore That Advice—Sometimes" (*FBI-LEEDA Bulletin*). Other articles, with emphasis from other agencies as well, include: "Setting Ethics Standards Early" (*Police Chief*) and "Implementing a Juvenile Impact Program" (*Police Chief*).

City Attorney Finds a Troubling Witness
—Anderson Case

A year or so into my tenure as the marshal in San Bernardino County, I was contacted to be a witness for the City of Los Angeles in a case brought against the city by the two sergeants in the Anderson case. I indicated my willingness to be helpful, but was pretty honest in my belief that the two sergeants had been treated unfairly and that they, and not Sergeant Anderson, were the victims of the situation.

The matter went to trial and a federal jury was unanimous in its ruling in favor of the two sergeants. The city appealed and the unanimous verdict in favor of the two sergeants was set aside! Later, however, the city recognized the merit to the claims of the two men and reached a settlement with them.

City Attorney Reaches Out Again
—Anderson Case

The city attorney again contacted me a year or so later. This time, however, it was to solicit my assistance in defending the city against a suit brought by Sergeant Anderson! It was clear to me, finally, that the city realized she was the primary problem. The city had settled with the two sergeants, and was well on the way to what struck me as a likely positive result for the city—then nothing.

I was aware of the strong evidence and witnesses on behalf of the city, and assumed the matter died some type of legal death when it became apparent that Sergeant Anderson could not prevail. Apparently, I was wrong; instead, my understanding is that she ended up with a sizable settlement! I shouldn't have been surprised, given her friends in high places, and the likelihood that those folks would be persuasive in distorting what had occurred for her benefit.

Realistically, the perspective of her supporters in the department that she was the victim of discrimination, and their tampering with the record to exclude information adverse to her claim (which occurred in this case), would leave the city attorney little choice but to settle.

The emotional pain I suffered for several months following the actions of Willie Williams and his cronies was just about as severe as it can get. However, there was never a time when I regretted the actions I'd taken, or even for one moment wished I could have the opportunity to do the things I'd done in a different way. There was an effort to compel me to do things that were wrong and unethical, and those were things I just could not do.

Clearly, I paid the price. But if I had it to do over again, I would take the same actions. I am not somebody who thinks that everything I don't like is unethical, because all of us find ourselves from time to time having to do things we don't agree with. However, there are times when the situation is truly one of serious integrity. The situations I was confronted with helped me to discover "my line in the sand;" a line I was not inclined across.

Quality of Leadership on the
Los Angeles Police Department

I am very critical of the performance of some of my former colleagues; however, my criticism is of a unique nature. We had all taken tests, worked hard, and participated in grueling processes to get to the positions we held. Notwithstanding, I think some of the folks at the top were lousy leaders for two reasons: they learned how to manage but not to lead, and frequently put their personal well-being ahead of that of the department.

I was let down by my chain of command, but realistically the way I was dealt with was more of a symptom than a problem. In the Anderson discrimination matter, those between Chief Williams and me knew I was correct, but decided that the situation wasn't going to be a hill they were going to die over. I clearly understand that it is wise to pick your fights; however, a situation where two sergeants were branded as racists and administratively transferred because of the questionable accusations made by a well-connected employee is a hill that I will die on if necessary.

In my judgment, that is the difference between selfishness and integrity.

As good as the LAPD is, in so many ways, it is a serious mistake to judge the law enforcement profession solely through the LAPD prism. Unlike many other agencies where a wide variety of various and sundry tasks—both personnel and operational—must be dealt with on a daily basis, the LAPD is a massive machine where many things emerge relatively effortlessly from the bureaucracy. Other people do the hiring, equip the troops, maintain the facilities, provide and repair the vehicles, do the budget, resolve the lawsuits, etc. The degree to which the average LAPD command officers typically deal with these and others issues pales in comparison to the roles played by their counterparts in most other agencies.

The fact that things previously taken for granted often become problematic issues can be a real eye-opener for LAPD retirees who move on to other agencies. From my experience, however, I would say that the greatest reason for LAPD alumni failures is the reality of many unforgiving climates for the type of leadership weaknesses that were often tolerated on the LAPD.

Weak and arbitrary command officers could survive on the LAPD. But when they left the department to become police chiefs elsewhere, they didn't last very long.

"Loose Cannons" or "Suppressed Stallions?"

While other people often know us better than we know ourselves, I believe that my reputation on the LAPD was largely a matter of whom you talked to. I know there were quite a number of folks who thought well of me in both personal and professional ways, and that the percentage of lower-ranking folks who thought well of me was mostly likely higher than the percentage of higher-ranking folks who felt similarly.

I know that to some, especially during my tenure in the Personnel Group, where I was in opposition to an increasing number of issues that I felt were wrong, I was perceived as a "loose cannon." However, in every other significant venue in my life, I have done pretty darn well (private to colonel in the U.S. Marines, Marshal of San Bernardino County, Chief on a Sheriff's Department, Executive Staff in the District Attorney's Office, nationwide leadership presenter for FBI-LEEDA, etc.). I must have done a few things right, and will gladly be compared with any of my detractors for multiple accomplishments, both within and outside the LAPD.

When I left the LAPD, despite my love for the department, it was the right time for me to go. My level of frustration was about as high as it could get. I have always wanted to do my best, but was in a position where some of the things I was expected to do were wrong, and the degree of confidence that I had in my leadership was close to non-existent. I was trapped in a very uncomfortable situation and not inclined to just exist with bozos as bosses.

As I look back and reflect on my final years in the LAPD, I think I was somewhat of a "suppressed achiever," essentially held back and reined in by some folks for whom leadership was merely a word they used, but not a strategy they practiced or even understood.

I can think of a few other extraordinary folks who were far more qualified and credible than their LAPD bosses at the time, and who went on to successful careers in other agencies. These people include Lieutenant Kathleen Sheehan, who went on to be the chief in Bishop and Port Hueneme; Commander Dan Schatz, who went on to be the chief in Prescott Valley (Arizona); Captain Rob Hauck, who went on to be the chief in Tomball (Texas); Lieutenant Larry Manion, who went on to be the chief of the Los Angeles Unified School District Police Department; Commander Bruce Hagerty, who went on to be the chief in Ridgecrest (California); Captain Pat McKinley, who went on to be the chief of the Fullerton Police Department; Commander Garrett Zimmon, who went on to be the chief of the San Bernardino Police Department (California), and then to the the U.S. Justice Department for international police education; Commander Dan Watson, who went on to be chief in the cities of South Pasadena and Mammoth Lakes; Deputy Chief Larry Fetters, who took a big job with the Transportation Security Administration; and others whose names do not immediately come to mind.

Is Top-Level Achievement on the LAPD a Guarantee of Future Success?

This is a complex question, but the short answer is no. Although the officers are better trained, more highly disciplined, and better equipped than ever, these advances haven't translated into the overall success of higher-ranking officers who seek law enforcement leadership positions elsewhere when leaving the LAPD. In some ways, this is very unfair, because there are many wonderful men and women with extraordinary skills who would do well beyond the LAPD, but who have been tainted by years of bad press (the Rodney King affair, the 1992 LA Riots, Rafael Perez and the Rampart Scandal, Consent Decree, etc.). Quite frankly, we have had a few jerks at the top, primarily those who floated up when the top leadership was not great, and that has hurt the better folks.

Also, the LAPD's disciples, those outside the department in positions of municipal leadership who play a role in police chief selection processes and who like the LAPD, are not all that plentiful these days. Too, there continue to be hard-core, anti-LAPD people who summarily reject LAPD applicants. I believe this reality is a reflection of the arrogance of some future command officers who were used to getting things their way because of the positions they held, and who crashed and burned when they no longer had the arbitrary LAPD security blanket to fall back on.

However, all is absolutely not lost. What this means is that LAPD applicants for chief positions need to be the best, brightest and most articulate, and have a solid record of achievement in everything they have done. Realistically, in the final analysis, except for isolated anti-LAPD situations, LAPD applicants will not be at a disadvantage. But the likelihood of a little boost in the process solely because of their coming from the LAPD, most likely isn't going to occur. Achievements beyond the department, such as in professional organizations, teaching, and military, can be of value. Another reality is that the LAPD "mystique" gets stronger and more positive the farther away you get from Los Angeles, with a concurrent increase in the likelihood of a "boost" in the process because of LAPD service.

I personally have both benefitted and suffered because of my LAPD background. In 1995, as one of two finalists to be the chief of police in San Bernardino, the anti-LAPD bias of the city administrator was a key factor in their selection of another person. A year later, my LAPD background, and quite frankly my actions in standing up to Chief Willie Williams, were positive factors in my selection to be the marshal of San Bernardino County. It can cut both ways.

THE ADMINISTRATIVE AND HUMAN RESOURCES ARENA

My criticism of the lack of ethical behavior of certain staff and command officers is narrowly focused, and not something that I considered to be widespread. The easiest and least controversial part of police work is catching crooks and investigating crimes; even with lousy leadership at the top, those things are often done reasonably well and without unnecessary meddling, other than budgetary constraints. The most immediate and heavily affected areas of weak top leadership are in the areas of hiring, firing, promotions, assignments, accommodations, and in the investigation and resolution of complaints of racism, sexism, and sexual harassment.

I reserve my greatest scorn for certain individuals who behaved un-ethically, and who failed in their leadership responsibilities, while in assignments that dealt with these subject areas. Were there some command and staff folks in the operations side of the department who did well, but who might have "caved" and compromised their integrity had they been in the administrative side of the department? Maybe. But such did not occur, so they deserve the benefit of the doubt because of the good jobs they did where they were. I cannot and will not allow my contempt over the few who were put to the integrity test, and failed, taint my respect for the majority of the department's command personnel.

What is Lacking in Leadership Training?

To be blunt, in my judgment the Los Angeles Police Department has never provided adequate leadership training to staff and command personnel. My sense is that there continues to be room for additional growth in this area. The LAPD's primary assumption is that command officers have attained a great deal of leadership training during their careers, and that the knowledge and skills allegedly attained prepare them for higher command.

A few good opportunities are offered, such as the West Point Leadership Program and the POST Command College. But a real deficiency exists in the area of practical instruction and mentoring in the more practical aspects of leadership. There are plenty of good resources out there on theory, long-range planning, strategic activities, and related issues. But there needs to be more, not on what to do, but in the details of how to do things. New captains need mentoring by very credible senior command officers regarding their actions, mannerisms, behaviors, reactions and other tangible issues that make a real difference in the areas of effectiveness and credibility. Had I advanced in the department to chief of police during the process that yielded Bill Bratton, this would have been my primary area of focus. This type of extraordinary leadership training would greatly strengthen the overall effectiveness of the staff and command personnel, and therefore vastly improve the performance of the department across the entire spectrum of challenging issues.

510

During my entire tenure with the Los Angeles Police Department, I felt that one of the agency's failures was to deal realistically with weak command officers who performed poorly. With very few exceptions, the unproductive command officers pretty much remained unproductive, with little department effort to either shape them up or ship them out. There were individual efforts by a few command officers to coach and mentor, but the only sanction for failure to perform amounted pretty much to nothing. Low performers remained in place until they were ready to retire, and the department suffered until that time came.

This situation inspired me to write an article, "The Unproductive Police Executive," that was published in *Police Chief* magazine in March, 1999. It describes the troublesome consequences of command officers who have decided to slow down to an unacceptable degree, and provides guidance on how to deal with such situations. I am flattered that I still get nice reviews about this article from many folks in the law enforcement community.

In all fairness to the LAPD of today, it is clear that command accountability is a very big thing—and that is a very good thing. From all indications, the Comstat process really keeps command officers' feet to the proverbial fire, and ensures they are knowledgable about the crime in their areas and that it is being dealt with. Without minimizing my absolute glee that this degree of accountability is occurring, my sense is that there remains significant opportunity for additional command leadership training and mentoring.

ONE OF MY FAVORITE SAYINGS

When asked what it was like to be a member of the Los Angeles Police Department, I frequently reply, "It was brutal, tough, ugly, vicious, and dysfunctional, and was also pretty tough once you left police headquarters!" For those familiar with the often dog-eat-dog culture at the upper levels of the Los Angeles Police Department, this expression has special meaning! I have always said that the easy part of policing is putting crooks in jail. The biggest challenges are internal.

BOB VERNON'S SAYING

Assistant chief Robert Vernon, long since retired, used to occasionally simulate a radio transmission that was funny: "Attention, all Central units in the vicinity and 1Adam12, handle a staff officer-initiated backstabbing at Parker Center, 150 N. Los Angeles St. Handle the call Code 3" (red lights and siren!)

Funny, but true.

Television "Talking Head" for Officer Randy Simmons' Funeral

In February 2008, Metropolitan Division Officer Randy Simmons was shot and killed during the service of a search warrant in the San Fernando Valley. Although we had exchanged pleasantries over the years, primarily in the locker room at the academy, we really did not know each other. Like most line-of-duty deaths, his services were long and complicated. I was flattered when invited to be the "talking head" on Channel 5 television for that day, as an "expert" to describe police procedures, details of the services, and related questions.

Application for Chief of Police

In 2002, I was among the forty or so applicants to replace Bernard Parks as the chief of police. In the end, William Bratton was selected over the rest of us. Although the headhunter from the firm that led the nationwide search was very complimentary about my background and accomplishments, and described me as a strong competitor, the selection committee apparently did not share his enthusiasm. I was among the majority of applicants who were not even called for an interview. I later developed the absolute belief that Mayor Hahn had decided on William Bratton before the application period ended.

Realistically, for political reasons, I didn't think I had much of a chance of being selected as the chief of police in Los Angeles. From the standpoint of personal and professional achievements, I had to be at the top of the pack, with experience that included turning around a troubled law enforcement agency and having had a number of experience-based articles published in key law enforcement publications. In a head-to-head competitive process, such as in interviews or an assessment center, I believe I could have risen to the top.

Unfortunately, however, I was associated with the past, which had been marketed in many unfavorable and unfair ways. I'm also afraid that the perception that I was a Daryl Gates clone, just like legal analyst Alan Derchowitz had said after my testimony in the O. J. Simpson case, was alive and well. The selection of Bratton, who I came to like and think well of, was just as much (if not more) of a political move as it was based on qualifications.

When William Bratton became the chief of police, he pretty much flushed out the last vestiges of those for whom I had no use. Most of them had survived the transition from Chief Williams to Chief Parks. But they were quickly recognized by Bratton for the lousy leaders they were, and wisely chose to retire as opposed to being demoted.

Although I was occasionally asked to speak before various LAPD groups (divisional training programs, promotional preparation groups, etc), it was still painful for me to visit the old alma mater. That all changed when Bratton came on board, as a great many of those who I had mentored and supported gravitated into the higher ranks and to other positions of increased responsibility. Among the activities I was invited to participate in was the Academy's West Point Leadership Program, where I continue to appear on an occasional basis as a guest speaker. It is a great program for aspiring command personnel, and I am flattered to be a part of it.

Guest Speaker at Los Angeles City Fire Leadership Program

Previous attendees at the LAPD West Point Leadership Program included a number of high-ranking Los Angeles City Fire Command (WPLP) officers. This group was the cadre that gave birth to the Los Angeles Fire Leadership Program. I was very flattered that the fire folks who attended the LAPD-WPLP were complimentary of my presentations. Consequently, I was asked and was pleased to accept my present status as a regular guest speaker at the Los Angeles City Fire Department's Leadership Program. I have completed an attractive cover for a fire leadership booklet, which I anticipate will be a modified version of my Command Leadership booklet, and hope to have it completed and provided to them during 2012.

There is a Courage Even More Difficult Than Physical Courage

I was honored to be the keynote speaker at the first graduation of the Los Angeles Fire Department's Leadership Program. For my topic, I emphasized a very special type of courage that is often more difficult to find than physical courage. I acknowledged the confidence I had that virtually everyone in that room, numbering around 400 persons, clearly had the courage to rush into a burning building to rescue a citizen or fellow firefighter.

But I then asked rhetorically how many of those present truly had the courage to immediately intervene and stop a colleague who was about to do something stupid; such as engaging in sexual harassment, discriminatory humor, or making a statement of an inappropriate nature? I discussed the organizational and individual consequences of the type of weak supervision that failed to intervene in these instances. The LAFD had been rocked with scandals stemming from these types of problems, with consequences that pushed at least one chief into retirement. It was clear that my remarks were resonating with those present, including all the chief officers.

VISIT TO THE SKELETON OF PARKER CENTER

Parker Center was built and first occupied in the mid-1950s. But by the early 1990s it was clear that the department had badly outgrown its headquarters, and that the building needed a number of significant repairs, including structural problems stemming from several earthquakes in recent decades.

Following all of the predictable municipal haggling and budgetary battles, in 2010 LAPD finally moved into its beautiful new headquarters complex, just a block or so away from Parker Center. At that time, Parker Center was all but abandoned, with just a couple of minor functions remaining (part of the Scientific Investigation Division, a portion of the Jail Division, part of Property Division, and the front desk). The rest of the building looked like a ghost town.

I couldn't resist the temptation to slip into the old building on two or three occasions, walk the halls, and to reflect on all of the things that occurred in that building, all of my experiences and all of the ghosts that most certainly have to be hidden in some of the closets! They were truly nostalgic experiences! Boy, if old Parker Center could only talk....

POSTSCRIPT ON MY DETRACTORS OVER THE YEARS

It should be pretty obvious that there were a few people on the LAPD for whom I had no use, primarily because of the way they abused their positions in order to gain personal advantage, and how they failed to exercise ethical leadership. For the most part, they all drifted in a downward manner when no longer still within the protective cocoon of the department.

514

The couple who did move to other organizations went because of unique allegiances, but ultimately even they didn't do particularly well. Despite truly exalted positions in one of the nation's premier law enforcement agencies, which can be a good launching pad to other leadership positions, a visit to Google reveals that most of the folks I lost respect for pretty much slipped into obscurity. Most of them managed to survive and thrive in the transition from Chief Williams to Chief Parks, in part because of their activities in undermining Chief Williams despite being some of his key people.

Chief Bratton saw these self-serving folks for who they were, and pushed them into retirement very shortly after he was named chief. Today they are, for the most part, pretty conspicuous by their absences at various LAPD activities or visits to the academy café. My assumption is that they avoid the department because they accurately recognize their legacies aren't good, and that they aren't well thought of by a considerable number of people who remain in the department, as well as by many of their fellow retirees.

Chapter Fourteen
SAN BERNARDINO COUNTY MARSHAL'S DEPARTMENT

Selected as the Marshal of San Bernardino County

Lady Luck must surely have been on my shoulder during this unbelievably difficult time. I was an emotional basket-case, so soon after the LAPD debacle, and really depressed.

Before the shit hit the fan (with my transfer and administrative charges for alleged inappropriate comments), I had applied for the position of marshal of San Bernardino County. But the selection process had not yet got underway. Actually, submitting my application was somewhat of a lark, as the position wasn't something I was all that passionate about. But it started looking real good when things at the LAPD turned sour, and even more so when it became obvious to me that the INTER-CON security position wasn't for me. About half of the forty or so applicants were invited to provide additional documents and were screened by San Bernardino County Human Resources, and about eleven of those were referred to a judicial interview panel. My appearance before the group of a dozen or so judges, around a conference table in a jury deliberation room at the Rancho Cucamonga Courthouse, went very well.

At the end of the hour or so of extensive interviews with all of the judges, I was asked if there was anything else I might want them to be aware of. Realizing that all the nastiness going on with my transfer and the pending discipline would come out during a background investigation, I decided to put the whole matter on the table for all present to be aware of. I told them everything that had occurred, the stances I had taken and my refusal to change my EOO findings, the alleged misconduct, and my transfer. I also explained I had retained documentation that would support the accuracy of everything I said, and that I would be pleased to make it available for judicial review. It was a somewhat touchy issue, but I took the position that it was my work product and that I could permit a judge to look at it if I so desired, but only after consultation with the city attorney's office. The interview went on for quite a while longer, as all the judges were clearly listening closely and considering all that was being said. I left with the tentative belief that the judges were favorably impressed with me because of the principled positions that I had taken. I was correct, and a couple of weeks later I was one of three finalists invited to appear before the full bench of San Bernardino County!

In mid-June 1996, I and the other two finalists appeared at the Rancho Cucamonga Courthouse for an oral interview before the full bench, consisting of approximately 100 judges from throughout the municipal and superior courts of the county. The other two finalists were Marshal's Captain Jim Williams and an LAPD captain (a former subordinate). One at a time, each of us made a presentation before all of the judges, seated in the witness box with the scores of judges in the gallery.

After our presentations, we sat in the lobby as the judges deliberated and ultimately voted. After a while, Judge Craig Kamansky approached the three of us, extended his hand to me, and congratulated me on having been selected as the marshal of San Bernardino County! Jim Williams and Dick LaGarra were gracious and congratulated me, but I soon learned that Jim Williams felt that he was the heir apparent, as the insider, and was deeply offended at not having been selected (later Jim did a fine job for me, and never let any personal resentment show).

The fact that I performed so well in these two interview processes is nothing short of amazing! During the time I was an emotional basket case, obsessed with despair over the circumstances of my departure from the LAPD. Still, I spent a great deal of time giving consideration to what I wanted to say to the interview panel and the full bench, and obviously identified the right issues and presented them well. As I look back, I was operating on emotional auto-pilot, but it worked.

BIG BEAR DEPUTY RUNS INTO THE NEW MARSHAL—LITERALLY!

The good intentions of Deputy Keith Kerns, of the Marshal's Big Bear Division, in making a good impression on the new marshal, went badly haywire. Shortly after my appointment Cathy and I were at our Big Bear home doing some chores around the property. Deputy Kerns called the house and asked if it would be all right to drop by and make my acquaintance; I was happy to hear from him, and told him to come on over.

Cathy was out in the driveway, having just put the finishing coat of varnish on our set of wooden outdoor chairs and table that she'd basically rebuilt. She was admiring her handiwork when the marshal's unit driven by Deputy Kerns roared into the driveway and turned Cathy's rebuilt furniture into splinters! Obviously, he was unaware of the furniture that Cathy had drying in the curve-around driveway, and destroyed it beyond any possible repair. Deputy Kerns was beyond embarrassed and humiliated, and probably felt that his career was over. Cathy and I got a big kick out of the incident and hopefully put Keith's mind at ease. Keith Kerns is a great fellow and a great cop, and to this day he remains a good friend.

My First Actions—Nothing

I think I did a very wise thing as the new marshal of San Bernardino County—NOTHING. I spent the first few weeks just learning about the organization and its people. I saw things that I felt should eventually be addressed, but resisted the temptation to make any changes until I truly understood the organization. I traveled to all of the divisions across the county and got to know my personnel. I also spent a lot of time getting to know as many of the judges as I could. After a couple of weeks, I had the budget analyst, Phil Coachbuilder, bring the entire budgetary document (several inches thick) into my office and sit there answering questions as I read through it and attempted to digest and understand what I was reading. Not immediately changing certain things was hard in certain instances, but it was the right thing to do. As I predicted, and constantly remind others, some issues were far more complicated than they originally appeared, and premature changes might have been wrong and harmful to the organization.

O. J. Simpson's Black Glove Misunderstanding

In 1996 the O. J. Simpson case was still pretty fresh in the minds of a great many people, and it was common for people to recognize me from the trial. In the first week or so of my employment in San Bernardino County, I was walking past the human resources offices when a man approached and asked if I was Commander Bushey. When I said I was, he became visibly excited and said that he and his wife had watched every minute of the Simpson trial, and that he couldn't wait to tell her he'd met me. He also asked if I could give him my autograph, to which I said I would do better than that and would be happy to give him an autographed 8x10 portrait, as I had quite a few printed up by LAPD's photo lab because of the demand after the trial. He was ecstatic and got his wife on his cell so that she could say hello as well.

I told him to drop by my office the following day to pick up the photograph. As a fun gesture, I also got one of the black slot machine gloves I had, attached an evidence tag indicating that it had been picked up by Detective Fuhrman at the crime scene, and put it in the envelope with the photograph.

I was not in my office the next day when he picked up the envelope. Unfortunately, he went crazy at what he thought was his unbelievable luck at being given the infamous black glove; I can't believe he didn't see it as a joke. Later that day he called, on the verge of hyperventilation, wanting to know if the glove was from the crime scene on Bundy or the Simpson estate on Rockingham. But he got very upset when I told him it was neither, that it was just a joke. We crossed paths a number of times in my subsequent years with the county, and his consternation remained alive as he always completely ignored me! That's okay, I don't want to associate with anyone who is that stupid!

How Could an Outfit that Reports to Judges be so "Unique?"

Except for a few individual personal exceptions, I have not previously had much experiences with judges. I always saw them as godlike creatures, full of wisdom and knowledge.

My previous impression didn't square with what I inherited in the Marshal's Department, where I found obvious sexual harassment and other unprofessional behavior. The person I replaced (a good and decent man) had a beard, didn't wear a uniform, and was widely recognized for having a few drinks at the noon hour and sometimes not being able to function well in the afternoon. How could this be, when this department was overseen by the Marshal's Oversight Committee, which consisted of about ten judges?

What I ultimately came to realize is that judges are just like the rest of us, and unless the judicial officer was someone who dealt with a particular subject such as discrimination or harassment, it was not likely they were any more knowledgeable in that arena than the average person. Also, I don't think the bench as a whole saw the Marshal's Department as much of a professional agency; rather, just a bunch of so-so cops getting a good salary for performing limited tasks. I still have a very positive impression of judges as truly great human beings who work hard to do a good job, but not necessarily vested at all times with all the world's wisdom. Also, I am very pleased for the role that I played in elevating the status of the marshal's personnel in the eyes of the judicial bench.

The presiding judges, Joe Johnson of the Superior Courts and Ray Van Stockum of the Municipal Courts, were very wise in denying the interim marshal the ability to make permanent promotions. The interim marshal, Andy, was a good man who attempted to exercise his best judgment and promote a number of people, but it was the wrong thing to do. Andy was aligned with the old marshal, who'd been forced into retirement, and was at odds with a number of people who had been aligned with the old marshal's adversary. It was a sorry state of affairs.

The presiding judges learned that Andy had promoted some personnal and felt, perhaps unfairly, that he was promoting his friends and disenfranchising his enemies. The judges made it clear that his promotions would be "provisional" (temporary) and would have to be ratified by the person selected to be the permanent marshal.

On arriving, I was immediately urged to ratify all of the provisional appointments, but I declined to do so. I made it clear that no promotions would be made or ratified for several months, until I had the opportunity to get to know the personnel. At that time I would seek to promote those who were the best, brightest, and most deserving. In December, after I had been the marshal for several months, I promoted a number of people to the ranks of captain, lieutenant, and sergeant. In making these promotions, I demoted a couple of folks who were holding provisional appointments, because I came to realize there were others who were more qualified and deserving. There were a couple of real unhappy folks (especially a lieutenant who had previously been a captain), but overall the promotions were well received by the men and women of the department. While I am aware that the lieutenant who I reverted back from captain never cared for me, he was truly a class act in that he never failed to perform to the best of his abilities up to the day he retired.

Bold Driving by the New Marshal

Early in my tenure I took two of my captains, Jim Williams and Richards Diggs, to lunch, and had some fun at their expense. I parked in the upper parking lot of a restrauant, which overlooked the lower lot of another restaurant, the two being separated by a dirt drop-off having about a six-foot difference in elevation.

As we departed the parking lot, I drove in the direction of an exit from the lower lot, but there was no driveway leading down to it. Either Jim or Richard made a comment to the effect that the driveway was not an option. At that point I commented that I had four-wheel drive, then stomped on the gas and headed for the drop-off. They both shouted Oh, shit! (or something like that) and grabbed something to hold onto. I can still picture the startled look on Jim's face as he lunged for the hand-hold. Obviously, I stopped before reaching the drop-off. We all laughed for a good five minutes and still re-live that incident from time to time.

SHOPLIFTING LIEUTENANT

A terribly difficult situation developed within just two or three weeks after my appointment as marshal. Lieutenant Ed Chasen (pseudonym) was the commanding officer of one of my divisions, a very personable and impressive man and well thought of by his subordinates and the judicial community. Ed also initially struck me as a strong candidate to fill one of two captain vacancies in the department.

One evening I received a call from Captain Andy Anderson, who had just been notified by the sheriff's department that Chasen had been named on a crime report for shoplifting at a tanning salon, and that his actions were clearly visible on the store's security videotape. It was a sad and painful investigation for all concerned, including me. I was under enormous pressure to consider the theft inadvertent, based on his alleged long-suppressed depression and absentmindedness caused by his wife's death from cancer a year or so earlier. I received petitions from all of his subordinates, from deputy district attorneys, deputy public defenders, and all sorts of others. A number of judges were on my case, including a not-so-subtle threat to revisit my selection for employment by one of the key judges who had supported my appointment. I wanted very badly to interpret Chasen's actions as unintentional, but the overwhelming evidence made clear that his actions were both intentional and criminal.

I grew quite a bit professionally during this incident, and came to understand why other chiefs often say it is "lonely at the top." I really liked my new position, and did not want to go sideways with the judges over this situation. But I took the position that the job would not be worth having if I could not do the right thing. I terminated the lieutenant.

Shortly afterward, I received a great deal of praise for the appropriate and professional way the matter had been handled—including from a number of judges who had taken a "wait and see" attitude. While I did what I did because it was the right thing to do, and certainly did not terminate Chasen because I was trying to strengthen my position, my actions in this case turned out to have been very beneficial in establishing a favorable reputation with just about every involved faction, including the rank and file in my department. It is my understanding that Chasen is now doing well; whatever he is doing, I wish him the very best.

Judge Borba Reached Out at the Right Time

Joan Borba was, and is, a superb jurist as well as an attractive woman who is the product of a prominent San Bernardino County family. A lawyer, she was appointed to the bench just shortly before I was appointed as the marshal. She struck me as soft-spoken, unassuming, and someone who was pretty much in the judicial background because of having been newly appointed. Right in the middle of the Chasen shoplifting matter, when it was obvious that I was taking some real flack from certain judges including one that was particularly prominent, she called my office and asked if I could drop by her chambers. When I went to her chambers, I was warmly greeted, and politely, but gently and firmly, told that she was impressed that I was doing the right thing and not to be dissuaded in my actions based on the statements and criticism of some of her judicial colleagues. He words of support could not have come at a better time, because I was feeling stressed over all that was occurring. I was and to this day continue to be appreciative for her reaching out to me in the way she did. Thank you, judge!

Deputy Cairns Had Nothing to Worry About

The Needles Division of the marshal's department was a small operation consisting of the officer-in-charge (OIC), a clerk, and an extra help (POST certified part-time) deputy. Deputy Chuck Cairns, the OIC, was a great fellow who had previously served about thirty years with the California Highway Patrol in the desert, and later became the elected constable in Needles.

Shortly before my appointment as marshal, all of the elected constables became deputy marshals as the result of new state legislation. Chuck was getting pretty long in the tooth, and at about 70 years of age was in mortal fear that I was going to force him to retire. He got pretty nervous during my first couple of trips to his division, fearing that the ax was about to fall. Linda, Chuck's clerk, whispered in my ear about his fear and level of anxiety. Shortly thereafter I took him for a cup of coffee and told him he had a job there as long as he chose to stay. I felt that his good judgment and diplomacy more than compensated for what he lacked due to declining physical prowess.

I was fortunate to have four great friends, all LAPD reserve officers, accept my invitation to become reserve deputies with the marshal's department. The first was Sarkis O'hanessian, a good friend of my son Jake. Sarkis was a reserve officer in Hollywood Division, someone who speaks more languages than I have fingers, and truly one of the finest young men I am privileged to be acquainted with. The second was another superb individual, close family friend, Air Support Division reserve, Hollywood personality and former producer of the Power Rangers, Ronnie Hadar. The third, another close family friend and medical unit reserve, was Bobby Sherman, a truly great fellow, teen singing idol from the 1960s and 1970s, and still very much a noted personality and performer. Last, but far from being least, is my very dear friend and physician, Ben Novak, who agreed to become the department's medical officer. These wonderful men did a great job with the marshal's department, and later with the sheriff's department after the merger. Except for Sarkis, they have since put away their San Bernadino lawmen's stars. Sarkis became a regular deputy marshal, then a regular sheriff's deputy, promoted to sergeant, and is now on the list for sheriff's lieutenant!

The Memo that Changed the Marshal's Department

When I became marshal, it was considered inappropriate for a deputy marshal to perform any law enforcement duties other than the department's primary duties. When I got there, it was not uncommon for a deputy to be called on the carpet for doing police work based on an observation. But this was a culture I found beyond troubling. While all good people, the leadership of the marshal's department was made up of those with a marshal's mentality of doing just marshal duties. I was very clear that, while our primary role was that delineated by the courts, our people were regularly-designated peace officers (not limited, like some specialized peace officers) and as such I absolutely expected them to perform the full range of law enforcement responsibilities when the circumstances arose.

I finally put out a memo, after first discussing the matter with Sheriff Gary Penrod, making it clear that whether helping a game warden with a bear up a tree, a sheriff's deputy with a robbery in progress, a highway patrol officer with a fatal traffic accident, or any other situation that our personnel came into contact with, I expected our personnel to be full partners in assisting those officers and agencies.

A few didn't like this, but it set well with the majority of my personnel. There were a few situations that I pretty much pretended didn't exist, such as fifty-plus, out-of-shape deputies who were not about to leave fairly sedate assignments. But for the most part I was serious about my directive. This change of mindset was probably the key issue, alongside increased professionalism, that moved the marshal's department into the mainstream of county law enforcement.

Seeking Every Possible School

I believed that the key to improving the department was to improve the quality of supervision and the quality of training. I sought out every school within a couple hundred miles, and had employees traveling all over the state attending professional courses. I had one lieutenant in particular who often resisted me, diplomatically and in good faith, believing that we couldn't afford to let so many people go to schools because we were running too lean in some of the divisions. I replied that if he thought training was too expensive, just wait and see the way the department would end up without that training. Somehow we managed to get by, and I knew we would. In a couple of instances, I came close to personally working a shift or two as a deputy because of having sent so many people to training. I was willing if it became necessary.

Sex Offender Sweeps

The county probation department would coordinate occasional sweeps under Section 290 of the Penal Code, to ensure that sex offender parolees were in compliance with registration requirements, keeping their addresses current, the same with employment, etc. Shortly after taking over as marshal, I let every law enforcement agency in the county know that the marshal's department would provide manpower for these and other types of operations. Within six months of my being hired, you couldn't find an operation or sweep of any nature in the county where the marshal's department did not have a uniformed presence.

An Unorthodox Approach to Discipline—Sometimes

Although the marshal's department was a fairly large outfit, I was able to be creative in some of the penalties for acts of misconduct. This was possible in part because the bargaining unit for marshal's personnel, the Marshal's Association, wasn't very strong, and because I developed a reasonably good relationship with its leadership. Some of my more creative disciplinary solutions included placing a thirty-day suspension (for a serious situation involving conduct unbecoming an officer) in abeyance, pending successful completion of an anger management course; and agreeing to turn a four-day suspension into a written reprimand, if the deputy would take two folks from another agency who he'd unnecessarily pissed-off, to lunch. Because of union rules, past practice, and meddling county counsel, these approaches aren't always possible. But in my judgment they should be used whenever the circumstances are appropriate and latitude exists to be creative.

Team-Building Seminars

The California Commission on Peace Officer Standards & Training (POST) provided funding for every law enforcement agency in the state to have a three-day team-building seminar every other year. I jumped on this great program, and conducted two of them during my tenure as marshal. I brought a friend from Los Angeles and the Command College, Tom Estensen, to conduct the training, and he did a fine job. This was a great process, and it was very helpful in developing priorities and direction for the discretionary parts of the department. This process was also helpful in providing me with personal feedback on my performance and credibility.

Dr. Novak and Witches' Panties

I started one of the department's training days with a personal presentation to all employees about my "zero tolerance" policy for any form of harassment, discrimination, sexual jokes, or any other type of behavior that had the potential to be offensive to any groups of people.

The second speaker was a very good friend whom I'd appointed the department's medical officer, Dr. Ben Novak, who was due to make a presentation on skin cancer. After I introduced Ben, I returned to my office. But when I walked into headquarters, every phone started ringing and every phone indicator light lit up. Several people were calling in an absolute panic. Just after my "zero tolerance" presentation, Ben started his talk by asking the 300 or so employees if they knew "why witches don't wear panties" (so they won't slide down the broomstick.)

It seems funny now. But it wasn't funny that day, because I was in a panic that Ben's joke would result in someone making a formal complaint to County Human Resources. Had this occurred in Los Angeles, there may well have been a couple of folks going off IOD ("injured on duty") for job-related stress/trauma, filing worker compensation claims for damages, and a lawsuit(s) by a shark attorney(s), not to mention a full-blown personnel investigation into not only what was said, but also the environment that allowed such dastardly behavior to occur!

I immediately returned to the auditorium and asked Ben to take a break. When he had stepped out, I apologized to all my employees for what occurred. Nobody seemed upset, and most just chuckled. Later that day, with Ben's blessing and understanding, I issued him a written letter of warning over the incident, mainly to cover my rear end if the issue ever went further. Fortunately, it died and there were no subsequent problems.

I did receive a petition signed by a considerable number of my female deputies urging that he not be disciplined for making an honest and good-natured mistake! Ben had my letter of reprimand framed and placed it on the wall in his home. We still laugh over this incident.

Learning about Those Mysterious People in Black Robes

Before I became somewhat of a colleague of over 100 judges, I really did not know much about them in general. While I was selected by and served at the pleasure of the bench, as were the court executive officer and the chief probation officer, I was generally treated very well and pretty much as an equal with the judges.

Not long after becoming marshal I came to a startling realization about a deficiency with judges in general: they are human, just like the rest of us! While generally smart people, they were not particularly knowledgeable in legal areas beyond those where they usually ruled, and—understandably—had to do a lot of self-education when unique cases arose. I developed a great deal of warmth and strong friendships with several of the judges, which continue to this day. While I liked some more than others, the vast majority were wonderful and dedicated individuals. There were only a couple who I really did not care for, but neither did most of their colleagues, primarily because they tended to be bullies when they slipped into their black robes.

"Keep Female Deputies Out of My Courtroom"

One day, one of my division commanders asked me to join him in what he thought was going to be a troubling meeting with a judge. He was right!

526

A very senior judge, who even though long gone shall remain anonymous, straight-out told me and the lieutenant that women are not suited for law enforcement. He wanted to make sure that we would never assign a female deputy to his courtroom as either a bailiff or custody officer!

First, I couldn't believe what I was hearing. Second, I couldn't believe he was so open in stating his troublesome beliefs and request. While remaining polite and respectful, I seized upon the opportunity to share my contrary belief that many of our female deputies (I did inherit a few who I really couldn't argue over) stood shoulder-to-shoulder with their male counterparts in physical and tactical prowess. I also suggested that if he really felt this way, he would be well advised to keep such thoughts to himself, or face potential sanction from the state bar if someone were to make a complaint.

While he was a pretty crusty old fart who was living in the social dark ages, he was a nice man and fairly gracious in accepting what I said.

Afterward, I asked the lieutenant not to share what we'd discussed with anyone, and to try to place only male deputies in his courtroom—not because the judge asked for them, but to not unnecessarily subject our female deputies to his potentially offensive comments or behavior.

Knowing When to Fold—Judicial Advocacy for Their Bailiffs

I had a great idea for a superb program, but it was retarded by realities including the judges' protection of their bailiffs. The serving of criminal arrest warrants was largely a discretionary task performed by the sheriff's department as resources permitted, which was not very often. I came to realize that it wasn't unusual for a number of courtrooms to "go dark" early in the afternoon because of judicial conflicts, appointments, etc. In these instances, the assigned bailiffs really didn't have anything to do, but usually remained in the empty courtroom reading books or whatever.

So I put together a plan where bailiffs of courtrooms that "went dark" would immediately be paired up, given a vehicle, provided a few arrest warrants, and sent out to hook up some folks. While my plan was solid, I failed to recognize the tight relationship between judges and bailiffs, and realistically how they look out for each other. Within a day or so of my new program, I started getting calls from judges explaining why it was necessary for their bailiffs to remain in the courtroom even when court went out of session for the day, supposedly to answer the phone, field inquiries and for other totally non-logical reasons.

I knew exactly who was responsible for these calls—the bailiffs who did not want to do police work. I was absolutely right, and the bailiffs and their protector judges were absolutely wrong, but I knew when to hold and when to fold, and this was not a battle that I could win. My new program never got off the ground.

Mass Confusion, and the "Code of Ethics"

For a sheriff's recruit graduation at San Bernardino Valley College, I was flattered as the new marshal to be asked to administer the oath of the Law Enforcement Code of Ethics to the new sheriff's deputies.

What I didn't know, was that the recruits on stage had been instructed to execute various maneuvers (stand up, do a half-left turn, raise their arms, etc) when I recited certain milestones in the oath and mentioned certain key words. This flew in the face of my way of doing business, because I don't read such things verbatim, and in the case of the oath I was speaking pretty much extemporaneously. What a cluster! Some of the kids stood up, some turned to the left, others did a half-turn to the right, about half their hands went up, etc!

Although badly screwed-up at the time, afterward we all had a good laugh over this. I wish I'd known those key words were intended to trigger certain movements on that stage!

The Marshal's Baker-to-Vegas Chase Vehicle

I have been a long-time supporter of the annual Baker-to-Vegas law enforcement relay race. It is sponsored and conducted by the Los Angeles Police Revolver and Athletic Club, and participants attend from several hundred agencies.

About twenty-four legs comprise the 120-mile course across the Mojave Desert, with a primary and back-up runner for each of the segments. Each team has a vehicle following its runner, containing water, first aid, communications, the back-up runner, and music to keep the runner entertained and motivated. A few teams have unique follow vehicles—such as a hearse for a sheriff's homicide team—but most are just rental vehicles with temporary lights and loudspeakers attached.

When I became the marshal, I decided we were going to have a team. While we had the runners, there had never really been the department leadership to encourage and support participation. I also decided that we were going to have the most awesome chase vehicle on the course. Then-Sergeant Russ Wilke caused it to happen.

Russ was most creative in what he could acquire and accomplish, and really did himself proud with the attachment (placed on top of a rental van) for our team. It was a large and long metal container full of lights, loudspeakers, floodlights, sidelights, and antennas. In the center was a very tall fold-over flagpole mast that, when extended, flew the marshal's flag about thirty feet above the vehicle, and it was illuminated at night with floodlights. Atop the flagpole was an antenna that gave us considerable distance for coordination on our radios. To have an adequate number of runners, we teamed up with our counterparts in the County Probation Department. We had the most awesome chase vehicle on the course!

The Worst Possible Nightmare for a Problem Tenant

As marshal for the entire county of San Bernardino (the largest county in the continental United States), I managed a department that really understood the eviction process. In fact, my name was printed on every civil enforcement document, including eviction notices, for the entire county, as personnel acting under my authority undertook all such actions.

My wife and I owned a rental home at Big Bear, and it was among the properties managed by a local realtor. She called one day to tell me about a problem she was having. Our tenant neither wanted to move out nor pay the rent. Without going into detail, the problem was solved almost immediately. When you are a problem tenant, it is not a good idea to screw with your landlord when he is the county marshal!

Haunted Houses

Being the county marshal was pretty cool in itself. But I was always looking for new things to do for the department to get more into the mainstream of law enforcement and the community. Downtown San Bernardino, where the marshal's executive offices were located, was not a great area at night. That also included the adjacent residential neighborhoods.

As an alternative to Halloween "trick or treating," I decided to use some of my personnel and a few work-release prisoners to turn an abandoned county building into the most awesome haunted house known to mankind. And that's just what we did. The effort was headed up by then-Sergeant Russ Wilke, and he did one heck of a job by creating a very scary haunted house that was just about beyond words to describe: coffins, ghosts, bloody creatures, scary music, decapitated heads, pop-up monsters, etc., etc., etc.

On exiting the exhibit, each person was chased by a bloody creature carrying a loud gasoline-powered chainsaw (its blade had been removed). My pal (and after the merger, my boss), Sheriff Gary Penrod, acquired all the candy we needed from his many resources in the business community. We developed and ran this event for the two Halloweens I was the marshal. It was really popular with the community, and had long lines, as the kids and their parents went through it time after time.

"Don't Pull Your Money Out of the Pension System!"

San Bernardino County had what I perceived as a weird loophole in its pension system: an employee could resign, pull all of his or her money out of the pension system, then be rehired without having to replace the money. The assumption (flawed in my judgment) was that the employee would get proportionately less on retirement. An employee could have thirty years of service and seniority, but only five years of contributions in the pension system because of premature withdrawals. This was crazy. It doesn't take much imagination to understand that people will retire, and that it will likely be a service-connected disability retirement if they don't have adequate funds saved for a conventional retirement. I had several employees who had quite a bit of seniority, but almost nothing in their pension accounts, because they saw it as a piggy bank and several times had cleaned out their retirement accounts then come right back to work.

I made it clear that anyone who quit the marshal's department could only return if they'd left in good standing, and either left their retirement funds in the pension system or put the funds back into the system at the time of their rehire. Except for a couple of people, this pretty much ended the abuse.

The last situation involved a marshal's technician, whose job it was to serve legal processes, who said she needed to resign to spend more time assisting a relative in Las Vegas. I all but begged her not to leave, and certainly not to take her money out of the pension system. I even offered to transfer her to our Barstow Division and place her on an adjustable work schedule, so she could spend substantial time with her allegedly sick relative. But she dug-in her feet and insisted she had no alternative but to resign, and that the money in her pension account was hers and she was going to withdraw it when she left. I made it very clear that the only way she could return was to return the money to her pension account if she did come back.

She resigned and took her money out on a Friday, then returned on

Monday to get her job back, insisting that I didn't have the right to not rehire her. The director of Human Resources sided with her, but I still declined to take her back. We did a quick and dirty update to her background investigation, and disqualified her on a key requirement for the position she'd held—financial responsibility! She ultimately got back into the county—but not with the marshal's department.

"Up Skirt" Investigation and Indignation—Kinda

As the county marshal, I was a member of the San Bernardino County Police Chiefs Association. In addition to all the police chiefs, the sheriff, marshal and district attorney were also members. At one of our monthly meetings, one of the police chiefs reported on the arrest of a pervert who had been taking surreptitious photos up the skirts of women at the large shopping mall in his city. This wacko would crawl under the dress racks to take pictures, attach a video camera to the bottom of his cane and take pictures, and ride up the escalator behind women in skirts and take pictures. In reporting on the investigation and subsequent arrest, this chief passed around various photos that had been taken into custody and were to be used in the prosecution of this sicko. All of us present were able to agree on two issues—our disgust at this guy's behavior, and our need to closely review the evidentiary photographs!

Fraternization—the Male Captain and the Female Deputy

The issue of workplace fraternization involving a romantic relationship between a superior and a subordinate, has always been particularly sensitive for me. On one hand, it can be very disruptive to the workplace and is usually based more on lust than deep and genuine affection. On the other hand, it can be deep and genuine, and not something I care to curtail if the relationship is meant to be.

I was put to the test on this issue when I learned that Captain Jim Williams was romantically involved with Deputy Blanca Castillo. Naturally, Blanca had to be in Jim's Valley command, as opposed to the desert region commanded by a different captain. I liked and respected both Jim and Blanca, felt there was genuine love and affection there, and that the relationship might well have the potential to be a lasting one. Against all conventional wisdom, as I should have transferred one of them or insisted the relationship end, I left them both in place. But I issued a written direction to the parties and supervisors involved that any and all actions involving Deputy Castillo be handled by the desert captain. I kept a close eye on the issue, as it could have caused difficulties in a number of ways, but no problems emerged.

Later, subsequent to the merger, Jim became the commander of the sheriff's Morongo Station and Blanca remained in Court Services at the Central Courthouse. Both are now retired, and in the second decade of being together. The thought of interfering with a relationship that was meant to be is a scary one, and obviously not something I was or am inclined to do.

Declined to Hire LAPD Officer
Whose Eye Had Been Shot Out

Several months after I became the marshal, I was contacted by a great guy and good friend, then-LAPD Captain Mike Hillman. Mike asked if I would consider hiring as a deputy marshal, a Los Angeles probationary police officer who had lost an eye in a gun battle. He was a fine young officer, and the department would liked to have kept him in a light duty status. But it was precluded because of his probationary status, and he was in the process of being medically retired.

I was very sympathetic to the situation, and felt he probably would do fine as a bailiff. But I chose not to hire him, because I didn't want to place my hiring standards in jeopardy. Moreover, I felt that I was a steward of the marshal's department, had been hired to do what was best for the county, and to take no actions based on personal beliefs. I could have hired him, but it would not have been the right thing to do.

Chief Patrick McKinley, another good friend and fellow LAPD retiree, ultimately hired the young man as a Fullerton police officer. My understanding is that he has done a fine job. Without passing judgment on what occurred, in late 2011 he and another officer were relieved of duty and filed on criminally for the death of a homeless man they had taken into custody. The resulting scandal has been very painful to that city, including the recall of three councilmen including Pat McKinley, who was elected to the council after his retirement as police chief.

Pat did not deserve that.

Humiliation of a Captain in an Oakland Elevator

The devil made me do this! While attending a marshals' conference in Oakland with members of my executive staff, I entered an elevator to descend for breakfast. Already in the elevator were an older couple and one of my captains, Richard Diggs. Richard is the consummate quiet and dignified professional.

532

After the door closed, I put my hand on Richard's shoulder and said something to the effect that he should hang in there and he would get though it. I saw panic in his eyes, and knew he was fearful of what I would say next, as he knew I was a prankster. By then I'd pushed the button for a lower floor that would take me off the elevator short of the lobby. When I exited and as the elevator door was closing, I said something to the effect that anyone could have mistaken the kid for eighteen years old, but the situation wouldn't be so bad if the kid had been female!

If Richard was a violent man, he'd probably have beaten me to a pulp when I joined him for breakfast. He said the woman moved away from him after I exited the elevator. But he told the couple that they'd have to know me understand why I seized the opportunity to poke some fun at him.

Trucker Pulled from Burning Vehicle

I don't believe I'm the type of person who frequently seeks recognition. The fact that I've declined three retirement recognition dinners is evidence of this statement. Having said that, I guess I wouldn't mind being recognized for doing something really good or heroic.

One afternoon I was driving in my marshal's unit accompanied by a member of my executive staff, when we came across a jackknifed big rig on the San Bernardino Freeway in the Ontario area. The engine in the tractor appeared to be on fire, and smoke was pouring out of the engine compartment. The driver was prostrate and slumped over the steering wheel.

I immediately ran to the tractor, climbed up into the cab, and wrestled the driver out of the seat. He regained some degree of consciousness, but remained in some type of stupor. After getting him out of the seat, I literally had to put him on my shoulders to extricate him from the cab and onto the ground, then pull him away from the burning rig. About the time I got him to the side of the road, the fire department arrived and dealt with the engine fire, and the CHP arrived on scene. Several citizens came up and complimented me for my actions.

After giving a statement to the CHP officer, my colleague and I resumed our trip. I felt a little puzzled that my subordinate, a key member of my staff and someone with whom I had a good relationship, appeared to feel awkward with the situation and didn't even discuss what occurred, or my actions. In hindsight, he should have helped me get the driver out of the cab. But I didn't even hint at his non-involvement. Perhaps he felt guilty? His actions in this matter have always puzzled me. While there is no way I would ever suggest that my actions merited recognition, he was well aware of our awards and decorations program, and quite frankly I would have appreciated him initiating formal recognition of what I did that day. The marshal's department had both a medal for valor and for lifesaving, and routinely made awards to our deputies. I guess neither occurred to my colleague.

PROMOTIONS BECOME SURPRISES AND FAMILY AFFAIRS

Promotions are a big thing, and I was determined to ensure that our ceremonies were memorable, enjoyable and unique for employees and their families. As openings occurred, I always gave eligible employees the opportunity to come to my office for the purpose of providing any new or applicable information that I may not already have been aware of. I tried very hard to ensure that my selections represented the most worthy and deserving individuals.

When I determined who I was going to promote, either I or another member of the executive staff contacted the employee's spouse and encouraged the family to participate in making it a fun and surprise event. We suggested that the spouse keep their kids out of school, and come to a meeting location the following morning with a new uniform shirt reflecting the new rank. We would surprise the employee by having him or her respond to a call at a location where his family and the department's leadership were waiting. I always had the kids hold the new badge while I administered the oath for the new rank, and then had the spouse pin the new badge on the employee's shirt.

I also immediately went to a phone and personally notified the other candidates that they hadn't been selected for this particular promotion, and thanked them for applying. I wanted them to hear from me that the promotion went to another person, and not through the grapevine.

HIRING THE SHERIFF'S DAUGHTER—A "TWOFER!"

As marshal, one of my best friends and supporters was Sheriff Gary Penrod, and to this day we remain close in our retirements. One day he called and asked if I would hire his daughter, Sandy Picotta, laterally from the sheriff's department, as a deputy. At the time, she was assigned to the West Valley Detention Center, but seeking a position that could offer a more stable home environment. I was happy to bring her across to my department, and within a week or so Gary and his ex-wife attended Sandy's swearing-in seminar.

The very next day Gary called me apologetically, and announced that they'd just learned that Sandy was pregnant! What a blow—the gal that I'd just hired would have to be in a modified light-duty position for the next year! I honestly believe they hadn't established that Sandy was pregnant until after I swore her in. But it was a big disappointment, because my manpower situation was precarious at the time. Sandy and her husband, both now retired deputies, are great people and we remain good friends.

Humiliation and Death for Deputy Chuck Montez

Chuck Montez (pseudonym) was a "steady Eddie" type of deputy, who was reasonably dependable and well-liked, and respected by his fellow deputies, judges, and court staff. He was on his second career, having previously retired from the Air Force.

But Chuck had a recurring problem with alcohol, and ended up with a second arrest for driving under the influence. While a second DUI was certainly grounds for termination, my goal was to get him cleaned up and back to work, and it included some discipline short of firing. The poor fellow was so humiliated and deeply ashamed of himself that he decided to resign from the department, anyway. I personally went to his home in San Bernardino on a weekend, and talked to him at length, trying to convince him to not resign and to get into a rehabilitation program. But in the end I felt frustrated because I just couldn't get through to him and beyond his shame. Despite my efforts, Chuck resigned.

Within a month he was in the hospital with jaundice, and had a skin color that was as yellow as a school bus. I was among the many employees who visited him in the hospital, where his embarrassment and shame continued to be obvious. A week or two later he was dead, and I stood among the many mourners at his funeral in Colton. I had tried so hard to get him back to work, and still consider Chuck to be among my failures.

Security Intern Program

During my tenure as marshal, we applied for and received a considerable amount of money to implement a weapons-screening program in the various courts throughout San Bernardino County. I saw this as a great opportunity to create a program for young men and women who aspired to careers in law enforcement.

Accordingly, I developed a security intern program, where all weapons screening positions were part-time during the morning and afternoon hours. We recruited and hired fine young men and women who were full-time college students, and gave them the opportunity to work one of the two shifts so they could continue their full-time studies. They were trained in weapons interdiction and searching procedures, and were issued uniforms and marshal's security badges. Managing the program was a bit of the pain because of all of the kids' conflicting schedules However, I felt the inconvenience was worth the effort because of the extraordinary pipeline we developed to identify individuals who appeared to have the greatest potential to serve as law enforcement officers, and to steer them in that direction.

During my time as marshal, I resisted a number of suggestions and efforts to turn the security interdiction program over to one of the prominent local private security companies, because of my enthusiasm for the security intern program. Unfortunately, when the marshal's department merged with the sheriff's department, one of the first things that Undersheriff Bob Peppler did was dismantle the security intern program and put the bid out to private security companies. Various private companies have performed the court weapons screening function ever since.

I remain enthusiastic about that security intern program, and can point to a number of fine peace officers in San Bernardino County today who got their law enforcement start as marshal's security interns.

THE "INFAMOUS" PRAYER

While attending a dinner banquet of the Footprinter's Association in Victorville, the master of ceremonies called on me to say a prayer before the meal. His request was completely unexpected, and I was really caught in one of those rare moments when I didn't know what to say. I made an effort and said a few things, but was no match for Billy Graham and must have sounded pretty dysfunctional.

Shortly after my lousy performance, a really good guy and nice friend, Judge John Martin, leaned over and whispered in my ear, "Didn't sound like you've done this very often!" He was right, and I was stuck between my laughter and my humiliation!

Subsequent to that dysfunctional performance, I organized my thoughts into an easily modified prayer format—adaptable to just about any set of circumstances—and have used it with success on several occasions since that humiliating evening in Victorville.

Chapter Fifteen
SAN BERNARDINO COUNTY SHERIFF'S DEPARTMENT

San Bernardino was among the last counties in California to maintain a separate marshal's department for court-related law enforcement. Because of a state-mandated shift in trial court funding, where monies that had previously gone to the counties for court functions would now be going to the state, and because all employee contracts and benefits were county-specific and the state was not required to honor them, marshals throughout the state sought to be absorbed into their respective county sheriff's departments. In October 1999, the San Bernardino County Marshal's Department ceased to exist, and all of its personnel and resources were taken over by the San Bernardino County Sheriff's Department.

MERGER—MARSHAL'S DEPARTMENT BECOMES THE COURT SERVICES BUREAU

Most of what had been the marshal's department became the Sheriff's Court Services Bureau. The merger also resulted in the elimination of a great deal of duplication of effort, as there were entities within the marshal's department such as communications, training and fiscal, that already existed and were much larger within the sheriff's department. With few exceptions, the former marshal's employees adopted the same titles within the sheriff's department (i.e., our dispatchers became dispatchers in the Sheriff's Dispatch Center, etc.) At the time of the merger I went from being the marshal of San Bernardino County to the seventh deputy chief on the San Bernardino County Sheriff's Department. My new title was the commanding officer of the Court Services Bureau. Although I didn't know it at the time, I was not to remain in that bureau for very long.

While I did not share my true thoughts with many people, I was absolutely ecstatic at the thought of becoming a deputy chief on the San Bernardino County Sheriff's Department. However, I was in somewhat of a difficult position both philosophically and outwardly. When I was hired as the marshal there was absolutely no inclination among the judges of San Bernardino County to ever have their court law enforcement function merge with or be handled by the sheriff's department. Although my secret desire was for the merger to occur, it would have been an abdication of my responsibility to outwardly lobby for it. In candid conversations with Sheriff Gary Penrod, we were both enthusiastic and looked forward to the merger at some point, but also realized that the time and climate would have to be right. Most of my personnel were happy with the marshal's department, and not necessarily in favor of the merger with the sheriff's department. In fact, a great many of them were previously with the sheriff's department and had lateralled to the marshal's department.

The time and climate became right in 1999, for two reasons. First, a merger became financially advantageous for the county when the responsibility for trial court funding shifted from the county level to the state level, and fewer funds became available to the courts. Thus, great economies were to be realized by merging duplicate functions. Secondly, in the three years I was the head of the marshal's department, that organization went from a third-class to a first-class organization, and one that the Sheriff very much wanted to absorb. It was also signicant that Sheriff Penrod was much better thought of by the bench than his predecessor. For me personally, while I enjoyed being the head of a department, I was anxious to once again be part of an organization that performed the full range of law enforcement functions. As good as the marshal's department was, the law enforcement tasks that we performed were fairly limited.

Internal Intrigue and Politics—Ignorance is Bliss

I just love the sheriff's department, and one of the reasons is that I'd never been involved in some truly nasty disputes and relationships that were part of that department's history. Like most agencies (probably all!), there were some people who really disliked others in the agency, which is not uncommon for sheriff's departments where loyalty was often tied to previous sheriffs. In my case, I pretty much liked and enjoyed working, at least initially, with everyone. As time went on, and over a period of the seven or so years I was there, there were a few folks (actually, very few) who I did not particularly care for. But that was to be expected with as many people as I interacted with. Even the folks who clearly did not like the idea of an outsider coming in at such a high rank treated me pretty well; the dislike for my appointment paled in comparison to their hatred for certain colleagues over old wounds.

Deputy Terminated for Computer Fatigue

To this day I continue to be troubled by my department's inability to solve this tragic situation. One of the bailiffs, Ken Tremby (pseudonym) was absolutely addicted to computers. He was an okay deputy and did a reasonably good job—until his computer addiction went into high gear. The situation got so bad that he would stay up on his computer until the wee small hours of the morning, then be late for work because he was fatigued and couldn't wake up. After several occasions when supervisors actually went to his house and got him out of bed, we turned to the disciplinary arena to try to get him squared away. After the many non-disciplinary visits to get him up, he received, in sequence, a reprimand, then a suspension, and ultimately was terminated. We did not want to fire him (and we tried hard not to) but we simply ran out of alternatives in dealing with his continuously troublesome behavior.

Sex With Spaniels?—What Do You Tell the Dad?

During my almost ten years with the county, I was involved with literally hundreds of employment applications. A number of these involved the sons and daughters of other cops, both the San Bernardino County Sheriff's Department and outside agencies, and there were times when the offspring turned out to be unqualified. Because of both propriety and the law, there was clear recognition and acceptance, often sad and painful, that just having a loved one on the department did not mean that the son or daughter would be hired. Not surprisingly, cop-parents would track the hiring process and often seek to intervene if problems arose, which became even more difficult because we could and would not reveal confidential information from either the background investigation or psychological evaluation.

One situation stands out in my mind because of its pain and uniquely sensitive circumstances. The son of a law enforcement official from another agency outside the county, who was long seen as a "shoe-in" to be a cop, failed the psych because of a strongly admitted fetish and fantasy for sex with cocker spaniel dogs! The dad was heart-broken at the rejection and obviously wanted to know the nature of the problem. I do not know what the father was told, but am glad I wasn't the person who had to deliver the news!

"Keep That Rock in Your Pocket"

Shortly after the marshal's department merged with the Sheriff's department there was a protracted labor dispute. During this dispute, the union, known as the San Bernardino County Safety Employees Association (SEBA), encouraged all sheriff's deputies to engage in a "professionalism campaign." This was actually a work slowdown, conducted under the auspices of being extremely careful to do everything right, cross every "t" and dot every "i", to allegedly ensure that everything was done with perfection. What this amounted to with respect to the courthouse, was taking three and four hours to move prisoners from the lockup to the courtrooms, a move that brought the court to its knees in terms of paralysis. The judges, understandably, were livid. I was loyal to the bench and shared their consternation. I was right on the verge of sending out an e-mail to all my deputies in the court services bureau (we had just become sheriff's employees), critical of the slowdown and encouraging them to work at their regular pace, as opposed to the guidance they were receiving from the union.

One of my captains, Richard Diggs, was aware of what I was about to do and gave me some of the best advice I ever received: he encouraged me to "keep that rock in your pocket!" I was influenced by Richard, took his advice, didn't send that e-mail, and am so glad I didn't. No other member of the sheriff's command staff took any action whatever; had I done so I might have been forever branded as an opponent of the union. As it turned out, the union became very supportive of me, and that support continues to this day in terms of their contributions to Devil Pups and other causes in which I'm involved.

It was of tremendous significance to me when SEBA reached out at the time Sheriff Penrod stepped down, and before they determined who to endorse, about whether I would be a candidate for sheriff. While it sounds terribly self-serving to say, it is important to be 100 percent honest in these memoirs. I was a popular chief with the men and women of the sheriff's department, and had tremendous support among the rank-and-file, including a number of people—several of whom were active on the SEBA board—who wanted me to throw my hat in the ring. Instead, I chose to support Rod Hoops, who was the incumbent anointed by

Gary Penrod to serve out the remaining two years of his term. There is no doubt in my mind—absolutely none—that had I indicated a desire to become sheriff, there is a reasonable chance I would have received the endorsement of SEBA instead of Rod Hoops, or at the very least triggered some real conflict on the SEBA board over whom to endorse. Let there be no doubt: I cannot think of anything I'd rather do than become the sheriff of that wonderful department. But I declined to seek the position because Rod Hoops is a good friend and I don't screw my friends!

OPERATIONS—REGION I
"WHAT WOULD YOU THINK ABOUT TAKING OVER REGION ONE?"

When the two departments merged, I become deputy chief over the Court Services Bureau. It consisted of what was left of the marshal's department, mostly just the bailiffs, custody officers, and security interns. I truly thought my fate with the SBSD was to remain in court services.

I never even bothered to raise another possibility with the sheriff or his key people, because I couldn't fathom that someone like I, though fairly well liked but still an outsider who had lateraled into the sheriff's department, would be considered for another key position.

Until strongly encouraged to move into my office at sheriff's headquarters, I maintained my old office at the now-court services bureau and spent most of my time there. Then, about two months after the merger a great guy and strong supporter, Assistant Sheriff Ron Bieberdorf, came into my office and asked what I thought about transferring into Operations and taking over Region I! You could have knocked me over with a feather. I told Ron I would kill for that assignment, and was flattered at even the consideration.

Region I at that time consisted of the sheriff's stations in Chino Hills, Rancho Cucamonga, Fontana, Central, Highland, Yucaipa, and Twin Peaks (Arrowhead, Crestline, etc); Big Bear was added later. Ron said he would get back with me. Unknown to me, Sheriff Penrod, a longtime friend and supporter, had called all his captains in Region I to a meeting in his office, to see what they thought of working for me. Later, I was told they all had positive remarks, based on my track record in the county. A couple of days later it happened, and I took over half of the full-service sheriff's stations for the largest county in the United States. I cannot begin to describe my happiness at this assignment, and my appreciation to Sheriff Penrod.

Without detracting from how happy and flattered I was, I strongly suspect there was another consideration as well. As marshal, I was very close to and well thought-of by most of the 100-plus county judges. I think that Sheriff Penrod, mostly likely strongly influenced by Undersheriff Bob Peppler, felt it was in the best interests of the sheriff's department to somewhat dilute my influence with the judges. The last thing the sheriff needed was a deputy chief who exerted more influence than he had with the judiciary, and I understood and couldn't argue with that premise (it was never really discussed, but I'm fairly certain it was a factor). No matter—I was enormously loyal to Gary Penrod and remain so to this day.

DEALING WITH HOME INVASION ROBBERS IN YUCAIPA

This caper was great! Not long after my assignment as the bureau commanding officer, Captain Bob Fonzi of Yucaipa came to my office one morning to tell me about an incident the night before. It was clear that Bob wasn't going to give me his assessment until he got an idea of what I thought about what had occurred.

That night there had been a series of home invasion robberies, and the suspects were driving a car they'd hijacked. The suspects were armed and had hit three or four mobile homes occupied by senior citizens. As the sun was coming up, two patrol units and one supervisor staked out on the back roads to try to apprehend the suspects. They were fortunate in going code 5 (stakeout) on the road the suspects were using to leave the city. One of the units stopped the suspects' car, and when the second unit and the supervisor arrived, the four suspects were ordered to exit the vehicle. But they ignored the officers' orders and remained seated in the car.

The supervisor, Corporal Dan McCarty, was not about to sit there and haggle with the suspects. So he picked up a very large rock and threw it through the back window of the suspects' car. They all immediately got out with their hands up! I thought this was absolutely great, and my glee was quickly perceived and replicated by Captain Fonzi.

Had this set of circumstances occurred in Los Angeles, and the suspects refused to exit their vehicle, it would've been a long and protracted situation with road closures, psychologists, helicopters overhead, hostage negotiators, a robot with a cell phone approaching the car, and God knows what else. I was pleased with the unique tactics and creativity exhibited by my personnel. For the next several weeks, as the opportunities presented themselves, I told all my friends in Los Angeles about this situation and how it was handled.

One night during a vehicular pursuit, one of the sergeants from Central Station tried unsuccessfully to apply the pit maneuver to stop a fleeing vehicle. The sergeant's vehicle missed the suspect's car, but caught a thick steel support cable for a large utility pole. The unit went about fifteen feet up the cable, then tumbled backward and landed on its roof! Fortunately, the only injury was to the sergeant's ego. He sheepishly told me what had occurred and indicated a willingness to take whatever disciplinary lumps he had coming. Actually, I thought it was kind of funny. There was no way he could have anticipated that cable being there. I decided it was just one of those things that occasionally occurs when you're out there trying to do a good job. I told him not to worry about it, as I didn't see it as a disciplinary issue.

Former Partners' Kids and Grandkids Work for Me!

Throughout my tenure in San Bernardino County with both the marshal's and the sheriff's departments, I continually ran across deputies who were the kids or grandkids of my old acquaintances and partners from previous lives. These included the son of retired LAPD Officer David Ziegler; the son-in-law of LASD Lieutenant Dennis Beane and his wife, Mary (with whom I'd gone to grammar school); Cindy Beaver, whose family lived across the street from us in Duarte; the grandson of Retired LAPD Officer and former partner Jerry Petevich; the son-in-law of another Duarte High alumni; the brother-in-law of deceased LAPD Officer Eddie Clark; the son of Retired LAPD Sergeant Richard Beardsley, etc., etc. I never ceased to enjoy these connections from my previous lives.

Nevada "Executive One" Inbound

Among my additional new responsibilities was serving as coordinator of the Rural Crime Task Force. In that capacity I was responsible for the planning and conduct of temporary operations to identify stolen livestock, fertilizer, and ranch and farm equipment. All sheriff's personnel had other assignments, but would temporarily come together for a day or so every two or three months for one of our task force operations. Two of my key people were then-Sergeant Errol Bechtel and then-Corporal Dan McCarty (who I later influenced, and kicked in the ass, to take the sergeant's exam that got him promoted).

About a half-dozen of us would take positions on a hillside overlooking Interstate 15, close to the Nevada border. It was a good operation. Our duties primarily consisted of watching the livestock trucks go past, then stopping and inspecting those carrying livestock to ensure they carried adequate documentation. In addition, I successfully used my influence with my former LAPD colleagues to obtain free rooms and free chow for my troops at a casino in Stateline, Nevada.

McCarty was pulling my chain, saying the sheriff's secretary, Lee Guerra, was calling and checking up on me for the sheriff. I knew it wasn't true.

So I decided to have some fun at McCarty's expense. He'd been telling everyone how helicopters would be coordinated, if a landing spot was necessary, in the event the Sheriff decided to come out and observe our operation. Again, I knew it wasn't the case. I called desert dispatch and asked them to contact McCarty on the radio and advise him that "Executive One,"—allegedly the governor of Nevada—was coming to our location with a twenty-minute ETA (estimated time of arrival). (Not true, of course.) McCarty went into a high-speed wobble and in a great panic had a bunch of truckers move their trucks to create a landing zone for the VIP he thought was enroute.

I let everyone else in on the joke, and it was all the rest of us could do to keep straight faces as McCarty ran around creating his landing zone! Finally, we told McCarty it was a joke. I have to say, he took it pretty well. By that time McCarty and Bechtel and I had become good friends and truly enjoyed one another's company—and screwing with each other, as well. The fact that I held a higher rank than them was interesting. They deferred to my rank when necessary, but our friendship seemed to be more important. To this day, most of the fine men from that task force remain good friends.

Director of the United States Marshal's Service?

Several months into the first term of President George W. Bush, a dear friend named Michael Ramon approached me. Mike was the former U.S. marshal for the Southern District of California, and also the former assistant director of the United States Marshal's Service. At the time, he was serving as a marshal's inspector in the Washington and Oregon regions.

Mike explained that the marshal's management association was seeking a person with extraordinary leadership skills and credibility, to support for appointment to the position of director of the entire U.S. Marshal's Service. It was a presidential appointment, which would re-

544

quire senate confirmation. He felt I was that person. I was honored and flattered beyond description.

It started a process that got pretty involved, with me ultimately gaining the support of the association, a number of federal judges I paid a visit to as part of the process, and several very key Republicans including Representative Jerry Lewis of San Bernardino County. My understanding was that the President wanted a Hispanic for the position, but the several who'd been nominated and started the process had ultimately fallen out because of problems with confirmation. At the time, according to what I was told, a former Texas police chief then in the pipeline was also about to fall out, again because of confirmation difficulties.

Everything (that I was aware of) was looking good for me to enter the formal pipeline for confirmation—when two hijacked airliners slammed into New York's World Trade Center towers on September 11, 2001, another hit the Pentagon in Washington, DC, and still another fatally crashed in a Pennsylvania field when the hijackers were overpowered by brave passengers.

Everything suddenly changed, including the relationship between the Senate and the White House. With all that was occurring being of gigantic severity, the White House correctly assumed that the Senate wasn't going to argue over some of the less-than-critical appointments. Thus, the former Texas police chief (who reportedly was about to drop out of the pipeline) was among the many appointments that, for the most part, were "rubber-stamped" by the Senate.

I felt disappointed, but far from devastated. Taking the director's position, had it worked out, would have been the apex of my career. It would not have been as financially lucrative as remaining in San Bernardino and retiring from the sheriff's department (though it would have meant a few more bucks' salary). But it would've required a temporary move to Arlington (Virginia), with no realistic likelihood of additional retirement income. Fate may have intervened to protect me from my selfish professional interests.

DYE PACK FOILS JAYWALKER IN HIGHLAND

A bank robber in Highland met Sergeant Eddie Finneran in a most unusual way. Things didn't go well at all for the crook that day. First, when he robbed the bank, the teller gave him a special packet of bills that contained an exploding dye pack. Second, the dye pack exploded and covered the crook with blue dye as he ran from the bank. Third, when the dye pack exploded the suspect was standing right in front of

Sergeant Finneran's unmarked vehicle. I was nearby and responded to the scene. I can still see the idiot, covered with blue dye, handcuffed and looking real unhappy in the back of Eddie's sheriff's unit.

MANNING CRIME PERIMETERS

I have never got tired of being a cop. However, I realize a couple of things. First, as the years go by, my physical abilities are not what they used to be, and if I get too rambunctious I might get hurt and place other officers in jeopardy. Secondly, the last thing cops want is to have a deputy chief take over a tactical situation.

With these realities in mind, it was very common for me to respond to situations where there was a search, and notify whoever was running the operation that I was available to take up a position on the perimeter. I didn't do this because I was trying to prove a point or impress the troops, but rather because it was a way for me to feel I was still a cop to some degree, and to provide reasonable oversight. As it turned out, I was the only high-ranking officer who did this. It appears the practice contributed to what I believe was a pretty good reputation I had with the troops.

"MY GOD, HE'S GOING TO CRAP ALL OVER YOU!"

One of my all-time favorite toys is the remote-controlled, battery-operated fart machine. My son Zak had just given me the super-duper latest model with fourteen exotic sounds, and a special high-resolution mini-speaker. Of course, I had to take it to work and try it out on the other members of the executive staff, including Sheriff Gary Penrod. After having been victimized, the sheriff clutched the device lovingly and said he would give it back to me in a few days. That night, in the executive conference room where the rodeo committee was meeting, Gary planted the device in the back pocket of one of his good pals, an attorney named Dave. On several occasions, Dave bent over the table with his fart machine-equipped rear end in the air. When former sheriff Floyd Tidwell walked by, Gary hit the button, which sent out a different fart sound every time the old sheriff came close to Dave's rear end. Each time the artificial farts sounded, Floyd reeled back in disgust. Finally he told another person who was walking past to "watch out before Dave craps all over you!" I wish I'd been there.

As I have said elsewhere in these memoirs, I believed then and now that Willie Williams' reign was one of the worst things that ever happened to the Los Angeles Police Department. I cannot think of many people I would rather have as a neighbor, but rather not have as a police chief.

The fault didn't really lie with him, but with the individuals and political processes that put such an unqualified person into such a critical position. While he was chief, a book came out under his name. *Taking Back Our Streets* was about American policing. Having worked under Chief Williams, I cannot began to describe how much contempt I had for anyone and anything suggesting that he knew how to run a police organization, much less be described as a leader in American policing. As a gag, someone had given me a large rubber, realistic-looking pile of crap. From that moment until my retirement, that pile of crap sat atop *Taking Back Our Streets* on the floor in a corner of my office.

Wounded Suspect Knew Where to Fall in Yucaipa

I still chuckle over this situation. Late one night, Sergeant Stan Urban got a call to the Stater Brothers market on Bryant in Yucaipa. A man was brandishing a knife. On arriving, the man made a serious mistake in lunging at Stan. Stan shot the guy, who then fell to the ground and right into the middle of a disabled parking space in the parking lot!

It turns out the guy was just a psycho and might not have actually stabbed the sergeant. But Stan did exactly what any cop would do when someone comes in your direction slashing with a knife. Fortunately, the gunshot wound wasn't very serious; in fact, it may have been the factor that finally resulted in the fellow's institutionalization. That disabled suspect sure knew where to fall!

Chief Bushey and the Big Angry Bird

I often joined my troops on raids and search warrant operations in early mornings, as that's the best time of day to catch suspects at home, most likely asleep and off-guard. I typically would take the rear of the dwelling, thus permitting the young guys to make the entries.

One foggy morning in Fontana was particularly memorable. I was at the back of a very large lot surrounded by a chain-link fence, poised to catch anyone who tried to exit a rear window. Then I heard a noise behind me. It was an angry emu, running in my direction! These big birds are like ostriches on steroids, have feet that look like boulders, and can be really mean. I didn't know what to do. I thought about grabbing it by its long neck, but that didn't seem like a good idea. So I ran like hell!

Finally, I got through a gate and slammed it behind me before the damned thing got to me. All my deputies got a big kick from my predicament, and were surprised their old chief could run so fast.

Since then I, and most San Bernardino County sheriff's deputies who occasionally encounter guard emus (kinda like the pit bulls we frequently encountered during narcotics busts), know to thwart the birds' attacks by waving a long stick at their heads. That day serves as a reminder that it's possible for someone to be scared shitless while laughing hysterically at the same time!

Horny Deputy and the Sex Fiend

One morning a deputy in one of the stations that was under my command responded to a family dispute. On his arrival the deputy learned that the husband had already departed the scene. The wife was a very live-wire and legitimate sexual goddess. She gave the deputy a tour of a house that was full of porno photos, sex statutes, and erotic toys. After the tour, the deputy graciously accepted a blowjob! Toward the end of his shift, the deputy decided to drop by for another dose of oral affection, but instead he was confronted by the hostile husband and a remorseful wife who had told her spouse all about her activities with the deputy.

A board of deputy chiefs terminated the deputy at the administrative hearing. The investigation clearly established that the woman was the aggressor in the matter, but we expect that our deputies should be able to rise above such foolish behavior and not become a part of it. Terminating a person who engages in this type of foolish behavior is certainly the appropriate course of action. But I always feel sorry for the fired deputy's spouse—and wonder what he told his wife about why he lost his job?

The Perfect Shooting on Alabama—Avoided

Late one afternoon, while in uniform and driving my sheriff's Tahoe, I was proceeding southbound on Alabama Avenue in a rural area just east of the old Norton Air Force Base. Suddenly, I observed a man with a knife chasing a woman. I immediately requested code 3 backup (red lights and siren), then drove between the knife-wielding suspect and the screaming woman. I exited the vehicle with my weapon drawn and ordered the suspect to drop the knife. But he refused to comply, and started walking toward me in a menacing manner. I thought I was going to have to shoot him. Everything would be on tape, as I was going to keep the mike open on my portable radio. It would be a classic "good" shooting.

But within a few seconds I also realized that I could easily avoid the shooting, at least temporarily, by just getting back in my vehicle and locking the doors, which is what I did. The suspect yelled at me and shook the knife at my closed window, but was soon taken into custody by a couple of deputies who arrived shortly thereafter.

Not surprisingly, both the suspect and the almost-victim were a couple of drunken low-lifes, and the woman almost immediately began begging us to cut her knife-wielding boyfriend loose. He went to jail, but since I never heard anything more, I suspect the matter was handled at the lowest level. I am not reluctant to use deadly force, but don't want to do so unless it is absolutely necessary. Had I shot the guy, it would have been justified and "in policy," but it wouldn't have been necessary. I'm sure glad I didn't!

Lone Voice on Rounds into Radiators

High-speed pursuits often occurred in San Bernardino County. Our deputies were aggressive, but also reasonable about bringing them to a safe and quick halt. When other agencies chased a suspect into sheriff's territory, it was somewhat accepted that the pursuit wouldn't last much longer. Our deputies were proficient in the pit maneuver, and used that technique frequently. Shortly after the merger, our aviation folks actually terminated a high-speed pursuit in the desert with gunfire from an automatic weapon carried in the helicopter. That was probably pushing the envelope a bit, but it worked out okay in that instance. I advocated developing a program where marksmen could be trained, under strict conditions, to place a round in the radiator of a fleeing vehicle, but found myself as the lone wolf on that issue. I remain in support of such a program, where a trained deputy could put a well-aimed bullet into a vehicle's radiator, most likely from the top of a freeway overpass. Oh well, seemed like a good idea (I still like it!)

Broken Bodies and Bouncing Cans at Onyx Peak

As the deputy chief over Region I, Big Bear was among the eight sheriff's stations I was responsible for. Because I owned a home in Big Bear, I spent a considerable amount of time in that part of the county.

One afternoon, with my nephew Richie as a ride-along, I stopped at our mountain home and picked up several hundred aluminum cans from the garage, with the intent of dropping them off at our house down the hill.

We were returning to headquarters via Highway 38 over Onyx Summit, and had just about reached the top of the hill when we came upon a serious rollover traffic accident. The victims, an elderly couple, were lying in the roadway. I immediately activated my emergency lights, radioed for medical aid, and positioned my county unit just below the scene to keep the couple from being struck by oncoming vehicles.

Then I opened the rear hatch of the county vehicle (a Chevy Tahoe) to get some road flares—but had forgotten all about all the cans crammed in there. You guessed it—hundreds of aluminum cans fell out the back and began rolling downhill in all directions! I was pissed—and amused—at the same time, and immediately put Richie to work chasing down all those damned cans while I attended to the victims and the situation. Thank goodness that both of the victims survived—and that Richie was riding with me that day!

Coffee and Rolls on a Rainy Night

One very dark and rainy Saturday night there was a massive search underway in the city of Fontana. The sheriff's department dedicated a considerable number of deputies to assist the officers from the Fontana and other police departments. I responded to see if I could be of assistance. Realistically, though, my rank would cause me to be more of a hindrance than assistance, especially in light of the fact that the command post was being run by command-level personnel from the Fontana Police Department. Some of these folks, including the chief, Frank Scaldone, were friends; nevertheless, the presence of a high-ranking sheriff's official wasn't needed. I finally thought of something I could do that would be well received—provide hot beverages and snacks to the officers on the perimeter. I went to the local convenience store and got about 40 cups of coffee and 40 Danish rolls, and delivered them to the officers participating in the containment. The hot coffee and rolls were well received by all those fine young officers (and a few old ones) who were out there standing in the rain. I liked doing things like this.

Commitment to Leadership Training

Other than the mandated POST training required for each rank, I wasn't aware of any continuing professional management or leadership education that recently had taken place within the sheriff's department.

Several years before while I was still with the LAPD, I had two SBSD lieutenants in my class (both were captains when we merged with the sheriff's department), and the undersheriff had also attended a number of years prior. The department had stopped sending people to the FBI National Academy, and the last person to go, although a great guy, was close to retirement and certainly wasn't the best investment for the department.

Iinitially, I worked hard and successfully to get the door kicked open again for the FBI National Academy, and got back a couple of dedicated spots per year that had been reallocated when the department stopped sending people. I also got the department to start sending folks to the LAPD West Point Leadership Program, and pushed several of my people into the POST Command College (Bob Fonzi, Sheri Stuart, and Paul Capitelli). I also created an organization, "The Inland Empire Chapter of the Command College Alumni Association," and put on several seminars at Glen Helen on leadership issues (Sheriff Penrod provided the lunch, which was really great). Toward the end of my tenure Undersheriff Bob Peppler decided the department could no longer afford to lose the manpower, and pulled the plug on most of this stuff. Included was cancelling Ron Perret's scheduled participation (all expenses paid by the FBI) in a two-week LEEDS (Law Enforcement Executive Development Seminar) session at Quantico.

Bob Peppler was a damn good guy, and I believe was the consummate undersheriff. He effectively ran the department, I believe he usually made wise decisions, and was appropriately frugal over fiscal issues. However, I remain puzzled as to why he, himself a Command College and National Executive Institute participant (one step up and related to LEEDS), put the brakes on such great, all-expense-paid training. SBSD is a great department, but the need for leadership training at the management and executive levels is very much evident.

"That Asshole Will Come Out of That Tree!"

One afternoon I got a call from John Hernandez, the captain of the Twin Peaks station (it covers Lake Arrowhead, Crestline, Running Springs, etc.) John informed me that one of his deputies had got into a foot pursuit with a possible burglary suspect, and the suspect had climbed to the top of a tall oak tree and refused to come down. This occurred shortly after a month-long media event took place north of Los Angeles, when a tree hugger climbed to the top of a tree and refused to come down, garnering days and days of press attention and celebrity supporters.

I wasn't about to let another spectacle like that develop, but feared it might well happen if we didn't get that shithead out of the tree before the media got wind of what was going on. John and I considered several options, many of which were not as practical as they initially seemed. When I called the fire chief and asked him to have apparatus respond with one of the large nets used to catch people who jump from burning buildings, I learned they hadn't been used for years!

We finally made a capture net out of canvas from the back of my unit, then sent a young deputy up as high as we could on a fire ladder, with directions to get that guy out of the tree. The plan worked just fine—the deputy grabbed a foot and pulled until the bozo broke loose and bounced from tree limb to tree limb, right into our impromptu capture net. I was determined that our suspect wouldn't remain in that tree, and wasn't going to leave until he was on the ground and in custody.

Working on the Colorado River

I really enjoyed working enforcement on the Colorado River out of our Needles Station, doing so on a great many of the big weekends during my tenure with the sheriff's department. Although I was in charge of all the desert stations, I did this from time to time when the Region II deputy chief was on vacation, as Needles was not typically under my command. A lot of flexibility existed within the department, and if I wanted to work the river, my name was added to the roster and I was assigned to a vessel.

I particularly enjoyed working the Personal Water Crafts (PWC), commonly known as "SeaDoos," and even completed a class for operators. Even though I was then getting long in the tooth, there was just something that really lit my fires about zipping around on a PWC equipped with red lights and a siren! While not officially in charge, my exalted rank of deputy chief meant that I was the senior person and, as such, responsible if something went badly sideways, which fortunately never occurred. I typically worked with young deputies and thoroughly enjoyed the experience. Although it wasn't by design, apparently I gained a considerable degree of credibility because of my uncharacteristic desire to do real police work. I could never believe I was getting paid to have so much fun—including lodging and meals being paid for by the department!

On one occasion, I served as the field commander for a RAVE concert held at an Indian reservation located on the California side of the Colorado River. The event started out bad and just got worse, when both the promoters (out of Los Angeles) and the tribal leadership insisted that the other was responsible for all safety and security measures the sheriff's department was requesting be provided.

In California, although the county sheriff is responsible for the enforcement of criminal laws, local governmental agencies have no power to compel Indian tribes to enact regulatory or safety/security measures. In this instance we received a great deal of lip service, but far less private security, traffic control, and other reasonable measures than we insisted were necessary. The event involved hundreds of people from Los Angeles, San Diego, and beyond, with the typical degrees of foolish behavior and drug abuse.

Six fatalities resulted from the event, including one kid high on drugs who stumbled into the desert and wasn't found for a week, one who died of an overdose, another who fell asleep while driving and crashed on the road to Needles, and yet another who fell asleep and killed an elderly couple when his car veered across the highway. I was saddened that the tribe and the promoters cared more about profits than safety, and disappointed that the tribal leaders failed to recognize that they were being exploited by the promoters from the big city. Obviously, I don't think RAVE concerts are a good thing, just a forum for foolish people to do stupid things.

Bear in the Basement—Unconscious Deputy

One very cold night, a deputy from the Twin Peaks station got a call of a possible burglary in the basement of a cabin in the Crestline area. Upon arrival, the deputy and a backup deputy deployed properly, with one deputy on the outer perimeter while the other carefully entered the basement. Before he entered, the deputy illuminated the basement with the beam from his powerful flashlight, to hopefully blind anyone down there. As he entered the basement door, the suspect decided to leave by exiting by the very same basement door. The suspect was a bear! The deputy was obviously startled and jumped back, struck his head on the doorframe, and was knocked out cold. The bear ran off. The deputy ended up with a big lump on his head and a great story to tell his grandchildren.

Paul Capitelli was one of my truly good investments. During my tenure with the SBSD he promoted to captain and became one of the eight station commanders who reported to me. I both "unleashed" and encouraged Paul in professional ways. As a new captain, he wanted to continue playing an active role in the California Peace Officers Association (CPOA). But for him to advance to the next step would require a time commitment to the organization that some others might oppose.

I told him to go for it, anyway, that I would deal with any opposition that might arise, and it worked out well. I encouraged Paul to participate in a variety of leadership development opportunities, and he did, including attending and graduating at the top of his California POST Command College class. He is now the executive director of the California Commission on Peace Officer Standards & Training (POST). I feel proud to be numbered among those who contributed to his development.

When Paul was fairly new as captain of the Chino Hills Station, he and his charming and fun wife, Cathy, hosted a Christmas party at their beautiful home in Rancho Cucamonga. My wife Cathy and I were invited, and no doubt part of the rationale for the gathering, in addition to having fun and spreading holiday cheer, was to impress me. Paul's Cathy had good reason to be proud of her home. To minimize the trauma to a home that a large number of guests can cause, she made part of the house off-limits to guests, including a particular bathroom. Not realizing that the bathroom was "off-limits," one of the guests went in. In the middle of that guest's actions in dealing with what a bathroom is intended for, an irate Cathy Capitelli pounded on the door and yelled: "Get out of there—NOW."

As the sheepish and apologetic guest emerged, Cathy was horror-stricken: the guest was Paul's boss—me! Luckily, Paul and Cathy recognized that I'm a pretty good sport, and after a nervous moment or two we all broke into laughter. To this day, when Paul and I chat, one of us always brings up that funny evening. I say that I'll visit if I can use that particular bathroom. Paul says I can use it anytime I drop by.

Death of Deputy Mike Tierney

Mike Tierney was a good guy and a fine cop whose demons got the best of him, being one of those few people who, in my opinion, suffered from a work-related substance abuse problem. Several years prior, subsequent to a legal and appropriate arrest operation, he, some fellow officers and the department were sued in federal court for false arrest, false imprisonment, violation of civil rights, etc. In addition to actual damages, the plaintiffs went after the deputies personally for punitive damages. Although the department stood solidly behind the deputies and assured them they would be fine, the thought of losing his house and everything else he owned took a very real and long-term toll on Mike. It led to his heavy drinking and taking meds for anxiety. As Mike started going downhill, so did his career, resulting in a demotion from corporal and reassignment to the jail. I stumbled across Mike and took a liking to him, had him transferred into my bureau and assigned to the Central Station. Unfortunately, the demons wouldn't go away, including some danger signs that we initially didn't recognize.

Laura Tierney called one day in a panic. She told us that her husband was suicidal, and she couldn't reach him. I launched an all-out search. This resulted in a big blow-out with a psychiatrist at a major health center who jacked us around unnecessarily, when all we were trying to do was verify whether or not Tierney had kept his appointment that day. We needed the information in order to make some of our search decisions.

Late in the afternoon we were notified that his best friend, a deputy involved in the search, found Mike dead of a self-inflicted gunshot wound to the head on one of the forestry roads that led out of Fawnskin to the high desert. It was a very sad scene. While I was standing alongside Mike's remains, the idiot psychiatrist called to complain to me that he was spoken to harshly by then-Sergeant Tom Hornsby (who later retired as a captain)! I told him that Mike was dead and, without suggesting that he was responsible, said that his unnecessarily foolish actions hindered our search for Mike. I abruptly terminated the conversation when he tried to rationalize his foolish actions as being professionally necessary.

I spent quite a bit of time after Mike's death, assisting Laura in what turned out to be a successful effort to have Mike's death ruled as "work related." I also spent time with Mike's grieving father, and sent him a pair of corporal's stripes that I believed would have been returned to his son had Mike not taken his own life.

I subsequently made a formal complaint to the hospital where the psychiatrist was employed, and also to the state medical board. After their investigation, the doctor received a "letter of instruction" from the state medical board. He was clearly told that it had been a police investigation involving a potential life-and-death situation. Yet he played silly-ass games with the courts and us over this issue. Unbelievably, at one point during the search and at his insistence, we got a court order from a judge and rushed it to him code 3 (red lights and siren). But he insisted it was on the wrong form, and still refused to simply tell us whether Mike had showed up that day for his appointment!

This was truly a situation where Mike found a permanent solution for a temporary problem. But he was suffering from acute depression, and his temporarily sick brain was telling him that the issues he faced were insurmountable. They absolutely were not. He left behind a wonderful wife and a couple of great kids.

Suspect's Suicide and Sheriff Penrod's Actions

This was unbelievable, and likely everyone who is reading this memoir watched it unfold on television—the gunshot suicide of a suspect who was in custody for shooting a cop!

A deputy out of Central Station was shot by the suspect in the community of Muscoy. After a massive search, he was apprehended by two San Bernardino police officers, then turned over to two sheriff's deputies and transported to Central Station. At the station he was turned over to two sheriff's detectives.

The two San Bernardino police officers hadn't adequately searched the suspect after he'd just shot the sheriff's deputy; even worse, the sheriff's deputies and detectives foolishly assumed that a through search had been conducted and didn't search him again. But he had a loaded .45 automatic pistol stuck way down inside his trousers. During a break in the interview when the detectives stepped out of the interview room, he pulled out the weapon and fatally shot himself in the head. He could easily have killed the two detectives when they returned, but thank goodness he chose not to. The whole episode in the interview room was recorded on the sheriff's video system, and released to the media. I doubt there is a cop anywhere in the free world who hasn't seen that video as part of an officer safety program.

Obviously, Sheriff Penrod and just about everyone else including me, was not happy. People were expecting heads to roll. Sheriff Penrod convened a meeting the following day in the large training room at headquarters, and mandated that everyone who'd had any role in the search and apprehension of the suspect be present. Some pretty nervous people were gathered in that room. The sheriff walked in, looked around, and started asking different people whether or not they had learned anything from what occurred. Obviously, those who he asked replied in the affirmative. Sheriff Penrod then stated the matter was over, and that he didn't want a situation like it to occur again! That was it.

This is a pretty dramatic example of how different departments handle things in different ways. Had this been the Los Angeles Police Department, it would have been bloody. Heads would have rolled, involving not only the involved negligent officers but potentially their supervisors and command staff, as well. I'm not sure I would have handled the matter with the same grace and understanding that Sheriff Penrod did, but the enormous respect that his employees had for their sheriff, and their obvious pain at having let him down, seemed to do the trick.

Holy Cow—It's the Chief!

I really enjoyed working the Colorado River on busy holiday weekends. On one of my many such occasions, I was partnered on a boat with a young deputy. Some type of what appeared to be a violent argument was occurring on a boat about fifty feet away, in a very crowded Copper Canyon. But we couldn't get over to it because numerous boats were in the way.

The young deputy said he'd be right back, took off his gun and handheld radio, dove into the water, and swam to the boat where the disturbance seemed to be taking place. But, as he was my partner, I wasn't going to permit him to go by himself! I divested myself of my weapon and handheld radio-talkie, jumped into the water, and followed him to the other boat.

He was incredulous that a deputy chief did that, and never stopped telling the other deputies about my actions. I didn't dive in to prove a point or to curry favor with the young deputies, but because my rank was secondary to my responsibilites to my partner. I kiddingly answered that I only went because of the big-breasted women in the boat where the disturbance was!

Matchmaking in Copper Canyon—USMC Style

When working boating enforcement on the Colorado River, the sheriff's personnel would typically be on the water earlier than the usual rush of recreational boats. It was usually necessary in Copper Canyon, in preventing recreational boaters from moving the buoys we'd placed to keep the channel clear for the numerous emergency situations that always occurred.

One morning while entering Copper Canyon, I spotted a large pontoon boat full of Marines, and started chatting with those hard-chargers who had just returned from Iraq. Two things were clear: they wanted to meet girls, and they were inexperienced in how to make the proper overtures. I directed (after all, I am a colonel!) six of them into the water, instructing three on each side of my SeaDoo to hold onto the struts. Then I towed the six Marines to another pontoon boat filled with young women, and asked them if the Marines could come aboard. Obviously, it was just fine with the girls. Within about an hour, the two boats were tied side-by-side and a great deal of romance was clearly underway. Given the forty or fifty folks involved, my guess is that some of the flirting may have blossomed into real relationships. I hope so, as they all seemed like nice young men and women. It was the least that I could do for my fellow jarheads!

Zero Tolerance and Deaths on the Colorado River

When I first started working the Colorado River, my impression was that the deputies were overly chickenshit in making arrests for boating under the influence, because it didn't take much for them to arrest a boat operator for it. But it didn't take long for me to realize that these fine young deputies were doing exactly what needed to be done to save lives.

In my many tours of duty on the Colorado River, on a number of occasions I witnessed the horrible aftermath of boating under the influence (BUI). Of all the propeller strikes, boat collisions and other serious injuries and fatalities, I cannot recall even one that did not involve alcohol. The sight of dead teenagers and young adults broke my heart, as just about all of them came from good and loving families. An image burned into my mind is the sight of the mortuary in Needles staying open well into the night to receive the bodies of young BUI victims. I honestly went into a rather depressed state, as I knew some parents were being given the worst news of their lives.

Death Off a Rock and Drunken Friends

Alcohol, impulsive behavior, steep cliffs and water can make for a lethal combination. Unfortunately, stupid people, especially when drunk, are not very good at accepting advice. One late afternoon, while idling on my SBSD PWC (personal watercraft, known as a "SeaDoo") at the base of a prominent rock in Copper Canyon, a loud-mouthed man, obviously under the influence (but not to the point of being so drunk that his arrest was warranted), was climbing up and down and jumping off the high rock cliff into the water. But after his last jump into the water he didn't come up!

His also-under-the-influence friends went crazy, and started screaming at me to go down and get him. Other deputies were there within seconds and all of us tried to find him, but he was apparently on the bottom and not visible from the surface, at least to the deputies who dove into the water. His pals were screaming profanities at us, accusing us of being responsible for his death, but finally backed off just before they would have got hooked up and carted off to our booking barge. The SBSD dive team was on the scene within fifteen minutes, and recovered the body after searching for about a half-hour. You cannot stop stupid people from their own self-destructive behavior.

CHEATING DEATH IN COPPER CANYON

My former wife Barbara and her husband are dear friends of Cathy's and mine, and reside in Lake Havasu. Most of my tours of duty on the Colorado River involved a visit with them, and they were always enjoyable. But they got me good one day, by doing some creative work to a photograph of me on a personal watercraft in Copper Canyon. Using a computer program known as "PhotoShop," they inserted an image of a shark that appeared to be lunging at me. The photo turned out great, and to this day is posted on the wall of the Colorado River Station (Needles).

I was fond of telling people that I had to work hard to "cheat death" in Copper Canyon. But many of them knew my biggest threat was eye strain—because of all the well-endowed women who went topless. Knowing that, they didn't buy into the dangers I described!

A TROUBLESOME LITTLE BUG AND THE MOUNTAIN FIRE TASK FORCE

Around the beginning of 2002, I started to become very worried about the potential for a particularly devastating wildfire in the San Bernardino National Forest. I certainly wasn't alone in my concern, because fire folks were getting concerned, as well, but more than anyone else I was responsible for evacuations should they become necessary.

These concerns were because of the severe impact that a parasite known as the "bark beetle" was having on thirsty trees, and we were well into a drought that resulted from far less rain than was necessary to maintain a healthy forest. Trees were dying at a disturbing rate, which made the forest more susceptible to fires, especially in late fall when the

Santa Ana winds annually arrive.

Based in part on the pain I'd witnessed during the Los Angeles riots, and the foolish actions I'd observed in their management, I decided to take the initiative and establish an early partnership between all of the public and private agencies that would play roles in the event the badly-feared wildfires were to occur. While the fire folks usually work well together, there was still room for an even closer relationship. As with most places, the cops didn't have much of a relationship with the fire folks, and there wasn't much of a relationship between some law enforcement folks either, especially with the CHP. There was no bad blood, and everyone liked each other okay; it was just that they were busy doing their own things and not spending much, if any, time on mutual aid and radio inter-operability.

In response to the need, I created the Mountain Task Force and scheduled regular meetings, always with a lunch involved, first monthly and as the threat continued to grow, every couple of weeks. We discussed every conceivable problem and possibility, and how we were going to cooperatively handle potential scenarios.

Some of the things I orchestrated included, but weren't limited to the following: under certain circumstances, cops would respond to potential "choke points" (i.e., stop signs on roads leading out of the mountains) to keep traffic flowing; authorized deputies would push disabled vehicles off the sides of cliffs if necessary; northbound lanes would be used as southbound lanes for maximum evacuation, in concert with the San Bernardino Police (who control the arteries at the bottom of the hill), and the CHP; authorized deputies would seize tour buses enroute to Las Vegas, take the passengers off, and use the buses for evacuations of the many youth camps up and down Highway 38 above Yucaipa; and (after the folks at Yucaipa station got the keys to the yard) seize and utilize Yucaipa School District buses for necessary evacuations.

The feared wildfires hit the San Bernardino National Forest in all their fury in October of 2003, and we collectively did a GREAT JOB! All of our hard work and coordination really paid off. Nothing happened that we hadn't developed a contingency for.

SAVING GLEN HELEN NORTH

During the devastating San Bernardino County wildfires in October 2003, known as the "Old" and the "Grand Prix" fires, I was at the fire camp located at Glen Helen Park, in the canyon below the Cajon Pass. I was the IC (Incident Commander) as part of the Unified Com-

560

mand, and my partners were the top folks from the U.S. Forest Service, California Department of Forestry and Fire Protection, and the San Bernardino County Fire Department. By choice, I took the twelve-hour night shift (because I got to sleep most of the night!) and my captain from the Fontana Station, Rich Beemer (later Undersheriff after my retirement), had the twelve-hour day shift. My assistant, who stayed in the Command Center after I hit the sack, was a fine young sergeant, Mike Newcomb.

About 2 a.m. one night, Mike woke me up and said the deputy who was patrolling the Glen Helen grounds (jail, driver-training facility, academy and ranges) reported that "Glen Helen North" (a good sized array of buildings we used as classrooms) was in imminent danger of being overrun by the flames, and he couldn't find anyone to respond. This wasn't surprising; at that time of the night, crews were either elsewhere on the fire, or bedded down, and the fire camp looked like a ghost town.

I immediately jumped up and started pulling on tents adjacent to several fire trucks, and roused a bunch of firefighters with my pleas to save our academy! Clearly, they weren't happy to be awakened, but realistically were pretty darn good about it. As was the case with the majority of the fire crews, they were from elsewhere (somewhere in Central California, I believe) and had responded due to mutual aid. They got up, put on their gear, manned their rigs, and followed me (in my emergency-equipped Chevrolet Tahoe) about four miles into the canyon where the northern part of our academy is located. I drove in first. The flames had almost surrounded the facility, and one structure was starting to burn. I pulled aside so the fire apparatus could get in and the firefighters could go to work. They did a great job in putting out the fires, and literally saved the entire complex. Since most of the surrounding area had already burned, the complex was no longer in jeopardy.

In hindsight, I wish I had identified the firefighters involved, to later restate my appreciation. But things were hectic, and it regrettably fell through the cracks. Several weeks later, in a fun and unofficial ceremony at the Glen Helen facility, I was honored with a firefighter's helmet for my actions in "Saving Glen Helen North." I look back on that incident with pride, and the helmet occupies a position of honor in my home office.

BURGERS, FRIES AND COKES FOR THE TROOPS

In addition to the massive "Old" and "Grand Prix" fires, there were a number of other fires that popped up from time to time that fall. In each instance, sheriff's personnel were required for containment and traffic control. I recall one such night. There was a fire in the area of Hesperia close to the top of Cajon Pass, so I drove to the location to see if I could be of assistance. While enroute I decided to stop at the McDonald's fast food restaurant off Highway 138 to get some chow for the troops. I picked up 50 or 60 cheeseburgers, a bunch of fries and of cokes, and took them to the fire perimeter. Boy, was I one popular person! The older citizen volunteers who were assisting our personnel were particularly grateful, as a few of them had medical conditions and they badly needed something to eat. I was happy to have been of assistance.

Honored by the Secretary of Agriculture

The role I played in planning and preparation for the potentially devastating wildfires, and the leadership role I played during those fires, are things of which I'm very proud. Major fires took place in both San Bernardino and San Diego counties at the same time. The San Bernardino County personnel received tons of compliments and accolades, but the San Diego County emergency services personnel were roundly criticized for a lack of preparation and performance. Toward the end of our fires, Secretary of Agriculture Ann Veneman came to our command post and personally presented several of us, including me, with very nice framed certificates commending our performance. Several days later the members of that same group were given similar awards from the President of California State University at San Bernardino.

Eloquent Speech at a Highway Patrol Retirement Ceremony

Richard Magyars is one of my best and oldest pals. He and I go back about forty years, to when I was a new sergeant. He is one of the nicest, funniest, and most generous men I have ever known. He is also one of the most unique (for reasons suitable only for discussion among my male friends, and only then when we've had a few drinks).

For many years before their merger with the California Highway Patrol, Rich was with the California State Police and assigned to dignitary protection. He was not pleased at the merger, went out of his way to not be productive when he became a CHP officer, and was proud of the fact that in the several years he was with the CHP he wrote only one ticket! He was well liked, but it was known that he wasn't among the CHP's most stellar performers.

I was among the guests at his retirement in Westchester. Among the other guests were the cremated remains of another pal (in an urn on display in the center of the Rich's table), who always said that he wanted to attend Rich's retirement! Also among the 150 or so guests was a CHP assistant chief who, although not acquainted with Rich, was sent from headquarters to wish a retiring officer well.

I was asked to speak, so in preparation I made a few notes on a cocktail napkin and then spoke, pretty extemporaneously, for about fifteen minutes. Everything I said (everything!) was in jest, and was the absolute opposite of how Rich really was. My comments were about his strong commitment to traffic enforcement; his commitment to traffic engineering; his high level of traffic enforcement productivity; his strong mentoring of new traffic officers; and other related lies! Just about everyone (with one exception, the assistant chief) chuckled, laughed and rolled their eyes, because they knew I was lying through my teeth. Overall, it was a great retirement and a fun event for a dear friend.

The next day I got a call at my office. It was the assistant chief from the CHP who'd been present a Rich's retirement. He thanked me for being present and representing the San Bernardino County Sheriff's Department, and said how much he enjoyed and appreciated the comments about one of his fine officers (Rich). He went on to say that occasionally he had to make comments at retirements, and requested a copy of my notes for future reference! He was a very nice and decent man and we had a good chat, but it pained me to tell him that most of my comments were false and pretty much came extemporaneously right out of the part of my body where the sun doesn't shine! While he didn't appear to be mad, he wasn't amused either; *confused* would be the way I would describe his reaction.

The Likelihood of Promotion to Assistant Sheriff

With accolades from the wildfires planning, and all my professional achievements prior to then, most would have agreed (a few grudgingly) that I was pretty close to the sharpest tool on the executive staff. From education to experience to credibility to achievements, there really wasn't anyone—although there certainly were other sharp and worthy individuals—who rose to my level of professionalism and achievement. While I never sought or lobbied for promotion to assistant sheriff or undersheriff, I was somewhat hoping it might occur.

But, by that time I had come to realize that the top promotions were always given to Sheriff Penrod's pals and loyal confidants. I never complained about this, or even hinted at any dissatisfaction. Realistically, during my entire tenure, Undersheriff Bob Peppler pretty much ran the day-to-day operations, often bypassing the two assistant sheriffs and dealing directly with the seven deputy chiefs. The two assistant sheriffs did some things, but the longer I was there I came to see those two positions as somewhat symbolic, and largely political rewards for the sheriff's closest pals.

No biggie—I remained grateful for the position I held and the superb way I was treated by just about everyone, including these special pals of the sheriff. On its worst day, the SBSD still beat the hell out of the backstabbing and selective political correctness of the LAPD!

Support Services Bureau

Just before I took time off for the first of two surgeries, Sheriff Penrod called me into his office and asked if I would hate him if he transfered me from Region 1 to the Support Services Bureau. He told me that newly-promoted Deputy Chief Rod Hoops would be an assistant sheriff before long, and it would be best if he could gain experience in Operations.

I told the sheriff, and meant it, that I supported the move. If he was going to fast-track Hoops, then he needed to fast-track his experience, as well. Personally, I was disappointed to leave Operations, but was grateful to have had Region 1 for almost six years. The Support Services Bureau consisted of the following divisions: Technical Services, Scientific Investigation, Communications, and a few other odds and ends. As we chatted, I told him that, since he was restructing a few things, perhaps he might want to give me aviation and the academy as well. He responded that those were viable possibilities. A few days later he added the academy to my command. As it turned out, I never returned to active duty after the two surgeries, and retired without spending much time in Support Services Bureau.

Surgery and Retirement

My initial intent was to return to work shortly after my first surgery and remain at work until my second surgery (both hands: carpal tunnel). But the lack of mobility and the time necessary for recovery were more than I'd anticipated. I had unfortunately waited far too long to address the carpel tunnel condition, and both hands were in bad shape. By the time I finally had surgery, I'd been spending a great deal of time continiously rotating the use of my hands, as I just about always had to be massaging and shaking them. I felt the surgical results were great and somewhat gave me my life back, but I never regained the ability to completely close my right hand.

When the surgeon declared my lack of flexibility to be "permanent and stationary," the department declared it was unable to accommodate my disability because all personnel were required to be able to perform "combative grasping." The SBSD processed and supported my application for disability retirement. I was on disability leave ("out on 4850 leave") for close to a year before the retirement application was approved. That was the end of my career with the San Bernardino County Sheriff's Department.

RETIREMENT FUNCTION

Kari Tessalar, a great gal and the sheriff's key administrative assistant, was really sweating my retirement. The burden of retirement celebrations usually fell to her. All of the people I knew from the various agencies I had served with and worked with, plus all my military contacts, caused her to recognize that in my case the usual big-shot retirement extravaganza could be all-consuming. However, that wasn't my style or desire. I opted to just have a luncheon with my captains and other members of the executive staff at the Mexico Restaurant. No speeches, no gifts, just good conversation. I was given an absolutely beautiful desktop cabinet containing my badge, which I continue to treasure.

CHAPTER SIXTEEN
POST-SBSD
THOUGHTS AND ACTIVITIES

POSTSCRIPT—AFFECTIONALY TOLERATED

As I reflect on my tenure with the SBSD, I think the best description of my acceptance (as an outsider who lateraled in at the rank of deputy chief) can best be described in two separate categories: Genuinely welcomed by most, and ultimately affectionately tolerated by others. Sheriff Penrod set the tone for my acceptance, which was very warm and welcoming, and the years that I spent there were among the most rewarding and enjoyable in my law enforcement career. I strongly believe that most of the department welcomed me with open arms, and saw me as exceptionally capable and worthy of the position. There was a percentage, including some of the assistant sheriffs, deputy chiefs, and captains, who were gracious and friendly, but also somewhat reserved in certain instances. They had worked together over the years, but I hadn't paid my dues and therefore was not part of their inner social circle. No sweat and no big thing—we still all got along well, and I had enough social circles of my own.

In the years since my retirement, several folks who I knew pretty well and have maintained a friendship with, have opined that I was treated poorly, especially by some higher ranking folks and a few others with a lot of seniority. This was not my perception. It was clear that I did things that most other members of the executive staff seldom did, especially by routinely engaging in field activities and being very conspicuous after hours, but I didn't perceive hostility over these actions. There was a great deal of latitude and discretion at my level, and my impression was that my colleagues pretty much took the position that if those actions worked for me, then so be it. I remain grateful, for the most part, for the goodwill that I continue to believe I was accorded.

Thank Goodness for that Sno-Cat!

Although retired, I continue to maintain close ties with my many friends, of all ranks, in the sheriff's department.

In fact, I was particularly grateful for my continuing friendship with the folks from the Big Bear Station during a heavy snowstorm in early 2010. I took my foster boys and their pals up to Big Bear, and foolishly thought I could make it all the way to our mountain house by using the four-wheel drive on my Suburban. In hindsight, I cannot believe I made it as far as I did: to the intersection of Antelope and Mount Verdi Road, just about fifty yards short of our house. The Suburban got stuck big-time. I fell into the deep snow twice when trying to make it to the house, and had to have Matthew pull me up and out of the snow. I finally gave up and called the Big Bear Station for assistance. They sent the giant Sno-Cat and before successfully pulling my car out, drove me to the house where I intended to get sleeping bags out of the garage. In my driveway, I jumped off the Sno-Cat and sunk up to my chest in snow! We spent the night in the Motel 6. I drove down the hill the next morning, and had to listen to Cathy happily tell me that she told me so! Thank goodness for the giant Sno-Cat, and my deputy friends.

Promotion of Errol Bechtel—Marker #1

Errol Bechtel was (and continues to be) a crusty old fart who does a great job. He was a sergeant who (in my judgment) was particularly worthy and deserving of promotion to lieutenant. I learned through the grapevine that his bureau commanding officer hadn't recognized his positive attributes and might not be pushing for his promotion; without that type of support he wasn't going to get promoted. So I went to Sheriff Penrod, shared my strong positive impression of Bechtel, and afterward felt I'd succeeded in strengthening Errol's credibility in the eyes of the right people. Bechtel was promoted to lieutenant not long after my chat with Sheriff Penrod. While there were certainly other factors, I suspect that my involvement didn't do him any harm. Errol is convinced that I'm the reason he got promoted. Since he claims he owes me a steak dinner, I don't think I'll tamper with that impression!

Evidence of Getting Old—Bushey Takes a Dive

Even though retired from the sheriff's department, I remain active in a quasi-reserve capacity. I am enrolled in the Specialized Services Bureau (SSB) as a reserve deputy and also as a civilian volunteer. Of course,

I am also an honorably-retired deputy chief with much POST training and credentials. I am also fortunate that I remain a fairly popular and respected person. This unique status enables me to pretty much work where and when I care to work, although my assignment is in the Administrative Support Unit (ASU) of Volunteer Forces. One of the things I really enjoyed before and after retiring was working either boats or the SeaDoos/Personal Water Craft (PWC) on the Colorado River during busy holiday weekends. But a sad situation occurred on such a weekend in 2008, and pretty much told me that my time as a deputy on personal watercraft had come to an end.

I was in the middle of the channel on the river between the Nevada and California sides, but the SeaDoo and I tipped over when I wasn't able to maintain balance in the wake of a larger boat that passed by rapidly. A couple of young deputies were there immediately to offer both assistance and good-natured ribbing. It didn't take me long to get back up on the PWC, but it really should never have occurred. It hurt me to acknowledge that age factored into a decrease in my balance, and that I wasn't as good at balance and confidence as when younger. It didn't take long to dry off (115-plus degrees!) but my hand-held radio was a total loss, and I immediately disassembled, cleaned and oiled my semi-automatic pistol. I think "Dirty Harry" (Clint Eastwood) said it best in one of his movies: "A man has to know his limitations!" I may work the river again, but my days of being a PWC deputy are a thing of the past.

Preston Leslie Not Permitted to Retire—Marker #2

Lieutenant Preston Leslie is among the finest cops and most decent men I have had the good fortune to associate with. When I became San Bernardino County marshal he was one of my sergeants who I quickly promoted to lieutenant. Preston was very loyal to me, but more importantly was fiercely loyal to both the marshal's department and, after the merger, the sheriff's department. Within the SBSD he was clearly worthy and deserving of promotion to captain, but as a lateral from the marshal's department it realistically wasn't going to occur. He had a couple of assignments with the SBSD after the merger, including several years as the executive officer of the Victor Valley Station, and was held in high regard for the good job he did.

When he transferred into a specialized unit as executive officer, Preston really went sideways with his new captain. I knew the captain and thought well of him. Even after hearing both sides of the story, I still don't know who was right or wrong. Preston felt he had to transfer out of the division, but was told by the executive staff there were no openings anywhere. Thus he was forced to either stay in a bad situation or retire.

He called and told me he had filed his application with the Retirement Board, but I knew his heart was broken. So I went and spoke to Sheriff Penrod and Undersheriff Rich Beemer (a great guy and former subordinate). I encouraged them to not permit Preston to retire under the circumstances, and to find a place for him to be reassigned. Further, I asked the sheriff to call the Retirement Board and have Preston's application pulled. That's exactly what Sheriff Penrod did! He reassigned Preston to the West Valley Detention Center, where he remained and did his usual great job for another couple of years before retiring on a positive note. I remain grateful for the actions of Sheriff Penrod and Undersheriff Beemer, in not permitting a wonderful man to retire under circumstances that would have caused his heart to be broken for the rest of his life.

A Flattering Call From SEBA—
Was I Going to Run for Sheriff?

Halfway through his fourth term, Sheriff Penrod announced his retirement, and urged the Board of Supervisors to appoint then-Assistant Sheriff Rod Hoops as his successor. There appeared to be some extended dialog over Rod, as the Board took quite a while before appointing him to the position. Apparently, there were also some folks hoping the Board would appoint me. But I maintained a low profile and opted to not throw my hat into the ring unless it became clear that Rod wouldn't be appointed.

Rod was appointed, and I sincerely wished him well. He and I go back to the early 1990s, when I was an LAPD captain and he was an SBSD lieutenant and we went through the California POST Command College together. Later, when I was appointed a deputy chief on the Sheriff's Department, Rod worked for me as a captain and commander of the Rancho Cucamonga Station.

In 2010, having been appointed two years earlier, Rod had to stand for election. He knew that I had substantial support within the department, and I realized he was concerned that I might run against him for the position of sheriff.

Before the board of the Safety Employees Benefit Association (SEBA—the union that represents Sheriff's employees) voted to endorse Rod, they called to determine my intentions, as there were some people on the board who were hoping I would seek the elected position of sheriff. While I would have dearly loved the honor of serving as the sheriff of San Bernardino County, and believe I would have had a pretty good shot at the job at the time, I don't believe in screwing my friends. Rod was a friend.

I again declined to seek the office, and endorsed Rod for re-election.

Pleased that Radio Interoperability Continues to Exist

A long-term impediment to inter-agency coordination in San Bernardino County has been the inability of California Highway Patrol officers to communicate via voice radio with their police and sheriff counterparts. This problem stems from the frequency spectrum used by the CHP, in the 38-42 Mhz range, in which no other county law enforcement agencies operate.

Communications interoperability has long been a concern and an interest to me, and while with the sheriff's department I was able to pretty much solve the problem for most rural portions of the county. With some money I was able to weasel out of the state and because of my good friend, Dave Seidel, who was the head of county communications, I was able to have a number of 800 Mhz sheriff's two-way radios refurbished, their long-term maintenance assured, and have them placed in the center console of every CHP car in the Barstow, Lake Arrowhead, Morongo Valley, and Needles CHP stations.

Although there were a few (fortunately, very few) crusty old CHP dogs who didn't bother to turn them on, the majority of the CHP officers plus our deputies saw it as a great resource, resulting in enhanced officer safety, faster coordinated responses, and many great arrests. In Morongo, this capability was credited with saving a deputy's life.

Although the program seems to be slipping a bit, it appears to still be alive, to some extent. I encourage the executive staff to apply the energy and creativity to find adequate radios, work out the maintenance issues, and work with their CHP counterparts to get them in the CHP vehicles, and all of our supervisors to provide the emphasis and leadership to make sure both departments use them. This is one of those types of extraordinary programs that, regardless of its value, can fall to the wayside without caring leadership. Our officers and the public are worthy of the effort.

Chapter Seventeen
CALIFORNIA DEPARTMENT OF FISH AND GAME

Basic Training to Be a Deputy Warden

Although all I ever really wanted to be was a conventional cop, I was always fascinated with the role of game wardens. One of my dad's brothers, Russ Bushey, had a long and successful career with the California Department of Fish & Game, (DFG) and at the time of his retirement around 1960 was a top official in northern California. His son, Russ Jr., was a career game warden living in Burney (California) who died in the line of duty of a heart attack. Later, Russ's son, Jake, was also a career warden, and is now (at the time of this writing) retired and the director of the state game wardens' association.

In 1980 then-Governor Edmund Brown, Jr., tasked various state agencies with the responsibility to develop volunteer programs. To my great delight, the Department of Fish & Game resurrected its reserve warden program after having been dormant for a number of years. As I was aware of the program and had always hoped it would be reestablished at some point, I was among the first to apply. Successful candidates had to have an existing peace officer's POST certification, and would be deputized as "deputy wardens." I was an LAPD captain assigned as the commanding officer of North Hollywood Patrol at the time. But the department had no problem with my volunteer participation and I was quickly accepted. The training consisted of two days of instruction at the headquarters in Long Beach. On the second afternoon, we were sworn in, given our badges, identification cards and citation books. We had to purchase our own uniforms, but would be paid all expenses for gas, etc., plus the stately salary of $1 per year. Because I indicated a willingness to work immediately in the San Gabriel Canyon, where there had been a regular warden vacancy for many months, I was also issued a portable radio.

I truly enjoyed working as a game warden! You could make the argument that there has to be something wrong with someone who works 10 to 12 hours a day as a cop, and then does more police work in his "leisure time!" However, I really enjoyed being outdoors, primarily in the forest, and as a warden I was directly interacting with people as opposed to my managerial and command role with the LAPD. It was kind of fun to be just a plain cop doing outdoors stuff, and not a big shot.

After being sworn in I was the only warden for the 5112 area, which was mostly the entire San Gabriel Canyon but also west to Pasadena and east to Mount Baldy. I worked alone most of the time and drove my personal vehicle, which was a green-and-white International Scout. I was reasonable with people, but did write quite a few citations and made a few arrests. Later my good pal and regular warden, Ken Walton, was assigned to the 5112 district. I worked regularly until the late 1980s, when my LAPD responsibilities became even greater, and when Cathy and I got married.

Over the years that I worked for Fish & Game, I met and worked with some really nice people, although there was a jerk or two. I gave some thought to retiring from the LAPD and going full-time with DFG when I hit my twenty-fifth police department anniversary. But the pay drop would have been far too much, and I really wasn't ready to leave the big city.

No Signs Where the Canal Was Entered!

One day a police lieutenant with whom I was acquainted, and who knew of my status with fish and game, approached me. He explained that he'd received a citation from a game warden for fishing in the California Aqueduct, and wanted to get my advice on the best way to contest the ticket. I suggested that he try to find a place where there was access but no posted signs. He replied there were no signs where he climbed over the fence! I still have a hard time believing a police lieutenant could believe that was some type of valid explanation. I suggested he pay the fine and not reveal his stupidity to anyone else.

Keith and the Bear at Barton Flats

Late one night I was on patrol in the Angeles National Forest with another warden and a good friend, Kenny Walton. We were in the Ranger Station at the Barton Flats Campground. Both Kenny and the forest ranger were inside the office having a cigarette. Not being a smoker, I stepped outside to get some fresh air, and for no particular reason walked a few feet into the forest. While standing and enjoying the silence and tranquility, a massive creature rushed past me like a freight train. It was big, fast, crushing all the brush in its path, and so close I could smell its body and breath. It was one gigantic bear! Obviously, it had been unaware of my presence, as I was pretty much standing still and leaning on the backside of a tree. It all happened so fast I didn't have time to be frightened—but sure was overwhelmed by the enormity of that animal.

No, You are Not Going to Cite Him!

As a deputy warden, I was officially subordinate to the full-time regular wardens with whom I often worked. However, as a long-time peace officer I don't believe I ever worked with anyone who had my level of law enforcement experience. As a result, most of my partners deferred to my tactical judgment and, at the very least, treated me pretty much as an equal.

One afternoon, accompanied by a female partner who was a regular warden, I was at Crystal Lake in the Angeles National Forest. We ran across an off-duty U.S. Forest Service fire patrolman who was fishing at an isolated spot. When we asked to see his fishing license, he apologized for not having one and identified himself as a forest service employee. My partner started berating him for not having a license and for not knowing better, and began the process of citing him.

It was too much for me! I whispered in her ear that citing him was not a good idea, that a warning would suffice, and reminded her that our only back-up usually was Forest Service employees. She angrily suggested I mind my own business and that she was going to give him a ticket. I snatched the ticket book out of her hand, told the guy to get a license, and walked back to our unit, with her following and pouting. We had quite a spirited conversation. I made it clear that I would never be part of a process that cited one of our essential partners for such a low-level violation, when a warning would suffice. I think (hope) that this incident shaped her enforcement philosophy under these types of circumstances. Since we went on to have a nice friendship, I think I got my point across.

While male wardens were not immune from foolish behavior, this is another stupid thing done by another of my female partners. It was close to noon on the opening day of deer season. Hunting was pretty much over for the day, as the deer that survived had bedded down. Louise (not her real name) and I came around a corner on a back road and observed about six or seven hunters gathered under a tree, talking. Several of them had placed their unloaded rifles, with actions opened, in various crooks of the tree. Technically, it is against the law to lean a gun against a tree, for safety reasons. In this instance, although technically a violation, it was no big deal. But Louise jumped out of the truck like a bolt of lightning and started screaming at the group for their egregious safety violations. As her squeaky feminine voice permeated the air, I was so embarrassed I could have slid under a rock. I took her aside and told her that I would handle the situation, which she mistakenly thought would be done through multiple citations.

After I'd warned the fellows I returned to a very angry partner who resented my actions. She was a vindictive person who was upset at my actions and, once again, I had a very spirited discussion with my regular warden partner. This person became one of the very few wardens who I declined to work with during my time with fish and game.

Snakes Everywhere!

I would occasionally work "pet shop patrol." Our job was to inspect shops to ensure that all fish, animals and reptiles were not native to California, and if they were, to ensure there was paperwork showing their importation from a state where personal possession was legal. On this particular day I was working with Warden Karen Longmore, a fine cop who was also a good friend. We went to several locations and seized a couple of dozen snakes—king, gopher, and garter types. We would typically release them in the wilds, and since my house was right up against the national forest, and because I liked to keep the rattlesnakes away and the type of snakes we seized were good for that, I just took the snakes home.

However, my son Jake wanted to keep and play with the snakes for a few days, and talked me into putting them—temporarily—in a large aquarium on a coffee table in the front room. Before hitting the sack that night, I made sure the top of the aquarium was secured by a screen with a weight on top. It seems that Jake wanted to play with the snakes after I went to bed, and he didn't adequately replace the screen. The next morning every one of the snakes had got out of the aquarium and was loose in our house! It took a couple of weeks before I found most of them, but there were at least two, including a beautiful king snake, that I never did find. It's a very good thing that I was single and there were no females living in my house at the time.

Uncle Clay's Deathbed Confession

Clay Bushey was one of my dad's brothers, and just a fun and wonderful man. He and his wife, my Aunt Riola, were among the finest folks I have known, as is their son, my cousin Tom Bushey. Clay was the consummate outdoorsman, and one of those folks who really loved to eat what he shot, especially venison and doves.

We chatted a great deal about my part-time position as a deputy warden. It was during one of our conversations, not long before he passed away, that he confided a long-kept secret to me pertaining to his employment and hunting. Clay was retired from Forest Lawn Memorial Parks (Hollywood Hills and Glendale), where he'd spent about forty years as an electrician. He told me that over the years he had killed and eaten scores of deer that he shot very early in the morning. The deer were easy to find, because they would come down out of the hills to eat the flowers on the graves. He said that he shot them with a .22, after placing a condom over the end of the barrel to muffle the sound of the gunshot.

Even after all those years (he had been retired from Forest Lawn for many, by then), it was obvious that he was still sensitive about his "poaching," and was a little reluctant to reveal his long-held secret.

Rest in peace, Uncle Clay and Aunt Riola. Thank you both for all the warmth and love you gave me.

Baited Field in Holtville

While nowhere close to my hunting dad and his brothers, I have been somewhat of a hunter all of my life, with a particular affinity for ducks and doves. Once, on opening day of dove season I was with my very good pal, Ben Staffer, a retired LAPD sergeant and World War II Marine veteran of the Iwo Jima campaign. We were hunting in a field where Ben knew the property owner and had obtained permission for us to hunt.

All of a sudden, several vehicles containing state and federal game wardens converged on us, demanded to see our identification, and started questioning us about our knowledge and experience in that field.

As it turned out, it was a "baited field," where some folks had spread feed throughout the field for several weeks prior to opening day, to unfairly lure doves into the trap. Ben and I knew nothing of that, nor would we have ever been involved in breaking any wildlife laws. It didn't take long for the various officers to realize that we were innocents caught in the dragnet intended for other people. I think the fact that Ben and I had next to nothing in our game bags was evidence of our innocence. It was astonishing that the feds had actually brought several federal game wardens all the way from the Hawaiian Islands just for this operation!

Just Kinda Faded Away

I never resigned as a deputy game warden, and I still have my badge and credentials. I worked less by necessity, and the folks I worked with transferred elsewhere, my DFG bosses transferred or retired, and I just faded away. As indicated elsewhere in these memoirs, I worked closely with the DFG in San Bernardino County, and managed to have a sheriff's radio placed into each Fish & Game vehicle in San Bernardino County. I look back with considerable fondness on my experiences as a deputy warden.

Chapter Eighteen

LOS ANGELES
DISTRICT ATTORNEY'S OFFICE

Honor to be Selected

Steve Cooley, the elected district attorney of Los Angeles County, and I have been close friends for many years. He was the student body president at California State College, Los Angeles, when I was an undercover policeman there and the president of the Students for a Democratic Society (SDS), a subversive and un-American organization.

During that time, Steve was unaware that I was a cop, and often said some pretty nasty things to me. Obviously, I couldn't reveal my true identify and thought he was a pretty good and spunky kid, including his actions on one occasion where he actually prevented a group of anti-war idiots from tearing down the American flag.

A couple of years later I was a sergeant at Rampart Division when he and another first-year law student, Kurt Hazell, came to the station and requested a ride-along. We had quite a fun conversation, and Steve was shocked to learn that his old nemisis was actually a cop. We've been good friends ever since, and I was honored to be among his strongest supporters when he ran for district attorney.

However, unlike a couple of his other strong supporters, Dominick Rivetti and Steve Simonian, I had no intention of ever working for Steve in the DA's Office. After retiring from the sheriff's separtment, I thought that working for Steve might be something I would enjoy, and a place where I might be able to do a pretty good job. I knew that Steve Simonian was going to retire, and was interested in the chief's postion in the Bureau of Investigation. However, Dominick Rivetti, a great guy and good friend, had already been tapped for that position. Instead, Steve offered me the position of law enforcement liaison, along with another person. I immediately accepted the offer.

Shortly after retiring from the sheriff's department, I met with a fellow SBSD retired command officer who I had long considered a good friend. He marketed himself as an expert in personnel issues and, although I became convinced he didn't know as much as he claimed to know, we still chatted often on personnel-related issues. Although I hadn't been able to remain with the sheriff's department because of a partially disabled hand, I was pursuing other options in law enforcement, including going to a small department in Los Angeles County as the police chief. I was also considering accepting a liaison position, the one I ultimately took, with the Los Angeles County District Attorney's Office.

I met with my pal, took him into my confidence about the positions I was considering, and asked if he believed I could still work as a police officer if the hiring agency was inclined to accommodate my disabled hand. Although lean on specifics, he insisted that I could not again have a badge or work as a peace officer in California because of my disability.

Not feeling comfortable with my pal's assessment alone, I reached out to a few other individuals and entities: Sheriff Gary Penrod, the San Bernardino County Council, San Bernardino County Retirement Board, Director of the California Commission on Peace Officer Standards & Training, and a law firm that specialized in law enforcement personnel issues, Lewis & Marenstein. What I learned was the my pal was wrong, and that I could once again be a peace officer in California if the agency was inclined to accommodate my disabled hand. Equally as important to me was that there was absolutely no opposition or ill-will from the SBSD if I did go to work elsewhere.

A few weeks later, while being processed to be a law enforcement liaison for the district attorney, one of the key aides told me the office had been contacted by San Bernardino County and advised that I was not eligible to be hired by the district attorney! I was flabbergasted, and replied that only one person, who I named, said that I was ineligible to be a cop again. The aide confirmed that the caller, who identified himself as calling from "San Bernardino County," was indeed my fellow SBSD retired pal! This guy and I were very close, our families were somewhat close and cordial, and I couldn't believe he stabbed me in the back like that. His call did set an inquiry in progress, which quickly established that I could be hired into the position. In later conversations with a few folks in San Bernardino, it turned out that they weren't surprised by his behavior. I am sometimes the last to see evil in others, and this was a good example. So much for integrity.

In Good Company at the District Attorney's Office

As it turned out, Steve Cooley ended up with three law enforcement liaisons. My civil service position was "detective." The other two were retired La Verne Police Chief Ron Ingels, who was also the former head of the California Association of Police Chiefs, and retired LAPD Detective and former president of the Los Angeles Police Protective League, Bob Baker. Both were very decent and competent men, who did a great job for Steve. Actually, it was a bit awkward for me, because I was hired to do many of the tasks that were ultimately assigned to Bob and Ron. But I really had no basis to complain because of their extraordinary backgrounds and contacts. While I did a lot of good for Steve and the office, I wish there had been the opportunity for me to do more.

Police Memorial Week—Washington, D. C.

The ceremony and festivities of "Police Week" in Washington, D.C., are extraordinary. Cathy and I were guests of Steve for this event in 2007, and it was something that we thoroughly enjoyed. We ran across a great many people we knew, met many new friends, and had the opportunity to acknowledge the memories of an unfortunately large number of fallen officers whom we had known.

Goodbye "Weiner Mobile"—Hello Crown Victoria

Steve Cooley took very good care of me. When first assigned to the DA's office, I was issued a take-home vehicle out of the surveillance fleet. While a nice car, it wasn't like the cars that the rest of the criminal justice command folks typically drove, which were mostly the Ford Crown Victoria. I still recall my first law enforcement funeral. I showed up as a VIP, was in a row of Crown Victorias, and ultimately had the only compact vehicle in the VIP parking area. Steve is a good guy and a good friend. But like the rest of us, there are some times that are better than other times to make requests. At the right moment, when Steve and I were alone, I asked if I could turn in my little "Weiner Mobile" for a big kid's police car, the coveted Ford Crown Victoria. Steve took good care of me, and for the rest of my almost five years with the DA's office I drove a late-model Crown Victoria. I know it may seem like a little thing, and either way it is not the end of the world, but it was important for me to have some degree of visual parity with my colleagues in the profession. The new vehicle, which had the usual array of antennas, also facilitated my entry into police scenes and facilities. When I left the

DA's office, it was tough turning in my badge—but it was really tough turning in my super-duper, low-mileage Crown Victoria!

Unique Presentations for Very Special Clergymen

One of my many thoughts over the years was to have made and present to Father Michael McCullough, a Catholic priest who the Los Angeles Diocese assigned to the LAPD, a large cross emblazoned with imbedded flat law enforcement badges. In 2010, I finally brought my vision into reality. I had a custom cross made by a craftsman in Tennessee, and had about fifteen or so flat badges, representing many of the departments that Father Mike ministers to, set into the wood. It was breathtaking and absolutely the first of its kind. The surprise presentation gathering included me, Steve Cooley, Mike Stone, Greg Meyers, Bob Taylor, Bob Baker and a host of other long-time law enforcement personalities. Father Mike was beyond grateful. He has since used it on a number of occasions, including at memorial services, funerals, and in conjunction with the Peace Officer's Desert Refuge in Joshua Tree, which he is the founder of (and recently conned me into becoming a member of the board of directors).

Since that time I have created and presented similar badge encrusted crucifixes to two additional wonderful clergymen, Reverend Harley Broviak at the Riverside County Sheriff's Department, and Episcopal Priest Mort Ward, a long time friend and badge collector.

Not Shattering a Son's Image

After one of my appearances for the DA where I was introduced as a retired LAPD commander, I was approached by a very impressive young man who was about to embark on a great career in a great organization. He asked if I had been acquainted with his dad during my service on the police department. When he mentioned his dad's name, it was obvious that he adored his father and was very proud of all he believed his dad had accomplished.

Although I'm confident my expression did not change, I was stunned to hear the name, and even more stunned that such an obviously fine young man could be the child of the man whose name was mentioned. Not only was I acquainted with the father, I played a major role in his termination and criminal prosecution. He was a rogue cop who had brought great discredit to the LAPD several decades earlier.

I responded that I was acquainted with his dad, asked him to convey my best regards to his father, and told him I hoped he could measure up to some of the great things his dad had accomplished. This was not a falsehood, as his dad had been a superstar at one time, and really did some great things before the misconduct occurred. I wasn't about to shatter this kid's image of his dad. At my next appearance at the same function, the dad was seated in the back of the audience. After the event, he approached me in the parking lot, we exchanged handshakes, and he said "thank you." What occurred many years ago had been pretty ugly, and as his commanding officer it had also caused some problems for me, but it was in the past. I hope that the dad's life has been a good one since those troubling days.

LEADERSHIP AND SUPERVISORY BOOKLETS TO COUNTY AGENCIES

Thanks to the generosity of Steve Cooley and the district attorney's great printing center, I was able to have several hundred bound copies of my very popular booklets printed. These booklets, with attractive full-color covers displaying scores of law enforcement badges, are titled *Command Leadership* and *Establishing & Maintaining Supervisory Credibility*.

Distribution of the command booklets included one to every staff and command officer on both the LAPD and LASD, as well as copies to many other agencies. The supervisory booklets went out by the hundreds. I remain flattered by the appreciative comments I continue to receive on the quality of these booklets, and am especially gratified when I'm told of how their lessons have been applied.

FBI COMMAND COLLEGE TRAINING—UNUSUAL OCCURRENCES

The training coordinator of the Los Angeles Office of the Federal Bureau of Investigation contacted me, in about 2008, with a request that I found interesting—to develop a presentation on the control of unusual occurrences, based on my many experiences. If it was a diversity of unusual experiences they were looking for, they came to the right person! Mine have included presidential visits, civil unrest, anti-everything demonstrations (as both a uniformed cop and while undercover), anti/pro-abortion, animal rights, love fests, RAVE concerts (including on Indian reservations), civil rights demonstrations, etc., etc., etc.

I spent some time reflecting, giving more attention to what went wrong as opposed to what went right, and ultimately developed a booklet that I used for that particular presentation and a few others. The name of the booklet is *UNUSUAL OCCURRENCES—Helpful Hints & Painful Lessons*. I strongly recommend it to other law enforcement leaders, as it consists of about twenty pages of discussion, by categories, of the most common mistakes made, the things that are most likely to go wrong, and how to prevent those problems. Thanks to Steve Cooley, it was also bound with a cool cover. I continue to use it in presentations. *Note: Books may be downloaded at www.KeithBushey.com.*

HUMANITARIAN OF THE YEAR!

Talk about a humbling experience! On November 17, 2010, at a massive luncheon at the Almansor Courts in Alhambra, with Cathy and most of our big and little kids in attendance, District Attorney Steve Cooley presented me with the 10th Annual Michael P. Noyes Humanitarian Award. The award was presented because of our long-time activities as foster parents. I was deeply grateful and humbled to be named a recipient of this coveted award.

PUSH FINALLY CAME TO SHOVE

Financial dark clouds started drifting over the County of Los Angeles within a couple of years of my employment as law enforcement liaison on the executive staff of the district attorney's office. Around 2009, I approached Steve Cooley and let him know that, while I was grateful for the opportunity to work for him, I would understand if he had to let me go. I specifically mentioned that if the choice was between retaining me and being able to hire a new deputy district attorney, he should go with the latter.

I was in a precarious position based on discretionary funding, but mostly I didn't want to become a potential political liability for him. He appreciated my overture, but said that we would ride it out for a while and hope the county's financial picture would improve. Nevertheless, in February 2011 he called me into his office and said that the "proverbial push has come to shove." It would be necessary to let me go.

I was not upset in the least. To the contrary, I was grateful for the opportunity to have served Steve and the county, and appreciative that he kept me on board as long as he did.

CONTINUED ROLE WITH THE DISTRICT ATTORNEY'S OFFICE

Even though I am no longer a paid employee, I offered and Steve accepted my offer to continue helping him in certain situations, and to represent him in several organizations. Although far less active than when I was an employee, as of June 2012 I continue to be of service to Steve in a reduced and volunteer capacity. I'll remain so until the end of his last term in office, at the end of the year.

CHAPTER NINETEEN

CITRUS COLLEGE

STRUCK AT THE RIGHT TIME

Timing is everything, and my visit to Citrus College to explore teaching opportunities truly occurred at the right moment, in 1976. I was a lieutenant in LAPD's Hollenbeck Division with a new master's degree, and thought I would see if I could possibly get a part-time teaching position at Citrus College, which is not far from where I live.

I went "cold" to the head of the Police Science Department. His name was Bart Bartel, and at the time he was also a sergeant on the sheriff's department assigned to the San Dimas Station. Teaching at Citrus had been his longtime off-duty job. Bart, who became one of my closest friends, thought that something might open up, and after a nice chat said he would get back to me.

I got a call from Bart just a day or so later, and was offered a part-time job teaching police science! Because he obviously wanted to ensure that I would do okay, he started me out with just one class. That first class morphed into over twenty years of part-time instruction, from roughly 1976 through 1998, at Citrus College.

BART BARTEL

Bart Bartel was one of the finest men I have ever known, and one of the best friends a person could ask for. I met him as he was in the process of retiring from the Los Angeles County Sheriff's Department, out of San Dimas Station, and assuming full-time duties as a dean at Citrus College. We quickly became close friends. We went through divorces with one another, laughed together, and cried together. He was very handy with household tasks, and was constantly helping me with various home maintenance chores. He lived in my yard in a series of increasingly large and exotic motor homes, before marrying the prettiest student (a divorcee) at the college.

Bart was a great "uncle" to my kids and someone who was always there for his friends. When in his early seventies he was diagnosed with cancer, and that horrible disease finally took his life in 2008. I had the honor of spending quite a bit of time with him as the disease progressed, and visited with him almost to the very end of his life. His wonderful wife, Jeanne, gave me the honor of delivering the eulogy at his funeral, and I also coordinated a fly-by over the services by the sheriff's aero bureau.

Rest in peace Bart. This world is a better place because you were part of it, and those of us who were blessed with having you in our lives are better because of your friendship and influence.

Three Classes in One Semester

I really overdid it one semester, but just the one. I taught three classes, each representing three credits, during a single semester. The day class was held three mornings a week from eight to nine, and the two full three-hour classes were on two evenings.

This really kicked my rear, and isn't something I would ever care to do again. I usually let the class out in the morning a bit early so I could be at the office no later than 9:30 a.m., but had get back to the campus in time for the evening classes. On the weekdays when I didn't teach at night, I remained at work longer to compensate for the three slightly abbreviated days. Realistically, it was hard on the school, the police department, and me.

Like the holocaust—never again!

Taught Without Pay

In about 1997, Citrus College fell into dire fiscal straights. Elective classes were cut from the semester that had just begun, and the school laid off a bunch of folks, including me. It was no big thing to me, but it certainly posed a problem for some of my students, and in a couple of situations jeopardized their anticipated graduation dates. It also threw a monkey wrench into some students' plans, who were on different types of scholarships that required them to take a minimum number of units to remain qualified.

I notified Bart Bartel that I would continue to teach for no pay, so that my students could complete the class. The college gratefully accepted my offer and I taught without pay for several months. Just before the semester ended, the college was able to hire some folks back. Because of my actions, I was the first instructor to be rehired.

A Substation for Workplace Fraternization

Bart Bartel was not my only big-shot pal at Citrus. I had another friend, very high up in the college leadership hierarchy, who was involved for quite some time in a really steamy relationship with one of his low-level female clerical employees. He was in about his mid-fifties and she was in her early twenties, but there was seemingly an unquenchable and passionate attraction between the two of them.

This pal, with my permission of course, actually parked a pickup topped with a really nice camper alongside my garage for their regular noontime passion sessions! As I recall, she was one of the underlings who reported to his executive secretary. It struck me as being a bit too close for comfort and, given women's intuition and feminine vindictiveness, seemed like a very risky situation. At noon, she and he would leave through separate doors at slightly different times, go to their respective parking lots, then separately drive to my house. She would get out of her car and make a beeline for that camper, like a thirsty person rushing to a water faucet. I don't know what magic the old fart possessed, but that young honey couldn't get enough of it. She continued to raise the possibility of marriage, which he insisted would not be a wise move. I believe it was the issue that ultimately caused them to go off in separate directions. He later ended up marrying another gal.

Fortunately, their relationship never developed into a problem at the college, because he remained there for quite a while after the affair ended, and continued to do well and be well thought of.

Brutal Assault on My Humiliation Rooster

For a number of years in my evening supervision classes, I had a rubber rooster that I called "Victor Verbatim." Each evening a different student would make a presentation to the class on a pre-determined subject. But I was death on verbatim presentations. When someone violated my "no verbatim" rule, I would place "Victor Verbatim" in a spot in front of him or her on the conference table.

It was a fun thing, intended to reinforce my seriousness about the need for the students to develop solid presentation skills. One evening when the class returned from our break in the student lounge, we encountered a horrible sight: Victor was hanging by his neck from an overhead light fixture, with a tampon sticking out of his rear end!

All of the students chuckled, and pled ignorance. But I knew exactly who was responsible, and later extracted a pound of flesh (fun stuff) on behalf of Victor.

Reservoir of Relationships for My Pals

I frequently invited guest speakers to my classes, and those presentations occasionally worked out well for some of my pals. The fact that most of my single friends who took the opportunity to make presentations were typically in their thirties didn't seem to pose a problem for the abundance of female students who weren't that long out of high school. I got the impression that some of those young ladies saw older men as their path to full womanhood, and I know that my friends were honored to assist in their transitions! The students always enjoyed my guest speakers, but I think the greatest enjoyment went to some of the speakers. Being a guest speaker for me had some real advantages. Such dirty old men!

Substitute Subjected to Coed Competition

Because of my military obligation, there were times when I had to bring in substitute instructors, sometimes for as long as three full weeks. During one of my absences, one of my substitute pals found himself the object of a competition between two coeds to see who could get him into bed first! This continues to be one of his best stories, and he delights in describing both the first- and second-place winners! Like all of my guest speakers, he could hit and run as a substitute teacher, engage in otherwise prohibited relationships, and not be subjected to the potentially adverse consequences that regular instructors might have incurred for similar behaviors.

The Teacher's Pension System

Although I didn't realize it until just about the end of my teaching career at Citrus, I could have gotten into the state teacher's retirement system. I'm sorry I didn't do that. I later learned that the school pretty much kept mum about this possibility for part-time instructors. Had I got into the system, I would be receiving another retirement check today!

586

My part-time teaching career at Citrus College was a very good and important part of my life for many years. The additional money had been helpful in the acquisition of four homes in Big Bear (two homes for each of my two wives!), and in paying child support after Barbara and I went our separate ways.

But the years and years of having to teach several mornings a week before school, and a full three hours at night once or twice a semester, finally took their toll. I got tired of the fatigue and inconvenience that went along with class commitments and the continuous frenzy of trying to get to the evening classes on time. So I decided to give up teaching at Citrus College.

Of critical importance to my decision was the fact that I really no longer needed the extra income. I finished up classes the spring semester in June of 1998, and that was it. I have been invited to return to Citrus on a couple of occasions, and have indicated that it would be my honor to come occasionally as a guest speaker or impromptu substitute. But I no longer want to be tied down to a regular schedule, and desire more free time for the family and leisure activities. I look back with great fondness to my days as both a student and instructor at Citrus College, and am grateful for the years of our pleasant affiliation.

My Students Seem to be Everywhere!

In thirty years of teaching typically two classes each semester, several thousand students passed through my classes, most of whom were from the local community. Today, I cannot go anywhere without running into former students, and it's always fun to encounter them. As I am writing this entry, I will soon attend the retirement of Corporal Glenn Purbaugh, who has completed thirty years of service with the Irwindale Police Department. Glenn was one of my police science students while he was still in high school! The fellow who owns the shop where I take my cars for servicing, and the assistant general manager of the local major recreational vehicle center, also number among my former students. Not surprisingly, every law enforcement agency within the area is full of former students of mine.

CHAPTER TWENTY
FBI-LAW ENFORCEMENT EXECUTIVE DEVELOPMENT ASSOCIATION

ATTENDING LEEDS

As the marshal of San Bernardino County, I was on the FBI's radar screen as a police executive with whom the bureau wanted to maintain a good relationship. Because of this, I was contacted by the local special agent-in-charge and given the opportunity to attend a two-week leadership course at the FBI Academy in Quantico, Virginia. The name of the course was the Law Enforcement Executive Development Seminar (LEEDS). It was a most enjoyable course, and led to my membership in the FBI's Law Enforcement Executive Leadership Association (LEEDA).

Several months later, I attended LEEDA's annual conference. At the conference I struck up a wonderful friendship with the organization's executive director, Tom Stone, a retired police chief from cities in Pennsylvania and Virginia. Tom and I, after much thought and planning, put together a leadership training package and went on the road, every month or so, to law enforcement agencies across the nation. As I write this entry in my memoirs, I have been traveling with LEEDA ever since that first conference. Predictably, our material has become greatly enhanced and we have grown to a number of instructors, of which I am considered a senior faculty member.

With the exception of Alaska, leadership-training opportunities have taken me to just about every state in the union, and as I write this entry I am sitting in a conference room at the Police Department in Hampton, New Hampshire. One of my colleagues, retired Police Chief Dean Crisp (Columbia, S. C.), is in the next room teaching; he and I are the team in this city this week (September 2011).

Obviously, LEEDA has become a big part of my life. It has also enabled me to carry out one of my life's passions: that of sharing my skills and experiences (many of which are based on some pretty painful lessons) with today's supervisors and managers in the wonderful profession of law enforcement.

Lecturing Throughout the United States and Canada

I have been on the speaking circuit for an average of one presentation per month since about 2000, and continue making presentations to this day. I have visited scores and scores of police and sheriff's departments and have made presentations to thousands of law enforcement officers throughout the United States and Canada. I am grateful to have leadership as my passion, and equally grateful that I seem to be effective in helping others to develop and exercise strong leadership skills. As I write this entry I recently returned from Kent (Washington) and have presentations scheduled next month in Harrisburg (Pennsylvania) and LaPorte (Texas). Very few people in this world get the opportunity to preach about their passion, and I am one of the lucky ones. For me, it is more of a calling and a professional responsibility than a job.

Visit to Slope County

Several years ago, Tom Stone and I provided training to the police department in Bismarck, North Dakota. The next day, after our training was completed, we were waiting for our evening flights back to our homes. As we had some time on our hands, we decided to drive to a town called Amadon (North Dakota), where Tom had been told the steak dinners were the best in the West. We drove to Amadon, a very small town in a very rural county, and the steaks were okay. But while there, we met the county sheriff, Tom Lorge, who made Tom and me honorary deputies. Now the Slope County Sheriff's Department consists of the sheriff, the part-time chief deputy, plus Tom Stone, Keith Bushey, and the uniformed mannequin in a worn-out police car parked along the highway running through town! Interestingly, Tom Lorge has a son who is a career Marine, and he and I have stayed in touch and maintain an ongoing friendship.

Late-breaking Slope County development: In late 2011 the department lost 20 percent of its staff, when someone stole the mannequin out of the parked sheriff's vehicle.

During the installation banquet at the 2009 FBI-LEEDA Conference in Tampa, Florida, I got quite a surprise. I was named the first recipient of the Tom Stone FBI-LEEDA Award of Excellence "In Recognition of Your Outstanding Achievement in Promoting the Science and Art of Police Management, Promoting the Exchange of Information between Police Executives, Expansion of Police Leadership Training, and the Growth of the FBI-LEEDA Organization."

Receiving an award is always humbling, but getting it from your friends and associates is about as good as it gets. I treasure the beautiful plaque I was presented. It will always occupy a special place in my office.

Chapter Twenty-One

BUSHEY & ASSOCIATES

Developing My Own Company

Like most people in my profession, I often get requests to do specialized training or investigations. When I choose to take on a task that falls outside of the LEEDA umbrella, I do marketing and billeting under the mantle of "Bushey & Associates." I am the only employee, but bring others on as necessary. In this capacity I have made scores of presentations that include, but are not limited to: regional command colleges, state police chief associations, specialized groups (custody, dispatch, forestry, etc.) Mostly, however, my presenations are made to police and sheriff's departments that want instruction tailored to address their unique needs. Not surprisingly, some of these opportunities come in the wake of department scandals.

Horrible Behavior at a Rural Sheriff's Department

This is one of those situations that I've waited for the involved parties to either die or retire! Many years ago I was retained to teach a three-day seminar on a variety of supervisory topics, by a rural sheriff's department (state and county to remain anonymous). The first clue that a problem existed should have been the lack of officers attending from surrounding departments, including the police department in the city that was the county seat of the sheriff's department that had retained me.

Shortly after my arrival, a sergeant walked up behind a female deputy who I was conversing with, reached around her with both hands, and started bouncing her breasts up and down! I was in shock, and he said, "That's how we say howdy around here." Shortly after our presentation, the members of the class, the leadership of the department, and my employee and I went to a restaurant for dinner. There the sheriff announced that we were all guests of the owner, and all but flat-out admitted that he had pressured the guy into giving us free chow.

At the conclusion if the training, the sheriff gave my associate and me each a large bottle of expensive scotch, and once again came just short of outright saying that the booze had been extorted from a local business. We couldn't get out of that place fast enough! Just before leaving, the sheriff said that he might try to bring us back to teach a course on sexual harassment (I swear it's true)! Over a dozen years have passed since that incident. The sheriff and all the employees I dealt with left after he lost the next election following our visit, but even now I wouldn't return to that department without ensuring that the culture has changed.

The "Baby Factory" Complaint

During one of the scores of presentations I've made throughout the nation, a female police commander complained about a comment I made. My presentation was in the area of human resources, and the topic dealt with abuses of the Federal Family Maternity Leave Act (FMLA).

In describing a troubling situation at a sheriff's department, where a female deputy had become a professional surrogate mother on multiple occasions while taking advantage of some extraordinary benefits for pregnant employees, I apparently made the comment that she had abused the FMLA and had become a "baby factory." The statement was made early in the training, and I had a cordial relationship with the woman commander during the subsequent training, with no hint of a problem.

But a couple of weeks later my office received a letter of complaint about my comment, signed by the woman's chief of police. While I certainly do not wish to offend anyone, I was troubled by her lack of inclination to say anything to me, as well as for the spineless actions of her chief in forwarding her complaint under his signature. If anything, he should have made a call to me regarding her concerns; but, in my opinion, he was afraid of her and wrote the letter to avoid further conflict with her. The matter did not go anywhere, but it was irritating nonetheless. Since that incident several years ago, I have returned to that area several times for various presentations, and felt relieved that she wasn't enrolled in my classes.

Acquisition of Badges for My Collection

Acquiring law enforcement badges for my collection has certainly not been the reason for my writing and teaching, but my constant interaction with police and sheriff officials from throughout the nation (Canada too!) has benefitted my museum. I've acquired literally hundreds of badges in conjunction with my teaching and visits. I'm careful about who I approach, and always subtle and not at all pushy, as I do not want a badge to be a factor in my goodwill or assistance to the hundreds of agencies I've dealt with. I really covet the badges that I've received from so many wonderful people who have become my friends over the years. The sad news is that, these days, I seldom go to an agency from which I don't already have a badge!

Unintended Consequences of Not Copyrighting My Writings

I have never considered copyrighting my booklets and articles. I am truly sincere in my long-term desire to make our workplaces better places, and to strengthen the leadership and supervisory skills of those who play the primary roles in bringing that long-term desire to fruition.

As such, I've always added this statement to my writings: "This material may be reproduced in whole or in part without permission. Attribution is appreciated." Others think I'm crazy not to copyright my material, but I remain steadfast in my determination not to do so. First, if I were to configure my material as a textbook, there would be the expectation that I would market it for sale, and if lucky, get a few thousand bucks in royalties. Then I'd be pressured to write an updated version a few years later, for additional revenue. No thanks! Second, as a Nevada police training manager found out the hard way, my material is very well-known, and plagiarizing it without giving me credit is immediately recognized and results in scorn and criticism from others in the profession.

The big, unintended consequence is that my material is used by hundreds of organizations and colleges throughout the United States and Canada; it is good and it is free, and easily found or simply downloaded from my website! I cannot go anywhere in the law enforcement community where I'm not known for my writings.

I'm continually flattered by the kind comments I receive for my materials, and never tire of hearing stories from other law enforcement leaders about how my material has affected their actions in positive ways.

CHAPTER TWENTY-TWO
DEVIL PUPS, INC.

A WONDERFUL ORGANIZATION

Devil Pups was formed in 1954 by a group of reserve Marine Corps officers who felt that certain portions of Marine Corps training, when provided to teenage boys, could strengthen their character and improve the likelihood that they would develop into responsible citizens. Visit the website: www.DevilPups.com.

UNABLE TO ATTEND—1956

I was beyond devastated as a twelve-year-old in the summer of 1956, when I was unable to attend one of the ten-day Devil Pups encampments at Camp Pendleton, California. At the time I was passionately involved in the San Gabriel Valley Junior Marines. The head of our outfit, Jim Smith, was affiliated in some way with the Devil Pups, and he had the ability to send kids to camp.

However, Smith decided to use Devil Pups as a membership incentive for some veterans organization (either the American Legion or Veterans of Foreign Wars, I don't recall which). If your dad was in the organization, or would join it, his kid could go to Devil Pups. My dad was eligible, but was too ill and unable to join. I still could have gone, as my older brother, Larry, was eligible to join. But he didn't care to.

This was really tough on me, in part because a group of the other junior Marines did go, including my best pal. I literally cried myself to sleep the night I learned I wouldn't be able to attend.

RECRUITED BY TOM VETTER

My longtime pal, Tom Vetter, had quite an impact on my Marine Corps life as an officer and a member of Devil Pups, Inc. I met Tom in 1968 while we were standing together in the registration line for classes at Cal State, Los Angeles. We started chatting, and learned that we both were Marines; he was in the reserves and I had already been discharged. Tom told me that he was a deputy sheriff, and I confided in him that I was an undercover LAPD cop assigned to Intelligence Division.

We became close and fast friends. He was in a Marine Corps Reserve counterintelligence team, for which I soon became a major source of valuable information while still working undercover. Tom is the reason that I returned to the Corps as an officer. He told me about a unique commissioning program, and motivated me through the process. After I surfaced and was commissioned, Tom recruited me into the Devil Pups. Both he and I serve to this day, as vice presidents. Tom is a wonderful man, a fine cop, a superb Marine, a great friend, and represents one of the most critical forks in the many roads that I have taken.

106 KIDS JAMMED ON THE BUS

Tom Vetter and I were liaison and recruiting officers for the Devil Pups. He represented the sheriff's department, and I represented the LAPD as well as the San Gabriel Valley. From the time we first worked together until well into the 1980s, Tom and I never failed to send a qualified kid to the camp, especially one who had a relative on one of our departments. If the youngster was qualified, we sent him without regard to whatever quota we were assigned. I think our record of "overshipping" peaked one year when we jammed 106 kids onto a 44-passenger bus, then told the driver his next stop was Camp Pendleton! Tom and I took a lot of heat for sending more kids than our quotas provided for, but we kept sending every one who was qualified. Finally, somebody got smart and increased our quotas! The Devil Pup organization is made up of truly wonderful people.

JAKE DECIDES TO ATTEND DEVIL PUPS!

Since he was just a little shaver, Jake would accompany me to the processing and shipping points for the Devil Pups candidates. But he never wanted to go himself. Then in the mid-1980s, with Jake at my side, I saw a bus-load of kids off from the Marine Corps Reserve Training Center in Pico Rivera. As the bus disappeared over the horizon, I said to Jake that I bet he wished he was going to the camp. He replied yes, he did wish he was on the bus! I immediately called a good pal, Sergeant Major Rudy Obad, who I knew was going to drive down to the base, and asked if he could take Jake. I quickly took Jake home to assemble the required clothes and items, met up with Rudy, and waved goodbye to Jake. He did a fine job, and for me it was particularly nice to attend the camp's graduation that year.

Pretty Much a Family Affair

Attending Devil Pups has long been a family affair. With the exception of Danny Bustamante, our oldest foster child and now a fire captain, who had to go to school every summer to graduate on time because he was so far behind academically when we became his legal guardians, all the other boys in the family have attended and graduated from Devil Pups.

Opened Up to Girls

I believe I was the first trustee to seriously raise the issue about opening Devil Pups up to girls. But I did it for the wrong reason.

I was convinced that Devil Pups wouldn't be at all attractive to girls, but was fearful of going sideways with the Department of Defense over the use of the Marine base if we didn't at least offer them the opportunity. The board meeting where I raised the issue turned really ugly; some of the older board members reacted like I was a liberal traitor and turncoat-feminist-women's-libber! Yet the majority agreed with me, both in opening it up to girls and believing that few, if any would apply. Wow—were we ever mistaken! My wife Cathy insisted that we should open it up to them, that many girls would apply, and was diplomatically persistent in chats with my Marine Corps pals. Since we opened Devil Pups to girls, we've had trouble accommodating all the applications, and recently had to add another female platoon. In recent years, some of our top graduates and performers have been girls! Next thing you know, they'll want to vote!

Fund-Raising Accomplishments

I'm pleased that I have been relatively successful, from time to time and often in spurts, in raising substantial amounts of money for Devil Pups. Without going into detail, because there may be a law against social extortion by suggestion, I have arm-wrestled some pretty decent amounts out of a few politicians and organizations. The long-term credible and quality organizations that typically are generous, and with which I have solid relationships, include the San Bernardino County Safety Employee's Benefit Association (SEBA), Los Angeles Association of Deputy Sheriffs (ALADS), Los Angeles Police Protective

League (LAPPL), and the San Manuel Band of Mission Indians. At the time of this entry, April 2012, I have some additional potential and very lucrative irons in the donation fire, and have my fingers crossed that they'll come to fruition.

MATTHEW AND SPENCER BECOME "EAGLES"

Colonel Ray Blum, a longtime friend going back to our Vietnam-era days, was for many years the camp commander for the two Devil Pups encampments we hold each year. Several years ago he had an idea to recruit older teenagers who were already Devil Pups graduates, to be assistants to the regular staff. They would wear distinctive shirts and hats, and be known as "eagles." This was a great idea, and it has become a great program. Both of the boys for whom Cathy and I are long-term legal guardians, Spencer Anderson and Matthew Saxton, have served as eagles. Like all of the kids who go through the program, Matthew and Spencer grew individually and profited from their Devil Pups experiences.

ELEVATED TO VICE PRESIDENT

I become involved in Devil Pups at the urging of Tom Vetter, in 1971, and have been involved ever since. Since that time, I have continuously been the liaison officer for the San Gabriel Valley, and have played various roles with LAPD and SBSD-related youngsters (kids of employees, Explorer scouts, magnet schools, etc.) Because of this, and also because of my fundraising accomplishments, I was elevated to "vice president" status about ten years ago, and remain one of the three or four vice presidents on the board of trustees. While enthusiastic about all the non-profit organizations that I am associated with, Devil Pups gets the bulk of my time and discretionary resources.

YEARS OF WONDERFUL FEEDBACK

Cathy and I constantly receive wonderful feedback about the positive impact that Devil Pups has had on the lives of the kids I've sent. The success stories include hundreds of men and women in the military, graduates of service academies, professional sports personalities, and leaders in government, industry and business, and they just keep coming. All of them, and their parents, express absolute praise for the impact that Devil Pups has had on their direction in life.

Chapter Twenty-Three
FAMILY STUFF & STORIES

Pop's Army Service

My dad joined the Army at the end of World War I, but never went overseas. He served after the "Great War," at a time when the military was drawing down and downsizing. I recall that Pop said he was in "Company B" of the First Gas Regiment (it would have been mustard gas in that era!), and that he did his service at Edgewood Arsenal in the state of Maryland. I believe his service lasted about one year. He said that he served as a bugler, and only played twice a day, in the morning and in the evening, then played cards all the rest of the time.

Larry's Marine Corps Service

My brother, Laurence David Bushey, entered the Marine Corps in 1950, when he was seventeen years old. His serial number was 1120485. Larry attended boot camp in San Diego, went to the Field Music School at the San Diego Marine Corps Recruit Depot (I don't know if he graduated or not, but don't recall him working in that specialty), and was first assigned to the Marine Barracks, Naval Shipyard on Treasure Island, at San Francisco.

He and another Marine were pictured on the cover of *Leatherneck Magazine* in July 1951, which is included among the photos in these memoirs. Larry later made buck sergeant and was accepted for Officer's Candidate School, which was really quite a feat for a high school dropout (I guess he earned a GED), even at that time, when there was a serious need for officers due to battle attrition during the Korean War. To get into OCS, he secretly used contact lenses to pass the entry physical, but washed out at the end of the course when he was given another eye test and didn't have his contact lenses with him. Failing OCS was traumatic for Larry. He then requested and got orders for Korea while the war was still going on. I recall visiting him at Camp Pendleton with my mom, and seeing hundreds of Marines in tents, cleaning weapons and preparing to ship out for the Korean War. My mom (and maybe my dad) and I went to San Diego and watched Larry's troop ship, the USS *Mann*, depart San Diego Bay enroute to Korea. It was a sad event for us.

My brother served for a period before the hostilities ended, in the First Marine Division Embarkation Section, which by then was his military occupational specialty. His awards and decorations reflect one campaign star for the Korean War. He returned to the States, where he was eventually discharged in 1955. He always loved the Marine Corps and was justifiably proud of his service. Larry played a major role in my attraction to the Marine Corps, and was proud of my service in that wonderful organization, too.

MOM AND POP: TWO OR THREE DIVORCES?

I always knew that my mom and dad were on their second marriage to each another, having divorced once in the late 1920s or early 1930s. But while recently reviewing the *Los Angeles Times* archives, I saw another divorce announcement (maybe just the filing?) for them in the late 1940s! While recognizing that it takes two to tango, it is my belief that my dad's actions were probably more at fault than those of my mom. I'm aware that my dad was a heavy drinker, gambler and womanizer for much of his younger years. Those qualities typically do not sit well with a wife!

THE RELATIONSHIP BETWEEN MY FATHER AND MY BROTHER

I loved my dad and my brother, but I don't think they had much use for one another. I have to assume there was some love between them, but it was not obvious to me. For years I've been of the impression that my dad was critical of the drama in my brother's life, primarily because Larry (my brother) continually shared his burdens and heartaches with our mom. While I'm sure this reality was a factor, I think the problems go back much farther than that. Dad and Larry just never had much of a relationship. In all fairness, my dad, with his earlier womanizing and excessive drinking for many years, certainly created enough drama himself. In assembling photos for these memoirs, I didn't find a single one of my dad and brother together!

"We Don't Live There Anymore, Mom!"

I was probably around five or six years old when this incident occurred. A policeman stopped my mom for some traffic violation. The officer, while in the process of issuing a citation to my mom, asked if we still lived at the address on her license, and I guess he mentioned the address. My mom said yes we did. But then I immediately corrected her, and blurted out that we no longer lived there! As I recall, that resulted in another vehicle code violation being added to her first citation. I'm sure that my mom would've liked to choke me, but to her great credit she took it in a pretty much humorous light.

Mom Stopped Smoking—Cold!

My mom was a regular smoker until sometime in the 1950s. Then one day she just stopped, cold. Mom was always grateful that she was able to stop smoking, and it probably added a few years to her life.

Pop Stopped Drinking—Cold!

My dad was a heavy drinker until the mid-1950s. I can recall terrible arguments over his drinking, and my mom being very upset. In one instance, when I couldn't have been more than ten or eleven and while we lived on Fourth Street in Alhambra, my mom clobbered my dad, who was drunk, with a frying pan. She drew blood, too.

Those episodes were pretty hard on me. I recall crying a time or two over their terrible arguments, but cannot say they had any real adverse impact on me, then or now. To his great credit, my dad stopped drinking, cold-turkey, I think sometime around 1955. I'm not aware that he took another drink until the day he died. But while taking his own life, he swallowed a lethal number of seconals and downed them with a quart bottle of beer.

Broken-Hearted Over an Ejection Seat

As a kid growing up, I was absolutely obsessed with military surplus. I loved everything green that had a musty canvas smell, and could think of no greater place I would rather be than in a surplus store. There were plenty of surplus stores around, and I loved every one of them.

On one occasion when I was about thirteen years old, I found the Holy Grail of surplus at a store in El Monte—an ejection seat removed from a military aircraft! I think the thing cost me five bucks, and I was thrilled beyond description. But there was a problem of how to get this thing home. My mom and I tried every possible way to get that ejection seat into the trunk of our 1952 Ford, but it just wouldn't fit. I finally took the seat back and got a refund. My heart was broken.

To this day, I still think of that ejection seat!

Larry Bushey's Law Enforcement Career

It is fair to say that I followed in my older brother's footsteps. Like my brother, I went into the Marine Corps as a seventeen-year-old high school dropout. Like my brother, I became a cop. Like my brother, my first law enforcement department was the Los Angeles County Sheriff's Department.

There, however, the similarities end. After a year or so with the sheriff's department, Larry quit and became a policeman in the newly-formed Baldwin Park Police Department, in 1956. He was there only a very short time when he and several other officers were fired. I really I don't know the reason why. He then went to the Buena Park Police Department, where I think he did a pretty good job before quitting and joining the Oakland Police Department. After a fairly short time in Oakland, he left and returned to Buena Park because he missed his family and wanted to try to reunite with his wife. He then got into a difficulty of some sort, and was terminated from that department. What followed were several insurance jobs before he returned to law enforcement as a policeman in the city of Blythe. In Blythe he was injured while making an arrest, and shortly thereafter returned to an insurance job in Palm Springs, where he had a home. While in Palm Springs he had a seizure that apparently was the result of a concussion he'd received when injured in Blythe. During the seizure, Larry broke his back, which was the beginning of the end in terms of his physical deterioration. After that, a series of brief jobs followed, and a lot of medical problems.

David Bushey Passes Away

On January 19, 1963, a Friday, I got early liberty from Camp Pendleton and drove up to our family home in Duarte. When I got there, my dad asked me if I would take him to the El Monte bus station. He wanted to go into downtown Los Angeles, as I recall, to get some medication.

My dad had recently declined another operation that the doctors at the City of Hope wanted him to go through for his cancer. When he declined the operation, he was discharged as a patient, and could no longer receive legitimate medications. As a result, my dad periodically went to downtown Los Angeles and bought Seconals on the black market.

I took him to the bus stop that day, we said goodbye, and that was the last time I ever saw him alive. In the late afternoon when my mother came home from work, she asked were dad was, and I told her I had taken him to the bus stop. She was visibly upset, but didn't say why. It turned out he had been contemplating suicide, and that is why she was upset at his absence.

At about 11 o'clock the next morning, a sheriff's car came to our home and reported that my dad had committed suicide at a motor lodge in Duarte, up on Highway 66. He'd apparently gone downtown, got a bunch of Seconals, returned to the motel on Huntington Drive, wrote a couple of goodbye notes, and washed down the pills with beer.

My dad was a very sick man whose life was more than a difficult existence. He'd had major cancer surgery that included having a portion of his neck removed, radiation treatment that killed his taste buds, he'd contracted tuberculosis as a result of a weakened system, and had emphysema. Toward the end of his life, he was in bed almost continuously, arising only to go to the bathroom or take some bullion as nutrition.

I loved my dad dearly. But, at the same time, I cannot fault his decision to end his miserable existence.

Uncle Reid, Gambling, Golfing and a Real Bad Decision

Reid Hood was one of my mom's younger brothers, and a great uncle to me and my cousin Diana. A life-long bachelor who was a very kind and decent man, he was also quite a good golfer, but not quite as proficient when it came to gambling.

For many years while I was growing up, Reid lived in my grandparents' home at 1011 South Fourth Street in Alhambra. As a twenty-five-year career employee of the Federal Reserve System, he was a typewriter and related equipment repairman. His frequent trips to the card clubs in Gardena reached a highlight one day, when he prematurely quit his job, took all of his retirement contributions out in cash, went to Gardena— and lost it all!

For the rest of his life, Uncle Reid drifted from one small job to another, and from one rooming house to another, with prolonged visits and stays in the homes of his sisters, Mary Bushey and Dorothy Twomey, and his brother, Keith Hood. He was a pleasant man and never stayed long enough to wear out his welcome. When visiting the home of his brother and sister-in-law, my Uncle Keith and Aunt Ilene, and our home, he always brought sock-fulls of pennies to my cousin Diana and me.

602

Reid was living in a rooming house in Rampart Division when I was a sergeant there, and we visited quite often. One day, he told me he was going into General Hospital for some exploratory surgery, and that he was frightened. His fears were justified, as he never regained consciousness after the surgery, and died. We buried him at Rose Hills Memorial Park in Whittier. But at the time we didn't have the discretionary money for a headstone. A few years later I came up with the money, and finally placed a headstone on his grave.

God bless you, Uncle Reid.

Not Remaining "Current" as a Private Pilot

I really enjoyed flying airplanes, but really didn't fly very much after I got my license. Because of the gasoline shortage crisis in about 1973, recreational flying was temporarily suspended for several months. During that time I lost a bit of my proficiency; but it was nothing serious, and could have been easily regained. However, with a growing family I really didn't feel it was fair for me to spend money on flying when I had a couple of little kids, Jake and Stacy. While dumb in many areas, I was smart enough to realize that if I continued to fly, I needed to do whatever I had to do to remain current and proficient. To do so would mean that my family would have to go without a few things.

Interestingly, over the following years I had a couple of Marine Corps buddies, both subordinates, who were certified flight instructors (CFIs) and who volunteered to bring me current. While I really wanted to get current and start flying again, it was all a matter of priorities, and I was not inclined to invest the time and money necessary to again become a safe pilot. The fact that first Barbara and then Cathy both made it clear they didn't want to fly with me was also a factor in not getting back into the cockpit.

I recently acquired a realistic flight simulation program, which is part of a large and high-quality new computer system, and will have to settle for having fun on computer flights.

Larry Bushey Passes Away

I lost my brother Larry on May 8, 1977. In all, it was a very painful and troubling situation. My brother's health had been deteriorating for some time, including having seizures. By then he was living at the Veterans' Administration domiciliary in White City, Oregon. His existence had to have been unbelievably emotionally painful. After a series of law enforcement and insurance jobs, he had pretty much squandered everything in life. He was divorced from his second wife, didn't see much of his son, and further was denied access to the son and daughter he'd had with his first wife for chronic failure to pay child support. His health was deteriorating badly, and he would have been pretty much homeless had it not been for the VA.

As difficult as it was, I'd written to the Department of Motor Vehicles and reported that Larry was having seizures and should not be driving a car. Again, the loss of his driving privilege must have been most painful for him. Toward the end he came down for a short visit, although everyone would have pretty much preferred that he remained in the domiciliary. On the way back to Oregon, he checked into a motel, and while there he passed away. The Sacramento County coroner spent a certain amount of investigative time trying to determine the cause of Larry's death in the motel, but everyone's best guess was that he'd had a major seizure that killed him in his sleep. Obviously, I hope and believe there is a heaven, and desperately hope I will see my brother again, and that we will have the type of relationship that really never existed on earth for us. God bless you, Larry.

KEITH AND THE TROUBLESOME GOAT

Having acquired an acre on a hillside overlooking the San Gabriel Valley, I had grand illusions about being a "gentleman rancher." My wife Barbara thought it would be nice to have horses (we did for a while), sheep (we did for a while), pigs (we did for a while), chickens (we did for a while), and goats (the topic of this story). I truly, and mistakenly, thought that goats would be the answer to keeping the formidable weeds and brush down—the goats would eat everything bad and ugly, and life would be good.

Yeah, right! I didn't realize was how difficult it is to regulate goats, and the reality is that what they want to eat isn't necessarily what you want them to eat! Just leading them to what I wanted them to eat didn't work; they just walked away. Tethering them on a leash in the area where I wanted them to eat didn't work; they came very close to hanging themselves when the rope became tangled. Constructing and placing a temporary corral in the yard to contain the goats where I wanted them to eat didn't work; they dragged and twisted the chain-link all over the acre and again almost hanged themselves (I should've let them!) In the end, I ran out of ideas and the goats had the run of the place, eating everything I didn't want them to eat.

604

The end of the goats occurred one afternoon. A male goat who I really didn't like very well, and who really smelled foul, came up on the front porch and looked at me through the large plate-glass window. I was seated on the couch and just glared back at the little bastard. He then turned around so his rear end was facing the glass, and let go with a truly vigorous bowel movement! With goats, their stool is in the form of circular pellets, and hitting the window those pellets sounded like a mini-machine gun (I may be exaggerating the sound just a tad bit). There was no doubt in my mind, absolutely none, that the goat was telling me what he thought of me. Within a day, all the goats were gone!

Lovely Linda and the Doberman

This tragic situation helped me realize that my ranching and animal-raising skills are not great. I had a nice lamb who I'd named Lovely Linda, and also a Doberman Pinscher dog whose name I don't recall. I had this thought that, if the two animals spent quality time together, with me holding and petting both simultaneously, they would become friendly toward one another.

Wrong! One morning I went to see Linda and found her torn open and bleeding badly. The Doberman had horribly mutilated her. I quickly took her to a vet. Of course, it was expensive, because it was a Sunday and he had to respond to his clinic in Pasadena, and because it took about 160 stitches to close Linda's wound! I probably should have put the animal to sleep, but felt guilty and opted to try to save her. Following the surgery I brought her home and gave her the best care I was able. But soon an infection set in and I finally had the lamb put down.

How foolish it was of me, to think I could tamper with nature and the natural tendency of a Doberman to slaughter small animals. I got rid of the Doberman. I was entirely at fault for this situation.

The Demise of Ozzie and Harriet

Another one of my ranching attempts turned tragic. I had two pigs, who I named Ozzie and Harriet. They were personable, funny and very smart. I don't recall how Harriett died, but at the same time I also had a nice and gentle Great Dane dog who I'd got from the pound. What I didn't know, was that Great Danes were originally bred to hunt wild pigs! One morning the dog teamed up with several local coyotes and slaughtered Ozzie. Again, I felt horrible at my ignorance while dealing with these animals.

Since my property was zoned "agricultural" and could legally acco-modate four horses, I decided to get horses. I had pipe corrals installed along the eastern front of the property, not thinking that the several avocado trees within the corrals would pose a problem. Wrong again! The horses loved avocados! They stripped the trees clean, including the bark, and ate every avocado they could reach or break loose. So much for guacamole!

Jake on Television Wheeling Dead Bodies Out of a House!

I was never sure where the line should have been drawn with respect to Jake's observations and experiences, and as a result there never really was a line. I made captain when he was eight, and even before then he would often accompany me to the station. As an LAPD captain and a single parent, I often responded to homicides, officer-involved shoot-ings, in-custody deaths and other related situations where my little kid could be found asleep in the back of my police car. Jake was always very forceful and inquisitive, and as a result he saw a great deal of death and trauma at an early age.

One day I was watching the news, kicking back because Jake was taking a tour that included the coroner's office. Then I saw Jake on live television, assisting a coroner's investigator in removing a body on a cor-oner's gurney from a house in Willowbrook, where several people had perished in a fire.

I had to chuckle—just another day in the life of Jake Bushey!

Stacy Takes Her Horse on a Walk Through the House!

One day in the early 1980s, I got a phone call from my dear friend Bart Bartel. Bart told me he didn't expect me to believe what he was about to tell me, but that he was serious.

Bart mentioned that, earlier in the day while driving past our house, he saw my daughter Stacy leading a horse out the front door of the house! Obviously, if what Bart was saying was true, Stacy had taken a horse into our home! Later, I confronted Stacy with what Bart told me. She indignantly replied that it was true, and that she'd done it because the horse had never seen the inside of our house!

I truly didn't know what to say. Where do you start with respect to that rationale? I probably just shook my head and asked her not to do it again. By that time, I think I'd learned that my loving and beautiful daughter was also a bit goofy, and trying to reason with her where an animal was involved was futile.

"Oh My God, Dad, You're Embarrassing Me!"

In the mid-1980s, I found and purchased the mechanical love of my life, a Vietnam era, three-quarter-ton Marine Corps personnel carrier. What a beauty! I enjoyed driving it around and basking in the glory of being thought of as a warrior just waiting for our nation's next conflict.

Unfortunately, my daughter Stacy didn't see it in the same light, and was humiliated to even get near my personnel carrier, let alone ride in it. Then one afternoon she lowered her standards and solicited a ride, knowing that my "warrior wagon" was the only vehicle available to take her anywhere. I guess she figured that the worst vehicle was still better than the best shoes! I took her to her destination, which she now recalls was a pizza restaurant.

But I'll never forget her action when we approached the destination, Stacy said something like, "Oh my God, I can't be seen in this thing," and ducked down so her friends couldn't see her! We laugh about it today, but it was pretty serious stuff for my little girl when she was in high school and obsessed with her social image.

Extraordinary Medical Treatment for a Mouse —at My Expense!

If I live to be 100, I know that I'll never completely understand how Stacy's mind works. While in her twenties, she had a gigantic (like fifteen feet long!) Burmese Python snake for a pet. It was kept in her room in a large glass aquarium. To feed the snake she had several white mice in a cage, which reproduced at a high rate of speed and thus provided a reliable flow of food for the reptile.

One day a glitch developed while Stacy was removing a mouse from the cage, and its little leg broke. What could possibly be a simpler problem to solve: a hungry snake and a mouse (which was raised for snake food) with a broken leg! However, that isn't the way Stacy thinks. The mouse instantly transformed from snake food to a victim in my daughter's mind. On top of her guilt-trip, the mouse was a female and apparently Stacy had only been offering up male mice to the snake!

Stacy took the injured creature to a veterinarian and had its little leg fixed and put in a cast—on my credit card! After several days, pneumonia apparently set in. Stacy took the mouse back to the vet and had it put in a specially-constructed oxygen tent in an attempt to save it—again, on my credit card!! As I recall, the medical treatment for that mouse cost me over $525. Predictably, the little creature didn't survive. Still, Stacy didn't feed it to the snake—as I recall it was buried in our yard. I'm surprised she didn't conduct a full-blown funeral with a hearse and internment—on my credit card!

No one argues that Stacy lacks compassion (except for my credit card).

Mary Bushey's Courage, Wisdom, and Thoughtfulness

Just about everyone thinks their mother was the best mom in the world. I know my mom was! I could write volumes about that wonderful woman and my love for her, but this paragraph is reserved to describe her wisdom and unselfishness as she moved up in years. The difficult and painful problems many people have with their parents in their senior years—of convincing them to curtail certain activities or embrace changing factors in their lives—was never a problem for me. Without any hint or suggestion, my mom knew when it was time to stop driving; a few years later knew when it was time to enter a retirement home; and a few years later, when it was time to transition into a nursing home. Although certainly it was always with my assistance, mom initiated each of those actions on her own. If it is possible for anything to match my love for my mom, it is my respect for her!

"Turn That Stuff Off!"

Before we got married, Cathy would occasionally comment favorably on my habit of listening to the radio while lying in bed at night. She felt that my listening to international short-wave transmissions, rescues in the nearby mountains, and the law enforcement stations that I commanded reflected a very positive quest for information. But her complimentary attitude lasted only as long as our engagement. Within days of our getting married, she started telling me to "turn that stuff off!"

"You Know How Dad Drives Close to the Right Side of the Road?"

Although this was a painful experience for our son Zak, there was also a comical dimension in the way he dealt with it. On the very day that he got his driver's license and was able to operate a motor vehicle by himself, he got into an accident when he drove too close to the right side of the road and scraped another vehicle.

Obviously, he was in great distress at the situation and how to tell his mom, me, and Cathy and Paul (my wife and Barbara's husband) what happened. When he notified us, he started out with a statement to the effect of "You know how dad sometimes drives too close the right side of the road?"

The little turd decided he would attribute his accident to having learned this particular bad trait from me! I was somewhere between irritated and amused, but we all agreed that Zak was the one at fault.

The resulting sanctions weren't really too severe on the kid.

Naughty Cowboys and Indians
From my Father-in-Law's Garage!

When Cathy's dad passed away, I just couldn't wait to get into his garage. There were rumors that everything up to and including hidden treasures were in there!

If rumor were fact, there was also a large amount of money on the premises. When we raised the long-sealed garage door, immediately in front of us stood a vertical wall of stuff! It was obvious there was a lot of junk in there, too, so we had a 40' by 12' by 12' dumpster delivered and parked in the driveway.

Some of the first things we found were bags upon bags of decades-old canned goods. A product of the Depression, for a long time Cathy's dad had been acquiring canned goods on sale (but the cans had rusted through and the food was no good). Included were all kinds of things, as her dad at one time or another had sold just about every type of unique trinket and novelty item ever produced, primarily to bars. There were boards and boards full of things like combs and lockets, to be removed and given away to buyers. Among the boards were two that were kind of unique. One had small viewers showing circa WWII nude women (when held up to the light), and the other was filled with cowboy and Indian key chains. During the estate sale I gave these away: the viewers went to the many men waiting for their wives and the key chains to all the kids who were running around.

But when Cathy saw I'd done that, she was really upset, and suggested I'd better take a closer look at the cowboy and Indian key chains. When squeezed, the cowboy produced a penis and sodomized the Indian! Oops!

Altogether, this was quite an experience. We spent the better part of two weekends pulling stuff out of the garage, and either throwing it in the dumpster or selling it to the hoards of South and Central American folks who congregated in the front yard and snapped up all of the bargains. We had to spend quite a bit of time stomping the junk on top of the giant dumpster in order to get the crap below its twelve-foot sides, before the company would haul it away!

BURNING DOWN THE PRAIRIE AND THE LITTLE HOUSE

Cathy's maternal grandparents spent most of their lives in the very historic small South Dakota town of DeSmet. This is the town where Laura Ingalls Wilder, author of the book series *Little House on the Prairie*, spent her formative years. Her books also gave rise to the long-running television series bearing the same name. The first of several trips that we took back there for family reunions was in 1989, and became memorable because of an incident where I feared I was going to burn down the historic town and the prairie.

It happened around the July 4th weekend. I had purchased a large number of fireworks for the kids to set off, so one afternoon I took Zak and another kid to the outskirts of town, where we started shooting off firecrackers and other fireworks. Unfortunately, I set off a wildfire, and was really afraid that the fire would spread out onto the prairie and grow into an inferno that could jeopardize structures and potentially the town. I immediately stripped off my new Levi's jacket and waded into the fire with a vengeance. Amazingly, I beat the flames down and finally got the fire out. I may have overreacted with my concerns, but really feared the fire would develop into an inferno. We all felt relieved when I'd put it out.

"HEY POP, I HAVE A BIRTHDAY COMING UP!"

I pulled off a great surprise fiftieth-birthday party for my dear friend Ray Sherrard. It was a lot of fun, well attended, and a complete surprise.

One of the little surprises for Ray was a well-endowed female stripper, who did a nice and tasteful dance and presentation, stripping down only to bathing suit-type of attire. My son Zak, who was about twelve or thirteen at the time, took great interest in the upstairs attributes of the stripper, to the point of staring somewhat unconsciously. As the party was ending, Zak reminded me that he too "had a birthday coming up!"

EXPLORER JAKE BUSHEY—"FREEZE!"

With a passionate interest in law enforcement since he was just a little kid, my son Jake was born to be a cop, and has become a great one.

Jake was anxious to become an Azusa Explorer scout, and by fudging about his age (and maybe because I was acquainted with a bunch of folks on the department), Jake became an Explorer when he was about twelve. He couldn't get enough of ride-alongs, and was a popular kid with the officers. Interestingly, at the time there were no significant differences between regular officers and Explorer scouts, except the Explorers wore cloth badges and no gun on their duty belt; other than that, a kid could be mistaken for a cop.

One night, Jake was riding with an officer who attempted to question two suspects. Both fled in opposite directions. The officer went after one of them and, unknown to the officer, Jake went after the other suspect! At an opportune moment, Jake, using a deep voice he found somewhere, ordered the suspect to stop and put his hands in the air, and lit him up with his powerful flashlight. The suspect, mistakenly believing that a cop pretty much had him contained, complied. We were proud of Jake; it was an example of his tenacious nature and interest in police work.

"The Stool Does Not Smell Right"

Dorothy and Matt Twomey, my mom's sister and brother-in-law, were the most wonderful aunt and uncle anyone could hope for. They were among my closest relatives while I was growing up, and I spent a great deal of time in their home. Matt had been a Navy Seabee during World War II, and returned home after the war with a lot of malaria still in his body. As a kid, I still recall the difficult nights at their house caused by his profuse sweating and unsettling behavior. As they entered their senior years and eventually went into a nursing home, it was my honor to visit with both of them on a frequent basis, right up until the end. The world is a better place because they were part of it.

Dot was a hypochondriac. Her condition was so acute that when calling or greeting her, you learned not to ask how she was doing, because you would get a long version of all of her ailments, potential ailments, and even remotely possible ailments. Dot and Matt had a daughter, my cousin Sue, who was my brother's age, and Larry and Sue grew up together. Sue married a fellowed named Tom, and they had a daughter, Lori, who was everything to Dot and Matt. Dot, the hypochondriac, was particularly sensitive to any medical problems with Lori, and really outdid herself with an inquiry to the family doctor because Lori's stool "did not smell right!"

Just before the fourth of July weekend in 1980, I was promoted to captain on the LAPD. Knowing the day was going to be pretty much administrative, I took Jake to work with me. I'd just gone into Personnel Division and was issued my new badge, when I got a call to report to the Central Bureau executive offices at the Central Facilities Building. When we got there, we were ushered into the office of Deputy Chief Ron Frankle. Ron, who later became a great friend and my immediate boss, presented me with a new set of captain's bars, which was a very thoughtful gesture.

As Ron and I were chatting, I noticed that Jake was actually sitting on the chief's desk! I was horrified, and told Jake to get off that desk. But Ron intervened and told me to leave the kid alone, that he was welcome to sit on the desk!

That's Ron Frankle, really a good and decent man.

Mary Bushey Slips Away

The evening of March 2, 1998 was one of sadness, relief, and enormous appreciation.

That night, I got the call that I knew was soon to come—my wonderful mom had passed away. Cathy, Jake, Stacy and I immediately responded to the Beverly Manor nursing home and spent some time with that wonderful woman before she was taken to Rose Hills Memorial Park. My sadness stemmed from the loss of the finest mom, grandmother, and mother-in-law who ever existed. The relief was because her diminished quality of life was over, and she was transitioning into eternal life. Finally, as I looked at her and reflected on my life, I was overcome with enormous appreciation for the wonderful life that my mom had made possible for me. I also felt deeply grateful for the love and support my mom had received from the wonderful staff at Beverly Manor.

I did something I never thought I would do—I went against her final wishes that her casket be closed at her funeral. At the visitation on the evening before the funeral, I absolutely couldn't believe how wonderful she looked. Unlike just about every deceased person I have seen—and I have seen plenty—she looked wonderful! Without exaggerating, she looked twenty years younger than she was, vibrant, free from the effects of aging, and at peace. Although sad at the loss of my mom, I was stunned and thrilled that she looked so good. Accordingly, contrary to her wishes, I had her casket opened at the services. If she'd had any idea that she looked so good, perhaps she wouldn't have been opposed to the open casket. I hope I did the right thing, and if not, that mom will forgive me.

STACY CHASES THE WEENIE WAVER!

Any man who exposes himself is well advised to stay clear of my daughter! In the pre-dawn hours on the day after the World Trade Center catastrophe in New York City (September 12, 2001), Stacy drove to a market in Huntington Beach where she believed she could get a copy of the *New York Times*. She was vaguely aware of a car behind her, but it was of no concern at that moment. She parked her car, walked into the market, learned they had no papers there, and returned to her car.

In the lot, parked next to her car, was the car that she'd previously noticed. As she started to drive off, she saw the driver was looking at her and whacking off! He then pulled away. But Stacy decided to give chase and hopefully have him arrested. The chase was on! She chased him all over the place while on the line with 9-1-1, while Huntington Beach police units raced to intercept the two speeding cars. Stacy is one sharp cookie, and when she told me of the dialogue she had with the dispatcher, providing descriptions and directions of travel, it occurred to me that the dispatch folks must have been amazed at her calmness and professionalism.

After about two miles, two marked police units intercepted both cars and stopped the suspect. He was a sex offender who had failed to register and was wanted for it. He was also in possession of drugs, pornographic materials, and stolen computer equipment. Stacy identified him in a field line-up, and made a private citizen's arrest. The suspect was hauled off, and Stacy was thanked for her tenacity. The officers speculated that Stacy wouldn't be required to go to court, and she wasn't. Way to go, Stacy!

ZAK COPIES MY NOTEBOOK OF JOKES

One of the many military courses that I attended created the opportunity to do something I'd long thought about: documenting in small notebooks all the jokes I could recall. For some reason, a lot of things go through my mind during prolonged lectures, and this two-week course in Quantico, Virginia, provided a fertile environment that enabled me to completely fill up two small notebooks with jokes, some of which were really ripe and nasty and certainly not things to be shared with children.

A month or so later, I caught my son Zak copying my jokes into his notebooks! I probably should have confiscated his little humorous stash, but as I recall I just chuckled and left well enough alone.

Bedroom Qualifies for Toxic Superfund Cleanup

To see our wonderful, clean, and articulate oldest foster son today, you would never guess that Danny was such a slob through high school and college. While a bit scraggly at times, he was usually at least clean. But his room was another matter. The heaps of candy wrappers, burger bags, old drink containers and other related worthless items had almost merged with each other, and were being held together by grime and old leaking liquids. Cathy just gave up and kept his door closed. When he got a real job as a firefighter and moved out, we were sad for two reasons: we hated to see him go, and we couldn't stand the thought of dealing with the disaster he left behind in that room! Today he is as neat as a pin (well, almost).

Jake and Military Bases

About 1980, after Barbara and I separated, I decided to start taking Jake with me when I went on military leaves of absence. Obviously, I couldn't pull this off when I was on prolonged maneuvers in the field or deployed overseas, but for training at domestic bases I thought I could make it work. To accomplish this, I had to feel comfortable with the assumption that I could solve whatever problems Jake's presence might create once I got on base. This turned out to be the case. I figured that once I got to a base, I could take advantage of childcare centers, or perhaps be able to have Jake spend days while I was in class with the permanent personnel I was sure to meet. As it turned out, even at a fairly young age Jake didn't need childcare.

Jake at Fort Bliss—Kicking Back with Potato Chips

Fort Bliss (Texas) is the first base I took Jake to. Before departing for the base on a two-week military commitment, I spent some time on the phone, exploring the possibility of a place where Jake could stay during the day. Pretty much, I got the bureaucratic shuffle and run-around. The childcare center said their facility was only for permanent personnel, and referred me somewhere else where no one answered the phone. The school command to which I had orders said there was no provision for dependents during my two-week stay. I then spoke to a Marine sergeant in the Marine Liaison Office (it was an Army base, but Marines regularly attended courses there), and he said Jake was welcome to stay at his house and play with his kids while I was tied up. Great!

On our arrival at Fort Bliss, the first thing I did was take Jake to the home of the Marine sergeant and drop him off. The sergeant and his wife were really nice folks, and I knew it would out work fine. Wrong! I spent the next couple of hours running around, going through processing, getting a vehicle, and acquiring lodging. But when I went to the sergeant's house to retrieve Jake, they said he was gone! Jake told them to say he would meet me at the bachelor officer quarters. Since I had trouble finding the quarters where I was going to stay, I couldn't imagine that an eleven-year-old kid could find them, and was more than a little worried about him.

Anyway, I drove to the quarters and what did I see—Jake kicking back under a shade tree, drinking a Coke and eating potato chips! That's when I began to realize just how independent and uniquely competent my son was.

"Keith Ate a Turd!"

One afternoon around the year 2000, two of Cathy's little nephews were at our house in Big Bear. Richie is the son of Cathy's sister, Nancy, and Michael is the son of Cathy's late brother, Raymond.

Earlier in the day I got some chocolate fudge, then saw the opportunity for some mischief. I took some of the fudge, rolled it into the shape of a dog turd, and put it out in the grass. Then I called Richie and Michael over and began educating them about how they could identify the type of animal that left a pile of crap by the turd's visible characteristics. I went to a lot of trouble to point out the unique shape and configuration of the "turd" on the ground, and even pointed out that its tapering was an indication of the size of the animal's rectum.

I encouraged both boys to get down on their hands and smell the turd so they could recognize its uniquely "pungent" odor. Then I explained how the turds from the animal I was describing, which I think I said was a coyote, had a very bitter taste. Both boys recoiled at the thought of even getting close to the "turd," let alone smelling or tasting it. But I reached over, picked up the "turd," and took a bite out of it! Both boys recoiled in horror and ran off screaming to Cathy that "Keith just ate a turd!"

I guess this helps illustrate my sick sense of humor, but I think it was pretty funny and have actually pulled the stunt on a couple of other occasions with other kids.

Farts Follow Maggie in Denver

This was just too funny! It involved one of my favorite pieces of technical equipment, my multi-sound fart machine. At some point in the early 2000s Cathy's family had a reunion, and everybody met in Denver. Among her relatives are Jerry and Maggie Bale, from Huron, South Dakota, both of whom are really nice and fun people.

One evening, we all took a walk in downtown Denver, where I managed to slip the fart machine into Maggie's very large straw purse. As she and Jerry walked several blocks I followed about forty or fifty feet behind them and activated the fart machine every time they passed someone. Surprisingly, Maggie didn't realize that the farts were coming out of her large bag, and Jerry's hearing is as bad as mine and he didn't hear the farts. Maggie is a pretty big gal (attractive and well proportioned), and the fact that her bag was so large and hung down quite a way contributed to the success of my treachery! When we got back to our hotel, and they were talking to the bell captain, I transmitted a gigantic fart. Maggie then realized what had been going on. Prior to then she'd heard the farts, but thought they were coming from me (she knew I had the machine). Maggie was horrified when she realized what had happened, but demonstrated her characteristically good humor through the whole affair.

A Little Boy Who Needs to Be Safe

In November of 2001, Cathy called and informed me that we were going to have a guest for dinner: a foster child whom she'd agreed to take into our home. Cathy explained that the social worker from the Department of Children & Family Service (DCFS) caught her at a weak moment, and the situation especially tugged at her heartstrings when the worker said "the little boy needs to feel safe."

We'd become Danny Bustamante's legal guardians when his mom died, but with Danny now off on his own, DCFS had us in their crosshairs as a home for foster kids. They really knew when to strike! That night we met eight-year-old Spencer Anderson, and he is still with us! But we had some pretty unsettling experiences around 2003, when, after helping his mother get him back by supporting her rehabilitation efforts, she re-offended. It got ugly. Some incompetent people with DCFS dropped the ball, and then the agency stonewalled us while standing solidly behind their problem employees.

Spencer went back with his mom but was in jeopardy most of the time. Finally, after about three years, in September 2006 I got a phone call from a DCFS social worker with whom I wasn't acquainted. She said they had just taken a boy into protective custody because his mother had overdosed and was in a coma and not expected to live. The little boy had a piece of paper in his hand with my name on it, and she wanted to know if I had any knowledge of the situation.

I informed her that we'd been waiting several years for her phone call, and that we would take him immediately as a foster child. But she replied it wasn't quite that simple, because of all the things people need to do to qualify as foster parents. I told her to enter our name into the DCFS computer. She was thrilled to learn that we were certified foster parents with DCFS, and that Spencer had previously lived in our home. Within two hours Spencer was back with us, and he hasn't left since.

Keith Bushey Conducts an Investigation

Spencer's mother remained in a coma for almost three months. She finally came out of it, but was in very bad shape. She was unsteady and almost totally deaf, but got some mobility back.

Then, after several months DCFS advised us that she wanted her son back, and that she might actually get him! It seems that, because everyone thought she wasn't going to survive, no investigation was done to establish and document all of the neglect that occurred during the three years that Spencer was gone from us! That did it! I decided I would conduct an investigation.

I interviewed over a dozen people who were familiar with Spencer and his mother. Each interview was typed, certified as accurate by me, included all contact information and indicated that each of the interviewees was available for future contact and/or court testimony. The report made clear that Spencer had continually been at risk at home, that his mother was continually under the influence, and that DCFS had badly dropped the ball. I had several copies of the report professionally bound at a stationery store.

Using my exalted position as a member of the executive staff of the district attorney's office, I then set up a meeting with the director of DCFS. At our meeting, she was joined by a few top members of her staff. I threw down the gauntlet by providing her and all the others present copies of the report. I also asked if she would take it and do something about the problems in her office—or should I give the report to a member of the Los Angeles County Board of Supervisors, which was clearly not a supporter of DCFS?

It turned out to be a very nice meeting. The director said she would take the matter seriously, and that she appreciated me providing her a copy of the report and the opportunity to address the issues. Within just a few days, the attorney for Spencer indicated there was no way that his mother would get Spencer back, and that he would be remaining in our home.

I Will Think of Nice Things. I'll Think of You!

When we took in two brothers, Daniel and Matthew, during December 2003, it was immediately obvious that Matthew had a morbid fear of darkness. Nothing I tried to break his fear seemed to work, and any time I covertly turned the lights off, or even down, he found a way to restore light. One night we had a long chat just before he went to sleep, and I encouraged him to just close his eyes and think about something nice. He replied that he would try real hard, and then said he would "think about me."

It was a very touching moment.

Could We Take a Little Girl for a Week or So?

On March 31, 2006, our social worker friend called and asked if we could take in a four-year old girl for no more than a week or two. She showed us a picture of the little gal, explaining that she had been living with two step-siblings and their grandmother. But then the girl's grandmother called out of the blue and demanded that the child be immediately removed from their home.

The picture was heartbreaking. It showed a child whose face reflected a combination of pain, anguish, unhappiness and sadness. We agreed to take in little Danielle Avila. But the weeks turned into months, and then into years, and her name is now Danielle Bushey! Some of the things that bring me tremendous joy are just watching her skipping, being happy, singing with the radio, singing along with karaoke on the computer, and just being a happy little girl.

Although another family would most certainly have come along and adopted Danielle, had we not done so, we provided a better life than she likely would have otherwise had. With us, she came and stayed. Had we not adopted her, she most likely would have been placed into one more, and possibly two more, homes. It would have been terribly traumatic to the wonderful little gal who needed time and stability and consistent love to recover from the bad experiences with her grandmother, the grandmother's boyfriend, and her two older step-siblings. We love her unconditionally and are grateful that she is part of our family.

The Joy of Foster Children

Before the untimely death of our first foster child's mother, I don't recall that Cathy and I gave any real serious consideration to taking in foster children. Danny's mom passed away while he was visiting with us one weekend, and he learned of her death only when we took him home. When we were notified by the Rampart watch commander about what had occurred, we never gave a second thought to not taking Dan into our home. After all, he'd been like a son to us ever since he was an infant.

When Dan grew up and flew the coop, we retained our foster home license. But again we didn't give much thought to taking in another kid. That all changed when DCFS told Cathy there was a "little boy who needed to feel safe," and Spencer came to us.

Taking in foster kids, especially being long-term guardians to some (Spencer and Matt) and adopting another (Danielle), isn't for everyone. But it works for us. We've found a great deal of satisfaction knowing that we are making a real difference in the lives of little people, and that because of us they have a much better chance of finding better lives as adults. Foster parenting is not without its challenges, though. Just about every foster kid brings emotional baggage. We've had several whose behavior was such that we chose not to keep them in our home.

"Mexicans Don't Eat Chocolate Pudding"

Danielle is one of the funniest little people whom I've ever met, and frequently comes up with expressions that I get a real kick out of.

After dinner one night, I suggested that she might like a bowl of chocolate pudding. She replied, "Mexicans don't eat chocolate pudding!" Where she came up with that I don't know, but apparently she has forgot her Hispanic heritage, because it's not unusual for her to eat chocolate these days.

Snuggles and Snot

Little Danielle came to our home as a foster child eligible for adoption, in March 2006, when she was four and a half. It wasn't long before she wormed her way into our hearts. But it took some doing for me to worm my way into her heart, because she had previously been mistreated by a man. So it was quite a while before she warmed up to me. For the first several months, she became disturbed when I attempted to show any physical affection. I thought she was starting to warm up after a few months when she snuggled up to me once in a while; then I realized she was snuggling up just to wipe her snot on my shirt! I didn't get upset in the least, a snuggle with snot is better than no snuggle at all! Besides, that unique initial snuggle was part of a long road that led to the father-daughter affection we share today.

Drying Out a Wet Newspaper—Burning Down the Kitchen!

This certainly wasn't one of my smartest moves. Around 2005, Cathy and I hired a contractor to do a great deal of work on our house. We added a second story, another bedroom, another bathroom, and had the kitchen remodeled.

About a month after the remodel was completed, one rainy day I was chagrined to find that the newspaper in the driveway was wet and therefore unreadable. In the past, I had dried the paper by lighting the oven and placing the wet paper on the open door. But, this day I decided to put the paper in the microwave for a minute or so. Not a good decision! The paper caught fire, I couldn't put it out, and the flames quickly spread to the surrounding cabinets. Cathy called 9-1-1 and the fire department arrived in about five minutes and quickly put out the fire. The damage amounted to something like $30,000 to our just-remodeled kitchen! We did a lot of eating out for the next month or so while the kitchen was being repaired. One of our first new purchases was a fire extinguisher!

Got a Big Part of My Life Back on December 31, 1999

For the better part of the 1990s, I spent a great deal of time visiting my mom, her sister and her sister's husband, in retirement and nursing homes.

My mom and Uncle Matt and Aunt Dot were among the most wonderful people in the world, and were always there for me in every way. As their lives wound down, it was my honor and pleasure to spend a considerable amount of time with them in both retirement and later in nursing homes.

But then it got real bad during the last three or so years, when Aunt Dot decided she didn't want anything to do with my mom because of a dispute they'd had over a boy back in the World War I era. Aunt Dot also tired of her husband.

620

Although all three lived in the same nursing home, Monrovia Manor, they were in different wings. So I had to visit each one separately, as opposed to my initial plan of visiting all of them in a nice family setting. It ate up more and more of my time, but I loved them dearly and spent quality time with each one. My mom was the first to pass, followed by her sister. On the last day of the 20th century, I went to the Arcadia Methodist Hospital to visit Uncle Matt, who had been temporarily transferred there from Beverly Manor. I found him deceased in his hospital bed. While of course it was sad to lose my uncle, there wasn't much of a person left in that pathetic shell, and I'll admit to feeling a tremendous sense of relief at no longer needing to spend time at Beverly Manor. I got a big chunk of my life back that day.

SPENCER'S POND

I doubt a more avid fisherman than Spencer exits! This kid loves everything about fish, from catching them to eating them to just watching them. Regardless of where we go, he wants to fish, and is good at it.

When Spencer was fifteen, with Matthew's assistance he built an absolutely beautiful and professional pond in our yard. He designed it, dug it out, modified it, lined it, installed lighting, installed and maintained a filtration system, then filled it with hundreds of fish. He knows fish very well, which species can co-exist with one another, and how to help them survive. He also constructed devices to keep raccoons, possums and predatory birds from getting at his fish.

Today. it's very common for Spencer to throw his sleeping bag on the ground and sleep next to his pond—that's how much he loves it. On several occasions, Spencer has continued to fish at Big Bear when it was bitterly cold and everyone else had gone inside. The kid would rather fish than eat, and doesn't let little details like the freezing cold keep him away from his beloved fish.

SPENCER SUSTAINS SERIOUS INJURIES AT DUMONT DUNES

In 2010, Spencer, Matt and I joined my good pal, Mark Adame and his son, Sampson, for a weekend at Dumont Dunes. The dunes are located in the rural desert of San Bernardino County, about forty miles outside of Baker.

The boys were riding their four-wheel quads and I was riding my side-by-side Polaris. Spencer rode my old Honda 450cc five-speed "Foreman" that was intended as a workhorse utility vehicle, while Matt was doing some fancy riding and jumping on his quad that had been designed for that type of activity. Spencer decided to follow suit on his quad, but it wasn't designed for jumping. He tried a jump that had a great take-off, but a really bad landing, and he "crashed and burned" big time!

It was clear that he was in pain and feeling pretty lousy. My first inclination was to keep an eye on him and take him to the hospital if problems began to develop. After some reflection, heavily influenced by the fact that I was at least an hour and a half from the nearest hospital in Barstow, I realized that taking the chance might not be a good idea. So I drove him to the emergency hospital in Barstow, and it turned out to be a wise decision. Spencer's pelvis was broken in two places, he had a crack in his back and a bruised liver, but fortunately no tearing. Because Kaiser is our health provider, they chose to do the treating, so we arranged for him to be taken by ambulance to the Baldwin Park Kaiser facility. He was in the hospital for a couple of days, followed by a few days of bed rest at home. Within about six weeks he was completely healed!

DANIELLE INVITES EVERYONE TO A PARTY

When she was about nine, Danielle decided we should have a party at our home. The problem was that her decision was made on the spur of the moment, and wasn't discussed with Cathy or me. Danielle posted an announcement on Facebook, about three hours before the "party" was to happen. Fortunately, people were curious about the posting and called Cathy and me. We quickly pulled the plug on Danielle's little scheme.

ZAK'S SENSE OF COMMUNITY

I am very proud of the person that Zak has become. He is friendly and outgoing, and ends up playing a leadership role wherever he goes. As I write this, he is a key person in his homeowner's association and well known within the Glendora Community. He is a master at using the computer to reach large numbers of people, and wisely uses this resource in his profession as a realtor.

STACY—THE PERSON WHO HOLDS HER OFFICE TOGETHER

Stacy definitely inherited her mother's invaluable organizational and management skills. Just like Barbara, Stacy is the hub of the wheel at her place of employment, and the person that pretty much coordinates everything that occurs. By virtue of her skills, dependability, and work ethic, Stacy has become an invaluable and close to irreplaceable employee. She is the ideal office manager.

Chapter Twenty-Four
SELF-ANALYSIS

I have always recognized that there are instances when other people know us better than we know ourselves. However, I pretty much know the person who I want and try to be. This section is devoted to letting others know the qualities that I value and have strived to achieve and demonstrate in my life.

Seek to Be Kind

Being a kind person is just about at the top of my list. I try very hard to be kind to others in all that I do. I recognize that every person I deal with is a living, caring human being who possesses all of the same internal thoughts and feelings that I possess. There are too many people in this world who appear not to be kind, or who are continually indifferent. Being kind to children, especially all of my kids (natural, adopted, foster, and grandkids) is especially important. Being described by others as a kind person is about as good as it gets for me.

I clearly recall my dad as having been a kind man. Although my paternal grandfather, Jacob Bushey, died before I was born and I never knew him, my mom always spoke well of him and described him as a very kind and considerate person. I hope I'm a kind person and, if so, it must be in the genes.

I must add a caveat: my kindness goes out the window when dealing with bad and evil people.

Genuine Fondness for People

I truly like people, and find them to be interesting. It is common for me to seize the opportunity to strike up a conversation with people, and we will almost always find common and familiar ground. While driving along a freeway, I occasionally glance at all the houses I'm passing and feel a tinge of sadness knowing that most of those houses contain wonderful people whom I'll never have the opportunity to meet. There is no doubt that some really bad people exist out there, but I believe that I've been successful in not forgetting they are but a very small percentage of humanity. I look for the good in people, and usually find it.

Making Your Part of the World a Better Place

I cannot change the world, or even a small part of it, but I have the ability to make the small part of the world that is my universe a better place for those who live in it. As an employee and boss, I accomplish this by taking my responsibilities seriously and trying to excel in leadership skills. I recognize that every person who works for and with me is the most important person in the world to somebody, and I always try to treat each employee the way I would hope someone would treat my son or daughter under the same circumstances. As a friend and neighbor, I hope I am kind, helpful and understanding, see the world for what it is as opposed to what it should be, and work hard to develop and maintain good relationships.

Last to See Evil in Other People

This is a real issue that helps to describe who I am, and realistically is something that has caused some close friends over the years to occasionally question my judgment. In many instances, while in personal and professional relationships, I have persevered with friendships and retained confidence in some when perhaps I shouldn't have been so charitable. Although certainly self-serving to say, I think this trait has been more of an advantage than a disadvantage throughout my lifetime. I am fond of saying that I look for the good in people, and usually find it. Also, I am aware that as a boss I have a reputation for being able to work with subordinates who have challenging and unique personalities. Still, I have been disappointed by a few folks through the years, especially when watching some of my long-time LAPD colleagues significantly lower their ethical standards for their own personal benefit while working for a weak and problematic police chief.

Premarital Understandings—Marine Corps

There are some issues so important, that a couple is wise to have a clear understanding about them before tying the knot. With my first marriage to Barbara and my last marriage to Cathy, there were pre-martial understandings with both that I intended to remain active in the Marine Corps Reserve. They included occasional prolonged absences due to training and, if required, mobilization to active duty.

As an interesting related comment, I have had discussions on this topic with scores, maybe hundreds, of men. I can't count the number of men who told me they didn't stay in the military because their wife or fiancé made it clear she would leave if he did. So they chose not to remain in the military. Often, the marriage didn't work out, anyway!

My advice, usually ignored, is that if she says it is either her or the military, tell her goodbye! It is not so much the military versus love or loyalty issue, but rather the need for a spouse to recognize and support a strong desire on the part of a man. Usually, this is the first in a long list of demands. Find someone else!

Do Not Take Advantage of Other Peoples' Ignorance

I would never be a good pawnbroker, because I don't have the inclination to take advantage of people. The best example can be found in badge collecting, where I'm candid with people and tell them the true value of a badge I desire to acquire, often when they have no idea of its value and are likely to blindly accept my assessment. Some of my fellow collectors are just the opposite and will gladly, if given the opportunity, pay a very small amount for a valuable badge, then turn around and sell it for many times what they paid for it.

Friendly

Some will say that I'm too friendly toward strangers, but that just happens to be my nature and I'm comfortable with who I am. It is rare when I don't go out of my way to be friendly and engage in fun or light-hearted conversations with people. For instance, when offered a receipt by a saleswoman, I will often tell her to "Keep it, to remember our good times together." There are far too many people who fail to recognize that fun and friendly people bring out the best in others.

Generous Tipper

I am definitely a generous tipper, and never refer to any scale in determining the amount to be left a server. I'm influenced because of my like for people, and also when I think of my daughter, Stacy, and her experiences as a waitress at a Sizzler restaurant while working her way through college (with our assistance). Stacy told us about a very large group that would come into the restaurant every Sunday after church, be demanding, and typically leave a one-dollar bill as a tip.

Maybe I'm compensating for those types of cheapskates!

Also, I'm aware that I typically get better service than most other people. Why? Because I go out of my way to be a fun and friendly customer, and servers almost always respond with great service and a good attitude. Some complainers need to realize that they are often contributing to mediocre service by virtue of their attitudes.

Do Not Lie

Honesty truly is the best policy, and as we mature it becomes very apparent. A lie is often today's solution, but tomorrow's nightmare.

We can fix broken bones, broken cars, and broken equipment, but it is much harder to repair someone's integrity. There are only four times when it is all right to lie: When someone is dying in your arms, and you tell them they'll be okay. You can lie to a suspect all you want. You can exaggerate someone's performance at their retirement celebration. Finally, you can tell a mother that her ugly baby is cute. Other than that, tell the truth. As all husbands can attest, remaining silent is not a lie, and it is often the best course of action in certain situations.

Courage to Personally Deliver Bad News

Everybody likes to deliver good news, and some people actually try to out-maneuver each other to be the first to pass on happy info. Unfortunately, the number of people who have the courage, or courtesy, or both, to personally deliver unpleasant information is much smaller. Throughout my careers, I have developed the perspective that delivering bad news in any manner other than face-to-face is an indication, to some extent, of a character flaw in someone in a position of leadership. Giving people information that is likely to be painful or troubling via note, text, e-mail or through another person, is cowardly. I do not enjoy delivering bad news. But when I do, it comes directly from my mouth and, unless impractical, when I am looking the recipient right in the eyes.

Afraid of Heights

Isn't this weird? I am both a pilot and a parachutist, but I'm afraid of heights. I have stood in the doorway of many planes, and on the skids and ramps of many helicopters, for prolonged periods, often in an aircraft that is bouncing up and down or doing some fancy maneuvers, waiting to bail out, and never had a problem. But to look over the edge of Hoover Dam or into the Grand Canyon, I get scared shitless and my knees turn to Jell-O.

This doesn't make much sense, but that's the way that I am. I have had some experiences where I had to set my fears aside, such as Marine Corps mountain warfare training and as a cop on fire escapes in tall buildings, but I suspect in those instances I didn't have the time to reflect on my fears. Certainly, I wasn't going to crumble in the eyes of my peers.

Writing as a Catharsis

A human trait is to talk a great deal about things that are important to us, both good and bad. With respect to the people and situations that have caused a great deal of pain in my life, I've found that I become pretty prolific and lengthy while writing about such things. I think this is probably more good than bad, at least in my case, because my pain has also resulted in a strong motivation to write about my experiences, and the lessons that others can learn from those experiences. Accordingly, in these memoirs there appear a few instances which, with the passage of time, I have chosen to discuss with far fewer words than were in the original draft.

Listen to a Radio at Night

I guess I must have inherited the trait of listening to a radio at night from my mom, who loved to listen to "talk radio" all night long. I have always been a "Type A" person, and listening to police and fire transmissions and shortwave broadcasts has been enjoyable and something I have done most of my adult life.

As I get older, and sleep becomes a bit more difficult, I find that listening to a radio is a good thing and usually helps me to fall asleep, as opposed to tossing and turning and trying to go to sleep without some type of assistance. Living on the West Coast in the Pacific time zone is great, because the really hot newcasts from the East Coast start at 6 a.m. East Coast time, which is 3 a.m. West Coast time. Whenever I wake up earlier than I want to, I just put on my earphones and listen to the satellite radio transmissions from the East Coast.

Minimize Repetitive Verbalization

When I was a sergeant in the Manuals & Orders Unit of the LAPD, I used to often use the expression, "that we have to recognize and appreciate." One day, when initiating a conversation with one of my men, he did a preemptive strike and said something to the effect of, "yeah, yeah, sarge, I know that we have to recognize and appreciate......!" Ever since that time, with the exception of fun phrases, I try not to use repetitive expressions in my conversations, but rather try to continually vary my words and expressions in the manner that I converse, at least to some extent.

Why? I don't know, I just do!

Minimize Use of Hands
in Verbalization

I think I would probably be a pretty good technical writer, because I try, both on the phone and in my writings, to clearly explain things. Obviously, in such instances no facial or hand expressions are possible. I would rather not use anything other than verbalization, for the most part, when I talk with other people. Why? Again, I don't know, I just do!

Changed With the Times

Most of us are not the same person we were several decades ago. I'm ashamed to admit that I did harbor some racial prejudices as a young person, but believe that I do not now, nor for many years have I harbored any of those types of bias whatsoever. I care only about a person's character, and work hard to instill the same belief in my children and others with whom I deal.

As a new policeman, I was pretty much in the mainstream of that era with fists that occasionally replaced verbal commands, but those tendencies began evaporating early in my career. I have long been an absolute crusader for verbalization and other methods of avoiding physical force, and for using only the force necessary when other methods fail.

Ethical

The only person I dislike more than someone who is unethical, is a hypocrite who exercises selective ethical behavior. To me, a reputation for consistent good character and unyielding ethics is everything. In raising this issue I am not suggesting opposition to everything I don't like, because there are many things that I don't care for that are not ethical issues, but rather just discretionary issues with which I disagree. Unfortunately, for some people loose ethics are like an outhouse—as time goes on you become accustomed to the odor, it becomes less offensive, and ultimately it ceases to be a consideration.

Passionately Loyal to Friends

I never forget a friend, and just about always try to be there for him or her in particularly trying times. While I certainly am not involved in every little issue involving my pals, when things really get tough they can count on my absolute support to the maximum amount of effort I can provide. When a loved one or a close friend is hurting, so am I.

Circumstances Certain to Bring Tears to my Eyes

Except for the loss of a loved one, I am pretty much a non-emotional guy. With a few exceptions. I moisten up a bit during a wedding when the happy couple walk down the aisle to the sound of "Here Comes the Bride," and at the birth of a child when I hear those first healthy crying sounds. However, my biggest emotions when I try to hide my tears occur at the sight of young (old, too!) servicemen and women coming home, walking through airports, and being greeting by their loved ones.

The worst such case, and I'm glad I was alone, was watching just-released prisoners-of-war from the Vietnam era exit the planes and rush to their families.

Respect the Girls I Have Dated

I honestly do not recall dating any girl or woman I didn't both respect and like as a person. I was never into "one-night stands," or "bar hopping." As I look back over several of my pleasant and relatively long-term relationships, I do so with continued warmth for those very nice ladies, and wish nothing but the very best for them.

Amorous Restraint

My life has created a great many opportunities for "amorous" encounters. Without suggesting that I'm a prude, I can say without reservation that I have successfully resisted some most attractive opportunities throughout my lifetime.

As a young Marine who traveled all over the world, I was in the minority in that I never availed myself of the many attractive (or unattractive!) prostitutes who were in absolute abundance for reasonable prices. As a Marine officer, although it was difficult on occasion, I followed the "no fraternization rules" (which, by the way, I believe are too stringent) and resisted the temptation to become romantically involved with several very appealing female enlisted Marines throughout my career. As a college instructor, I rarely dated students, and only then when the semester was coming to an end and the grades had been finalized. Finally, as the commanding officer of the Communications Division within LAPD, with several hundred female employees, many of who were single and continually signaled their availability, I stayed clear of my employees until the very end of my tour, when I picked one out and married her!

My Many Aches, Pains, Back Injuries
—From an Active Life

I wish that my lower extremities were as enthusiastic as my mind! As I climb the ladder of life, and get closer to the top, I am starting to daily experience the consequences of an active, reckless, and occasionally violent life! As a thirty-nine year Marine (especially a parachutist), a forty year-plus cop, and an avid outdoors person who has fallen off my share of trails and tumbled down my share of slopes, I am pretty much like the aging former rodeo rider. Add to this, in addition to the usual cop experiences, the trauma that we now know results from years of wearing a Sam Brown gun and equipment belt.

If I had the opportunity to start over again—I cannot think of anything that I would do differently. I bear my aches and pains as a reflection of the fun and satisfaction I have experienced in life, along with the things I am fortunate to have accomplished.

The Prosperity I Have Achieved

I have got to be one of the luckiest guys around. Never in my wildest dreams did I ever think I would attain the prosperity that I now enjoy. While I am not a millionaire in terms of available cash, I am able to provide (especially with Cathy's retirement income, as well) a very comfortable existence for my family and me.

Realistically, as a kid I don't recall having any goals beyond just becoming a Marine, and certainly harbored no thoughts of the absolutely-unattainable feat of becoming a commissioned officer. As a cop, I just wanted a badge, a car-full of radios and antennas, and free donuts. Like many of us, I just kind of lucked into where I ended up, and often wonder what my future might have been if I hadn't failed Arcadia's oral examination for policeman. Or, more bizarre, if I had been hired as a cop in Blythe? What would have happened if I hadn't gone sideways with Willie Williams and his pals, and didn't go to San Bernardino? What would have happened if I had not had a solid reputation with the sheriff's department at the time of the marshal-sheriff merger—would I have been eliminated from the picture as occurred in several other counties? What would have happened if I had not met Tom Vetter, and ultimately returned to the Marine Corps as a commissioned officer?

I am extremely grateful for the life I have, and continue to enjoy. I'm also grateful for the positive consequences of my past and present activities and accomplishments—and for not totally crashing and burning when some of my actions weren't all that great!

Be the Best at Whatever Your Are

This comment is attributed to Abraham Lincoln. As with so much of Lincoln's wisdom, it is true and applicable and powerful and essential to any man or woman of character. A person of character who continues to do his or her best, especially in the face of adversity, and ends up with a few titles and material objects, is a person I would much rather associate with than someone who "fell into" their prosperity. People who always do their best and continue to "lean forward" are my heroes!

Chapter Twenty-Five
FAVORITE THINGS

United States Marine Corps

By now, it should be obvious that I am very high on the Marine Corps. Any doubts can be eliminated by a quick trip to my home in the middle of the night, to see the well-illuminated American and Marine Corps flags atop an industrial flagpole in my front yard. I was about five years old when my brother, Larry, joined the Marine Corps. My fascination for the Corps has been strong ever since. Enough said.

Uniforms

I have always been fascinated with military uniforms. As a little kid, I loved going to surplus and second-hand stores, where I frequently purchased uniforms. I would put them on, sew on or move around their insignias, and just have a great time. It wasn't until about the eighth grade that some of the uniforms actually fit me, and by then I had stopped playing in that manner. But Halloween was a favorite time because I could wear a uniform without being out of place. As mentioned elsewhere in these memoirs, my pal Don Middleton and I actually dressed up like sailors and went hitchhiking at about the age of fourteen or fifteen, and of all things, we got picked up by a real Navy chief petty officer!

On November 13, 1961, the Marine Corps gave me a whole duffle bag of uniforms—and they were all mine! My entire subsequent life has involved uniforms: military, police, sheriff, marshal, and game warden!

Medals & Insignias

I have always had a passion for collecting medals and insignias. Even as a little kid, I scoured second-hand and thrift shops, and was always buying patches, badges, and insignias. On a couple of very short family vacations to San Diego, I would walk up and down Broadway, visiting all the tailor shops and asking for the patches on the floor that had been taken off uniforms when new ones were sewn on. The tailors were always nice, and told me to help myself.

War Surplus Stuff

As a kid growing up, there was no place on earth I would rather be in than a war surplus store. Fortunately for me, there were tons of surplus available from World War II and, to some extent, from the Korean conflict. The wonderful smell of all that canvas was intoxicating to me. Gas masks, helmets, leggings, cartridge belts, tents, insect netting, patches, boots, uniforms, insignias, etc.—what could have been more appealing? When I grew up and went into the military, the bases I was assigned to merely became big surplus stores (really big ones!)

Sleeping Bags

Ever since I was a little kid, I really enjoy snuggling up in a sleeping bag. Among my earliest recollections are a new flannel sleeping bag, along with toy guns and a red wagon, under the Christmas tree. As an old fart these days, I never get through the night without getting up a few times to relieve myself. When we're out camping, getting up is a real pain, but crawling back into that warm flannel sleeping bag is about as good as it gets!

BB Guns

I grew up with a gun in my hand, from toy guns to BB guns to pellet guns, and as an adult I've owned and used a whole variety of weapons. Throughout my younger years and up into high school, I became absolutely deadly with my BB gun and, without fear of contradiction, I fired thousands of BBs and pellets. From about 1957 until almost the time I went into the Marine Corps in 1961, I prowled the Santa Fe Dam with my dog and my BB gun, blasting away. In hindsight, I am truly sorry (actually, ashamed) for all the innocent birds and lizards that I shot, and I have plenty to be sorry about.

Scanner Radios

I have been a radio nerd for my entire life. I have always found police and fire radio transmissions to be of tremedous interest, and fascinating. As a teenager, I listened whenever I could when some transmissions were at the bottom of the AM broadcast band. As a new cop, I bought the latest in scanners. In the late 1960s, while visiting the Radio Product Specialities (RPS) store at 1501 South Hill Street (downtown Los Angeles), I became absolutely estatic on discovering the brand-new Uniden 210 digital entry programmable scanner radio! Before this, only single-band crystal control scanners were available. As I recall, it was about $200. I immediately drove to the police credit union, took out a signature loan, and went back and got one of those radios! I later became an amateur radio operatior, first KA6KJS (technician and general class) and later KF6UJ (advanced class), and spoke all over the world on the low bands. To this day, my car and home are full of scanner radios.

Industrial Sewing Machines

As a little kid I was always sewing military patches on my clothes. As mentioned elsewhere in these memoirs, when I was kicked out of the Cub Scouts I immediately removed the scout patches from my uniform and replaced them with Marine Corps insignias. When in junior high school, I purchased an old Singer treadle sewing machine, and sewed everything and anything with it. Besides patches and uniforms, I earned a few bucks here and there making covers to mask tires for auto body and paint shops, and also custom carpenters' aprons for tradesmen working at construction sites.

When I first went into the Marine Corps, I bought a portable sewing machine and made a few bucks at promotion time by replacing chevrons on other troops' uniforms. As a young adult, I started acquiring industrial sewing machines for various applications, and ended up with a heavy-duty sewing shop second to none. For years I had great fun making outdoors equipment such as survival vests and military tactical pouches and related items. I submitted entries every year in the Los Angeles County Fair, and always took home blue ribbons. Because of their difficulty in determining what category to place my stuff, the fair staff actually created a category just for me: "Outdoor Men's Action Wear."

Unfortunately for me, but good for the rest of the world, was the explosion in companies that started making tactical items beginning around the year 2000. Not only was the great stuff that I made no longer unique, but these new items were made well and sold cheaply by the various companies. I got rid of most of my equipment, but still have a few machines and a bunch of material and hardware in case I get the urge to make some more stuff in the future.

This is really a big issue for me. At present, I have what most of my fellow collectors believe is the biggest and arguably best collection of U.S. law enforcement metal breast badges. I got my first badge when I was just five or six years old, and have been an avid collector ever since then.

By the time I went into the military, I probably had a dozen or so badges, and then picked up a few more, mostly foreign, when I was on active duty as an enlisted Marine. My collecting really went into high gear after I became a cop, and has been going full-speed ever since. I am not a casual collector, but someone who takes my collecting very seriously and really works at it. As these memoirs reflect, I seize every opportunity to acquire badges. I've done well, and have a collection that numbers in the thousands.

One badge story (believe me, there are plenty of badge stories) is so funny it is worth putting in these memoirs. I always tell people I like old beat-up badges, and the older and more beat-up the better. In a chat with a buddy of mine who was then the chief of police in Southfield, Michigan, he asked what kind of badges I preferred. I responded with "the more beat-up, the better." A couple of weeks later I got a box from him containing badges that had been worked over with a hammer!

Now I just say "worn out," when describing the type of old badges that I prefer!

FART MACHINE

The battery-operated, remote controlled fart machine, especially the new models with various sound options, is absolutely one of my most favorate items. These memoirs contain a few fart-machine stories, and I hope that readers will find them amusing.

Although probably terrible to discuss publicly, I have one dear friend whom I've told that I intend to put a fart machine inside his casket if he pre-deceases me, then trigger a series of farts as people approach him to pay their last respects. There's a chance that I might just get to do this!

FOUR-WHEEL DRIVE VEHICLES

There has never been a time, since I was about twenty years old, when I haven't had at least one four-wheel drive vehicle. My first, second, third, and fourth were Scouts made by International Harvester. I have also had a couple of surplus military vehicles, a Jeep and a three-quarter-ton Dodge personnel carrier. All of my official vehicles with the County of San Bernardino, both marshal and sheriff, were Chevrolet Tahoes. At present, we have a Chevrolet 4x4 Suburban, a Chevrolet 4x4 Silverado pickup truck, and a Polaris 4x4 side-by-side, off-road utility vehicle. I have always enjoyed the outdoors, and four-wheel drive vehicles come in pretty handy.

DONUTS

Although I don't eat many donuts these days, I must admit that my perfectly tuned, masculine masterpiece, aerodynamic and scientifically-calibrated body has had more than a few donuts pass through it in my over four decades of law enforcement service.

Actually, donuts aren't among my favorate foods—but they are among my favorate topics when joking with other people about police officers.

Chapter Twenty-Six
SPECIAL PALS
(Alphabetical)

This is a difficult and sensitive part of my memoirs, because I have so many good and wonderful friends. But, for the reasons discussed following each of the persons below, I absolutely have to specifically mention certain people. I hope that the scores of other folks who I think the world of will not be offended.

Jim Collins

If there were individual photographs in the dictionary as examples of verbs, Jim Collins' photo would precede the words loyal, decent, and caring. He is such a good and decent man, with an extraordinary sense of fairness and knowing right from wrong. I first met him when he was a probationary Azusa patrolman. We remained the closest of friends through his career to lieutenant, where he served with absolute honor and distinction. He is now retired with his second wife Robin (like all my pals, second is best), and lives in Texas. Along with Ray Sherrard and Gary Hoving, Jim is an essential component of my support system of fellow men and law enforcement officers. Although I had already known him for several years, he really popped up on my radar screen as an extraordinary friend and remains there for his assistance and loyalty, when what he had to offer in advice and support was exactly what I needed at the time of my deep consternation when retiring from the LAPD under painful circumstances. Jim has only one agenda, and that is being the most decent man he can be. He has far exceeded those expectations, if possible, for as long as I have known him. Although he is in Texas, if I had a problem and needed him, there is no doubt that he would be on a plane coming my way within hours. Thank you, Jim, for being such a great pal and integral member of my support system.

PAUL GREENWALD

Paul and Isabelle Greenwald are two of the finest folks I have ever known, and their great kids, Seth and DJ (who I've been calling "Della Joella" since she was a little girl) are also the best. They live in Orange County, where Paul practices law. Unfortunately, we don't get to visit as often as all of us would like. I met Paul when I was the commanding officer of West Los Angeles Patrol Division. Paul came to my office and volunteered to do free legal work (within bounds) for my officers, did a great job and became a fine resource. We became fast and great friends, to the extent that he and Isabelle provided their home for our ceremony and reception when Cathy and I got married. I hope the future will provide us with more frequent visits.

GARY HOVING

Gary is a relatively new friend. I've only known him since about 2001, but couldn't ask for a better one. Along with Ray Sherrard and Jim Collins, Gary is a key member of my support system and inner circle. I met him when he was a chief deputy on the San Luis Obispo County Sheriff's Department, and we became fast friends. It soon became obvious that we share near-identical perspectives on both personal and professional issues.

Gary and I seriously considered a couple of chief/sheriff opportunities, one with him as the boss and me his number-two, and another with me as the boss and he my second-in-command. While neither of those situations materialized, we took them seriously; either or both were definite possibilities, but the timing just didn't work out. What I say, I don't say lightly: there is no person I can think of, based on shared perspectives and my enormous respect for his extraordinary leadership abilities, who I would rather have as a partner at the top of a law enforcement organization! Time is drawing short, and my teeth are getting longer ("long in the tooth"), but at the time of this entry I haven't given up completely on one more top leadership possibility. As the old cowboy might say, "there's a chance that I have one more rodeo left in me!"

RICHARD MAGYAR

In reflecting on our behavior over four decades ago, if my daughter ever brought someone like Rich Magyar home to dinner as a suitor, I would shoot both of them. If she brought him home as a husband, I would shoot myself! Having said that, Rich has long been one of my best and favorite friends! I love the guy. He is one of the finest and most loyal friends a person could ever ask for, and someone for whom honor to his friends is not only desirable, but also as essential as oxygen. He and I go back over forty years; we met when I was a new patrol sergeant in Rampart. Some people are generous to a fault; he is generous beyond a fault. This wonderful man has all but given me valuable badges that he could have sold for considerable sums. Instead, I needed them, and he is my friend. Hopefully, I have responded in kind. If I have something he needs and it isn't absolutely essential to my displays, regardless of its value, it's his! I have no shortage of dear friends, but Rich Magyar is clearly in the small group at the top of the list.

Art Mattox

Art Mattox is one of the most decent and genuine persons I have ever met—but not someone who would logically appear to be a dear friend. I met him when I was the commanding officer of Northeast Area, and he was reaching out from the gay community. Art emerged as a representative of that community. He was an extraordinary voice of reason who quickly developed equal rapport with the cops as well as gay groups, and played a strong and positive role in breaking down barriers and helping each camp develop mutual respect. Art's actions while assisting Northeast Area (and me) elevated him in the eyes of a number of folks, including Mayor Richard Riordan, who appointed him to the five-member Board of Police Commissioners! We didn't visit often when he was on the board, but he immediately came to my aid, personally and not as a representative of the department or the commission, when I was getting screwed-over by Willie Williams and his top disciples. While I don't recall the context, at one point Art stated clearly that our friendship was more important than his position on the board, and he would resign that position if a conflict arose. Art has been among those at my side during difficult times, then and since, and is someone for whom I have deep respect and affection. He is close with Cathy and me, and will be strongly considered as godfather to Danielle at her baptism. Thank you, Art, for being such a great friend to the Bushey family.

Ben Novak

Dr. Ben Novak, M.D., is as fine a man as has ever walked the face of this earth. I am fortunate to have him as a dear friend. He has a military background as a Navy physician, and is every bit a law enforcement supporter. I met Ben when I was the commanding officer of the Personnel

Group of the LAPD, and head of the Reserve Corps. He became a reserve physician for the Air Support Division, and quickly earned the love and respect of all personnel. I also introduced him to then-Sheriff Mike Corona of Orange County. Ben became and remains a reserve to this day, while former Sheriff Corona sits in a federal prison in Colorado for unethical actions and crimes (having been found guilty on only one of many counts, because of statutes of limitations) while in office. Ben was also the sworn physician (with a very cool badge) for the San Bernardino County Marshal's Office and the San Bernardino County Sheriff's Department, while I was with those agencies. Ben's loyalty extends far beyond the workplace, and a better friend to my cop friends and me doesn't exist. There was a time when Ben saved my life. He knows why, and I will never cease to be grateful.

RAYMOND SHERRARD

Ray is as close to a genetic brother as could possibly exist. He and I have been the closest of friends for about forty years. We first met as fellow badge collectors when he was a young special agent with the U.S. Treasury Department (Internal Revenue Service—Criminal Investigation) and I was a young sergeant in the LAPD Manuals & Orders Unit. Ray has literally been with my entire family as it developed and grew, and there has never been a time when "Uncle Ray" has forgotten or not been there for my kids, especially Jake. We are both at the top of the varsity pool of badge collectors, although he is exclusively a federal collector. Except in the instance of dividing the assets of the Orval Davis collection (which Ray purchased for $150,000, and needed to recoup his investment), we have never charged one another for a badge. If I acquire something he needs or wants and it isn't essential to my display, it is his, no questions or conversation. The same is true when he acquires items to my liking. Although our friendship trumps our collecting, the latter has provided each of us with some extraordinary badges. Ray married and divorced early in life and, after several decades of bachelorhood, married a great gal he'd known for years and who was the widow of a long-time friend. Ray did well, and she is a pleasure to have as my best pal's spouse. In the introduction to my memoirs, I mention some things from my single days that are best not written about on these pages, being only suitable for a night out with the boys (and even then only after a few drinks). Ray plays a leading role in some of those stories, as they were his single days, as well.

Thank you, Ray, for being such a great pal.

CHAPTER TWENTY-SEVEN
MY HEROES

DAVID & MARY BUSHEY

My mom and pop (that's what I started calling my dad when I was around ten or eleven—why, I don't know, I just did!) are at the top of my heroes list. By the time I was old enough to comprehend my surroundings, however, our family had fallen on hard times.

My pop took ill at about that time, and from then on until his death in 1963 he was in and out of the City of Hope Medical Center. But there was never a time, within his physical and financial limitations, when he wasn't there for me. My remembrances are many, including him always driving me to and from places where I wanted to go, often to movies on Saturday afternoons, and always waiting up for me when I was a teenager and went out at night. When dad died, his wallet contained three photos of me. He never went beyond the seventh grade in school, but was very wise and intelligent.

I cannot imagine a mom that was more caring or loving than mine. She was an integral part of every phase of my life, from my birth until her passing, and her memories still influence my daily actions. My triumphs, dreams, accomplishments, heartaches and worries were hers, as well. She was both my launching pad and my support system, someone who I loved dearly and spoke to just about every day of my life. When I was serving overseas in the military, she wrote to me just about every day. I am so grateful to have had such a wonderful mom, and hope and believe that I reciprocated her love and attention during the twilight years of her life. I visited her just about every day; first in the retirement home, and later in the the nursing home where she passed away.

My wife is a saint, and I couldn't possibly have found a better spouse or mother. While there is often some "conversation" involved about it, there's very little I want to do that I'm not able to do, and I work hard to ensure that she also gets to pursue her dreams and interests. She is the loving and ideal "step-monster" to Stacy and Zak, and their affection for her is equally devoted. Cathy is a wonderful mother, tutor and friend to many of the foster children (especially Spencer and Matthew, who have been with us for a number of years) who have come into our home (there were several whose deplorable behavior caused us to have them removed), and the absolute most loving and devoted mom in every way to our beautiful, fun and smart daughter, Danielle. Thank you, Cathy, for being you.

RONALD REAGAN

I worship the ground that Ronald Reagan walked on. I don't need to go into a lot of detail about this, as those who read this and also cared for him know exactly how I feel. Those who read this and feel differently, after all the history that occurred and the perspective provided since his service as our president, are not likely to be swayed by anything I might say.

God bless you, President Reagan.

TOM STONE

In 1999, because of my exhalted status as San Bernardino County Marshal, the Federal Bureau of Investigation hosted my attendance at the two-week Law Enforcement Executive Development Seminar (LEEDS) held at the FBI Academy in Quantico, Virginia. That experience led to my association with the FBI-Law Enforcement Executive Development Association (FBI-LEEDA), where I first met Tom Stone. At that time, Tom was (and still is!) the executive director of FBI-LEEDA, and had previously served with a number of law enforcement agencies in Florida, Virginia and Pennsylvania, in most instances as the chief of police. Tom and I hit it off right away, and before long we launched the FBI-LEEDA Training Program. Over the next several years we made literally scores of presentations on leadership to law enforcement agencies throughout the United States and Canada. Under Tom's leadership, FBI-LEEDA has grown into a professional law enforcment powerhouse, offering what I believe is the best such training in the nation. I remain affiliated as both a strong participating member and as a senior instructor, and typically travel somewhere every month or so for several days, teaching on behalf of the organization. Tom Stone is the reason why, and a better friend would be impossible to find.

Tom Vetter

Tom has been a good pal over the years, and is one of my heroes because he is the reason I returned to the Marine Corps as an officer. As mentioned elsewhere in these memoirs, Tom and I met while standing in a registration line at Cal State LA when I was undercover. We learned that we both were Marines, and he provided the guidance and inspiration for me to apply to an officer program. I did, and the rest is history. The Marine Corps has played an enormous role in my life, ever since I was honorably discharged as a corporal. Such would not have been the case, had I not had that chance encounter with Tom Vetter. He was an enormous fork in one of my many roads. Thanks, Tom!

Sheriff Gary Penrod and
Assistant Sheriff Ron Bieberdorf

Moving laterally into a high-ranking position in a law enforcement agency is seldom done, and when it does occur it usually becomes ugly. The reason is that people work for years to advance in grade, then in comes a stranger at the highest level, which typically results in resentment and hostility.

It occurred once before me within the San Bernardino County Sheriff's Department, and it wasn't a good experience for either the department or the person involved. He was a great guy, and a well-seasoned former police chief, but he was pretty much "dead on arrival" because of so much hostility directed at the sheriff who had appointed him.

In my case, when appointed directly to the rank of deputy chief, I had the advantage of previously being a known commodity as the county marshal. But it still could have become pretty unpleasant for me, and probably wouldn't have been a very good experience. The keys to my great experience were Gary Penrod and Ron Bieberdorf. These two wonderful gents set the standard and expectations for how I was to be treated when I entered the department, and I shall be forever grateful for the measures they took to ensure that I was made to feel welcome, and that others saw and dealt with me just as they would any other deputy chief. There were occasional glimpses and hints of resentment, but they paled in comparison to the overwhelming warmth I received from the men and women of that department.

CHAPTER TWENTY-EIGHT
ODDS & ENDS

WHEN ONE DOOR CLOSES—OFTEN A BETTER ONE OPENS

I believe that I've just about always been one who attempts to make the best of the hand he was dealt in life, and always "keeps leaning forward" and trying to make the best out of difficult situations. In this vein, I have to say that my life, with but a few glitches, is a good example of how when one door closes, another one, often even better, opens.

The high school educational door closed (because I was such an idiot), but the Marine Corps door opened and I retired as a colonel. In the Marine Corps Reserve, virtually every time I failed to obtain a billet I'd applied for, I ended up with an even better assignment.

As a police sergeant who wasn't selected for assignment to Internal Affairs, I obtained an even better position as officer-in-charge of the Manuals & Orders Unit. After a bitter battle with the police chief who put me in a humiliating assignment that resulted in my decision to retire from the LAPD, I landed the position as marshal of San Bernardino County. When the marshal's department was eliminated, I was appointed a sheriff's deputy chief. When the hiring process for the police chief of Sierra Madre was put on hold for budgetary reasons, I got an even better position as personal law enforcement liaison to the Los Angeles County district attorney, and at a much higher salary. While luck and timing certainly played some role in these achievements, hard-working people with optimistic attitudes have better luck than their sluggish and pessimistic counterparts!

NO WORK-RELATED PHYSICAL FEAR

What I am about to say, I say without intending bravado or sounding courageous. I truly cannot recall a time in my law enforcement career when I was frightened! Like anyone who has been a cop for a long time, I have found myself in more than my share of dangerous and difficult situations, and have clearly faced severe physical danger on many occasions. But again, I do not recall ever being afraid. Why? Good question! My guess is that it was a reaction, or better yet a lack of reaction, based on a combination of confidence and learned bravado. Since Marine Corps boot camp, I have always believed and practiced during difficult situations, that the best defense is a good offense and that "running into the eye of the storm" is often the best approach. As an adult, I never backed away from a physical confrontation and have shown—often feigned—absolute confidence that I would prevail and that it would be disastrous for any adversary to engage me in a physical confrontation.

In my early adult years, especially as a new cop, I was involved in literally scores of fights and arrests, and I always prevailed! My confidence, my training, and the fact that I was a policeman (and on the right side of the law) were most likely the key factors. These early experiences have served me well, in terms of confidence and a lack of fear, throughout my life.

McIntyre Senior Becomes Lucid For a Short Period

In 1999, I had a next-door neighbor named Tom McIntyre. Tom was a good friend, and his elderly father lived in the same nursing home as my uncle Matt. Tom's dad was clearly in the advanced stages of either dementia or Alzheimer's disease. When I visited my uncle, which was fairly frequently, I would always take the opportunity to say "hi" to Tom's dad, and would even take him chocolate malts from time to time. Tom's dad just sat there in a wheelchair, stooped over, and had little to say that was coherent.

One afternoon when I went to visit my uncle I learned that Tom's dad had suffered a fall, as he had a bandage on his head. When he saw me he very coherently said: "You are Matt's nephew; how are you doing?" I was shocked because this man had never said anything anywhere near that coherent in the couple of years I'd been acquainted with him. Then he and I went on to have a normal and detailed conversation, where he told me about Tom's childhood and how he and Tom had worked on cars together, and he actually provided specific information about boring out the cylinder on one of their cars!

I couldn't believe what I was seeing and hearing: a man who I knew to be in full-blown dementia was now as coherent as I was, the apparent result of an injury to his head. I rushed home and found Tom in his driveway, told him that his dad was "back" mentally, and suggested that he might want to literally rush to the hospital and have a conversation with his dad. I opined that his dad's condition could potentially be temporary and that Tom should take advantage of the situation. Tom did, but by the time he arrived at the hospital his dad was back to his same old self, in advanced dementia.

I have never forgotten this incident, nor have I ever really received an explanation from any physicians I've spoken to about my observations. Amazingly, this man went from full-blown dementia to being absolutely coherent, temporarily, as result of a head injury. This certainly tells me that his brain cells were not dead, but rather masked as the result of some other medical condition.

Futile Efforts to Keep "Bill" from Crashing and Burning

Bill is the grandson of a very dear friend and former LAPD lieutenant, now deceased, who was instrumental in helping me during the course of my police career. At the time, Bill was in his early forties and a lawyer. But he'd fallen on hard times after being laid off from the law firm that lured him away from a public defender's office.

Because Bill was bipolar he had to be on medication to remain stable. I was contacted by my friend's widow with a plea to somehow assist Bill, as he had stopped taking his meds and was engaging in foolish and bizarre behavior in court that was jeopardizing his stature and standing as an attorney. I arm-wresled him to a psychiatrist, got him back on his meds and stabilized, then contacted the presiding judge of the courthouse where he practiced, with the gentle notification that Bill had been ill but was now getting the assistance he needed. (Although my overture to the judge was apparently of some value, the judge lashed out at me for inappropriately contacting the court!)

I then spent several days babysitting Bill to keep him from making calls and saying stupid things until the meds kicked in and he became stable. But after a couple of months he stopped taking his drugs again, and again I hauled him off to the psychiatrist and got him stabilized. The third time he stopped taking his meds was the final straw. I tried to get him back to the psychiatrist; but he made it clear, while doing and saying stupid things, that he wasn't going to take his meds.

The last I heard of Bill, he was bouncing around the nation, sponging off acquaintances and acting bizarre. Even if Bill gets stable again, there is no assurance he'll stay that way. I fear that he has irreparably damaged his law standing by essentially walking away from some of his clients while off his meds. Watching such foolish behavior, which could have been so easily resolved by just taking his meds, broke my heart.

Among the very strong needs of the medical community is time-released psychotropic medication. Bill's case was just one among the many examples in my life of this need.

KEITH REPAIRS THE FURNACE

On a scale of one to ten, my household repair skills are probably somewhere around six. When I put my mind to it I can do a decent job around the house, in terms of fixing things up and performing minor repairs.

In about the mid-1980s, on a very cold night, I just couldn't get the furnace in the basement to work. I called one of my closest friends and somebody who was very handy with respect to fixing things. That person was Bart Bartel. With the phone in my hand, Bart had me just about completely disassemble the furnace to find the problem; we probably spent forty-five minutes on the phone troubleshooting the darn thing.

When we had tried just about everything he could think of, Bart asked me to make sure that it was plugged in! Well, it wasn't! Once we put the furnace back together, and plugged it in, it worked just fine!

FINALLY, A HEALTHY TAX RETURN—OOPS!

In the early 2000s, Cathy and I got some really great news: we were getting several thousand dollars back from our taxes! We couldn't believe our good luck, as we usually had to pay. But Lee, our tax man, re-ran the numbers and assured us that we were getting a substantial refund.

We had been talking about purchasing a couple of quads (off-road four-wheeled recreational vehicles) for the foster kids who were coming and going from our home, and this seemed like the right time. So we went to Berts, the local off-road recreational dealer, and bought a couple of nice quads.

On Monday, Lee called us with bad news: his numbers were right, but he had miscalculated them as a refund. We owed the amount he had previously indicated was a refund! What could we do, other than tighten our belts?

It was what it was.

In the late 1960s, while undercover, I decided that I wanted to obtain a private pilot's license. I enrolled in a program at Brackett Field in Pomona, completed ground school on my own, and ultimately obtained my private pilot's license. In fact, before marrying Barbara, I extracted a commitment from her that I would be able to complete my flight training, and also remain in the Marine Corps Reserve. During my short career as a pilot, because I did very little flying after obtaining my certificate, I had a few noteworthy situations that may be fun for others to be aware of.

During one of my solo cross-country flights I flew to Blythe, California. The airstrip was an old World War II airfield without any a tower or support facilities. As I approached the field I was having a great deal of difficulty keeping the aircraft straight because of high winds. I lined up on the runway and descended and, even though I was doing everything possible to keep the plane straight, it was still flying sideways. While about ten feet off the ground I realized I couldn't land the plane sideways, so I applied power, went around the landing pattern and tried to figure out what to do. Another aircraft approached and requested the information from UNICOM (an airport advisory provided by one of the airport tenants). Then I realized I was trying to land on the wrong runway, and was fighting a fierce crosswind! With the right information and the appropriate runway, I landed without further incident.

On another of my solo cross-country flights I flew to Montgomery Field in rural San Diego County. This was a controlled field with a tower. I was given permission to land, then directed to what I thought was the appropriate runway. After I'd touched down the air traffic controller, in not-so-pleasant words, directed me to report to the tower. When I went to the tower I got a pretty good "chewing out," because I'd landed on the left runway when I should've landed on the right runway.

As mentioned previously, I'd put myself through ground school. Not until this incident did I became aware that some fields have parallel runways that have the same number, but are distinguished by the designation of either "right" or "left" (such as "runway 26-left"). Apparently another aircraft had to abort its landing and go around the pattern again, because I had inappropriately placed myself in front of that aircraft after it was given permission to land on the left runway. I felt bad about my mistake. But I certainly learned a valuable lesson in the process.

After obtaining my license, I took flights from time to time. One of the more memorable flights was to and from Las Vegas with another badge collector friend, Jim Burton, to visit a mutual friend. We went over early in the morning when there were few winds aloft and it was a smooth ride. However, coming back in the late afternoon was a different issue altogether. While it didn't bother me, there was a lot of turbulence. Although I didn't notice it at the time, my friend Jim was continually puking in his jacket!

Then I encountered some problems when entering the airspace above Cajon Pass, while transitioning from the high desert to the inland valley. I actually got lost and couldn't see where we were because of all the smoke and haze! I was fearful of flying into a mountain. So I started flying in circles and climbed to a higher elevation where I knew I was higher than any of the mountaintops in that vicinity. We then flew back to Apple Valley, and landed. I approached a man who was obviously a tenured pilot and explained my dilemma. He was very helpful and explained that, even though you cannot see either to the right or left, you can always see straight down. His advice was for me to literally fly through the pass by looking down and remaining directly above Interstate 15. His advice was good, and that is the way I flew back to Brackett Field.

I sure felt sorry for my friend Jim, though, and know that he was very happy to get his feet back on the ground.

Loose Bowels and an Even Looser Mother

There are stories attached to just about every foster child who has ever come into our home. Many of them came into our hearts. Little Kaitlin, who was about six years old, didn't stay long. But her story is most memorable.

Because of her mother's mental illness, the symptoms of which included seeing non-existent bugs on her body and Kaitlin's, a physician felt the little girl was at risk being with the mother and recommended that she be taken into protective custody. Since the father, who was divorced from the mother, had just been in an accident and couldn't immediately take custody of his daughter, DCFS asked us if we could take the very nice little gal for a week or so until the dad could get back on his feet and take the child.

DCFS did bring to our attention a troubling issue that we needed to be aware of: Kaitlin had a medical condition, with a long medical name, which essentially meant that the child wasn't always able to control her bowels. Thus she had to wear a diaper at night. As is our custom, immediately after taking Kaitlin into our home Cathy had her call her mom just to say that she was okay. Then Cathy spoke to the mom to reinforce the well-being of her child. During their conversation, the mom was concerned that Kaitlin hadn't taken her "medication" with her—laxatives!

We certainly solved that "medical problem"! We could only assume it was the mother's way of purging the bugs or demons or whatever from that little girl's body.

Winning a New Mustang Convertible

As far as weeks go, the week of September 10th, 2012 was about as good as it gets for Cathy Bushey. Early in the week, at the Los Angeles Police Protective League golf tournament, she won a beautiful pearl necklace and earrings set for making the longest drive in the women's category.

The following Saturday night, at the annual Jack Webb dinner hosted by the Los Angeles Police Museum and Historical Society, I held the lucky winning ticket for a brand-new 2013 Ford Mustang convertible! Cathy was truly stunned when I handed her the winning ticket and told her to go up on stage and get her new car—but it wasn't long before she broke out into a really big smile.

Before we even left the banquet that evening, we were getting congraulatory emails from all over the country, including one from our former exchange student in Germany. Within moments of winning the car, Cathy had posted the good news and a picture of the car (on display in the banquet's lobby) on Facebook!

Early the following week, we went to Galpin Motors (great folks and longtime supporters of law enforcement) in the San Fernando Valley. There, Cathy, our daughter Danielle and foster son Will picked out a metallic green Mustang convertible. The color is nice, but not something I would have chosen. However, it was made very clear to me that my job was just buying the tickets—and that all future decisions involving the car will be made by Cathy and the kids!

I hope they'll at least let me ride in it occasionally.

Chapter Twenty-Nine
MY VIEWS ON
CONTROVERSIAL ISSUES

Nature of Our Democracy

Whoever said democracy is dysfunctional and fraught with downfalls really knew what he (or she) was talking about. No truer words could ever be spoken. Those who govern are often far inferior to those they lead. The law enforcement profession is a great example: because of rigid standards in all of the states, new officers have to meet certain background standards that do not apply to the elected officials in their cities, counties and states.

In the past twenty or so years, we have had two American presidents who, because of background issues involving drugs, would likely not be qualified to be cops—yet they were arguably leaders of the entire free world. In my extensive travels throughout this wonderful country, I am continually impressed at the personal qualities of our police executives, but the troubling behavior of large numbers of elected officials. In many of our cities, counties and states, the law enforcement officials are the sharpest and most credible individuals in their communities.

No example of this is more striking than the selection of Willie Williams to be the chief of the Los Angeles Police Department, in the wake of the Rodney King tragedy. The collective appointed and elected officials who brought a decent but wholly unqualified individual to lead one of the nation's finest organizations were, in my opinion, largely less qualied and—along with the chief they brought to Los Angeles—possessed skills that were generally less than those of the average LAPD command officer!

Democracy can be very problematic. But it is still the best thing that any government has come up with. In my opinion, the very difficult answer to strengthening our democracy lies in addressing the many factors that distort the information that is fed to the electorate.

I am strongly pro-choice and pro-life! But, like all of us, I am influenced by my own observations, experiences, and beliefs. I always reflect on two pregnancies that could not have occurred at worse times, and for which abortion was considered: my son Zak and my grandson Matthew.

I love these two more than I can say, and the thought that either or both might never have been part of my life is unbearable. The choice of whether to continue a pregnancy has got to be one of the most difficult decisions a person can make, but it has to be that person who makes it and not something or someone driven by society or its laws. To say that I have seen thousands of instances where a child had little or no chance to lead a good and criminal-free life, would be an understatement. Our prisons serve as a constant testament to children who are the by-product of alcohol- or drug-addicted parents in criminal environments.

While I have no right to play God, by suggesting who should and who should not be born, a visit to our prisons yields much to consider. I must confess particular disdain for those individuals who scream the loudest that the answer is to be found in foster and adopted homes, but who themselves have no foster or adopted children. This is a terribly serious and sober issue. But I believe it is one most appropriately decided by those personally involved in each situation.

Physician-Assisted Suicides

While I strongly believe that suicides are most often a permanent solution to a temporary problem, I make an exception for someone who is in pain, terminally ill, and whose death is imminent. My wonderful father was such a person, and he ended his life with an intentional overdose of drugs.

I honestly don't know anyone who would desire that his or her life be maintained when they are in a horrific physical state and close to death. Besides the horrible existence of a person on the verge of death, the impact on their loved ones is awful, as well. From a practical standpoint, what is accomplished (and look at all that is lost) when thousands (and sometimes hundreds of thousands) of dollars are spent to keep a terminally ill and suffering person alive? Although safeguards are certainly necessary to ensure that the end is truly imminent, and to avoid potential criminal and unethical activities (such as accelerating death for the purpose of harvesting organs when death is not imminent, etc.), I am completely in favor of physician-assisted suicide.

Recognizing the oath that physicians take to preserve life, I am nevertheless okay with a medically trained non-physician performing these terribly difficult, but in my judgment compassionate and common-sense, acts.

A very critical issue in physician-assisted suicides is to absolutely ensure that the patient's terminal condition is truly physical, and not psychological. Key symptoms of depression are feelings of helplessness, seeing issues as worse than they might be, and believing one's problems to be insurmountable. The assertions or insistence of the person who seeks to end his or her life must not be the deciding factor; medical confirmation is essential.

GAY MARRIAGE

In over four decades as a peace officer, serving six different agencies and goodness knows how many communities, I have come about as close as is possible to being able to say I have seen it all! I doubt that society has any underbellies that I have not only seen, but policed, as well. I have seen incredibly good things come from incredibly bad environments, and vice-versa.

With respect to sexual orientation, I have encountered some real jerks who are gay, but not in a greater proportion to those who are straight. As I have ascended to positions of increased responsibility, and interacted with a wide variety of interests and communities, I have encountered no shortage of truly wonderful persons who, other than being gay, are no different from the other folks for whom I have goodwill and respect.

This journey has been a long road. But I have reached the point where I believe that, in the vast majority of instances, sexual orientation is genetic. Just as we are all a bit different on the outside, we are also a bit different on the inside. Stemming from this belief is another belief: that persons whose sexual orientation is different from mine have the same rights to happiness and what society has to offer, as I do. If a couple of people who happen to be gay desire to sanctify their relationship under the auspices of their religious beliefs, it doesn't detract from me in any way. It is not something that I find objectionable. Besides, gay couples suffer like the rest of us when it comes to divorces and separations.

Further, the issue of a gay couple taking in foster children, and adopting children, is worthy of brief mention. Let there be no doubt, the ideal situation in my judgment is an "Ozzie & Harriet" household, as depicted on TV at least, within a happy and wholesome heterosexual family environment. Unfortunately, not enough of these ideal situations exist for all of the parentless children who need loving and nurturing homes. It seems to me that a happy and wholesome home where both parents are of the same gender, is preferable to a group home, or to bouncing from one foster home to another, oftentimes where the monthly stipend is more important that the best interests of the child. I am inclined to accept as valid—in the absence of credible research to the contrary—the studies which indicate that the overriding considerations in the development of a child are character and affection, and that the sexual orientation of the parents is not typically a factor in the sexual orientation of children.

I realize there are many folks, including personal friends, with differeing perspectives on these issues, and I respect their beliefs. I am not driven by social concerns or ideology. Rather, I'm just trying to be practical based on years of observations and the tendency to see the world as it really is, as opposed to how some people would like it to be.

Gun Control

I am and have always been a strong advocate of a person's right to keep and bear arms. However, I have spent a good portion of my life witnessing the tragedy of gun violence, especially when weapons are permitted to fall into the hands of those with evil intentions.

I believe that good and decent citizens who are mentally competent and who have been trained in safe firearms operation and self-defense should have the ability to possess firearms. I am also not opposed to permitting such persons to carry concealed firearms, the thought being that criminals may be less inclined to commit crimes because they cannot know which citizens, from old men to pregnant women, might have a gun and know how to use it.

With respect to "assault rifles" as well as fully-automatic weapons, I see no legitimate purpose for them and have no problem with laws prohibiting their possession. I don't want them accessible to being stolen, then used for criminal purposes. I do believe that convicted felons, and those with a history of multiple petty offenses, should be prohibited from possessing firearms. Those convicted of using firearms during the commission of a crime should be severely punished. Finally, I support laws mandating very secure containers, such as gun safes, for storing weapons.

The key problem with immigration lies not with the people who understandably want to come to this country to make a better life for themselves and their families, but with the politicians at all levels throughout the last half-century or so, who have failed in their responsibility to seal our borders.

Immigration is a good thing and just about all of us, aside from Native Americans, are here because of the migration of our families to this country.

Unfortunately, because these politicians, for any variety of reasons, essentially turned their back to the problem, we are now in a very difficult position as a nation. Most families, including mine, have loving relatives who are either themselves illegal or the offspring of someone who came to this country illegally. Nevertheless, we love them, they are part of our family, most consider themselves to be loyal Americans, and we sure as heck don't want them deported!

I believe that at this time we should slam our borders shut—but act with realism and compassion by permitting the continued LEGAL immigration of folks, with a strong emphasis on family unification. Further, we are a big and generous nation, and in fact have a need for immigration. But we should be steadfast in permitting only good and productive people, who must commit to embracing the American form of government and mastering the English language, to have the honor of coming into this wonderful country.

MILITARY TRADITIONS AND HAZING

I experienced some pretty rough stuff while in the military, and think I am a better person because of those experiences. However, as institutions and society evolve, I am regretfully in favor of the fairly recent restrictions put on some activities that used to be commonplace. The activities that I refer to include, but are not limited to, "pinning" stripes on newly-promoted Marines by having them walk a literal gauntlet of fists slugging their arms where the stripes will be attached, and slugging new corporals and above on the upper leg where the NCO stripe is placed on the dress trousers. Also, "pinning" the coveted Marine Corps Parachutist badge on one's shirt, with the pins literally sticking into one's chest, by slugging the wings with considerable force; and the Neptune ceremony on ships while crossing the equator; and other, related painful traditions.

In all of the above I experienced not only the indoctrination, but also some excesses. Unfortunately, there is typically a jerk or two who uses these types of events to satisfy a brutal proclivity, and who slugs his victim so hard as to truly harm him. Pinning the wings on the chest of new Marine parachutists is a good example: every slug draws blood as the pins pierce the flesh, but a savage blow from a sadistic person, which we have all experienced, can really do damage.

I would be in favor of permitting the continuation of these traditions, if there was some way to ensure that only mature and reasonable persons participated. But I regret that it isn't possible. While it goes against my grain when these activities are discredited as unacceptable "hazing," I understand and must regretfully support their prohibition.

STEM CELL RESEARCH

I strongly support all forms of stem cell research, and that includes those of an embryonic nature. I am troubled that this topic has been tied to the abortion argument, and that there are people whose philosophic opposition to abortion has translated into opposition for this very worthy and necessary type of research. Anyone who knows anything about the subject is aware that there are embryonic stem cells that will never otherwise be used for anything. It is a waste—just a total and tragic waste—to not use those cells for research purposes, in pursuit of medical breakthroughs for some of our worst physical diseases and conditions.

IS TODAY'S LOS ANGELES POLICE DEPARTMENT BETTER OR WORSE THAN WHEN I JOINED THE FORCE?

This is a good question, and I'm pretty certain that I know the answer. Overall, it is neither better nor worse, but certainly a lot different. When I was a new cop, all of the old-timers criticized the "new" department, and were quick to say that the department wasn't as good a place as when they were first hired. During my entire career, and even now, I continue to hear almost these exact words.

Realistically, the equipment today is absolutely superb and mind-boggling, as opposed to the limited-channel radios, lack of walkie-talkies, and dependence on the Gamewell telephone system when I was first hired! Today's training is second to none, and people at all levels are more proficient in their ranks than was the case many years ago.

A big issue of criticism is the argument over hiring standards. But it is hard to credibly argue in support of retaining procedures that didn't enable the development of a workforce that resembles the unbelievable face of the city's present-day workforce. Anyone who thinks that all of the cops of yesteryear were sterling personalities, or that most of today's officers are not fine young men and women, has to be crazy, blind, or both. Sure, things are different. But that is the case with just about every segment of our society.

If I could start all over again with the LAPD, I would be at the front of the line of applicants. I hope that all present employees recognize how great the department is. Despite issues that cause all of us concern, it is still a great organization, made up primarily of the best that our society has to offer.

I wish the typical politician had the ethics and integrity of the typical Los Angeles police officer.

WHY PEOPLE BECOME WHO THEY BECOME

I have seen some of the best people come from some of the worst homes and environments, and some of the worst people come from some of the best backgrounds. It is clear to me that who a person becomes is primarily the result of two things: their internal biological make-up and their environment. There is no doubt in my mind that some people are born inherently bad and evil, and I have encountered a number of such folks in my long law enforcement career. We are all a bit different on the outside, and it is only logical to realize that we are all just a bit different on the inside, as well. Except for the few who are just plain evil, I think that most people are pretty much genetically predetermined to develop into decent folks, if raised in a positive environment.

CHAPTER THIRTY
REGRETS

UNDERESTIMATING MY CAPABILITIES

In my adolescent and teen years, I told myself that I didn't have the capacity to understand certain subjects, particularly mathematics and chemistry. As I look back on those days, I now realize that my limitations were self-imposed. Probably, I could've done just fine in those topics if I had applied myself. Now in my senior years, I do find there are topics that I struggle with, especially automation and computers. But it may be somewhat of a generational thing, because my kids seem to do just fine in these areas—probably because they grew up using these devices.

NOT FIGHTING BACK SOONER

While I had the typical experiences with conflict as a young boy, those experiences were actually minimal until my family moved to Duarte when I was in the sixth grade. From almost the minute I arrived at my new school, Beardsley Elementary, I found myself being "chosen off" by a few bullies. For several months, I continually declined to fight and tried to avoid conflict. That turned out to be a real mistake, because the more I said no, the more I was chosen off by an increasing number of young thugs who saw me as vulnerable and somebody whose refusal to fight bolstered their egos.

Finally, one day I'd had enough, and accepted the challenge of a kid named Laverne Wetzel to fight. We met in the dirt lot after school and exchanged blows, while several other kids stood around. I held my own and actually drew blood, which Laverne did not. Almost from the moment we stopped exchanging blows, my life changed for the better. Laverne was complimentary of my fighting skills, shook my hand, and we became good friends. After that, I was never chosen off again in Duarte. Later, as a United States Marine, a lack of aggressiveness was never a problem with me!

Not Spending More Time With Stacy

When Barbara and I split up in 1980, it was agreed that Jake would live with me and Stacy and Zak would live with their mother. Although I saw a lot of Stacy and Zak, it wasn't the quality time that it should have been. Zak and I visited quite often, but in hindsight it wasn't often enough.

With Stacy, I look back with great regret and realize that I should have made a greater effort to spend time with my daughter. The fact that she is female meant that we had different interests, but still I wish I had been more active in her life. I think what I really missed were many of the cute and subtle little things that kids do as they're growing up.

As I write this, I reflect on the funny little things that our adopted daughter Danielle does, and continually remind myself that I missed a lot of these activities with Stacy. Stacy has developed into a wonderful woman, and I am very grateful that today she and I have a close and loving relationship. Stacy brings a great deal of happiness to my life.

Missing Zak's Baseball Games

My LAPD duties made it really difficult to attend Zak's baseball games. But I should have tried harder to attend more than the very few that I did. A staff or command officer, absent unique circumstances, seldom left the office before 5:30 p.m., or so. Add to that the commute, which was typically no less than forty-five minutes, and the problem of my attendance at his games becomes obvious. Still, had I planned a bit better than I did, I could have attended a few more games than I did. Zak was fortunate to have his mom and stepdad attend most of his games, but his dad should have been there, too. I never go to the games of my foster boys or adopted daughter, without feeling pangs of guilt for attending more of their games than I did of my biological children.

Not Having a Better Relationship with My Late Brother

The twelve-year age difference between my brother and me, in our early years, might as well have been 100 years. Where I pretty much followed in Larry's footsteps with the Marine Corps and law enforcement, I somehow managed to excel in both fields.

But success was not always possible for him. Due to weak eyesight, he failed to be commissioned as a Marine officer, and I know he was troubled at being denied that honor. In law enforcement, he bounced from department to department, with a few very painful bumps in the road, while I was doing well with the LAPD. I became a cop about the same year that he left his last law enforcement job. He was plagued by ill health and bad luck, and his fortunes fell as mine rose.

During a very big portion of Larry's adult life, his problems translated into terrible anxiety for our mom. He leaned on her heavily for both financial and emotional support; as a result, mom was constantly in a state of stress and despair. Although he loved his children dearly, Larry's failed marriages and inability to pay child support resulted in him having very little contact with his kids, especially Tommy and Nancy, which weighed heavily on his mind.

My brother was a good and decent man, who had a long string of bad luck. Although there was tension between us, particularly because of the toll that his problems took on our mom, I loved him dearly and regret that we didn't have a better relationship. Hopefully, the future will provide for the relationship that eluded us on earth.

Wasted Time on Worry and Anxiety

I have been a worrier, especially as it pertains to my employment, for most of my life. I look back with tremendous regret on the days and weeks that I spent worrying about things at work that I really shouldn't have worried about.

I think that a major contributor to my worrisome nature was the supercharged, dog-eat-dog political climate of the Los Angeles Police Department. In that organization, actions and perceptions, especially as I gained considerable rank, could make a real difference. Also, there were a few people who held very high rank but who seemed to relish making others uncomfortable; if that was their goal, it worked with me.

I especially remember the many visits to Washington, D.C., when I was the LAPD's liaison to Congress and to the Federal Communications Commission. I should have been having the time of my life (and realistically did have a number of really fun times), but I also spent an awful lot of time worrying about the actions of my boss back in Los Angeles.

In worrying about a situation, I always constructed and worried about the worst potential scenario, but those terrible scenarios just about never came to fruition. My worrisome nature has caused me to be sensitive to the potential that others may be worriers, as well. It's been very common for me, in the executive positions I've held, to go out of my way to set people's minds at ease, so they can enjoy themselves and not constantly worry about the petty politics that often take place in the workplace.

Being Too Quick to Respond to Troubling Situations

The irritation that stems from receiving troubling information, and the natural desire to quickly resolve problems, often causes people to act prematurely, when they are better off to let some time pass before acting.

I normally want to eliminate anxiety, but this is often easier said than done. Nevertheless, it is something I wish I'd done nore often in my career. Problems usually aren't as bad as they initially appear. But our minds often initially think the worse, and we sometimes act prematurely based on evil that may not exist, or on mistaken interpretations. I have had a good life and good careers, but my life would have been even better and my careers even more successful, if in many instances my first course of action had been nothing! I encourage people in the classes I teach to avoid the temptation to solve a problem or to resolve a situation until they truly understand the issues. Most often, it means letting some time pass before taking action.

Not Reuniting a Father and Son on the LAPD

Joe was a wonderful man, the best man at my first wedding, and one of my former supervisors. He had a son, Dudley, who, like his dad, was also on the LAPD. Because of a divorce, Dudley and Joe went sideways and didn't speak for years. At one point, long after Joe retired, Dudley worked for me. Over a period of several years, in chats with both of them, I got the impression that they might be able to break down their barriers if I put them together in a room. It was my intention to do so, but I never put enough effort forward to make it happen. Then Joe moved to another state, and died of cancer. I worked with Dudley in the district attorney's office. After Joe died and his widow gave me his badge, I offered it to Dudley, and he accepted. Not putting forth more of an effort to reunite Joe and Dudley is among the things I sincerely regret.

That There are Not More than Twenty-Four Hours in the Day!

There are not enough hours in the day to do all the things I would like to do. At present as I work on my memoirs, I also need to spend time (but have trouble finding it) to do the following: finish a book on LAPD badges; write a "white paper" for a security firm I'm associated with; finish several articles I'm writing for publication on the topic of leadership; pursue historical research on a number of badges in my collection; install additional radios in my vehicle; ride my side-by-side, four-wheel-drive Polaris in the mountains above my house; etc., etc., etc. When my time comes, I'm likely to croak with my boots on!

Failing to be SCUBA Certified

I had four personal achievement goals, at least of a recreational nature, that I hoped to attain as an adult. One, to become a parachutist—accomplished. Two, to become a private pilot—accomplished. Three, to become a licensed amateur radio operator—accomplished (KF6UJ). And four, to become SCUBA qualified—*not* accomplished. I guess three out of four isn't bad. And who knows—maybe I'll still get that SCUBA qualification one of these days!

Not Recommending Joe DeLadurantey for the Medal of Valor

During my early tenure as a sergeant in Rampart Divison, during the eartly 1970s, Joe DeLadurantey was a pal and a fellow supervisor.

One day, a woman was intent on committing suicide by jumping from the Benton Way overpass onto the Hollywood Freeway. Her initial attempt was thwarted by fast-thinking officers, and she was committed for being mentally unstable and unable to care for herself. However, almost immediately after her release, she returned to that overpass, jumped into the freeway lanes during rush hour traffic, and was killed by one or more of the several vehicles that struck her. Sergeant Joe DeLadurantey got to the scene, and, despite significant personal risk, rushed out into the traffic and pulled her to the side of the freeway, only to learn that she was dead.

Joe should have been nominated for the LAPD's medal of valor. While he and I were peers, any such recommendation technically should have come from our lieutenant. But there was nothing to prevent me from making the recommendation, and I'm ashamed that I failed to do so. Joe is a great guy who, after retiring from the department as a captain, became the police chief at both Torrance and Irwindale. Having recently obtained his doctorate, he is now "Dr. Joe," and remains a good friend and is a board member of Devil Pups, Incorporated.

Sorry I let you down, Joe.

This situation occurred over forty years ago, and I'm still ashamed at the way I handled it. I was driving southbound on Pasadena Freeway around Stadium Way, and saw a large tractor-trailer rig pulled to the side of the road. I stopped to see if I could be of assistance. The driver told me that he had once again mistakenly got on the freeway, where he wasn't supposed to be. He explained that he'd previously been stopped by a CHP officer and given directions off the freeway, which he now realized he hadn't understood. He asked me if I could help him get off the freeway.

As I was assisting the trucker, the same CHP officer pull up behind my unit and started yelling at the driver for being on the freeway. It was clear the driver was confused and had made an honest mistake. But the CHP officer was very verbally forceful, told me that he would handle the situation, and that I was no longer needed. So I left.

Within a very short time, I felt awful for having permitted that pushy CHP officer to handle the situation the way he handled it, probably including issuing a citation to the trucker. Plain and simple, I backed down and failed to behave as I should have, and was inappropriately influenced by the CHP officer's forceful personality. The fact that I still remember the situation so many years later is an indication of the shame that I felt, and still do. In every pile of horse poop there is a pony, and the pony in this poop is that I truly learned from this situation. To the best of my recollection, I never again permitted myself to be influenced by the force of someone's personality.

NOT INITIATING A SEARCH

Many years ago I was told a story by a young woman. It made me aware of the possible existence of a white slavery ring operating out of a storefront on Robertson Boulevard in the West Los Angeles area.

She told me about a job she had, selling magazines door-to-door with other kids in California and Arizona. She explained that a Middle Eastern-appearing woman, working out of the storefront on Robertson, had recruited her and other young people, who often were taken to other states for the door-to-door sales.

She then said that one morning her best girlfriend had just disappeared, the answers given to her inquiries made no sense, and she was fearful that her friend had been taken to one of the Arab countries for immoral purposes. But no identified victim existed—nothing other than the perceptions of this young gal.

Many people have disappeared over the years and were never accounted for. I believed that this situation, the recruitment of wayward kids for out-of-state, door-to-door solicitations, might be the perfect way to abduct them. I went first to the FBI, and later to the commanding officer of the LAPD Juvenile Division, but could stimulate no interest whatsoever. Although it was outside my sphere of investigatory authority at the time, I regret not pushing harder for some entity to look into the issue and to determine if there was merit to a full-blown investigation.

Because this situation was early in my career as a command officer, I was being very careful to not stray outside the perimeters of my authority. Today, I would have no reluctance to push the propriety envelope to look into a matter I find troubling or suspicious.

Trying to Sway Plaintiffs' Attorneys

If this wasn't stupid! For several years after I became a cop, I actually foolishly believed that I could reason with a suspect's defense attorney and convince he or she that their client was guilty. My additional mistaken belief was that such a realization would cause the attorney to be less tenacious in defense of their client.

What was wrong with me? Defense attorneys are paid to defend and be advocates for their client, not to be convinced of their client's guilt by some young cop. I guess I was just revealing the idealism of youth.

Not Taking More Photographs Throughout My Life

I wish so much that I had taken more photographs during the course of my lifetime. In one instance, because it was color film and then (the 1960s) so expensive to develop, I actually threw away a complete roll of undeveloped film from a Marine Corps visit to Hawaii.

For those who read these memoirs—Take More Photographs!

Seeking Safe Legal Advice

For a number of years I did something that I have now long realized was pretty stupid: seeking safe legal opinions, and acting on that advice. Attorneys are staff advisors, not decision-makers, and often give safe advice that is today's solution and tomorrow's nightmare.

Today I spend a great deal of time on this subject in the seminars and presentations that I present. I encourage managers and executives to solicit legal perspectives, but for them to decide what is best for their organization, and to have their legal advisors help them achieve what the chief or sheriff believes is most appropriate. As I look back on my career, I can think of a number of situations where I solicited and acted on advice, which, in the big scheme of things, wasn't very good for the organizations over the long run.

Not Reaching Out to Rod Bernson

Somewhere around 2004 while on an ocean cruise, Rod Bernson was accused of sexual improprieties with a couple of young girls in a hot tub on the ship. I considered Rod a friend, but really didn't know him very well. What he was accused of didn't strike me as something he would have done, but I chose to reserve judgment.

Eventually, Rod was completely exonerated of the charges and, after what had to be months of absolute hell, got some of his life back. I believe he lost a good job when the allegations were initially made, and that he will never recover completely. I'm sure that he is deeply grateful to those men and women of strong character who stood by him during those difficult times, and wish I had been one of them. I think something like these allegations takes a permanent toll on a person, even when found to be untrue. Rod is a good man, and did not deserve the heartache.

Not Serving in Iraq

My desire to get back into the Marine Corps and deploy to Iraq was fulfilled, or so I thought, in 2004 when Major General James Amos, then commanding general of the 2nd Marine Division, approved my request for recall from the retired list. I was to be on his battle staff and involved in intelligence activities. I took part in all the preparations, was on the computer net for staff updates, had my orders, purchased all my new desert-digital camouflage uniforms—but just before reporting to the mobilization station, the Marine Corps cancelled my orders because of my age.

Between the time of my selection and reporting, the Marine Corps closed the door on the return of any retiree who had reached sixty years old. I was really bummed out, and remain disappointed that I was denied the opportunity to serve my Corps and my country one last time. Volunteering to return to the Corps for a tour in Iraq was probably among the most selfish and foolish things I have done, but the honor of putting that wonderful green uniform back on was more than I could resist. Now all I can do is put on one of the desert-digital camouflage uniforms I purchased for Iraq, then crawl around the flood control area behind my house and pretend that I am still a warrior.

Not Seeing More Combat in the Marine Corps

This is a sore and painful point with me. The reason I don't share too many "war stories" with my kids and grandkids is because I don't have many to share! In Cuba during the missile crisis, there was some insurgency and hostile contact with Cuban military forces, as evidenced by my torn hands from communications wire that had been sabotaged by enemy infiltrators. For Vietnam, I flew in and out on several occasions as a communicator and classified message courier and cryptographer. When I returned to the Corps as an officer on a leave of absence from the LAPD, Vietnamization (turning the prosecution of the war over to the South Vietnam military) was in full swing, and my services in theatre were not required. During the first Gulf War (1991), the unit that I commanded was deployed to Kuwait; the advanced party got into action and did a great job, but I was enroute with the main body of the unit when the fifty-six hour war ended. I received great accolades for my leadership and the performance of my people, but I didn't see combat in that war. I volunteered to deploy to Iraq as a "retired recalled reservist" in 2005, had orders in my hand to the Second Marine Division in Iraq, but just before reporting to Camp Pendleton for processing my orders were canceled when the Marine Corps ceased to activite retirees who had reached sixty years of age.

I have a chest-full of medals and decorations, up to and including the Legion of Merit, with enough expeditionary medals to qualify as a combat veteran for purposes of all veterans' organizations. But I wish I had seen more action during my career in the Marine Corps.

Not Having Sooner Developed My Leadership Skills and Expertise

While admittedly self-serving to say, the reality is that I am, and have been since about 1990, a pretty decent leader who has a solid record for leadership achievements and strong credibility. Being equally candid, there were times prior to 1990, give or take a few years and activities, where there was room for improvement with respect to my leadership knowledge and skills. If I had to use a scale, I would rate myself about a solid seven on a scale of one to ten, for my first couple of decades in a leadership role, with a few bursts into the 9-ish category. I don't think I was bad, and in fact I think I was pretty good; but not as good as I wish I had been.

This self-assessment, more so than any other factor, is why I work so hard to mentor others, and to instill mentoring and development skills in other law enforcement leaders.

Probably Not Able to Enjoy Danielle's Children

Now that I am beginning to see the end of the tunnel in writing these memoirs, I am sixty-seven years old. My beautiful and witty adopted daughter, Danielle, is ten years old. While I hope that I and the rest of the family will live forever, or at least be physically and mentally viable well into our nineties, I realize that neither may be the case.

By doing the math, I have to be honest and realize there is a chance that I will never, or barely, know my grandchildren from Danielle. This reality also holds true for my grandchildren (Alyssa, Matthew, Addison, Nathan, and Serena)—that I may never get to know my great-grandchildren from those wonderful kids. I may make the transition to eternal life, hopefully in the northbound lane, before I would prefer to. Should that occur, I want all those great kids who I may never meet on earth to know that I'm looking over them (hopefully, looking down!), that I love them, that I wish them all the best health and happiness, and wish I was physically present to spoil them rotten! Having married a much younger woman, I have every confidence that Cathy will use our resources to take as good care of them as she has all the kids in our extended families.

Not Being Able to Live My Life Over Again!

Like just about everyone else, I've had a few rough times in my life, experienced some things I wish hadn't occurred, and a few things I wish I could do over again. However, all things considered, I am pretty satisfied with my life and wish I could do it all over again. All I ever wanted to be was a cop and a Marine, and I got the opportunity to do both to the max. I have the best wife in the world, and the best ex-wife in the world, and all of my kids are people who I like as much as I love. For hobbies and interests, I have always had four-wheel-drive vehicles; when I was into making industrial-grade canvas gear I had a shop second to none; and with a lifelong interest in law enforcement badges I have a collection that is about as good as it gets.

With respect to my life, does it get any better than this?

Chapter Thirty-One
FAVORITE QUOTES

"These are the Best Years of Your Life!"

This is among my favorite expressions. I use it often, in both my writings and in my presentations. In far too many instances, we spend too much time thinking about the future when we should really be focusing on all the things we have to be thankful for in our present lives.

"The Leader With Scar Tissue Has a Special Perspective that the Unblemished Will Never Know."

I have a special reason for liking this quote: I'm the author! Just about everybody carries scar tissue to some extent, but some of us have real deep and genuine scar tissue. In my case, the deepest stems from my painful departure from the LAPD. I am convinced that the actions and styles of some of our best leaders are related to their scar tissue. Some people wither up in the face of adversity, while others get back up and continue to charge forward in life. I believe I fall into the latter category.

"The Difficult We Do Immediately, The Impossible Takes a While Longer!"

A great and favorate Marine Corps expression. Obviously, this is great bravado that implies that the impossible is possible, which is not actually possible. However, in some ways, there is a lot of truth to people being able to accomplish things they thought were impossible! As examples, there is no way the Marines should have prevailed at places like Iwo Jima, Tarawa, Inchon, and Khe Sanh, but it was the indomitable spirit and "can do" attitude of young Marines that enabled them to accomplish things that others saw as impossible.

I think that I'm a good example of this: a dead-end kid who was not in great physical condition, who had dropped out of high school, and who certainly was not a stud. Four months later (after boot camp and infantry training) I was a Marine honor graduate who could run miles without being winded, and who was willing to fight any aggressor!

"You Can't Change the World, But You Can Make Your Part of It a Better Place!"

This is a very big issue with me, and a pillar of my leadership training. I try hard to make the part of the world that I have influence over a good and fun and healthy place. I am continually telling police supervisors and managers that, while they might not be able to change some things they don't like about their departments, they do have the ability and the responsibility to develop and maintain a wholesome environment to create a workplace where people feel good about themselves, their colleagues, their department and their profession. People need to understand that lousy leadership affects not only the employee, but also his/her spouse and kids, as well. Further, because we often share our consternation with our parents (if still alive), when the employee is suffering there is a pretty good chance that the mom or dad whose shoulder is cried upon is suffering, too.

"Don't Waste Time Worrying About the Things You Cannot Control!"

This is a great and absolutely valid concept, and something that I very much wish I could have complied with during most of my life. This is related to the concept of not worrying about something until the issue actually arises and becomes a problem, which is another great goal. A number of years ago I had a boss, Bill Rathburn, who was able to put potential problems out of his mind, and to give them attention only when and if they materialized. In support of these concepts, it is helpful to remind ourselves that most of what we fear and worry about never comes to fruition.

Enjoy the "Now!"

It is a mistake to always be looking for greener pastures. While it is fine and appropriate to look toward improving oneself, it is important to also enjoy who and where you are, and what you have at the time.

"Among Our Greatest Challenges is Dealing with the Young Officer Who Acts His Age!"

This is a true and sincere statement! Most young officers still have a lot of growing up to do, and at times they can be very immature. In most of my training I ask the participants, typically senior command officers, to reflect on some of the foolish and immature things they did as young officers, and remind them that today's young officers still do foolish things. As I remind supervisors and command officers of their special responsibility to provide oversight to young officers, there is always unanimous agreement with the above. Most of us, me included, did things that we could have been fired for, but were saved from ourselves by a senior partner or supervisor who pulled our chestnuts out of the fire.

"Think in Terms of Responsibility—Not Authority."

This is a cornerstone of my personality, beliefs, value system, and the leadership training that I provide. The authority is always there and an option, but is not something that needs to be asserted except in truly necessary situations.

"Every One of Your Employees is the Most Important Person in the World to Some Other Person!"

A term that I have continually used in my leadership teachings and mentoring. I think it is pretty self-explanatory.

"Always Treat Each of Your Employees, Regardless of the Circumstances, the Way You Would Want Your Son or Daughter to be Treated Under Those Same Circumstances."

A saying that I have continually used in my leadership teachings and mentoring. I think it is also self-explainatory.

"I Don't See an Anchor on Your Ass!"

I have used this term many times when someone has challenged me to fight, always with confidence and bravado. It usually had the desired effect of causing the instigator to back off.

"If You Feel Froggy, Go Ahead and Jump!"

I have also used this term many times when someone challenged me to fight, again always with confidence and bravado. It too usually had the desired effect of causing the instigator to back off.

"No Bad News on Fridays!"

A term that I have continually used in my leadership teachings and mentoring. As someone who has had many weekends and days off ruined by foolish and unnecessary remarks, this is an issue for which I have great passion.

"If It Doesn't Kill You, It Will Make You Stronger!"

No truer words were ever spoken. As the years have gone by, I no longer give a second thought to issues that I would have stayed awake nights worrying about earlier in my careers.

"Darkness is Your Friend!"

This has long been a big and serious issue with me. With decades as a Marine and a cop, I have long realized that a person who is acclimated to darkness can see a great deal, yet not be seen. Certainly there are times when a flashlight is appropriate, but they are badly overused. A flashlight provides good vision within a small field of view, and pretty much eliminates everything else, because the eyes are not acclimated to darkness. I have always used flashlights sparingly.

"Suicide is a Permanent Solution to a Temporary Problem!"

This is so very true, and an expression that I frequently use in my training when the issue of suicide is discussed. Again, no truer expression has ever been said. I have had far too much experience with workplace and personal suicides in my life and, except for situations involving ill-health and suffering (such as my dad), every suicide I can think of was a permanent solution to a problem that could have been solved. In many instances, the suicide stemmed from clinical depression that could have been treated with psychotropic drugs, which are true life savers.

"You Cannot Hurry the Creative Process!"

To the extent that I have any creative qualities, I find this to be very true. In the articles I've written, I really have to be in the right creative mood, as well as in the right time of the day, usually midmornings. There have been times when I haven't made any contributions to my manuscripts for several weeks at a time, because the mood just hadn't struck me. There have also been occasions where, almost out of the blue, I've gone full-speed ahead on a couple of different manuscripts, one after the other. For the booklets I have written, as well as these memoirs, any time is pretty much acceptable because creativity is not really a factor in creating a factual paragraph. Along with my wallet, watch, cell phone and wedding ring, I also carry a small notebook with which to capture thoughts that often occur, sometimes at the darndest times, for potential inclusion in my writings.

"First I Was Afraid that I Would Die Now I'm Afraid I Won't!"

Among my fun expressions.

"I Used to be Afraid that People Would Talk About Me Now I'm Afraid They Won't!

Among my fun expressions.

"Busy Hands are Happy Hands!"

Among my fun expressions.

Things are Seldom as They Initially Appear!"

Another of the expressions I frequently use in my leadership instruction. Most often, when some supervisor or mananger really gets upset or "flames out" over an issue, he or she is reacting to something that is likely to actually be different than what was initially perceived. True leaders avoid the human temptation to over-react, and wait for the facts to be known.

"I Have a Lot of Stories, and Some of Them are Even True!"

Among my fun expressions.

"Idle Hands are The Devil's Workshop!"

Among my fun expressions.

"CHILDREN OF THE WORLD: 100 years from now it will not be important what kind of car I drove, what kind of house I lived in, how much was in my bank account, or what my clothes looked like—only that the world may be a little bit better because I was important in the life of a child!"

A wonderful expression, especially for foster and adoptive parents.

"Nothing Changes if Nothing Changes!"

(Al-Anon)

No elaboration is necessary. Related to the reality that it is foolish to continue to do the same thing and think there will be a different outcome.

"I Did Not Cause It and I Cannot Cure or Control It!"

(Al-Anon)

I am hopelessly addicted to Al Anon, and this is one of the key tenets of that wonderful organization. It helps bring serenity to the loved ones of people who are substance abusers.

"There is Always Free Cheese in the Mouse Trap!"

A great expression to illustrate that someone is being intentionally led down a path, or lured in a particular direction.

"I'm Not Just a Pretty Face!"

A fun expression that I often use to describe myself. Truly humorous and just the opposite of my aging face and body.

In recent years I almost always start my presentations with a discussion of "peaks and valleys." I indicate that there is likely a person or two in the room who is "hurting" very badly, because of obsessive concern or worry over some issue so severe that the person(s) is having trouble even focusing on the presentation. To a sea of nodding heads, I indicate that we have all been in that state before, and that now those unknown person(s) are having their "turn in the barrel" as part of life's peaks and valleys.

I then remind everyone that we all have additional valleys ahead of us, and to enjoy the peaks while we can. I finish with the comment that understanding the realities and absolute predictability of peaks and valleys somehow makes the valleys just a little less difficult to deal with when we slip into them.

"Your Rank or Title Does Not Mean That You Have the Skills to Do the Job!"

In my years of teaching leadership to law enforcement executives, I have come to the absolute reality that one of the great crises facing American policing is the very high percentage of police chiefs and sheriffs who do not have the leadership skills they need to do a credible job in their positions.

Worse yet, far too many of these skill-challenged individuals fail to recognize their weaknesses. I cannot even begin to guess at the number of situations where weak executives have sought training for their subordinate managers and supervisors, but have failed to recognize, or accept, that in many instances the weaknesses of their people are often driven by their, the top executive's, lack of professional competence.

Too many executives see those stars on their uniforms as symbols of extraordinary command leadership abilities. Unfortunately, just the opposite is often the case.

CHAPTER THIRTY-TWO

PRESENT ORGANIZATIONS AND ACTVITIES

EMPLOYEE SUPPORT FOR THE GUARD & RESERVE

I am relatively active in this association, known as ESGR. It is part of the Department of Defense. Well-trained volunteers, on behalf of the Secretary of Defense, perform a variety of tasks intended to support men and women in the National Guard and military reserves, as well as provide recognition and advocacy for those who employ them. My activities include briefing military units in the process of deploying, or returning from deployments, making presentations to supportive employers, and acting as an ombudsman in cases of termination or other adverse employment situations.

INTERNATIONAL ASSOCIATION OF CHIEFS OF POLICE

I have been a member of the IACP since about 1985. A massive conference takes place every year in some major city; those who are not department heads are considered associate members. This is a major professional organization for police chiefs in the United States, as well as police executives from many other countries. There was a time when I was active on one of the organization's many committees, but I departed over frustration when nothing much seemed to be getting done (at least to my liking). The monthly publication is *Police Chief*, and I feel honored to have had several articles published in this prestigious magazine. IACP is a fine outfit, but I have been relatively inactive for the past several years.

CALIFORNIA PEACE OFFICERS' ASSOCIATION

For whatever reason, although a longtime member, I do very little with this outfit. It is a good organization, commonly known as CPOA, which provides top-notch training to law enforcement officers in California. I guess with the extensive training that I provide in other states, plus what I do for local agencies through Bushey & Associates, and the Los Angeles County Peace Officers Association, there just isn't much of me left for CPOA.

There was a time, in the 1980s, when I taught various supervisory classes and promotional preparation quite a bit for them. But people change, new people come and go, and I just pretty much drifted to the sidelines. When with the San Bernardino County Sheriff's Department, I strongly endorsed the extensive participation of one of my captains, Paul Cappitelli, who was a member. Paul moved through the chairs, and ultimately became the president for a term. I also pushed Paul into the Command College. Paul is now the executive director of the California Commission of Peace Officer Standards and Training (POST). If I wished to get back actively involved in CPOA, it wouldn't be difficult. My problem is that there aren't enough hours in the day!

Los Angeles County Peace Officers' Association

I was a periodic and largely inactive member of the LACPOA for many years. Then I became particularly active, and a member of the board of directors, subsequent to going to work for Steve Cooley in the DA's Office. I was Steve's representative to this group, and remained involved after I left his office. At the time of these memoirs, I remain a member of the board, and also periodically put on supervisory and leadership presentations for the group. I do it *gratis*, and the fees for my classes go into the association fund.

Marine Corps Mustang Association

Being a former enlisted Marine who advanced from private to colonel is among the things in my life of which I am extremely proud. I served a four-year active duty enlistment, with overseas tours, then was released from active duty and remained in the inactive reserves as a corporal. At the height of the Vietnam War I applied for a commission, which came to pass toward the end of that conflict. I was commissioned as a second lieutenant in the summer of 1970 and retired as a full colonel in December of 1998.

Very few enlisted Marines become officers, and even fewer go all the way to full colonel. The Marine Mustang Association is made up of the few of us who have achieved the distinction of Mustang—an enlisted Marine who became an officer. In the Marine Corps, an officer who has a good conduct medal in his array of awards, indicating prior significant enlisted service, enjoys exceptional status and credibility.

Veterans of Foreign Wars

At the urging of my older brother, who became briefly active in the Monrovia post in the late 1960s, I joined the VFW. But I let my membership lapse when my brother ceased to be involved. In the mid-1990s, another pal asked me to join him in the post in Big Bear City, where I also had (and continue to have) a home. Cathy signed me up as a life member. But I never got around to going to a meeting, and my pal became disillusioned with the post and dropped out. Then the post was dissolved. I transferred my membership, and am now a member of the post in Azusa. While I have never attended a meeting, I sometimes go by at noon for a hot dog and soda, and also attend some other functions, especially the good breakfasts they host once a month. There is no reason, other than just being very busy, that I'm not more active. I enjoy visiting with other veterans, and hope to become more active one of these days.

American Legion

I have been a continuous member of the Los Angeles Police Post #361 since 1967. That year, Officer Norm Conn, a great fellow who was truly the face of the American Legion with the LAPD for many years, signed me up. As another entry in these memoirs describes, Norm gave me a World War II submachine gun in return for me enrolling in the organization! Since joining, I have attended two or three meetings, all within the last couple of years. I like the outfit, the guys, and the mission, but just haven't found the time to get more involved. Most of the time, meetings are held on a weeknight in the San Fernando Valley, which pretty much has ruled out my involvement. Like the VFW and the American Veterans, perhaps the future will enable my greater participation.

American Veterans

I am a fairly new member of this organization, known as AMVETS. I joined largely because the Irwindale Chapter, Post 113, has been so supportive of the Young Marines, in which Matthew and Spencer were involved for a while, but both boys lost interest and dropped out. AMVETS seems like a pretty good outfit. As is typically the case, it is always enjoyable to visit and chat with other veterans.

Los Angeles Police Historical Society

I have been interested in the history of the department almost from the moment I was sworn in. As another entry in these memoirs describes, at one time I was the department's archivist and literally rescued just about all of our historical items from the trash heap. I am one of the charter members of the Los Angeles Police Historical Society, and count its founder, Richard Kalk, as one of my good friends. I remain very active and presently serve on the board of directors.

Los Angeles Police Associates

This is primarily a social club for retired LAPD employees, with monthly luncheons held at Taix's Restaurant on Sunset Boulevard. My two terms as president give some indication of how the outfit works. After missing meetings for over a year (and even then my attendance was sporadic), one afternoon I entered the meeting room a few minutes late—right in the middle of the process of electing new officers. The moment I walked in the room, someone yelled "I nominate Keith Bushey!" Someone else provided a quick "Second," then someone else yelled "Call for a vote!" Before reaching my seat, I was the president of the outfit! I served two terms, each one year, before declining a third term due to time constraints. It is a fun group, a most enjoyable luncheon, and truly a walk down the LAPD memory lane.

San Bernardino County Sheriff's Historical Society

I don't make many meetings these days, but I am happy to be a member of this organization. They are all friends and good folks, with a real interest in the history of the department and the county. I have a number of "to kill for" SBSD badges in my collection, which will someday be displayed by this group when a true SBCSHS museum comes to fruition.

Los Angeles Police Command Officers' Association (COA)

This is the organization and bargaining unit for LAPD captains and above, active and retired. Other than soliciting money for Devil Pups (they don't give much) and attending the annual Christmas Holidays celebration receptions (great heavy hors d'oeuvres!), I don't have much contact with them, as the association's issues primarily deal with active command officers.

Los Angeles Police Revolver and Athletic Club

Every LAPD cop, active and reserve, is a member. This outfit manages the academy grounds, including the café and the shops. LAPRAC also coordinates the department's sports program.

Other than my participation as the head of emergency communications for the annual Baker to Vegas Relay Race in 2011, I haven't played much of an active role. But I do appreciate all that the association does.

San Bernardino County Safety Employees' Association

This is the bargaining organization, essentially a union, for sworn sheriff's employees of all ranks. It is commonly known as SEBA. I have always had a good relationship with its leadership, and am honored to have been considered among the most fair and reasonable of the command officers.

When Sheriff Penrod stepped down and "anointed" Rod Hoops to replace him, SEBA first called me to determine if I intended to run for sheriff, as part of the process to determine who the organization was going to support. I told them that I supported Rod Hoops, which I believe influenced their decision to support him, as well. Sometimes I wish I had decided to run for sheriff, and believe I would have had a reasonable chance at being elected, had I chosen to do so.

California Law Enforcement Historical Society

My very good friend Gary Hoving formed this outfit around 2005. Gary has done a great job, which has included all the legwork involved in a mobile museum and a monthly CLEHS newsletter. Gary also sponsors a yearly CLEHS badge show. I am proud to be a life member, and to support Gary in any every possible way. In 2006, I was flattered to be designated "Police Historian of the Year" by this group of my friends and fellow law enforcement buffs and collectors.

Desert Refuge for Peace Officers

This wonderful facility is the dream and product of Father Michael McCullough, a dear friend and a Catholic priest who has been assigned full-time to the LAPD ministry by the Los Angeles Archdiocese.

"Father Mike" took a five-acre parcel of desert in Joshua Tree, and is gradually building it into a refuge for peace officers and their spouses, for healing and reflection. Father Mike has been a friend and resource for many years in my dealings with police employee tragedies, and has been there a time or two during my own difficult times. Cathy and I have been reasonably generous to his effort, and in late 2011 I was honored to become an active member on the board of directors.

This is a wonderful endeavor, and I have decided to make time for it, along with Devil Pups and the ESGR.

First Marine Division Association

I served in the First Marine Division, both overseas (Cuba) and at Camp Pendleton.

One day my good friend, Tom Vetter, who at the time was the president of the 1st Marine Division Association, asked if I had one of the new platinum American Express cards. When I replied in the affirmative, he asked if he could see what it looked like. A month later, I got a card and letter thanking me for enrolling and paying the fee to be a life member of the association! That damn Tom had copied down all the info when he "looked" at my card, and signed me up! I guess the $185 was worth it, to be part of this fine outfit. It sure gave me a good story to tell about Tom!

Marine Corps Heritage Foundation

I love the Marine Corps, and everything (well, there are a couple of things I would probably change!) about it, especially its history. It is my honor to be an active member of the MCHF, and hope one day soon to visit its new museum in Quantico. I have visited the San Diego Recruit Depot Museum on several occasions, and never tire of looking at the Corps' heritage.

Marine Corps Reserve Association

When I was first commissioned, the professional group that lobbied on behalf of reserve officers was the Marine Corps Reserve Officers Association, known as MCROA. I was an active member of MCROA, and felt grateful for its advocacy.

A few years ago scandal was caused by the MCROA leadership being involved in serious improprieties. As a reuslt, the organization was dissolved. It was reborn as the Marine Corps Reserve Association, with the mission to advocate on behalf of all reservists, both officer and enlisted.

I am happy to be a member and supporter, but have had no involvement, and really don't know much about the MCRA's activities. Since retiring from the USMCR, and having my orders to return to active duty canceled, I haven't paid as much attention to the intricate details of the Corps as I did during my active years.

SAN GABRIEL VALLEY FOSTER PARENTS' ASSOCIATION

This membership goes hand-in-hand with our foster parenting. Cathy and I were invited to participate in workshops and parties, and we did. It is good for networking, and for foster parents to exchange information on programs, grants and other opportunities. At the time of this entry in my memoirs, Cathy is the president.

U. S. FOREST SERVICE—ANGELES NATIONAL FOREST

I am a volunteer with the Forest Service. My duties are to patrol in the off-highway area above the East Fork Bridge in San Gabriel Canyon. When time permits, I patrol in my Polaris four-wheel drive, side-by-side, utility vehicle. My Polaris is totally tricked-out, with numerous radios, custom cab, and a gigantic USMC flag. Patrolling consists of providing information, access control, and applying gentle persuasion when people do stupid things.

WILLIAM H. PARKER FOUNDATION

The role of the Parker Foundation is to raise money, through donations, for the purpose of funding critical issues for the Los Angeles Police Department in areas where conventional funding is not available. It also provides interim funding in advance of regular funding. In April 2012, I was invited and accepted an invitation to serve on its board of directors, and was honored to do so.

LONG BEACH POLICE HISTORICAL ASSOCIATION

I have never done anything with the LBPHA, or attended a meeting. When the outfit was established, I was among the "law enforcement historical experts" who were recruited as technical advisors, complete with a unique badge and identification card. I feel a little guilty, because I have some really rare and valuable Long Beach badges (three chiefs' badges, two of which are solid gold, and the other was worn by the first chief!) that should be in their museum. But I paid a great deal of money for them, and am not inclined to make that generous a donation. That said, my artifacts will always be available to the Long Beach Police Historical Association (not to an individual, but to the association) for exactly the amount I paid for this extraordinary grouping (approximately $20,000).

CHAPTER THIRTY-THREE
THE FUTURE

I really have no idea of what the future may hold for me, in terms of extraordinary opportunities. Perhaps none.

My primary concern is and must be the welfare of my family. Anything I might do that would affect them would certainly include them in the decision-making process. Some of my most unique opportunities have come my way unexpectedly. Who's to say whether or not other interesting situations might arise?

Several potential opportunites have arisen in the past several years. For one reason or another—not the least of which was a loss of interest and enthusiam on my part—none of them materialized as initially envisioned. At the time of this entry in my memoirs, there are a couple of situations that I am watching closely, either of which have the potential to be of possible interest to me. I am in idle mode, but poised to pounce if something tickles my fancy! Although it's not completely out of the question, however, I remain reluctant to relocate.

A very big factor is the resolution of the continuing argument between my mind (that says I can do just about anything) and my body (that insists my mind is overly optimistic). Whatever I do, or don't do, in the future will represent a compromise between these two forces.

The future may be influenced by these memoirs. As with Facebook, once something is out there in the public domain it has the potential to become a liability. In writing these memoirs, I've resisted the temptation to be politically correct and to exercise too much restraint. On occasion I sought legal advice, and followed that advice in areas where there was the potential to face litigation for libel or slander. Nevertheless, I pretty much had my say in just about every area that occurred to me.

It is entirely possible that my candor, positions, beliefs, actions and salty expressions may render me unwelcome in certain venues. Should that be the case, so be it; these memoirs are intended to be an accurate and comprehensive accounting of my life.

Like the optimistic old cowboy once said, "I may have one more rodeo left in me!" For now, I intend to keep my options open, and see what the future may bring!

— END —

Made in the USA
Coppell, TX
23 December 2021

69943464R10383